Hermann Gebhardt, John Jefferson

The doctrine of the Apocalypse and its relation to the doctrine of the Gospel and Epistles of John

Hermann Gebhardt, John Jefferson

The doctrine of the Apocalypse and its relation to the doctrine of the Gospel and Epistles of John

ISBN/EAN: 9783337283278

Printed in Europe, USA, Canada, Australia, Japan

Cover: Foto ©Thomas Meinert / pixelio.de

More available books at **www.hansebooks.com**

CLARK'S

FOREIGN

THEOLOGICAL LIBRARY.

NEW SERIES.

VOL. LVIII.

Gebhardt on the Doctrine of the Apocalypse.

EDINBURGH:
T. & T. CLARK, 38 GEORGE STREET.
1878.

THE DOCTRINE

OF

THE APOCALYPSE,

AND ITS RELATION TO THE DOCTRINE OF THE GOSPEL AND EPISTLES OF JOHN.

BY

PASTOR HERMANN GEBHARDT.

Translated from the German

BY THE

REV. JOHN JEFFERSON.

EDINBURGH:

T. & T. CLARK, 38 GEORGE STREET.

1878.

PREFACE.

I AM aware that the title of the following volume leaves the reader to some extent in doubt whether he has to do with a treatise on biblical theology or on biblical criticism, or with a work of a mixed character. But instead of prefixing a tedious title, which would still need explaining, I have expressed myself briefly, and feel under obligation to define my meaning in a preface.

According to Keim's preface to the third volume of his *History of Jesus of Nazareth*, John is "historically vanquished." Such great words, often easily uttered, frequently fail to justify themselves. For me there exists no historico-philosophical necessity to reject beforehand the portrait of Christ as sketched by John; and the generally learned and acute attacks on its authenticity,—far more than all modern defences, whether with or without limitations, more even than the thorough and ingenious researches of Weizsäcker,—and, though it may seem strange, above all, the attempt of Keim, surprising in many respects, to construct the life of Jesus exclusively from the synoptical Gospels, have made it to me increasingly improbable that the ecclesiastical tradition respecting the origin of John's Gospel is untrue. But should this avowal be understood to mean that, according to my own statement, the difficulties of the question were gradually overcome in this way, I must strongly protest against such an interpretation; for, on the contrary, the more unacceptable the negative solution became to me, the less did the various attempts at a positive solution—Weizsäcker's not excepted—succeed in satisfying me. My own thoughts and efforts originated and cherished the suspicion that the key to the enigma must lie in the Apocalypse; this book—it was before the late crusade against the residence of the Apostle John in Ephesus — was still unanimously and energetically, and, as it seemed to me, with the fullest justice, ascribed by the Tübingen criticism to the beloved disciple; and these opponents of the Gospel of John still recognised a relation between it and the Apocalypse, even as impartially as its apologists, though with reluctance, everywhere felt themselves compelled to do.

Whichever of the two sides the solution might be nearest, in order to escape the dilemma between the unsatisfactory nature of the negative criticism and the not less imperfect character of all positive attempts at a solution of this question, I began a comparison between the doctrine of the Apocalypse and that of the Gospel and Epistles of John. It was very soon clear to me, that the individuality of the first of these three was such as to render this comparison impossible before I had fully wrought out for myself its doctrinal ideas; and though at first led only by personal interest, I did not permit myself to be intimidated either by the entire absence of a precedent to any considerable extent, or by the testimony of Baur and others respecting the great and almost unconquerable difficulties presented by the style of the Apocalypse itself. Only when, in the course of my labours, I found that the obstacles to a doctrinal representation of the Apocalypse, though considerable, and partly from other causes than its symbolic character, were not in any way insurmountable, did I decide to write with a view to publication, and thus, according to my ability, to help to supply a want in New Testament theology.

There should certainly be no need for the assurance, though I may here most expressly give it, that in my examination and representation of apocalyptic doctrine I have designedly withdrawn my attention as much as possible from the Gospel and the Epistles of John, and with all the means in my power have endeavoured to make myself thoroughly at home in the apocalyptic world of thought. That which during a series of years, in the little time left by the ordinary duties of my office and many additional interruptions caused by sickness, domestic occurrences, change of place, and teaching, I have been able gradually to examine and verify as the doctrinal contents of the Apocalypse, forms the chief part of the following treatise.

I am aware that the representation of apocalyptic doctrine here given departs considerably, and in various ways, from the standard forms of biblico-theological monography. Some of these departures were required by the peculiarities of the Apocalypse, and the difficulty, partly lying therein, of its doctrinal treatment. To this cause may be attributed the rather frequent exegesis, which, notwithstanding modern and most recent labours, including the solid work of Düsterdieck, was—like the polemics occurring at almost every more important point—not to be omitted. Mostly, however, that in which my representation differs—and under this head will be found the close connection of the arrangement with the material, the prominence given to the least important doctrinal features, the avoidance, almost without exception, not only of parallels from other New Testament writings, but also of the usual dogmatic categories and assumptions—is connected with my view of the task of special biblico-theological writings as independent preparatory labours, and not fragmentary expositions of biblical theology. May its contents prove to be justified! The results which I have attained in this way differ throughout from many, and in important points from all, previous conceptions of the Apocalypse. In case these results should attract general attention, I expect attacks from directly opposite sides. Against these, I may beforehand plead, and I do it with all sincerity, that I can hardly hope that it has been given to me to have entirely avoided or obliterated all repetition, prolixity, insufficiency of statement, formal errors, and the like; and I trust, therefore, that they may be ascribed as much to the numerous and profound questions in dispute as to my personal treatment. On the other hand, I can the less honourably seek shelter from opposition to my conclusions behind the difficulties of the Apocalypse, as I am firmly convinced that in all *essential* particulars I have found and presented the real sense of the book.

Strictly as I avoided, during these doctrinal researches, even a side glance at the fourth Gospel, I could not help remembering the original cause of my labours; and the result was well adapted to tempt me to a supplementary comparison of that result with the doctrine of the evangelist. I undertook that also, and though conscious of the essential difference between a biblico-theological and a critical examination, and though apprehensive, and not without reason, that on many sides there would be seen in this comparison "the kernel of the matter," and with it the evidence of the "apologetic tendency" of the whole of my work, I have not on that account been able to withhold the publication of my comparison as an appendix. That in this appendix I have omitted polemics and expositions of the literature almost entirely, will hardly call forth objection, for even without such an addition it may yet seem too dull. I do not give my comparison as final; still I believe that if it be extended and deepened by others,—to me a desirable result of my labours,—they will arrive essentially at the same conclusion.

I send forth *The Doctrine of the Apocalypse, and its Relation to the Doctrine of the Gospel and Epistles of John* with sincere thanks to the authors of *The Apocalypse and the Fourth Gospel*, which, whether I agree or differ with them, are justly due,—the new edition of Weiss' *New Testament Theology* I have not been able to use,—with the further humble hope that my labours may be regarded both by friends and foes as not altogether worthless; and, finally, in these times, and especially in this case, with the very earnest wish that at least some of my readers, instead of beginning with the sentence of condemnation, either on account of "free" ideas respecting the Apocalypse, or of a fixed position with respect to Johannine and other questions of New Testament criticism, will, without prejudice, *test* the aim, spirit, and results of my treatise, for it has been written in the candid and earnest pursuit of truth.

THE AUTHOR.

MOLSCHLEBEN, GOTHA,
March 9, 1873.

CONTENTS.

THE DOCTRINE OF THE APOCALYPSE.

INTRODUCTION.

REPRESENTATION OF DOCTRINE.

FIRST PART.

MORE REMOTE PRESUPPOSITIONS.

SECOND PART.

NEARER PRESUPPOSITIONS.

THIRD PART.

PROPHECY.

THE RELATION BETWEEN THE DOCTRINE OF THE APOCALYPSE AND THE DOCTRINE OF THE GOSPEL AND THE EPISTLES OF JOHN.

THE DOCTRINE OF THE APOCALYPSE.

INTRODUCTION.

THE historico-theological treatment of any book of the New Testament writings would be most profitable if exposition and representation of doctrine were not carried on separately. The same writer, after an introduction embracing only the history and authorship of the work, might next give the exegesis, and then on this foundation: first, the original readers in all their relations as discoverable from the text; secondly, the author in his personality and motives, the time and place of authorship, so far as the previous exposition shed any light upon it; and thirdly, the doctrinal contents, represented in a simple grouping of the materials lying before him. Since the distribution of labour in this sphere still continues, and especially, since existing expositions of the Apocalypse, however variously we may have to object to them, both in general and in detail, even to those coming nearest us, do not leave any necessity for an entirely new exposition, we think it comparatively the best to make the whole direct and indirect statements of the book which are of any theological value, in the widest sense of the word, the subject of our doctrinal representations, and by way of *introduction* to precede those representations with a discussion of the statements of the Apocalypse concerning itself. They have to do with the author, the time and place of composition, the origin, meaning, and form of the book. To the consideration of these the four sections of the Introduction are devoted.

1. *The Author.*

The author of the Apocalypse calls himself John, i. 1, iv. 9, xxii. 8. He describes himself more particularly as " a servant of

Jesus Christ," "a brother and companion" of his readers in "the tribulation, and kingdom, and patience of Jesus Christ," i. 9; an angel said to him: "I am thy fellow-servant, and of thy brethren the prophets," xxii. 9, comp. xix. 10.

Who is this John? Ecclesiastical tradition replies, *the Apostle John;* and so early, so firmly, and so unanimously does this reply come to us, that even Düsterdieck (*Kritisch-exegetisches Handbuch über die Offenbarung Johannes,* 2d ed. p. 88) compares the testimony to a strong bulwark. Holtzmann (Bunsen's *Bibelwerk,* VIII. p. 469) describes it as ancient and forcible; and still more recently (Schenkel's *Bibellexikon,* III. p. 337) gives prominence at least to the antiquity of the tradition which testifies the Johannine origin of the Apocalypse. It is indeed only an appropriate representation of the real state of the case, when Keim (*Gesch. Jesu v. Nazara,* p. 162) says that from the time of Justin Martyr to that of Irenaeus and the great Fathers, the Apocalypse was recognised as a production of the apostle. At the same time, the apostolic origin of the Apocalypse has been disputed even from the third century, and much more frequently and decidedly in later times. With reference to this question modern criticism has changed its position in the most remarkable manner. Until within a few years the attacks on the genuineness of this book proceeded almost exclusively from the moderate theology, on account of its supposed lack of harmony with the received Gospel of John; Neander, Lücke, Ewald, Bleek, Düsterdieck, and others denied it to be the work of the apostle, and ascribed it to some prominent person of the same name in Asia Minor. By a few it has been ascribed, after the example of Eusebius, conjecturally at least, to the Presbyter John; and by Hitzig (*Ueber Johannes Markus und seine Schriften*), whose opinion Weiss, and recently Hausrath (Schenkel's *Bibellexikon,* art. "Apocalypse"), have endorsed, to John Mark. On the other hand, the historico-critical school, with Baur at its head, in unsought union with traditional theology as here represented, especially by Hengstenberg, regarded the contents of ecclesiastical tradition as affording important evidence against the genuineness of the fourth Gospel. Wholly isolated until a short time ago, Volkmar (*Kommentar zur Offenbarung Johannis,* p. 41 et seq.) declared the Apocalypse to be a forgery, written during the life of the apostle by a learned Christian, and as in the name, so also in the spirit—"under the shield"—of the

Apostle John, in an anti-Pauline sense, unmistakeably a compromise between the wish to deny the Christology of the Apocalypse to one of the original apostles, and to maintain intact the evidence of their anti-Paulinism. Then appeared Keim's inquiry into the authorship of the fourth Gospel (*ut ante*, p. 156), in which, in connection with earlier unimportant and less noticed remarks, he says that "the residence of the Apostle John in Asia Minor melts away in the presence of historical evidence, and to that extent indeed, that not only is the question decided with respect to the Gospel, but also with respect to the Apocalypse and the supposed apostle of the Ephesian revelation; and so the authorship of the Gospel by the son of Zebedee is driven from its last refuge." Since then, a fierce struggle has been carried on respecting the abode of the Apostle John in Asia Minor. While Keim immediately found an imitator in Wittichen (*der geschichtliche Charakter des Evangeliums Johannes*), an adherent in Holtzmann (Schenkel's *Bibellexikon*, the article, "über den Apostel und über den Presbyter Johannes"), and, finally, one who far exceeded him in Scholten (*der Apostel Johannes in Kleinasien*), Riggenbach, Ewald (*Göttinger Anzeiger*, 1867), Steitz (*Studien und Kritiken*, 1858, p. 468 et seq.), Krenkel (*der Apostel Johannes*, p. 133 et seq.), and Hilgenfeld (*Zeitschrift für wissenschaftliche Theologie*, 1872, p. 373 et seq.) are opposed to him and his companions. Probably in the transition already begun the denial of the apostolic authorship of the Gospel will, with growing unanimity, be extended to the Apocalypse; it remains to be seen whether, on the other side, with a similar evolution even now apparent, the defence of the authenticity of the Gospel will, with increasing firmness, associate itself with the recognition of the apostolic origin of the Apocalypse.

I do not consider it part of my task to treat here *the question of the residence of the Apostle John in Asia Minor in its details.* But since I cannot entirely agree with any of the defenders, and still less with any of the opponents, of this view, I must give expression to my judgment. To me it appears that an unprejudiced consideration of the well-known fragment of Papias in Eusebius would certainly lead to the conclusion that he distinguishes a disciple of the Lord of the same name from the Apostle John as the presbyter, and also that Papias did not know the apostle personally. When Eusebius reports that Papias declared himself a hearer of the presbyter, which, though not expressly stated in the fragment, is in evident agreement with it, and as there is no proof of the contrary, the inference must therefore be that the presbyter himself lived in Asia Minor. When, now, Irenaeus, apart from the words ascribed to the Lord concerning the millennial kingdom,—for Eusebius does not expressly say Papias heard them from the presbyter,—makes Papias a hearer of the apostle, it must be conceded that there is here a confusion of the apostle with the presbyter, and it follows that the general testimony of Irenaeus to the residence of the apostle in Asia Minor may possibly rest on this confusion, or be unhistorical. But the assertion of Keim, "that through the working together of misunderstanding and the lapse of time, Irenaeus, a native of Asia Minor, about 190 A.D., first proclaimed John the apostle of that country," is false throughout. For the Apocalypse, as Keim himself says, "distinctly enough points to Asia Minor and Ephesus." In other words, no one in the second century *could* believe that the Apostle John was the author of the Apocalypse, without at the same time believing that he lived in Asia Minor; and in like manner, the acknowledgment of the Apocalypse as the apostle's, from the time of Justin Martyr downward, made prominent by Keim, is an acknowledgment of his residence in Asia Minor, and inferentially at Ephesus. Therefore Scholten also has entirely given up explaining the Johannine tradition by the mistake of Irenaeus, and affirms instead that this tradition owes its existence "solely to the apparent claim of the Apocalypse to have come down from the Apostle John." But when he finds it evident "that not another John, but, as already current in Justin's time, the Apostle John, was regarded as the person who received this revelation,"—when he expressly affirms that "by the name John, Rev. i. 1, 9, xxii. 8, the apostle is meant," and notwithstanding charges tradition with being erroneous, the question we must next consider is whether internal evidence decides that the revelation recorded in the Apocalypse was not received by the apostle? The assertion of Scholten, that the author of the book does not identify himself with the seer and the apostle, but in the manner of an introduction, Rev. i. 1, gives a report of a revelation which John had received, as an assertion already offered by Volkmar, and resting as it does upon the obvious confusion, due to prejudice, of title with introduction, is hardly worthy of serious reply. Or we may ask, Would such a reply be thought necessary should it occur to some one to reject the first Epistle to the Corinthians, because from such passages as 1 Cor. i. 13 it does not follow that the author identifies himself with Paul, but gives, 1 Cor. i. 1, 2, after the manner of an introduction, a report of an epistle which the apostle wrote? That in tradition, John, the apostolic disciple of the Lord, may have absorbed the non-apostolic, and that in the Johannine tradition many things, apart from exegetical and other myths, may have to be referred to the presbyter, may be the more readily admitted, inasmuch as such abatements can in the end only be advantageous both to the Apocalypse and the Gospel. But seeing that the abode in Asia Minor goes along with the apostolic authorship of the Apocalypse, the tradition respecting it must be regarded as essentially historical so long as this authorship is not disproved by internal reasons.

But even the *internal reasons* are led into the field with great certainty of victory. And, in fact, "if even the *Apocalypse* of John about the year 70, and the Gospels of Luke and Mark between 40 and 100, believe in the death of the apostles" (Keim, I. p. 156, note, comp. Scholten, p. 10), what further proofs are needed against the apostolic authorship of the Apocalypse? Supposing, however, that the editors of Mark's and of Luke's Gospel, in quoting the passages referred to, had any regard to the question whether all the apostles were dead or not, Steitz is manifestly right in his conclusion, that at the time of the editorship some of the apostles must still have been living. The references made to Rev. xviii. 20, xxi. 14, by Keim and Scholten, prove nothing. In the first passage there is as little evidence of the decease of all the apostles as there is of the death of all the saints and prophets; and Scholten's question to Hilgenfeld, whether from the continued existence of prophets and saints in later times it should follow that the seer cannot have meant those who had already died as martyrs, may with similar justice be applied to the case of the apostles. The inscription of their names upon the foundation of the New Jerusalem, spoken of in the second passage, affords no more evidence of the death of the Twelve than the picture of the new world does of its descent from heaven.

But "in the relation of the seer to the churches to and for which he wrote there appears no trace of apostolic authority. He wrote, not from plenitude of power as an apostle, but from a special revelation. — The apostle would hardly need the full and express attestation which the prophet exhibits in his special calling," Rev. i. 9 et seq. (Düsterdieck, *Commentar,* p. 65 et seq.).—" Of the intimate relation which existed between the Lord and the Apostle John there is not the slightest trace" (Ewald, *die johanneischen Schriften,* b. 2, p. 57; comp. Hoekstra, " die Christologie der Apokalypse," in *Theologisch Tiidschrift,* III. 4, p. 366). " When the seer places the names of the twelve apostles upon the foundations which bear the walls of the New Jerusalem, xxi. 14, comp. iv. 4, 10, what is to be observed is less the fact that such a mode of view was lacking in modesty (Ewald), than the perfect objectivity with which the number twelve as a designation of the apostles presented itself to the seer." Comp. xviii. 20 (Düsterdieck, p. 66; comp. Ewald, p. 56; Hoekstra, p. 366; Weizsäcker, *Untersuchungen über die evangelische Geschichte,* p. 238; Hausrath, *Neutestamentliche Zeitgeschichte,* II. p. 654; Scholten, pp. 10, 129).—" The Revelation of John is the work of the prophet; at all points it affirms that it is not the work of the apostle;" and to this Bleek, Lücke, Ewald have given their assent. The author calls himself *only* a servant, i. 1, xxii. 6; a companion, i. 9; a prophet of the church with the spirit of the prophets, xxii. 6, ix. 10. He speaks objectively of the apostles, indeed of the holy apostles, and though not directly of Peter and Paul, of those who were put to death by Rome, xviii. 20, xxi. 14 (Keim, I. p. 159 et seq., note). Thus the tradition is contradicted by *the manner in which the seer speaks of himself and of the apostles!* But if we miss every trace of apostolic authority in the Apocalypse, it must still be granted that for the first circle of readers the description of himself given by the author must have been sufficient; indeed, it must be admitted also that among Christians of Asia Minor the author must have possessed considerable authority; and if we begin with the assumption that the author was the Apostle John, does he not speak to his first readers with that authority throughout the entire book? Moreover, Scholten, p. 6, like Volkmar before him, finds that when the writer distinguishes himself from other servants as " the servant of Christ" honoured of the Lord by a special revelation, and commissioned to be the bearer of letters to the churches, dictated to him by Christ Himself, and then emphatically speaks of himself as " I, John," it is hardly like the language of one who was not an apostle; and, indeed, as the same writer justly remarks, it could scarcely be doubted by any one that the receiver of the Revelation was the apostle, did not a prepossession in favour of the fourth Gospel lead to that result. Certainly the author expressly calls attention to his apostleship as little as he does to his earlier confidential relation to the Lord, and he speaks of the apostles entirely in an objective sense; but has he written the book as an apostle? No; he wrote it as a prophet; and if we should not have the slightest objection to a prince who wrote as a poet if he were to lay aside court, or government, or military language, and speak simply as a poet, and if he were to make no reference to his rank, and speak objectively of princes, need we object to the apostolic authorship of the Apocalypse because as a prophet he speaks in prophetic language? The Apocalypse declares itself not to be the work of an apostle, in the same sense as Schiller's poetry declares itself not to be the work of a professor of Jena. I doubt whether a historian of literature, without theological prejudice, would reply to the objections against the genuineness of the Apocalypse, above quoted, otherwise than with ridicule.

The objections urged by Volkmar, Hoekstra, and Scholten, *from the character* of the Apocalypse, are more important. The first mentioned says (*Commentar zur Offenbarung Johannis*, p. 42): "The rabbinical learning and art which predominate throughout the book can scarcely be referred to an apostolic fisherman" (comp. Holtzmann in Schenkel's *Bibellexikon*, III. p. 337). Scholten, p. 8 et seq.: "The picture of Christ which here comes before us seems to presuppose a conception so perfectly free, that it can only belong to a later Christianity." Comp. Scholten, p. 9: "The apotheosis of Christ is too strong to be ascribed to a contemporary and disciple of Jesus." "The fire of enthusiasm, the youthful power of imagination, which inspire a book written A.D. 68, are scarcely natural for a contemporary of Jesus surviving until then." Hoekstra (p. 367 et seq.) remarks, that "the whole spirit and learned contents of the book speak against the authorship of the beloved disciple; not only because, according to this book, Jesus, compelled by the circumstances of the times, unwillingly refrained from laying upon His followers, so far as they had escaped it, the burden of the Mosaic law, ii. 24, but because it expresses not a single thought which elevates Christianity in principle above the dispensation of Moses. And then, too, as far as the spirit and character of the historical Christ—as John had personally learned to know Him—were the foundation upon which he based his representation of the heavenly Christ, there is scarcely anything left of the picture of the loving and amiable Son of man as sketched by the Synoptics" (comp. Scholten, pp. 9, 130). To all this Scholten has added (p. 10) the charge, that the author of the Apocalypse represents himself as at enmity with the Gentile Christians, while the Apostle John recognised the propriety of the mission to the Gentiles, and gave to Paul the right hand of fellowship. We find, however, that powers of production, as they are shown in the Apocalypse, have been possessed and exercised by a few favoured spirits even in modern times at even a more advanced age. What is called the rabbinical learning and art of the book has more than one analogy in the history of the church,—for example, the writings of the tinker Bunyan. If the portrait of the historical Christ proposed by certain critics is not to us certainly supposition, so also may the wholly independent opposite of such portrait, the strong intuition of the Apocalypse concerning Christ, be no evidence against its apostolic origin; moreover, the Christ of the Apocalypse must be regarded in His relation to the apocalyptic Christ of the synoptical Gospels and of Paul, and then it may be asked whether He still appears a perfectly independent conception of the seer? The objection drawn from ii. 24, as well as those found in the supposed absence of specific Christian thought, and the difference between the writer as opposed to the Gentile Christians and the friendly apostle, can be considered only when we come to an examination of the doctrine of the Apocalypse. With respect to Hoekstra's "loving and amiable Son of man," if I am not wholly mistaken, He is found as little in the eschatological portions of the synoptical Gospels as in the Apocalypse. Holtzmann, to whom we can hardly ascribe a prepossession in favour of the apostolic origin of the Apocalypse, says, *ut ante*, p. 337: "It cannot be denied that much of what we know of the character and history of this disciple—the Apostle John—is in harmony with the spirit, contents, language, and style of this book" (comp. Mark iii. 17, Luke ix. 49, with Rev. ii. 2, 9, iii. 9; Luke ix. 54 with Rev. xv. 7; Luke ix. 50 with Rev. ii. 6; Matt. xx. 21 with Rev. xx. 4 et seq. Comp. Krenkel, p. 10, note 1, p. 121). The objection of Weizsäcker (p. 235 et seq.), that while in the circle of the apostles the prediction of Jesus respecting the destruction of Jerusalem was held with remarkable definiteness and precision, the author of the Apocalypse departs from it, can be best considered when we come to the exposition of the statements of the book with respect to that subject.

Those who, on the one hand, have no desire to maintain the genuineness of the fourth Gospel, or, on the other, to deprive the apostolic origin of that Gospel of its last refuge, as well as no desire to retain an original apostolic anti-Pauline author, or to be rid of an original apostolic Christologist, will probably agree with us when we give our final judgment respecting the authorship of the Apocalypse. The contents and style of the book, especially the introduction, the letters, and the conclusion, undoubtedly show that the John who wrote it must have been a man of very high authority in the Christian circles of Asia Minor. The memory of such a man could not possibly vanish without leaving some trace behind it. Now there comes down to us no information of any other John who, at the required time and place, held a more important position, besides the apostle and—though only indirectly and scantily—the Presbyter John; and we must, in case the tradition of the residence of the apostle in Asia Minor is proved to be false, ascribe the Apocalypse entirely to the presbyter of Papias, who is perhaps to be identified with John Mark. But the tradition of the residence of the Apostle John in Asia Minor is not contradicted either on external or internal grounds, so that we have our choice between the apostle and the presbyter. From internal grounds a prophetic book does not enable us, with entire certainty, to decide between an apostolic and a non-apostolic disciple of the Lord, though the style, especially at the beginning, tells more in favour of an apostolic authorship than it does on behalf of the authorship of one who was simply an "elder." Since the presbyter has not the slightest advantage over the apostle,—passing over the words ascribed to the Lord Jesus respecting the vine and the ears of corn, so little in harmony with the Apocalypse,—we need only appropriately and provisionally avoid all reference to the result as it affects the fourth Gospel, and we cannot then hesitate to give the preference to the apostolic authorship, attested as it is by a comparatively ancient, entirely unanimous, and remarkably decided tradition (comp. Krenkel, pp. 144–165), rather than to the authorship of the presbyter, suggested for the first time centuries after the origination of the Apocalypse by a notoriously biassed criticism, and even by that only conjecturally, and acknowledge the Apostle John as the writer of the Apocalypse.

2. *Place and Time of Authorship.*

According to Rev. i. 9, the author "was in the isle that is called Patmos, for the word of God and for the testimony of Jesus Christ." He was there "in the spirit on the Lord's day," i. 10 (comp. iv. 2, xvii. 3, xxi. 10). Those expositors who, as Züllig, and more recently Volkmar, regard the ecstasy in which the revelation was received as nothing more than a literary form, after the example of Dan. viii. 2, x. 4, naturally consider the residence of the author on the isle of Patmos merely as part of the drapery. From the account he gives of himself as a man well known to his readers, as well as from the accompanying matter of course assumption that he was really in an ecstasy, we conclude that his sojourn on Patmos was an actual event. That which he refers to as the occasion of his being there,—"for the word of God and for the testimony of Jesus Christ,"—as we shall have opportunity of pointing out in the section on the "Work of Christ," may in itself equally well mean that he was at Patmos to preach the gospel, or to receive the revelation contained in our book, or, finally, that he was there as a martyr, either as banished or as a fugitive. The insignificance of the island is against the supposition that he was there to preach the gospel. That the reference is to the reception of the revelation, is certainly favoured by the fact that not long before, i. 2, similar expressions are used which undoubtedly describe it. Since, however, his actual residence there being taken for granted, it is impossible to understand how he found himself there, or rather how he came thither (ἐγενόμην) in order to receive the revelation, unless we suppose that, unlike Paul, he may, in a spirit of dislike, opposition, or even defiance, have taken up a position of antagonism to the prevailing heathen tendency at Ephesus, and "have had to retire to the quiet Patmos if the Spirit of the Lord was to speak to him,"—I decide for the interpretation justified by Rev. xx. 4, that the author came to Patmos as a martyr. Whether as a captive, or more probably as one banished, which was in accordance with the practice of Rome in Domitian's time, and which also agrees with one form of tradition, or whether as a fugitive, which another tradition asserts (Eusebius according to Düsterdieck, p. 93), cannot with certainty be decided from the "tribulation" of i. 9, and the "leading into captivity" of xiii. 10, or from the general contents of the book.

As to the day when he received the revelation, he speaks of it as "*the Lord's day*," which, on account of its connection with i. 17, 18, is the festival of the resurrection of Christ, and certainly not the annual one or Easter, but that which the name usually meant with the Fathers of the Church—the weekly or Sunday celebration.

Evidently John did not wish by the isle of Patmos and the Lord's day to direct his readers merely to locality or time, but to a definite locality,—it was the place of banishment or refuge,—and to historical circumstances,—it was on that day of the week on which the resurrection of the Lord, in its meaning, was vividly present to his mind, and on which, in the spirit, he communed with the risen Saviour (comp. i. 17, 18)—in which the revelation came to him, and by which it was externally conditioned, and from which it proceeded. We need therefore expect no express information respecting the year in which this book was produced; it was written "in this year," as it sometimes stands on the title-page of pamphlets written at the period of the Reformation. But this year is so clearly indicated by the description of the Beast, in complete agreement with everything else in the book, that, as we shall show in the sections on nearer doctrines, the choice can only be, whether it was written under the government of Galba, between August 68 and January 69, or in the time from the accession of Vespasian to the destruction of Jerusalem, between the end of December 69 and the spring of the year 70. And as in the same sections we find nothing in favour of Vespasian, but on the contrary very important considerations in favour of the time of Galba, we conclude, with Volkmar and others, that the Apocalypse was written in his reign, toward *the end of the year* 68, *or early in the year following.*

3. *Its Origin and Meaning.*

The author was in the spirit, or became in the spirit (ἐγενόμεν), i. 10, comp. iv. 2, xvii. 3, xxi. 10. "The Lord God of the holy prophets sent His angel to show unto His servants the things which must shortly be done," xxii. 6. Jesus sent His angel to bear witness to the readers of the book respecting the things therein written concerning the churches, xxii. 16. John received a revelation of Jesus Christ which God gave unto Him to show His servants things which must shortly come to pass, i. 1. What Jesus Christ showed to His servant John, i. 1, he has seen, i. 2, seen in a vision, ix. 17, heard and seen, xxii. 8. Suddenly, at the beginning, he heard "a great voice as of a trumpet, saying unto him, What thou seest write in a book, and send it unto the seven churches which are in Asia," i. 11. The Lord said to him again, "Write the things which thou hast seen, and the things which are, and the things which shall be hereafter," i. 19. When the seven thunders had spoken, the author was about to write, but he heard a voice from heaven which said, "Seal up those things which the seven thunders uttered, and write them not!" x. 4. After he had eaten the little book, the voice said to him, "Thou must prophesy again before many peoples, and nations, and tongues, and kings," x. 11. He heard a voice from heaven saying unto him, "Write!" xiv. 13; and at last the angel said to him, "Seal not the sayings of the prophecy of this book, for the time is at hand," xxii. 10. The author "bare record of the word of God, and of the testimony of Jesus, and of all things that he saw," i. 2. He counts him blessed who reads and hears the words of this prophecy, and keeps those things which are written therein, for the time is at hand, i. 3, xxii. 7. The angel said to him, "I am thy fellow-servant, and of thy brethren the prophets, and of them which keep the sayings of this book," xxii. 9. The author testifies, to every one who hears the words of the prophecy of this book, that if "any man shall add unto those things, God shall add unto him the plagues that are written in this book; and if any man shall take away from the words of the book of this prophecy, God shall take away his part out of the Book of Life, and out of the holy city, and from the things which are written in this book," xxii. 18, 19. Once more the angel said, "These are the true sayings of God," xix. 9. God Himself said to him, "Write, for these words are true and faithful," xxi. 5. And lastly, the angel said to him, "These sayings are faithful and true," xxii. 6.

There can be no doubt that the author declares the contents of the book to be a revelation *received from God through Christ*; and since the assertion that this is only a literary form falls to the ground with the untenable hypothesis of a pseudo-John, that he himself so regarded it. But, on the other hand, the author must have *erred* when he expected that in a short time Nero, as the antichrist, would return from Hades, and that his appearance would bring the end. Instead of, as is most commonly done, denying either side of this contradiction, the only just course seems to me to be to endeavour to *reconcile* both sides. Referring at the same time to the section on the "Spirit," I here observe the following:—The spirit of prophecy is the Christian vital principle on the side of knowledge, and of knowledge as far as it is new (*mysterium*), and equally, whether it belongs to the present or the future, to things internal or external. Such new knowledge completed itself in apostolic times, like all other manifestations or operations of the Christian life-principle, in the way of sudden illumination, consequently in a miraculous manner. The subjects of it were, with good reason, conscious that it did not proceed from themselves, that they had not themselves produced and given it, but rather that they had received it. Objectively it came to them as vision and revelation; they saw and perceived in a state of inspiration and ecstasy. That at the same time their subjectivity and individuality took part, they themselves understood, or at least others did. Hence the words of the apostle, "Prove all things; hold fast that which is good," 1 Thess. v. 21; hence also the gift of "discerning spirits," 1 Cor. xii. 10. Especially does it appear, and I find it very conceivable, that this fellowship of the subjectivity is acknowledged in prophecy where it has to do with the future, the time or the hour, or with the signs of the times. Comp. Matt. xxiv. 32–36; 1 Thess. v. 1–3; 2 Thess. ii. 1–3. Comp. 1 Pet. i. 10–12. It was manifestly not injurious to the standing of a prophet when he miscalculated with reference to the future; comp. 1 Thess. iv. 13–15; 1 Cor. xv. 51, 52. It need not therefore surprise us when the author of this book speaks indiscriminately of its contents as prophecy, seen and heard in the spirit, received from God or Christ, while, according to the manner of apostolic times, he still assumes as self-evident that his interpretation of the signs of the times, and his estimate of the future, require to be justified by the result. Moreover, the seer himself sometimes clearly gives us to understand that he wishes to see a distinction made in the contents of his book, a difference of which he is of course conscious himself; and he gives this intimation, not as Volkmar, speaking of xix. 9, thinks, through a distinction between the spirit and the word; nor can I, with others, prefer a distinction between the general outline and the individual features. It is not to be denied, indeed, that the author clearly distinguishes between the predictions peculiar to himself and to the Old Testament prophetic word,—it may be the word of a Daniel, or a proverbial eschatological sentence,—nor that he really derives the contents of his book generally from God, though he speaks, xix. 9, xxi. 5, xxii. 6, of the faithful and true words of God, which gives a good meaning only when referred to what immediately precedes, but which, by implication, modifies the certainty and real divinity of the remaining portions. I may venture on the whole, I think, to affirm that precisely this peculiarity of the seer, namely, the way in which he interprets "the signs of the times and points to the landmarks within his historical horizon, by which we may count the steps to be made by the developments of the last time until the final catastrophe" (Weiss, *Lehrbuch der biblischen Theologie des Neuen Testaments*, p. 515), was not to him really the absolute; and all the expressions which describe the contents of his book as absolute spring essentially, first, from eschatological truths come down to him as such, and then from their application or realization through the Apocalypse before us.

But should I say how *I represent the circumstances of the origin of the book*, my opinion is, and I do not give it for more, that, in view of the persecution of Nero, the surging waves of which reached as far as Asia; in view also of the state of the Christian churches, and of his flight or banishment to Patmos; being on the Lord's day absorbed in devotion to the exalted and, notwithstanding the ardent longing of the earlier, and the palsying, cooling doubt of the later Christian generation, still only coming Lord; thinking of the enigma of the course of this world, and carried away by various powerful emotions, he passed into a state of ecstasy, and the Roman empire in general, and the hateful Nero in particular, appeared to him as the fulfilment of the predicted Antichrist, as the Beast of Daniel; and from this central point he saw present, past, and future grouping themselves around it in a series of eschatological scenes. Christendom and its accompanying circumstances were the foreground, and became the preliminary picture; and, on the other hand, the whole vast eschatological background became the principal view. Thus the author actually saw and heard in ecstasy the entire essential contents of his book; he received it as a "revelation of God or of Christ," the same was shown to him, and he has borne witness to the word of God and the testimony of Jesus Christ (comp. Weiss, "Apocalyptische Studien," in *Theologische Studien und Kritiken,* 1869, vol. i. p. 1 et seq.).

4. *The Form.*

In chap. x. an angel appears with a little open book. At his cry, seven thunders utter their voices. When the seer was about to write, a voice from heaven said to him: "Seal up those things which the seven thunders uttered, and write them not!" The angel swore by Him that liveth for ever and ever that time should be no longer, but in the days of the seventh trumpet the mystery of God should be finished, as He had declared to His servants the prophets. A voice from heaven bade him take the open book from the hand of the angel; and as he did so, the angel said: "Take it and eat it up, and it shall make thy belly bitter, but it shall be in thy mouth sweet as honey." He did so, and found it as the angel had said; he was then assured that he "must prophesy again before many peoples, and nations, and tongues, and kings."

Various as have been the expositions of this scene, I cannot adopt any of them; but I submit an original one, which I confidently hope will prove itself to be true. The author has begun, vi. 1, *in mediam rem,* in the style of a genuine epic, and introduced the visions of the seals, after the sixth of which comes the episode of the seventh chapter. Out of the seventh seal he unfolds the visions of the seven trumpets in chap. viii., ix.; and then, standing before the sounding of the seventh trumpet, another episode interposes as in the former case. At this point he becomes conscious that, to continue the method of representation hitherto pursued, he must sketch in too broad a manner the judgment being prepared and foreshadowed. He resolves, therefore, to strike into another path, and to refrain from a further exposition of the judgment scenes, and instead of bringing on the winding up of the past, or the beginning of the end, by individual episodes, to do it rather by a connected representation, that is, by the contents of chap. xii. and xiii., and then to pass on to the final catastrophe. Of this change, or rather this modification of his original plan, the author, in apocalyptic style, gives us notice in chap. x. The seven thunders, that is, the divine voice, the revelation of God in the thunder (comp. Ps. xxix., l. 6), can only mean the publication of judgment as the burden of the seal and trumpet visions. The seer is commanded to seal up and not to write what is spoken (comp. Dan. viii. 26, xii. 4, 9). But when he then enters upon another course, will not the reader be deceived in his expectation that the catastrophe is near? It is for this reason that the angel (comp. Dan. xii. 7) swears that with the sounding of the seventh trumpet the end shall certainly come. But the seer may have received a special direction (Ezek. ii. 8) for this modified course; he ate the little book,—reminding us of the book in chap. v., yet still somewhat different, perhaps a part of it, but in a special form,—which was sweet in his mouth—that is, the reception of the revelation—but bitter in his belly,—that is, the perception and examination of the revelation received,—and was thus commissioned to continue his prophesying, but in a different manner. He does it, however, not by an abrupt departure from his preceding course, but by bringing next the prediction concerning Jerusalem, xi. 1–14, or the Jewish people, which on one side by the apocalyptic time-space of three and a half years, xi. 2, 9, 11, and the mention of the beast from the bottomless pit, xi. 7, shows itself to be homogeneous with the prediction in chap. xii.; while on the other, by the declaration, "The second woe is past, and behold the third woe cometh quickly," xi. 14 (comp. ix. 12), it formally attaches itself to the earlier prophecy. True, in xi. 15–19, he records the sounding of the seventh trumpet, and celebrates in anticipation the fulfilment of the divine mystery; but in chap. xii. he entirely forsakes, even in form, his earlier course, only in the vision of the vials to return to it. The construction of the Apocalypse, then, presents itself thus: chap. i. 1 to iii. 32, and chap. xxii. 6–21, need no exposition of their connection. In the great principal vision, extending from chap. iv. 1 to xxii. 5, only chap. vi., viii., ix., to some extent also chap. xi., xv., xvi., xviii., xix. 11, etc., and the chapters following, are connected in time; on the other hand, with the exception of the introductory chapters iv. and v., and also the tenth, chap. vii., xii., xiii., xiv., xvii., xix. 1--10 are, chronologically, not to be limited more definitely than by the apocalyptic conception of the last times. Ewald's distribution into seven—three seven-membered sections (iv.–vii., viii.–xi. 14, xi. 15–xxii. 5), the third again divided into three (xi. 15–xiv. 20, xv.–xviii., xix.–xxii. 5); the preface and dedication in seven members (ii.–iii.); the introduction of four, and the conclusion of three parts—betrays less the art of the seer than the refinement of the expositor, and in any case is for us unimportant.

But if our interpretation of chap. x. be correct, even in general only, there follows a result which *reaches* far beyond the mere architecture of the book. Decidedly as we have declared ourselves against the origin of the Apocalypse from reflection, to say nothing of an artistic purpose, and in favour of the full subjective truth of its revelation, with equal decision we must declare against the view that it is a dictation or protocol written in the ecstasy itself, or that it is only a direct reproduction of what was seen or heard "in the spirit." Much rather, as it seems from chap. x., has the author treated the whole contents of the revelation given to him in an artistic and independent manner. And here he was bound—which for the most part is not recognised—even more strictly than the poets of ancient or modern times, by the laws of the kind of literature he employed. As a seer, he had *to observe the rules of apocalyptic authorship or art*, and to clothe his ideas in apocalyptic language,—that is, in Old Testament rabbinical forms of representation. If, now, the language of the book is almost throughout composed of Old Testament and Old Testament rabbinical expressions and images, and so far forms a kind of *cento*, we are not obliged beforehand to find in it the subjectively corresponding expressions for the views of the author, and with this the proof of his Old Testament theocratic standpoint, as in the crudest manner is done by the Tübingen school; on the contrary, we are justified, having regard to the words and symbols of the book, in inquiring whether as a seer the author, according to the laws of apocalyptic art, has clothed his thoughts in the variously limiting but reverential and only suitable drapery of ancient sacred language and symbolism, in the conviction that the reader would penetrate the veil and reach the sense.

REPRESENTATION OF DOCTRINE.

AFTER having discussed in the Introduction the statements of the Apocalypse concerning itself, its so to speak subjective contents, we now proceed to consider its objective contents—its doctrines, its direct and indirect statements—in their theological significance. To examine these in their full extent we must not limit ourselves to that which is peculiarly *apocalyptic or prophetic*, but must take into consideration its *nearer and more remote presuppositions;* and if we desire to represent these contents organically, we must not exhibit them in categories brought from without, but must group them according to the ideas of the author himself. We have therefore, in the first part, to consider the more remote presuppositions: on the one side, God, angels, and heaven; and on the other, the devil and hell; and then the middle sphere, the earth and its inhabitants. In the second part we shall review the nearer presuppositions: Christ, the Spirit, the gospel, the saints and their works (Christian life), the churches (Christendom). In a third part, the prophecy of the book, including the beast, the false prophet, Babylon (Antichrist), the seals, the trumpets, the vials (the preliminary judgments), the saints in the great tribulation (Christians in the last time), the Holy City during the forty-two months (the Jewish nation in the last time), the impenitence of men (the heathen in the last time), the fall of Babylon, the coming of the Lord, the millennial kingdom, the judgment, and the new heaven and the new earth (the final issue of all things).

FIRST PART.

MORE REMOTE PRESUPPOSITIONS.

1. God.

THE name of Him who is feared by the devout, xi. 18, etc., blasphemed by the beast, xiii. 6, as well as by men when they suffer from the plagues, xvi. 9, is simply God; or rather, it is the name of the nature of God as made known by Him to men, and understood by them in His word. The name of God, which Christ will write upon those who overcome, iii. 12, and which the 144,000 who are with the Lamb, xiv. 1, and which the servants of God bear upon their foreheads, xxii. 4, whether we understand it to be the sacred name of Jehovah or not, is of little importance so far as the doctrine of God is concerned.

The so-called *gods* of the heathen are to the seer, in their external manifestations, the work of men's hands, idols (εἴδωλα) of gold and silver and iron and stone and wood, which neither see nor hear nor walk; but in their nature they are demons (δαιμόνια), *i.e.* supernatural evil beings, ix. 20 (comp. ii. 14, 20, xvi. 14, xviii. 2; see section on the devil). It is evident that, to the author, the true or real God, a Being as much opposed to an idol as to a demon, is in His physical nature eternal and almighty, and in His moral nature holy. But frequently and impressively as he brings forward these two sides of the divine nature, it so happens that, comparatively, he seldom brings them into contrast with false gods; and Köstlin is mistaken when he affirms (*Lehrbegriff des Evangeliums und der Briefe Johannis*, p. 482) that, in the doctrine of the Apocalypse concerning God, it is especially prominent that He is the μόνος ὅσιος whom all must fear and adore; that He created the whole world by His will; and that He is called the God of heaven, in opposition to idol gods. Certainly, when the angel with the everlasting gospel says to those who dwell on the earth, "Fear God, and give glory to Him; for the hour of His judgment is come: and worship Him that made heaven and earth, and the sea, and the fountains of waters," xiv. 7, the Creator of the world is, according to the sense afterwards to be explained, as well as according to the analogy of the Old Testament (Jer. x. 11 et seq., et passim), placed in contrast with powerless idols. In like manner, God, as the "only holy" (ὅσιος), xv. 4, is placed in contrast with demons and heathen gods, their immorality and untruthfulness, and with the lies and frauds of witchcraft, as much by the "only" as by the connection. Almost immediately before, xv. 3, God is called, after Jer. x. 7, "King of nations." While the nations serve false gods, He is the only true God whom justly they must solely worship. But here all the places are quoted where He is contrasted with idols. Baur, indeed, affirms (*Verlesungen über neutestamentliche Theologie*, p. 227) that He is spoken of as the God of heaven, in xvi. 11, in opposition to heathen gods; but He is designated in a similar manner in xi. 13, where it is impossible to conceive a contrast between Him and the gods of the heathen.

There is another *contrast* which determines the utterances of this book concerning God. While the course of this world contradicts ever more sharply and fiercely the Christian idea, John has to testify, x. 7, for the comfort and admonition of Christ's disciples, that the mystery of God shall speedily be finished, and how. May we not, then, expect beforehand that he will give prominence to that chiefly, if not exclusively, in the nature and operations of God, wherein lies the pledge of the truth of the prophecy given by him against the existing position and course of the world as it lies before men's eyes? We find, in fact, that the general statements of the Apocalypse concerning God are easily explained from this standpoint. Another question is, whether it will particularly appear to us, as it does to Baur, p. 226 (comp. Köstlin, p. 482 et seq.), from the idea of God as the highest theological idea, how greatly the Apocalypse rests on the standpoint of Old Testament Monotheism and Theocracy, of which naturally it is no proof in an apocalypse that almost exclusively Old Testament predicates are made of God.

(*a*.) *The Nature of God.*

He is called simply God (ὁ θεός), in i. 1 for example; in the mouth of Christ, "my God," ii. 7 (n.r.l.), iii. 12. On the lips of the inhabitants of heaven He is "our God," iv. 11, vii. 10, 12, xii. 10, xix. 1, 5; and speaking of the inhabitants of the New Jerusalem, He is said to be "their God," xxi. 3 (comp. Ex. xxix. 45; Lev. xxvi. 12; Ezek. xxxvii. 27). He stands also in a special relation to Christ, to the inhabitants of heaven, and to Christians.

He is called "the Lord" (ὁ κύριος). The victors sing, "Who shall not fear Thee, O Lord!" xv. 4; the elders cry, "Thou art worthy, O Lord!" iv. 11; and the great voices in heaven say, "The kingdoms of this world are become the kingdoms of our Lord," xi. 15. He who is thus revered is God; and for worshippers in heaven and on earth, He is the Lord, or their Lord. Not of equal importance, but convenient to mention here, is the fact that the martyrs, vi. 10, cry to God, "How long, O Lord, holy and true, dost Thou not judge and avenge our blood?" They recognise Him as their Master or Lord (δεσπότης), because, in His acceptance of them as His possession, His servants (see fellow-servants, vi. 11), is their security that He will not permit them to be slaughtered unavenged.

He is also called "the Lord God" (κύριος ὁ θεός). This name is synonymous with the Old Testament Adonai Jehovah (compare, for example, Isa. xl. 10), or Jehovah Elohim, and in like manner denotes the God of Israel and of Christians, though it is not brought into conscious and prominent contrast with heathen gods, but is more solemn and emphatic than the simple term "God." To some extent, the terms "Lord God" meet us as a proper name in connection with the words, "which is, and which was, and which is to come, the Almighty," i. 8 (n.r.l.), iv. 8, xi. 17, xxi. 22. Also in the words, "for strong is the Lord God who judgeth her," xviii. 8, the "Lord God" is only a more full proper name of God. In the passage, "The Lord God of the holy prophets sent His angel to show unto His servants the things which must shortly be done," xxii. 6, there is evidently a union of the terms "the Lord God" and "the God of the spirits of the prophets." Comp. Num. xvi. 22.

Sometimes independently, i. 4, xvi. 5, and sometimes preceding or following "the Almighty," as an attribute of the Lord God, i. 8, iv. 8, xi. 17, the description of God appears as *He who is, and was, and is to come.* The passage in i. 4, where the author wishes for his readers grace and peace "from Him which is, and which was, and which is to come," in its designed method of construction (ἀπὸ ὁ ὢν κ.τ.λ.), admits of no doubt that John intended by this rabbinically developed paraphrase and interpretation of Ex. iii. 13–15 to represent synonymously the sacred incommunicable name of Jehovah, who in the past, present, and future equally, therefore eternally exists; and just as little, in view of the two passages, "We give Thee thanks, O Lord God Almighty, which art, and wast, and art to come, because Thou hast taken to Thyself Thy great power, and hast reigned," xi. 17, and "Thou art righteous, O Lord, which art, and wast, and shalt be, because Thou hast judged thus," xvi. 5, can it be affirmed—as Ewald does, p. 108—that John has merely appropriated the rabbinical formula. The omission in these two places of "who art to come" can have no other ground than that the completion of the divine kingdom is celebrated proleptically. It must be remembered, too, that John does not use *ἐρχόμενος* as synonymous with *ἐσόμενος*, but in the sense of coming to judgment for the final completion of the eternal world-plan. In the rabbinical formula for expressing the eternal existence of God, he has found a formula for His living or energetic eternity. He who was, and is, and is to come, is the God who, as He has revealed Himself in the past in the creation of the world and in the leadership of His people Israel, as also in the present, to the eye of faith, He is active in the government of the world, so in the future He will manifest His power in the decision of all conflicts, the solution of all contradictions and strifes, in the complete establishment in the world of a state of things in harmony with His nature, His purpose, and His promise. He will appear for the judgment of the world and the completion of His kingdom.

Nearly related to the rabbinical name Jehovah in the conceptions of the seer, only of more special application, is the designation of God as "*the Alpha and Omega, the first and the last, the beginning and the end.*" Of these expressions, which all affirm the same thing,—though the first is symbolic, the second Old Testament, and the third more philosophic,—the middle one gives us the key by which we may understand the whole three. It is taken from Isa. xli. 4, xliv. 6, xlviii. 12 (comp. xliii. 10), where God calls Himself the first and the last, that He may encourage firm confidence in the promise given through the prophets. The seer represents God as using in the same sense the above words concerning Himself, "I am the Alpha and the Omega, the

First and the Last, the Beginning and the End,"—that is, "I am He from whom all being proceeds, and to whom it will return; who, as the source of all history, am also the end; who, having called the world into existence, will also terminate it;—I therefore know equally what has happened and what will happen; both are my act and deed, and on what I publish through the prophets as being yet to take place, you may rely with perfect confidence!" It is the Lord God of the spirits of the prophets who thus speaks of Himself, and the predictions of this book are faithful and true, xxii. 6. It is remarkable that we find this self-expression on the part of God only at the beginning and the end of the Apocalypse. It occurs at the beginning, where the Lord God, "which is, and which was, and which is to come, the Almighty," i. 8, confirms the theme-like contents of the preceding verse by the words, "Even so, Amen. I am Alpha and Omega." At the close we find it, xxi. 6, where the prophecy has terminated, and God, repeating His early assurance, says, "I am Alpha and Omega, the beginning and the end." In chap. xxii. 13, where the summary repetition of the prophecy in the verse before is followed by the assurance, "I am Alpha and Omega, the beginning and the end, the first and the last," it is usually supposed that Christ is speaking, but, as we shall see later on, without foundation.

With the two last-mentioned names of God is connected that designation which speaks of Him as *the living God* (ζῶν), as the God who *liveth for ever and ever*. The foundation of this is the Old Testament expression, the living God (comp. Deut. xxxii. 40; 2 Kings xix. 16); but the antithesis to lifeless idols, into which it is almost everywhere brought in the Old Testament, is nowhere to be found in the Apocalypse. The living, or living for ever, here rather represents God as the personal absolute life, in distinction from created, impotent, and temporary life. The living creatures, the representatives of the animated creation, bring to Him who sits on the throne, and who lives for ever and ever, glory, and honour, and thanks, iv. 9; and then, at the same time, the four and twenty elders, the representatives of the first-fruits of all animated creation, worship Him who liveth for ever and ever, and cast their crowns before the throne, and say, "Thou art worthy, O Lord, to receive glory, and honour, and power; for Thou hast created all things, and for Thy pleasure they are and were created," iv. 10. Here God is spoken of as living for ever and ever, because all created, subordinate relative life comes from Him. When the angel, x. 6, swears by Him that liveth for ever, who created heaven and the things that therein are, and the earth and the things that therein are, and the sea and the things which are therein, that there should be time no longer, He is described, as He is also in xv. 7,—where one of the living creatures gives to the seven angels the seven vials full of the wrath of God, of Him who liveth for ever and ever,—as the eternally-living God, because as such He has created all things, and does not stand before the world He has made dead and powerless, or passive, but is angry with the evil which opposes Him, and in His own time must affirm Himself in an active and vigorous manner. Finally, the designation "living God," whose seal the angel has, vii. 2, to seal His servants,—the only place in which the "for ever and ever" is omitted,—can only be based on the principle that He, as the living God, gives such life to His servants as will survive all suffering, and even death itself. The twenty-four elders in their songs of praise, and the servants of God in their being sealed, unquestionably understood Him to be the living, or the eternally-living God, the possessor and giver of eternal life, in the highest sense of these words.

In addition to what has already been mentioned, there appears, often parallel with the predicate, "which is, and which was, and which is to come," and with special emphasis, the designation of God as "*the Almighty*" (comp. i. 8, iv. 8, xi. 17): "I am the Alpha and the Omega," says God, "which is, and which was, and which is to come, the Almighty," i. 8. The living creatures say, "Holy, holy, holy, Lord God Almighty, which was, and is, and is to come," iv. 8; the elders cry, "We give Thee thanks, O Lord God Almighty, which art, and wast, and art to come," xi. 17. The victors sing, "Great and marvellous are Thy works, Lord God Almighty," xv. 3. From the altar there comes forth a voice, saying, "Even so, Lord God Almighty," xvi. 7. The kings of the whole earth are gathered for "the battle of that great day of God Almighty," xvi. 14. The multitude cries, "Alleluia, for the Lord God *Omnipotent* reigneth," xix. 6. Christ "treads the winepress of the fierceness and wrath of Almighty God," xix. 15. John sees no temple in the New Jerusalem, for "the Lord God Almighty and the Lamb are the temple of it," xxi. 22. The designation "Lord God Almighty" represents the Old Testament "Lord God of Hosts," after the example of the LXX. (comp. Amos iv. 13); and that this omnipotence, or absolute power of God, is placed by the seer frequently and emphatically in express contrast with the seemingly unconquerable power of the wicked in the world, hardly needs pointing out.

In a similar position to that of "the first and the last," in its relation to "which is, and which was, and which is to come," there stands, according to the sense, but with a more special application, the designation of God as "the Strong One" (comp. LXX. Deut. x. 17), with reference to that which describes Him as "the Almighty." "Strong is the Lord God who judgeth her," xviii. 8. Connected with this is the might (δύναμις), the power (κράτος), and the strength (ἰσχύς) of God. He has this power even now; it is manifestly so in heaven,—the temple is filled with smoke from the glory of God and from His power, xv. 8,—but He has it not yet for the world; therefore we read, iv. 11, "Thou art worthy, O Lord, to receive—or to take—power," v. 13; "Power for ever and ever is ascribed to Him who sitteth upon the throne, and unto the Lamb," vii. 12; "We give Thee thanks, because Thou hast taken to Thyself Thy great power," xi. 17; "now is come the strength of our God," xii. 10; "power unto the Lord our God," xix. 1. We may also mention here the power (ἐξουσία) ascribed unto Him where men under judgment "blaspheme the name of God, who hath power over these plagues," xvi. 9. Riches (πλοῦτος) are only in one instance ascribed to God, v. 12, in connection with His power.

Again, in a similar manner as the phrase "who liveth for ever" is associated with the words "who was, and is, and is to come," as the more common with the more solemn designation, so "*who sits upon the throne*" is connected with the predicate "Almighty:" "Behold, a throne was set in heaven, and one sat on the throne," iv. 2. Immediately after, God is described as He "who sits on the throne," iv. 9; and this predicate, with the addition of God in vii. 10, xix. 4, is constantly repeated in the course of the visions, and evidently describes Him, in opposition to the visible ungodly course of this world, as the true Lord and Ruler, Judge and King, who, as such, must and will assert Himself. We may here add a few of those predicates of God which are related in meaning. He is several times called the *God of heaven*. By this rendering of the אֱלֹהֵי הַשָּׁמַיִם, found in the later writings of the Old Testament, Ezra i. 2, God, in His exaltation above the earth, is represented as manifesting Himself through His powerful magisterial judgments upon it. It is by this exposition at least, and not by that of Baur (*ut ante*, p. 227),—that He is so called in opposition to the heathen gods,—that we get an acceptable sense of xi. 13, " the remnant" of the holy city " were affrighted, and gave glory to the God of heaven " after the occurrence of a great earthquake in which the tenth part of the city fell, and 7000 men were slain; or of xvi. 11, where " men," evidently the heathen, blasphemed " the God of heaven because of their pains and their sores;" just as, immediately before, xvi. 9, they had blasphemed the name of God, who had power over these plagues. Once He is called "*the God of the earth.*" According to xi. 4, the two witnesses of Christ are " the two olive trees and the two candlesticks standing before the God of the earth." He is so spoken of in this rendering of Zech. iv. 14, because in the name applied to Him lies the truth taught in what immediately follows,—that God can and will, even on earth, arm the two witnesses, as His servants, with miraculous powers, and there protect them from their foes. In like manner, only once, in harmony with Jer. x. 7, is God described as "*King of nations.*" Those who have " gotten the victory " sing, " Just and true are Thy ways, Thou King of nations," xv. 3. While the nations wonder after the beast and worship the dragon that gives him power, xiii. 3, 4, while all the inhabitants unite in paying him homage, xiii. 8, God is still really the King, the righteous Lord, the actual Ruler even of the nations; and when He begins to give proofs of His supremacy through the last plagues, the victors recognise His ways as just and true.

Hitherto we have, so to speak, represented the divine nature according to the statements of this book; we turn now to a consideration of His ethical *character*, and in the first place there comes prominently before us the *holiness* of God. By this the writer understands not merely the opposition of the Divine Being to all evil as that which is against Himself, nor merely His exaltation above all creaturely impurity (Weiss, *bibl. Theol.* p. 616, note), but also the essential difference between Him and all created, imperfect ethical being; therefore His ethical perfection and absolute goodness. " Holy, holy, holy, Lord God, which was, and is, and is to come," iv. 8, exclaim the living creatures (comp. Isa. vi. 3), the representatives of creature life generally, in recognition of the truth that God is for ever exalted over all created and mortal beings; that He is perfect, and as such continually reveals Himself to His creatures. "How long, O Lord, holy and true," say the martyrs, "dost Thou not judge and avenge our blood on them that dwell on the earth!" vi. 10; because, being opposed to evil and against the supremacy of the wicked, He could not regard the oppression of the good with indifference.

It is not the same thing, as Weiss (*bibl. Theol.* p. 616, note), with an entirely unjustifiable appeal to the phraseology of the Apocalypse, against Hahn, p. 102, affirms, though it always expresses some relation to the holiness of God, when He is called the "*only holy*" (ὅσιος); for this expression, which represents the Old Testament חָסִיד or יָשָׁר, and signifies among men conscious reverence for God and the relations ordained by Him, and refers to *religiositas* and *pietas*, can affirm nothing of Him beyond regard for His own sacred ordinances, faithfulness to His own holy laws. This regard or faithfulness—this, so to speak, holy reverence on the part of God—appears once distinctly in contrast with the violation of moral order by demons, when it is said, "Who shall not fear Thee, O Lord, and glorify Thy name? for Thou alone art holy (ὅσιος, *fromm*): for all nations shall come and worship before Thee; for Thy judgments are made manifest," xv. 4. On the other hand, when the angel of the waters says, "Thou art righteous, O Lord, which art, and wast (καὶ ὁ ὅσιος), because Thou hast judged thus," xvi. 5, the holiness of God approaches nearer to a definition and affirmation of His justice as manifesting itself, against existing pretensions, through His righteous judgments.

As *just*, God is spoken of only in the passage above quoted, xvi. 5. His ways are said to be "just and true," xv. 3; His judgments are "true and righteous," xvi. 7, xix. 2. What the writer understands by God's justice we learn from xiii. 10, xiv. 9–11, xviii. 6–8, xxii. 12. It is retribution strictly and accurately corresponding to desert; and the individual acts in which He exercises His justice are called His judgments (δικαιώματα), xv. 4.

By the martyrs God is called the "Lord, holy and *true*" (ἀληθινός), vi. 10. The victors cry, "Just and true are Thy ways," xv. 3. The angel of the waters says to Him, "True and righteous are Thy judgments," xvi. 7; and after the fall of

Babylon, xix. 2, it is said of Him, "True and righteous are His judgments." To the seer it is said, "These are the true sayings of God," xix. 9; and God says to him, "These words are true and faithful," xxi. 5; and once more, in xxii. 6, we find the same affirmation. If we add that Christ is called "the holy and the true," iii. 7,—not the truly holy,—"the Amen, the faithful and true witness," iii. 14, "faithful and true," xix. 11, we have all the places in which "true" occurs. Düsterdieck on iii. 7, appealing to Meyer on John vii. 28, remarks that all interpretations of *ἀληθινός* are false which rest on the supposition that it means as much as *ἀψευδής* or *ἀληθής*;—"real, corresponding with its idea, its name." But he contradicts himself when he affirms that such passages as xxi. 5, xxii. 6, xv. 3, are to be explained according to this representation, for which he quotes the LXX. Isa. lxv. 16; on the other hand, he refers to xv. 3, also to the LXX. on Deut. xxxii. 4. It hardly needs to be shown how, according to his view, the "true" in vi. 10 gives a weak, in xv. 3, xvi. 7, xix. 2 a scarcely tolerable, and in xxi. 5, xxii. 6 no sense at all; nor especially how the writer, with the single exception of xvi. 7, subjects the "true" to the co-ordinate predicate, while in the sense of "real" it should precede it. For this reason I understand "true" in the ethical sense, in opposition to the morally false, not giving place to the deceptive, word-breaking, traitorous, but applied to the true Lord as to one who fulfils His promises and threatenings; to the true ways and judgments of God as such, in which both promises and threats have accomplished themselves; to the true words of God as such, whose contents of promises and threats will be fulfilled; and it is applied in a similar sense to Christ as it is to God Himself. If we thus understand the "true," we get a good sense in all the places where it is found; we see how the author everywhere, excepting xvi. 7, makes it a subordinate predicate, and also how he can in a single instance make it the predominant one; even when this solitary exception comes before us in the Old Testament in Düsterdieck's sense,—as, for example, in Jer. ii. 21, Zech. viii. 3, —it is still undeniably the moral import that is prominent there, and, as by our author, is equally presupposed (comp. Deut. xxv. 15, xxxii. 4; Isa. xxv. 1, xxxviii. 3, lxv. 16; Job ii. 3, viii. 6).

God Himself is never called *faithful* (reliable, sure, certain) (*πιστός*) in the Apocalypse, but it is said, xxi. 5, that the words spoken immediately before by Him who sits on the throne, and which include the contents of the prophecy, are "faithful and true;" the same assurance is given, xxii. 6, by the angel concerning what has preceded, which, according to i. 1, is a revelation from God.

The *wisdom* of God is twice mentioned in doxologies, v. 12, vii. 12.

Of the *emotional* characteristics, states, dispositions, and excitements in God there is hardly anything mentioned in the Apocalypse, except wrath (ὀργὴ, πρόσωπον), indignation (θυμός), fierce anger; and certainly these are mentioned very frequently and emphatically, vi. 16, 17 (comp. Ps. ii. 5, xxxiv. 17), xi. 18, xiv. 10 (comp. Ps. lx. 5, lxxv. 9; Isa. li. 17–22; Jer. xxv. 15, xlix. 12), xiv. 19 (comp. Joel iii. 18; Isa. lxiii. 1-6; Jer. xxv. 30–33), xv. 1, 7, xvi. 1, 19, xix. 15, xx. 11 (comp. xviii. 3, 6). Baur (p. 227), with some plausibility, affirms that the most prominent attribute in the Apocalypse is the avenging justice or wrath of God (comp. Köstlin, p. 483); for where can we find mention of His love, grace, compassion, long-suffering, etc.? But has the seer really omitted all reference to these features of the divine character? The face, the anger, the wrath, the fierce indignation of God is directed against the godless world, and therefore cannot but be regarded as love, grace, and mercy toward His servants. Indeed it is the holy God, their Lord and Ruler, who is angry, and whose anger burns against His enemies, who are their persecutors and oppressors. If He were not angry, they might doubt His love; and the more displeased He is, the more heartily do they rejoice in Him as their God. Comp. vi. 9–11, xix. 1–5. When we think of this, we find that the Apocalypse, from beginning to end, is really full of indirect assurances and proofs of the love of God, and that it is so even in the repeated publication of terrible judgments. At the same time, much as the direct mention of God's love is suppressed, and great as the necessity was, from the nature of the book, that it should be, it is not entirely wanting, if we keep in mind God's relation to His people in the past, the present, or the future. He had communicated to His servants the prophets His secret, His designs with respect to the world and mankind, as a joy-inspiring message, x. 7. After the child, a symbol of Christ, had been taken up to God and His throne, the woman, the church, fled into the wilderness, where she had a place prepared by God, that she should be nourished there 1260 days, xii. 6. There were given unto her two wings of a great eagle, that she might fly to her place in the wilderness, that she might be nourished a time, and times, and half a time, from the face of the serpent, xii. 14. The serpent cast out of its mouth water as a flood after the woman, that it might carry her away; but the earth helped the woman, and opened its mouth, and swallowed up the flood, xii. 16. The author wishes "grace and peace" to his readers "from Him which is, and which was, and which is to come," i. 4. An angel comes from the east with the seal of the living God, and says to the four angels to whom it was given to hurt the earth and the sea, "Hurt not the earth, neither the sea, nor the trees, until we have sealed the servants of our God in their foreheads," vii. 2, 3. Those who overcome are in heaven, clothed in white before the throne of God, and serve Him day and night in His temple: and He that sits on the throne shall dwell among them. They shall hunger no more, neither thirst any more; neither shall the sun light on them, nor any heat. For the Lamb, which is in the midst of the throne, shall feed them, and shall lead them unto living fountains of waters; and God shall wipe away all tears from their eyes, vii. 15–17. It is said of the heavenly state, "Behold, the tabernacle of God is with men, and He will dwell with them, and they shall be His people, and God Himself shall be with them, and be their God. And God shall wipe away all tears from their eyes; and there shall be no more death, neither sorrow, nor crying, neither shall there be any more pain," xxi. 3, 4. He who sits on the throne says, "I will give unto him that is athirst of the fountain of the water of life freely. He that overcometh shall inherit all things; and I will be his God, and he shall be my son," xxi. 6, 7. With all this we may compare the promises at the close of the book, and observe how the seer conceives of the relation of Christ and of God, and speaks of the connection of the former with His people, and it will be with difficulty that any one will say that John knew nothing of a God of love; or affirm, with Baur, p. 229, that the Christian idea of the Fatherhood of God, much as it goes against the Old Testament doctrine of His sovereign power, may still have come into his consciousness through His being called the Father of the Messiah. Certainly God bears the name of Father only in a Messianic sense, but He cherishes the fatherly disposition to all who belong to Him through Christ. (See also what follows.)

There only remain for consideration the *symbolic representations* of the divine nature. It is said, "Behold, a throne was set in heaven, and one sat on the throne. And he that sat was to look upon like a jasper and a sardine stone: and there was a rainbow (ἶρις) round about the throne, in sight like unto an emerald," iv. 2, 3. For this representation the author is dependent mainly upon Ezek. i. 26–28 (comp. viii. 2, x. 1; Dan. vii. 9, 10); but for the bow, upon Gen. ix. 12, 13. That the colours should not merely represent the glory of God in general, but should each have a special signification, is clearly in harmony with the manner of the book. Expositors agree, and with tolerable unanimity, that the author means by a sardine stone, a precious stone of a red colour; by a jasper (comp. xxi. 11, 18, 19), a transparent and brilliant crystal, probably our diamond; and that by the emerald a green stone is meant. The appearance as of jasper is designed to represent the holiness; that of a sardine stone, the anger or avenging justice; and that of the bow, like an emerald, the grace of God. Düsterdieck has unquestionably given the meaning of the whole when he says, p. 219, "Here, where the eternal and personal cause of what follows is represented, the glorious holiness and justice of God appear in the closest connection with His unchangeable grace, so that the entire approaching development of the kingdom of God and the world until the end of time, as decided by the wonderful, unique nature of the holy, just, and gracious One, as well in its course as in its end, must correspond to this threefold glory of the living God." With iv. 2, 3 we associate xv. 8; after one of the living creatures had given to the seven angels the seven vials full of the wrath of God, who liveth for ever and ever, it is said the temple was filled with smoke from the glory of the Lord, and from His power; so that no man was able to enter the temple until the seven plagues of the seven angels were fulfilled. Here such passages as Ex. xl. 34, 35 (comp. Ex. xix. 18, 19, xx. 18; Num. xiv. 10, xvi. 19; 1 Kings viii. 10, 11; Isa. vi. 3, 4) must have been present to the mind of the writer. The smoke with which the temple was filled proceeds from the presence of God in His glory and power; and since He cannot be approached, no one can enter the temple while He is there, which will be until the seven last plagues are fulfilled. Thus the author clothes the thought that the prayers of Christians (comp. vi. 9, 10, viii. 3, 4, xv. 2, 3) are heard, and that now the last and most terrible judgments of God will certainly come, and, as Ewald says, all prayer and labour and effort end. Naturally, in distinction from iv. 2, the grace of God becomes subordinate. His glory (δόξα) is here the appearance of God as a consuming fire, and with fierce anger, of one powerfully executing His displeasure, and therefore with the glory there is expressly mentioned the power of God. Again, we connect with iv. 2, 3 and xv. 8 a few passages in chap. xxi. and xxii. In the description of the New Jerusalem, it is said, xxi. 11, to have "the glory of God;" its light—rather its light-giver or illuminator (φωστήρ, comp. the LXX. Gen. i. 14, 16; Wisd. xiii. 2; Sir. xliii. 7)—was like the most precious stone, the brightness of crystal or crystalline jasper. "The city had no need of the sun, neither of the moon, to shine in it; for the glory of God did lighten it, and the Lamb is the light thereof," xxi. 23. "There shall be no night there; and they need no candle, neither light of the sun; for the Lord God giveth them light," xxii. 5. Very naturally, again, the red sardine stone of iv. 3, or the glory and power from which the smoke goes forth, xv. 8, as well as the bow, like a green emerald, iv. 3, disappear, and only the jasper of crystal clearness remains as an image of God; for, with the end of the old world and its sins, the nature of God can no longer manifest itself either as wrath or as grace, but as holiness. We see from this threefold representation of the divine glory—for the δόξα is also represented in iv. 2, 3—that to the seer, as indeed the thrice holy of the four living creatures distinctly says, holiness is the ethical basis of the divine nature. But, generally, holiness—symbolized by the crystal jasper, the rainbow, the smoke, and the luminary of the New Jerusalem—is with him in meaning similar to light, or the nature of light. But of the ethical nature of God, sun and moon and the light of the candle are only transient and insufficient images, and in the final state fall away. God is light—light which to evil is like a consuming fire, to a sinful world like a rainbow of mercy after the storm of avenging justice, bringing consolation and peace, and which, in the consummation of all things, will stream forth still more brightly, inspiring with life and happiness.

(b.) *The Works of God.*

God *created* the world. The elders say, "Thou hast created all things (τὰ πάντα), and for Thy pleasure (θέλημα) they are and were created," iv. 11. The angel swears "by Him that liveth for ever and ever, who created heaven and the things that therein are, and the sea and things which are therein," x. 6. "Worship Him," said the angel, "that made heaven and earth, and the sea, and the fountains of waters," xiv. 7. Twice we find the words, "since the foundation (καταβολή) of the world," xiii. 8, xvii. 8.

God *governs* the world. As already observed, Christ speaks of the throne of His Father, iii. 21; and John, iv. 2, sees a throne standing in heaven, and one sitting upon it; so almost throughout our book God is called "He who sits on the throne." He is *King*, in all the ancient meaning of the word, over all things which He has made. Therefore all that transpires in the world is willed of God, and a necessity; hence the oft-recurring expression δεῖ (comp. i. 1, iv. 1, xi. 5, xiii. 10, xvii. 10, xx. 3, xxii. 6), and especially the interchange of μέλλει and δεῖ, i. 19 and i. 1, xvii. 8 and xvii. 10 (comp. xx. 7 and xx. 3), and ἐδόθη or δώσω (comp. vi. 4, 8, vii. 2, ix. 1, 5, xi. 3, xii. 14, xiii. 5, 7, 14, xvii. 17). Here also may belong that which was said to the martyrs, namely, that they should "rest for a little season, until their fellow-servants and their brethren that should be killed, as they were, should be fulfilled" (full numbered, πληρώθωσιν; comp. Rom. xi. 25). It is a fixed number who, according to the divine will, will suffer martyrdom. But certain as it is that God is truly King of all the earth, still He is not so in manifest reality, neither in the existing condition of the world nor in the acknowledgment of men. The cause of this is in the devil, who deceives the whole world, xii. 9, as will be more fully shown in the sections on the devil, and on the earth and its inhabitants. The aim of the divine government is therefore opposed to him, bringing to men deliverance or salvation (σωτηρία), and to God Himself the sovereignty, or the kingdom, the real kingship over the world (βασιλεία). Both, in their full significance and perfection, form the contents or subject of the mystery, the mystery of God (μυστήριον), which, as glad tidings, He has communicated (εὐαγγέλισε), x. 7, to His servants the prophets, and since the birth of the predicted child, chap. xii., gradually more fully unfolded until it is complete (ἐτελέσθη, x. 7; comp. xv. 8, xvii. 17; γέγοναν, xxi. 6). At every stage of its development this completion is, by anticipation, celebrated in heaven. After the casting out of the dragon, a loud voice says in heaven, "Now is come salvation, and strength, and the kingdom of our God, and the power of His Christ," xii. 10. At the sounding of the seventh trumpet there are voices in heaven saying, "The kingdoms of this world are become the kingdoms of our Lord and of His Christ, and He shall reign for ever and ever," xi. 15; and the elders also say, "We give Thee thanks, O Lord God Almighty, which art, and wast, and art to come, because Thou hast taken (εἴληφας: received and taken) to Thyself Thy great power, and reigned," xi. 17 (ἐβασίλευσας: become and made Himself King). After the fall of Babylon, the seer heard much people in heaven saying, "Alleluia; Salvation, and glory, and honour, and power, unto the Lord our God," xix. 1; and "Alleluia: for the Lord God omnipotent reigneth," xix. 6. But as, at every stage of the development of the whole, the inhabitants of heaven thus express themselves, so also departed Christians, as they enter heaven, anticipate the completion of the divine purposes, and exclaim, "Salvation unto our God, which sitteth upon the throne, and unto the Lamb," vii. 10; and the angels joyfully unite in their song of praise, vii. 11, 12. But by what means does God work out this salvation and the establishment of His supremacy? By His "just and true ways" xv. 3 (comp. Ps. cxlv. 17; Deut. xxxii. 4). His "true and righteous judgments," xvi. 7, xix. 2 (comp. xviii. 20). His "judgments," xv. 4 (comp. Ex. ix. 16, xiv. 17, 18; Ps. cxxvi. 2; Mic. vii. 16–18). This is symbolically represented to us when John sees going out from the throne lightnings, and thunderings, and voices; and seven lamps burning before the throne, which are the seven Spirits of God: and a sea spreading out before it as clear as crystal, iv. 5, 6. The lightnings, and thunderings, and voices represent God's avenging justice or manifestations of wrath in the world (comp. Ex. xix. 16; Ps. xviii. 8–10, xxix. 3, 4, l. 3, xcvii. 1, 2), and correspond to the red sardine stone in the picture of the divine majesty. The seven lamps John himself interprets; he tells us they are the seven Spirits which, according to v. 6, are sent into all the world through the mediation of Christ, and correspond to the green emerald, iv. 3, the image of grace in the representation of God;

and finally, the sea of glass, clear as crystal, which appears in xv. 2 mingled with fire, is a representation which originated in a combination of Ezek. i. 22–28 with Ex. xxiv. 10, perhaps also with the narrative of the passage of the Israelites through the Red Sea and the destruction of the Egyptians; and as a sea represents immeasurableness and profundity, comp. Ps. xxxvi. 6, as a sea of glass, the holiness of God (comp. xxi. 11); as mingled with fire, holiness manifesting itself in wrath, but as a whole reminding us of the righteous deeds of God resulting on the one hand from the avenging judgments of God, and on the other from the Spirit's work, and so corresponds to the crystal sea of the former representation, iv. 6. Just as the description of God directly represents the personal author, so the symbolism of the lightnings, the voices and thunders, the lamps and the sea of glass, pictorially represents the real contents of what follows. According to another view, namely, that of a secret purpose of God, which is revealed by Him to Christ, and through Christ to His prophets, these contents appear under the image of a book. This book the seer, being in the spirit, sees in the right hand of Him who sits on the throne, and finds it written within and without, that is, on both sides, or full of writing, and sealed with seven seals—that is, securely sealed or perfectly secret, v. 1; but the Lamb receives or takes the book from the hand of God, v. 7, and one after the other opens the seals, vi. 1. This sealed book relates to the mystery of God, which He made known to the prophets of the Old Testament, x. 7, in a similar manner as the little open book which the seer afterwards took from the hand of the angel and ate, x. 8–10; it interprets the counsel of God in a special revelation. The "mystery" is the contents of all Old Testament prophecies; the "book" contains the entire predictions of the Apocalypse; "the little book," the predictions concerning the antichristian powers, as they appear onward from the twelfth chapter. As the contents of "the book" unfold themselves in the several visions of the Apocalypse, so our representation will introduce them in the course of its various sections; we need not, however, expect to hear of the work of God in sending Christ, which is certainly presupposed by the Apocalypse, and is, as it were, recalled only in one aspect in chap. xii., and that merely from the point of eschatology at which the seer, chap. iv. and v., placed himself.

2. Angels.

To the dragon and his angels, xii. 7–9, the seer opposes Michael and his angels, which he calls the *holy* angels, xiv. 10, "the armies of heaven" following Christ at His coming, and elsewhere simply "the angels." Expositors are not agreed whether the four angels which stand at the four corners of the earth, and which hold the four winds, and to whom it is given to hurt the earth and the sea, vii. 1, 2; further, whether the star which falls from heaven, and to whom is given the key of the bottomless pit, ix. 1,—where, as in xii. 4, Düsterdieck *in loco* correctly observes there is a union of the symbol of a star with that of an angel, as in the Old Testament conception of the heavenly hosts, Ps. ciii. 21, Jer. xxxiii. 22, Job xxxviii. 7 (comp. Ewald, p. 202); and further, whether the angel of the bottomless pit, the leader of the locusts, called Abaddon and Apollyon, ix. 11,—not to be confounded with the fallen star, ix. 1;—and lastly, whether the four angels bound in the great river Euphrates, who, on their liberation, lead an army of horsemen, ix. 14,—are to be understood as good or evil, the angels of God or of Satan. Individual expressions may be quoted in favour of the latter idea;—it was given to them to be injurious (comp. ix. 10, 19, and xiii. 5); a star fell from heaven (comp. xii. 4, 9). On the other hand, see xx. 1, Apollyon (comp. xvii. 8, 11) bound and loosed (comp. xx. 2, 3). At the same time, these angels do not evidently belong to the angels of Satan, xii. 7–9, nor to the demons, ix. 20, for they are not in the service of the dragon, but in the service of God. I think the seer himself would have been perplexed had the alternative been placed before him: good or evil? angels of God or of Satan? Decidedly, as with him God and the devil, the kingdom of God and the kingdom of the world, stand over against each other, he has still not carried out this dualism to its ultimate results. In the sphere of evil there is rather a certain indefiniteness; while it originates in departure from God, it must still serve His sacred purposes. Thus the angels of the destructive winds, the fallen star, the angels of the Euphrates, are not the holy angels of God, but fallen angels, to whom the liberty is given to bring upon men the plagues decreed of God. They have the same significance as in the Old Testament, for example, the Destroyer in 2 Sam. xxiv. 16.

The *multitude* of the angels serving God seems to the seer innumerable. He writes, v. 11: "And I beheld, and I heard the voice of many angels round about the throne, and the beasts, and the elders; and the number of them was ten thousand times ten thousand, and thousands of thousands" (comp. Dan. vii. 10). He represents them as differing from each other: he sees "a strong angel proclaiming with a loud voice," v. 2. "Another mighty angel comes down from heaven, clothed with a cloud, and a rainbow upon his head, and his face as it were the sun, and his feet as pillars of fire," x. 1 (comp. i. 14, 15). In xviii. 1 he says: "I saw another angel come down from heaven, having great power; and the earth was lightened with his glory;" and in ver. 21 of the same chapter we read that "a mighty angel took up a stone like a great millstone, and cast it into the sea." That these "strong angels," as Hoekstra, p. 373, note, finds probable, are the seven archangels who stand in the presence of God, does not follow from the term "strong;" rather, as Weiss (*bibl. Theol.* p. 618) thinks, and especially from the fact that their features are suggestive of the divine glory, x. 1, xvii. 1, they belong to higher *orders* generally. The acquaintance of the seer with the Jewish angelology is shown in viii. 2: "And I saw the seven angels which stood before God; and to them were given seven trumpets" (comp. ver. 6, xvii. 1, xxi. 9), for by these can be understood only the seven angel princes or archangels (comp. Dan. x. 13; Tob. xii. 15; 1 Thess. iv. 16). When Hoekstra (p. 370, note), after the example of others, declares that the seven angels are doubtless identical with the seven Spirits of God, i. 4, iv. 5, v. 6, his conclusion is based upon a common misconception of the "Spirits" in the Apocalypse; where these are accepted in their true meaning, no refutation is needed.

But while the same angel is evidently charged by God, now with one mission and now with another,—to this class certainly belong the angels who showed visions to the seer, xvii. 1 (comp. xxi. 9), interpreted, xvii. 7, symbolically represented the future, x. 1–11, xviii. 21, or made announcements, xiv. 8–10, 15, 16, xv. 1–3; further, the angel with the seal of God, vii. 2, the angel with the key of the bottomless pit, xx. 1 (against Hoekstra's *Seal and Key Angel*, p. 373), is evidently also the angel who presents the prayers of saints before God, viii. 3, 4,—other angels have undeniably their distinct office, their fixed position and *special calling.* Such we have already found in the four angels who stand at the four corners of the earth and hold back the four winds, vii. 2, and the angel of the bottomless pit, ix. 11, and the angels bound on the river Euphrates, ix. 14, also the angel who comes out from the altar and had power over fire, xiv. 18,—not merely the fire of the altar, viii. 5, which is not here in question, but fire in general, in its judicial signification as the image and means of the divine displeasure. In addition to these, there is the angel of the waters, xvi. 5. The Rabbis speak of angels placed over earth, sea, fire, and other departments of nature; indeed, they know their very names. Not only have the various elements and kingdoms of nature their own angels in the Apocalypse, but so also have the various spheres in the world of men. Michael appears, xii. 7 (comp. Dan. x. 13, xii. 1), as the guardian angel of God's people, or the church; and then, again, each individual church has its own angel, for, according to i. 16, Christ holds in His right hand the seven stars; and we find in i. 20 that these stars are angels of the seven churches; and to these angels the seer writes seven letters, each of which begins, "To the angel of the church at ——, write!" These angels of the churches are personified representations of the spirit of the churches. It is common to give other interpretations. Bunsen (*Ignatius,* p. 85) sees in them monarchical bishops; Rothe (*Anfänge der Kirche,* p. 423) finds them to be the expression of the idea of a monarchical episcopate. Ritschl (*Entstehung der Altkatholischen Kirche,* p. 409) conceives of them as superintending colleges. Ewald, *ut ante,* p. 115, takes angel in the sense of mediator or messenger, as in Hagg. i. 13, Mal. ii. 7, Eccles. v. 5, and considers the angels of the churches to be their representatives (comp. Köstlin, *ut ante,* p. 487). Ritschl grants, however, that the relation of the superscriptions, and the conclusions of the letters, favours the idea that the angel may be regarded only as a symbolic representation of the church, after the analogy of the guardian angel. Each of these views fails when it comes to be considered in detail; and the only thing that can be said against the interpretation I have offered is, that both churches and angels have already their symbols,—one the candlestick, the other the star,—and that a symbol cannot again be symbolized; but this difficulty disappears when we consider that the angel of the church is not the symbol of the church, but is the church itself in one of its two aspects. While "the church" is an assembly in one place of individual Christians of every variety, and who are therefore variously regarded and treated by Christ, "the angel of the church" represents it as a unity, an organization, as a moral person, a living whole, in which one member depends upon and affects the others, and where all are mutually responsible for each other, in which a definite spirit reigns, and by which one church is distinguished from another. The angel of the church is the general spirit of the church personified. A leaning to the rabbinical doctrine of the ἄγγελος ἔφορος is not to be mistaken (comp. Düsterdieck's full and striking exposition of i. 20, p. 132, etc.).

According to i. 1, Jesus Christ sent and signified by *His* angel to His servant John what should shortly come to pass. In xxii. 16 it is said: "I, Jesus, have sent *mine* angel to testify unto you these things in the churches;" and in xxii. 6 we read that "the Lord God of the holy prophets sent *His* angel to show unto His servants things which must shortly be done." It has been perplexing to expositors that the *angelus interpres* supposed to be mentioned in these places does not appear everywhere in the book; it is also disputed whether he may be regarded as the conductor of John in all the visions where he is not mentioned, or where another appears; or whether he had nothing more to do than to place John in the ecstasy; or whether he is to be taken generically, and is intended to include all the angels which in the various visions discharge the duty of interpreting signs; or whether we are only to think of him as the angel who in chap. xvii. expounds to John the chief subject of the whole revelation, speaks with him in xix. 9, shows him the bride, the Lamb's wife, and the last great feature of the book, xxi. 9, the river of the water of life, xxii. 1, also announces himself as an angel sent of God, xxii. 6, and who is mostly intended where the heavenly voice speaks with the prophet, as in i. 10–12, iv. 1, x. 4–8, xiv. 3, xxi. 3, or where the speaker is not definitely distinguished, xix. 9 (?). Recently Hoekstra has endeavoured to prove, pp. 373, etc., 397, etc., that the angel who appears in x. 1 represents Christ, and is His angel in a special sense, as it were, a second self (comp. xiv. 14, 17), and therefore after the Old Testament manner speaks as Christ Himself (comp. xi. 3). So far as I can see, an angelic representative of Christ never comes into the book; even the angel of the tenth chapter is not shown to be a representative of Christ either through his symbols—the rainbow (comp. iv. 3), the cloud (comp. i. 7, xiv. 14), his appearance as the sun (comp. i. 16), his feet as pillars of fire (comp. i. 15)—or by his deeds —he holds in his hand the little book (comp. v. 6), gives commandment to prophesy, swears that there should be delay no longer,— but appears as a messenger of God who discharges his commission with corresponding glory. There are no internal grounds for thinking of the angel of Christ as interpreter only from chap. xvii. onward; and the idea is utterly destroyed when we remember that one of the vial-angels cannot at the same time be a specific angel of God or Christ. The mere translating into ecstasy cannot be regarded as showing the future. Nor is it possible, moreover, in those visions where another speaks, to think of the angel of Christ, in addition, as the companion of the prophet. The generic conception of the angel of God or of Christ avoids these difficulties, but leaves it unexplained how this angel can show all, and even speak to the seer in voices and persons which do not belong to angels (see especially xi. 3). There seems to be no alternative but to regard xxii. 8 as not referring to the angel of the Lord and the general contents of the revelation, but only to the last mentioned vial-angel and his interpretations,—which, by the way, sheds an important light upon the different position of the seer with relation to his own and to ancient predictions,—and by the angel of Christ or of God to understand the *personification so far as it respects the seer of the whole revealing activity of God or Christ.* With this idea alone can we reconcile the fact that now this angel and now that, sometimes indeed a voice, the voice of God or Christ Himself, speaks to the seer; and it is only on this principle that we can explain the manner in which, xxii. 6, the angel speaks of the angel of God being sent; and finally, this alone gives a representation in harmony with itself.

Twice John falls at the feet of the angel who had spoken to him, to *worship him,* xix. 10, xxii. 9; and at the first time the angel said to him: "See thou do it not: I am thy fellow-servant, and of thy brethren that have the testimony of Jesus: worship God!" The second time he said: "See thou do it not: for I am thy fellow-servant, and of thy brethren the prophets, and of them which keep the sayings of this book: worship God!" Köstlin,

p. 483, finds in these places a protest against angel-worship, for which there may have been frequent occasion, Col. ii. 18 (comp. Baur, p. 227, also Ewald, p. 330, who applies here the words: "the measure of a man, that is, of the angel"); but if we notice the two passages immediately preceding those quoted, xix. 9, xxii. 7, and consider that the angel does not found his objection upon the circumstance that the offered worship would affect the honour of God, but rather that of the seer, and if we remember that the latter makes the angels speak of *their* God, and also that he thinks of them as in a specially near and intimate relation to Him, —indeed, Hoekstra, p. 373, on account of v. 11, vii. 11, would place them among the redeemed, since they stand nearer the throne; but this reason, founded upon local symbolism, would also place them amongst the four living creatures,—it appears simpler to abstain from side blows or innuendos, for which there is no reason in the connection, and to seek the cause of the seer's falling down in the supposition that, overcome and carried away by a sense of the importance of the message, he testified his reverence for the messenger, and to find therein, as well as in the refusal of the angel, the reply to the question: Is it possible that a man should know the true word and counsel of God? Answer: Yes, wonderful as it is, the prophets, and through them, Christians generally, become acquainted even with the mysteries of God. It is not against the worship of angels that the seer protests; but he thus symbolizes the glory of the Christian, and especially of those among them who are the instruments of the Holy Spirit.

Should any man, from the nearness of the numberless angels to the elders and the living creatures, v. 11, which, at all events, we must recognise as real *symbols*, draw the conclusion that the author regarded the angels as nothing different, he would shoot far beyond the mark. John decidedly believed in the existence of angels in the sense of supernatural personal beings, concrete spirits, engaged in the service of God; and not merely in angels generally, but in angelic orders, angels of the waters and of fire. But, on the other hand, he who, every time an angel comes on the scene, assumes an angelic appearance to the seer, or at the word "angel" thinks of a concrete personality, has certainly not formed a correct idea of the matter. These representations rather move to and fro in easy transition between the vision of an operative idea and that of an instrumental personality. What

Baur says, p. 228, is certainly true, though in a different sense than he intended, that "angels play a leading part in the Apocalypse." And when Lücke (*Versuch einer vollst Einleit. in die Offenbarung des Johannes*, p. 740) finds serious difficulty in the fact that in this book angels are the bearers of revelation, it is important to observe that the angel of the Lord is not the bearer of revelation, but the personally represented revelation itself, so to say, the spirit of revelation; while all the rest, without prejudice to the question of the existence of angels, in the view of the writer, are here, as in so many Christian poems since, used as poetic methods of representation.

3. Heaven.

The creation, as a consistent whole, is described by the seer in the following expressions as the *world:* "the kingdoms of this world," xi. 15; "the foundation of the world," xiii. 8, xvii. 18. Speaking of its various parts collectively, he designates it "all things," iv. 11. In frequent descriptions of the same, according to its principal divisions, there are at the bottom two different conceptions, which to some extent remind us of Paul's dichotomy and trichotomy of man, which stand side by side with each other (comp. 1 Cor. vii. 34; 1 Thess. v. 23). According to the ancient popular conception, all created things are divided into heaven and earth, Gen. i. 1. From this originates the apocalyptic idea of earth and heaven fleeing before the face of Him who sits on the throne, xx. 11; and the appearance of a new heaven and a new earth, xxi. 1. It is not an essentially different idea, but only a poetical modification, when the seer represents the angel as swearing "by Him that liveth for ever, who created heaven and the things that are therein, and the earth and the things that therein are, and the sea and things which are therein," x. 6; also when he writes, xxi. 1, "The first heaven and the first earth were passed away, and there was no more sea;" and when he represents the angel as demanding homage for Him who "made heaven, and earth, and the sea, and the fountains of water," xiv. 7. With these passages we may compare the subjects of the four first trumpet and vial plagues, viii. 7–12, xvi. 2–9. On the other hand, when the seer writes: "No man in heaven, nor in earth, neither under the earth, was able to open the book, neither to look thereon," v. 3, he expresses, even if his tripartite division flows from Ex. xx. 4 (comp. Ewald, *ut ante*, p. 165), a later and more learned conception, which divides the universe into heaven, earth, and the lower world. Again, it is not an essentially different, but the same idea poetically modified, when he says, v. 13: "every creature which is in heaven, and on the earth, and under the earth, and such as are in the sea, and all that are in them," etc.

Far more seldom do the names of the various spheres of creation serve our author to distinguish all sensible things in their principal divisions, than to symbolize locally the different departments of being. In this sense he generally makes only a twofold division, *heaven* and *earth*; but here and there he adds to these two a third, not, however, under the name of the under world,—we use the term only in its natural sense,—but under that of the "*abyss*" or pit. According to this, all existence appears to the seer to be divided generally into heaven, or the superearthly, divine, and ideal sphere of existence; earth, or the earthly, human, middle sphere; and the abyss, or the subearthly (infernal), diabolical, anti-ideal sphere: the earth is the theatre and subject of the history, of the unfolding and development of the struggle between heaven and hell, God and the devil, the ideal and the anti-ideal. For the present we have to do with heaven, the first or highest of these spheres.

By *heaven* with its sun and moon, vi. 12, and stars, viii. 13, its "midst" or zenith, viii. 13, xiv. 6, xix. 17, and birds xix. 17, under the heaven, the stars of which fall to the earth, and which departs "as a scroll when it is rolled together," vi. 13, 14, is unquestionably to be understood the heaven *perceptible to the senses*; and with this signification it is often mentioned. But more frequently, where the seer speaks of heaven poetically (comp. Isa. xliv. 23, xlix. 13), not dogmatically (comp. 2 Cor. xii. 2; Eph. iv. 10),—Ewald finds, p. 217, a distinct reference to the seven heavens in x. 2–4,—he means heaven in the peculiar, tropical, higher, and spiritual sense of the word, the one and indeed the *highest and chief region of all existence.*

How does this heaven appear? It is the tabernacle or dwelling, or, according to the Mosaic designation, the sanctuary of God, xiii. 6, xxi. 3, xv. 5 (comp. vii. 15, xii. 12; comp. Ex. xxvi. 1–3, xxxiii. 7–9 et passim). It has a door which is opened, and by which the seer being in the spirit enters, and becomes acquainted with the things to be seen there, iv. 1. In it there stands a throne, a semicircular divan (comp. iv. 6, vii. 17), upon which God is seated, iv. 2; around this throne are twenty-four thrones, upon which sit the twenty-four elders, iv. 4. From the throne proceed lightnings, and thunderings, and voices, iv. 5, and before it are seven lamps of fire, iv. 5, and also a sea of glass like unto crystal, iv. 6. In the midst, before the throne, and around the throne, are four living creatures, iv. 6. In the midst of the throne and of the four living creatures, and in the midst of the elders, is a Lamb, v. 6, vii. 17, and around them John heard the voice of many angels, v. 11. We read also that the temple of God, iii. 12, vii. 15, xi. 19, xiv. 15, 17, xv. 5, 6, 8, xvi. 1, 17,—comp. xi. 1, the temple of the tabernacle of the testimony, that is, the temple pertaining to and having within it the Holy of Holies,—is in heaven, xv. 5. We hear more particularly of the ark of testimony, xi. 19; of the altar of burnt-offerings, vi. 9, viii. 3, 5, xiv. 18, xvi. 7, comp. xi. 1; and of an altar of incense, distinguished from the other as "the golden altar," viii. 3, xix. 13. Many expositors suppose that these altars are the same, corresponding completely neither to the altar of incense nor to the altar of burnt-offering in the earthly temple. But we cannot understand why the seer should speak of the same altar sometimes with the adjective "golden" and sometimes without; and still less why he should confound the two well-known altars in the earthly sanctuary, when he intends by the altar only that which belongs to the altar of burnt-offering, and by the golden altar what belongs to the altar of incense (comp. Winer, *s.v.*). Most expositors understand Mount Sion, xiv. 1, upon which John saw the Lamb and the 144,000, in a literal sense. But the passages vi. 14, xiii. 1, 11, xii. 1, 7, quoted by Düsterdieck, p. 462 *ut ante*, are inconclusive. That the seer heard a voice from heaven, xiv. 2, does not compel us to suppose an earthly locality when he deals so freely with the heavenly topography; and there is nothing in the contents of ver. 3 which suits the hill of Sion. All that is said by expositors in explanation presupposes an ideal region. The choice can only be between De Wette's idea, according to which Mount Sion is the earthly mountain of that name, not, however, in reality, but in apocalyptic vision; or, more correctly, and according to the analogy of the holy city and the temple in chap. xi., the ideal locality of the church of God on earth, and the conception according to which we have to look for Mount Sion, analogous to the New Jerusalem, in heaven. The striking parallel in Heb. xii. 22 decides in favour of the second; the undoubted contrast to the sea, xiii. 1, and to the earth, xiii. 11, prepares the mind to expect a heavenly locality; and the harpers and singers of ver. 2 certainly do not differ from the 144,000 who alone (comp. ii. 17, xix. 12) could learn the new song; consequently the 144,000 are conceived of as in heaven, with which alone the aorists "defiled," "redeemed," and "found," in vers. 4, 5 agree; so I decide for Mount Sion as a region in heaven. From this heaven and from God John saw the New Jerusalem descend in the final state, xxi. 2 (comp. ver. 10, iii. 12; comp. Heb. xi. 10, 16, xii. 22, 28, xiii. 14; Gal. iv. 26). Certainly, in view of all these particulars, there is strong temptation to construct a topography of heaven, as the Rabbis did for themselves on the basis of such passages as Ex. xxv. 9, 40; Isa. ii. 2; Mic. iv. 1; Joel iii. 5; Zech. i. 8–10: heaven the archetype of Jerusalem, the hill of Zion, the city of the King, the sanctuary with all its parts. The fact cannot be denied, that this rabbinical topography of heaven, everything that is holy, sublime, and beautiful on earth, a copy of things in heaven, the embodiment of an idea, the representation of an ideal, has been recognised and used by the seer. But when we notice how, in ii. 7, he speaks of the tree of life in the paradise of God, and, vii. 17, of the living fountains of waters, which involve a wholly different representation than the usual one; how he places, viii. 3, the altar of incense before the throne; and how he, xvi. 17, hears a great voice out of the temple of heaven from the throne, and combines the representation of a temple and a royal city; how he almost always, without any hint of a change of place, gives those local representations which best suit the events then transpiring; how he says expressly that in the New Jerusalem he saw no temple, xxi. 22; and, indeed, how, according to xxi. 9, he will not have us by the New Jerusalem to understand anything local;—when we observe these things, we should do him decided injustice should we ascribo to him the doctrine that heaven, archetypally, has the same local forms as the earthly seat of the kingdom of God. Rather must we say, that as for the vision itself, so also for its representation, John needed local images of heaven, and in this sense he has made the most abundant and at the same time the freest use of traditional material. But he desires, for example, that we should understand the temple in heaven as a concrete image of the sacred presence of God, the throne as an image of the authority of God, Mount Zion as an image of the exaltation of Christ and of the elevation of His people above the world with its temptations; in a word, he will have us regard every locality of heaven as a symbol of the idea shadowed forth by corresponding localities on earth. On the other hand, he has never given us any right, but rather endeavours, as far as possible, to guard us against ascribing to him an actual knowledge of heaven as a substantial part of his doctrine.

As it is with the scenery of heaven, so it is with its *inhabitants.* After the seer has beheld in heaven the throne of God and the glory of Him who sits upon it, iv. 2, 3, he sees immediately around the throne the twenty-four elders, then the seven burning lamps, which are the seven Spirits of God, and lastly the four living creatures. We shall speak of the seven Spirits of God in the chapter on the Spirit. Here we are concerned to know what is meant by the elders and the living creatures. Let us begin with the latter.—" In the midst of the throne, and round about the throne," —the throne is represented as a half circle; one in the midst before the open side, the other three around it,—John saw " four *living creatures* full of eyes before and behind." The first was like a lion, the second was like a calf, the third had a face as a man, and the fourth was like a flying eagle. Each had six wings, and they were full of eyes within,—that is, not merely on the surface of the body, but also under the wings,—and they ceased not day and night crying: " Holy, holy, holy is the Lord God Almighty, who was, and is, and is to come," iv. 6–8. It is evident that in these four living creatures the seer has combined the cherubim of Ezek. i. 5–14, x. 12–14, from which he has taken the name, the fourfold faces,—only not united as in Ezekiel,—as well as the whole body full of eyes, and the seraphim of Isa. vi., from which come the six wings and the song of praise. If now we consider that man, the eagle, the calf, and the lion are the heads of four classes of the animated creation representing intelligent existence, birds, tame and wild animals (comp. Düsterdieck, p. 228), there can be no doubt that John intended by the four living creatures an ideal representation of living beings in general. It is in striking agreement with this, that when the plagues are descending upon the animated creation, vi. 1, one of the four living creatures always invites the seer to "come and see;" and that, xv. 7, one of them hands to the seven angels the "golden vials full of the wrath of God," which were to be poured upon the living creation. There being four, represents the totality of created life. The six wings which, Isa. vi., they use for covering their faces and their feet, and for flying, indicate the reverence by which creatures, according to their idea, are led not to venture to look up to the holy God, the humility with which they cover themselves in the presence of His glory, and the obedience they render to His commands; the eyes covering the whole body may be most simply referred to the ever restless activity of organic life, or the vivacity of the organic creation (comp. the eyes in v. 6); the praise of God ceasing not day or night, is emblematic of the fact that He is, according to the idea, acknowledged and honoured by His creatures as their Lord (comp. Ps. ciii. 22). Should we conceive of the living creatures as concrete realities, we should entirely mistake the intention of the author; we should rather think of them as representing animated nature collectively in its idea, as, indeed, is abundantly shown in the fact that on the arrival of these blessed times in which the idea of the creation becomes a visible reality, the living creatures disappear from the book.—Our understanding the meaning of the *twenty-four elders* is dependent upon a correct interpretation of the living creatures. Before John perceived the latter, he saw around the throne twenty-four thrones, upon which sat twenty-four elders clothed in white—that is, shining garments, and wearing golden crowns, iv. 4; and as often as the living creatures gave glory, and honour, and thanks to Him who sat on the throne, the twenty-four elders fell down before Him, and cast their crowns at His feet, and said: "Thou art worthy, O Lord, to receive glory, and honour, and power; for Thou hast created all things, and for Thy pleasure they are and were created," iv. 9–11. Later on, one of the elders says to the thrones: "Weep not," v. 5. When the Lamb had taken the book, the twenty-four elders fell down with the living creatures before Him, having every one of them harps and golden vials full of odours, which are the prayers of saints, and they sung a new song in His praise, v. 8–10. After the seventh angel had sounded, "the twenty-four elders which sat before God on their seats fell upon their faces and worshipped God," xi. 16, 17. In like manner, after the fall of Babylon, "the four and twenty elders and the four living creatures fell down and worshipped God that sat on the throne, saying, Amen, Alleluia," xix. 4. In explanation of the four and twenty elders, most expositors start from the number twelve, and interpret the doubling of that number either so as to represent the Old and New Testament church, more definitely the patriarchs and the apostles, or so that they find in them the representatives of the Christian church gathered from Jews and Gentiles. Against the former of these two expositions is the fact that on the gates of the New Jerusalem the names of the twelve tribes, the names of the patriarchs, are written, and on its foundations the names of the twelve apostles, xxi. 12, 14; but neither on the gates nor on the foundations do we find the two associated. It is entirely foreign to the thoughts of the seer to conceive of the two side by side with each other. They are the same, but one as the type, the other the fulfilment. The song of Moses and the Lamb, xv. 3, which is quoted in favour of this interpretation, is neither a double song, nor is it sung by Old and New Testament believers; it is one, and ascends from the lips of conquerors in the Christian life. Against the second view is the consideration that, with the writer, believers from the Gentiles never, not even in chap. vii., as will be shown in the section on Christendom, constitute a second Israel by the side of believers from the seed of Abraham; there is only one Israel which continues itself in the Christian church, into which the believing Gentiles are adopted (comp. Hengstenberg, I. p. 269). Baur, p. 227, regards the elders as Christian martyrs, according to Matt. xix. 28, Rev. iii. 21; but the martyrs are often expressly mentioned, and, vii. 13, are distinguished from the elders in the most decided manner. We notice also that in the millennial state the elders are as little mentioned as the living creatures, we therefore do not regard the former as concrete realities any more than the latter; but as the living creatures are a symbolical representation of the animated creation of God in general according to its ideal, so are the elders a symbolical representation of the people of God according to their ideal, or, in other words, of redeemed humanity. They are clothed in white raiment; but, as Hengstenberg shows, I. p. 271, white in the Apocalypse is not simply white, but radiance, the whiteness of the light or of snow, the colour of pure brilliance, the symbolic adumbration of their glory, especially the glory of manifesting or manifest holiness (comp. i. 14, iii. 4, 5, 18, vi. 2, vii. 9–14, xiv. 14, xix. 11, 14, xx. 11, xv. 6, xix. 8). The elders are also holy, glorious; they sit on thrones, and have golden crowns on their heads; thus they are kings, for on account of their connection with thrones their crowns cannot be merely garlands of victory, as in iii. 11, but kingly crowns, as in Matt. xxvii. 29; John xix. 2, 5. They worship God, and cast their crowns before His throne; they have harps and golden vials full of odours, and sing a new song to the Lamb; they are also priests to Him and to God. We shall find later on, in the section on Christian life, that the holy, priestly kingdom of God and Christ is peculiarly the seer's representation of the character and dignity of Christians. That the representatives of this priestly kingdom are twenty-four, is very simply explained from the priestly classes or courses of Israel, 1 Chron. xxiv. (comp. Luke i. 8, 23), probably in union with 1 Chron. xxv. When the seer permits the elders to stand beside the conquerors in heaven until the millennium, it is not without good reason. They represent the people of God in their ideal completeness; the victors in heaven are only actual, individual members of the same. It tends only to confirm our view, that, according to iii. 5, vii. 9, the victors also are clothed with white garments; that, according to iii. 21, they are received to sit with Christ on His throne; and, according to vii. 15, they are before the throne of God, and serve Him day and night in His temple; and in xiv. 2, 3, xv. 3, they are said to have harps like the elders. In the millennium, or, more correctly, at the beginning of the thousand years' reign, the elders disappear, evidently because the church of God is then in reality what before it had been only ideally as symbolized by the elders (comp. xx. 4–6, xxii. 3–5).—As the elders and the living creatures stand around the throne of God, so again the angels, of which we have already spoken, stand around them.—Of the victors in heaven, and of the saints in the great tribulation, we shall find occasion to discourse in the section on the Christian life.—But who are those to whom it is said, "Rejoice, ye heavens, and ye that dwell in them," xii. 12, and of whom is it said, "He opened his mouth in blasphemy against God to blaspheme His name, and His tabernacle, and them that dwell in heaven"? xiii. 6. In the former of these two places the heavens and their inhabitants stand in express contrast to the earth and the sea, and these are undoubtedly realities of the earth, the sphere of the struggle, the scene of coming events and historical developments; the latter places the habitation of God and those who dwell therein in still more striking antithesis with the earth and its inhabitants as estranged from God, with the fallen world and that which belongs to it. We may therefore think of the inhabitants of heaven as consisting not only of the holy angels, and the elders, representatives of the ideal church, and of Christians who stand before the throne, but, with Hengstenberg, perhaps even of Christians below, inasmuch as they are essentially separated from the world; according to a few places, at least xii. 10 (comp. ver. 12), xviii. 20, it almost seems as if the seer considered Christians even here as in one sense the ideal, as belonging to heaven, or as heavenly inhabitants.

There remains for us to consider the heavenly *state*, and what happens there. God is seated on His throne, iv. 2–6; the four living creatures incessantly adore Him, iv. 8; the elders, without ceasing, worship Him, iv. 9–11; and both celebrate the praises of the Lamb, v. 9, 10; the angels also swell the song, v. 12; and the whole creation brings its homage to God and the Lamb, v. 13. On the contrary, Satan rages on the earth, xii. 13–15; he deceives the whole world, xii. 9; he gives his power to the beast, xiii. 2, who blasphemes God, xiii. 6, makes war against the saints, and overcomes them; and all the inhabitants of the earth worship him, xiii. 7, 8. Men blaspheme God on account of His plagues, xvi. 9. We see that it is in heaven as it should be on earth.—But it is also in heaven as it will be on earth. From heaven and for heaven Satan has already been cast down, xii. 9, and he rages the more terribly on the earth until he is bound, xx. 3, and cast into the lake of fire and brimstone, xx. 10. In heaven it is already said: "Now is come salvation, and strength, and the kingdom of our God, and the power of His Christ," xii. 10; and on earth the judgments of God, whereby He will establish His authority, are gradually unfolded (xi. 17, 18, xiv. 7, 8, 14-20, xv. 3, 4, xvii. 1, xix. 6–9). In heaven there is the crystal sea, iv. 6, xv. 2, an image of the righteousness of God which shall be fulfilled upon the earth. Heaven is generally regarded as the region of being beyond time and space, the region of the supersensuous, super-historical, eternal, absolute existence. Hence the writer, as we shall subsequently find, sees the travail of the woman, the birth and taking away of the child, Michael's struggle with and conquest over the dragon,—events which, for the earth and history, have passed away,—as present in heaven; and therefore also all that is to happen, or must shortly come to pass, as transpiring there. — Further, heaven is the sphere of existence which limits and controls the visible reality. There the book with seven seals is opened, vi. 1; the seven trumpets are sounded, viii. 2–7; the vials are poured out, xvi. 1; the temple of God is opened, and the ark of the testament is seen, xi. 19; by His glory the temple is filled with smoke, so that no man can enter, xv. 5, 8; and after each event the judgments of God descend upon the earth (comp. viii. 5, xi. 19, xv. 5–8). —Further, heaven is also the region of real being, in contrast with that which is apparent; thus John saw under the altar of burnt-offering, vi. 9–11, the souls of those who were slain for the word of God and the testimony they held; the blood of the sacrifices was poured at the foot of the earthly altar (comp. Lev. iv. 7, v. 9); thus—for it is not of the spirits of the slain nor of their place of sojourn that the seer speaks (comp. xx. 4)—the entire representation is a dramatizing of the idea of Gen. iv. 10 (comp. Heb. xii. 24); Christians slain on earth are slain for God, or are, in reality, a sacrifice, and their blood cries to Him for vengeance. The representation in viii. 3–5 signifies that the prayers of saints on earth, the sum of which is, "Come, Lord Jesus!" (comp. xxii. 17, 20), are valued in heaven as incense (comp. v. 8), are acceptable to God and heard by Him, and, though powerless in the eye of the world, are really efficacious (comp. ix. 13, 14, xiv. 18, xvi. 7).—Again, heaven is the place for that which earth has lost, as well as for all future ideals: the paradise of God, with the tree of life, ii. 7; the living fountains of waters, vii. 17, once on earth, are now in heaven. So it is with the hidden manna, ii. 17. We may understand the term "hidden" simply of existence in heaven, in distinction from the common visible reality, or as a change of the Jewish legend of the concealment of the ark of the covenant and its sacred contents by Jeremiah or Isaiah, until the times of the Messiah, into a representation of the removal of the manna to heaven. In the latter case the ark of the covenant also would probably be included here, though still more probably both it and the temple and the altars owe their place in heaven to the above-mentioned use of Ex. xxv. 9, 40, and the rabbinical theory of an original pattern, founded on these passages. On the other hand, the New Jerusalem, iii. 12, which one day is to descend from heaven, xxi. 2, is even now there, and generally all that millennial times are to reveal; for example, the exaltation and honour of Christ's disciples is considered as being already realized there.—If, now, we take the heavenly topography of the book in its true meaning, namely, that heaven is the region of the original types of all that is beautiful, and great, and holy upon earth, the issue shortly conceived is this, that the apocalyptic doctrine of heaven is, that it is in the widest sense the idea or the ideal world—not, indeed, as conceived of in distinction from the real world, but as real though invisible or hidden, in contrast to the actual or visible world of sin and sorrow, in distinction from the real but visible world of perfection, the new heavens and the new earth.

At this point, as being the most convenient, we may consider the use made in this book of the word "*new.*" Christ promises to those who overcome that He will give to them "a white stone, and in the stone a new name written, which no man knoweth save he that receiveth it," ii. 17; that He will write upon him the name of His God, and the name of the city of His God, New Jerusalem, which comes down from heaven from His God, and to write upon him His new name, iii. 12. The twenty-four elders sing a "new song," v. 9. John heard a "new song" before the throne, xiv. 3; he saw a "new heaven and a new earth," xxi. 1; and "the New Jerusalem coming down from God out of heaven," xxi. 2. God says to the seer, "Behold, I make all things new," xxi. 5. The Old Testament also has this expression (comp. Isa. xlii. 9, 10, xliii. 18, 19; Ps. xxxiii. 3, xl. 3, xcvi. 1, xcviii. 1). According to xxi. 1, 4, 5, the new contrasts with the former; but the former signifies the present evil visible reality, with all that belongs to it; the new therefore means the future perfect visible reality and all that belongs to it, which is even now in heaven, only hidden, together with everything heavenly or ideal.

4. The Devil.

The Apocalypse names the personal principle of evil, the Devil, ii. 10, xii. 9, 12, xx. 2, 10; Satan, ii. 9, 13, 24, iii. 9, xii. 9,

xx. 2, 7; the Serpent, xii. 14, 15; the Old (ἀρχαῖος) Serpent, xii. 9, xx. 2; the Dragon, xii. 4, 7, xiii. 16, 17; the great Dragon, xii. 9; the great red (πυῤῥός) Dragon, xii. 3.

The form of the vision recorded in xii. 7–9 was, according to Düsterdieck, moulded in the mind of the seer by his recollection of the biblically-revealed fact of the overthrow of the apostate angels: "Certainly," he says, "this fact in itself, and as such, has nothing to do with the connection before us. The special representation to which he gives expression here, clothes itself in his mind in the same form, but does not concern itself with doctrinal definition, only with a deeply-penetrating intuition of the wrath of the arch-fiend against the faithful." In Weiss, *bibl. Theol.* p. 619, we read: "He, the devil, was, according to xii. 9, one of the heavenly inhabitants; and when, as xii. 4 says, 'his tail drew the third part of the stars of heaven, and did cast them to the earth,' it can only mean that he led away from God part of the angels, which in i. 20 are symbolized by stars, so that now they are described as *his* angels," xii. 9. We shall afterward show that the paragraph in question does concern itself with doctrinal definition, and that the doctrine is something entirely different from the proposition that Satan was originally one of the heavenly inhabitants. It is true, however, that the seer would not have chosen the form of xii. 7–9 (comp. xii. 4) for the fact represented, nor would it have presented itself to him in this form, if, on the one side, the standing of Satan before God, in the Old Testament, and on the other the fall and expulsion, as well as the leading away of part of the angels, according to Jewish representations, had not lain in his memory. Little as xii. 4 and 7–9 are supposed to teach or even to express the doctrine, it is still certain that in them as well as in ix. 1 it is witnessed that the seer received it: originally, the devil belonged to the inhabitants of heaven, but fell, and in his fall carried with him a part of the angels. Certainly this does not stand in the foreground of his Satanology; not only according to individual predicates, such as "seat" (θρόνος), "might," "power," ii. 13, xiii. 2, "wrath," "worship," xiii. 15, "synagogue," ii. 9, iii. 9, and to his relation to Antichrist, which runs remarkably parallel with that of God to Christ, but, according to the entire dualistic conception of the book, Satan has far less of the fallen angel and angelic prince than of the Antitheos.

The consideration of the *characteristics* and *activities* of the Evil Principle may be best carried on in connection with the various symbols and names under which the same appears in our book. The devil is called the *Old* primeval *Serpent*, or, more briefly, the Serpent,—a name which refers us to Gen. iii., and which corresponds to the rabbinical הַנָּחָשׁ הַקַּדְמוֹנִי or הָרִאשׁוֹן, according to the manifestation which he has given of himself in the history of the fall as the tempter of man. This aspect of his character is often emphatically brought forward: "The great dragon was cast out, that old serpent, called the Devil, and Satan, which deceived the whole world," xii. 9. The angel "cast him into the bottomless pit, and shut him up, and set a seal upon him, that he should deceive the nations no more, until the thousand years should be fulfilled," xx. 3. "He shall go out to deceive the nations which are in the four quarters of the earth," xx. 8. "The devil that deceived them was cast into the lake of fire and brimstone," xx. 10. How and to what the devil tempts men we shall learn later on, especially in the sections on the earth and its inhabitants, the churches, and the false prophet.

Another principal feature of the devil is brought before us by the name "*great red dragon,*" LXX. Isa. xxvii. 1, Ezek. xxix. 3, and often appears as the equivalent of the leviathan, or as the image of a conquering world-power. When we read in the Apocalypse: "There appeared another wonder in heaven; and behold a great red dragon, having seven heads and ten horns, and seven crowns upon his heads," xii. 3, the reference to the beast with seven heads and ten horns, and upon his horns ten crowns, xiii. 1, and to the "scarlet-coloured beast full of names of blasphemy, having seven heads and ten horns," xvii. 3, 7–9, is unmistakeable. This beast, as we shall afterwards see, signifies the Roman Empire. When the seer clothes the dragon with the emblems of that power, he gives us to understand that the devil is the principle of all world-power, the real world-ruler. In what way the dragon works will come under notice in the sections on "the earth and its inhabitants," "the churches," and "the beast." For the present we have only to notice that he is called "great" on account of his power, that he is said to be red—fire-red (πυῤῥός);—this epithet may possibly refer to desolation and destruction (comp. ix. 17, 18), but more probably to rage and murder (comp. vi. 4, xii. 4, 12, 13, 17, xiii. 7, 11, 18, according to the LXX. 2 Kings iii. 22),—in order, as also by the drawing away of a third part of the stars of heaven, xii. 4 (comp. Dan. viii. 10), to characterize him according to his raging and murderous or persecuting disposition.

Amongst those above mentioned, the names Devil and Satan, preceded by the words "called," xii. 9, "which is," xx. 2, are clearly distinguished as proper names. To distinguish these, again, and to find in Satan the antagonistic, and in the Devil the slanderous, as Züllig (*Johannes des Gott besprachten apokalypt. Geschichte*), Hengstenberg, and Ewald do, is forbidden by the comparison of ii. 9, xiii. 3, 9, with ii. 10, and xx. 7 with xx. 10. The term "devil" is the same from the Greek as "Satan" is from the Hebrew. The above places show, however, that by these proper names of the evil principle the seer wished sometimes to present one particular feature,—namely, the blasphemer, calumniator, and instigator. But this feature, as the passages quoted also show, is very closely concerned with temptation, and not less so with accusation. When cast out of heaven, a loud voice is heard saying, "The accuser of the brethren is cast down, which accused them before God day and night," xii. 10. At the foundation of this there is doubtless the representation of Job i. 6–11, ii. 1–5, Zech. iii. 1, 2, in its rabbinical form:—Satan, *κατήγωρ*, *ille semper stat tanquam delator coram rege Israelis*; Michael, *συνήγωρ*, the agent of the pious (Düsterdieck). Instead of objecting to this representation borrowed from the Old Testament, or, in its concrete form, from the Jewish theology, and which appears to us, from what immediately follows, very harmless, we rather draw from it the doctrine that, until the overthrow of the devil through Christ's saving work, even the brethren in heaven, true members of Christ's church, though in a manner different from that of the inhabitants of the earth, were before God in a state continually open to accusation,—in other words, they were in the state of the unatoned, and as such chargeable with sin.

The last-mentioned work of Satan naturally leads us to a consideration of his *position in heaven*. After the taking away of the child to God and to His throne, there occurs a conflict in heaven. "Michael and his angels fought against the dragon; and the dragon fought, and his angels, and prevailed not; neither was their place found any more in heaven. And the great dragon was cast out, and his angels were cast out with him,"

xii. 7–9. In these words, as in vers. 10–12, many expositors find that the devil and his angels were first driven out after Christ's birth or ascension, and that until then he had a place or standing in heaven (comp., for example, Baur, p. 228; Keim, III. pp. 12, 14). Without doubt, such expositors have the sound of words in their favour; but it is equally certain that by such a representation of Satan's presence in heaven the seer would have placed himself in hopeless contradiction to all his other representations of the same place:—or has he really thought of the devil as an inhabitant of heaven before Christ? (comp. xii. 12, xiii. 6). The enigma may be solved in the following manner: in the passage quoted, he desires in the form of a vision to represent the significance of Christ's saving work, or the complete subjugation of the evil principle in the ideal reality, the heaven of his doctrine. For this representation there offered itself, first, the Jewish idea of the struggle between Michael and the devil (comp. Dan. x. 13, 21, xii. 1; Jude 9); then the kindred representation of the fall of Satan from heaven, Luke x. 18; and finally, as an image of the meaning of this overthrow, Job's picture of the devil as an accuser of the pious before God, ii. 1; Zech. iii. That the heaven from which the devil was expelled at the exaltation of Christ was the sphere of power, but not the ideal reality, and that the accuser of the brethren before God is not his, but the Old Testament devil, the seer has not noticed, and thus the overthrow of Satan in the ideal reality has come to have the false appearance of an expulsion from it. We may therefore with justice ascribe to the seer, at this point, incongruity in the choice of the means of presenting an apocalyptic vision-scene; but we may not burden him with the impossible representation of a pre-Christian residence of the evil principle in heaven.

In xii. 7–9, in addition to the dragon, there are also *his angels*. There can be no doubt they are beings who in other parts of the book are called demons (*δαιμόνια*), ix. 20 (comp. LXX. Deut. xxxii. 17; 1 Cor. x. 20; Rev. xvi. 14, xviii. 2), and unclean spirits, xvi. 13, 14, xviii. 2. The seer conceives of the devil as surrounded by fallen angels (comp. xii. 4), who execute his commands, as holy angels discharge commissions received from God. They are called demons on account of their supernatural character, as in xvi. 13, 14 it is said, "I saw three unclean spirits like frogs come out of the mouth of the dragon, and out of the mouth of the beast, and out of the mouth of the false prophet. For they are the spirits of devils, working miracles, which go forth." The seer seems also to regard the devil himself as a demon, but the chief of all. The unclean spirits in the passage just quoted are distinguished from the demons, and probably as potencies or powers of those beings, in a similar manner as we shall find it in the relation of the Spirit to God and to Christ. On the other hand, when he writes, xviii. 2: "Babylon the great is fallen, is fallen, and is become the habitation of demons, and the hold of every foul spirit," unclean spirits and demons are with him identical, or demons are a particular class of unclean spirits. According to this passage, as already with the LXX. Isa. xiii. 21, xxxiv. 14, Bar. iv. 35, and the synoptical Gospels, their dwelling and operations are preferably in waste, desolate regions and places; probably also in idolatrous images, ix. 20. Their activity consists in helping the devil in his struggle against God and His kingdom, and especially in tempting men to worship them as idols, instead of the true God, ix. 20; for while the images of idols are with our author the work of men's hands, the worship of them has always a demoniacal background (comp. xiii. 15). They are in possession of powers for carrying on this and other temptations (comp. xvi. 13, 14), and the seer also gives them credit for working real wonders (*σημεῖα*), xvi. 13, 14 (comp. Matt. xxiv. 24). Why the unclean spirits are said here to go forth as frogs, whether in allusion to Ex. viii. 1–5, or more probably with reference to the signification of frogs and toads, in magic, cannot with certainty be decided. We have spoken of the fallen angels, who have to execute the judgments of God, in the section on angels.

5. The Abyss.

The seer beheld a star fall from heaven unto the earth, and to him was given the key of the abyss (*ἄβυσσος*) or the bottomless pit. He opened it, and "there arose a smoke out of the pit, as the smoke of a great furnace; and the sun and the air were darkened," ix. 1, 2. According to ix. 11, the locusts which issued from the smoke had over them as king the angel of the bottomless pit, whose name is "in the Hebrew tongue Abaddon, but in the Greek tongue hath his name Apollyon." "The beast that ascendeth out of the bottomless pit" appears in xi. 7. It is said of him, "he shall ascend out of the bottomless pit," xvii. 8. An angel comes down from heaven having the key of the bottomless pit, and he casts the dragon into it, and shuts him up, and sets a seal upon him, xx. 1–3. "The lake (λίμνη) which burneth with fire and brimstone" is a designation which occurs not less frequently; and into it are cast the beast and the false prophet, xix. 20, the devil, xx. 10, and those whose names are not found written in the book of life, xx. 15. Those who worship the beast and his image "shall be tormented with fire and brimstone in the presence of the holy angels, and in the presence of the Lamb: and the smoke of their torment ascendeth up for ever and ever," xiv. 9–11. "The fearful and unbelieving have their part in the lake which burneth with fire and brimstone," xxi. 8 (comp. xix. 3, ix. 17). All these expressions are based upon rabbinical representations, originating from such Old Testament statements as Ps. lxxi. 20, cvii. 26, Isa. xiv. 15 (comp. Isa. v. 14, xxx. 33), according to which there is under the earth an abyss or bottomless pit, with a lake or sea in which brimstone and fire seethe together. From this abyss goes a channel with a mouth, after the manner of a cistern, a narrow passage as from a scarcely visible spring, to the surface of the earth. This pit, like an ordinary cistern, can be opened and closed, or sealed. From the mouth, when opened, the smoke, which continually rises from the fire and brimstone, and fills the abyss, ascends, after the example of Gen. xix. 28, to the surface. But when the seer expressly says, "This—the lake of fire—is the second death," xx. 14, and "the lake which burneth with fire and brimstone: which is the second death," xxi. 8, he shows his relation to the rabbinical topography of the abyss not less clearly than in its place his familiar knowledge of heaven may be traced to the same source.

As an *inhabitant* of the abyss, one expects first of all to find the devil; and Düsterdieck, p. 319, regards it simply as the present abode (comp. on the contrary, xx. 10) of the devil and his angels; while Weiss, *bibl. Theol.* pp. 619, 620, note, after xii. 9, 12 on the one hand, and ix. 1, 2, xi. 7, xvii. 8, xx. 1–3 on the other, supposes a twofold view, according to one side of which, Satan, cast upon the earth, has power there for a season; but, according to the other, his proper seat is the abyss, with temporary power to work from it on the earth. But manifestly, according to John, the devil is thrown into the abyss, xx. 3, after he has hitherto been cast down to the earth only, and has been raging there, xii. 12. He does not appear at all as the leader of the infernal plagues; and the ascent of the beast from the abyss only shows that the devil is operative there. Certainly, according to his nature, he belongs to the abyss, and it is his true home; but as Christ during His sojourn on earth was at home only in heaven, though He had not His residence there, so the devil abides until the end not in his own place, but on the earth among men; indeed, we may say, that according to the doctrine of the Apocalypse the whole course of the history turns upon the fact that he is not where he belongs, but at length must be banished thither. But he is, as we may sum up the sense of the Apocalypse, from the beginning of human history until its close, active on earth; and thus the various productions of hell—all the supernatural, or rather the unnatural, horrible, and destructive appearances—come from the abyss: the locusts which come from the smoke of the opened pit, and torment men for five months, ix. 1–7; "the horsemen with their breastplates of fire, and of jacinth and brimstone;" the horses with heads of lions, out of whose mouths proceed "fire, and smoke, and brimstone," ix. 13–18, all point to an origin from the abyss. Thence ascends the beast which was and is not, xi. 7, xvii. 8, 11; and as Christ since His departure to heaven still lives and will reappear, so Antichrist after his banishment to the abyss still lives and will come some day to the earth, and then go into destruction.

The abyss in its *signification* is a perfect antithesis to heaven. The latter is an invisible but real ideal world, which one day with the new heaven and earth, and the New Jerusalem, will become a visible reality. So also the former is the invisible but real world of the anti-ideal and the ungodly, which also will become a visible (comp. "in the presence of the holy angels and in the presence of the Lamb," xiv. 10) reality in the lake of fire and brimstone, with its torment and its smoke which ascends for ever and ever; just as the New Jerusalem is now in heaven, so the lake of fire and brimstone is now in the abyss. Heaven, according to the statements of the seer, may be expressed in one word—life, eternal life, relatively—salvation; so he says that the angel of the bottomless pit hath his name in the Hebrew tongue Abaddon,—which in Job xxvi. 6, xxviii. 22, is translated by the

LXX. *ἀπώλεια*, the region or kingdom of destruction, described by the Rabbis as the lowest sphere of the under-world,—but in the Greek Apollyon, ix. 11. He also says of the beast, that he goeth into perdition, xvii. 8, 11, and that with the false prophet he is cast alive into a lake of fire burning with brimstone, xix. 20; and that being cast into this lake is the second death, xx. 14, 21.

Death and the kingdom of the dead, nearly as they are connected with the subject just considered, we must, according to the idea of the book, leave to the next chapter.

6. The Earth and its Inhabitants.

The word "earth," like the word "heaven," often occurs in the Apocalypse in its *proper sense;* sometimes in the wider signification, which embraces the general surface of the earth, as in vii. 1, vi. 4, 8, 13; at other times in the narrower one, of land in distinction from water, vii. 2, x. 6, xii. 12, xvi. 2 (comp. ver. 3); and again in the still narrower meaning of land in distinction from water, as well as from what grows upon it, vii. 1-3, viii. 7 (comp. x. 6). Instead of an enumeration of individual parts, the surface of the earth is described as "the whole earth," v. 6, xiii. 3, or "the whole world" (*οἰκουμένη, orbis terrarum*, the whole known world, the Roman Empire and what belongs to it), iii. 10, xvi. 14. Still these expressions have a meaning corresponding to our "world;" "all the world"—the population of the world, or *mankind;* "all the world" has this meaning, indeed, continually (comp. v. 6, xiii. 3), and "the whole world" is used in the same sense at least in xii. 9. The seer very often calls its individual members "men," ix. 20, xxi. 3; and not much less frequently, after the manner of the Old Testament, they are "those who dwell upon the earth," iii. 10, vi. 10, viii. 13, xi. 10, xiii. 8, 12, 14, xiv. 6, xvii. 2, 8 (comp. Jer. x. 18; Ps. xxxiii. 8; Isa. xviii. 3). They are also collectively represented by an enumeration of the various sorts of men; at one time they are grouped according to their national varieties,—"tribe (clan or horde), and tongue, and people (*λαοί*), and nation" (*ἔθνη*, the non-Jewish peoples, the Gentile nations), v. 9, vii. 9, x. 11, xi. 9, xiii. 7, xiv. 6, xvii. 15,—the fourfold signature for the whole earth. At other times they are described by varieties in the relations of life—"the kings of the earth, and the great men (the bearers of honours, courtiers, and the like), and the rich men, and the chief captains, and the mighty men (warriors, comp. 1 Kings xi. 28; 1 Sam. xxxi. 12), and every bondman and every freeman," vi. 15. "The small and great, rich and poor, free and bond," xiii. 16 (comp. xix. 18).

The *anthropological* wealth of the Apocalypse is small. When the two witnesses are slain by the beast, their bodies (πτῶμα) lie on the street, xi. 8, 9. But "after three days and a half the spirit of life from God entered into them, and they stood upon their feet," xi. 11. The false prophet gave life (πνεῦμα) to the image of the beast, that it should speak, xiii. 15. An angel called the fowls of heaven together that they might eat the flesh (σάρκας) of kings, and the flesh of captains, and the flesh of mighty men, and the flesh of horses and of them that sit on them, and the flesh of all men, both free and bond, both small and great, xix. 18; and all the fowls were filled with their flesh, xix. 21. The ten kings and the beast will hate the whore, Babylon, and will make her desolate and naked, and will eat her flesh, and burn her with fire, xvii. 16. At the sounding of the second trumpet the third part of the creatures in the sea which had life (ψυχάς) died, viii. 9. At the pouring out of the second vial the sea became as the blood of a dead man, and every living soul died in the sea, xvi. 3. At the fall of Babylon the merchants of the earth shall weep and mourn over her, that no man buyeth any more, horses, and chariots, and slaves (bodies, σωμάτων), and souls of men, xviii. 13. The brethren of the heavenly state have not loved their lives—souls—unto the death, xii. 11. With the fall of Babylon "the fruits that thy soul lusted after are departed," xviii. 14. After the opening of the fifth seal John saw "under the altar the souls of them that were slain for the word of God, and for the testimony which they held," vi. 9. At the coming of Christ he "saw the souls of them that were beheaded for the witness of Jesus," etc., and they were living; but the rest of the dead were not yet living, xx. 4, 5. According to ii. 23, all the churches should know that Christ is "He who searches the reins and hearts," ii. 23. God put it into the hearts of the ten kings to fulfil the will of the beast, xvii. 17. The whore says "in her heart, I sit as a queen," xviii. 7. Who hath understanding (νοῦν) is to count the number of the beast, xiii. 18. "Here is the mind (νοῦς) which hath wisdom," xvii. 9.—We see that men have flesh in common with animals, xix. 18, 21 which at death becomes corpse or carcase (πτῶμα), xi. 8, 9 (also σάρκες in the plural, xvii. 16, xix. 18, 21). But in distinction from animals man is a body or *corpus*, a person or personality, xviii. 13. How? While in animals there is a living soul, xvi. 3, viii. 9, there is in man a living spirit from God, xi. 11, xiii. 15. The soul is therefore, first, the principle of the animal life; the spirit is the principle of the human, super-animal life as it manifests itself, for example, through the power of speech, xiii. 15. Certainly in xii. 11 the soul expresses only the sentient life principle, or life in man. In xviii. 13, "souls of men," in the sense of living men, the significant Hebrew expression for slaves (comp. Ezek. xxvii. 13; 1 Chron. v. 21), as an epexegesis of bodies, the significant Greek designation of slaves, may, however, possibly be also the "immortal" souls as intensive of the "personal" bodies. In one of the remaining passages, xviii. 14, the "soul" means the principle of the sentient perceiving life, the life susceptible to pleasure and pain, to aversion and desire. Finally, in vi. 9, xx. 4, the soul is used in contrast with the flesh, which perishes in death, and is the principle of the super-fleshly life in man, which is imperishable and does not pass away in death, but, according to its condition, enters into the death state of the grave until the general resurrection, or into heaven until the first resurrection. The heart once describes, in contrast with that which is visible, ii. 23, the inner sphere, xviii. 7, as it were the region of the emotions, desires, resolutions, and intentions, xvii. 17. The understanding is the intellectual sense by which men acquire wisdom, xvii. 9, and which enables them to solve difficulties; for example, the enigmas of prophetical representations, xiii. 8.

By the words earth, xii. 9, 13, earth and sea, xii. 12, earth and heaven, xx. 11, the first heaven and the first earth, and the sea, xxi. 1, the seer also describes the sphere of existence lying between the ideal and the anti-ideal—this world; and the whole earth, xiii. 3, the whole inhabited earth, xii. 9, men, for example, xvi. 9, the inhabitants of the earth, iii. 10, designate those belonging to this sphere as its occupants collectively and individually—the "*world*" in the personal sense of the term. This middle sphere of existence, the visible reality, is in its entirety created by God, iv. 11, x. 6; and all things were created for His good pleasure, iv. 11, and therefore originally without sin, and without suffering and death. But by reference to Gen. i., to the tree of life in the midst of the paradise of God, ii. 7 (comp. xxii. 2), to the living fountains of waters, vii. 17 (comp. xxii. 1), to the Old Serpent, xii. 9, etc., we learn that by the influence of Satan through his temptations, xii. 9, man, and with him the whole middle sphere of being, has been changed and brought into its present state. Everywhere in this book where the above quoted expressions have a *religious* rather than their proper natural sense, we have in them to think of the visible reality and that which belongs to it, not in its original state, but in that subjectively and objectively altered condition to which it has been brought by the fall.

In what, more closely considered, does this consist? According to its *subjective* side, described generally, in the injustice of men, xxii. 11. Its individual features are "unrighteous deeds," xviii. 5, "sins," i. 5, xviii. 5;—and according to the latter passage, ver. 4, a man may be a partaker of the sins of others—"works" in an evil sense, xviii. 6, and these again are variously particularized; thus it is said, ix. 20, 21, "the rest of the men which were not killed by these plagues yet repented not of the works of their hands,"—that is, idolatrous images (comp. Deut. iv. 28; Ps. cxxxv. 15–18; Isa. ii. 20, xvii. 8),—that they should not worship devils, and idols of gold and silver and brass, and of stone, and of wood, which neither can see, nor hear, nor walk (comp. Ps. cxv. 4–8; Dan. v. 23 *et passim*); "neither repented they of their murders, nor of their sorceries (mingling of poisons), nor of their fornications, nor of their thefts."—God says that "the fearful and the unbelieving, and the abominable, and murderers, and whoremongers, and sorcerers, and idolaters, and all liars, shall have their part in the lake which burneth with fire and brimstone," xxi. 8. Into the New Jerusalem there shall not enter "anything that defileth, neither whatsoever worketh abomination or maketh a lie," xxi. 27. It is written, "without are dogs" (comp. Prov. xxvi. 11; Matt. vii. 6; Phil. iii. 2; Deut. xxiii. 18), "and sorcerers, and whoremongers, and idolaters, and whatsoever loveth and maketh a lie," xxii. 15. We see from the first of these passages that sins against the frequently mentioned commandments of God, for example in xii. 17, xiv. 12, xxii. 14, are in the view of our author prominent features of the world: as breaches of the first table, various forms of idolatry; and as breaches of the second, murder, whoredom, sorcery, and theft. The other passages show us that he was disposed to distinguish in the nature of the world the inward and the outward, or thought and deed, and to conceive of the former as falsehood, and the latter as abomination, xxi. 27; or of the former as the love of falsehood, and of the latter as its practice, xxii. 15 (comp. xxi. 8). According to the position of "lying" in xxi. 8, 21, 27, after idol-worship, and its being coupled with the universal expressions occurring there, we may indeed perceive that falsehood is the general counterpart of true religion, or of truth in theory and practice (comp. xiv. 5), inwardly and outwardly; it serves, however, to describe only the first. As for our author, the devil is a deceiver and a murderer, or persecutor, though in several places (comp. xii. 9, xx. 2, 3) the persecutor is conceived of in the deceiver; so he considers wickedness and sin as lying and abomination, or as the opposite of truth and holiness; still with him the inward contains the outward, the disposition involves the action, and falsehood is abomination in itself.

The image by which the Apocalypse most commonly represents sin is that of *uncleanness* in the Levitical sense of the word. "Thou hast a few names even in Sardis which have not defiled their garments," iii. 4 (a statement with which we may compare what is said, vii. 14, of the white garments washed in the blood of the Lamb). "These are they which were not defiled with women," xiv. 14. The filthy continue their uncleanness, but on the contrary the holy remain pure, xxii. 11. The dogs are without, xxii. 15. Into the New Jerusalem there shall in "nowise enter anything that defileth," xxi. 27. Essentially the same image meets us in "the abominable," xxi. 8, in that which "worketh abomination," xxi. 27, and when, xxii. 3, it is said, after Zech. xiv. 11, "there shall be no more curse."—Very closely associated with the image of uncleanness in its various forms is that of *whoredom*, as appears from "the filthiness of her"—Babylon's—"fornications," xvii. 4. Still, the fornication of Jezebel, ii. 21, adultery with her, ii. 22, the fornication of Babylon, and the leading away of kings, cities, and nations by her, xiv. 18, xvii. 2, 4, xviii. 3, 9, xix. 2, must, after the manner of the Old Testament, be regarded as descriptive of sin, as apostasy from God, and unfaithfulness to Him. It is also in rather close connection with this image of impurity that it is said of the Laodiceans, iii. 17, "Thou sayest I am rich, and increased with goods, and have need of nothing; and knowest not that thou art wretched, and miserable, and poor, and blind, and naked." Their sin is represented as *wretchedness*, the pitiful condition of *poverty, blindness*, and *nakedness* (comp. ii. 18). Sin is represented under the figure of nakedness or shame also in xvi. 15, "Blessed is he that watcheth, and keepeth his garments, lest he walk naked, and they see his shame." To the image of wretchedness is related that of *death*, or the state of death, as it meets us in the letter to the church at Sardis, iii. 1, 2, "Thou hast a name that thou livest, and art dead: be watchful, and strengthen the things which remain, that are ready to die."—Another principal image, though not occurring so often, is that of *bondage*. Apart from i. 5, which, according to one reading, says of Christ that He hath delivered us (λύσαντι) from our sins, He is often praised as having redeemed us with His own blood, v. 9. According to the ancient representation of the relation of subjects as one of servitude, the doctrine of the book respecting Satan and his kingdom leads to the same image of sin. The Egyptian bondage, which in many places lies unmistakeably at the bottom of the figure, shows how the author came to think of sin in this aspect.

How the author has regarded the actual state of the world on its *objective* side, the two passages, xxi. 3, 4, and xxii. 1–5, though *e contrario*, very fully show us. In each of these places two prominent features present themselves: in the first, principally, and in more literal language, the habitation of God with men; in the second, subordinately, and more in symbol, the throne of God: in the first, consequently and negatively, "God will wipe away all tears, etc., for the former things are passed away;" in the second, principally and positively, "a pure river of water of life." The first thing which will pass away in the final consummation, is the present objective state of the world; and its main features are, first, that God does not dwell with men—His throne is not in their midst; He has withdrawn from them, and they are under His displeasure (comp. above on God): the second is, that the water of life and the tree of life are absent; tears, death, sorrow, crying, and pain are prevalent, and the trials of the present find their climax in the grave. Evidently these two chief features in the objective state of the present world are not treated in an abstract manner, nor according to their ordinary appearance, but in the concrete, and in that order in which the last times will bring them. In the descriptions of the plagues there will meet us the climax of the objective state of the world, corresponding to the climax of the subjective state.

This state, entering with the fall and the loss of paradise, has prevailed not only *continuously* (comp. xii. 1–6), but *universally.* According to xii. 9, the devil has deceived the whole world; and when the author, in Christian times, often speaks of mankind in contrast with God and the people of God and His kingdom or heaven, simply as the earth, the whole earth, the whole world, xii. 9, xiii. 3 (see also i. 5, 7, v. 10, vi. 15; comp. Ps. ii. 2), and of the ungodly simply as men, ix. 20, xvi. 8–11, or as "inhabitants of the earth," vi. 10, viii. 13, xi. 10–12, xiii. 8, 12, 14, xiv. 6, xvii. 2, 8, and since men in general, mankind in the gross, appeared to him to be ungodly,—we may certainly, without hesitation, apply the same principle to pre-Christian mankind.

But what the writer says of the condition of pre-Christian humanity generally, cannot be *understood of all men without exception.* Can he have reckoned among the inhabitants of the earth in this sense—we take these only as types—a Moses, whose song the victors sing, xv. 3; the prophets, the servants of God to whom He has communicated the joyful message of His merciful purposes, x. 7; the children of Israel, comp. vii. 4, xxi. 12; the worshippers in the temple, xi. 1; or the citizens of the Holy City, xi. 2? No; for the same distinction which now exists between the saints and the "inhabitants of the earth" existed from the beginning; Christendom and Christianity on the one hand, heathendom and heathenism on the other, as now in mutual opposition, and coming into more direct conflict, are only the consummation of the *antagonism* running through all history —derived by Baur from a view of the world analogous to the Manichaean dualism (*ut ante,* p. 229)—between the huge multitude of devil-tempted *men, the inhabitants of the earth,* and the *servants of God.* This antagonism appears to the seer in the concrete, in the great world-empires as Daniel described them, and as they formed in his conceptions a series of *Satanocracies* in opposition to that the aim of which was gradually developed in the *Theocracy* among the people of Israel. This view meets us in the most striking manner in chap. xii., where a woman appears clothed with the sun, and having the moon under her feet, and upon her head a crown of twelve stars: and, being with child, travails in birth,—an evident symbol of the

Old Testament church; and a great red dragon, with seven heads and ten horns, and upon his head seven crowns, who draws away a third part of the stars of heaven, and casts them to the earth, and stands before the woman ready to devour her child as soon as it is born. The dragon may be differently interpreted; but in any case it is clear how for the seer the antagonism between the kingdoms of the world and the kingdom of God runs through the whole, and is the primary moving power of everything, as well as the true meaning of the history.

But does the seer class the *heathen world* in pre-Christian times with the *kingdom of the devil, and the Jewish people with the kingdom of God*, in a merely outward and mechanical manner? After all the kings of the earth and their armies have been destroyed, xix. 19–21, he represents the nations from the four corners of the earth as deceived by Satan at the close of the millennial reign, and gathering together for battle against the saints, xx. 6–9; from which it follows that by "the world" and "the inhabitants of the earth" he had immediately in view only the Roman empire, if extending by its influence beyond the political borders, still only the known race of mankind, almost covered by the extent of the imperial power; on the other hand, he thinks of the nations at the four corners of the earth as behind or outside the Satanocracy properly so called. Still further, our author manifestly makes distinctions within the heathen world of the Roman empire. Not only does he represent those who overcome as singing: "all nations shall come and worship before Thee," xv. 4, but the saints who have their part in the first resurrection live and *reign* with Christ on earth a thousand years, xx. 6. Thus in the heathen peoples of the Roman empire, beside a multitude of the incorrigible servants of the devil, the enemies of God and Christ, the writer sees a great number of men, the nations proper, from which individuals and individual circles have been won for God and Christ (comp. v. 9, vii. 9, xiv. 3); but the masses of the same are as *nations* converted only in the accomplishment of the earthly history, or in the thousand years' reign. But must not the seer, in harmony with such conceptions of the present and the future, have distinguished different classes of the heathen existing before Christ? for the individual conversions of the Old Testament, as well as the expectations of the heathen nations, must have been known to him. When Baur writes, p. 213, that according to the view of the seer the heathen are without a receptive faculty for the divine, and form in the universal contrast of principles an established antagonism to the people of God, it is indeed true of heathenism as a principle, but not, as he takes for granted, of heathendom in its totality, or of the heathen nations. As for Köstlin's assertion, p. 490, that in places where the book of life is mentioned, xiii. 8, xvii. 8, the worshippers of Antichrist, and therefore the heathen, are represented as not written in the book, or as reprobate, we miss the proof that, according to the apocalyptic conception, not merely heathendom in the gross, but heathens individually and collectively, were involved in this guilt. As the heathen world, in the view of the writer, was not an indistinguishable mass, so the theocracy and the Jewish people were not regarded by him as a perfect unity. The twelve tribes certainly represented in general the children of Israel, the people or church of God, in contrast with the heathen in general. But as among the heathen there were those who were not really heathen, and as in the future their number would increase; so among the Jews there were those who were falsely so called, who, while regarded as the church of God, belonged to the congregation of the devil, and were his servants, ii. 9, iii. 9. Indeed, as a temporary condition, and until the great final catastrophe, the heathen nations in general are unbelieving, so also is Israel until xi. 13. Hitherto Christendom, the true Israel, consists of individual Jews and Gentiles, and only in the future there lies, on this side of the final catastrophe, the conversion of Israel, and on the other the conversion of the nations. Is it possible, then, that in the Jewish people before Christ—certainly regarded by the writer as being in general the people of God—he can have mistaken the difference between the true Israel and the congregation of Satan, or Sodom and Egypt (comp. xi. 8), the Israel according to the flesh, which the Old Testament, and especially the history of the prophets, brings so prominently forward?

Having found that the Apocalypse teaches that the present contrast between Christianity and Christians on one side, and the world and its inhabitants on the other, is only the consummation of an antagonism existing from the beginning of human history between the people or servants of God, essentially the people of Israel, and the earth, or the world led astray by the devil, substantially the heathen nations, there arises the question, how the two sides of this contrast, in its pre-Christian form, relate to their fulfilment?—in other words, how the *pre-Christian world* and the *pre-Christian church* of God differ from the world and the church since Christ? While the woman, who symbolizes the Old Testament church, is in travail, the dragon stands before her ready to devour her child as soon as it is born, xii. 4; there arises a struggle in heaven between Michael and the dragon, and the dragon is cast out, xii. 7–9; he then comes down to the earth in great wrath, knowing that his time is short, xii. 12, and persecutes the woman, xii. 13, and goes to make war with the rest of her seed, xii. 17, an account of which is given in the following chapter. Thus, with the appearance of Christ, the crisis comes. As since Christ the world has, through unbelief, become decidedly hostile to Him, so it is a state of things of which the condition of the world before His coming was but the prelude. The Old Serpent has indeed always seduced the whole world; the dragon has always been red, and has ever stood in a threatening attitude in the presence of the woman; but the obduracy into which the world has now fallen, and into which it continues to fall irretrievably, notwithstanding mercy and judgment, and the rage with which it persecutes the people of God, was earlier not so,—it was then typical, after the manner of prophetic facts. On the other hand, the position of the pre-Christian church was also only a symbol of its state after the introduction of Christianity. That which Christendom really has, and for which it jubilantly offers praise to God, for example, in chap. iv. and v., and in v. 7, 10,—salvation realized in principle,—the Old Testament church painfully waited and hoped for; but what Christendom has really to suffer from persecution, only threatened the Old Testament church. We must not, however, allow it to mislead us that our author speaks of Christianity, and individual Christians, and the church, almost entirely in Old Testament phraseology; the distinction between the pre-Christian and the Christian church is not, therefore, less important to him. For Christians only the devil was cast out, xii. 9, 10, and it is by them that he is overcome, xii. 11. The devout men of pre-Christian times, little as they served the devil, feared him who accused them day and night before God, xii. 10, and were unable to overcome him, xii. 11. Instead of being reconciled, they were guilty before God, and could not cleanse themselves from sin, and could only long for deliverance; trusting in the promises of God, they had to content themselves with type, and symbol, and preparation. Thus those who come out of the great tribulation, and have washed their garments in the blood of the Lamb, vii. 14, and those who rise for the thousand years' reign, xx. 4, are not the souls of Old Testament saints, but of Christians. The former will certainly rise at the judgment, xx. 12, will be found written in the book of life, xx. 15, and will be citizens of the New Jerusalem, chap. xxi.; but they neither go at death into heaven, nor will they share with Christians in the first resurrection, xx. 5,—to both classes of which belongs real, in distinction from the typical Christianity of Old Testament saints, and, so to speak, from the non-personal Christianity of the converted heathen nations,—but, like the inhabitants of the earth, they are dead from the moment of death until the general resurrection.

What representation has our book to give of *death?* According to i. 18, the risen Christ has the keys of death and hades, or the kingdom of the dead. At the opening of the fourth seal John sees a pale horse, vi. 8, and the name of him who sits upon it is Death; and Hades follows him, and power is given them over a fourth part of the earth to kill with sword, and with hunger, and with death (*θάνατος*), and with the beasts of the earth. In xx. 13 the sea gives up the dead which are in it, and death and hades deliver up the dead which are in them; and in xx. 14 they are cast into the lake of fire. According to this, as death is distinguished from the second death, eternal damnation or destruction (comp. on the abyss), so also it is distinguished from death, dying, and plagues, vi. 8 (comp. ii. 23, xviii. 8). On the other hand, death and hades are not wholly separated from each other; for while, vi. 8, xx. 14, hades seems to be as personal as Death, his companion and helper, in i. 18, xx. 13, death has evidently the same local signification as hades; still in the Old Testament we read not only of the gates of hades, for example, in Isa. xxxviii. 10, but also of the gates of death, Ps. ix. 14, Job xxxviii. 17; and there is also the same personification of hades as of death, Hos. xiii. 14 (comp. 1 Cor. xv. 54–56). More important, however, than the relation between death and the kingdom of death, is the relation of both to the devil and the abyss. Their appearance in vi. 8 forcibly reminds us of the powers of the devil and of the products of the abyss; and their being cast into the lake of fire, xx. 14, shows distinctly that the seer, where he personifies them, had in his mind what we call death, and regarded it as a demon, a power of the evil principle, belonging to the anti-ideal sphere of existence. Not less important is the relation of death and hades to the sea. It does not follow from xx. 13 that the author expresses the view that the souls of those who had perished in the sea never reached hades, but wandered about in their grave of water; still it is significant, that with death and hades he classes the sea as an abode of the dead. We may compare with this v. 3, "no man in heaven, nor in earth, neither under the earth, was able to open the book," also v. 13, "every creature which is in heaven, and on the earth, and under the earth, and such as are in the sea, and all that are in them," and must then conclude that where the seer speaks of death and hades in a local sense, of that which we call the "realm of death," the under-world, or, according to the Lutheran form of expression, "hell," hades was for him the grave, or rather the grave-world, the graves conceived of as one. It lies under the surface of the earth; the sea, in which there are so many dead, he regards as another place of the dead in addition to hades; and—which is the principal thing—he conceives of those who died before and without Christ, "the rest of the dead," xx. 5, as in their graves, or in the world of the dead, until the judgment; while, at the same time, as we shall afterwards show, he regards "the souls" of Christians as in heaven from the time of their departure, vi. 9–11, and Christians as living at the beginning of the thousand years, when the spirit of life comes into their dead bodies, xi. 8–11, and body and soul are reunited.

SECOND PART.

NEARER PRESUPPOSITIONS.

1. Christ.

(a.) *The Evangelical History.*

IF those expositors are right, who, with Hengstenberg, pp. 595, 599, 607, Ewald, p. 240, note, Düsterdieck, p. 401, etc., believe that the seer, in xii. 1–6, had before him in some form or other Christ's birth of the Virgin Mary, the intrigue of Herod, and the Bethlehemitish child-murders, we possess in this passage, though indirectly, a confirmation of several important particulars *of the birth and childhood of Jesus,* recorded in the histories of the evangelists Matthew and Luke. Without, however, reversing the relation, as Volkmar does (pp. 186, 188, note), and finding in the Virgin birth, Herod the Great, and the flight into Egypt, a narration of the images of Rev. xii. 1-6, I am unable to recognise in this place a reference to the birth and childhood of Jesus. The seer does not desire—and here expositors are unanimous—to give the history itself; and for the explanation of that which he does desire to give, it is sufficient to refer to the Old Testament representation of the church as the spouse of God, and to the rabbinical figure of the travail of the Messiah. Certainly, according to this, the entire historic product of xii. 1–6, with respect to the childhood of Jesus, consists in the fact that He came from the church of the Old Testament, and appeared on earth as an Israelite. Still more strictly is the origin of Jesus defined when one of the elders says: "Weep not: behold, the Lion of the tribe of Judah, the Root of David," v. 5; and when Christ Himself says: "I am the root and the offspring of David," xxii. 16. These two passages, the former resting on Gen. xlix. 9, the latter on Isa. xi. 1–10, describe Jesus directly only as He in whom the Messianic predictions of those Old Testament words are fulfilled; but it is evident that the writer could see those predictions fulfilled only when of his own knowledge Jesus had really sprung from the tribe of Judah, and more particularly from the royal family of David. According to this book, Jesus was an Israelite, of the tribe of Judah, of the family of David.

Not only is the Apocalypse silent respecting the *birth and childhood of Jesus,* but it has generally *very little to say respecting His life.* The expressions, "the Amen, the faithful and true witness," iii. 14; "the word of God and the testimony of Jesus," i. 2, 9; "the word of my patience," iii. 10,—a more careful consideration of which will follow,—show that, according to the representations of our author, Christ during His earthly life was active as a teacher, and that among His words there were such as exhorted to patience. We may infer the miracles which Christ wrought, as well as His predictions, from the imitation sketch of the two witnesses, xi. 3–7. On the foundations of the walls of the New Jerusalem are written the names of the twelve apostles of the Lamb, xxi. 14; whether also in the other places where the apostles are mentioned we are to understand the Twelve, will be seen in a later section. When the dragon stands before the woman to devour her child, xii. 4; when it is caught up to God, xii. 5; when it is said, "the Lion of the tribe of Judah hath prevailed," v. 5; and when Christ Himself says, "as I also overcame," iii. 21, —we learn that from the beginning to the end of His earthly course He had to contend with evil, and also to suffer on account of it. In these few particulars, almost everything recorded in the Apocalypse concerning the life of Jesus may be included.

There are only two events in the evangelic history which the Apocalypse brings forward repeatedly and most impressively, namely, Christ's *death on the cross,* and His subsequent resurrection. The living creatures and the elders praise the Lamb, and say, "Thou art worthy to take the book, and to open the seals thereof; for Thou wast slain (ἐσφάγης), and hast redeemed us to God by Thy blood," v. 9; John sees standing, "a Lamb as it had been slain," v. 6. The angels say, "Worthy is the Lamb that was slain" (ἐσφαγμένος), v. 12. The blood of Christ is mentioned also in i. 5, vii. 14. It is said of the two witnesses, that "their dead bodies shall lie in the street of the great city, which spiritually is called Sodom and Egypt, where also our Lord was crucified," xi. 8. "Behold, He cometh with clouds; and every eye shall see Him, and they also which pierced Him," i. 7. That

Christ was slain, or, more correctly, allowed Himself to be slain, like the "blood" of Christ, historically considered, tells us nothing further than that He voluntarily surrendered Himself to a violent death. Both expressions receive a narrower limitation only when it is said that Christ was crucified, and in that way met the termination of His life. When we find later that the seer perceived in the slain Lamb chiefly the fulfilment of the passover-type, or the complement of the paschal sacrifice, the supposition lies very near, that he had seen this type fulfilled in Christ with respect to the time of its being offered; in other words, that, according to his representation, he died on the day, and at the hour, when the paschal lamb was slain. When He is said to have been crucified in the great city, spiritually called Sodom and Egypt, it is evident that the reference is not purely local, nor a declaration that Christ was crucified by the Jews, but is, as a comparison of xi. 7 with 8 shows, a hint that the degenerate Jews stood in the same relation to the actual murderers of Jesus as they will stand to the beast, the actual murderer of the two witnesses, namely, that of spiritual originators and authors of the murder. The piercing of the body of Jesus, i. 7, resting directly upon Zech. xii. 10, is, on account of John xix. 37, in a very conceivable manner, to many expositors, a great difficulty, which they endeavour to remove, especially by the supposition that the seer does not refer to the particular fact of His being pierced by the spear of the soldier, but to His death generally, as the final result of unbelief; and on behalf of this view they refer to the use of ἐκκεντεῖν in Num. xxii. 29; Judg. ix. 54; 2 Macc. xii. 6 (comp. Düsterdieck, p. 117; Ewald, p. 112). But these passages by no means prove that ἐκκεντεῖν points to death indefinitely; the idea expressed is always death by piercing. The words of the Apocalypse do not, however, enable us to say decidedly whether the writer had in his mind the piercing of the hands and the feet of Jesus, or the wound in His side, or whether he intended both. When these expositors refer the words: "they also which pierced Him," to the Jews, they are mistaken; and we shall show in the section on the coming of Christ, that they refer to the Gentiles.

But He who died on the cross *rose from the dead,* and is said to be "the first-begotten of the dead," i. 5. He Himself says, "I am He that liveth and was dead; and, behold, I am alive for evermore," i. 18. It is said of Him, "These things saith the first and the last, which was dead, and is alive" (ἔζησε), ii. 8. According to this, it was for the seer as really a historic fact that Christ was dead, as that He rose to a new life which would not again be subjected to death. Those passages here come into prominence which speak expressly of the resurrection of Christ, and chiefly of the meaning of the fact: they and others permit a conclusion as to the way in which the resurrection was conceived by the seer. We are instructed, at least by one of the passages quoted, which describes Christ as the "first-begotten of the dead," especially when it is taken in connection with the saying that He was dead and now lives for evermore, that the author conceived of the resurrection of Christ as he did of the resurrection of the dead generally, after the analogy of birth in the earthly life, not as a return to life merely, but as an entrance into a higher condition of existence. Of the highest importance in relation to the representations of the Apocalypse respecting Christ's resurrection, is the passage in chap. xi. 3–12. Everything which is to happen to the two witnesses, as predicted in this chapter, is, according to the correct interpretation of most expositors (comp. Volkmar, *die Religion Jesu*, p. 79, etc.), but an intensified picture of the history of Christ. In addition to the unmistakeable parallelism in the series and character of the facts, the express remark, "where also our Lord was crucified," is in favour of this view. Though, according to the manner of the seer, there are undoubtedly and repeatedly evident combinations of various types, we shall still, as in their prophesying, miracles, and violent death, vers. 3–7, so also in the latter part of the narrative, vers. 8–12, recognise the type of Christ as being most prominent. The first feature which strikes us is, that the bodies of the two witnesses slain by the beast lie like carrion on the street of the great city, and that the people see them for three days and a half, and will not suffer them to be buried. We are not permitted to infer from this that Christ, after His death on the cross, remained unburied, for in that case the exposure of the witnesses on the street would no longer be an intensified picture; but we may conclude that the writer saw something special in the manner of Christ's burial, something disgraceful, unseemly, and humiliating,—at least, something unsuitable. The three and a half days between the death and resurrection of the witnesses point, both by their number and their meaning,—a limited season of misfortune,—so distinctly to the three days intervening between the death and resurrection of Christ, that notwithstanding objections from several quarters (comp. Düsterdieck, Hoekstra, p. 386), this sentence needs neither proof of its relation, nor, as intensive, any exposition of its sense. Not less certainly, from a consideration of the bodies and their non-burial, as well as from the joy and gift-sending of those "that dwell upon the earth" after the death of the witnesses, may we conclude that the seer refers to the unsubdued rage and triumph of the world after the crucifixion of Christ. The entrance after three days and a half of the Spirit of Life from God into the dead bodies of the witnesses, and their standing upon their feet, reminds us of Ezek. xxxvii.; but still more forcibly does the number of the days direct our thoughts to the resurrection of Christ on the third day. The great fear which fell upon those who saw them belongs to the entire connection, and is added to strengthen the picture. Finally, the ascent of the witnesses to heaven contains a reference to the translation of Elijah; but the expression "in a cloud" (comp. Acts i. 9), though originating from Dan. vii. 13, can scarcely be applied to the two witnesses otherwise than through Christ, and does not admit of a doubt that the seer had in mind his ascension, supplemented by the "great voice from heaven," saying, "Come up hither," as well as by the ascent in the sight of their enemies. But the ascension of the two witnesses, though in time most decidedly distinct from their resurrection, follows it, judging from the "and" five or six times repeated without more definite limitation, and from the words, "and the same hour," also from the general impression of the whole, rather directly. Precisely because there is no "immediately," a climax cannot here have been intended, and consequently the seer does not regard the ascension of Christ as divided from His resurrection by a long space of time, but conceives of it as only a continued manifestation of the same. We have next in chap. xi. 3-12, and especially in xx. 4, a disclosure of the author's conception of the resurrection of Christ: for when he sees in the first resurrection "the souls of them that were beheaded for the witness of Jesus and the word of God, and which had not worshipped the beast, neither his image, neither had received his mark upon their foreheads, or in their hands, and they lived and reigned with Christ a thousand years," similar expressions concerning Christ, namely, that "He is alive," ii. 8, the description of Him as "the first-begotten of the dead," i. 5, and the sense of the first resurrection, justify us in reasoning back from it to the resurrection of Christ. According to this, the seer thinks of Christ, from His death to His resurrection, as being, with respect to His body, in the grave, but with respect to His soul, as in heaven (comp. vi. 9–11). He must have considered His resurrection body as beyond the possibility of suffering,—"blessed is he that hath part in the first resurrection," xx. 6,—still by no means inaccessible to the perceptions of the senses, for the millennial kingdom is on earth. Of some value for our inquiry is v. 6. The writer saw standing "a Lamb as it had been slain." Its standing, as Düsterdieck remarks, shows that it was living; its standing as slain, as having been once led to the slaughter and put to death,—in other words, the Lamb standing there as slain, means that Christ lives; but the marks of His wounds show that He has been crucified. Let us, in conclusion, gather up the results, and we have the following representation of the resurrection of Christ:—After His crucifixion at Jerusalem, He was for a short but important period in the embrace of death; His body was disposed of in an ignominious manner, and His enemies triumphed over His fall. While His body was in the grave, His soul, free from all suffering, rested in heaven. After the appointed time the Divine Spirit of Life entered into His body. He lives, and has been born to a new life, exalted, it is true, above the earthly, but still not inaccessible to the perceptions of the senses; bearing upon Him corporally the marks of the death of the cross. His ascension followed without further delay, after the manifestation of His resurrection.

(*b*.) *The Person of Christ.*

He is called Jesus, i. 9, xii. 17, xiv. 12, xvii. 6, xix. 10, xx. 4, xxii. 16; the Lord Jesus, xxii. 21 (comp. ver. 20); Jesus Christ, i. 1, ii. 5; the Christ, xx. 4, 6; the Christ of God, xi. 15, xii. 10.

He is the *Messiah* in the Old Testament rabbinical sense. He is described as such, partly by express statements, and partly by tacit but easily recognisable leanings to Old Testament or rabbinical representations, and by most of the names, attributes, and activities which in this book are ascribed to Him. To quote these in detail would hardly be possible, without destroying their connection with several later sections. Having, therefore, generally recognised the statements belonging to this part of the subject, we must limit ourselves to a *confirmation of the Messianic sense of those passages to which a different sense has been erroneously assigned.* When Christ calls Himself "the bright and morning star," xxii. 16 (comp. ii. 28), the title has no reference to xxi. 23, but either distinguishes Him as the Messiah who precedes the great day of God (comp. 2 Pet. i. 19), or, as is more probable from ii. 28, it refers to Him as the bearer or possessor of the Messianic kingly glory, and is to be regarded as a rabbinical Messianic expression borrowed from Num. xxiv. 17 and Isa. xiv. 12. "The Prince of the kings of the earth," i. 5; "The Lord of lords, and King of kings," xvii. 14, xix. 16, is a title applied in the Old Testament to God Himself, Deut. x. 17, Ps. cxxxvi. 2, 3 (comp. 1 Tim. vi. 15); but it is affirmed also of earthly rulers, Ps. lxxxix. 28; Ezek. xxvi. 7; Dan. ii. 37; Ezra vii. 12. Thence comes also "the golden crown," xiv. 14, and "the many diadems," xix. 12 (comp. also 2 Sam. xii. 30; 1 Macc. xi. 13). Christ has the key of David; He opens and no man shuts, He shuts and no man opens, iii. 7, which is obviously a play upon Isa. xxii. 22, but containing also an evident departure from the original idea, inasmuch as Christ has not, like Eliakim, the key to the house of David, but the key of David, involving personal rights in the whole Davidic kingdom. From Christ's mouth there goes "a sharp two-edged sword," i. 16, ii. 12, xix. 15, 21; but God's magisterial power is also described by this symbol, Wisd. xviii. 15, 16; still Isa. xi. 4 (comp. xlix. 2) uses the same with reference to the Messiah.

But throughout the Apocalypse, in constant interchange with many direct and indirect Messianic expressions, we find not a few *predicates of Christ* which *cannot be referred to rabbinical Messianic representations of the Old Testament.* We shall arrange them in different classes.

We begin with i. 13 and xiv. 14. John sees in "the midst of the seven candlesticks one like (ὅμοιον) a Son of man"—"upon the cloud *one* sat like unto a Son of man." There can be no doubt that Christ is intended in both places, and that in each there is a reference to Dan. vii. 13 (comp. x. 16, 18). De Wette and Hengstenberg find in the expression, the superhuman glory of Christ; for, as De Wette remarks, to affirm of a man that he is like a man, is to say nothing; or, as Hengstenberg expresses it, if Christ only resembles a Son of man, there must be another side of His nature which surpasses the human; Düsterdieck thinks that this dogmatic thought is not in the expression, but acknowledges that *ὅμοιον* does not correspond with the simple *ὡς* of the Septuagint in Daniel; and that if, for its explanation, John must write *ὅμοιον*, so far the typical nature of the form of the Son of man is recognised in the divine majesty of the appearance (comp. xiii. 2), and there follows what the connection of both passages demands, that John expressly and designedly represents Christ not *as* a Son of man, but *like* a Son of man, that is, as a divine person in human form.

We may take at this point those texts in which Christ is *spoken of in parallel with God, or in which something is affirmed of God and Christ in common, or where both are spoken of as one.* Men are represented as saying to the mountains and rocks, "Fall on us, and hide us from the face of Him that sitteth on the throne, and from the wrath of the Lamb," vi. 16; and we read, "Now is come salvation and strength, and the kingdom of our God, and the power of His Christ," xii. 10. The whole creation ascribes "blessing, and honour, and glory, and power unto Him that sitteth upon the throne, and unto the Lamb, for ever and ever," v. 13. The great multitude before the throne cry, "Salvation to our God which sitteth upon the throne, and unto the Lamb," vii. 10. Great voices are heard in heaven, saying, "the kingdoms of this world are become the kingdoms of our Lord, and of His Christ." According to xiv. 4, the 144,000 "redeemed from among men" are "the first-fruits unto God and to the Lamb." The temple of the New Jerusalem is "the Lord God Almighty and the Lamb," xxi. 22 (comp. xxiii.). The river of the water of life proceeds out of the "throne of God and of the Lamb," xxii. 1. In the New Jerusalem is "the throne of God and of the Lamb," xxii. 3 (comp. i. 4–8, iii. 12, xiv. 1). In vi. 17 we read of "the great day of *His* wrath," and the verse preceding tells us it is the wrath of God and the Lamb. He shall reign, that is, our Lord and His Christ, xi. 15. He who hath part in the first resurrection "shall reign with Him," namely, with God and Christ, xx. 6. "The throne of God and of the Lamb shall be in it, and *His* servants shall serve Him," xxii. 3.—When Hoekstra remarks, p. 373, that several times the angels are mentioned in the same breath with God and the Lamb, iii. 5, xiv. 10; and

p. 380, that the 144,000 sing a new song "before the throne, and before the four beasts and the elders," xiv. 3,—we willingly yield to him all those passages where something is said to be done "*before* Him who sits upon the throne, and before the Lamb," also those symbols or affirmations common to angels, elders, saints, and Christ; but, on the other hand, we ask him to produce predicates of angels and men parallel with those we have quoted respecting Christ. He constantly endeavours to show, p. 378, etc., that Christ is not the *σύνθρονος* of God in relation to His throne, as the throne of the King of heaven and earth, but only in relation to it as that of the King of the theocratic people of Israel,—a relation continued in the Christian church, or kingdom of God (comp. Jer. iii. 16, 17; Rev. xxi. 22); that the theocratic kings, from the standpoint of their office, are, in a certain sense, placed on a level with Jehovah (comp. Zech. xiii. 7; 1 Chron. xxviii. 5, xxix. 23; 2 Chron. ix. 8; Ps. xlv. 7); that the Lamb is not literally seated on the throne, v. 6; and that only in the New Jerusalem is the throne of the Lamb, as the *rex vicarius Dei*, naturally identified with that of Jehovah. But, in fact, it is not the throne of Christ, as Hoekstra insinuates, but Christ Himself, who appears as mediator between the throne and the living creatures and the elders, v. 6, as also in vii. 17, "in the midst of—before—the throne." He meets us in other situations, each time with a significance corresponding with the connection; for example, i. 13–16, xix. 11–13 (comp. i. 7, xx. 4, 6). But, according to xii. 15, the child is "caught up unto God and to His throne;" and in iii. 21, Christ is set down with His Father on His throne; and that this throne is the throne of God as the Ruler of the world, and not merely as the King of His church, is satisfactorily proved by the homage of the four living creatures (comp. iv. 6–9, v. 14); nor is the throne of the Lamb, as that of the *vicarius rex Dei*, "naturally" identical in the New Jerusalem with the throne of God, much rather, according to Hoekstra, must God alone sit on the throne there. Sharing the throne of God in the New Jerusalem manifestly distinguishes the Apocalyptic from the Pauline Christ (comp. 1 Cor. xv. 28), and an expression which so clearly and forcibly testifies to the superhumanity of Christ, as hardly any other in the New Testament does, cannot be set aside by merely saying that it is "natural."

A further departure beyond the Messianic, appears in the fact that frequently the same *attributes, actions, and conditions are ascribed to Christ as to God Himself.* Not to mention such predicates as "master," "lord," which have nothing in them specifically divine, Christ is certainly never described as "the Lord God Almighty," never as "He who sits on the throne," never as "He who is, and was, and is to come;" in other words, He is to the seer not the absolute God. It is also to be observed that the phrase, "which is to come," is not of equal import with the words, "I am," and that Christ in the Apocalypse is strictly "the coming one," or "He which is to come" (comp. for example, i. 7, xvi. 15, xxii. 12, 17, 20). The "new name," known only to Himself, is not the inexpressible name of Jehovah, as assumed by Baur, p. 215; nor does it in itself affirm of Christ an ontological divine nature, as Beyschlag finds, p. 123; but it is the expression, elsewhere receiving its supernatural contents, for the ideal meaning of the person of Christ, yet unknown in the manifest reality, but revealed in the final state. This is taught by a comparison of iii. 12, xix. 12, with ii. 17 (comp. also the "new" in the section on heaven). When God calls Himself "the Alpha and Omega, the beginning and the end, the first and the last," i. 8, xxi. 6, xxii. 13, we do not find that Christ applies literally the same terms to Himself. Not to mention xxi. 6, which Köstlin, p. 483, refers to Christ, but which, according to the connection, can be understood only of God, it is tolerably common to ascribe xxii. 13 to Him; but Düsterdieck justly observes that the words of ver. 12 come from Christ's own mouth, while those of the following verse (comp. xxi. 5, vi. 1, 8) read like the words of God Himself; that neither of these two passages is to be ascribed to the angel, nor are we to think of Christ or God as speaking directly, but that John, in the old prophetic manner, having at the beginning, i. 8, struck the keynote, in God's words here at the close adheres to the essential thought of his prophecy in two summary quotations of the divine apothegm (comp. Hoekstra, pp. 373, 396, note). But Christ distinctly speaks of Himself as "the first and the last," i. 17, ii. 8. God is He "who liveth for ever and ever," iv. 9, 10, x. 6, xv. 7; and Christ says, "I am the first and the last. I am He that liveth and was dead; and, behold, I am alive for evermore," i. 17, 18. When the living creatures "rest not day and night, saying, Holy, holy, holy, is the Lord God Almighty," iv. 8; when the martyrs say to God, "O Lord, holy and true!" vi. 10;

when, according to xv. 3, xvi. 7, xix. 2, God's ways "and judgments are true and righteous;" and, according to xix. 9, xxi. 5, xxii. 6, "these words," the words of God, "are true;" and when it is also said that Christ is "holy and true," iii. 7; "the Amen, the faithful and true witness," iii. 14; "behold a white horse, and He that sat upon him was called Faithful and True," xix. 11,—in the "holy" of iii. 7 we do not see "the Holy One of God," Luke iv. 34, nor "the Holy One and the Just," Acts iii. 14 (comp. ver. 13), nor "God's "Holy One," Acts xiii. 35; and, with Düsterdieck *in loco* (comp. Hoekstra, p. 371, note), understand the "holy" as opposed to the slander of the Jews (comp. iii. 9), and as simply affirming that Christ is absolutely holy, and what is involved therein, that He is the "true," the real and genuine Messiah, the heir and Lord of the real and abiding theocracy; but as certainly as "the holy and the true" was not for John the slain criminal and deceiver of Jewish calumnies, but the genuine Messiah, so certainly would he describe Him as "the holy and the true," just as "the holy" describes God in His ethical nature, and as "the true" describes Him in the affirmation of this ethical nature through the fulfilment of His promises and threatenings. We mistake the meaning of the predicates, which in the introductory letters Christ ascribes to Himself, if we suppose that they are covered by the contents of those letters; for, as Düsterdieck himself remarks, p. 178, they contain only special applications of universal predicates. God is often mentioned as judging, vi. 10, xix. 2. He is righteous, xvi. 5; His ways are just and true, xv. 3, xvi. 7, xix. 2; and apart from individual magisterial acts, especially as ascribed to Christ in the letters, it is said of Him, "that in righteousness He doth judge and make war," xix. 11. According to xxii. 6, "the Lord God of the holy prophets sent His angel to show unto His servants the things which must shortly be done;" and, according to i. 1, "Jesus Christ has sent, and signified by His angel unto His servant John," "things which must shortly come to pass" (comp. xxii. 16).—The same acts and states are often ascribed to God and Christ, and at other times only to God: "The city had no need of the sun, neither of the moon, to shine in it; for the glory of God did lighten it, and the Lamb is the light thereof," xxi. 23; but we also read, xxii. 5, that they "need no candle, neither the light of the sun; for the Lord God giveth them light" (compare, for instance, the exercise of authority in xi. 15, xii. 10; the redemption of Christians in xiv. 4, 3; their priesthood, xx. 6, i. 6, v. 9). The saying in xxii. 13 we have regarded as God's, and without doubt the preceding verse contains the words of Christ; and if the connection is also a summary repetition and injunction, it is significant that the words of Christ and the claims of God are side by side, without any indication of a change of subject. Christ is the object of the ascription, "to Him be glory and dominion for ever and ever," i. 6. When the Lamb took the book, "the four living creatures and the four and twenty elders fell down before the Lamb, having every one of them harps, and golden vials full of odours, which are the prayers of saints: and they sung a new song, saying, 'Thou art worthy to take the book, and to open the seals thereof,'" v. 8, 9. With a loud voice, numberless angels say, "Worthy is the Lamb that was slain to receive power, and riches, and wisdom, and strength, and honour, and glory, and blessing," v. 12. With these passages we may compare iv. 8–11, vii. 11–17, xi. 16, 17, xv. 2–4, xix. 1–7, where similar homage is presented to God. The seer hears the whole creation say: "Blessing, and honour, and glory, and power be unto Him that sitteth upon the throne, and unto the Lamb, for ever and ever. And the four beasts said, Amen. And the four and twenty elders fell down and worshipped Him that liveth for ever and ever," v. 13, 14. The multitude, whom no man could number, stood before the throne and before the Lamb, and cried with a loud voice, Salvation to our God which sitteth upon the throne, and to the Lamb! vii. 9, 10. In the New Jerusalem is the throne of God, and the Lamb and *His* servants shall serve Him, xxii. 3. Finally, we may compare the manner in which Christians are described as servants of Christ in i. 1, ii. 20, with the description of them in other places, vii. 3, xi. 18, xix. 2. Hoekstra, p. 380, is exceedingly angry with Düsterdieck's exposition of i. 18, and finds that all the emphasis is placed upon "I am alive" (comp. ii. 8), and affirms that ζῆν does not distinguish Christ essentially from others, and that He is ὁ ζῶν only as "the first-begotten of the dead," i. 5 (comp. Hoekstra, p. 384, etc.). But in his zeal he seems to have entirely overlooked the fact that Christ calls Himself the first and the last, and the living, and declares that He lives for evermore; surely this is not merely as the first who rose from the dead! The same expositor says that God is the only ὅσιος, xv. 4, xvi. 5; but, on the other hand, the predicate ἅγιος is applied to Christ, and angels, and believers. But ὅσιος is evidently nothing less than a specific divine epithet, and the μόνος unmistakeably expresses a contrast with heathen gods; if Christ were distinguished as ὅσιος, we should have quoted it above under non-super-Messianic expressions. With respect to the "holy" angels, xiv. 10, and the "holy" of xxii. 11, for example, the seer does not thus name the individuals; and the "holy" of xxii. 11 is, through the parallelism and the predicate, distinctly shown to be "the sanctified." Can Christ have spoken of Himself in iii. 7 in the same sense?—How the expositor can attach importance to the circumstance that once God, and several times His ways and judgments, are called righteous, I cannot understand, in the presence of "in righteousness He"—Christ—"doth judge and make war," xix. 11. On the contrary, it is not difficult to understand when the same expositor, p. 379, emphasizes the proof that God is the proper object of worship. Certainly neither the prostration of John at the feet of Christ as if dead, i. 17 (comp., for example, Dan. viii. 17, 18, x. 8, 9), nor the expression προσκυνεῖν (comp. iii. 9), can be made available for the divine reverence of Christ; and it is also true that the angel said to the seer, xix. 10, xxii. 8, 9, "worship God, not God and the Lamb," and that everywhere we read only of the fear of God (comp. xiv. 7, xv. 4, xi. 13–18, xix. 5). But this does not set aside the fact that the glorification of Christ, above referred to, is not shared in by angels, nor elders, nor saints, but by these, in union with the whole creation, glory is given to Him, nor that it is remarkably like that given to God, and, indeed, is sometimes expressly ascribed in common to both. The angel said to the seer, who fell down to worship him, "See thou do it not;" but from the mouth of the Lamb, before whom the elders fall down to worship, we hear no such injunction; and the golden vials full of odours, signifying the prayers of saints, can be presented to Christ only in the sense of divine homage;—or, according to biblical religion, is prayer offered to man? That the seer does not wish to give the divine glory to another is evident; whether by individual differences in the representation, such as casting the crowns before the throne, he has indicated a distinction between the homage paid to God and Christ, seems to me doubtful. Throughout the book the reverence paid to Christ appears to be divine, that is, such as is suitable only to be rendered to God or His other self. Especially is this the case in xxii. 3 (comp. vii. 15). Hoekstra has taken all possible pains to show that, since divine predicates are several times affirmed of angels, the church, elders and saints, the same, when applied to Christ, cannot imply a metaphysically divine nature; and that, on the other hand, there is a great difference between God and Christ, especially that God alone, without the interposition of a middle person, is the Creator, sole King and Judge, and the sole object of proper worship. To the objection, that divine predicates are affirmed of angels and men, we have already replied, and have nothing further to say respecting Hoekstra's remark, that the Apocalypse never represents Christ as the absolute God,—a statement neither difficult to establish nor of much importance, inasmuch as we are not aware that John's monotheism has ever been disputed. When he says that specific divine predicates are not generally affirmed of Christ, and often not even verbally, no admission so difficult, and yet so worthy, could give us more surprise, except its opposite. It comes therefore, in truth, to this, that qualities, actions, and conditions which belong specifically to God, are also ascribed to Christ, and to Him only; and Hoekstra has not been able to prove it otherwise.

After what has been said, it will not surprise us if we find that *in Old Testament expressions things which otherwise belong to God are frequently affirmed of Christ.* It is said of Christ that "His head and His hairs were white like wool," i. 14; and in Dan. vii. 9, God is so represented. The eyes of Christ are as a flame of fire, i. 14, ii. 18, xix. 12; and in the same words God's omniscience is symbolized as directed with holy indignation against all unrighteousness, Dan. x. 6. The feet of Christ are "like unto fine brass, as if they burned in an oven," i. 15, ii. 18; the same image represents God's power in treading down the wicked, Dan. x. 6; Ezek. i. 7. The voice of Christ is as the voice of many waters, i. 15; and we find a similar representation of God's power against His enemies, Dan. x. 6; Ezek. i. 24, xliii. 2; Ps. xciii. 3. Christ's countenance is as the sun shining in his strength, i. 16; and so it is said of God, Dan. x. 6 (comp. Judg. v. 21). The seer fell down before Christ as if dead, i. 17; a similar effect was wrought by the appearance of God,

Ex. xxxiii. 20; Isa. vi. 5; Ezek. i. 28; Dan. viii. 17, 18, x. 7–9. Christ says, "I am He that searcheth the reins and hearts, and will give unto every one of you according to your works," ii. 23; and we read that "the righteous God trieth the hearts and reins," Ps. vii. 9, and that He "renders to every man according to his work," Ps. lxii. 12. Christ says, "As many as I love I rebuke and chasten," iii. 19; and in Prov. iii. 12 we read, "whom the Lord loveth He correcteth." Christ calls Himself "the Amen," iii. 14; and the same expression is used of God, Isa. lxv. 16. The Lamb has "seven horns and seven eyes, which are the seven Spirits of God sent forth into all the earth," v. 6; and in Zech. iv. 10 we read of "the eyes of the Lord, which run to and fro through the whole earth." According to vii. 17, the Lamb will feed His people, and lead them to living fountains of waters; and the same thing is said of Jehovah in Isa. xlix. 10. What is said of the anger of Christ, xix. 15 (comp. xiv. 10, 14–16), is drawn from a similar passage respecting God in Isa. lxiii. 1–6. The "vesture dipped in blood," worn by Christ, xix. 12, is said to have been worn by God, Isa. lxiii. 1, 2. Hoekstra affirms, p. 400, that the application of the picture of the seven Spirits and of the seven eyes of the Lamb, borrowed from Zech. iii. 9, iv. 10, may have been directed by Isa. xi. 2. We admit that this may have been the medium, but do not see that the significance of the image for our purpose, namely, the ascription to Christ, in Old Testament expressions and symbols, of those predicates which otherwise belong to God is in the least prejudiced. The remaining passages of this class, which to us appear in the highest degree worthy of consideration, Hoekstra has not noticed.

On the ground of a greater or less proportion of the passages hitherto quoted, and, indeed, on the ground of others also which, being less conclusive, we have not mentioned, several expositors admit that *the Christology of the Apocalypse far transcends the Messianic representations.* Reuss (*Histoire de la Théologie Chrétienne,* I. p. 346) writes: "Il faut reconnaître sans hésiter, que Christ, dans l'Apocalypse, est élevé au niveau de Dieu." Ritschl, *ut ante,* p. 120, etc., says: "Like Paul and James, the seer recognises the full divinity of the exalted Christ, to which idea the Jewish-Christian representation of the pre-existence and higher nature of Jesus as the original man and archangel does not reach." Weiss (*bibl. Theologie,* p. 623) says: "Of the process by which

Paul and the Epistle to the Hebrews were led to the conclusion of the divine glory of Christ, to the idea of His original divine nature, there is no trace in the Apocalypse; still the fact that the Messiah was *originally* divine stands firm from the beginning." It is otherwise, however, with the Tübingen school. Baur, *ut ante*, 244 et seq., grants that in the Apocalypse Christ has ascribed to Him titles which differ from those of Jehovah only as the derived differs from the original; indeed, in view of xxii. 13, he regards it as undoubted that the Apocalypse gives names of Jehovah to Christ. But he labours all the more diligently to weaken the force of the dangerous instances, and comes to the conclusion that, "taking all this together, the Christology of the Apocalypse has the peculiarity of ascribing to Jesus as the Messiah the highest predicates, but they are only names borne outwardly by Him, and are not associated with His person in any inner unity of nature; there is still wanting the inner connection between the divine predicates and the historical individual who is the bearer of the same. Hence it is remarkable how the Christian consciousness at this point feels the impulse to place the person of Christ so high as it does; and yet at the same time it cannot fail to be seen how the entire conception of these predicates is a transcendental form which, in the concrete, the personality of Jesus Himself lacks established contents. They are not immanent definitions springing originally from the substantial nature of his person; they are only the great eschatological hopes for the sake of which the Messiah, as their chief object, must have an adequate position. All metaphysics are outside the circle of the seer's vision; he takes his standpoint entirely from below, in order to carry over to the Messiah, after his death, what His divine dignity gives him," etc. (comp. Köstlin, p. 483 et seq.). A refutation of Baur would be an anachronism after Hoekstra has recently again adopted his view, not merely freeing it from several unnecessary admissions, but also placing it upon a broader, and, at first sight, upon a more solid basis, and consistently carrying it out. I fully admit the diligence and acuteness with which, in the interests of his school, or tendency of thought, he has endeavoured to evade the fatal objection which can be offered to a denial by the hyper-Tübingen Christology of the apostolic origin of the Apocalypse, a book coming into existence before the destruction of Jerusalem, namely, "that at this time many of the first Christian generation must have been living, certainly also apostles and other witnesses of Christ's person and life, even if the writer of the Apocalypse himself belonged to the second generation; that he wrote not for Pauline or Hellenistic, but for the circle of Judaizing Christians; and that the imagination could only have free course in the glorification of a man were he the most extraordinary conceivable, if it had not seen him at all otherwise than from a distance. In other words, that in a man a divine being could be recognised and honoured only when all concrete and obvious proof showing him to be similar in origin to ourselves had entirely disappeared from the representation" (comp. p. 368). I cannot find that this objection, so destructive to a certain school of theology, has been successfully met by Hoekstra's labours. What he offers, after a depreciatory remark respecting the proof for the metaphysical divine nature of Christ built up by the earlier theologians from the names, works, attributes, and honours ascribed to him, p. 370, in favour of his opposite view, namely, that we have to do in the book before us with an Apocalypse, and not with a dogmatic handbook, and that the difference between apocalyptic word-painting and doctrinal definition must not be forgotten, is an undoubted truth recognised and acted upon by all scientific expositors. But from this there follows nothing further than that the symbols in which the book abounds must be interpreted in such a way that those, the meaning of which is still seriously disputed, should provisionally not be applied in the representation of doctrine. But it by no means follows that in the presence of those plain expressions of the book, which differ from the theological intuitions brought to it from without, we should fall back upon its symbolic character. That we have to do, as Hoekstra further observes, with a description of the glory of the exalted Christ, is also perfectly true; but that this must therefore assume a metaphysical character because all in heaven is conceived of in that character; that distinct as the idea of the "superhuman" and the "divine" may be, the representation of the superhuman is at best separated by the uncertain limits of the representation of the divine, that the picture of a person who stands higher than those men who have reached the highest glory possible for them, will necessarily appropriate those predicates which, strictly understood, belong only to God,—all this bears simply no relation to a notorious and manifest consciousness and representation growing out of the Old Testament and the Jewish theology. In the next part of this section we shall review in detail those expositions of Hoekstra's which relate to the work of Christ. To the objection that angels and men are classed with Christ in the predicates above referred to, and that a very great difference is made between God and Christ, we have already in the earlier portion done ample justice. Unmistakeably Hoekstra himself has not been able to suppress a feeling of the weakness of his position; for, after apparently concluding, he has said: "The martyrs are placed more or less on a level with Christ, though the distance between the Messiah-king and His subjects, who receive their rank from Him, remains great," p. 395; he nevertheless starts the question whether the names given to Christ imply His metaphysical divinity, and whether it results from what He testifies of Himself in the seven letters to the churches. He finds a partial reply to this inquiry only in the discovery of Baur, that, according to a Talmudic tradition, three things, the righteous, the Messiah, and Jerusalem, are called by the names of God; and he supplements this with the remark, that in the Scriptures persons who represent God (or Christ) really appear in the person of God (or Christ), and speak as if God Himself were the speaker; often, however, with a certain abrupt change of the subject, so that here and there in the same discourse "I" indicates God Himself and His almighty power (comp. Gen. xviii. 13; Ex. iii. 1, 4; Gen. xxxi. 11, 13; Ex. xiv. 16 (19?), 24; Gen. xviii. 13–33; Ex. iii. 6, xxiii. 20; Josh. v. 13, vi. 2; Isa. lxiii. 9, 10). In proof that this method is followed by the seer, he appeals to x. 1, xi. 3, where, according to his exposition, in the first case, the angel is Christ and not Christ, and in the second, God and not God; we thus have to do with the representing angel. He then finds it easily explicable that Christ, who, according to His office, or in relation to the church, represents God Himself, also speaks words which properly can be uttered by God only, and therefore that He speaks in the person of God without its proving anything respecting His divinity. This result of Hoekstra's statement of proof is really so brilliant that one cannot but wonder why he gave himself further trouble, and did not confine himself to this decisive argument, if it is as forcible as he represents it to be. Hardly any one will dispute—the question of the relevancy of the passages quoted being left in abeyance—that the Old Testament angel of the Lord and the super-Messianic Christ stand in a certain relation to each other. But, as we have found in the section on angels, the angel of the eleventh chapter does not show that the seer has generally followed the method according to which those who represent God or Christ really appear in the person of God or Christ. We may remark further, that on the supposition that the seer has applied this method to Christ, it would be as unaccountable on the one side that he should have made a "very great" difference between God and Christ, as it is on the other that he has almost throughout placed God and the Lamb beside each other, and made Christ, where He stands alone, speak so often of God as His God and Father. When the eleventh chapter, as the middle term of the argument, fails, Hoekstra may furnish the proof that the angel of Jehovah in the Old Testament stands in the same relation to God as Christ does in the Apocalypse; until then, we must maintain that when Christ utters words which properly can be spoken "by God only," that it proves something in favour of His divine nature. Hoekstra gives the result of his researches, p. 399 et seq., in the words: "between Christ and His followers there exists essentially only a difference in degree. The glory of Christ is essentially only Messianic; it consists in the kingly office which He holds in the kingdom of God. To Him will be committed by God the execution of the Messianic judgments upon the enemies of the people of God, and royal authority in the Messianic kingdom itself, as now over the decisions relating to it" (comp. 395 et seq.). "The martyrs are more or less placed on a level with Christ; still the difference is great, because Jesus as the Messianic king is naturally high above His subjects, who receive their rank from Him." On the contrary, we have found that the glory of Christ is in no way merely Messianic, but, according to our idea, super-Messianic, because divine. We have no difficulty in denying, and, indeed, do so emphatically, that on one side Christ in Himself is not God, and that Christians may and will be through Christ like Christ, and that, not merely in a Messianic, but also in a super-Messianic sense, as we shall show in the next and later sections. But we believe that in what has been said we have unanswerably shown that on the other side Christ has in the Apocalypse a great number of predicates, which differ not merely in degree, but specifically from those ascribed to believers and martyrs,—in a word, from those ascribed to man,—and are specifically divine. Whether, according to the categories of the new theology and philosophy, upon whose Procrustean bed the self-styled historical criticism lays the New Testament writers, there is a discrepancy between the two sides of the apocalyptic Christology, does not trouble us; we have to do with the historical,—that is, in the case lying before us, with the categories in the thoughts of the seer.

We now proceed to the question, *What constitutes the inner unity of the various super-Messianic expressions of the Apocalypse concerning Christ?* Weiss, *bibl. Theol.* p. 623, justly remarks that Baur's idea of these expressions as merely titular for a consciousness of God springing from the Old Testament, is not admissible; and with equal justice, as it seems to us, notwithstanding constantly renewed antagonism, that Old Testament presuppositions, and the impression of the historical Christ, in no way suffice for the explanation of these expressions, and that there is lying beneath, some substratum which must be accepted as a link in the thoughts of the seer between these expressions and the Old Testament idea of God. If we notice in Matt. xxii. 41–46 a hint respecting the position of the prevalent Jewish theology with regard to this question, and consult, wholly without prejudice, the history of the philosophy of religion in those times, and finally, the above quoted group of super-Messianic expressions both individually and as a whole, the *Logos-idea* forces itself upon us as the required substratum, and the only reconciling medium. Here we find against us not only our old enemies, but not less decidedly, though from different motives, almost all those upon whose friendship we have been hitherto accustomed to lean. Let us consider the two passages with which this question is concerned.

In iii. 14 Christ is called "*the beginning of the creation of God.*" Baur, p. 217 et seq., grants that if Jesus, as "the beginning of the creation of God," was only the first created, the expression still appears to involve clearly enough the idea of pre-existence, but says that it is not very evident whether the Apocalypse describes the Messiah Himself, or only His name, as having been prepared before the foundation of the world. He finds it to be very probable that this description contains no dogmatic definition, but is merely a title of honour in the sense of the highest creature to which by "the beginning of the creation" reference is made; moreover, immediately before (iii. 12) the heavenly name of the Messiah is called a "new name," and nowhere else in the book is His pre-existence clearly expressed; it is further sustained by the fact that the expression in Prov. viii. 22, which the seer doubtless had in his thought, is figurative, and that the rabbinical theology is very liberal with the predicate: "before the foundation of the world." Hoekstra, p. 376 et seq., adopts Baur's view, and strengthens it by two reasons: first, that Christ is expressly called "the beginning of the creation *of God*," from which no one can infer anything but that the creation was the work of God, and that Christ was the beginning of that work, and in any case the creature of God; second, that if in these words the pre-existence of Christ were expressed, it would not prove His metaphysical divine nature, since the question would still remain whether we must understand an ideal or a real pre-existence, for the former is not foreign to the Apocalypse, xiii. 8; and with respect to the latter, according to Baur's remark, Jewish theology, is liberal with the expression: "before the foundation of the world," and speaks of seven things created with the world, among which are the names of the Messiah. Köstlin, p. 484, finds a great difference between the expression in iii. 14, "the beginning of the creation," and "Thou, Lord, in the beginning hast laid the foundation of the earth," in Heb. i. 10, and thinks it most probable that only the first should be referred to rank (comp. Ewald, p. 151, note). According to Weiss, *bibl. Theol.* p. 623, the expression does not describe Christ as the principle of the creation, which appears here to be God's, but as one who existed, according to the Book of Proverbs, earlier than the whole creation, without being placed on a level with it. Ritschl, p. 120, note, finds that since the passage has to do with Christ's appearance as a judge, the predicate *ἀρχὴ τῆς κτίσεως τοῦ θεοῦ* refers to Christ's magisterial function. It would carry us too far should we follow in succession these widely differing explanations, and we must satisfy ourselves with simply asking the question, What exposition is demanded by the laws of language? Without further delay I reply, that had the seer written "the beginning of the creatures (*κτίσματα*) of God," or had he written "the first, or the first-born, or the first-fruit (*πρῶτος, πρωτότοκος, ἀπαρχή*) of the creation of God," then the expression might be understood to denote the first created, or that which precedes all things, the first creature in time and rank. But the seer has written ἡ ἀρχὴ τῆς κτίσεως τοῦ θεοῦ, which can mean nothing else than *principium creationis*, the principle, the ἐν ᾧ, δι' οὗ, εἰς ὅ, of the creation of God. After this affirmation of the literal sense, I may remark that it finds confirmation in i. 17, 18, ii. 8, the first of which Hoekstra must wholly have forgotten, or he would not so readily have written, p. 400, "nowhere is this—the glory of the exalted Christ—brought into connection with His original metaphysical nature." Must we then understand "the last" to signify the last creature in time and rank? Much rather, has not the first, in connection with the last, undeniably the sense of "the beginner of the world development"? When Hoekstra, p. 377, finds in Düsterdieck's confirmatory exposition of xxii. 13 as many errors as words,—first, because the passage contains God's own words; second, because, according to the Apocalypse, not Christ, but God, terminates the old creation, and calls the new into being (comp. xx. 11, xxi. 1, 2–5); and thirdly, because Christ is expressly called "the ἀρχή of the creation of God,"—it was certainly an oversight of Düsterdieck that he has appealed to xxii. 13 rather than to i. 17, 18, ii. 8; but does the "creation of God" exclude a divine creation-principle distinct from the originator or founder? or does "the creation of God" demand that the ἀρχή, the principle of the same, must be a creature? But why give prominence to detail? Are not all the expressions concerning Christ, quoted above, so many proofs that John, by "the beginning of the creation of God," cannot have meant the earliest and greatest of creatures, but a Being above creation? We need only add, that while we have said above that the contents of the apocalyptic letters do not exhaust the contents of the predicates of Christ which precede them, so on the other side it is evident that the contents of the letters must harmonize with these predicates. But if "the beginning of the creation of God" is conceived of after the manner of our opponents, it will not permit a relation to be shown, to say nothing of an inner correspondence, between this predicate and the succeeding letter. To a church in which Christ not only discovers self-blindness, but which He threatens to spue out of His mouth, which He counsels to seek help from Himself for its disease, to which He says that He rebukes and chastises those whom He loves,—in a word, to a church to which He reveals Himself as to no other in His fullest and highest significance, and we must remember that we have to do with the last of the seven letters, "the first creature" has not in any of its possible meanings a really satisfactory sense, and we find that sense only when we understand it to mean the principle of the creation of God, that is, the personal, mediatorial essential ground and end of the creation.

Thus simply explained, according to the laws of language, the passage iii. 14, taken in connection with those quoted before, furnishes us with a very remarkable result, namely, that the seer has expressed the Logos idea itself in its highest meaning,—pre-existence and creative activity,—only not by name. Has he done the latter also? In xix. 13, describing the advent of Christ, he writes, "and His name is called *the Word of God*," ὁ λόγος τ. θ. While Hoekstra gives to this passage no thorough consideration, but regards it, p. 401, as a description of the moral character of the apocalyptic Christ, he finally says, "His vesture is stained with blood, and He is called the Word of God, the Judgment of God, the Word which, as a sword, goes out of His mouth to smite the nations," xix. 15. Baur and Köstlin labour hard to paralyse the meaning of xix. 13. With both, the treatment of this one passage takes an equally disproportionate space in the representation of apocalyptic doctrine. According to Köstlin, *ut ante*, 484 et seq., the expression "Word of God" has here much more resemblance to the παντοδύναμος λόγος of the Book of Wisdom than to that of Philo and John; Christ is here the Word of God, as He who efficiently administers the divine will on earth,—or, in other words, He is the bearer or holder of the Divine power. Baur, *ut ante*, 215 et seq., affirms that we must take the predicate "Word of God" as the well-known paraphrase of the name of Jehovah often occurring in the Targums, and the Messiah will then be called ὁ λόγος τοῦ θεοῦ only in the sense in which the Jehovah name is given to Him, iii. 12, xix. 12, even as the same name is given in an old Talmudic tradition to the righteous, and to the city of Jerusalem. This interpretation does not appear to have been entirely satisfactory to Baur himself, for he immediately proceeds to a second, according to which the seer saw from the point of view of the λόγος τοῦ θεοῦ the whole manifestation of Jesus, so far as the Word of God was revealed as well as fulfilled through Him, and according to which Jesus, as revealing and fulfilling the purpose of God, may be called "the Word of God." Other expositors also wholly fail to recognise the Logos in xix. 13. Hofmann (*Schriftbeweis*, I. p. 106) refers the name "Word of God" to ver. 9, and explains it as "the contents of the divine promises." Ritschl (*die Entstehung der altkatholischen Kirche*, 2 Auflage, p. 120, note) understands by "the Word of God" the name by which Christ will be known at His second coming, and remarks that it refers to His magisterial functions (ver. 11), which He exercises not merely instead of God, but which God Himself carries on through Him. Düsterdieck, p. 542, *ut ante*, says the name "Word of God" corresponds to the mediatorial position of the Lord, as described in i. 1–3, comp. xix. 10, iii. 11. According to Weiss, *bibl. Theol.* p. 623 (note), the name which Christ bears as He goes out to the last conflict has no reference to His pre-existence, nor to the Alexandrine doctrine of the Logos, but rather to Him in relation to the function by virtue of which He bears it as the minister of the divine—magisterial—will, so far as, according to the Old Testament doctrine (Heb. iv. 19), the Word of God, as a living word, directly fulfils what it predicts. But it would lead us too far to quote all the expositions of xix. 13, and, apart from the portions of truth they contain, individually to confute them. To some extent they are mutually destructive, and their variety is a strong reason for suspicion that there is an attempt to escape from a too obvious fact. We content ourselves with the question, Why this passage in particular should not be understood of the Logos? Köstlin, p. 484, replies that ὁ λόγος τοῦ θεοῦ being written, and not ὁ λόγος, shows that we have here no independent hypostasis distinct from God (comp. Baur, p. 217, *ut ante*); and similarly Düsterdieck says, p. 57, "The limiting genitive, τοῦ θεοῦ, differs somewhat from the manner of the Apostle John; but it is wholly inconceivable that the Apostle who wrote John i. 1–5 could represent the Logos under any form." But we have to do with a writer who was led by the laws of the literature upon which he was engaged to speak of the Logos after the manner of the Old Testament, and therefore as λόγος τ. θ., and directed by his art, to give form to the invisible, as he has also done to the Holy Ghost, and to a certain extent even to God Himself. Moreover, I think the genitive case might in Philo be against the independent hypostasis, but not so in an original Christian writer who could not conceive of Christ in His pre-existence otherwise than as an independent hypostasis distinct from God. Another objection Köstlin formulates thus: "The name 'Word of God' is directly ascribed to Christ only in His state of exaltation, and when, and only *in so far* as He comes down to the earth as an avenging judge" (comp. Baur, p. 217, *ut ante*). But does the seer at any time speak at all of Christ in His humiliation except in the beginning of the twelfth chapter, where for the sake of consistency it was impossible to describe Him as the Word of God? And though this name is first ascribed to Christ when He comes as judge, it is nowhere said that it is so ascribed to Him only in that character. According to this principle of interpretation, most of the predicates of Christ in the introductions of the letters must have attributed to them a narrower meaning than they have, either according to the literal sense, or according to the view of the expositor himself; the analogy of these introductions compels us much rather to understand the name "Word of God" in such a sense that the judicial function in which Christ appears is included in it, but it does not compel us to regard that function as the only one, or as being in the thoughts of the seer the full contents of that name, when the word sense or other circumstances are against such an interpretation. As Düsterdieck, *in loco*, correctly remarks, the idea of the formula *καὶ κέκληται* shows that a definite name (comp. ver. 12) current with believers, which the Lord had received and continually bears as a significant name (comp., on the other hand, the more appellative designations in vers. 11, 16), is here pointed out. Further, the connection of xix. 11–16 generally, and especially the name of Christ, which "no man can know but He Himself" (comp. Beyschlag, *Christologie des N. T.* p. 132), shows that the author desires not merely to represent Christ as appearing in His judicial capacity, but briefly and forcibly, in all those attributes which give real and full significance to His final appearance as judge; and lastly, from xix. 1, the seer unmistakeably sketches the single aim of all His predictions, the great world catastrophe through which all discrepancy between the reality and the ideal, or all conflict on the part of the world against God and His purposes, will be destroyed. On one side this catastrophe is regarded as the coming of Christ, and on the other as the coming of God. We may compare what we have already recognised as the sense of "which is to come," for example in i. 4, and in so doing must acknowledge that it was precisely where His coming, who comes as God, should be placed as such in the fullest light that it was impossible to ascribe to Him the name "the Word of God" with such evident emphasis and with such manifest brevity, in a different sense from that of the personal principle of the self-revelation of God, the Mediator in an absolute sense, in whom God appears, and through whom God works as in and through His other self. If in my conception of "the Word of God" I stood entirely alone, I should still be disposed to maintain it against all the subtilties of exposition. It has, however, been to me a source of satisfaction to find myself in agreement with at least a few expositors. To say nothing of Neander, who (*ut ante*, p. 481, note) speaks of the harmony of the Apocalypse with the doctrine of the Logos, which cannot by any ingenuity be explained away, Ritschl, *ut ante*, p. 120, note, on xix. 13 and iii. 14, recognises "the Word of God" as the starting-point of the Johannine conception of Christ. Hase (*die Tübingen Schule*, p. 29) writes: "The substance of the Logos doctrine is not wanting, nor the verbal element and harmony." Schmid (*bibl. Theol.* II. p. 362) says: "The idea of the Logos is found in the Apocalypse, but it is applied only in special relations." Lechler (*das Apostolische und Nachapostolische Zeitalter*, 2 Auflage, p. 200) finds that, according to xix. 13, Christ Himself is the "Word, the personal bearer of the divine wisdom and power, the medium of the divine self-revelation." Beyschlag, *ut ante*, p. 133, recognises a relation of reciprocal complement between "the Word of God" and "the beginning of the creation of God," and remarks "that only a world-creative Word of God, and not a mere world-judging Word, can be called the beginning of the creation." Understand "the beginning" as we please, it is evident that a mere world-judging Word might be a τέλος, but in no sense an ἀρχή. Further, the name "Word of God" confirms our decision with respect to "the beginning of the creation," that it does not mean the first creature, but can mean only "the principle of the creation," for the latter only, according to Gen. i. 3, and according to self-evident conceptions, can be called λόγος τοῦ θεοῦ. Both names are essentially congruent, only that in "the beginning of the creation of God" the relation expressed is to the world, but in "the Word of God" it is to God.

We also, without restriction or hesitation, trace to the doctrine of the Logos, as their inner unity, their substratum, their connection with the idea of God, all those expressions of the Apocalypse which go beyond Messianic representations. *But how did the seer arrive at that doctrine?* The book itself gives us no reply to the question. Almost in every word it shows us that its author must have sprung from Palestinian Judaism, and the inquiry then arises which of the two Christological phases, the Messianic or that of the Logos, was the earlier, and, as it were, originally familiar, and which was subsequently appropriated as supplementary. Further, the Apocalypse does not contain anything which might be regarded as the starting-point for the formation of the doctrine, it gives us simply the doctrine itself; and thus all such expositions as those of Baur, and especially of Köstlin, which tell us that, for the sake of the great eschatological expectations, the Messiah, as the chief subject of the same, must have an adequate position, fall away of themselves (comp. Baur, p. 219; Köstlin, p. 485). But we could as easily believe that the doctrine of the Logos came to the author in its original Alexandrian form, as that it was for him already associated with the Messianic idea, or that he met with it already applied to Jesus. In like manner, the Apocalypse leaves us in doubt how its author may have been prepared for the independent application, or for the acceptance of the Logos doctrine when it had already been applied, whether through acquaintance with a Palestinian Christology, surpassing the popular Messianic representation and its reference to Jesus, or through the contents of his faith in Jesus having passed the limits of the popular Palestinian theology. When he applies so many Old Testament descriptions both of Jehovah and the Covenant, or presence angel, to Christ, it may as easily be that the Christological significance of the Logos doctrine may have come to him first from the related passages, as that they had the same for him before his becoming acquainted with that doctrine.

On the other hand, the Apocalypse does not leave us entirely in the dark respecting the *relation in the mind of the seer of the Messianic idea and the doctrine of the Logos to each other*, especially if we consider the pervading peculiarity noticed above, according to which, with well-sustained art, he clothes

Christianity, in its facts, ideas, and circumstances, in Old Testament forms, though not with artistic licence; for Christianity, in all seriousness, was for him the fulfilment or the full truth of Old Testament types. We shall not be tempted, by the multitude and preponderance of Messianic predicates, to conceive of the Apocalypse as if it contained, besides the Messianic idea, only a few isolated traces, or germs, or starting-points of the doctrine of the Logos. And just as little shall we think, with Beyschlag, *ut ante*, p. 138, that, with the seer, the Logos was that which pre-existed in heaven; but, on the other hand, that which existed on earth, in Israel, was the parallel maturing manifestation, each only a factor in the future Messianic personality, the former the ideal, the latter the historic; and by the union of both factors the personality, as such, comes into existence; in other words, the paternal share in this Son of the Eternal God and the Old Testament church is the Eternal Word, the divine self-revelation, personally realizing itself in history; the maternal share is the Israelitish recognition of God and the Messianic idea. Much rather, according to the analogy of the book, we should represent the relation to ourselves thus: the seer perceived in the doctrine of the Logos the realization or full truth of the Messianic idea, and in the Messianic idea the doctrine of the Logos in its holy and typical form; Jesus is for him the Messiah; but the Messiah, in the full sense of that sacred name, is no other than the Logos. I confidently affirm that had the writer not thus regarded the relation between the idea of the Messiah and the doctrine of the Logos, he could not have appropriated the latter in its entire individuality. But from the way in which alone he could appropriate it, and really has done, namely, through its identification with the Messianic idea, we have a solution of that which has been an enigma to many expositors, namely, how the Messiah has ascribed to Him the very highest, even Logos-predicates. Not less simply is it thereby explained why the Logos is only once mentioned by name, and even then, in Old Testament phrase, "the Word of God;" also how, only once, and again in a quotation from the Old Testament, "the beginning of the creation of God," the Logos is characterized according to His peculiar nature. He ventures to describe Him only in sacred language, therefore, with such predicates as are applied to the Messiah, the angel of God, the angel of the presence.

By the last circumstance, and still more by the purely presuppositional and occasional character of the Christological statements of our book, an *organic representation of the apocalyptic doctrine of the person of Christ* is clearly rendered impossible. We venture, therefore, to sketch it according to its peculiar nature, or according to its idea. The Logos is the real self-revealing principle of the absolute God; He mediates God with that which is not God; in other words, He is both for the world to be created and for the created world of the last times—the real personal medium of God. The Messiah is the restorer of the kingdom of God promised to Israel and expected by Israel, in other words, the mediator, the salvation as well as the perfection of man fallen from God. Through the identification of the Messiah and the Logos, the former becomes to the seer the creating, governing, and perfecting principle of God to the universe; the latter, the saving, judging, and perfecting mediator to fallen humanity. Jesus is the Messiah-Logos. To Him as such, not to Him merely as the Messiah, belongs all that we have quoted above as the Messianic expressions of our book; to Him as such, and not merely as the Logos, are ascribed all the expressions to which we have referred as super-Messianic. According to xxii. 6, "the Lord God of the holy prophets sent His angel to show unto His servants the things which must shortly be done." In xxii. 16 Christ says of the same thing, "I Jesus have sent mine angel to testify unto you these things in the churches;" and it is still of the same that in i. 1 we read, "The revelation of Jesus Christ, which God gave unto Him, to show unto His servants things which must shortly come to pass; and He sent and signified it by His angel unto His servant John." It was to the author perfectly valid whether he said that God had given him the revelation, or that Jesus had given it him; but when he wishes to express himself with complete accuracy, he says that God gave the revelation to Jesus, and that Jesus gave it to him. We may therefore, reasoning from the particular to the general, describe the nature of Jesus as that of the Messiah-Logos. He is as really one with God as He is distinct from God; as really related to God as to the world. He is, has, and does all that God is, has, and does; but what God is in Himself, that is He as having become; what God has from Himself, that has He as received; what God does independently, that He does according to the will of God. There is little difficulty in showing this from a series of examples. We may compare xv. 3, 4 with xii. 5, and ii. 27 and x. 2 with xix. 11 and xix. 15; also i. 4 with xvi. 15 and xiv. 14–16; and further, iv. 8–11 with v. 12 and v. 13, especially xxi. 23 with xxii. 5. Though, on the other hand, while it is explained how many things are affirmed, sometimes of God and at other times of Christ, or of God and Christ at the same time, we remain in the dark as to the different relations of both to the common predicates,—we may compare the above quoted Messianic expressions,—it can hardly be a difficulty to the unprejudiced, for they will naturally not expect that the seer would furnish a dogmatic theology, but that he would present now one and now the other of various sides of the relation of the Messiah-Logos to God—resemblance, difference, and transferred possession—as he really does.

We shall now be able to judge correctly how our author has conceived of the pre-existence, the earthly history, and the exaltation of Christ, or in other words, the various *positions* of Christ in their contrasting relations. Beyschlag, with whom alone we have here anything to do, says, p. 137, *ut ante*: "*The difference between the pre-existence and the historical existence must be sought* in something else than, with the orthodox, in the human nature, namely, in the relation of reality and ideality. What the author, by his direct application of predicates of pre-existence to the historical Christ, has left out of consideration is the difference between that which is still to be realized and that which is already so historically; the eternal idea, the pre-existent principle which has unfolded itself in this historical person, he has, without hesitation, made the name of the same." At this point we see how difficult it sometimes is to get a correct understanding of individual particulars apart from their connection with the complete doctrine, and at other times how the application of modern dogmatic categories to New Testament doctrine avenges itself. Beyschlag, with his distinction between ideality and reality, is near the truth, but has not succeeded in grasping it, because neither has he disengaged himself from the modern doctrine of personality, nor does he understand ideality and reality otherwise than in the modern sense. Then certainly must the seer have left the difference between that which is not yet realized and that which is, without notice, and overlooked the manifest difference between historical and pre-historical being—between ideal and real existence. But first, our notion of personality was evidently unknown to him, or one might still attempt to bring his statements and representations with respect to angels under the categories "personal" or "impersonal," or into both. Secondly, as we have seen in the section on heaven, ideality and reality are with the seer not opposites; rather does he distinguish between ideal and historical reality. He has therefore not overlooked anything when he calls the exalted Christ, with whom only he everywhere has to do, "the Word of God," "the beginning of the creation of God," and speaks of those who, since the foundation of the world, are written in the Lamb's book of life, xiii. 8. *Ideally*, the Messiah-Logos was realized in Jesus from eternity, as in the fulness of time He was *historically* realized in Jesus; not in historical, but in ideal reality is Jesus the Word of God and the Principle of the Creation from eternity; and the Messiah-personality has not two factors, one ideal and the other historical, but before its entrance into the historical it had real actuality; before the child was born of the woman, He existed in heaven in ideal real actuality, and prepared for His appearance to Israel by prophecy in word and deed as through preliminary manifestations (comp. Weiss, *bibl. Theol.* p. 623). It is with the relation of the pre-existent and the historical Christ as with the state of the perfected in heaven and in the New Jerusalem, where also the distinction is not between realized and to be realized, but between the ideally real and the historically real perfection. Instead, therefore, of speaking here, with Beyschlag, of biblical modes of thought and speech being distinguished not so well dialectically as understood mystically, I submit whether we have not probably something to learn from the seer's distinction of ideal and historical reality in Christology.

But how has the seer conceived of the *relation of the historical to the pre-existent Christ?* Beyschlag, *ut ante*, p. 129, formally protests against the idea that anywhere in the Apocalypse the God-like glory of Christ is described as a pre-existent and voluntarily surrendered possession. In the only place which speaks of the coming of the Messiah into the world, xii. 1, 2, the seer says nothing of such a surrender. Indeed, the thought of such a thing seems to be at variance with the fundamental representation of the author, that the historical Christ showed Himself to be the Messiah-Logos. Yet such a surrender is distinctly expressed in i. 17, 18, where He says, "I am the first and the last: I am He that liveth, and was dead (ἐγενόμην, became); and, behold, I am alive for evermore." As the first and the last, as the living, He died not according to human lot, but voluntarily; He did not therefore lose His life, but gave it: in His death the writer undoubtedly sees a surrender on the part of Christ. But how explain the contradiction? Simply by the consideration that the Logos-Messiah has not entered into the future complete, but into the present imperfect historical reality, and that therefore He has shown His Messiah-Logos nature in the voluntary surrender of His glory. According to the representation of the seer, there must have been in the life of Jesus harmonious parallel revelations of His Messiah-Logos nature in manifestations of glory, for example, as "the living one;" and in self-humiliation and self-surrender, for example, as "the Lamb," who permits Himself to be slain; in other words, the historical Christ has both manifested His pre-existent Godlike glory, and voluntarily surrendered it, and has in both equally shown Himself to be the Messiah-Logos, so that even the self-surrender is regarded as a manifestation of his glory.—Was *Christ* to the seer *a real man?* We look at such expressions as, "where also our Lord was crucified," xi. 8; "as I also overcame," iii. 21, and are inclined to reply in the affirmative. On the other hand, we remember the evident design—discussed above—with which the author, in his use of the passage in Daniel respecting the Son of man, instead of ὡς, corresponding to the Hebrew and to his own frequent practice, twice writes ὅμοιος, which differs from the former in that ὡς implies a similarity of appearance without reference to a similarity of nature; it describes, indeed, a similarity of appearance with a difference of nature, and so we feel inclined to reply in the negative. It appears to me that in ὅμοιος there is the thought that Christ, according to His appearance and demeanour, was throughout a man, but that according to His nature He was not a man; and thus that docetic views of Christ, and all views of human development, uniqueness in the midst of the whole race, and the final deification of Jesus, were entirely foreign to the seer. When Beyschlag, p. 130, *ut ante*, says that Christ was far from regarding His heavenly glory as an exclusive privilege of His person, and that He promised to communicate it to His disciples, and has in principle already done so; that He treats Himself in everything, even in things the loftiest and most sublime, not as an original, divine I, but as the head of humanity, the Son of man, who has attained what He possesses, and as having attained it not for Himself only, but for all,—he again applies modern categories which are not adapted to the author of the Apocalypse. While we now regard " human " and " divine " as excluding each other, the seer knew nothing of such exclusive contrast; indeed, the " real " men, the inhabitants of the earth, humanity fallen from God, the kingdom of Satan on the one side, and on the other the dwellers in heaven, to whom Christians even here essentially belong, stand opposite each other in the very rudest manner (comp. sections on heaven, and on the earth and its inhabitants). Can Jesus then have been to the writer a man in his sense of the word ? No. Did he therefore conceive of Him in the manner of the doceti ? Also, no. The Messiah-Logos was like a Son of man, that is to say with Paul, He appeared "in the likeness of sinful flesh," became flesh that He might change the earthly into the heavenly, or make it like Himself. It is worthy of remark, that while Paul says, " when all things shall be subdued unto Him, then shall the Son also Himself be subject unto Him that put all things under him, that God may be all in all," 1 Cor. xv. 28, the seer, according to xxi. 23, xxii. 1, 3, thinks of Christ in an entirely different relation to God, and knows nothing of Beyschlag's idea of a head of the human race.

Neither am I able to regard *the seer's conception of the relation of the exalted to the pre-existent and historical Christ,* as Beyschlag does when he says, p. 129, " The divine glory of Christ is never described as possessed before time, and as being taken again after a voluntary surrender, but is everywhere considered as having been acquired on earth and given by God, and therefore, instead of excluding dependence on God and subjection to Him, implies it." Baur also says, p. 200 : " For Christ, death was the way in which He acquired the highest divine power and glory " (comp. Köstlin, p. 487) ; and according to Weiss, *bibl. Theol.* p. 621, Jesus, who rose through His resurrection to the throne of God, was exalted to a Godlike authority, and so has become a Godlike being. But of the passages quoted in proof of this, such as " Thou art worthy to take the book," v. 9, and " Worthy is the Lamb that was slain to receive power," etc., v. 12, prove nothing, for in iv. 11 we read, "Thou art worthy, O Lord (God), to receive glory," etc. It is different, however, with the words, "even as I received (εἴληφα) of my Father," ii. 27; "even as I also overcame, and am set (ἐκάθισα) down with my Father on His throne," iii. 21; "Behold, the Lion of the tribe of Judah, the Root of David, hath prevailed to open the book," v. 5. In all these places the divine glory of Christ appears to have been acquired on earth, and to be described as given to Him by God. In the meantime, however, we notice that it is said in xi. 15 that "the kingdoms of this world are become the kingdoms of our Lord, and of His Christ; and He shall reign for ever and ever;" in xi. 17, "We give Thee thanks, O Lord God Almighty, which art, and wast, and art to come; because Thou hast taken (εἴληφας) to Thee Thy great power, and hast reigned (ἐβασίλευσας)," comp. xii. 10, xix. 6. Such expressions cannot be understood as if God had not been Lord and ruler before, or as if He had not till then possessed His great power; but rather, that now in historic reality He will gradually become and take to Himself that which in ideal reality he is and possesses eternally. We notice further, that as we shall find below the "reward" of the Christian finally consists in nothing else than the perfection of his Christian character, so without further evidence we shall not be able to assign to the seer in the above words concerning Christ the meaning that what he then received he had not earlier possessed, and that he had not been earlier what he then became. How little the modern antithesis in this matter agrees with the views of the author may be learned, for example, from xii. 5, ii. 26, 27, xix. 15. According to the analogy of the passages respecting God, we cannot place similar expressions concerning Christ, such as "received" or "given," in antithesis with "possess."—The Messiah-Logos has all that God has, but He has all as received; He is all that God is, but God has given it Him—rather, we must regard the representation of the seer as being that—all that Christ in His exalted state properly is, and has, and does, that has He also been, and has had as received and given, and done in His pre-existence, and during His earthly course; but while to these states in ideal reality, He has come historically, only in His exaltation, and only then received and taken, it is still not in such a way as if the historical reality were already perfected, but it completes itself gradually, so that according to the idea the completion is involved in the beginning, but the same must and will come to pass only historically.

(c.) *The Work of Christ.*

Instead of exhausting the contents of the name of Christ, "the Word of God," xix. 18, and the self-designation, "the beginning of the creation of God," iii. 14, and thus construing the author's representations of Christ's *pre-existent activity,* we shall for the present only show that according to these names the Christ of the Apocalypse, as the real divine or God-principle of all revelation of God generally, and especially of the creation and government of the world from the beginning, has been mediatorially active. We turn at once to the works of Christ in a narrower sense, namely, *to those of His earthly life.*

Here we have first to explain a number of statements connected with this part of the subject, and then to estimate their value. Christ is called "the faithful Witness," i. 5; "the Amen, the faithful and true Witness," iii. 14 (comp. xxii. 16, 20). John says that he "bare record of the word of God, and the testimony of Jesus Christ, and of all things that he saw," i. 2. He also says that he "was in the isle that is called Patmos, for the word of God, and for the testimony of Jesus Christ," i. 9. He "saw under the altar the souls of them that were slain for the word of God, and for the testimony they held," vi. 9. The dragon went to make war with the remnant of the woman's seed which keep the commandments of God, and have the testimony of Jesus," xii. 17. In xiv. 12 we read: "Here is the patience of the saints: here are they that keep the commandments of God, and the faith of Jesus;" in xvii. 17, "until the words of God shall be fulfilled." The angel says to the seer, "These are the true sayings of God," xix. 19; "I am thy fellow-servant, and of thy brethren that have the testimony of Jesus," xix. 10. John saw alive the souls of them that were beheaded for the witness of Jesus and for the word of God," xx. 4. "He who testifieth these things saith, Surely I come quickly." And according to one reading, John writes, "Blessed are they that do His commandments," xxii. 14. Christ says to the church in Philadelphia, "Thou hast kept my word," iii. 8; "thou hast kept the word of my patience," iii. 10. First of all, the question arises, What is the meaning of "the word of God and *the testimony of Jesus Christ*"? It is said of the two witnesses, "when they shall have finished their testimony," xi. 7; and of the brethren in heaven, that "they overcame him—the dragon—by the blood of the Lamb, and by the word of their testimony," xii. 11; and in both places we are no doubt to understand *their* testimony: in the first, that of the witnesses; in the second, that given by the brethren (comp. i. 2, xxii. 18). In like manner must we understand the testimony of Jesus as that given by Him, and not, as many expositors understand it, as the testimony concerning Him. It is evident, therefore, that by "the word of God and the testimony of Jesus," there are not meant two different things, but the same in different relations. The word of God is the testimony of Jesus as far as it is expressed by Jesus: the testimony of Jesus is the word of God as far as it is given by God. "The word of God and the testimony of Jesus" are thus related to each other as God and Jesus are related; what God says, that Jesus says, as spoken by God to Him, i. 1. Thus there is no essential difference between the expressions, the testimony of Jesus, and the word of Jesus, and "the word of my patience," iii. 8, 10, only there is the absence of express reference to God as the giver of the same, as occurs also in a similar case, xxii. 16, i. 1. Again, "the word of my patience" is the word of Jesus, with the special intimation that it demanded constant patience in the midst of all opposition (comp. Matt. x. 22, xxiv. 13; Luke xxi. 19). On the other side, we have in the "commandments of God," xii. 17, xiv. 12, xxii. 14, and "the words of God," xvii. 17, nothing different from the word of God—by "the commandments of God," some, with Hoekstra, p. 389, understand the law of God in the Old Testament in distinction from the New,—except that, perhaps, in "the commandments of God" there is prominence given to God's word on its preceptive side, and in "the words of God" we have reference to the same word in its prophetic aspect; and instead of saying, with Baur, *ut ante*, p. 223, that our book regards the essence of religion on its subjective side, as keeping the commandments of God, and the true worshippers of God as those who keep His commandments, to which, if they are at the same time to be described as Christians, there must be added the testimony of Jesus, or faithfulness to Jesus, we much prefer to find in the commandments and in the words of God the Old

Testament form for the word of God. But what is that which, only according to its various relations, is called "the word of God and the testimony of Jesus"? In i. 2 the seer can have meant nothing else than the revelation given to himself, and in xix. 10, only that given to the prophets. On the other hand, i. 9, vi. 9, xx. 4, xii. 17, iii. 8, 10, give a good sense only when we understand the expression to refer to the teaching of Jesus, or the gospel in the usual sense of the word, and not, as Baur, p. 207, and even Weiss himself, *bibl. Theol.* p. 627, note, to prophecy, the prediction of the advent. But must not the seer, when he thus uses the same expression to describe the word which Jesus spoke on earth, and that which He uttered after His exaltation, have considered both as essentially one? How he comes to regard Christian prophecy in its origin, like the historical words of Jesus, as the word of God and the testimony of Christ, will be explained in the section on the Spirit; at present we are content with the fact that he does so regard it. After having learned the meaning of "the word of God and the testimony of Jesus," we can be no longer in doubt why the seer speaks of Jesus as "the Amen, the faithful and true Witness," iii. 15. Neither i. 5 nor iii. 14 is exhausted by the reference of these names to the revelation contained in the Apocalypse, and certainly just as little by the teaching of Jesus contained in the Gospel. On the contrary, with respect to both passages, all is clear as soon as we associate them with the correspondence found above; they unite, and say, Christ is the faithful or genuine and true Witness, or the Witness whose word perfectly agrees with the fact (comp. Isa. lv. 4; Jer. xlii. 5). He is Amen, or True (comp. Isa. lxv. 16), as far as His testimony reaches, whether He speaks in the flesh, or in His exaltation through His prophets (comp. xix. 11, xxi. 5, xxii. 6). But does not the "faithful and true Witness" forcibly remind us of the doctrine of the Logos? The name "faithful Witness," both in i. 5 and iii. 14, is introductory to the highest predicates of Christ; and as "the word of God and the testimony of Jesus" so fully represent the relation of the Logos to God, we cannot doubt that in both expressions the seer had in his mind the Logos nature of Christ. The question now arises, are we to limit "the word of God and the testimony of Jesus" to the words of Jesus in the Gospels and the Apocalypse? Must we not rather extend the meaning of these phrases to the law and the prophets, and say that the seer held that the same Messiah-Logos-Jesus, who during His earthly life testified the word of God, did the same before through the Old Testament prophets, and still did it through the Christian prophets? It is in favour of this that by the words of God, xvii. 17 (comp. x. 7, xix. 9, xxi. 5, xxii. 6), the writer had undoubtedly chiefly in mind the prophecies of the Old Testament, and by the commandments of God, xii. 17, xiv. 12, xxii. 14, it is in the highest degree probable he meant the Old Testament commandments; that, as we shall find in the section on the Gospel, Old and New Testament prophecy was for him one complete whole; and, as we have already seen, and shall see still more clearly, that, according to its all-penetrating intuition, Christianity is simply the Old Covenant in its fulfilment, and the Old Covenant was simply Christianity in type, in preparatory predictions, in antecedent germ and principle. Must, then, the testimony of the historical and the exalted Jesus not have been to him Old Testament prophecy in its fulfilment? And on the contrary, must not Old Testament prophecy have been to him the testimony of Jesus respecting the future?—As the point to which we now come, we affirm from our discussion, that according to the doctrine of this book the work of Christ consisted prominently in His testifying the word of God; He was the faithful and true Witness. But we must not omit calling attention to the remarkable circumstance, that, as the expressions "witness" and "testimony," used equally of Christ and His disciples, i. 5, iii. 14, ii. 13 (comp. xvii. 6, xi. 3), i. 2, xii. 17 (comp. xi. 7, xii. 11), show, like those works of Jesus which point so clearly to His Logos nature, besides the divine there is also a human side, according to which the Logos-Christ is as it were the first-born, the beginner and founder of the testimony which, as received from Him, His followers, His witnesses continue after His example and in His strength.

Certainly not in express words, but not the less plainly, the seer gives us to understand that another prominent feature in the life of Christ was His *conflict with the devil.* According to xii. 3–9, the dragon, whose tail draws away the third part of heaven and casts them to the earth,—symbol of his rage and zeal,—stands before the woman to devour her child as soon as it is born. It is said, xi. 8, of Jerusalem, "where also their—the two witnesses—Lord was crucified." The Lion of the tribe of Juda overcame, v. 5; Christ says, "To him who overcometh will I grant to sit with me in my throne, even as I also overcame, and am set down with my Father on His throne," iii. 21. Thus even before the Messiah-Logos-Jesus had come forth from the bosom of the Old Testament church, the devil, threatened in his empire, as may be seen in xii. 3 et seq., made ready to destroy him. That he really attacked Him, and that Jesus really entered into conflict with him, is expressed in the statement that Jesus overcame, v. 5, iii. 21. According to outward appearances, Christ was overthrown by the devil in this struggle, for He was crucified, xi. 8; and of this crucifixion the devil is said to be the author, xi. 7. But the overthrow of Christ was only in appearance, really he had overcome—we may notice how the slain Lamb appears immediately, v. 6, after the mention of the victory of the Lion of the tribe of Juda—he was caught up to God and His throne, that is, in Old Testament phrase (comp. Isa. liii. 3), not merely to the delivering God and to His throne, as the safest and most sublime refuge, but to a condition which, while it was completely and for ever withdrawn from all suffering, is, at the same time, one of divine honour and power, xi. 8, iii. 21.

This *victory of Christ over the devil* is differently represented in the scene sketched in xii. 7–12. Its form we have already explained in the section on the devil, and in the same connection we have stated the meaning of the whole, namely, that the result of Christ's conflict with the devil is the expulsion of the dragon from heaven, or the conquest of the evil principle. But what sort of a conquest? After the devil and his angels are cast out, a loud voice is heard in heaven, saying, "Now is come salvation, and strength, and the kingdom of our God, and the power of His Christ: for the accuser of our brethren is cast down, which accused them before our God day and night. And they overcame him by the blood of the Lamb, and by the word of their testimony; and they loved not their lives unto death. Therefore rejoice, ye heavens, and ye that dwell in them. Woe to the inhabiters of the earth and of the sea! for the devil is come down unto you, having great wrath, because he knoweth that he hath but a short time," xii. 10–12. By this victory of Christ the devil is not yet "cast into the lake of fire and brimstone," as in xx. 10; he is not yet imprisoned for a thousand years in the bottomless pit, as in xx. 3.

The devil is indeed expelled from heaven, and thereby for the inhabitants of heaven the kingdom of God is already in its glory, and the subject of pure joy; and also, indeed, for the brethren of the heavenly inhabitants, Christians on earth as related to the ideal world, the conquest of the devil, ideally considered, has become an objective,—the accuser is cast down,—and in so far as they have by faith appropriated the work of Christ, the ideal has also become a subjective accomplished fact, they have overcome him "by the blood of the Lamb, and by the word of their testimony; and they loved not their lives unto the death." But the earth and the sea, as the sphere of the historical reality, are called to woe, because the dragon has come to them with fierce anger. In other words, in the invisible ideal reality, and for the same, the power of the evil one is entirely and for ever broken by the conflict of Christ; but in the historical reality his activity in temptation and persecution is only gone with the victory of Christ, and the nearer it comes to an end,—the Lord is at hand,—the more fiercely his power rages in a last despairing effort, the more frightfully he pours out, as if for a final display, the evil that is in him. In this lies the explanation why and how the seer presents in the conflict of Jesus, as he does also in His testimony, a human as well as a divine side. Christ's conquest of the devil does not relieve, and in its nature cannot relieve, His followers from the burden of the same conquest, which, for such an expositor as Hoekstra, is to say that the victory of Christ was only typical, and as such had an encouraging power for His followers. An unprejudiced reader will acknowledge that it is perfectly consistent, if we suppose that the seer regarded the conflict with the devil, on one side as a specific saving work of Christ, and on the other as a work in which His followers imitate His example.

We must, by the testimony of Jesus, which we have represented as the first prominent feature in His work, think more of what precedes that part of the evangelic history, which is a history of suffering; the conflict and the victory have led us from His birth to His death on the cross and His exaltation to heaven; thus the third principal feature in His work, His *sacrifice or self-sacrifice*, most directly relates to His sufferings and death. Hoekstra, in his examination of the doctrine of the Apocalypse respecting the death of Jesus, p. 387, affirms that, according to the Old Testament, the place of the sacrifice will be taken by prayer, especially where opportunity for a proper sacrifice might fail, and that the Apocalypse knows no other sacrifice than that which consists in the worship of God, v. 8, viii. 3, 4. But besides the altar of incense, there was in heaven the altar of burnt-offerings (compare the section on heaven), and below it John saw the souls of those who had been slain for the word of God and the testimony of Jesus, vi. 9; here the expression used for "slain" is confessedly not that used for mere death, but that which expresses sacrifice. Instead, therefore, of taking away from the death of Jesus its sacrificial character, we should be disposed to say rather, that in the eye of the seer the martyr death of the Christians was a sacrifice also; not implying, however, that the death of Christ was only a martyr's death, but that on the human side He is a sacrifice, that is, He has not loved His life unto death, but permitted Himself to be slain by the world for God, as His followers have not loved their lives unto death, but have allowed themselves to be slain for God. But this is only one side of the sacrificial meaning of Christ's death; the other is peculiar to Himself, and Christians are not in any way its imitators, but its objects. In relation to this side, we have to consider the sufferings and death of Christ, first in symbolical representation and description of Christ, then in a few figurative expressions representing the significance of the blood of Christ.

John saw, v. 6, in the midst of the throne and the four living creatures, and in the midst of the elders, a Lamb as if it had been slain, which had seven horns and seven eyes. This Lamb is Christ; and under this image and name He henceforth appears—with the addition of "slain," v. 6, also v. 12, xiii. 8 (comp. v. 9, vii. 14)—very often, and almost exclusively (comp. v. 8, 12, 13, vi. 1, xvi. 7, 9, 10, xiv. 17, xii. 11, xiii. 8, 11, xiv. 1, 4, 10, xv. 3, xvii. 14, xix. 7, 9, xxi. 14, 22, 23, 27, xxii. 1, 3). The use of the less common diminutive *ἀρνίον* instead of *ἀμνός* is simply explained in v. 6, from the design to sharpen the contrast between the announced Lion of the tribe of Juda, and the actual appearance of Christ Himself. Possibly because the writer had once introduced Christ by it, for reasons of authorship he continues its use. It may be also that he preferred it because he desired continually to bring into prominence the contrast between the appearance of Christ and His real importance, therefore between the idea and the visible reality of Christianity, through the contrast between the glory and activity of Christ and His standing symbol. It appears to me, with Hoekstra, p. 388, most likely, only not solely on account of the "wrath of the Lamb," vi. 16, but on account of the rather frequent incongruity of the symbol and the activities of Christ, that we must accept the word "Lamb" as being to the seer almost a name of Christ, and therefore as furnishing a proof that he ascribed the very highest significance to Christ's death. It is almost universally admitted that the name and symbol of the lamb here, as well as in 1 Pet. i. 19 (comp. Acts viii. 32, 33), may be traced to Isa. liii. 7. Ritschl, p. 121 (comp. Reuss, p. 477), grants that in the above passages of the New Testament the expression of Isaiah is applied to Christ, but considers it more than improbable that the prophet's passing use of the image of the gentle lamb called forth John's description; his representation of the "wrath of the Lamb" is out of harmony with it; in that case, the common apostolic representation that Christ has died as the true paschal Lamb (comp. 1 Cor. v. 7; 1 Pet. i. 19; comp. Ex. xii. 5; John xix. 36; comp. Ex. xii. 46), decides that this type rules in the Apocalypse also; further, ancient Christian literature generally attests its value to the extent that the image of Isaiah was first applied to Christ through the medium of the paschal lamb; finally, if all these New Testament passages refer to the type of Isaiah, it would be natural to expect that Isaiah's word *πρόβατον* would be used, and not *ἀμνός* and *ἀρνίον*, which belong to the language of sacrificial ritual. From the circumstance that the standing form under which Jesus appears is that of a lamb, and of a lamb that has been slain, it is indeed by no means certain, as Weiss has recently observed, *bibl. Theol.* p. 621, that we are not to think of the paschal lamb, but of the Messiah, who, according to Isaiah, goes quietly and patiently to the slaughter. Baur, p. 223, in direct opposition to Ritschl, affirms that "the wrath of the Lamb" is not inconsistent with the reference of the term to Isa. liii.; for if there be in this wrath nothing un-Messianic, it may be ascribed even to the meek and gentle lamb of the prophet; that nowhere in the Apocalypse is there any allusion to the paschal lamb, unless the expression "slain lamb" can be referred to it, an expression which may be just as easily referred to Isaiah; and finally, that the passage in Isaiah is often referred in other relations to Jesus; and even where He is called the paschal Lamb, it describes Him not as the slain paschal lamb, but as the Lamb of the prophet led to the slaughter. Without entering into a lengthy discussion of all the reasons for and against, I remark that the seer in the course of his representation unquestionably often uses the expression, "the lamb," without any special signification, but only as a standing designation of Christ (comp. xvii. 14); the decision, therefore, lies solely in the place where the lamb first appears, v. 6–14. But not a single word or feature reminds us of the lamb-like patience of Isaiah; on the contrary, the expressions used, such as, "in the midst of the throne and of the four living creatures, and in the midst of the elders"—"as it had been slain"—"Thou hast redeemed us to God by Thy blood"—"kings and priests"—"we shall reign on the earth," give a good and consistent sense only when we think of the paschal lamb. And to me it appears very significant, that in the only other place where "the Lamb" is expressly mentioned as having been "slain," it seems to lie far from the type of Isaiah; while, on the other hand, the thought of the deliverance of Israel and the paschal sacrifice, finds spontaneous expression. Egypt, the Egyptian plagues, the salvation of Israel, the foundation of the Old Testament church, the sojourn of the people of God in the wilderness, and other things in the same connection, lie as types at the bottom of many of the representations of the Apocalypse. Can it be that the passover alone has presented no type to the writer? These reasons, apart from subordinate ones, such as, for example, the undeniable prominence of the temple service in the symbolism of the book, and the comparatively few references to Isaiah, are to me decisive in favour of the view that the ground-type for the name and symbol of the Lamb was the paschal offering. But it is also certain, and that not merely on the ground of the few undoubted references to Isaiah, as in xii. 5, xiv. 5, but more on account of the author's habit of combination, that in his representation of the lamb led to the slaughter, the figure of the prophet has a share (comp. i. 9, iii. 10; comp. Beyschlag, p. 126). Such passages as vii. 14 (comp. 1 Pet. ii. 22–25) make it probable that the lambs offered at the cleansing of the leper (comp. Lev. xiv. 10–13) form an integral part in the lamb-symbols of the Apocalypse (comp. Lechler, p. 200); and, indeed, when Hoekstra, p. 388, on account of the word *ἀρνίον*, thinks it not impossible that Jer. xi. 19 (*ἐγὼ δὲ ὡς ἀρνίον* ἄκακον ἀγόμενον τοῦ θύεσθαι) was in the thoughts of the seer, I cannot but agree with him. But the statement of Baur, p. 233, that the lamb, in the symbolic language of the Old Testament, is the most pregnant expression for the idea of sacrifice and atonement, as based upon the historical fact of Christ's death, ought not to have been called in question by the writer above mentioned, as it is when he says, "it would have been so if the Apocalypse had, like Paul, regarded the death of Christ as our propitiation," for the question here is neither anything about the Pauline expressions,—"propitiation, forgiveness, non-imputation of sin, justification by grace,"—nor about the Pauline view of the meaning of the death of Christ with reference to sin, and the relation thereby disturbed between God and men; but whether His death was in the esteem of the seer, as Hoekstra affirms, p. 394, only the highest and most perfect martyrdom, and at the same time the necessary fact for our deliverance from Satan's most trying weapon, the fear of death, and was thus merely symbolic and subjective in its significance; little as there may be available for the explanation of the lamb-symbol in detail, in any case it exalts the doctrine of the author respecting the death of Jesus above the purely typical and subjective.

Interpretation in detail finds a place only in the figurative expressions of the book concerning the *blood* of Christ. In our judgment, Hoekstra, p. 389, would take us captive *à priori* when he affirms that, if the seer teaches the atonement of our sins through the blood of the cross, and therefore, though not in the same words, justification by grace, this doctrine not only does not stand in connection with any of the other representations of the writer, but it would be with him a decided *nonsequitur*, since his doctrine of the way of salvation—he distinctly takes the standpoint of works—entirely excludes such a theory of the atonement. In the section on the saints and their works, we shall show that the "works" of the Apocalypse do not exclude the sacrificial significance of the death of Christ, but rather presuppose it. Moreover, such men as Baur, who regard "the works" in the same light as Hoekstra, find nothing illogical in the fact that the seer ascribes to the death of Christ an objective and sin-atoning power. Let us, however, hear and endeavour to understand the author himself.

We read in v. 9, "Thou wast slain, and hast *redeemed us to God by Thy blood* out of every kindred, and tongue, and people, and nation; and hast made us unto our God kings and priests: and we shall reign on the earth." It is said of the 144,000 on Mount Zion, "These were redeemed from among men, being the first-fruits unto God and to the Lamb." In that they are redeemed to God, or God and the Lamb, they become His possession, His servants, His people; from their previous slavery they are redeemed by a price. Therefore they were before not His possession: they belonged to the earth, to men, to the world, which did not give glory to Him as their Lord, but served the devil; they were previously in a condition of slavery, because deceived by the devil (comp. xii. 9), to whose kingdom, subjects, and servants they were attached; or—and this representation is interwoven with the other—because (comp. xii. 10), on account of their sins, they are accused by him whose bond-slaves and prisoners they are. But Christ, with His blood, that is, by the surrender and sacrifice of His life, has paid the price or ransom, the penalty or debt. He has—for this is implied—put Satan's accusation to silence, and discharged his claim on the sinner; He has thus delivered all whom He has made free and acquired, from subjection to the devil; or freed them from his claims, separated them from the earth, and made them God's, not merely as subjects or servants, but as kings and priests, first-fruits unto Him. The entire representation reminds us of such places as Matt. xx. 28; 1 Pet. xviii. 19, ii. 9, 10; Acts xx. 28, xxvi. 18; Rom. vi. 17–19; Gal. iii. 13, iv. 5; 1 Cor. vi. 20, vii. 23; Col. i. 13; Tit. ii. 14; 2 Pet. ii. 1; it comes, indeed, from a combination of the Old Testament idea of the sin or expiatory-offering, which, as payment, penalty, or ransom, redeemed from indebtedness to God, with that of the peculiar or acquired people which He had taken from amongst the nations, Ex. xix. 5; Deut. vii. 6, xiv. 2, xxvi. 18; Isa. xliii. 21; Mal. iii. 17; ideas, though incongruous in themselves, reconciled by the later idea of the kingdom and rights of the devil. The type with respect to deliverance from sin may be Isa. lii. 4, 5, 7–12; but the type of the passover, which not only atoned for the people, but also delivered them from servitude and separated them from the world for the service of God, is pre-eminent. When Hoekstra says, p. 394, from the standpoint which he assigns to the seer, that the death of Christ may be represented as a price which He has paid to redeem a divinely-consecrated church for Himself and for God, the divines and preachers of our day furnish striking proof that, while they regard the death of Christ as a martyrdom and as an event delivering from the fear of death, they can also speak of redemption through the blood of Christ. The seer was not a speculative Rationalist; and when he regards and represents the blood of Christ as the purchase-price or ransom, His death cannot have been to him anything else than a sacrificial death.

We meet with another representation in vii. 14, where it is said, "they have washed (ἔπλυναν) their robes, and have *made* (ἐλεύκαναν) *them white* (bright) in the blood of the Lamb." While Hengstenberg distinguishes the washing from the making white, and refers the former to the forgiveness of sins and the latter to sanctification, Düsterdieck declares it to be against the nature of the image, which he regards as describing a washing by which the garments are made white; and he sees in it a fine trait of genuine ethics, namely, that they who, in their earthly life, have washed their garments white in the blood of the Lamb, shall in the future life appear clothed in white raiment (comp. iii. 4, xix. 8). But the passages quoted do not refer to that life at all; and the "white" of the Apocalypse, as Hengstenberg justly remarks, is not simply white, synonymous with καθαρός, but the brilliant, shining white of the light, synonymous with λαμπρός (comp. xv. 6, xix. 8). Consequently, in the idea of the seer it cannot be the result of washing. To wash makes clean; to make white, is to make bright or shining. What, then, is the representation involved in washing and making garments white in the blood of the Lamb? Impurity, defilement, uncleanness, are in this book the most frequent designations of sin (comp. iii. 4, xiv. 4, 5, xvii. 4, xxii. 11–15); and when Christians are said to have washed their garments in the blood of the Lamb, it is meant that they have appropriated the death of Christ to themselves, and that His death has cleansed them from their sins—taken their sins away from them, or brought to them deliverance from them. When Christians are said to have made their garments white in or with the blood of the Lamb, it is intended to say that, having appropriated the death of Christ, the same has sanctified them, that the white garments are the symbols of holiness, and making them white, of the process of purification, as we shall show in the next section, pointing out, at the same time, the close connection of these symbols with the idea of the priestly and kingly office of Christian men. Purification from sin, expressed by washing the garments, the washing which is frequently mentioned both in the Old Testament and the New under the images of forgiveness, atonement, deliverance, and justification, springing from the sphere of law and social life, and under others arising from the natural bodily life, must be distinguished from that occurring in Jas. iv. 8, 2 Cor. vii. 1, which comes to the same thing as the legal and social images, as far as on both sides the negative phase of becoming a Christian is made prominent. In the one case it is evident that, through grace, sin is put away on the part of God, and on the other that it is put away on the part of man: in the former case the result is happiness; and in the latter, holiness. Making the garments white in the blood of the Lamb relates to washing, not as the positive to the negative aspect of becoming a Christian, but it describes positively the practical realization of the same in the principle of life given by the death of Christ, the essential appropriation of which the washing negatively symbolizes. The whole representation reminds us of Acts xv. 9, xxii. 16, 1 Cor. vi. 11, 2 Pet. i. 9, and has doubtless originated in a combination of the Old Testament ideas of the sin-offering (comp. Lev. xii. 8, xvi. 30–34) and the washings, especially of the priests (comp. Ex. xix. 10, xxix. 4; Ps. li. 4–9). Isa. liii. is not to be accepted as the type; much rather, as shown by the white garments, the clothing of priestly kings, the passover in its meaning as a sin-offering, together with the lamb as an offering of purification, and the washings, have led to the representation of washing the garments in the blood of the Lamb. Moreover, there hardly needs any statement of proof that the seer, in this washing, thought of *baptism*, or rather, by this biblical expression desired to represent in its signification baptism itself. According to Hoekstra, p. 394, there was in the mind of the seer the idea that the blood of Christ is the power which prepared the martyrs for martyrdom—the self-washing of their garments. What he adduces in support of this, namely, that in the words, "these are they which came out of great tribulation," vii. 14, the persons mentioned are designated as martyrs, and that the white robes decidedly permit us to think of them as such (comp. vi. 11), fails in presence of the fact that martyrs are not the only persons who come out of the great tribulation, xx. 4, and that white raiment is worn by non-martyrs also (comp. iii. 4, 5). It would have been different if John had done certain expositors the favour of writing, "they have washed their robes, and made them white in or with their blood;" but he has written, "in or with the blood of the Lamb;" so that it is always partially right, that from a Pauline standpoint it cannot be said, "We have delivered ourselves from our sins through the blood of Christ, or have reconciled ourselves to God, or cleansed ourselves from evil;" but this does not hinder that, according to the view of the seer, the death of Christ has power to deliver and sanctify those who avail themselves of it.

In i. 5, two readings, each with strong claims, stand opposed to each other: λούσαντι ἀπό and λύσαντι ἐκ. If we read, "who loved us, and *washed* us from our sins in His own blood," it reminds us forcibly of vii. 14; only λούσαντι does not refer to the robes, but to the wearers, and the washing is ascribed to Christ, and not, as in vii. 14, to Christians. In the latter difference I cannot, with Hoekstra, p. 394, find a reason against the reading which gives λούσαντι, and the less so, as the washing of the body is a different image from the washing of garments. If, on the contrary, we read, "who has loved us, and *redeemed* us from our sins by His own blood," we are led to v. 9, xiv. 3, 4; only I would not say, with Köstlin, p. 486, that "ἀγοράζειν adds to λύειν the positive idea that the redeemed belong to God and His Son." But while ἀγοράζειν expresses the negative and the positive side, freedom from the power of the devil, and subjection to God as His, λύειν expresses the negative side. Better still, if we say that the phrases, "redeemed from the earth" unto God, and "redeemed us from our sins," are different images. In the latter, sins are conceived of as bonds which hold men under debt and slavery, from which Christ, through His death, as that which removes the debt, or propitiates, or delivers from servitude, saves them. And though part of the reading in i. 5 may be disputed, this is certain, that it emphatically expresses what similar passages tacitly imply, namely, that the motive by which Christ was led to give His life was His *love* for His people. How Hoekstra can say, p. 394, that the breaking of the power of temptation, through the martyr-death of Christ, is, in fact, a deliverance of believers from the bond which binds them to sin, can be explained only on the assumption that he supposed the seer to regard sin, and slavery to sin, as destroyed by good example, or, more strictly, by enlightening instruction,—a view so utterly foreign to a consciousness springing from the Old Testament and Judaism, that the unprejudiced reader will require no special proof.

It is said in xii. 11, "*they overcame him by the blood of the Lamb, and by the word of their testimony;* and they loved not their lives unto the death." To give the final blow, Hoekstra, p. 395, has reserved this passage until the last, and he triumphantly assures us that his interpretation is the only one it will bear. Why? Because it is said of "our brethren" that they themselves overcame Satan their accuser before God, and not that Christ has done it for them. They are also said to have overcome him,—not through, which *διά, c. accus.*, does not signify, but on account of, or in virtue of the blood of the Lamb and the word of their testimony; and it is expressly stated that the conquest consists in their not having loved their lives unto the death, so surrendering themselves as martyrs. But it seems to me that his triumph is premature. The sense of the passage is not that they overcame him in that they did not love their lives, but died a martyr's death, for which the blood of the Lamb gave them strength, and of which the word of their testimony was the cause. If it were, the passage would certainly sustain Hoekstra's position. But the words affirm that they overcame him on the ground of three things: the first of which is, the blood of the Lamb; the second, the word of their testimony; the third, the sacrifice of their lives: for it is as certain that *διά* in both cases belongs to *ἐνίκησαν*, as that *οὐκ ἠγάπησαν τὴν ψυχήν* implies a third, only in a somewhat looser connection. The blood of the Lamb is not, therefore, the motive to martyrdom, but the first causal power of their conquest over Satan, upon which the other two are based. The words, "by the blood of the Lamb," have no special importance in relation to the doctrine of our book concerning the death of Christ. Neither in themselves nor in their reference to the conquest of Satan, nor in their connection with the testimony and the martyrdom, do they tell us whether the writer had in his mind the representation of v. 9 or that of i. 5 or vii. 14, or some other.

If, in xxii. 14, we should read *πλύνοντες τὰς στολὰς αὐτῶν* instead of *ποιοῦντες τὰς ἐντολὰς αὐτοῦ*, we then have only a parallel with the first half of vii. 14, though conceivably containing within it the second.

The words, "whose names are not written in the book of life of the Lamb slain from the foundation of the world," xiii. 8, as Hengstenberg remarks, ascribe the book of life directly to the slain Lamb, and thus make all salvation, even that of the devout men of the Old Covenant, dependent upon the sacrifice of Christ. Beyond this, the passage does not give any information respecting the connection between the death of Christ and eternal life. Schmid, *bibl. Theol.* II. p. 361, thinks that, with the predicate of Christ, "the Word of God," a statement is associated which points to the atonement, "He was clothed with a vesture dipped in blood," xix. 13. We may notice, however, an unmistakeable reference to Isa. lxiii. 1–4, and the impossibility of finding the atonement in the latter leads us to regard Schmid's supposition as untenable.

The seer, says Köstlin, p. 483, agreeing with Baur, p. 220, belongs to those who attach great importance to the fact of the resurrection. And, indeed, the *resurrection* of Christ undeniably stands with Him in the same rank as His death on the cross. Christ says: "I am the first and the last: I am He that liveth and was dead; and, behold, I am alive for evermore, Amen; and have the keys of hell and of death," i. 17, 18. In ii. 8 we read: "These things saith the first and the last, which was dead, and is alive;" and Christ is also called "the first-begotten of the dead," i. 5. Hoekstra has endeavoured to show, pp. 380–382, that, though it fell to Christ's lot to rise soon after His death, His resurrection in the idea of the writer did not differ from that of believers. It is true that the word ζῆν is used of the resurrection of others as well as of that of Christ (comp. xx. 4); in the account of the two witnesses, xi. 7–12, it is in the highest degree probable that we have indirect evidence of the views of the seer concerning Christ's resurrection. Christ does not appear in either of the resurrection scenes described in xx. 4, 5, xx. 11–15; this, however, does not exclude the possibility that for the seer His resurrection might have a different meaning than that which is common to the resurrection of others; and that it really had a higher meaning, he has distinctly shown. According to i. 17, 18 (comp. ii. 8), Christ is the first and the last, that is, the self-eternal beginner and finisher of all created being. He is "He that liveth," the eternal and absolute Life, from which all created life proceeds, and in which it consists, and to which it tends.

He was dead, or became dead (ἐγενόμην νεκρός), but the historical fact of His death is followed by the historical fact of His resurrection; He is alive again (ἔζησε), and lives for evermore, that is, having regard to the "behold!" He is revealed as the eternally living One. This fact has for Christians the signification that Christ as the risen "first and last," as He who liveth for ever, has the keys of hell and death; that is, He possesses power over both, and can deliver from them, and can subject to them (comp. ii. 10, 11, xxii. 3–5, xiv. 13). When Christ is described as "the first-begotten of the dead," i. 5, it cannot be intended merely that He was the first to rise, but that He was the first-fruits, the beginner and forerunner, the Head and Lord of all who are dead, or will die, and rise again to eternal life. Thus, though Hoekstra entirely ignores the ownership of the keys of death and hell, and declares it to be at least doubtful whether by "the first-begotten of the dead" we are to understand anything more than that Christ was the first to rise; or whether the writer intended to represent His resurrection as *nativitas quaedam*, and so arrives at the conclusion that Christ rose first of all, and immediately after His death, but that there is no essential difference between His resurrection and that of others,—we have found that He, as raised from the dead, and thereby declared to be alive for evermore, is, on one side, the possessor of the keys, and has power to punish men with death and to deliver them from death, to kill and to make alive — undoubtedly a divine prerogative; and on the other side, as "the first-begotten of the dead," He is made known as sharing in that eternal life which, like Him and through Him, His followers shall ultimately enjoy. Here, again, we evidently meet with that quality in Christ which to modern critics appears to be a contradiction, but which does not seem to have presented the slightest difficulty to the seer, namely, that in Him there is a revelation of the absolute divine nature as well as of the absolute human nature, or of what human nature may and will become, wholly corresponding to the Logos nature of Christ in His twofold or mediatorial capacity.

In what does the activity of the *exalted* Christ consist? That, according to v. 8, the seer, as De Wette thinks, appears to know nothing of an interceding Christ, hardly needs to be expressly questioned. It is certainly not without meaning that the Lamb, v. 6, stands "in the midst (ἐν μέσῳ) of the throne and of the four living creatures, and in the midst of the elders;" and that it is said, vii. 17, "the Lamb which is in the midst of the throne" (ἀνὰ μέσον, the throne, an open half-circle). In the former passage John does not intend merely to define the limits within which the Lamb stands, namely, the space whose centre is the throne and the four living creatures, and which is surrounded by the elders (comp. Düsterdieck *in loco*); nor could his design be only to present the Lamb in the highest place, which the Messiah, standing next to God, and exalted far above the elders, could take (comp. Ewald *in loco*), but, as Düsterdieck himself, p. 297, observes, whether the Lamb is seen in the midst before the throne of God, or (?) whether in the midst of the representatives of believers who surround the throne, He has always the same position between Him who sits on the throne and the living creatures and the elders who stand around; that is, His appearance as a Lamb, as well as the position in which He stands, indicates His atoning, mediatorial character; or we may rather say, with special reference to His state of exaltation, that the position of the Lamb, v. 6, vii. 17, teaches that as Christ from eternity has been the mediator between the Creator and the creation, and as in time He sustained the same office, so He does also in His exaltation, and thus continues in its *propitiatory* aspect His Logos-Messianic activity.

But this mediatorial office has two other sides, one of which is the *revelation* of God to the world. John sees "in the right hand of Him that sat on the throne a book written within and on the back side, sealed with seven seals," v. 1–3. It is the book of the future and of destiny, the secret purpose of God concerning the world. A strong angel cries with a loud voice, "Who is worthy to open the book, and to loose the seals thereof? And no man in heaven, nor in earth, nor under the earth, was able to open the book, neither to look thereon." At this John wept; but one of the elders said to him, "Weep not: behold, the Lion of the tribe of Judah, the Root of David, hath prevailed to open the book, and to loose the seven seals thereof;" and John saw that "in the midst of the throne and of the four living creatures, and in the midst of the elders, stood a Lamb as it had been slain, having seven horns and seven eyes, which are the seven Spirits of God sent forth into all the earth; and He came and took the book out of the right hand of Him that sat upon the throne," and one after another opened the seals. The sense is, that the Messiah, who is completing His saving work, has looked into the secrets of the divine counsels (Weiss, *bibl. Theol.* p. 629), or that God reveals to Christ alone His hidden purposes, and that Christ makes them known to men through the prophets (comp. i. 1, xix. 10, xxii. 16). So in His exaltation Christ is called "the faithful Witness," i. 5; "the Amen, the faithful and true Witness," iii. 14. The two prophets in chap. xi. are witnesses of Christ; and when He is said to have the seven Spirits of God, who are sent forth into all the earth, iii. 1, v. 6, what can it mean, if not that Christ is the medium through whom the Holy Spirit is sent, and, as the possessor of all communications of life from God to the world, as the personal principle of all revelation of God, is continually active?

The third side of this mediatorial activity is the *government of the world.* Christ has sat down with His Father on His throne, iii. 21; He is "the Prince of the kings of the earth," i. 5; He is "Lord of lords and King of kings," xvii. 14; "He hath on His vesture and on His thigh a name written, King of kings and Lord of lords," xix. 16. The Lamb has seven horns, the symbol of divine power, v. 6. Christ has received from His Father authority to rule the nations with a rod of iron, and to break them in pieces like a potter's vessel, ii. 27; and He is a sharer of the divine throne, not merely, as Hoekstra says (comp. "The Person of Christ"), in a limited Messianic sense, but in a universal sense; as the Logos-Messiah He takes part in the divine government of the world; He rules or governs the world with omnipotent power, in that God rules or governs it through Him. But what is true of God's government of the world, namely, that it is perfected in the ideal reality, and in the historical reality is still struggling and future, is naturally entirely so with the mediatorial world-government of Christ; for even in the places where the heavenly inhabitants rejoice that the kingdoms of this world are become the kingdoms of God, the same is also said of the Lamb, xi. 15, xii. 10, though at the same time the book predicts that in the future Christ is to be the ruler of the whole world; once it is said that it has been given Him to rule the nations, ii. 27; and at other times it is affirmed that He must or will exercise this authority, xii. 5, xix. 15.

The same *duality* in the relation between Christ and Christians, —I do not say men, but Christians,—according to which He is as well the author of salvation as He is the head and type of the saved, while His followers are both its subjects or receivers, and followers or imitators, of the works of Christ,—the same duality, which in so many particulars I have pointed out, reaches even to the exalted state of Christ. It is symbolized by the position in which He is placed, v. 6, vii. 17, as the reconciler and mediator in the narrower sense of the word. We need only compare the position of the elders, v. 11, vii. 11, and their insignia, iv. 4, with the priesthood of Christians, i. 6, v. 10, and it will be with difficulty that we can avoid the conclusion that, in the representations of the seer, Christians have, through Christ, received a mediatorial standing. Christ appears especially, v. 1–7, as the personal principle of all self-revelation of God; so in view of chap. x., and the expressions concerning Christian prophecy, it must be that the possessors of the Spirit also bear witness as Christ does (comp. xix. 10). Christ sits with His Father on His throne, but those who overcome shall sit with Christ on His throne (comp. iii. 21, ii. 26, also i. 5, xvii. 14, with i. 6, v. 10). Does this mean that between Christ and His people there exists only a difference in degree?

Christ's activity in the already existing kingdom of God, or His relation to Christianity, is a separate and narrower sphere within that of His general operations as world-reconciler, revealer of God, and mediatorial ruler of the world. In it we find three distinct features, that of *the prophet, the high priest, and the king*, which, according to the manner of our author, are frequently combined. It may therefore be wiser, instead of classifying them, to consider them genetically. We read, "These things saith He that is holy, He that is true, He that hath the key of David, He that openeth, and no man shutteth; and shutteth, and no man openeth," iii. 7 (comp. Isa. xxii. 22). The house of David is a symbol for the kingdom of David (comp. Ps. ci.), and David and his kingdom are actual predictions of Christ and the kingdom of God. Christ "is the root and offspring of David," v. 5, xxii. 16; He possesses and exercises in the kingdom of God the power of David in his house; He is Lord of the kingdom of God; irrevocably receives men into it, and irrevocably excludes them; and that, not with the distinction of the earthly kingdom, either in one case or the other, but without distinction both here and hereafter. Christ makes the Christian; makes blessed, and takes away both Christianity and blessedness. The Lamb, as slain, stands "in the midst of the throne and of the four living creatures, and in the midst of the elders," v. 6. When we rightly understand the meaning of the elders, it is evident that here is meant the efficacy of Christ's sacrificial death, and His priestly intercession for His people. But as the priesthood of Christ is thus described on its atoning side with reference to God, so the same appears, i. 12–16, more from its kingly governing side with reference to Christians. John sees one like a Son of man, i. 12, 13, in the midst of the seven golden candlesticks. He describes Himself as He "who walketh in the midst of the seven golden candlesticks," ii. 1; and the seven candlesticks are explained to mean the seven churches, i. 20. Christ has in His right hand seven stars, i. 16, and He speaks of Himself as "holding the seven stars in His right hand," ii. 1; and the seven stars represent the angels of the seven churches. He is also ever present with the churches, and always active among them (περιπατεῖ); they are in His power, and no man can deliver them out of His hand when He is disposed to rebuke and chasten; nor, when He resolves to protect, can any one rend them from Him. He also searches the reins and hearts, and gives to every man according to His works, ii. 23. He knows the works of Christians, ii. 2, etc., and sometimes finds them not perfect before God, iii. 2. He hates the works of the Nicolaitanes, ii. 6; and where their doctrines are professed among Christians, ii. 14, where they are quietly endured, ii. 20, where Christians have left their first love, ii. 4, there He has somewhat against them. He, however, gives time for repentance, ii. 21, exhorts to reformation, ii. 5, and return, iii. 2; but if they will not repent, ii. 5, xvi. 22, and watch, iii. 3, then He will come upon them as a thief, at a moment of which they know not, iii. 3, xvi. 15. He then removes the candlestick of one of the churches out of its place,—that is, He rejects it, and takes the gospel from it, ii. 5. He fights with the sword of His mouth against the adherents of error,—that is, in judgment He turns His omnipotent word destructively against them, ii. 16 (comp. Isa. xi. 4; Wisd. xviii. 15, 16). He casts the false prophetess into a bed, and them that commit adultery with her into great tribulation, and destroys her children with death, ii. 22, 23 (comp. Lev. xx. 10, 11). He spues the lukewarm out of His mouth, iii. 16. On the other hand, the church is His bride, xxii. 17; He loves those who belong to Him, i. 5, iii. 9; He rebukes and chastens them, iii. 19; He gives them counsel, iii. 18; He stands at their door and knocks, and goes into those who hear His voice and open the door (the thought of *the Supper* lies very near to this), and eats with them and they with Him, iii. 20. Those who have not defiled their garments shall walk with Him in white, iii. 4 (comp. the section on the saints and their works). Before the church, which has a little power, and has kept His word, and not denied His name, He sets an open door, which no man can shut. He gives to the synagogue of Satan those who say they are Jews and are not, and makes them come and worship and acknowledge that He has loved His people; that is, they will humbly acknowledge that they are the true Israel, amongst whom salvation must be sought, iii. 8, 9 (comp. Isa. ii. 3, xliii. 3–7, xlv. 14, xlix. 23–26, lx. 14; Ps. xviii. 45, lxxii. 9; Zech. viii. 20–23). Because one of the churches has kept the word of His patience, He will keep it in the hour of temptation, iii. 10. Upon the faithful He will put no further burden, ii. 24. To those who are faithful unto death He will give a crown of life, ii. 10 (comp. the closing passage of the seventh letter, also vii. 17, xiv. 1–5). How Christ knows the works of Christians, how He regards them, and how He does and will stand in relation to them, He testifies through His prophets (comp. i. 11, xix. 20, xix. 10, xxii. 16).

It will be evident that, in what has been said above, our aim has not been to exhaust, but merely to sketch a subject which must find its completion in the following sections. I will only add a word here respecting Hoekstra's judgment of the *moral character of Christ* as represented in the Apocalypse. With reference to De Wette's utterances, in the introduction to his Commentary, p. 5, Hoekstra says, p. 401: "The moral dispositions of God and Christ toward men are sharply divided between love and wrath, but of a sympathizing, forbearing, forgiving disposition toward the erring and the sinful; of the disposition of Jesus, who wept over the blindness and misery of His stiff-necked kinsmen, we do not find much in the book. The basis of Christ's character is the theocratic King; He is much less the

Saviour, who does not break the bruised reed, the spiritual deliverer, who was kind to His enemies that He might win them for the kingdom of God, than the powerful prince and warrior, the victorious general, who crushes his foes." Very justly Hoekstra has drawn a parallel between the disposition of God and Christ. What we have said in the section on God, respecting His love as represented in this book, is essentially applicable to Christ also. The seer has, in no sense of the word, aimed to give a picture of the character of Jesus, for in the Apocalypse He is no longer the evangelist; and in our opinion the impression of sentimental tolerant modern liberalism is not left by the Christ of the synoptical eschatology. If the statements of our book respecting the disposition of Christ are sharply divided between anger and love, historical criticism will perhaps find a similar division in the Christ of history when it no longer pleases it to indemnify to its utmost Him whom it represents as a man, "though an exceptional one," by assimilation with a free-thought theologian of the latest date.

But how can we contend with those who at one time proceed upon the "settled fact" that we have no historical sources concerning Christ, and know as good as nothing about Him certainly, but at another time, with virtuous indignation, oppose to the revengeful seer the Christ of the Gospels praying for His enemies?

2. The Spirit.

In the use of the word "spirit," the trilogy of our book is to a certain extent repeated: God, the devil, man; heaven, the abyss, the earth. The "spirit of life," which after three days and a half came from God and entered into the two witnesses, so that the dead stood upon their feet, xi. 11 (comp. vers. 8, 9), as well as the "spirit" which the second beast gave to the image of the first, so that it spoke, is nothing more than life, or the breath of life,—in the first passage, described after the manner of the Old Testament (comp., for example, Gen. ii. 7),—by which the flesh is animated; in a neutral sense, the *natural*, human, earthly life-principle, but which appears in the words "from God" as supernatural, and by its relation to the false prophet as subnatural. Everywhere else in the Apocalypse the spirit is the principle of that which influences the natural, human, and earthly, affirming itself therein, potentializing the same, and not the natural life. But this separates again, on the one hand, into the *supernatural*, the holy, and the divine; and on the other, into the *subnatural*, the unholy, and the devilish. "Spirit," as the principle of the latter, certainly occurs only once in the Apocalypse, and then only in a peculiar case, where the writer sees three unclean spirits like frogs go out of the mouth of the dragon, and out of the mouth of the beast, and out of the mouth of the false prophet; and says, "they are the spirits of devils working miracles," xvi. 13, 14.

In all other places of the Apocalypse the term "Spirit" is used of the *Holy Spirit or the Spirit of God*, the principle of supernatural life. It is certainly not generally granted, that in all passages not quoted which speak of the Spirit, the Holy Spirit or the Spirit of God, in an ethical sense, is meant. Yet Düsterdieck's explanation of the Spirit in i. 10, as meaning the higher spiritual nature of man, stands alone, as also the exposition which makes the spirits of the prophets to mean their own human spirits, xxii. 6. De Wette, on iv. 5, finds in the seven lamps an image of the continuous, calm revelation of God, in distinction from the thunders and lightnings as symbols of the critical, powerful manifestations of Himself, and affirms, therefore, that the Spirit is to the seer the principle of physical and mental life through which the inner influence of God comes into contact with the world of nature and men. But the thunder and the lamps do not describe different aspects of the Spirit: the first is rather a symbol of works of power; and the second, of the Spirit of God (comp. v. 6). Hoekstra says, p. 370, note, "the Spirit of God (or the seven Spirits) is in this book not conceived of ethically, but physically, as a revelation of the power of God, as in the Old Testament, while His purely spiritual operations consist in the communication of the gift of prophecy;" and Weiss, *bibl. Theol.* p. 629, writes: "The sevenfold Spirit which Christ also has, appears to be conceived of after Zechariah, as the world-pervading power of God; but in the sphere of salvation it has its peculiar significance as the medium of revelation, and appears in men exclusively as the principle of prophecy." But as the seer distinguishes the Spirit as clearly as possible from the revelation of power, by the contrasting images of thunder and lamps, he has also done the same by the distinction of the horns and eyes, v. 6; and we shall soon learn why it is that, amongst all the activities of the Spirit, prophecy appears so prominently in the foreground of this book. Still less than the ethical signification of "the Spirit," is its nature acknowledged as the principle of supernatural *life;* on the contrary, almost all expositors (comp. Köstlin, p. 488) regard it as the principle of revelation. And yet, I think, against such a conception of the Spirit, which beforehand makes it impossible to understand the doctrine of the Spirit, it is sufficient to mention that the Logos is the revealing principle, and is yet not identical with the Spirit. It is almost superfluous to remark how, for example, in iii. 1–3, it cannot, on the supposition that the Spirit is the principle of revelation, be explained why Christ is introduced as "He that hath the seven Spirits of God;" but if we regard the Spirit as the principle of divine life, it is clear enough, for then we find a reference to the condition of sleep and death which prevailed at Sardis.

But the seer at one time speaks of "*the seven Spirits* of God," iii. 1, iv. 5, v. 6 (comp. i. 4); at another, of "*the Spirit,*" ii. 7, etc.; and then again, of "*the Spirit of prophecy,*" xix. 10; of "*the spirits of the prophets,*" xxii. 6, and of being "*in the Spirit,*" i. 10. The question arises, How are these various expressions related to each other? According to De Wette on i. 4, the sacred, perfect number describes the manifoldness of the Spirit in His relation to the world, inasmuch as the same one Spirit is everywhere present, and penetrates all things (comp. v. 6; Wisd. vii. 22). Düsterdieck on the same passage says, "John's example is Zech. iii. 9, iv. 6, 10. The Spirit cannot be perceived in His essential unity, as He is before the throne of God, or as sent into all the earth; for that, there needs the concrete form (comp. Matt. iii. 16; Acts ii. 2–4), associated with the sacred number, which symbolizes the fulness of the divine perfection; and thus the one Spirit, which, as with Zechariah, is the safety of the church, appears as 'seven eyes,' 'seven lamps,' or even as 'seven Spirits.'" Weiss (*bibl. Theol.* p. 629, comp. p. 616) thinks that the "seven Spirits," like "the spirits of the prophets," may be regarded as the one Spirit of prophecy in His various manifestations. Züllig's exposition appears to me the simplest (I. p. 255); going back to Isa. xi. 2, he points out how the later Jewish theology, in its efforts to produce a complete list of the prophetically-revealed perfections of

God, attaches great importance to this passage, and partly from a predilection in favour of the number seven, and partly from the fact that, for example, in Num. xi. 25–29, Isa. xliv. 3 (?), and Joel ii. 28, 29, the Spirit of the Lord has the more special meaning of the Spirit of prophetic gifts, or the Spirit of prophecy, has conceived of the Spirit of the Lord, so prominent in that passage, in the sense of this more special signification, and has brought out of it seven perfections of the Spirit of God, or the seven Spirits of God, and so laid the foundation for rabbinical speculation. This doctrine they found confirmed by such passages as Zech. iv. 10, where it is said of "those seven," that "they are the eyes of the Lord, which run to and fro through the whole earth" (comp. Rev. v. 6); and Ex. xxv. 37, Zech. iv. 2, where the seven lamps are mentioned (comp. Rev. iv. 5). The seer has everywhere used this figure when he wishes to represent the Spirit of God in the whole fulness of His nature; and it is equally the case when he speaks of Him independently of God or Christ, i. 4, iv. 5, and also when he considers Him as the Spirit which Christ has, iii. 1, v. 6. He speaks solely of the Spirit, for example, in ii. 7, xiv. 13, and understands thereby what he expressly says in xix. 10, and unmistakeably points out by the association of the Spirit and the bride in xxii. 17, namely, the Spirit of prophecy, the prophetic Spirit, the Spirit of God, so far as, in distinction from other manifestations of the Spirit, He reveals Himself to and through the prophets. The Spirit of prophecy also affirms itself in manifold variety in the individual prophets, hence "the spirits of the prophets," xxii. 6. Finally, the condition which the Spirit of God, especially the Spirit of Prophecy, renders prominent in various individuals is evidently Spirit, the condition of the Spirit, the being "in the Spirit," i. 10.

Köstlin (*ut ante*, p. 488) acknowledges that the exalted Christ has a specially close relation to the Spirit, and that an important position is given to the latter in this book, as he also acknowledges that the Spirit is there threefold: first, with God and Christ, but in an impersonal form; then in Christ; and finally, in the whole earth, that is, in believers and people of every tongue, and especially in the prophets; but he thinks the Spirit is not distinguished from the Son, not, indeed, as a separate *personality*, and admits only a somewhat independent definition of the same. We will pass over the expression "personality," and—which will lead us to a similar result—ask whether the seer decidedly distinguishes the Spirit, as a Being distinct from God, from Christ, and from Christians? When he, i. 5, speaks of "the seven Spirits which are before the throne" (comp. iv. 5), the Spirit is represented clearly enough as distinct from God. When, in xxii. 17, the Spirit and the bride say to Christ, "Come!" does there need any proof that, for the writer, the Spirit is independent of the Son and of the church? Could it be said of the Spirit conceived of as an actual principle, "he that hath an ear, let him hear what the Spirit saith unto the churches"? ii. 7; or, "yea, saith the Spirit, that they may rest from their labours"? xiv. 13. If we may not desire from the seer that he should have expressed his views in doctrinal rather than in symbolical language, I do not see what more he could have done to cause the supposed somewhat independent definition to appear perfect and complete.

But what is the relation of the Spirit to *God*, to *Christ*, and to *Christians?* Let us begin with the last. The Spirit is expressly distinguished from the bride, the church, xxii. 17; the Spirit speaks to the churches, ii. 7, etc. But the Spirit does not, therefore, stand outside the Christian, for the testimony of Jesus is the Spirit of prophecy; and that testimony, and thus the Spirit of prophecy, is possessed by the brethren of the seer, xix. 10; and the spirits of the prophets, xxii. 6, are the witnessing acts of the Spirit to the individual prophets. In like manner, the Spirit's independence in relation to Christ is clearly expressed in xxii. 17. But the Spirit does not stand outside, and with Christ, but He *has* the seven Spirits of God, iii. 1; the Lamb has the seven eyes, which are the seven Spirits of God, v. 6, and the testimony of Jesus is the Spirit of prophecy. We find, too, that while the prophet always has only a spirit, an individual feature of the Spirit, Christ has the Spirit in His entire fulness. The prophet only comes into Spirit ἐγενόμην ἐν πνεύματι, i. 9. Christ has the Spirit already; it belongs to His nature, and is, as it were, born with Him, as the eyes with the body, v. 6. The prophet is the instrument of the Spirit, or the Spirit speaks, witnesses through him (comp. i. 19, x. 9–11, xxii. 18); Christ speaks, or testifies continually through the Spirit, xix. 10. Evidently Christian prophecy has, for the seer, fully the same significance as the testimony borne by Christ during His earthly life. But why are the two perfectly equal? Because prophecy is nothing but the continued testimony of Jesus

Himself, xix. 10. Therefore, at the commencement of the letters, it is said that Christ speaks; and for the same reason, it is said, at the close of each, that it contains "what the Spirit saith to the churches." The seer symbolically represents the relation of Christ to the Spirit, when, in v. 6, the Lamb has seven eyes, which "are the seven Spirits of God sent forth into all the earth." I have nothing to add when Köstlin, p. 488, says of this passage—"The exalted Christ constantly sends forth from Himself the Spirit; the presence of the Spirit on the earth is, as it were, an effective looking down upon it on the part of Christ, a streaming forth of His light;" but when he continues, "The Spirit, the principle of revelation, is the self-opening, and the being open, of the heavenly to the earthly, through which the human perceives the divine, as through the eye of a man, we believe ourselves to be able to perceive his inward thoughts," he rests on the false conception of the Spirit as the revealing principle; but the apparent support which this idea finds in the "eyes" and the "lamps," fails when we consider that light in this book appears not as revelation, but as the nature of God; and the Spirit is light, not as the revelation, but as the life-principle of God. In like manner, when Köstlin remarks, p. 485, that, "according to iii. 1, v. 6, the Spirit of God is in the Lamb, the Spirit is the divinity which Christ possesses in addition to His humanity," it is hardly necessary to point out, after what has been said, that, v. 6, the Lamb has seven horns as well as seven eyes. The correct interpretation is rather that Christ has received the Spirit as well as the power from God; while God has both, not as received, but in Himself. But because the Spirit is the Spirit of God, it does not the less take an independent position in relation to Him; much more does the Spirit in Christ, in this respect, hold a similar relation as it does to God, and as in the prophets it does also to Christ. Chap. iv. 5 is symbolic, and is anticipated in i. 4, and states, that before the throne of God seven lamps burn, which are the seven Spirits of God, and that they are sent into all the earth.

Keeping in mind this relation of the Spirit to God and to Christ, it will not surprise us when John, i. 4, 5, wishes for the seven churches in Asia "grace and peace from Him which is, and which was, and which is to come, and from the seven Spirits which are before His throne, and from Jesus Christ." The principle of grace and of peace, as generally of all "spiritual," holy, supernatural, divine life for Christians, has for the writer also a threefold distinction—God, who has the same absolutely; Christ, who has received it mediatorially, but in its entire fulness; the Spirit, who has also received it for its realization among men, for individual Christians as well as for universal Christendom; but, again, according to its nature, not three but one, namely, the spiritual life-principle which is absolute in God, mediatorially in Christ, derived in the Christian. That the author, in i. 4, 5, has not indulged in pleonasm, nor mentioned the Spirit with God merely as a more strict definition, but that he thought and spoke really in a *Trinitarian* sense, in the wider acceptation of the term, need not, after all that has been said, be specifically proved. But when he, very remarkably, at the first glance, mentions the Spirit in the second place and Christ in the third, the tacit reason may certainly be, that he intended a varied testimony of Christ; but more probably we may find the ground of this in the consideration that the seer passed in thought from the absolute to the present active principle, and then returned to that which is mediatorial.

But wherein consists the *activity* of the Spirit? It would be decidedly too narrow a conception of v. 6, if, with Düsterdieck, we should think of the Spirit principally according to the measure of the eye-symbol, as the all-seeing, and say, "since Christ has the Spirit He knows all things, even things on the earth, whither the Spirit is sent,—the movements of His enemies, the condition of His friends," etc. It has the much deeper sense already given above, and which Köstlin has clearly seen, namely, that of representing generally Christ's relation to the Spirit. But the words, "sent forth into all the earth," mean that the Spirit, having gone out from Christ, and continuing to go out, is operative in all the earth, or in every land. The seer, according to his manner (comp. ii. 6, 15), here indicates beforehand what he afterwards, v. 9, expressly states when he says, "Thou hast redeemed us to God by Thy blood out of every kindred, and tongue, and people, and nation." During His earthly life Christ's activity was limited to Israel; but in His exaltation He sends the Spirit into all the earth,—in other words, since His exaltation the principle of the divine or spiritual life has become active in the widest circles. But if the relation of v. 9 to v. 6, according to the manner of the writer elsewhere, is unquestionable, so also the words, v. 10, "and hast made us unto our God kings and priests: and we shall reign on the earth," will not be without connection with sending the Spirit into all the earth; it is, however, only an Old Testament conception when the seer regards the communication of the Spirit as an anointing, and those who receive it as priestly kings. Accordingly the writer traces the sublime position of Christians in relation to God and men, their priestly kingdom, to the Spirit which is sent to them; so, on the other hand, he sees in the Spirit the source of all Christian salvation and happiness, and wishes grace and peace, Christian salvation and happiness, as given and experienced, i. 4, for the seven churches from the seven Spirits which are before the throne of God. But as this wish respects churches rather than individuals, so by his description of Christ as He who has the seven Spirits and the seven stars, iii. 1 (comp. i. 16–20), he expressly gives us to understand that the stars, the Christian churches, are such through the work of the Spirit, or as holders or possessors of the Spirit; that the Spirit and the church, as a living whole, stand in the closest relation to each other. Thus the whole Christian, spiritual life in individuals, as well as in the church, and not, as Weiss, *bibl. Theol.* p. 629, repeatedly assumes, prophecy merely, is to the seer the result of the Spirit's work, or, rather, of the self-affirmation of the Spirit. But the Spirit is to him sevenfold; he recognises, therefore, in Christendom a manifold variety of powers or existence-forms, gifts, or modes of manifestation of the one Spirit, which in their union express His entire fulness.

From the manifoldly various gifts of the Spirit, from the universal activity of the Spirit in Christians and Christendom, from the individual peculiarities of the Christian life in their relation to the divine principle, or, as the seer himself would express it, from the number of the seven Spirits, the Spirit comes before him especially and almost exclusively as the *Spirit of prophecy*, xix. 10. As the prophetic Spirit is a special Spirit by the side of the other, so that again has many distinctions, and every prophet has his individual Spirit, xxii. 6. Those who have the Spirit of prophecy, xix. 10, xxii. 9, x. 7, enter into the Spirit, or a state of inspiration (γίγνεσθαι ἐν πν.), i. 10, iv. 2 (comp. xxi. 10). As long as the prophet is in this condition he does everything, and everything happens to him in the Spirit,—that is, not being subject to the senses, but in an ideal manner corresponding to the nature of the Spirit; thus John is carried away by the angel in the

Spirit into the wilderness, xvii. 3; and to a great and high mountain, xxi. 10. He sees and hears, i. 2, 10, etc.; but he sees in a vision (ἐν τῇ ὁράσει, בֶּחָזוֹן), ix. 17. But what does he see and hear? "The things which are, and the things which shall be hereafter," i. 19, iv. 1; "things which must shortly come to pass," i. 1; not things existing and present to the senses, but the things, persons, and conditions of the present and the future in their ideal meaning; or the hindrances and state of development of the kingdom of God in the present, the completion of the same in the future, or the present in the future, and the future in the present, as it appeared to him in signs (σημεῖον), that is, in significant pictures, xii. 1, 3, xv. 1. According to a somewhat different conception, God gives to Jesus Christ a revelation to show (generally δεικνύειν, comp. iv. 1, xvii. 1, xxi. 9, xxii. 1) what must shortly come to pass, and Christ sends by His angel and shows it (σημαίνειν, specially through significant signs and words, comp. i. 1) to His servants the prophets. The subject-matter of the revelation is the mystery (μυστήριον); either the mystery of God as He has shown it (εὐηγγέλισε) to His servants the prophets, x. 7,—that is, the purpose of God respecting the completion of His kingdom; or the mystery of the seven stars and of the seven golden candlesticks, i. 20,—that is, the condition and prospects of Christendom; or the mystery of the woman and the beast which carried her, of which the angel spoke to the seer, xvii. 7 (comp. ver. 5),—in other words, the meaning of Rome and the Roman empire in its relation to the kingdom of God. Instead of the detailed statement that God gave the revelation to Christ that He might show His servants what must shortly come to pass, and that He made it known to John by an angel, it is said more briefly, either that "the Lord God of the Spirits of the prophets hath sent His angel to show unto His servants the things which must shortly be done," xxii. 6 (comp. x. 1–7); or, "I, Jesus, have sent mine angel to testify unto you these things in the churches," xxii. 16. But as "mystery" corresponds as a name, so also the book sealed with seven seals, held in the right hand of God, and opened by the Lamb, and from which successive figures go forth, corresponds as a symbol to what has already taken place, and to that which is still future, v. 1–5. But what is so communicated to the prophet he receives that he may make it known, and he does this when he prophesies, x. 11. It is pointed out to him that a part of what he sees and hears is to be sealed,—that is, not to be made known or written, x. 4. But he is also told that the rest is not to be sealed, but written, xxii. 10, i. 11, 19 (comp. ii. 1, xiv. 13). Thus originates a book of prophecy, xxii. 19; its contents are words of prophecy, i. 3, xxii. 7, x. 18. That which stands in such a book, and generally that which is spoken by a prophet, is spoken by the Spirit, ii. 7 and xiv. 13, as being really spiritual,—that is, things are named not according to their empirical nature, but according to their signification, xi. 8. According to another idea, Christ speaks of the same things. The seven letters which close with the words, "He that hath an ear, let him hear what the Spirit saith to the churches," are introduced by the formula, "These things saith He,"—Christ,—or elsewhere, "testifies" (comp. xxii. 16, 20). The same things, only differently conceived, are spoken by God. He has "sent His angel to show unto His servants the things which must shortly be done," xxii. 6. "These are the true sayings of God," xix. 9 (comp. xxi. 5, xxii. 6). We may also remember what was said in the section on the works of Christ respecting "the word of God and the testimony of Jesus;" in a few places, such as i. 2, xix. 10, these terms can mean nothing else than recent revelation given by God, mediatorially through Christ, to the Christian prophets. Predictions will be fulfilled as the words of God, xvii. 17 (comp. x. 7); therefore the angel declines the homage of the prophet, saying, "I am thy fellow-servant, and of thy brethren that have the testimony of Jesus: worship God," xix. 10; and in xxii. 9, "Do it not: for I am thy fellow-servant, and of thy brethren the prophets, and of them which keep the sayings of this book: worship God;" therefore is it said, "Blessed is he that readeth, and they that hear the words of this prophecy, and keep those things which are written therein," i. 3; therefore the prophet "testifies unto every man that heareth the words of the prophecy of this book," xxii. 18, 19, concerning what is written therein (comp. Deut. iv. 2, xii. 32). Certainly there are not only true prophets, but those who, like Jezebel in Thyatira, say they are prophets, and seduce the servants of Christ; indeed, there is a false prophecy which seduces the whole earth (comp. section on the false prophet).

The seven Spirits of God are sent into all the earth, v. 6, and are *operative* even among and upon *non-Christians*, the unbelievers, the inhabitants of the earth. But how? Expositors contend over iv. 5, "there were seven lamps of fire burning before the throne, which are the seven Spirits of God;" and the question is, whether, on account of the expression "lamps," and the parallel with v. 6, we are to understand the all-enlightening, all-seeing, all-searching Spirit, and therefore His universal (comp. Ps. cxxxix. 7), holy, and efficacious jurisdiction; or whether, on account of what precedes, and the expression "fire" (comp. Isa. iv. 4), those operations of the Spirit are meant which bring into the world punishment and destruction. From the position of the seven lamps of fire between the lightnings, and voices, and thunders, and the sea of glass, as well as from the evident relation of the whole passage to the ways or judgments of God, it seems to me certain that the seer intended the Spirit, in His inward convicting and condemning work, adapted for the conversion of the world; that as in the lightnings, and voices, and thunders, he represents the contents of the following seal, trumpet and vial visions; so in the lamps he thought of the accompanying everlasting gospel, with its repentance-call to the world, xiv. 6. By the sea of glass the writer represents the result of both classes of works, the justification of God, xv. 4 (comp. vers. 2, 3).

3. The Gospel.

An angel swears by the living God, x. 7, that in the days of the voice of the seventh angel, when he shall begin to sound, the *mystery of God* shall be finished, as He *hath declared* (εὐηγγέλισε) to His servants *the prophets.* According to the connection, the mystery of God can mean nothing else than His glorious purpose concerning the completion of His kingdom, which, after the seventh angel has sounded, is, xi. 15–18, celebrated in anticipation by the heavenly inhabitants, and described in detail from xix. 11 to xxii. 5. This purpose God has also communicated to the prophets — here can be understood only Old Testament prophets—as a joyful message. It is also said: "And I saw another angel fly in the midst of heaven, having the *everlasting gospel to preach* (εὐαγγελίσαι) unto them that dwell on the earth, and to every nation, and kindred, and tongue, and people, saying with a loud voice, Fear God, and give glory to Him; for the hour of His judgment is come: and worship Him that made heaven, and earth, and the sea, and the fountains of waters," xiv. 6, 7. This gospel cannot be called everlasting, as assumed by expositors, with reference to the eternal purpose of God respecting what is made known therein, but only on account of its having always existed, or on account of its continuance for ever; but since the latter has no sense, it must be only because it has existed, and proceeds and is published from eternity.

With reference to that which the angel utters in a loud voice, it cannot be, as, for example, Düsterdieck says, that the result of the message, which is to the faithful a real gospel, is intended to be for the ungodly inhabitants of the earth something different from its contents; the angel publishes the gospel itself according to the word-sense, its real contents, though only in its substance or in a single aspect. The question now arises, whether by the gospel in the two places quoted, and by the gospel of God to the prophets, and the gospel of the angel to the inhabitants of the earth, we are to understand the same thing. The same name, the related contents,—comp. xiv. 7, "the hour of His judgment is come," with xi. 18 in connection with x. 7,—and the expression everlasting, which evidently points to the Old Testament prophets, decide for their identity.

Another question is, how *this gospel is related to that which is designated by the same name in other parts of the New Testament?* It is surprising how, almost without exception, expositors have failed to perceive that the seer, xiv. 6, desires to represent neither a mere formally significant fancy picture, nor an isolated event of the future,—according to Weiss, *bibl. Theol.* p. 628, the announcement of the judgment of Babylon, necessary for the bringing in of the final consummation, is an everlasting gospel,—and that he has rather represented apocalyptically, on one side the entire principal feature of the eschatological process, and on the other the entire apocalyptic plagues; in other words, he has considered in a plastic manner, and has described what the Gospel of Matthew, xxiv. 14, predicts in the words, "This gospel of the kingdom shall be preached in all the world, for a witness unto all nations; and then shall the end come." The absence of the article before *εὐαγγέλιον αἰώνιον* is no objection to this view; for, on account of the visionary nature of the representation, it was not necessary, and then it was only by the omission of the article that the term gospel could be used, for the seer must use it as an Old Testament expression. And just as little does that which appears as the contents of the gospel in x. 7 and xiv. 7 militate against this interpretation. It certainly consists in the mystery of God, that is, in the purpose of God in relation to the completion of His kingdom, and is therefore of an eschatological nature; but if we compare the statements of the Acts of the Apostles, such as ii. 14–21, especially vers. 17, 21, 34, etc., ver. 40, iii. 19–23, x. 42, 43, xiv. 15, xv. 15–18, xvii. 30, 31, as well as of the earliest Epistles of Paul, for example, 1 Thess. i. 9, 10 (comp. ii. 5), the resemblance to Rev. xiv. 7 cannot be doubted, and we must conclude that the seer in this place has briefly but fully characterized the gospel in its original and apostolic nature. If it should be objected that the other New Testament writers expressly state the contents of the gospel to be the requirement of faith in Jesus, it may be replied that the single passage, xi. 13, "and the remnant—the Jews—were affrighted, and gave glory to the God of heaven," satisfactorily shows that the seer intentionally avoided faith in Jesus, as a New Testament expression, while he clothed it in the Old Testament forms, fearing God and giving glory to Him.

What now, after this, appears to be the *general idea of the gospel as expressed* by the author of the Apocalypse? He understands by the gospel the announcement of the purpose of God concerning the completion of His kingdom, though, from its various aspects, he at one time presents to believers the consolatory, x. 7, and at another time to unbelievers the admonitory side (comp. the sweet and the bitter, x. 9, 10); but in both respects it is to him the gospel, the good news. As this good news, since Christ's appearance, has gone forth to Jews and Gentiles; so, before His appearance, it was made known to the prophets of the Old Testament. It is an everlasting gospel; it began with the protevangelium after the fall. This application of everlasting lies near, on account of the position occupied in the doctrine of the author by primitive history, and especially by the fall. The distinction between the publication of the gospel in the New and in the Old Testament, that in the latter it was the announcement of a gospel still future, and in the former of a gospel which had already appeared, as well as of a Christ yet to come, the seer has certainly passed over, as sufficiently shown in the doctrine of Christ's work,—not, however, because the appearance of Christ already realized, in comparison with that still expected, had no great importance, but for a threefold reason: first, because for him, as a seer, the publication of the future, and thus the aspect of the gospel common to both Testaments, stands in the foreground; secondly, because, and again as a seer, he had an interest in conceiving the New Testament gospel as identical with that of the Old; and thirdly, since, from his doctrine of the Logos, he could and must teach that Christ as really appeared to the prophets of the Old Testament as He had done since His exaltation, both to himself and other New Testament prophets, the distinction of New and Old Testament gospel must have been for him a vanishing one. One difference he certainly recognises, and brings it prominently forward, namely, that the gospel, which had proceeded from eternity, and which God had made known to the prophets in Israel, was now, by an angel flying in the midst of heaven, over all the inhabitants of the earth, preached, in ever-widening circles, to the whole world. After what has been said, there needs no circumstantial refutation of Köstlin, who (p. 491), with reference to the doctrine of the Apocalypse respecting Christian life, says that in this "everlasting" gospel, above all, is its hold on Monotheism, xiv. 6, 7. The question here is not at all respecting its hold upon anything; still we may, with the same justice, claim Monotheism as the content or the meaning of the everlasting gospel, as we can claim it to be the meaning of Paul's preaching among the Gentiles. It is said of the jailor at Philippi: "He rejoiced, believing in God, with all his house" (comp. Acts xvi. 31, 32). In preaching the gospel, there would naturally be involved the worship of God, who created the heavens and the earth, the judgment, and obviously faith in the only true God, who, through the Christ predicted in the Old Testament, manifested in the last time, crucified and raised from the dead, will judge the world, and offers forgiveness to all men in His name. If we call this Monotheism, the everlasting gospel of the seer may be always described by the same term.

Since we have now to do with the publication of Christianity, we need no longer adhere to the term "gospel," but may turn to the "*word of God and the testimony of Jesus*" already referred to in the section on the work of Christ and the activity of the Spirit. We have there said that, in i. 2, xvii. 17, xix. 9, 10, "the word of God and the testimony of Jesus" has the narrower sense of prophecy concerning the completion of the divine purpose concerning the world. We now add that, especially in such places as i. 9, vi. 9, xx. 4, there might be substituted for the "word of God and the testimony of Jesus," the word "gospel," according to its use in Mark viii. 35, x. 29. Seeing that the latter is an Old Testament expression, and is therefore apocalyptic also, while "the word of God and the testimony of Jesus," as we found above, is undeniably connected with the doctrine of the Logos, it is at the first glance very remarkable that the seer uses this so much more frequently than that. But the enigma is very easily solved when we remember that these twofold names for the publication of Christianity are, in the view of our author, essentially related to each other, as the names Messiah and Logos are to Jesus; but when he wrote this book the word "gospel" had no longer the mere Old Testament and original Christian sense, it had already gained the later New Testament signification which so often meets us in the passages quoted from the Gospel of Mark and elsewhere, from the publication of God's purpose, for the completion of His kingdom, through His Anointed, Christianity had come, as the already apparent kingdom, or as the specific Christian conception and doctrine of the kingdom of God. Thus the term "gospel" had, for the seer, generally fallen into disuse, and was still applicable only in those cases where it is self-evident that it occurs in its Old Testament sense (בַּשֵּׂר); in other words, where he speaks of the promises made through the prophets of the Old Covenant, and of the preaching of the apostles and evangelists to Jews and Gentiles in the sense of Mark xvi. 15. On the contrary, wherever he speaks of the gospel in its later sense as that for which suffering is endured, as in i. 9, vi. 9, xx. 4, or of Christian doctrine, whether in its precepts or its promises, whether of Christ during His earthly life or in His state of exaltation, as, for example, in i. 2, xii. 17, xix. 9, 10, he was compelled, as a seer, to substitute for the Old Testament "gospel," with its limited signification, the later "word of God and the testimony of Jesus," which, though containing the narrower meaning, had a much more comprehensive bearing, and at this point to show us how consciously and designedly he used expressions and representations for his purpose.

4. The Saints and their Works.

(a.) *The Christian Life in its Origin.*

The seven Spirits of God are sent out into all the earth, v. 6. The angel which John saw flying in the midst of heaven with the everlasting gospel, had it to preach unto them that dwell on the earth, and to every nation, and kindred, and tongue, and people, xiv. 6. The Lamb that was slain redeemed men to God with His blood out of every kindred, and people, and tongue, and nation, v. 9 (comp. vii. 9). Christianity has already, hyperbolically expressed, been published in all lands and in every nation, and will, in ever-widening circles, be preached among men; and it has, moreover, no national limits, no particular, but a common human *universal* signification (comp. Köstlin, *ut ante*, p. 489).

Thus far, Christianity has not been received by any nation in the gross, but only *by individuals, and comparatively by very few from the various peoples.* According to vii. 9, the great multitude of believers is, in comparison with the number of unbelievers, so small, that the seer, as we have seen in the section on the earth and its inhabitants, designates the latter by the simple terms, "all the world," xiii. 3; "the men," ix. 20, xvi. 8, 9; "them that dwell upon the earth," iii. 10, vi. 10, etc.

If we ask what the author, in this respect, *looks for in the future,* the answer, in the predictions of xi. 1–14, as we shall show in the section on "the Holy City during the forty-two months," informs us that he expects the conversion of Israel as a nation before the second advent. And when, in xv. 4, the victors say, "all nations shall come and worship before Thee, for Thy judgments are made manifest," John does not put such hopes into their mouths merely that the subsequent obduracy of the world, in the presence of God's righteous judgments, may appear in a more striking light; but he brings them before us as seeing and saying what, according to his views, really will happen after the advent. But we shall have frequent opportunity of pointing out how the seer distinguished between the converted before the advent, the individuals from amongst Gentiles and Jews on the one side, and on the other the converts after the advent, the Gentile nations as such. He does not see full Christians in these; and if we take the words "conversion," or "becoming a Christian," "believer," or "Christian," in their full sense,—and for the sake of simplicity we do so,—we must say that the seer expected that, in addition to individuals from various nations, the people of Israel would be converted to the Christian faith, and that concerning the rest of mankind he cherished a hope which reached beyond the advent, but not to the conversion of individuals.

But, *according to the purpose of God, should all men become Christians?* With respect to this, our book presents us with a threefold view. To the church in Philadelphia the Lord says, "I also will keep thee from the hour of temptation, which shall come upon all the world, to try them that dwell upon the earth," iii. 10. The plagues, accordingly, have the tendency, either of leading the world to turn to God, or wholly against Him. We find also that in this hour of trial the everlasting gospel, with its call to repentance, is proclaimed to all the inhabitants of the earth, xiv. 6, 7 (comp. xv. 3, 4). Of the results of the trial, it is said repeatedly that the "men repented not," ix. 20, 21 (comp. xvi. 9, 11). In such statements God is undoubtedly conceived of as offering salvation to the penitent and the impenitent, and men as voluntarily accepting or rejecting it. It is thus that the seer looks at the matter in relation to *the world;* he expects that generally it will be lost, but by its own fault. God is not unfaithful; He does everything to help it, and if it is not saved its ruin is self-caused.

But it is otherwise when He looks upon *Christians.* He writes, xvii. 14, "The Lamb shall overcome them,—the ten kings,—for He is Lord of lords and King of kings; and they that are with Him are called (κλητοί), and chosen (ἐκλεκτοί), and faithful (πιστοί)." The first and second of these expressions differ widely from the usual style of the book, and at the first glance remind us of Paul. Hengstenberg, with most, translating πιστός by "believing," remarks (*in loco*): "The expressions are among those ascribed to John but enfranchised by Paul, and are to be regarded here as proper names." But in other places of the book where πιστός occurs, it evidently has the meaning of "faithful." And then, in the Pauline sense, choice or election does not stand between calling and belief (comp. Rom. viii. 28–30). Finally, it is hardly possible to point to a specific Pauline phrase outside the salutations, i. 4, xxii. 21. It will be more correct if we take the expressions "called" and "chosen" in the sense of Matt. xx. 16, xxii. 14 (comp. xxiv. 22–24; 2 Pet. i. 10). When John treats of the perfected Christian, which he does in the above passage, he considers his nature as consisting of three things. He has been called,—that is, apart from his own volition, God by His grace has invited him to be a partaker of the Messianic salvation. Then he has been chosen; he who has obeyed the gracious call, or accepted the offered salvation, is, as one who has come out of the world, received by God as His, and appointed or ordained to salvation. Finally, he has been faithful,—that is, he has held fast the offered and communicated grace in his struggle with the temptations of the world and the flesh; he has proved himself by his deeds, and is therefore counted worthy of eternal life. When it is said, "Blessed are they which are called (*κεκλημένοι*) to the marriage supper of the Lamb," xix. 9, judging from the connection, the call appears (comp. especially vers. 7, 8) not merely as issued, but as accepted and confirmed; consequently, for the sake of the figure of an invitation to a wedding feast, the single term is to be conceived in a wider sense, embracing within it the other two; still, in the passages in Matthew, with an evident similarity in the essential conception of the Christian nature, it is distributed in a somewhat different manner, to the two ideas of calling and choice. We can hardly venture to say, with Weiss, *bibl. Theol.* p. 625, note (comp. p. 593, note), that choice and calling describe the same divine act from different sides, and that calling may be considered as a destination to complete salvation. But how does the purpose of God with respect to Christians show itself? What is trial to the world is here grace, the bringing salvation near, or offers or inducements and drawings to it; briefly, the calling of grace, as the bestowment or award of salvation, separation from the world, and acceptance, in a word, the election of grace is an affair of Christian fidelity.

Still otherwise does this relation appear to the author when he refers the contrast between the world and Christians, perdition and salvation, to the everlasting and almighty God and His absolute will. Christ said that He would not blot out the name of him who overcame from the book of life, iii. 5. We read that "all that dwell upon the earth shall worship him—the beast—whose names are not written in the book of life of the Lamb slain from the foundation of the world," xiii. 8; and that "they that dwell on the earth shall wonder, whose names were not written in the book of life from the foundation of the world, when they see the beast," xvii. 8. John "saw the dead, both small and great, stand before God: and the books were opened; and another book was opened, which is the book of life: and whosoever was not found written in the book of life was cast into the lake of fire," xx. 12, 15. According to xxi. 27, "there shall in no wise enter into" the New Jerusalem "anything that defileth, neither whatsoever worketh abomination, or maketh a lie; but they which are written in the Lamb's book of life" (comp. Ex. xxxii. 32, 33; Ps. lxix. 28; Isa. iv. 3; Dan. xii. 1; Phil. iv. 3; Luke x. 20). The image of the book of life has come from the registers which the authorities kept of the citizens, and from which the dead were blotted out. It is the symbol of divine appointment to eternal life revealed and realized through Christ. Düsterdieck is certainly mistaken when he says, p. 185, "A man is written in the book of life when he becomes a partaker of new spiritual life (comp. iii. 1), when he receives life-giving truth (comp. iii. 3), or becomes a child and heir of God through faith in Christ (in baptism)." According to xiii. 8, xvii. 8, those who are ordained to eternal life are written in the book of life from the foundation of the world. Weiss, *bibl. Theol.* p. 625, on account of these passages, acknowledges that it seems as if the gift of eternal life were bestowed through an eternal divine predestination, but concludes from iii. 5, xx. 12, 15, that no irrevocable divine purpose is involved with respect to individuals, and refers only the calling of Christians to the eternal purpose. The irrevocableness of the divine purpose is certainly excluded by the word-sense of iii. 5; but, on the other hand, xx. 15 (comp. ver. 12) will hardly show that in the judgment it will then be seen what names remain standing in the book of life (see section on the judgment). To refer only the calling of Christians to the eternal purpose, cannot possibly be the signification of the book of life, for it goes direct to the individual. Much rather, according to the views of the seer, God, in the plenitude of His power, has from eternity resolved, through Christ, to save a number,—the 144,000, and again, an innumerable multitude, vii. 4, 9,—to bless them with eternal life; and they, or their names, are written in the book of life, or the Lamb's book of life. This record, or this divine appointment to salvation, reveals itself, or becomes a manifest reality, when a man avails himself of the salvation of Jesus: it shows itself to be firm and abiding when he remains faithful to Christ; it proves to be just and righteous when in the judgment the names of those who on account of their works do not pass, are absent from the book of life, and the names of those who do are present, so that what has been, and what will be,—absolute predestination, and salvation or perdition; God's eternal purpose, and the result of the whole history,—ultimately cover each other. When Christ promises to him who overcomes that He will not blot out his name from the book of life, iii. 5, there remains—provided we neither ascribe to the book of life a twofold signification, nor admit that those who from eternity are written in the book of life may fall way—nothing for us but so to understand the assurance of the Lord, that they who fall in the time of trial show by their fall that they did not stand in the book of life; those who overcome are thus assured by their victory or their faithfulness of the blessed certainty that their names are in the book of life, and naturally cannot be blotted out; so that instead of expressing the matter with absolute accuracy, and saying, "I will give him the certainty that he is written there," it is said loosely, "I will not blot his name from the book of life." The terrible nature of the temptations in the last time is nowhere more strikingly shown than in the prediction that only those recorded in the book of life from the foundation of the world, or ordained to salvation by the eternal purpose of God, remain faithful, xiii. 8, xvii. 8 (comp. Matt. xxiv. 24). But as they who are written in the Lamb's book of life are those who are faithful to Christ until death, and hold fast His works to the end; so the righteous, as partakers of eternal life, are said to be written in the book of life, in contrast with the common mass of the abominable and the false, xxi. 27.

To attempt to reconcile the differences in the representation of the book of life, between this and the two above mentioned, and again between these themselves, would be for us an entirely superfluous labour.

We may ask, What sort of men become Christians? Not merely Christians in name or profession, but in reality; in other words, upon what *conditions or presuppositions does conversion depend?* On the side of God it is His will that man should have life. "Blessed are they who are called to the marriage supper of the Lamb," xix. 9. Christians are said to be "called, and chosen, and faithful," xvii. 14. In the first of these two passages the seer evidently takes calling in a pregnant sense—the publication of the gospel as designed of God for salvation, and its having become a saving power. The called are here those men to whom God has sent the gospel, with the intention that they should receive it, and who therefore have received it. They are those whom God has earnestly invited to the acceptance of the gospel, and therefore the invitation has not been rejected. In the second passage the author uses the word in a weaker sense, merely that of the publication of the gospel as accepted or rejected; thus with respect to God, as designed in one case for faith, and in the other for unbelief. Here calling being insufficient for salvation, the writer adds choice, according to which God, with respect to a part of those who hear the gospel, wills that they should really accept it and be saved, and therefore they do not merely hear it, but receive it also. But the being chosen, absolutely considered, is the same thing as being written in the book of life. Thus on the side of God the condition of becoming a Christian is that a man in the full sense be called, or that, in the narrower sense of the word, he be called and chosen, or written in the book of life. For this reason the victors, vii. 10, ascribe "salvation to our God which sitteth upon the throne, and to the Lamb." Christians owe their deliverance from sin and destruction, their sanctification and heavenly blessedness, not to themselves, but to God and Christ. Indeed, God says to the seer, "I will give unto him that is athirst of the fountain of the water of life freely," xxi. 6; and at the close of the book the writer cries to those who thirst, "Let him take the water of life freely," xxii. 17. Christians have paid no price, have no claim or merit, that they should be saved; their happiness is the unmerited gift, the free bestowment of the grace of God in Christ. On the side of man, the condition of becoming a Christian is his will so to do. This condition is expressed in the oft-recurring expression, "He that hath an ear, let him hear what the Spirit saith to the churches," ii. 7, etc. Certainly these words are always addressed to men who are already Christians; but if he uses the same expression for becoming a Christian again as for becoming a Christian, namely, "repent," we may surely suppose that he regards the condition of becoming a Christian as being the same,—namely, that man must have an ear to hear, that he must also meet the gospel with a healthy organ, possessed of its attendant sense, with a true receptivity, with the understanding, and with an open heart. The human presuppositions for becoming a Christian are also pointed out when God says, "I will give unto him that is athirst of the fountain of the water of life freely," xxi. 6; and when it is said that those who thirst may come and take of the water of life, xxii. 17. Should thirst in the first of these places be limited to the disposition of the Christian in his earthly life, the second will doubtless suffice to reach those who are not Christians; and when they receive the water of life, they have nothing to pay, nothing to bring; they obtain it freely; it comes from the free grace of God; the only condition is, that they thirst for and desire (*θέλειν*) salvation. Negatively, the same condition is expressed in the words of the Lord to the church of Laodicea, iii. 17, 18, which, for reasons stated above, we may refer also to those who are not yet Christians. "Thou sayest, I am rich, and increased with goods, and have need of nothing; and knowest not that thou art wretched, and miserable, and poor, and blind, and naked: I counsel thee to buy of me gold tried in the fire, that thou mayest be rich; and white raiment, that thou mayest be clothed, and that the shame of thy nakedness do not appear; and anoint thine eyes with eye-salve, that thou mayest see." On the side of man there is thus the condition of receptivity for the truth of the gospel, a longing after happiness and the true life, an unsatisfied sense of his condition in the world, subjectively as well as objectively.

But how does a man become a Christian, or in what does the process of *conversion consist?* According to the analogy of other New Testament writers, we expect to find, as a common designation, the expressions *πιστεύειν, πίστις*. But the first is not used at all, and the second occurs only in ii. 13, 19, xiii. 10, xiv. 12. We meet with *πιστός* rather more frequently, i. 5, ii. 10, 13, iii. 14, xvii. 14, xix. 11, xxi. 5, xxii. 6; and once we find *ἄπιστος*, xxi. 8. Weiss, *bibl. Theol.* p. 627, writes: "That faith is not more frequently mentioned as the fundamental condition of salvation, arises from the fact that what is admonitory in the book is governed by the thought that the whole development is a struggle carried on by Satan and his instruments against the church." In these words he has correctly pointed out the reason why the seer has spoken so little of that which precedes conversion, and of its conditions, or, more strictly, of its means or instrumentality; but with faith, in particular, it is somewhat different. Is there, after all, nothing in this book respecting *faith*, in the sense of an inward act grasping and appropriating salvation? It is certainly remarkable that πίστις nowhere occurs in the sense of the corresponding verb πιστεύειν. The adjective πίστος everywhere, even in xvii. 14, where De Wette hesitates between fidelity and faith, means fidelity or faithfulness. In xxi. 8, the ἄπιστοι, according to the arrangement of the sentence, belong to the δειλοῖς, and consequently describe, not, as Düsterdieck thinks, the inhabitants of the earth considered as enemies of Christianity, but those who have fallen away, the unfaithful or untrue. There must, then, be special reasons, if we are to take πίστις in an entirely different sense. If, in ii. 13, xiv. 12, we take the genitive subjectively, the word bears none of the three possible interpretations—belief of, confidence in, or faithfulness to any one; nor can we understand "faith" objectively in either place, for it would be against the usage of the writer elsewhere, if in the former passage he regarded holding fast the name of Jesus as one member of the parallelism, and, as the other, the not denying His faith, thus describing the contents of the first negatively, and referring both to a single case; and if in the second passage he intended keeping the commandments of God as the first, and faith in Jesus, though, in relation to the commandments of God, logically prior, as the second object "kept." Again, the interpretation by "confidence in" is destroyed in the first passage by the words, "hast not denied," and in the second by a comparison with the undoubted parallel in xii. 17, where keeping the commandments of God, and having the testimony of Jesus, cannot, in the second member of the sentence, be explained as parallel to confidence in Jesus; and it is destroyed equally in both by the impossibility of conceiving confidence to be subordinated to activity. In ii. 19 the writer cannot have understood faith, for he subordinates it to love; and for the conception of πίστις as confidence, the eschatological connection fails. Finally, on the same grounds as xiv. 12, the passage occurring in xiii. 10 is decidedly against the interpretation of πίστις by faith. There remains, then, nothing for us but to understand by it fidelity or faithfulness. And has it not a good sense, if in ii. 13, in addition to the name of Jesus as the objective, fidelity to Jesus as the subjective side is meant? And is there not beauty in the arrangement of ii. 19, if in love and service, fidelity and patience, two pairs are represented, in each of which the first proves itself by the second? When fidelity here stands before patience, and in xiii. 10 after it, we thereby learn that patience may be regarded as a proof of fidelity, as much as fidelity may be considered a proof of patience. That keeping the faith of Jesus with respect to keeping the commandments of God, xiv. 12, and having the testimony of Jesus with respect to keeping the commandments of God, xii. 17, are as closely related subjectively as the testimony of Jesus is related to the word of God objectively, and that xiv. 12 and xii. 17 run parallel in the second member with the meaning of having the testimony of Jesus, as it appears from vi. 9, only when *πίστις* is understood as faithfulness, needs no further illustration. It is to me a source of gratification to be able, on this point, to agree with Baur, who expressly declares, p. 224, that *πίστις* in the Apocalypse is not to be understood in the Pauline sense, but in the sense of fidelity in the confession of Jesus. Our agreement, however, is at an end when he thinks that to the true worshippers of God, who keep His commandments, if at the same time they are to be described as Christians, there should be added the *μαρτυρία Ἰησοῦ* or the *πίστις Ἰησοῦ*; for, apart from his misunderstanding of *μαρτυρία Ἰησοῦ* as a testimony of Jesus, keeping the commandments of God does not describe the Old Testament commandments, nor does having the testimony of Jesus, or fidelity to Jesus, describe those of the New,—the book nowhere makes such a distinction, and least of all in xv. 3,—but there meets us there in subjective Christianity the same parallelism corresponding to the Logos doctrine as in objective Christianity meets us in God and Christ, xii. 10, and in the word of God and the testimony of Jesus. Just as little can I agree with Baur, when he says that *πίστις* expresses a fidelity in the confession of Christ, suitable to the times sketched in the Apocalypse, when Christianity had to maintain so great a struggle with heathenism. From the state of the times, it may certainly be explained why the seer gives much less prominence to the reception of Christianity than he does to its retention, but it will not explain how he could have brought over the name of the former to the latter. The truth is, the seer, in his usual manner, avoided expressing in New Testament style the event of becoming a Christian, and uses the word which in the New Testament writings signifies "faith," in the Old Testament sense of fidelity. It follows, therefore, that, according to the view of the writer, πίστις does not belong to this part of the discussion, but to a later stage in the section, namely, where we treat of the conditions upon which they "overcome."

We have now arrived at the representations of the Apocalypse concerning the process of becoming a Christian. We are at once met by the phenomenon which we have often noticed before,—in the foreground an artistic Old Testament form, but here and there coming into prominence an entirely different appearance. Let us at once consider the *Old Testament form.* It is said, "the rest of the men which were not killed by these plagues yet repented not of the works of their hands, . . . neither repented they of their murders," etc., ix. 20, 21; "they blasphemed the name of God which hath power over these plagues, and they repented not to give Him glory," xvi. 9 (comp. Jer. xiii. 16); "and they repented not of their deeds," xvi. 11. The obdurate do not submit themselves; they do not repent, nor do they glorify God. In these statements we learn, by implication, what is done by those who are susceptible to religious impression, namely, that which the Lord demands from apostate Christians when He says, "Repent!" ii. 5, 16, iii. 3; that which is said of the remnant after the judgments of God, "they were affrighted, and gave glory to the God of heaven," xi. 13; that which the angel, with the everlasting gospel, required, when he cried, "Fear God, and give glory to Him," xiv. 6, and which is described as the evident result of God's righteous judgments: "Who shall not fear Thee, O Lord, and glorify Thy name?" xv. 4. They are seized with fear, or they fear God, that is, they are plunged into a state of terror and anxiety by the judgments of God threatened or experienced; they give God the glory, or glorify His name,—that is, they confess His justice and power, His pity and His grace; they repent, and turn from their neglect of God, and opposition to Him. That the seer, by these things, really represents the transition to Christian life, we cannot doubt, after what has been said in the section on the gospel, as the true interpretation of xiv. 6, 7, and after what we have learned in that on the works of God (comp. also the section on the works of the Spirit), respecting the relation between the plagues and the proclamation of the gospel, or the offer of salvation. After what we have seen of the uniform manner of our author, there needs no special illustration of the fact that, on account of the character of his book, he intentionally represents conversion to Christianity in the style of the Old Testament; and though not mentioning it by name, he manifestly implies and includes faith in Jesus.

But from a few faint and occasional indications, we may discover that John has, in his *ordinary* language, otherwise described the process of conversion. To the church in Sardis the Lord says, "Remember, therefore, how thou hast received and heard," iii. 3 (comp. "he that hath an ear, let him hear," for example, in iii. 6; and, "if any man hear my voice, and open the door, I will come in to him," iii. 20). To the church in Philadelphia he says, "thou hast kept my word," iii. 8, and "thou hast kept the word of my patience," iii. 10. The writer sees under the altar in heaven "the souls of them that were slain for the word of God, and for the testimony which they held," vi. 9. The dragon is wroth with the woman, and goes "to make war with the remnant of her seed which keep the commandments of God, and have the testimony of Jesus Christ," xii. 17. We cannot here accept the idea of Baur (*ut ante*, p. 207), that the seer intends by their "having the testimony of Jesus" to designate all true Christians as prophets; thus, according to the passages quoted, in the esteem of the author, a man is in the way of becoming a Christian when the word of God and the testimony of Jesus is proclaimed to him; when he receives, and, in the pregnant sense of the word, hears, so that he now has it as his own. Would it seem far-fetched if, from the oft-mentioned words of the Lord to the church in Laodicea, iii. 17, 18, we should conclude that the seer represented to himself the process of becoming a Christian as one in which a sinful man discovers himself to be, in a spiritual sense, wretched, and miserable, and poor, and blind, and naked, and turns to Christ, who offers to make him rich, to clothe him in white raiment, and to enable him to see? We may compare what is said on this passage in the section on the earth and its inhabitants.

(*b.*) *The Christian Life in its Meaning.*

By a rapid transition we pass from the process of conversion to its *meaning*; from the inquiry, how a man becomes a Christian?

to the question, what becomes of the man when he is a Christian? The victors cry with a loud voice, "Salvation to our God which sitteth upon the throne, and to the Lamb," vii. 10. After the overthrow of the dragon, a voice is heard saying in heaven, "Now is come salvation, and strength, and the kingdom of our God, and the power of His Christ," xii. 10. We refer to what has been said in the section on the works of God about salvation, and content ourselves here with the remark that lost men, who have fallen before the devil, become partakers of the salvation or deliverance which God wills and accomplishes through Christ; they are saved when they become Christians.—Salvation describes, *very generally*, the result of embracing Christianity. We therefore seek for a *more definite* statement, and find several by a reference to the sections on the condition of men without Christ, and on the works of God; for that which belongs to the subjective and objective states of non-Christians ceases, on their acceptance of Christianity, and whatever the work of Christ signifies, in that the Christian has a share. From the former point of view, what is it that happens to the sinner on his becoming a Christian? He turns from the works of his hands, and no longer worships idols; he also ceases from murder, sorcery, witchcraft, whoredom, and theft, ix. 20, 21 (comp. xxi. 8, 27, xxii. 15); in a word, he ceases to transgress the first as well as the second table of the commandments of God; turning from all abomination on the one hand, and from all falsehood on the other. He is washed from his former uncleanness (comp. iii. 4, vii. 14, xxii. 11, 15, xxi. 27, viii. 22, 3). He has turned from his fornication (comp. ii. 21, 22, xiv. 8, xvii. 2, 4, xviii. 3, 9, xix. 2). From misery he passes to happiness, from wretchedness to gladness, from poverty to riches, from blindness to sight, and from nakedness to being clothed in bright array, iii. 17, 18 (comp. xvi. 15). From death he is awoke to life, or enters into life, or rises to life, iii. 1–3. He is delivered from slavery to the devil, and from the bondage of sin, i. 5, v. 9, xiv. 3, 4. Those who are separated from God are brought into closest union with Him; and the sufferers in this life, who await death as its climax, are made heirs to life eternal, xxi. 3, 4, xxii. 1, 2. What, considered from the second point of view, has Christ done for the men who became Christians? He who is a follower of Christ has received, heard, and possesses the word of God. and the testimony of Jesus, iii. 3, vi. 9, xii. 7

(comp. xix. 10). He shares in the victory of Christ over the devil, and in Christ has overcome him; for him the Accuser is cast out, iii. 21, v. 5, xii. 9–11. He is redeemed by God from the earth, and from among men, v. 9, xiv. 3, 4. He has washed his robes, and made them white in the blood of the Lamb, vii. 4. He has experience of the love of Christ, and has been delivered by Him from his sins, i. 5, iii. 9. He has become identified with Him who has risen from the dead, and has thereby been delivered from death, and has obtained the resurrection life, i. 5, 17, 18. In all things Christ has become for him the pattern, or, more correctly, the operative type, ii. 26, iii. 21, xi. 8, xiv. 4. —And that these things are, in the mind of the seer, associated with baptism, we may the more readily believe, when, as remarked in the section on the work of Christ, the washing or making the garments bright in the blood of the Lamb, vii. 14, as also the white or shining garments in iii. 4, 5, 18, vii. 9, 13, 14, refer not to the baptismal robes only, but are rather a double reference to these and to the priestly attire, in which reference the former has an essential part. But when, in xvi. 15, it is said, "Blessed is he that watcheth and keepeth his garments, lest he walk naked, and they see his shame" (comp. iii. 4, v. 18), the image of washing or making bright is certainly changed into that of receiving garments or being clothed; still, however, it points distinctly to baptism, for this rite alone, in its then existing form, could have led the author to symbolize conversion to Christianity by receiving white raiment, as well as by washing, and making them bright.

The Apocalypse gives us yet another representation of the meaning of becoming a Christian, in the *names* or predicates which it awards to the followers of Christ. By far the most frequent designation of Christians is that of "*saints*," v. 8, viii. 3, xi. 18, xiii. 7, 10 (comp. Dan. vii. 22, 25), xiv. 12, xvi. 6, xvii. 6, xviii. 20, 24, xix. 8, xx. 9. The passage xxii. 11, "he that is holy, let him be holy still," does not apply here, for it is spoken of a saint, and not of the saints. Nowhere do we find any reference by the saints to the sins from which, or to the world out of which, they have been sanctified. The seer has evidently used the honourable Old Testament name of Israel to some extent as a proper name to designate Christians as the true Israel,—a circumstance which as much implies consecration and nearness to

God (comp. v. 8, viii. 3, xvi. 16) as characteristics of saints, as it does their separation from, and opposition to, the world (comp. xiii. 7, xvii. 6).

Next to the designation of saints, the most frequent name applied to Christians is that of "the servants of God," vii. 3, xi. 18, xix. 2 (comp. Ps. cxxxv. 1; Gen. l. 17; Isa. lxi. 6). They are called "fellow-servants," vi. 11, xix. 10, xxii. 9; also "the servants of Jesus Christ," i. 1, ii. 20. We do not here consider the question whether these names are applied in a pre-eminent sense to a particular class of Christians, and confined exclusively to them. Christians are sometimes called the servants of God or of Christ, because they have been redeemed for God and the Lamb, and thus properly belong to God and to Christ, vii. 3, xix. 2, xxii. 6 (comp. v. 9, xiv. 4; also vi. 10, for the designation of God as δεσπότης or proprietary Lord). In other places they are servants of God, because they keep His commandments, xii. 17, or do them, xxii. 14, or wait upon Him in priestly service, vii. 15, xxii. 3. According to the same Old Testament conception, from which we have the designation servant of God for the individual, we have the collective title "*people of God*," xviii. 4. The servants of God in their collective capacity belong to Him in distinction from all other gods; they are chosen by Him, and honour and worship Him. With reference to the misunderstanding which springs from the modern use of language, and which leads to the supposition that the names "servant" and "people of God" imply rights rather than honours, there needs only the remark that the seer speaks as much as possible after the manner of the Old Testament, and that there, both names are titles of honour to Israel and the Israelites.

The twenty-four elders say to God, "the time is come that Thou shouldest give reward unto Thy servants the prophets, and to the saints, and them that fear Thy name, small and great," xi. 18. A voice is heard from the throne saying, "Praise our God, all ye His servants, and ye that fear Him, small and great," xix. 5. In the first place, those who *fear the name of God* are mentioned in addition to the saints; and in the second, those who fear God are spoken of with His servants. Since the author in Old Testament style describes conversion to Christianity in the words, "fearing God, and giving glory to Him," for example, in

xiv. 7, it would not in itself be remarkable if in Old Testament language he represented the chief feature of Christian life to be continuance in the fear of the name of the Lord, as Köstlin, *ut ante*, p. 491, explains the disputed expressions; and in that case we should have to treat of them in a later section. But they appear only in the two places above mentioned, and in the form quoted, and undoubtedly belong to the present part of the discussion. This is not without meaning; for, since Ps. cxv. 11 undeniably in equal measure underlies both passages, and we have always found so far that in the use of Old Testament language the seer has special reasons, we must seek the reason in this case also. Very forcibly we are reminded of Acts xiii. 16, 26, and of proselytism. If we had only the expression: "them that fear Thy name," in xi. 18, I should not hesitate to affirm that the seer there distinguishes from the saints as those who had already been converted, or would be converted before the coming of Christ,—those men who accept Christianity at the time of the thousand years' reign, who would then not be citizens properly so called, but subordinates of the New Jerusalem,—briefly, those who would stand in the same relation to Christians as the proselytes did to the Jews. For when Düsterdieck on this passage affirms that the expression: "them that fear Thy name," embraces conclusively and summarily the whole multitude of the pious, whether prophets or simply saints, whether small or great, the position of the words, as well as the *καί* before *τοῖς φοβουμένοις*, is wholly against such an explanation; and what then could "ye that fear him," xix. 5, mean? Even this place forbids us to understand by those who fear God any other than Christians. There remains, therefore, nothing for us but to regard those who fear God in both places as Christians from among the heathen, in distinction from Christian Jews. Certainly we may not, as Volkmar does, ascribe to the writer the meaning that converts from among the Jews were the only true Christians, and that Gentile Christians were only proselytes or subordinates. Prophets, saints, and those who fear God will alike receive the reward. Servants of God and those who fear Him are alike engaged in His praise; the predicates are the same for both classes; and elsewhere Gentile Christians include servants of God as well as saints, and Jews become Christians when they fear Him, xi. 13 (comp. ver. 11). "Small and great" do not correspond, however, as we shall afterwards see, to the saints and those who fear God. The case stands thus: The seer knew, and that without anti-Pauline fanaticism, that the early Christians were partly Jews and partly Gentiles; and while he has described both elsewhere by the title of "saints" or "the servants of God," in the two places mentioned he has, in order poetically to express universality, taken the pre-Christian relation as a pattern, and has conceived of the saints or the servants of God in a narrower sense, and has thus designated the Christian Jews, but has spoken of the Gentile converts as those who fear God.

We read that "the dragon was wroth with the woman, and went to make war with the *remnant of her seed*, which keep the commandments of God, and have the testimony of Jesus Christ," xii. 17. The remnant of the woman's seed has been variously interpreted. One class understands thereby individual Christians; in the woman they find the whole, and in the remnant of her seed its individual members. Others see in the remnant those disciples of the Lord who remained after the earlier persecutions, ii. 13–16, who, having partially escaped their pressure, were to be found in the dispersion, outside Palestine or Jerusalem. Others, again, refer the remnant to the Gentile Christians, as those who with the woman, the true Israel, belong to the same seed. Some see symbolized in the remnant the Gentile Christians as part of the seed of the woman, the church of God, and so far the brethren of the Messiah, the other line of Christ-worshippers having become in Christ another branch of Israel. If we are to stand by the words, Züllig's exposition unquestionably deserves the preference. He says: "The remnant of the woman's seed are the Zionites on earth, in contrast with the child caught up to heaven" (comp. Hoekstra, p. 399). The seer would then consider Christians as children of the same mother as Christ, brought forth after Him from the maternal bosom of the same church; brethren of Christ; He the first-born, and they the younger children (comp. i. 5). Who can deny that this view of the question has strong analogies in the doctrines of this book? Still, to the unprejudiced reader the relation of the remnant to the born and exalted child, ver. 5, would hardly present itself spontaneously. Much rather will he involuntarily contrast the remnant of the woman's seed with the woman herself, and that not as a part contrasted with the whole, for the whole is persecuted in its members, but as Gentile Christians contrasted with the believing Jews. We notice how, in the course of the twelfth chapter, the woman is silently transferred from the Old Testament church into that of the New, into the church of the first or Jewish Christian times; and the author in vers. 13–16 has passed in thought to the concrete, the Jewish Christians. We thus understand how it is, that where he speaks of the New Testament church in the later or Gentile Christian times, he describes these Christians as the remnant of the woman's seed, as if in 13–16 he had spoken of Jewish Christians as her seed. It is not the mere expression in itself, for which in such a signification Düsterdieck vainly seeks a parallel in the Old Testament, but the inner connection of chap. xii., which compels us to understand by "the remnant of the woman's seed" Christians from the Gentile nations. But the predicates demand that we should regard that remnant as full born, though, as Christians of the second period, later born; for they keep the commandments of God, and have the testimony of Jesus,—that is, they do and have that which the Jewish Christians do and have, and are true Christians.

We come now to the *royal-priesthood* or *priestly-royalty* of Christians. It is disputed whether in i. 6 John wrote ἡμᾶς, or ἡμῶν, or ἡμῖν, and whether in v. 10 we should read ἐποίησας ἡμᾶς τῷ θεῷ ἡμῶν βασιλεῖς καὶ ἱερεῖς καὶ βασιλεύσομεν, or ἐποίησας βασιλείαν καὶ ἱερεῖς καὶ βασιλεύσουσιν, or the last reading with the difference of βασιλευούσιν. We have already said, in speaking of the twenty-four elders, that in the second passage, ἡμᾶς τῷ θεῷ ἡμῶν and βασιλεύσομεν must be false. With respect to the remaining discrepancies in v. 10, βασιλείαν or βασιλεῖς, βασιλεύσουσιν, or what is more probable, βασιλεύουσιν, and in i. 6, ἡμῶν, or ἡμῖν, or ἡμᾶς, may be the original; for, according to i. 9, John is a companion of his readers "in tribulation, and in the kingdom," or the authority, "and the patience," or stedfastness, "of Jesus Christ," and so there can be no doubt of this at least, that the book recognises the royal dignity of Christians even on earth, and regards them as kings. Certainly, it is not thereby proved that βασιλεία, i. 6, and probably v. 10, may be explained as a kingly people, or a kingship. It must be admitted that this word is to be understood in the Apocalypse as it is everywhere else. Therefore, with De Wette, we understand βασιλεία, i. 6, to mean the kingdom of God, the holy and blessed community in which all are united, and through which every individual enters into the position and holy dignity of priests; or with Düsterdieck, that the redeemed are the kingdom of God, the subjects, but at the same time the blessed partners, in the kingdom with God; or with the same writer on v. 10, that they are God's possession, redeemed for a *βασιλεία* to Him—"as God's possession they are also gathered into His kingdom." So also Köstlin, *ut ante*, p. 404, says: "Christians are the priests of God, forming a kingdom which governs the earth, and has God Himself for its immediate Ruler;" and thus we arrive at another of the peculiar views of the seer concerning the importance of Christians. But, first, *βασιλεία* in this book means kingdom, in the sense of the subjects of a king, only in one place, xvi. 10. In all others except i. 6 and v. 10, for example in xi. 15, xii. 10, xvii. 12, 17, 18, it signifies kingly authority. Secondly, the words: "and we shall reign on the earth," in v. 10, are in no way, as Düsterdieck thinks, superfluous to the conception of *βασιλεία* as kingship; for to be a king, and to exercise kingly authority, are different things, as we have already found with regard to God and Christ. Thirdly, it does not read kingdom of God, as many expositors seem to suppose. But if we may not interpret it by kingship, and only by realm or kingdom, the seer has expressed himself in very important places insufficiently or indistinctly. But, finally, while we can hardly fill up this idea as expressed by kingdom from the contents of New Testament conception given elsewhere, which the seer so carefully avoids, the reference both of i. 6 and v. 10 to Ex. xix. 6 (comp. Isa. lxi. 6; Dan. vii. 27) is so striking, that, taken in connection with other reasons, we are certainly justified in regarding *βασιλεία* in these two places not as it is misrepresented as a nation of kings, but as a kingly people, or a kingship. Züllig is doubtless right when he (I. p. 263) traces this designation of Christians to the rabbinical exposition of Ex. xix. 6, according to which it is there predicted that the Israelites should one day be kings and priests, and this at the same time, consequently, priest-princes,—as the high priests were,—in such a way, however, that each of these princes or kings had not a special sovereignty, but a sovereignty in common under God, the supreme King. Ewald also, *ut ante*, p. 111, says, our prophet has followed the exposition of 'מ' כ, Ex. xix. 6, attempted elsewhere in the Jewish school, according to which both words are placed loosely beside each other; for all three Targums translate either "kings, priests," or "kings and priests." With Hengstenberg, we may venture to say, even on account of the relation to Ex. xix. 6, that the seer starts with this view of the priesthood, and from it infers the kingship, since by the priesthood he evidently understands their direct communion with God, in which they present themselves before Him, offer their petitions, and generally give themselves to Him in holy obedience and spiritual service (comp. xxi. 22, the New Jerusalem without a temple, Düsterdieck on i. 5); and by the kingship of Christians, their thereby inwardly-conditioned sovereignty over the world; or, so far as he describes them by the name of priests, he conceives of them more in their relation to God, and by the name of kings, more in relation to the world (comp. xxii. 3, 5). But it is to be carefully noticed, that he does not consider Christians to be first priests and then kings; nor does he regard them as Köstlin does when he says, *ut ante*, 494, "they are priests of God, because they live to honour God, especially in bringing as offerings their prayers to Him; they are rulers on the earth, because to them even in the present, and notwithstanding all afflictions, its possession in the millennial reign is assured," i. 9. But Christians as such are now priests and kings, kingly priests and priestly kings; as Baur says, *ut ante*, p. 220, so far as through Christ's death they are consecrated to Him and to God His Father for a special possession, they are called kings and priests; and as kings and priests they are the governing power in the world, the centre around which it turns. Attention has already been called to the connection between the priestly kingship, or kingly priesthood, of Christians, and washing their garments and baptism, and it needs only to be mentioned here, that we have before us in this priestly kingship the whole specific designation of the dignity of Christians, the carrying over of the New Testament idea of sonship to God into the Old Testament; and in the relation of Christians as priestly kings of God to Christ, as the real priestly king, there is a close parallel to the relation of the sons or children of God to the Son of God.

With the priestly kingship of Christians is closely associated the idea of their being *first-fruits*. "These were redeemed from among men, being the first-fruits unto God and the Lamb," xiv. 4.

Many expositors see in the 144,000, of whom these words were spoken, Christians from amongst the Jews only. Ritschl, *ut ante*, p. 141 (comp. p. 147), refers to this text as a proof that the apostles held it to be a privilege resting on Old Testament prophecy (comp. Isa. ii. 49, 60; Mic. iv.; Jer. iv. 1, 2), by virtue of which Israel, as a nation, would be received into the Christian church before the Gentiles (comp. Acts ii. 39, perhaps also Jas. i. 18). Other expositors, as Düsterdieck *in loco*, see in the 144,000 an election from the Gentiles; while some regard them as the first-fruits chosen from believers, or from the blessed dead. In the section on the churches, we shall show that the 144,000 represent Christians generally, as the elect. But in what sense are Christians called "the first-fruits unto God and the Lamb"? It seems natural to understand the word in the sense of Rom. xi. 16, xvi. 5, 1 Cor. xv. 20, 23, xvi. 15, as related to what is to follow, and all the more so because xv. 4, xx. 4, 6, xxi. 24–26, xxii. 5, show that the seer really looked for such a succession; that, as appears also from vi. 11, he expected in the present dispensation, in common with all who believed the second advent to be near, including Paul, the conversion of a comparatively small number of the Gentiles, as he expected also that of Israel at the twelfth hour, as a nation; but the great efficiency of Christianity, only from the setting up of the kingdom of Christ on earth. Yet certainly as the author cherished this expectation, he does not refer to it in his use of the word "first-fruits." Neither "the redeemed from among men" (comp. v. 9), nor the "being without fault" which follows (comp. 1 Pet. i. 19), leads us beyond the idea of a consecration or an offering. Nor is the relation of Christians to the converted nations in chap. xx. and xxi., as we shall show in its place, a relation of first-fruits. I therefore follow De Wette and Hengstenberg, the former of whom understands "first-fruits" merely in the sense of a consecrated selection from the mass of mankind; and the latter considers the point of agreement between "first-fruits" and Christians to be consecration, holiness, conceived in contrast with the common, or with the rest of men (comp. Jas. i. 18).

"I, John, who also am your brother and companion in tribulation, and in the kingdom and patience of Jesus Christ," i. 9. To the martyrs white robes were given, "and it was said to them that they should rest for a little season until their fellow-servants also, and their brethren that should be killed, as they were, should be fulfilled," vi. 11. The words of the angel to John are, "I am thy fellow-servant, and of thy brethren that have the testimony of Jesus," xix. 10. Christians are servants of God and of Christ, but in relation to each other, *fellow-servants.* By their redemption from among men, xiv. 4 (comp. v. 9), chiefly by the common renewal of their nature accomplished in them by their reception of Christianity, they enter into the closest mutual relation of heart and life,—a relation symbolized by one of the nearest in natural life, they are *brethren.* Thus their religion is represented in three main aspects, as tribulation or suffering in Jesus (comp. ii. 9, 10, vii. 14), as authority or kinghood in Jesus (comp. i. 6, v. 10), and, mediating between these two opposite poles, stedfastness or patience in Jesus (comp. ii. 2, 3, iii. 10, xiii. 10, xiv. 12). Christians have these three features in common, and are *companions* therein.

To the passages quoted above (xix. 10, xxii. 9) we add xii. 10, 11, "I heard a loud voice saying in heaven . . . the accuser of our brethren is cast down," where we think that by "brethren" is meant only believers in their earthly life (comp. Düsterdieck *in loco*); and thus it appears that the seer considered real Christians (comp. xxii. 9) as not inferior in dignity to the *angels,* or to the inhabitants of heaven generally, for they are their *fellow-servants and brethren.*

(*c.*) *Christian Life in its Activity.*

In passing from a consideration of the meaning of being a Christian to a discussion of the activity of the Christian life-principle, we notice, first, how much more prominently this appears in the Apocalypse than the *continued saving operations* of God upon Christians. Not, however, as if the seer regarded men as being left to themselves after they have become Christians, for from first to last they ascribe their salvation to God and the Lamb, vii. 10 (comp. xii. 10, xix. 1). So John at the beginning of the book wishes for the churches grace and peace from God, from the seven Spirits, and from Jesus Christ, i. 4; and he closes with the prayer, "the grace of our Lord Jesus Christ be with you all!" xxii. 21. We find also that Christians continually need the mercy, and grace, and love which God shows toward the sinner, and that only thereby can the state in which all disturbance of spiritual life by depravity and sin is abolished, be maintained for them, in them, and by them, progressively toward perfection (comp. also xxi. 6, xxii. 17, "freely"). Otherwise the tendency of the Apocalypse is to place the independent activity of the *Christian life-principle* prominently in the foreground.

In the consideration of this activity we have, in the first place, to establish the author's doctrine of *works*. We read of the works of God: the victors sing, "Great and marvellous are Thy works, Lord God Almighty!" xv. 3 (comp. Ps. cxi. 2, cxxxix. 14); of the works of Christ he says, "he that overcometh, and keepeth my works unto the end;" of the works of Christians: at the beginning of each of the seven letters the Lord says to the church concerned, "I know thy works," ii. 2. The church at Ephesus is exhorted to do its "first works," ii. 5; the "last works" of the church at Thyatira are more (πλείονα) than the first, ii. 19; the works of the church at Sardis were not found perfect (πεπληρωμένα) before God, iii. 2; those who die in the Lord are followed by their works, xiv. 13. But we also read of the works of the Nicolaitanes, ii. 6; of the works of Jezebel, ii. 22; of the works of their hands of which the rest of the men do not repent, xvi. 11. Babylon is rewarded double according to her works, xviii. 6; and finally, the Lord says, "I will give unto every one of you according to your works," ii. 23; "Behold, I come quickly, and my reward is with me, to give every man according as his work shall be," xxii. 12. "The dead were judged out of those things which were written in the books, according to their works," xx. 12; "every man according to their works," xx. 13 (comp. Prov. xxiv. 12, 29). Köstlin, *ut ante*, p. 490, affirms that in the doctrine of the Christian life the seer lays the greatest stress on the ἔργα. He does not, however, mean thereby the works of the Mosaic law, for the entire sentiment of the church, to which, for example, genuine faith belongs, is summed up in ἔργα, iii. 1, 15; but even this summing up is characteristic, since the Christian life is conceived of from the standpoint of the judgment, according to an absolute standard which it should cover, and is everywhere interrogated according to what is really present and actual, and has assigned to it proportionate reward or penalty. In the great emphasis which the seer lays upon works, Köstlin, pp. 482, 486, sees the chief argument for the theocratic view of life, and the Old Testament prophetic and anti-Pauline character of the Apocalypse. Baur also says, *ut ante*, p. 224, that since the essential definition of the religious consciousness is described as the fear of God, it must practically manifest itself, and thus the chief feature will be works; in the Apocalypse all things terminate in works; there must be some definite, actual, present results to which a man can appeal before God. He also sees in these works a proof that even on the subjective side the standpoint of the Apocalypse is that of the Old Testament religion. Hoekstra, p. 389, says, "the writer rests wholly upon the standpoint of works, though by 'works' he understands only moral and religious works, not ceremonial works, which for him had lost their value." Passing over ix. 20, where, by "the works of their hands"—according to Old Testament usage, 2 Kings xxii. 17; 2 Chron. xxxiv. 25—idols of their own making are to be understood, as well as those places where the works of God and Christ are the subject, we must not only acknowledge that the "works" of the Apocalypse everywhere refer to something actually done by men, and really existing, but we must regard as significant that comparatively they are so often mentioned. Evidently the seer did attach great importance to works. But when Köstlin and Baur speak of the emphasis placed by the Apocalypse on works as an emphasis of the greatest strength, they must have had in view ii. 19 and iii. 2. Certainly, in the first of these passages, the greater number, and in the second—according to the analogy of vi. 11—the complete number is the subject of remark; but if we should conclude from this that the seer regarded Christian life from the point of view of a pattern number of works, we should overshoot the mark. He has, in a poetic manner, used a numeral to express in the former case the relation of the present to the past; and in the latter, the relation of that which actually existed to what ought to have been "before God." Further, when the above writers find in the manner in which the Apocalypse treats the question of works an argument for its theocratic, Old Testament prophetic, and anti-Pauline character, they first overlook the fact that here, as elsewhere, the writer was bound by literary art to clothe his ideas as much as possible in the forms of Old Testament prophecy; and secondly, they fail to notice that, according to the nature of the subject, he has far less to do with the origin of the Christian principle than with its exercise, efficiency, verification, and confirmation (comp. Weiss, *bibl. Theol.* p. 627). If the "works" of our book were approached without prejudice, it would be seen that the seer treats as such those which flow from the Christian as well as from the anti-Christian principle, almost exclusively according to their activity, development, and manifestation; to express these, and again as a seer, he does not use an abstract term, but the concrete "works;" and whether in its use he means the Christian or anti-Christian principle, he leaves us to discover from the connection. Where he intends Christian works, he classes, not characteristically, but consequentially, not only the πίστις, or fidelity, but Christian activity in general, under the name of works. Düsterdieck, on ii. 2, explains works as meaning the general conduct of the church, including its demeanour in suffering; on iii. 2, as the collective activity of the inner life in external acts; and certainly he comes nearer the truth than Köstlin or Baur, though the "works" of the Apocalypse do not express the outward life as distinct from the inner, but the life-principle in its activity, whether internal or external, as distinct from the principle itself.

In what do the works of Christians consist? Comparatively, but self-evidently, little—or may we, with Baur, *ut ante*, p. 226, regard it as a reproach to the writer, that where in the progress of events the idea of Christianity realizes itself, the inner side of Christian life is with him very subordinate to the outer, and that the inner immanent development of Christianity, as well in the life of the individual as in the great course of history, lies outside the circle of his vision?—is said of the activity of the *Christian principle apart from its reference to occurring hindrances.* If we first inquire with respect to it in *general,* the writer replies: "He that is righteous, let him be righteous"—or exercise righteousness—"still; and he that is holy, let him be holy (ἁγιασθήτω) still;" and according to the common reading, "blessed are they that do His commandments," or according to another, "blessed are they who wash their robes," xxii. 14 (comp. vii. 14). The Christian is as such holy; conceived of in a different relation, he is righteous; figuratively expressed, he is clad in garments clean and bright; he unfolds, developes, and gives expression to the Christian life-principle present within him when he continually sanctifies himself, or exercises righteousness, or, conceived of in the concrete form, keeps the commandments of God, or when he continues to cleanse his garments and make them bright. The individual acts in which the exercise of righteousness completes itself are the righteous acts (*δικαιώματα*) of saints, of which it is said, "to her," the Lamb's bride, "was granted that she should be arrayed in fine linen, clean and white: for the fine linen is the righteousness of saints," xix. 8. The maintenance of their fidelity on the part of the saints is not to be found, as Düsterdieck remarks, in this passage; just as little can we find in the words, "to her was granted," as the same expositor does, a reference to the grace of God as the original source of the righteousness of saints; nor is there any ground for the remark of Baur, p. 225, that the good works of individual Christians are here conceived of as a unity; and that if not regarded as the treasure, they are considered as the ornament of the church, and in anticipation a beginning is made to distinguish between works and their moral subjects, from which as moral acts they cannot be separated, and to ascribe to them in themselves a moral worth. If the activity of the Christian life-principle is real, then, as the Lord says of the church at Thyatira, "the last works are more than the first," ii. 19; there is addition, growth, progress; then Christians are truly rich before God. "I know thy poverty, but thou art rich," ii. 9 (comp. the contrast in iii. 17, 18); the aim is that the Lord may find the works of Christians—as He did not find them in the church at Sardis—complete, in full measure, and weight, and number, iii. 2; in other words, that the activity of the Christian principle, judged not merely according to appearances, and from a human standard, but according to an absolute rule,—a divine, true, and righteous judgment,—should be wholly as it ought to be.

If we inquire after the non-antagonistic activity of the Christian principle in the *individual*, the reply of the seer is in the one significant word *love*. The Lord had somewhat against the church of Ephesus, in that it had left its first love, ii. 4. He knew the "works, and love, and service, and faith, and patience" of the church in Thyatira, ii. 19. If we had only the first of these texts, we should understand merely love to God or Christ, on account of its near relation to Hos. ii. 15, 16, Ezek. xvi. 8–15, as well as to the analogy everywhere occurring in the Scriptures, and especially in the Apocalypse (comp. xix. 7, xxii. 17), between the relation of believers to God and that of the wife to the husband. If we had only the second, we should understand it to mean brotherly love, for the parallelism of love and service with fidelity and patience points to that love which proves itself in service to those needing help. We do not desire, however, unnecessarily to attach different significations to the same word, and must therefore say that love to God or to Christ, and love to the brethren, are the same thing, presented to the reader at one time in its relation to God or Christ, and at another in its relation to the brethren; or perhaps better still, it is love to God and Christ manifesting itself in love to the brethren. When Köstlin, *ut ante*, p. 493, says that with the seer love never fails a church, but it is not exalted to the highest practical principle, and indeed is entirely denied to the outer Jewish and Christian worlds, I acknowledge that I can understand how the seer, ii. 19, can have, on account of its relation to the brethren, associated love with fidelity as a specially prominent feature of the Christian life, but I cannot understand how love can have been to him in its full signification anything else than the all-embracing practical principle. Love to the world, the world in its ungodliness and opposition to Christ, is in the Apocalypse nowhere to be found, except, indeed, that which a Christian understands intuitively, an example of which we have in the publication of the everlasting gospel, xiv. 6, 7, and especially in the bitterness of the little book, x. 9,—pitying, seeking love to the lost, or those who are not partakers of the salvation of Christ.

Prayer in our book is the transition of the Christian life-principle toward antagonistic development. When the Lamb has received or taken the book, "the four living creatures and the twenty-four elders fall down before Him, having every one of them harps, and golden vials full of odours, which are the prayers of saints," v. 8. "An angel came and stood at the altar, having a golden censer; and there was given to him much incense, that he should offer it with the prayers of all saints upon the golden altar which was before the throne. And the smoke of the incense, which came with the prayers of the saints, ascended up before God out of the angel's hand. And the angel took the censer, and filled it with fire of the altar, and cast it into the earth: and there were voices, and thunderings, and lightnings, and an earthquake," viii. 3–5. "The Spirit and the bride say, Come!" xxii. 17. John writes: "Amen: even so, come, Lord Jesus!" xxii. 20. The connection of v. 8 decidedly forbids us to understand the prayers of saints as special petitions. The seer must either intend the prayers of Christians generally, by the offering of which they show their reverence for the Lamb, or—and the context favours this—the special praise and thanks of Christians of the kind which immediately follows, v. 9, 10. On the other hand, the connection of viii. 3–5 shows just as decidedly that by "the prayers of saints" the seer there thought of supplication only. Taking the usual view of the identity of the altar and the golden altar, we may represent the event by saying that the angel fills his censer from the same altar-fire which consumed the incense, and then casts it to the earth (comp. Ezek. x. 2); or, more correctly, distinguishing between the altar and the golden altar, the event then appears to us thus: After the angel who stood at the altar of burnt-offering, the symbolic offering-place of the saints, had filled his censer with incense, and burnt it at the golden altar, he took the same censer and filled it with fire, the image of divine wrath, from the altar of burnt-offering; and then followed the signs of the coming judgments of God (comp. Ezek. x. 1–8). In each case the prayers of saints and the divine judgment stand in causal connection, and are therefore understood as petitions for the coming of Christ, as expressed in xxii. 17, 20. The seer also "heard a voice from the four horns of the golden altar," the locality symbolizing the prayers of saints, "saying to the sixth angel which had the trumpet, Loose the four angels which are bound in the great river Euphrates," ix. 13; the saints have achieved the liberation of the angels by their prayers. We learn the contents of Christian thanksgiving and prayer, not merely from the few words of xxii. 17, 20, but also from the petitions to which expression is given in heaven. The adorations of the four living creatures, iv. 8, 9; of the twenty-four elders, iv. 10, 11, v. 9, 10, xi. 16, 17; of the angels, v. 12; of the victors, vii. 10, xv. 3, 4; and the heavenly inhabitants, xii. 10, 11, xix. 1–7, we may certainly regard, even as much as the cry of the slain for vengeance, vi. 10, (comp. Ps. lxxix. 10) as praise and prayer, as in reality they are offered by saints or Christians on earth. The prayers of Christians, as the passages quoted show, are sometimes addressed to God, sometimes to the Lamb, and sometimes to God and the Lamb at the same time. They are symbolized by the golden vials full of odours, v. 8. Incense is given, and it ascends for them before God, viii. 3–5; when incense is given, then they are made acceptable to Him, and are admitted to an audience; when the smoke of the incense ascends before God, they are accepted and heard (comp. Ps. cxli. 2; Ezek. viii. 11, x. 2). The elders and the angels have here no independent meaning. That the prayers of saints are heard and answered depends on the will of God and their supplications; they do not need priestly mediation, for through Christ, the perpetual Mediator and High Priest, they are themselves a royal priesthood to God and the Lamb. The writer sees in the petitions of Christians the activity peculiar to this priesthood; as suppliants who have always access to God and the Lamb, and approach Him with praise and prayer, they show their priesthood; and as suppliants whose praise and prayer is always acceptable and audible, and who thus control the destiny of the world, they prove themselves to be kings on the earth (comp. what is said above on the royal priesthood of Christians).

When we inquire respecting the *form which subjective Christianity assumes in relation to its opposites, the result is unusually rich.* The seer is as well acquainted with the dangers and difficulties of the Christian life, which are found in the *subject* himself, in his own flesh, the world within him, as he is with those which spring *from without*, from the surrounding world, and which are the cause of his fall. The latter, again, come partly from the Jews and partly from the Gentiles, and consist not merely in *persecutions* by word and deed, but also in tempting *delusive doctrinal error.* In the letters to the churches of Ephesus, Sardis, and Laodicea, the subject is neither persecution nor the influence of erroneous doctrine. Ephesus had left its first love, the love shown at the time of its foundation, ii. 4, and its members had fallen from the high position in which they then stood, ii. 5. In Sardis they had a name as if they lived while they were *dead*, iii. 2; a part of the church was *ready to die* (ἔμελλον), iii. 2, —terms which, when taken in connection with watching and strengthening, in ver. 2, must be interpreted in the sense of slumber and sleep. On account of their profession of the true faith, they presented the appearance, and had the credit of possessing Christian life; but they were on the way or near to complete spiritual inactivity and sloth; indeed, the church generally had already sunk into spiritual death. The same church had a few names which had not defiled their garments, iii. 4,—that is, either there were a few members of the church who did not live an impure, sinful life; or, with reference to washing their garments and making them white through the blood of the Lamb, as represented in baptism, there were a few persons in the church who had not gone back to their former sins, or fallen into the sins of the heathen. A different image is used when the Lord says: "Blessed is he that watcheth, and keepeth his garments, lest he walk naked, and they see his shame," xvi. 15. The righteousness of the saints is the fine linen given to the bride wherewith to clothe herself, xix. 8; and they who do not watch and care for righteousness fall back again into the natural condition of the unrighteous, and expose themselves to shame. Finally, in Laodicea they are neither cold nor hot, but lukewarm; they say: "I am rich, and increased with goods (πεπλούτηκα) (comp. Hos. xii. 8), and have need of nothing; and know not that they are wretched, and miserable, and poor, and blind, and naked," iii. 15–17 (comp. xvi. 15),—that is, they are neither attached to the Lord by ardent love (comp. ζήλωσον, ver. 19), nor altogether estranged from Him by enmity and opposition. They had fallen into a state of indecision, half-heartedness, and indifference, and in this condition had come prominently before the Lord for rebuke,—not in its essential nature, as many expositors think, but in its consequences, the satiety, self-satisfaction, and haughty self-deception in which they imagined themselves rich in Christian feeling and conduct, as needing no improvement, while their real condition was the opposite. Hoekstra, p. 391, thinks that a man must be forsaken of all the gods if he explain the self-glorification of the Laodiceans by self-righteousness. From the standpoint of the seer (comp. iii. 4) self-righteousness does not appear in such dark colours as in Protestant dogmatics, and we have rather to think of a degenerate Pauline liberalism, which, indeed, might very easily overtake those whose glorying in grace and knowledge (comp. 1 Cor. viii. 1) was associated with abated religious zeal and relaxed morality. But we think that a contradiction between the doctrine of salvation, as taught in this book, and the censure of an unjustifiable self-satisfaction, as here expressed, can be found only when we bring with us the categories of Protestant dogmatics. That this self-satisfaction, or rather its cause, the lack of zeal, had its origin in a degenerate

Pauline liberalism, is not implied by a single syllable. Why, indeed, should the seer have avoided every indication of it, if he had Nicolaitanism in view? Or what is there to compel us, in the entire absence of any indication, to derive from a single original all the improprieties in the Christian churches which caught the eye of the seer? But Christians are not only overcome by the flesh, but also by the pressure of false doctrine. The Lord says to the church in Pergamos, "I have a few things against thee, because thou hast there them that hold the doctrine of Balaam," ii. 14; and "thou hast also them that hold the doctrine of the Nicolaitanes," ii. 15. There is thus indolence, weakness, and delay in the correction or rejection of the adherents of doctrinal error. To the church at Thyatira it is said, "Thou sufferest that woman Jezebel, which calleth herself a prophetess, to teach and to seduce my servants to commit fornication, and to eat things sacrificed to idols," ii. 20; and, "behold, I cast her into a bed, and them that commit adultery with her," ii. 22; that is, those who are sharers with her in this false prophetic nature, and thus in the theocratic sense of the word violate the marriage vow, ii. 22, those who patiently endure it, and unite in many things taught and practised by it. Finally, persecutions are also regarded as temptations. "Behold," says the Lord to the church at Smyrna, "the devil shall cast some of you into prison, that ye may be tried; and ye shall have tribulation ten days," ii. 10. On account of the expression, "that ye may be tried," rather than "that he may try you," we are led to differ from many expositors, who suppose that there was on the part of the devil a temptation designed for their destruction,—though it is certainly to be maintained that the work of the devil is under divine control,—rather than a trial on the part of God which, according to His purpose, should serve not only for the establishment and advancement, but for the separation of genuine Christians from the counterfeit; for then, to the latter, the tribulations which they have to endure for the sake of Christ become temptations in an evil sense, inducements to apostasy. Such are afraid of the things they shall suffer, ii. 10; they do not hold fast the name of Christ, iii. 8; they worship the beast, and receive his mark in their foreheads and hands, xiii. 8, xv. 16, xx. 4; they are cowardly and faithless, xxi. 8.

What happens to those who *fall before the power of such*

temptations? The Lord says of Jezebel, "I gave her space to repent," ii. 21; and where such space for repentance is not used, then, as we have seen in the section on the work of Christ, He comes in judgment. But He desires that men should repent, ii. 5, 16, iii. 3, 19, and brings those who are His to this condition. He says, "As many as I love, I rebuke and chasten," iii. 19. To the church in Ephesus He says, "Remember, therefore, from whence thou art fallen, and repent and do the first works," ii. 5; to the church in Sardis, "Be watchful, and strengthen the things which remain that are ready to die: . . . remember, therefore, how thou hast received and heard, and hold fast and repent," iii. 2, 3; that is, the church regarded as a unity should arouse itself in its relatively healthy members from the prevalent spiritual indolence or torpor, to an active and vigorous life, to a holy walk and conversation, and thus strengthen those who were approaching spiritual death. They were therefore to remember how, that is, with what zeal and living faith, they once received Christian truth, and so to embrace it with fresh ardour, and turn away from their present state. The church in Laodicea is counselled by the Lord to buy of Him gold (comp. Isa. lv. 1) tried in the fire, that she may be rich; and white raiment, that she may be clothed, and that the shame of her nakedness do not appear; and to anoint her eyes with eye-salve, that she may see, iii. 18. He exhorts her to be zealous and repent, iii. 19; that is,—it is altogether arbitrary to refer the gold, and the raiment, and the eye-salve to individual features of the Christian life; yet, with Düsterdieck, the gold and the raiment are the blessings of salvation, the eye-salve is the enlightening gift of the Holy Spirit; with Hoekstra, p. 392, the gold is fidelity to the truth, the white raiment is chastity, and the eye-salve pure doctrine,—the Lord exhorts to burning zeal in contrast with lukewarmness; to repentance springing from zeal, in contrast with self-righteousness, originating in lukewarmness, which is expressed in the three symbols—gold, bright raiment, and eye-salve, closely corresponding to those of the false condition, poor, blind, naked. The words "of me" do not express, as Hoekstra supposes, a contrast with false apostles; but they direct the Laodiceans to Christ as to one whom they had disgracefully forsaken, and to whom they must return if they are to receive help. The church in Pergamos, which numbered Nicolaitanes among its members, is simply called upon to "repent," ii. 16. Manifestly, when the author wrote, no Christians had fallen through persecution; for while, in relation to those who endured it, he has words of approbation and encouragement, there are no exhortations to repentance.

We come naturally to the remark, that, according to the conception of the seer, Christians do not yield or sink under any kind of persecution, but in all, and over all, obtain the victory, or *overcome*, as Christ overcame, iii. 21. A voice from heaven declares, "The accuser of our brethren is cast down, which accused them before God day and night. And they overcame him (ἐνίκησαν) by the blood of the Lamb, and by the word of their testimony; and they loved not their lives unto the death," xii. 10, 11. That is, as the devil is overcome by the death of Christ objectively, so they have overcome him subjectively who have, and because (διά) they have, by faith appropriated the death of Christ, and proved their faith by their testimony, or Christian confession of Jesus, even to the surrender of their lives. Düsterdieck *in loco* says that "the ἐνίκησαν is accomplished only when the conflict, continuing until death, and demanding the surrender of life, is at last fought out, and the garments washed in the blood of the Lamb have been kept pure notwithstanding all the temptations and oppressions of Satan. That, although the jubilant host in heaven know the struggle against the dragon to be still before their brethren on earth, they can yet celebrate the victory as already won, because the battle fought in heaven has made Satan a conquered foe for the faithful on earth; in the meantime, the celebration in heaven of a victory as achieved which has yet to be accomplished by believers on earth must have given to the latter the most efficient encouragement." But this expositor has failed to notice, or at least has not given sufficient prominence to, the fact that according to the ideas of our author, just as the conquest of Satan through Christ, and the authority of God and the Lamb wherever they are celebrated as already present, are by no means conceived of merely as present, but present in ideal reality; so also the conquest of the dragon by Christians, by the appropriation of the blood of the Lamb, by the word of their testimony, and by the surrender of their lives, and by subjective Christianity at every step of its realization from the beginning onward, is also ideal reality. In ideal reality

Christians have even as Christians overcome the devil. This is the plain statement of the seer, a statement in complete harmony with the whole doctrine of the book; and when Köstlin, *ut ante*, p. 492, says in one breath, "the victory is completed only with the successful self-prosecution of the conflict even unto death," and "only he who has successfully passed over has conquered," he makes two very different assertions, of which the first is as true as the second is false. But as in the thoughts of the seer there is given to those who have overcome a continued conquest, so it is distinctly expressed in the remainder of the passage quoted—"Therefore rejoice, ye heavens, and ye that dwell in them. Woe to the inhabiters of the earth and of the sea! for the devil is come down unto you, having great wrath, because he knoweth that he hath but a short time," xii. 12; that is, as Düsterdieck says, "To the inhabitants of heaven alone belongs pure joy; to the earth and those who dwell on it there is woe; even to the faithful on the earth, for with the raging dragon they have now to struggle even unto blood;" or, as I would rather say, the victory objective and subjective is still only ideal; in heaven, real; on the earth, or visibly, yet to be realized; therefore, as the visible reality is the theatre of the despairing efforts of the ideally overthrown Satan, so Christians, as far as they still belong to the visible reality, are liable to temptation and suffering, the subjects of the angry attacks of Satan. The Apocalypse does not contain a direct exhortation to Christians to overcome in such a struggle, but indirectly it is given at the close of each letter, ii. 7, xi. 17, 26, iii. 5, xii. 21, and also in xxi. 7.

But what must the Christian *do in order that he may overcome?* The Lord says to the church in Ephesus, "I know thy works, and thy labour, and thy patience, and how thou canst not bear them which are evil: and thou hast tried them which say they are apostles, and are not, and hast found them liars: and hast borne, and hast patience, and for my name's sake hast laboured, and hast not fainted," ii. 2, 3. When Düsterdieck *in loco* finds in the words "thou hast tried," etc., the exposition of the sentence, "canst not bear them which are evil," and in the words "hast patience" the exposition of "thy labour and thy patience," and in "hast borne" a striking antithesis to "and canst not bear," and then says, "the labour and patience refers to all in which believers fulfilled their peculiarly holy task with divine spiritual strength and endurance,—a labour which must always be associated with suffering in every form, and which therefore can never be accomplished without patience,"—it seems to me that the exposition is forbidden by the words immediately following: "Nevertheless I have somewhat against thee, because thou hast left thy first love," ii. 4. These words demand that we should understand the labour and the patience mentioned in the former part of the paragraph in a special rather than in a general sense, as referring to false teachers. The individual statements, in their fulness of meaning, then at once arrange themselves. The Ephesians had labour,—that is, they experienced difficulty and trouble with false teachers,—but they had not become weary, nor spared themselves; they possessed patience (comp. ii. 19), and thereby showed that in their struggle with error they had borne for Christ's sake, and had not fainted; but "them which are evil"—probably standing in the same relation to the liars as the righteous to the saints—they could not bear; they could not therefore suffer (comp. ii. 20) those who said they were apostles, and were not, but proved, tried, put them to the test, and found them liars. Thus there was an indictment against teachers of error, in the labour they undertook, in their not fainting, in their having patience for the sake of Christ, but not bearing the evil, in their close examination and searching scrutiny of falsehood. Hating the works of the teachers of error, for which the Lord praises the same Ephesian church,—"thou hatest the deeds of the Nicolaitanes, which I also hate," ii. 6,—differs little from not being able to bear their authors. To the church in Thyatira the Lord says: "I know thy . . . faith (fidelity), and thy patience," ii. 19; and to as many as have not this doctrine He says: "I will put upon you none other burden but that which ye have already; hold fast till I come," ii. 24; and, "he that overcometh, and keepeth my works"—that is, either the works which I require of him; or, in still sharper contrast with the works of the Nicolaitanes, "my example, or the activity of the Christian life-principle manifested in me and springing from me"—"unto the end, to him will I give," etc., ii. 26. It is thus against the teachers of error, and in favour of the Christians, that the latter have not suffered themselves to be moved away, but have held fast that which they had of subjective Christianity, and under every temptation preserved the Christian life-principle within them from adulteration, deterioration, or destruction. With respect to persecution in word and deed, the Lord says to the church in Smyrna: "Fear none of these things which thou shalt suffer . . . be thou faithful unto death," ii. 10. To the church in Pergamos He says, "Thou holdest fast my name, and hast not denied my faith (comp. ii. 10), even in those days wherein Antipas was my faithful martyr, who was slain among you," ii. 13. To the church in Philadelphia Christ says, "Thou hast kept my word, and hast not denied my name," iii. 8; "thou hast kept the word of my patience," iii. 10; "hold that fast which thou hast, that no man take thy crown," iii. 11. The remnant of the woman's seed, with which the dragon went to make war, is described as consisting of those "which keep the commandments of God, and have the testimony of Jesus Christ," xii. 17. Where the subject is the conflict of the beast with the saints, and divine retribution coming upon the persecutors, xiii. 7–9, it is said, "Here is the patience and faith of the saints," xiii. 10. It is the same where retribution is predicted as coming upon the faithless, xiv. 10, 11. "Here is the patience of the saints; here are they that keep the commandments of God and the faith of Jesus," xiv. 12; and accordding to one reading, xxii. 14 gives us, "Blessed are they who keep His commandments." We have already shown that we are not to understand the commandments of God in the Old Testament law in distinction from those of the New Testament, but the word of God on its preceptive side; the remaining expressions have also been explained. They overcome the dragon by the blood of the Lamb, and by the word of their testimony; and do not love their lives unto death, xii. 11 (comp. vi. 9, xi. 3, 8, xx. 4). Thus they hold fast that which they have; they hold fast the name of Jesus; they do not deny His faith; they keep the word of His testimony, they keep the word of His patience; they are not afraid of suffering; they do not love their lives; they are faithful unto that death which overtakes those who overcome in the midst of persecution. With reference to the temptations which come from the flesh, the Lord says, "Blessed is he that watcheth and keepeth his garments (comp. iii. 3, 4), lest he walk naked, and they see his shame," xvi. 15 (comp. iii. 17, 18); so also we read: "Come out of her—Babylon—my people, that ye be not partakers of her sins, and that ye receive not of her plagues," xviii. 4. We may add here that the writer, conscious of uttering the word of God, says, "Blessed is he that readeth, and they that hear the words of this prophecy, and keep those things which are written therein," i. 3; and hears the angel say, "I am thy fellow-servant, and of thy brethren the prophets, and of them which keep the sayings of this book," xxii. 9 (comp. xxii. 18, 19); and so also are described the chief features of those who overcome the temptations of the flesh. Those who overcome are lyrically depicted, both according to their nature and their conduct, in the words: "These are they which were not defiled with women; for they are virgins. These are they who follow the Lamb whithersoever He goeth. These were redeemed from among men, being the first-fruits unto God and the Lamb. And in their mouth was found no guile: for they are without fault," xiv. 4, 5. We omit the exposition of this picture here, that we may not separate it from its connection in the section on the saints in the great tribulation. It remains only to point out that—not in the almost entirely presupposed neutral activity of the Christian life (comp. "love" and "service," ii. 19, with "my works" in the same letter, ii. 26), but in its activity against its opposites, and, indeed, in overcoming generally (comp. the frequent conquests of Christ as those of Christians, and particularly iii. 21), especially in overcoming persecutions, in patience (comp. iii. 10, ii. 10, with ii. 26), in fidelity (comp. ii. 10 with iii. 14), in testimony or confession (comp. xii. 11, vi. 9, with iii. 14), in voluntary self-sacrifice (comp. vi. 9, xx. 4, with v. 6, 9, also xi. 3, 8); we may notice, moreover, the significant "with me," iii. 4—it is distinctly evident that the seer regarded the activity of the Christian life as an imitation of the example of Christ (comp. xiv. 14).

(*d.*) *Christian Life in relation to its Promises.*

What *prospects* have those who overcome? or what is promised to subjective Christianity? We stand here before one of the decisive questions. According to Düsterdieck, p. 196, the closing promises to the victors refer in all the letters to the time of the eternal glory after the coming of the Lord; and according to the same writer, p. 294, there is given beforehand to the seer, in vii. 9–17, a glimpse of the final glory of all true believers, in which it is shown to him how, after the great tribulation of the last days, they will be perfected, and stand before the throne of God and the Lamb. Köstlin says, p. 494, "There certainly prevails in the Apocalypse no such dualism of the present and the future as that of James, who demands humiliation, sadness, and poverty; but goodness, according to the law of recompense, brings its good results only after death (comp. the closing verses of the seven letters)." But are these assertions well-founded? With absolute certainty, I say no. The future tense, "I will give," at the close of the letters, is, for a book with the style and purpose of the Apocalypse, the only possible form of promise. It is forbidden beforehand, by the laws of apocalyptic language, to say, "He that overcometh eats of the tree of life," or "I have given him to eat of the tree of life," etc.; nor is it said to the combatant who is admonished to fidelity and patience, "thou eatest of the tree of life," or "I have given thee to eat of the tree of life." The future means nothing more than that, according to the view of the seer, the contents of the promise belong not merely to the past or the present, but must be a prediction not yet wholly fulfilled. If we conclude, from the form of the promises, that they belong to a period after the coming of Christ, there is certainly a frequent agreement with the pictures of the heavenly state. But first, there are not wanting contradictions which, if we limit the promises to the latter, are inexplicable. We need only compare the promise of being "a pillar in the temple of God," and the assurance of the seer that he "saw no temple therein," iii. 12, xxi. 22. It is evident, further, from a rather numerous group of promises, that while they reach to the perfect or the heavenly state, they refer also to life on earth. We may compare the statements of xiv. 3, 4, where those in heaven are said to have been "redeemed from the earth" and "from among men," with v. 10, where the same thing is said of those "on the earth." Those who are in heaven wear white raiment, vii. 9–13, and so do those who are below, iii. 4 (comp. ver. 5). In heaven they stand "before the throne of God and the Lamb, and serve Him day and night in His temple," vii. 15 (comp. xxii. 3, 4); but in the earthly life they are already servants of God and of Jesus, ii. 20, vii. 3. The heavenly inhabitants bear the name of God and of the Lamb on their foreheads, xiv. 1, xxii. 4, and also on earth they have on their foreheads the seal of the living God, vii. 3. In heaven they serve God as priests, and rule over the world as kings, vii. 15 (comp. xxii. 3–5); and even here they are a kingdom, or a kinghood, and a priesthood to God, and reign on the earth, i. 6, v. 10. In heaven they follow the Lamb, vii. 17, xiv. 4; and here also they walk with Him in white, iii. 4 (comp. also vii. 17 and iii. 20). The promise of Christ is, "I will give thee a crown of life," ii. 10; and He also gives the admonition, "Hold that fast which thou hast, that no man take thy crown," iii. 11. The works of Christians follow them in heaven, xiv. 13; but Christ says that true Christians are rich even here, ii. 9; comp. also vii. 10 and xii. 10. In the presence of such a number of witnesses, which might be easily multiplied, can it be seriously affirmed that the promises of our book, made to those who overcome, belong exclusively to the heavenly state? How does the case really stand? When Köstlin, p. 494, speaking of an earnest of eternal life, and bringing into prominence the royal priesthood of Christians even on earth, says, "still there is in the *νικᾶν*, which in every struggle with the world has already triumphed, a feeling of superiority over it," he had at least a glimpse of the truth. But we must go deeper, and say that the seer, in strict analogy with his entire views, and more immediately with those respecting the triumphs of Christians, regards the promises as being on the one hand *fulfilled*, as well in the conversion of the man, with a view to the conquests of the Christian, as on the other in his being a Christian and a gradual victor over evil. They are continuously fulfilled,—in this life, amid struggle and conflict with the external reality; in heaven, in the ideal or hidden reality; and in the final perfect state, in ideal manifest reality. Useless as it is to contend against the meaning of the book, it would be not less so if, on the ground of a few modifications in the imagery of its promises for the earthly life, for heaven, and for the final state, we should endeavour to prove an essential difference in their nature. The contents of the promises are everywhere the same; but the measure of their fulfilment in the different stages is various, yet always more complete and glorious. The question thus arises, whether we should throw the promises together into one place, and into what place; and though it would not be out of order should any one treat together the entire substance of the promises considered in itself, our representation demands that we should distribute it, and for the present confine our remarks to that portion complicated neither with heaven nor the final perfect state.

And what are the *particulars* in which this consists? We simply return to the letters to the churches. "To him that overcometh will I give to eat of the tree of life, which is in the midst of the paradise of God," ii. 7,—that is, the Christian shall have eternal life in blessed communion with God. "Be thou faithful unto death, and I will give thee a crown of life," ii. 10. Life is here the crown, and the Christian shall have eternal life as the reward of victory. "He that overcometh shall not be hurt of the second death," ii. 11. The second death is the opposite of eternal life—condemnation, misery, and perdition; but it shall not harm the Christian, for he shall have eternal life. "To him that overcometh will I give to eat of the hidden manna, and will give him a white stone, and in the stone a new name written, which no man knoweth saving he that receiveth it," ii. 17. The hidden manna, in distinction from the manna in the wilderness, means the ideal or the heavenly manna. The Christian shall enjoy the ideal food, the heavenly bread; he shall have eternal life. The gift of the white stone cannot here be regarded, with Hengstenberg, I. p. 200, as having an independent signification, but must be taken in connection with the inscription of the new name; and certainly the gift of the tablet, as the medium upon which to write, and its being bright or white, as material corresponding with the inscription, are to be associated; but the new name (comp. Isa. lxii. 2, lxv. 15) is the ideal glory of believers; the Christian as such shall have a standing or personal relation with God and Christ, which, though incomprehensible to the world, is perfectly known to himself. "He that overcometh . . . to him will I give power over the nations"—the heathen—"and he shall rule them with a rod of iron; as the vessels of a potter shall they be broken to shivers; even as I received of my Father. And I will give him the morning star," ii. 26–28. The possession of power over the nations (comp. Ps. ii. 8, 9) denotes earthly dominion (comp. xii. 5, xix. 15); but the morning star, according to Num. xxiv. 17, Isa. xiv. 12 (comp. Dan. xii. 3, Matt. xiii. 43), is equivalent to great glory and splendour of authority. The Christian shall, with power and glory, rule the world (comp. v. 9). "Thou hast a few names even in Sardis which have not defiled their garments; and they shall walk with me in white: for they are worthy. He that overcometh, the same shall be clothed in white raiment; and I will not blot out his name out of the book of life, but I will confess his name before my Father, and before His angels," iii. 4, 5. The bright or white garments symbolize positive purity, holiness, or righteousness (comp. xix. 8). The Christian, as holy, shall stand in the closest personal community of life with Christ: he shall become holy, ver. 4; he shall be recognised, declared, and honoured as holy, ver. 5 (comp. xix. 8, it was given to her tc be clothed with white byssus). Being written in the book of life, describes the divine election to eternal life; on account of his holiness the Christian shall be assured of eternal life or blessedness (comp. Luke x. 20); and the confession before God and the angels is the absolute declaration of their connection with Christ; the Christian shall, with divine certainty, be recognised by Christ as His (comp. Matt. x. 32). "Behold, I will make them of the synagogue of Satan, which say they are Jews, and are not, but do lie; behold, I will make them to come and worship before thy feet, and to know that I have loved thee," iii. 9,—that is, Christians shall win unbelievers to repentance and faith, and thus be the means of extending Christianity to others, and saving them. "Thou hast kept the word of my patience, I also will keep thee from the hour of temptation, which shall come upon all the world, to try them that dwell upon the earth," iii. 10; by which the seer intended to say that Christians, through the grace of Christ, shall be delivered from the great tribulation which is to precede His coming, for John xvii. 15 shows that there is no essential difference between τηρεῖν ἀπό and ἐκ; "to try them that dwell upon the earth" does not mean that the temptation should come upon these so far as they were not kept,—that the tribulation which is to precede the coming of the Lord will come upon all believers, will be shown later on to be unfounded,—but that Christians should be spared the plagues which should come upon the world to try whether it would repent or not (comp. vii. 1–3). "Him that overcometh will I make a pillar in the temple of my God, and he shall go no more out: and I will write upon him the name of my God, and the name of the city of my God, which is New Jerusalem, which cometh down out of heaven from my God; and I will write upon him my new name," iii. 12. The pillar in the temple of God is a distinguished part of it,—a support,—and its not going out indicates its continuance there; which signifies that the Christian is a support, an important member of the kingdom of God, and shall remain there immoveably. The inscription of the three names relates to three aspects of the life of the Christian,—his consecration to God, his citizenship in the New Jerusalem, and his belonging to Christ, with all its endless significance (comp. xiv. 1, xxii. 4). "Behold, I stand at the door and knock: if any man hear my voice, and open the door, I will come in to him, and will sup with him, and he with me," iii. 20,—that is, Christ enters into the most complete and blessed life-relation and life-communion with the true Christian, and the true Christian enters into the same relation with Christ (comp. Cant. ii. 8, 9, v. 2). "To him that overcometh will I grant to sit with me in my throne, even as I also overcame, and am set down with my Father in His throne," iii. 21. Here the throne of God and of Christ represents the divine power and authority; the Christian shall share in it with Christ, as Christ does with God. How each of these promises was adapted to the condition of the church concerned in it, is the business of the expositor to point out. We refer to it here only to show that they do not form a perfect whole, but only individual features, without claim to completeness. We may, however, refer these promises to a few general heads; and the following are distinctly recognisable—those relating to God, or personal communion with Him, ii. 17, iii. 12; those relating to life and love, and even to nature and honours, in common with Christ, ii. 17 (comp. iii. 12, xix. 12), iii. 5, iii. 21, based upon that which is more prominent than all—life, eternal life, ii. 7, 10, 11, 17, iii. 5; and further, the divine features—holiness, happiness, glory, and power, ii. 17–27, iii. 5, 12, 20, 21.

Let us now look back to the meaning of becoming a Christian, and compare, for example, the walking in bright garments, iii. 4, with the washing and making those garments white or bright in the blood of the Lamb, vii. 14; the names of the saints, the inscription of the names of God and Christ upon Christians, iii. 12, with the names servant of God and Christ, their being made permanent pillars in the temple of God, and the inscription upon them of the name of the New Jerusalem, iii. 12, as well as their ruling over the nations with a rod of iron, and their possession of the morning star, ii. 27, 28; their sitting with Christ upon His throne and upon the throne of God, iii. 21, with the priesthood and kinghood of Christians, i. 6, v. 9. Let us notice also that several of the promises—for example, "I will not blot out his name out of the book of life," iii. 5; "I will make him a pillar in the temple of my God," iii. 12; and, indeed, most others—appear in a remarkable manner to be more or less mere artistic variations of what the Christian, as such, is and has; for instance, his name stands in the book of life; he is a pillar in the temple of God; he has life, etc.; and we must confess that, while the promises of the seer are usually referred to the future, and not at all to the present, even his promises for the present are essentially nothing different from the import or *meaning of becoming a Christian, only not represented by formal statement or predicate, but as promise of reward, or as an end to be achieved.* Those who have not recognised this constant peculiarity of the seer, who conceives and represents these things as being present, and yet future,—as still to be attained, and yet possessed; as actual, and yet not actual; as reward (comp. xi. 18, xxii. 12), but, at the same time, as the result of a man's own nature,—want the master key for understanding this book.

5. The Churches.

The seer recognises not merely individual saints or servants of God,—*names*, as he says, iii. 4 (comp. xi. 13; Num. i. 2, 18, 20), —but single communities, consisting of individuals, and a living union of all these single communities, or a collective church. Our representations must begin with the latter; and we shall consider, first, its *names and symbols;* then, its *constituent parts;* next, its *organization;* and after that, its *history;* and finally, its *present position.*

(*a.*) *Christendom according to its Designations.*

First, the *names* and *symbols* of the church in general—"Come out of her—Babylon—*my people*"—was the injunction heard by the seer, xviii. 4 (comp. Jer. li. 45); and a voice from heaven said, "Behold, the tabernacle of God is with men, and He will dwell with them, and they shall be His people," xxi. 3 (comp. Num. xxiii. 21, 22; Ezek. xxxvii. 27). As the parallel passages show, the expression drawn from the Old Testament closely agrees in meaning with the name "servant" of God or of Christ, mentioned in the former section as descriptive of individual Christians. The designation "people of God" does not describe Christendom in distinction from Israel, but the organic whole of the servants of God, as in the predictive fact of the Old Covenant it had already existed, as realizing its time fulfilment in Christendom, and as it will find its eternal accomplishment in the New Jerusalem. When, from the various tribes, there are sealed 144,000 of the *children of Israel*, vii. 4, and when the names of the twelve tribes are written upon the gates of the New Jerusalem, xxi. 12, we are to understand, as we shall afterwards show, neither the Jews in contrast with the Gentiles, nor the Christian Jews in distinction from the Christian Gentiles; but Christians, —the true Israelites,—whether Jews or Gentiles. The twelve tribes of the children of Israel are therefore identical with the people of God; only the latter are described in Old Testament style, or typically, and as a great living organism.

In chap. xii. there appears to the seer "a great wonder in heaven, a woman clothed with the sun, and the moon under her feet, and upon her head a crown of twelve stars" (comp. Gen. xxxvii. 9, also the description of Christ, i. 12–16, especially ver. 16). "She, being with child, cried, travailing in birth, and pained to be delivered," xii. 2; "the dragon stood before the woman which was ready to be delivered, for to devour her child as soon as it was born. And she brought forth a man-child, who was to rule all nations with a rod of iron: and her child was caught up unto God, and to His throne. And the woman fled into the wilderness, where she hath a place prepared of God, that they should feed her there a thousand two hundred and threescore days," xii. 4–6. After the conflict with the dragon and his overthrow have been narrated, we read, "And when the dragon saw that he was cast unto the earth, he persecuted the woman which brought forth the man-child. And to the woman were given two wings of a great eagle, that she might fly into the wilderness, into her place, where she is nourished for a time, and times, and half a time, from the face of the serpent. And the serpent cast out of his mouth water as a flood after the woman, that he might cause her to be carried away of the flood. And the earth helped the woman; and the earth opened her mouth, and swallowed up the flood which the dragon cast out of his mouth. And the dragon was wroth with the woman, and went to make war with the remnant of her seed, which keep the commandments of God, and have the testimony of Jesus," xii. 13–17. The church of God is represented by the figure of a woman in the Old Testament (comp. for example, Isa. liv. 1, 13, lxvi. 8; Mic. v. 1–3). The question now arises, whether we are here to understand the church of the Old Testament or the New. Instead of entering upon a consideration of the various expositions, we affirm that, from the first verse of the chapter to the last, the woman without doubt represents the same personality, and the seer cannot have understood by the woman the New Testament church in distinction from that of the Old Testament; the general statements of vers. 1–6 are against it; nor is this interpretation helped by limiting the meaning to the Jewish Christian church. On the other hand, it is utterly impossible to understand by the woman the Old Testament church in distinction from that of the New, for then not only vers. 13–17, but even ver. 6, would be without meaning. What, then, are we to understand by the woman? Simply the church of God, which already existed in the prophetic fact of the Old Covenant, and which now exists in its time fulfilment in Christendom, and will exist in its eternal completion in the new heaven and the new earth.

We read, "Let us be glad and rejoice, and give honour to Him: for the marriage of the Lamb is come, and His wife"—ancient for *bride* (comp. Gen. xxix. 21)—"hath made herself ready. And unto her was granted that she should be arrayed in fine linen, clean and white: for the fine linen is the righteousness of saints. And He saith unto me, Write, Blessed are they which are called unto the marriage supper of the Lamb," xix. 7, 8. In xxi. 2 it is said, "And I John saw the holy city, New Jerusalem, coming down from God out of heaven, prepared as a bride adorned for her husband;" and the angel said, xxi. 9, to the seer, "Come hither, and I will show thee the bride, the Lamb's wife." It is written also, "the Spirit and the bride say, Come," xxii. 17. The entire figure, with which also xxii. 2 is probably connected, rests ultimately upon the Song of Solomon (comp. Jer. ii. 25; Isa. lxii. 4, 5; Hos. ii. 19; Ezek. xvi. 8; Matt. xxv. 1–12). Weiss, *bibl. Theol.* p. 610, though alone in the opinion, thinks that the church which is to constitute the perfected kingdom of God is now the bride of the Messiah; but against this xxii. 17 is decisive. Generally, expositors consider the bride of the Lamb to be the New Testament church; and, in fact, it is difficult to find a feature which speaks in favour of the church of the Old Testament. But if we first fix our attention upon xxi. 2 and 9, and then read how the New Jerusalem, xxi. 12—the bride,—has twelve gates, and at the gates twelve angels, and on them twelve names, which are the names of the twelve tribes of Israel, the conviction forces itself upon us that the seer, even by the bride of the Lamb, does not mean the New Testament church in distinction from the church of the Old Testament, but here also the church, which already existed as a prophetic fact in the Old Testament dispensation, which at present finds its time fulfilment in Christendom, and which will come to perfection only in eternity.

If, now, we take in at one glance the three names and symbols, —"people of God," pointing to the twelve tribes of Israel, "wife," and "bride,"—we shall see once more confirmed, in an important particular, our remark that the seer is mostly not in harmony with the usual categories. He is superior to the alternatives, according to which the woman in chap. xii. must be either the Old or the New Testament church. Such a view as Köstlin's—who says, *ut ante*, p. 489, "the woman, who is the subject in xii. 1–6, 13–17, is the Jewish and the Christian church in one person; Christianity is thus nothing different from Judaism; it can at most be only a new form of the same"—is not far from that of the seer. We would rather say that as, according to him, God sits upon the throne from eternity, and yet becomes Ruler only by progressive stages; that as salvation and deliverance in the ancient sacred records was through Moses, but has been fulfilled in Christ, and will become absolutely complete through Him (comp. xv. 3, the song of Moses, the servant of God, and of the Lamb, sung by the victors); that as the Christian, at the time of his conversion, has overcome, and will continue to do so to the end; in other words, that as the ideal is for the writer always already actual in its sphere, but, from one step to another, more fully realizes itself, until it has reached perfection,—so also the church of God, the ideal of humanity, was in the true Israel of the Old Covenant already realized, is so, more fully, in Christendom, and will be perfectly so in the final state. The distinction between the church in the Old and the

New Testament stage, which, as chap. xii. plainly shows, he knew very well, and did not fail to make prominent by different names and images for the two dispensations, can hardly have been to him so great as to necessitate the designation of Christian things by specific New Testament names. As to the clothing of Christian doctrines in Old Testament forms, which are indeed still the same, only in an earlier stage, he had, according to his views, the right and, with his purpose, the obligation of pointing out, by names and symbols, the church of God as the true Israel, which is really nothing else than Christendom before and after the appearance of Christ,—than Christendom which at an earlier stage expected the appearance of the man-child, and which in the present expects His coming to judgment. But it is thereby obvious, that while the idea of the people of God permits no modification, the image of the woman must form itself into harmony with the connection. In chap. xii., where "the travail," that is, the painful hopes of the church of God in the Old Dispensation, are represented, she naturally appears as a wife and mother; and the same form is maintained where she is represented as persecuted under the New Covenant; but in chap. xix. and xxi., where the subject is the marriage of the Lamb, the much-desired entire union of the church with God, or Christ, or the blessed completion of the church, she is just as naturally represented as a bride. Should it be said that in the image of the wife the Old Testament, and in that of the bride the New Testament, predominates, there can be no objection; only it may not be understood as a preponderance of the Old or the New Testament church, but only of the two sides of one and the same church of God, as related either to Christ in the flesh or to Christ in His glory; for, from the connection, we cannot fail to see why the seer could not symbolize the church of God in the Old Testament stage rather as a bride, and in the New Testament stage as wife and mother.

An entirely different symbol for the general Christian church appears in i. 12, 13, and 16. In the first passage, John sees "seven golden candlesticks; and in the midst of the *seven candlesticks* one like unto the Son of man." In the second, he sees the same person having in His right hand "*seven stars.*" The seven stars are afterwards said to be the angels of the seven churches, and the candlesticks are explained as meaning the seven churches.

We have already shown, in the section on angels, that the angels of the churches signify the churches themselves as religious unities, or bodies or persons; but the seven churches represent the churches as the sum of the manifoldly various religious individualities. The sacred number seven leads us to see in the candlesticks and the stars, Christendom in Asia (comp. i. 4); and beyond this, Christendom in its entire extent (comp. xxii. 16), for the book was undoubtedly intended for the whole church. When John represents the angels of the seven churches by stars, and the churches by candlesticks, we need not, with Düsterdieck, p. 132, find in the latter symbol merely the representation that the churches have their light from Christ, and are kept continually by the Lord, who walks in their midst, and in the former a kindred idea; but by the image of the candlesticks we shall, with Hengstenberg, I. p. 124, go back to Ex. xxv. 37 and Zech. iv., and in the oil as a symbol of the Spirit of God, and in the light as a symbol of spiritual light, we shall see the operation of the Spirit of God, and ascribe to the seer the representation that Christendom—the seven candlesticks—is filled by the Spirit of God, and with its spiritual life shines into the darkness of the world (comp. Matt. v. 14, 15; Luke xvi. 8); while by the symbol of the stars, which correspond to the angels signified by them, we are to understand less the light that is in the world, than the heavenly, light-like, glorious, in a word, God-related, or divine nature of Christendom itself.

Another entirely different image is given in the *New Jerusalem*; but this local symbol of the church in its final state will be better illustrated in the section which relates to that period.

(*b.*) *Christendom in its Constituent Elements.*

We are now in presence of the question, In what relation, in the view of the seer, did the *two elements* of the Christian church —*the Jewish and the Gentile* Christian—stand to each other? The four living creatures and the twenty-four elders say to the Lamb, "Thou art worthy to take the book, and to open the seals thereof: for Thou wast slain, and hast redeemed us to God by Thy blood out of every (πάσης) kindred, and tongue, and people, and nation; and hast made us unto our God kings and priests: and we shall reign on the earth," v. 8, 9. The writer sees an "angel fly in the midst of heaven, having the everlasting gospel to preach unto them that dwell on the earth, and to every nation, and kindred, and tongue, and people," xiv. 6, 7. In these passages it is unmistakeably declared that not Jews only, but men from all nations, had become Christians; and that, without distinction of nationality and religious antecedents, men might and should embrace the Christian faith; in other words, they undoubtedly express the *universality* of Christianity; and so decidedly does this feature belong to the entire tenor of the book, that amongst expositors there is no sort of difference with regard to it. On the contrary, with respect to the *relation of Jewish and Gentile Christians to each other*, in the Apocalypse there are three different views. De Wette, on vii. 4–8, says, "The seer makes no distinction between Jewish and Gentile Christians, and sometimes describes Christians as Israel, and at other times as the chosen out of all nations and tongues, or from off the earth." Hengstenberg, on vii. 4, remarks that in the Old Testament the wicked, notwithstanding their natural descent from Jacob, appear as rooted out from among their people; but that, on the contrary, under certain limitations, native Gentiles could, on account of their faith, become children in Israel; and that, according to the announcement of the prophets (comp. Isa. lvi. 6–8; Ezek. xlvii. 22, 23), at a future time these limitations would fall away, and the adoption of the believing Gentiles, going hand in hand with the exclusion of the false seed, would follow on the grandest scale. He therefore takes the tribes of the children of Israel in the Israelitish-Christian sense; they are to him the Christian church, as the legitimate continuation of the earlier Israel. The disciples of the Tübingen school think entirely otherwise. Baur, *ut ante*, p. 211 (comp. Köstlin, *ut ante*, p. 489), certainly finds the universality of Christianity so far recognised by the seer, that he represents Christians as divinely consecrated kings and priests, redeemed from all peoples and nations; but that he considered the Gentiles as being citizens of the New Jerusalem, equal in birth and privileges, cannot, according to Baur, be affirmed. "It is true that, in vii. 4, Jewish and Gentile Christians are conceived of together, and the innumerable multitude of ver. 9 does not differ from those already mentioned; but it is easy to see how the Gentiles belong to the Christian church only so far as they are received into communion with the Israelitish race. The Jews still have the absolute privilege of being the people of God; they are the root and stem of the whole theocratic community, and the Gentiles stand to them only in a secondary relation and in a subordinate rank (comp. chap. xi. 11, 12). The seer admits the Gentiles into the Messianic kingdom and into the New Jerusalem; but a perfect equality of Jew and Gentile does not come within the circle of his vision. When those only can enter the New Jerusalem whose names are written in the book of life, we know not whether this category has a full application to the Gentiles (comp. xxi. 24–27)." According to Volkmar, *ut ante*, p. 146, the Christian community has for the Jewish-Christian seer two different sides—the strictly citizen community of the kingdom of God, consisting of the Israelites who are faithful to God in their acceptance of the Messiah, xv. 3, xi. 3, 4, vii. 1–8, xxi. 12, 19; and, on the other hand, the unenfranchised believers from among the heathen. The former are the numbered citizens of the twelve tribes; the latter, the one mass of the innumerable multitude, vii. 9–12, xxi. 24–27. Certainly this distinction does not imply that the two sides cannot and shall not meet. Ritschl, *ut ante*, p. 134, sees in the fact that John describes the sum of those chosen from the twelve tribes as the first-fruits of the saved, as the true Israel, vii. 4, xiv. 1–4, and that he points to the privilege of the Old Testament people within the New, evidence that he thinks of the reception of the Gentiles, vii. 9, solely on account of their faith. By a third class of expositors, such as Neander, Bleek, and Düsterdieck, it is acknowledged that in this book Jewish and Gentile Christians are distinguished from others; but they deny that any preference is shown for the former. With these I agree, though not for the same reasons. It seems to me that, in the consideration of this subject, it is above all important to distinguish and to keep separate two pairs of ideas which Baur, and, after him, Köstlin, continually confound with each other, namely, Jews and Christian Jews, Gentiles and Christian Gentiles. That the writer saw in the Israelites before Christ essentially the people of God, the type of the Christian church, and in the Gentiles before Christ essentially the people of the devil, we have shown in the section on the earth and its inhabitants; and that he expected in the future the conversion of the Jews in the gross, but amongst the Gentiles only increasing obduracy, I shall point out in the sections on the holy city during the forty-two months, and the continued impenitence of men. In the section on "The New Heaven and the New Earth," I shall discuss the question of his placing the great mass of the Gentiles who, only after the revelation of the judgments of God, give glory to Him, in eternal subordination to the true Israel, the priestly kingdom of God. But we have not to do here with Jews or with Gentiles, as Baur, *ut ante*, p. 212, ambiguously writes, but with members of the church coming from Jews and Gentiles; and are we beforehand to expect that the seer would give preference to Christian Jews, and assign to the Gentiles only a secondary position? No; certainly we need expect only that, considering the time in which the book originated, there would be here and there a distinction made between the two component parts of the Christian church; but whether one is preferred and the other subordinated, we expect to learn only from the statements of the book which relate to the subject. In this expectation we are not deceived, for in a former section we have shown that in the juxtaposition of the "saints" and "them that fear the name of God," xi. 18, and of His "servants" and them that "fear Him," xix. 5, as well as in "the remnant" of the woman's seed, xii. 17, there undeniably meets us —though with the exception of the last-mentioned passage, which is misunderstood by most expositors—a distinction between Jewish and Gentile Christians. But since nothing different is affirmed of those who fear God and the remnant of the woman's seed, than is affirmed of the saints, the servants of God, and the woman's seed, we are able to recognise in the two first passages only a poetic classification of Christians according to their origin, borrowed from the pre-Christian relation of Jews and proselytes, and corresponding to the grouping found elsewhere in the book; and in the third, only a designation of Christian Gentiles suggested by the connection, as of those who became Christians historically later. This distinction perfectly agrees with the addresses to the seven principal Gentile churches; with the name of the Christian church, which in itself has no distinction between the Jewish and Gentile elements; and with the repeated and emphatic prominence given to the origin of the church from various nationalities. It would be otherwise if here and there the two classes of Christians were placed in a position of superiority and subordination. But is that the case? I deny it, and deny even that in any other than the passages quoted they are distinguished from each other. The places which here come into question are, vii. 1–8, vii. 9–17, xiv. 1–5, xxi. 12, 24–27. The relation between vii. 4–8, vii. 9–17, and xiv. 1–5, is conceived in a threefold manner, either so that in the first and third passage believers from the Jews, and in the second believers from the Gentiles, are meant; or so that in the first believers from the Jews, and in the second believers from both Jews and Gentiles, are intended; and in the third, an election from the Gentiles included in the innumerable multitude of the second; or finally, so that believers generally are understood in all three places, without reference to their origin. Against the first of these views it is decisive that the words of vii. 9, "of all nations, and kindreds, and people, and tongues," and of v. 9, x. 11, xi. 9, xiii. 7,—thus wherever they occur in this book,—describe mankind in general, and without the exclusion of the Jews or contrast with them; that in the whole paragraph contained in vii. 9–17 there is nothing specifically Gentile-Christian; and that, on the other side, there is not in xiv. 1–5 a specially Jewish-Christian feature to be discovered. The second idea is wrecked, first, upon the impossibility of explaining why, on the one hand, vii. 9–17 should be affirmed of Jewish and Gentile Christians, and on the other, why vii. 4–8 should be referred only to Jewish Christians; and further, upon the impossibility of separating the subjects of vii. 4–8 from those of xiv. 1–5. The want of the article before the 144,000 in the latter place, to which Düsterdieck attaches importance, has its reason, as Hengstenberg, *ut ante*, I. p. 115, justly observes, in the fact that in our book the groups oftener formally maintain their independence than refer definitely to those which are earlier (comp. i. 13 and xiv. 14, chap. xiii. and xvii. 3, 4, 6, and xv. 2); and though the name-sign of xiv. 1 has a different signification than the seal-sign of vii. 1–8, it can hardly be disputed that the same persons in different situations may bear different emblems. Moreover, both conceptions are alike incapable of making it even distantly probable that, according to the expectation of the seer, 12,000 from the twelve tribes of the real Israel should certainly remain protected when such an actual twelve-tribed people had in his day long ceased to exist; still less, that from each of the twelve tribes an equal number of souls were or should be faithful. All difficulty vanishes before the third interpretation, for, as De

Wette observes, it gives a very good sense if, where the mercy of God and the love of the Lamb are praised, Christians are represented as an innumerable multitude; and where the purpose is to confirm Christians in their confidence in God, or to impress on the mind their high dignity, they are represented as the true Israel, as the numbered or chosen 144,000 (comp. vi. 11, πληρωθῶσι). When, therefore, in vii. 1–8, xiv. 1–5, he treats of protection, he has chosen the latter mode of representation; but where he speaks of the results of the same, he has chosen the former, vii. 9–17; the number 144,000 serves to present the idea of appointment and election in contrast with rejection; and, indeed, it offered itself to the seer very naturally, since he retained for the saved in each tribe the number twelve, so significant with Israel, only multiplied a thousand-fold. The reference to the individual tribes owes its origin entirely to the effort of the author to make the election evident, and in our opinion has its analogy in many of the widely extended plastic images of the book. The passages found in xxi. 12, 24–27, differ from those of which we have hitherto spoken. The subjects are not the same, and there can be no doubt that those of the latter are subordinate to those of the former. But in the section on the new heaven and the new earth, we shall show that by "the children of Israel," who inhabit the New Jerusalem, not merely Christian Jews are intended, but all who have become Christians before the advent of Christ, consisting for the present of individual Jews and Gentiles, but finally, of Israel in the gross, and adopted Gentiles; on the other hand, of Gentiles who dwell around and frequent the New Jerusalem; all those who are converted during the thousand years' reign, the "nations,"—the Gentile peoples in the gross. That between these two constituent parts of those who share in the perfect kingdom of God there is a distinction in the representations of the Apocalypse, as between the citizens and the dwellers around the city, as between priest-kings and a holy nation, as between Israel and converted Gentile nations, cannot be questioned. But that by the citizens, or the priest-kings, or the true Israel itself, in its descent from Jews or Gentiles, a relation of superiority or subordination is intended, there is no proof.

But the seer distinguishes Christians not merely according to their descent, but also according to their position or dignity, according to their importance. Even in those places where, in addition to the saints, he mentions those who fear the name of God, xi. 18, and besides the servants of God, those who fear Him, xix. 5, he also speaks of "*small and great.*" That we are not to regard this distinction as in apposition with those from Jewish and Gentile Christians, as might be suggested by the absence of "and" (comp. xiii. 16, xix. 18), is shown by the position of small before great, which, though according to xx. 12, was verbally not necessary, follows also from what has been said before. But certainly the absence of "and" shows that we are not to conceive of the distinction of small and great in Christendom as we do in the world, as a distinction placing the subjects side by side, and in this case placing by the side of each other Jewish and Gentile Christians, as analogous, but yet different, and referring therefore to dignity, significance, and position. Nor does the seer leave us in the dark with respect to what he means by the distinction of small and great. As we have already seen, all Christians are to him what true Israelites are in the Old Testament, namely, servants of God. But when he writes: "The revelation of Jesus Christ, which God gave unto Him, to show unto His servants things which must shortly come to pass, and sent and signified it unto His servant John," i. 1, and that God hath as a joyful message "declared it unto His servants the prophets," x. 7, that the time has come "to give reward to Thy servants the prophets," xi. 18; and when in xi. 18, xvi. 6, xviii. 24, with the saints, he expressly refers to the prophets,—we must acknowledge that with him, just as in the Old Testament, *the prophets* are distinguished as God's servants in a prominent sense from Christians generally, who are all His servants. Instead of saying, with Baur, *ut ante*, p. 207, "all true Christians are to the seer, as such, also prophets; true Christians are those who have the testimony of Jesus, but this itself consists in a man having all his thoughts and wishes directed toward the advent of Christ; in the same proportion in which the consciousness of the Christian is filled by the idea of the advent of the future, has he the Spirit of prophecy in himself," xix. 10,—we should more correctly represent it thus: all true Christians are servants of God and Christ; angels are their fellow-servants, xxii. 9; they have the testimony of Jesus, xii. 17; but the prophets are servants of God and Christ in an eminent sense; with special significance the angel calls himself their fellow-servant, xix. 10; they have the testimony of Jesus in a special manner, xix. 10; and the difference between the prophets and saints in general is, that the former have received the Spirit of prophecy, therefore the testimony of Jesus directly, and for communication to others, xix. 10; the latter, on the contrary, do not possess the Spirit of prophecy, the testimony of Jesus directly, but they possess it through the service of the prophets, and keep the word of the prophecy, xxii. 9 (comp. i. 3).

Another question is, whether the seer understood by the prophets only those who are usually described by that name. He writes, "Rejoice over her, thou heaven, and ye holy apostles and prophets!" xviii. 20. Had he, in those places where he mentions the prophets with the saints, no thought of the apostles? Is it not more probable that under the title of prophets he has included all those whom in xviii. 20 he distinguishes as *apostles and prophets.* This supposition harmonizes perfectly with what we have found above respecting the word of God and the testimony of Jesus, namely, that to the author the word of Jesus sojourning on the earth, and the word of Jesus exalted to heaven, was the same thing; must not apostles and prophets, therefore, have for him essentially the same meaning, and be classed together, not under the conception of "apostles," which was historically limited, but under that of "prophets"? (comp. Matt. x. 41). Certainly, where he speaks only of prophets, as, for example, in xxii. 6, and even where prophets and apostles stand side by side with each other, as in xviii. 20, the seer intends prophets in the narrower sense of the word, the organs of the *exalted* Christ; on the contrary, where, as in xi. 18, xvi. 6, xviii. 24, he mentions prophets with saints, he understands by them all who are generally the organs of Christ to the church, whether as apostles, or as prophets in the narrower sense, they have directly received the testimony of Jesus, in distinction from other Christians who possess the same through their mediation. That "Asia Minor was the region where we early find the prophetic Spirit as the direct leader of the church, where it had not its rest in apostolic tradition, where the Paraclete could manifest itself" (Köstlin, *ut ante*, p. 495), need not, so far as it expresses the importance of the prophets as a peculiar class, be disputed. But we shall not say, "thus was the church consistently formed after the reality of the Old Testament theocracy" (Köstlin),—in fact an inadmissible idea!—but thus the seer consistently used the theocratic form for the representation of the church.

Thus we have found, with the seer, the distinction, existing from the beginning, between apostles and those converted by them widened in a peculiar manner into a distinction between prophets and saints, the Christian productive and the Christian receptive: let us now advance with him to another of these peculiar distinctions. It is true that he describes all Christians as those who keep the commandments of God, and have the testimony of Jesus, xii. 17. But when Jesus speaks of Antipas as "my faithful martyr who was slain among you," ii. 13; when John "saw under the altar the souls of them that were slain for the word of God and the testimony which they held," vi. 9; when it is said by the inhabitants of heaven, "they overcame him by the blood of the Lamb, and by the word of their testimony; and they loved not their lives unto the death," xii. 11; when John "saw the souls of them that were beheaded for the witness of Jesus, and for the word of God," xx. 4,—we can hardly fail to see that he means "having the testimony of Jesus" in an eminent sense. Look now at xvii. 6, where the writer sees "the woman drunk with the blood of saints and the blood of the martyrs—witnesses—of Jesus" (comp. xviii. 24), and we shall not be able, with Düsterdieck, to explain this juxtaposition of saints and the witnesses of Jesus by saying, "the witnesses are not separated in kind from the saints, but the former designation is prominent, inasmuch as the witness or testimony of Jesus borne by the saints was the cause of their death" (comp. xi. 3, 8). We prefer saying that, corresponding to the time in which the book was written, and the peculiar demands it made upon Christians, those of them who had the testimony of Jesus in an eminent, or, we may say, in an energetical sense, that is, who testified the gospel to a persecuting world by their word, xii. 11, as well as gave themselves to death for its sake, ii. 13, vi. 9, xii. 11, xx. 4, are distinguished by the author from the mass of Christians as witnesses—*martyrs*, xvii. 6. There was for the seer a distinction between those Christians who simply had the gospel, and those who bore testimony in word and deed, with patient suffering (comp. iii. 10), and with the sacrifice of life, xii. 11 (comp. ii. 10). That the martyr-death, as a repetition of the death of Christ, purified; that the bleeding confessor sprinkled himself as it were with Christ's own blood, and that this cleansed his garments, as Köstlin, *ut ante*, p. 493, after Ewald's example, infers from vii. 14,—has in this passage, which speaks of Christians in general, no foundation whatever. There is not in the Apocalypse even the most distant indication that the seer regarded the "prophets" clerically, or the "witnesses" as "martyrs in the catholic sense;" and yet, as certainly, there are present the historical connecting points of hierarchy and saint-worship.

(c.) *Christendom in its Organization.*

In what has been said above respecting the distinction of prophets—referring also to apostles—from saints, and still more in what was said earlier in the sections on the Spirit and on the Gospel respecting the activity of the prophets and the publication of the Gospel, we have greatly anticipated the inquiry into the *organization* of Christendom. When Köstlin, *ut ante*, p. 482, remarks that in our book the church appears perfectly organized, he is right so far as the two constituent elements of different origin, Jewish and Gentile Christians, are amalgamated; the churches in general were already an organic whole. But with respect to the individual members and functions of the church organism, we do not glean from the Apocalypse much information,—a very conceivable result when we remember the prophetic contents, and consequent Old Testament drapery of the book. What is certain may be given in few words. The symbols of the seven golden candlesticks, in the midst of which Christ walks, i. 12, 13, 20, and the seven stars which He holds in His right hand, teach, as we have already remarked, both by their number and their form—the garland—that the seer regarded, first, *the Christian churches in Asia, and then all the Christian churches on earth, as a great living unity.* He represents this organic whole of Christendom in its manifoldness of Christian condition by the seven churches to which the book was addressed, i. 4, 11, xxii. 16, and the variety of its Christian principles or fundamentals by the twelve apostles, xxi. 14, 19, 20. Those who infer from the names of the twelve apostles of the Lamb being written upon the foundations of the New Jerusalem, the denial or rejection of the Apostle Paul, must as a consequence call in question every reference of the book to any other than the seven churches expressly mentioned. Whether we are to seek the reason why just these and not other churches in Asia were selected as representatives, beyond the concrete condition of the individual churches and in a near ecclesiastical relation to the church at Ephesus, an already formed metropolitan connection, is at least very doubtful. It seems to me that such a supposition is very much like that which regards the seven churches as having been chosen—only possible to a very lively imagination—on account of their garland-like situation with respect to each other, and is wholly incompatible with the unmistakeable ground of choice found in the peculiar conditions presenting the most various colours in the Christian life. Of course, it is not denied that at the time of the authorship of the Apocalypse the position of the Ephesian church in relation to the Asiatic churches, in the germ, probably tolerably well developed, may have contained the same metropolitan relation which we see perfected in somewhat later times, but which we find already in the Acts of the Apostles.

The supposed connection of the angels of the churches with their *individual organization,* found by those who hold a different view, falls away by our exposition of them. To refer the twenty-four elders to the elders of the churches, the presbyters, is far-fetched; nor is it the manner of the seer to use Christian names in a New Testament sense; rather, it might be concluded from the names of the ideal church-representation, that in Asia the leaders of the churches were called bishops. Still less have we occasion from the service (*διακονία*), ii. 19, of the church at Thyatira, to think of the diaconal office. On the other hand, it is easy to see that the evangelist is represented in the angel with the everlasting gospel, the joyful message to every nation and kindred, xiv. 6, 7.

When Volkmar, *ut ante*, p. 132, on v. 8–13, remarks that worship by the representatives of the priestly people in the upper sanctuary has an aim beyond itself, and that the seer desires to represent all Christian worship on earth, I agree in so far as that he would certainly not have permitted such songs of praise in heaven if the same had not been raised in the Christian churches as well as in the temple and synagogues; but to reconstruct the form of Christian worship, or even that of Christian praise only, from the devotions of the heavenly hosts, must ever be a very uncertain task. Only two particulars of Christian worship come clearly to the front in this book. One of them is given in i. 10, "I was in the Spirit on the Lord's day." As we have pointed out in the introduction, the Lord's day can only be the day of Christ's resurrection, the *dies dominica*, the Christian Sunday; and John could only speak of it as he does on the supposition that at least in the churches of Asia, Sunday was already held as a special weekly festival for the celebration of the resurrection. The other less important particular is given in the words, "Blessed is he that readeth (readeth to), and they, that hear the words of this prophecy, and keep those things which are written therein," i. 3. This blessing, taken in connection with other statements of the New Testament, shows that in the churches for which the apostle wrote there was a public reader, and that in their assemblies such writings as this book were read by some one of the Christians present (comp. Volz, "über die Anfänge des christl. Gottesdienstes," in *Stud. und Krit.* 1872, p. 61, etc.).

(*d.*) *Christendom with respect to its History.*

The *history* of Christendom is distinctly divided by the seer into two separate periods. Certainly, regarded from its eschatological point of view, instead of speaking of a history of Christendom, we should more correctly speak of a struggle between the church of God and Satan, and in this distinguish three periods. The first of these is pictured in xii. 1–12, and includes the conflict of the dragon with the Messiah, and closes with the expulsion of the former from heaven, already considered in the section on Christ. The second period of the struggle, the *first period* of the history of Christendom, is represented in xii. 13–16. As in xii. 6, in summary anticipation, it is said, "and the woman fled into the wilderness, where she hath a place prepared of God, that they should feed her there a thousand two hundred and threescore days;" so in xii. 13–16, a resumption and further statement of ver. 6, we read, "and when the dragon saw that he was cast unto the earth, he persecuted the woman which brought forth the man-child. And to the woman were given two wings of a great eagle, that she might fly into the wilderness, into her place, where she is nourished for a time, and times, and half a time, from the face of the serpent. And the serpent cast out of his mouth water as a flood after the woman, that he might cause her to be carried away of the flood. And the earth helped the woman; and the earth opened her mouth, and swallowed up the flood which the dragon cast out of his mouth." In this picture Ewald finds a representation of the flight of the Jewish Christian church across the Jordan to Pella; and this view is common, especially in popular expositions of the Apocalypse. It has also the great superiority over the older allegories, in that it recognises past history in the related section of the twelfth chapter. But, apart from all impossibilities in detail, Ewald's interpretation is met by the insuperable difficulty of supposing that the seer has given a prominent place in his magnificent picture to such a fact as the flight to Pella. Even if the individual features required a reference to that episode in the Jewish war, which they did not, we should still only say that in painting the first period of the Christian history the seer has borrowed the colours of that particular event, or has used its outline as apocalyptic drapery for his picture. The design of xii. 13–16 is —as xii. 1–12 sketches the history of Christ, but only on the side harmonizing with the book, namely, as the conflict of the dragon with the woman's child—to represent the first development of this history, or the history of Christendom on Jewish ground, but again only according to the side suitable for the purpose of the Apocalypse, namely, as the conflict of the overthrown dragon with the woman who bore the child. If we do not firmly hold that the author as a seer must in the course of his representations, on the one side bring up episodically the entire historical premises of his predictions, but on the other had not as a seer the slightest inducement to disclose in the Christian history anything else than the premises of his prophecy, that is, the course of the conflict hitherto between Satan and the people of God, especially with the Messiah, the twelfth chapter in its second half, as in its first, must remain an enigma. How simple, on the other hand, is every detail from the point of view of the writer himself! After his overthrow, the dragon "persecuted the woman which brought forth the man-child;" in these few words he presents, as before in the words, "the dragon stood before the woman which was ready to be delivered, for to devour her child as soon as it was born," less the history of Jesus than the meaning of that history from an eschatological standpoint; so, again, less the history of the Jewish Christian church, or Christianity among the Jews, than the meaning of this history from an eschatological standpoint, and that is persecution, and on account of the defeat suffered through Christ, only the more fierce persecution, ver. 12, of the church of Christ by the Jews: the rich concrete basis of his brief words the author takes for granted as known. But what is the result of the persecution of Christianity among the Jews? As "her child was caught up unto God," so the woman fled unto "the place prepared of God;" that is, Christianity escaped the destruction threatened among the Jews, while, through the divine arrangement, it spread among the Gentiles. This important transition the seer represents by a skilful use of Old Testament symbolism. He represents the Gentile world by the wilderness of Sinai, with its double antithesis to Egypt, the image of unbelief and persecution of the people of God, and to the worldly Jewish people (comp. xi. 8), as being the region of security, as well as the region of poverty in resources. It is not to our author the natural ground, but the asylum of Christianity, wonderfully prepared by God. The woman is to be nourished in her place in the wilderness 1260 days, or 3½ times, far away, and safe from the serpent; nor does he regard the Gentile world as the new and abiding home of the kingdom of God, but as the seat of Christianity during the time of tribulation appointed by Him; and naturally during that time the significance of Israel is not in its being the seat of the kingdom of God, but in that which the eleventh chapter explains. The two wings of a great eagle given to the woman have their type in those of Ex. xix. 4 (comp. Deut. xxxii. 11). There are for the seer wondrous ways and means of divine power and grace by which Christianity is transferred from the Jews to the Gentiles. The flood is, according to Ps. xviii. 4, 15, 16, cxxiv. 4, 5, Isa. viii. 5–8, Jer. xlvi. 7, 8, xlvii. 2, the figure of great and pressing danger; and from the symbolic language of the Old Testament he has, as it were, produced bodily forms, eagle's wings, and the flood of water. When "the dragon casts out of his mouth water as a flood after the woman," the writer can hardly have intended anything else than the difficulties which the Jews cast in the way of the publication of the gospel, and the formation and growth of Christian churches among the Gentiles. Whether the swallowing of the water by the earth, which came to the help of the woman, and which reminds us of Num. xvi.

30–34, Isa. v. 14, is to be explained merely as a symbolic representation, harmonizing with what precedes it, of the vanity of Jewish opposition; or whether by the name and image of the earth we are to understand the Roman empire as a protection of Christianity against the Jews,—it is difficult certainly to ascertain.

The *second period* of the history of Christianity, or the third period of the conflict between Satan and the people of God, is summarily pictured in xii. 17: "And the dragon was wroth with the woman, and went to make war with the remnant of her seed, which keep the commandments of God, and have the testimony of Jesus." As the purpose of devouring the child represents the history of Jesus, and the persecution of the woman the history of Christianity among the Jews in Palestine and in the Hebrew form; so "making war with the remnant of her seed" signifies, in apocalyptic style, the history of Christianity among the Gentiles, in the countries beyond Palestine, and under the preponderance of the Gentile-Christian element, until the turn of events introduced at xi. 13. The two earlier periods have been sketched with only few lines, but the third appears in a more complete picture of the past, the present, and the future. In this place we have to do only with the past; and even in the consideration of that, we limit ourselves to the indications of the letters, apart from the related data in the description of the beast, the false prophet, and Babylon; and, indeed, on a double ground, first, because from this description the historical can hardly be certainly and accurately separated; at the best, we rend asunder things which belong to each other; and secondly, and chiefly, because the absence of all reference in the letters to the beast and to the false prophet shows that the seer himself has not completed the connection of the previous persecutions and false doctrine in his Asiatic circle with the past activity of the anti-Christian powers. Therefore, instead of saying, with Neander, *ut ante*, p. 474, that the Apocalypse everywhere testifies of the flowing blood of the martyrs, and of the oppressions which threatened Christians in prison, as of the still fresh memories of Nero's cruelties; and instead of combining, like other expositors, the false prophecy of the letters and the false prophet of the beast,—we acknowledge that John, in the conduct of the beast generally, and in the persecution of the Asiatic Christians especially, has recognised different things as little as he has in the doings of the false prophet generally, and in the erroneous doctrine amongst the Asiatic churches in particular; but we find it very conceivable that he has not therefore directly applied the vision of the anti-Christian powers which came to him on Patmos to the past history of his ecclesiastical circle, but has rather, in his conception and representation, only placed the relations of that circle and those of Christendom in general side by side with each other. From this we infer the propriety of limiting our reflections in this place to the indications of the letters concerning the war of the dragon, hitherto carried on with the remnant of the woman's seed, in the seer's own circle.

Let us now hear what is said there concerning opposition or *persecution* from without. To the church in Smyrna—with respect to its external relations as well as to those of the apocalyptic churches generally, comp. Hausrath, p. 654—the Lord says, "I know thy works, and tribulation (comp. i. 9), and poverty; but thou art rich; and I know the blasphemy of them which say they are Jews, and are not, but are the synagogue of Satan. Fear none of those things which thou shalt suffer: behold, the devil shall cast some of you into prison, that ye may be tried; and ye shall have tribulation ten days," ii. 9, 10. But to the church in Philadelphia the Lord says, "I know thy works: behold, I have set before thee an open door, and no man can shut it: for thou hast a little strength, and hast kept my word, and hast not denied my name. Behold, I will make them of the synagogue of Satan, which say they are Jews, and are not, but do lie; behold, I will make them to come and worship before thy feet, and to know that I have loved thee," iii. 8, 9. We see that the anti-Christian Jews had on their side not failed to persecute the Christians; certainly they had not the power to carry their rage against them into actual ill-usage; therefore, as far as possible, they caused them to be suspected of the Gentiles. In what such slanders consisted is not said; and when Ewald, *Geschichte*, VI. p. 636, supposes that the Jews may easily have used the privileges still left them under the Roman empire against the Jewish Christians as apostates, and punished them even in their own synagogues, it is at least not expressed in the passages, ii. 9, 10, iii. 9, quoted by him. In Smyrna, as in Philadelphia, the Christians had to suffer from such slander and hunting down on the part of the Jews; at the latter place they had already maintained their ground when tempted to forsake the word of Jesus, and to deny His name. To the church in Pergamos the Lord says, "I know thy works, and where thou dwellest, even where Satan's seat is: and thou holdest fast my name, and hast not denied my faith, even in those days wherein Antipas was my faithful martyr, who was slain among you, where Satan dwelleth," ii. 13. We see that the Gentiles, in their enmity to the Christians, could go more openly to work, and that they were not backward in it. Still their hatred and persecution were not everywhere equally fierce. The city of Pergamos, probably as the seat of the worship of Esculapius, and of a medical school, as the locality of a supreme court of justice, and probably also as the residence of certain specially fanatic heathen, was among all Asiatic cities the headquarters of Gentile opposition to Christianity. This is indicated by the "seat" and "the dwelling" of Satan,—possibly, as Hausrath, II. p. 656, thinks, with special reference to the statue of Esculapius, upon which a serpent entwined itself. There they had not only held fast the name of Christ, and maintained their fidelity to Him, but a faithful witness called Antipas had suffered death. Frightful things had happened also elsewhere. Certainly it cannot be decided whether the poverty of the church at Smyrna, of which the Lord speaks, ii. 9, was caused by persecution, or whether it made the Christians helpless against the bribery of Gentile magistrates and officials by rich Jews (comp. Jas. ii. 5–7), or whether it is added to the calumnies of the Jews and the cruelties of the Gentiles as an aggravating circumstance; but when the church is admonished not to fear those things it would have to suffer; when it is warned beforehand that some of them would be cast into prison, and that for a short time—meant by ten days—they should have tribulation; when it is exhorted to be faithful unto death,—it may undoubtedly be assumed that things similar to those predicted had already passed over them; that as, according to Düsterdieck's remark, the warning of the prison, more than the mention of death, shows that here the Gentile authorities, incited by the Jews, had begun to persecute. Very justly Neander, *ut ante*, p. 455, note, says that the expression "beheaded," xx. 4, points to something different from mere popular tumult, which would not have satisfied itself by beheading the Christians; and that it rather shows that, in the administration of Roman justice, this punishment was already applied to Christians. While by the use of the term "beheaded," John may have had in his eye the persecution of Nero, the "prison" at Smyrna places beyond doubt that also in Asia,—though, indeed, the result of this persecution at Rome,—not only the Gentile people, but the Gentile authorities also, were already opposed to the Christians when this book was written.

We will not here follow any further the statements of the Apocalypse concerning the existing persecutions of the Christians by Jews and Gentiles, but, under reference to the section on Antichrist, turn to a consideration of what is said about seductions or about *heresies.* To the church in Ephesus the Lord says, "I know thy works, and thy labour, and thy patience, and how thou canst not bear them which are evil: and thou hast tried them which say they are apostles, and are not, and hast found them liars: and hast borne, and hast patience, and for my name's sake hast laboured, and hast not fainted," ii. 2, 3. And to the same church He says, "But this thou hast, that thou hatest the deeds of the Nicolaitanes, which I also hate," ii. 6. In the letter to the church at Pergamos He says, "But I have a few things against thee, because thou hast there them that hold the doctrine of Balaam, who taught Balak to cast a stumbling-block before the children of Israel, to eat things sacrificed unto idols, and to commit fornication. So hast thou also them that hold the doctrine of the Nicolaitanes," ii. 14, 15. In the letter to the church at Thyatira He says, "Notwithstanding I have a few things against thee, because thou sufferest that woman Jezebel, which calleth herself a prophetess, to teach and to seduce my servants to commit fornication, and to eat things sacrificed unto idols. And I gave her space to repent of her fornication; and she repented not. Behold, I will cast her into a bed, and them that commit adultery with her into great tribulation, except they repent of their deeds. And I will kill her children with death; and all the churches shall know that I am He which searcheth the reins and hearts: and I will give unto every one of you according to your works. But unto you, and unto the rest in Thyatira, as many as have not this doctrine, and which have not known the depths of Satan, as they speak, I will put upon you none other burden," ii. 20–24.

By these indications we are led to ask whether we have to do with *one heresy or several.* Though De Wette, speaking of the false apostles, ii. 2, says that it does not with certainty anywhere appear what error is meant, and that it is evident from ii. 15 that the Nicolaitanes and the followers of Balaam, though similar to each other, were yet different parties, and that even Jezebel appears to point to a special position, most expositors refer the various expressions of our book, with respect to heresy, to a single false doctrine. I do not find the truth on either of these two sides. What Jezebel taught the servants of the Lord in Thyatira, and to which she seduced them,—namely, to eat idolatrous sacrifices, and to fornication,—is doubtless identical with the doctrine held by the members of the church at Pergamos,—"the doctrine of Balaam, who taught Balak to cast a stumbling-block before the children of Israel, to eat things sacrificed unto idols, and to commit fornication." Again, we find that *οὕτως καὶ σύ*, of which *ὁμοίως* is the only possible philological interpretation, identifies the doctrine of the Nicolaitanes with that of Balaam. On the other hand, I fail to recognise, in the commendation of the Ephesian church, that they hate "the deeds of the Nicolaitanes," a repetition of the praise already bestowed, ii. 2; much rather do I see in the false apostles and the evil a reference to a heresy different and, indeed, opposed to that of the Nicolaitanes.

But this point needs a searching discussion. It is well known that the Tübingen school refers ii. 2, 3 to the *Apostle Paul.* We may compare Baur, *ut ante,* p. 214, who, however, expresses himself carefully and inquiringly when he says, "Since, on the foundations of the New Jerusalem, only the names of the twelve apostles are written, xxi. 14, we may properly inquire whether among the apostles here the Apostle Paul is included, and whether the seer regards as a true and genuine apostle one who took such a mild view of eating flesh offered to idols, and did not utterly condemn it." Köstlin, *ut ante,* p. 486, according to whom the seer, ii. 2, evidently had Paul in his eye; Schwegler in *Nachapostolischer Zeitalter;* and Volkmar, *ut ante,*—beyond all doubt, on account of ii. 2, ascribe to the writer an entirely different controversy with the apostle. Keim, *ut ante,* I. p. 160, finds that the Apocalypse presupposes the Twelve, and thus also John himself, as kindred in sentiment, and pillars of the future Jewish Jerusalem; just as, on the other hand, in recognisable opposition, it disowns and denies the position of Paul; and he adds the remark, that we must certainly not go with Volkmar so far as to see Paul in the false prophet, chap. xiii., which is very arbitrary; but in the letters, and chiefly in that to the Ephesian church, ii. 2, reference to the Paulites and their apostle is undeniable (comp. 1 Cor. ix. 1, 2; Acts xv. 25, 26; Rom. xvi. 17–20) (comp. Hausrath, II. p. 645, etc.). I cannot, with Ritschl, *ut ante*, p. 120, describe the proof of the anti-Paulinism of the author, drawn from xxi. 14, as at the least ambiguous, because "twelve is a round symbolic number which alone is suitable to the type founded on the Israelitish tribes, and was so conventionally established, that even Paul speaks of the Twelve, 1 Cor. xv. 5, where only eleven were really concerned;" for, certainly, he did not number himself with the "Twelve," nor did others so number him. But is it not also exceedingly plain that the seer brings as a supplement to the Old Testament symbol of the twelve tribes of Israel, a corresponding New Testament symbol, and that he chooses as such "the twelve apostles of the Lamb," as most nearly related to Christ's choice of, and promises to, the apostles? It almost appears as if the seer, to escape the suspicion of the Tübingen school, must make Paul an original apostle, or obliterate the distinction between him and the others. Very justly, Hase (*Tübing. Schule*, p. 25) refers to the supposed opposition of the seer to Paul, in the words, "Highly as Paul's importance may be rated, his place was not among the apostles, the Twelve, in the genuine historical sense."—We find that ii. 2 relates to something different; and we cannot pass over it with so light a step as Neander, when he says, *ut ante*, p. 474, "Falsifiers of the original truth, who gave themselves out for apostles, became prominent;" and in a note he adds, that the polemic is not directed against one, but several, and their character must be learned from the remaining contents of the apocalyptic letters, which will lead us to think of an opposition entirely different from that said to be offered to Paul; nor, as Düsterdieck, who, p. 148, after he has characterized the Nicolaitanes as ethnistic libertines, says that, on the other hand, he will not affirm that they, ii. 2, usurped an apostolic authority; for when they, perhaps in the Pauline sense, proposed to make Christian freedom a reality, they would be apostles in a similar manner to Paul. But we do not therefore get away from ii. 2 so easily, because the name apostle, even with Paul, or in a Pauline sense, by no means, as Düsterdieck assumes, coincides with the name prophet; and inasmuch as a vision of the Lord, as well as a commission from Him, belongs to the apostolic office as well as to the office of the prophet, the difference can only be, that the apostle has seen and heard the Risen One in the body, the prophet in the spirit; consequently, the Gentile Christians could very well use the name prophet, but under no condition that of apostle. Have we proof of this? If, now, these false teachers, who called themselves apostles, were identical with the Nicolaitanes, they could only have been Jewish Christians who by the assumption of apostolic authority were led to fornication and eating of sacrifices offered to idols; and what other Jewish Christians could the seer have had in his eye, than the Apostle Paul and his allies from among the Jews?—It is an entirely different question, however, a question which should have been seriously considered before ii. 2 was used as an important and sure ground upon which to construct the times of the apostles, namely, whether in the passage under consideration the apostle and his associates *could* be intended. To an unprejudiced student it must have already appeared impossible, because it would place the seer, as far as we have understood him, in absolute contradiction with himself, if he declared, as some would gladly have it, that Paul was not only not true and genuine, but that, as the words according to the interpretation of our opponents demand, he was a lying or false apostle, a seducer like Balaam and Jezebel. That the Apostle John was not capable of this, is granted even by the opposite side. But even another John would not have been able to do it, simply because, according to the unequivocal and complete statement of the first Epistle to the Corinthians, from the fifth to the tenth chapter, Paul opposed in Achaia exactly the same thing which, according to the ideas of our opponents, he taught in Asia. So long as the views and principles contested by Paul in the first Epistle to the Corinthians are not proved to be his own, it is simply impossible to refer Rev. ii. 2 to him. But does the seer describe the false apostles as identical with the Nicolaitanes? It is said that ii. 6 has a good sense only when there is seen in it a repetition of the commendation of ii. 2, and consequently the Nicolaitanes here, and the false apostles there, are the same. Notwithstanding, there occurs in the letter to Sardis, iii. 4, and also introduced with "but," not a repetition of ver. 1, but something entirely new. Is there, indeed, in any one of the seven letters, such a concluding repetition as it is thought must be supposed in ii. 6? Will not the assertion, that without such a supposition the Nicolaitanes in this place are unexplained, and must remain so, immediately fall away if we compare the mention of the beast from the bottomless pit, xi. 7? Is it not very significant that the author places the approval of their unmasking false prophets at the beginning, and the commendation of their hatred of the deeds of the Nicolaitanes at the close, of the letter, if the temptations by false apostles, as the aorist, and still more the fixed recognition of time in the Apocalypse, permit us to suppose (we may remember that false apostles can have existed only as long as the true), belong mainly, or more probably altogether, to the past, and the works of the Nicolaitanes, on the contrary, to the present, or principally to the future? On our view of the case, what a significant and wholly unsought coincidence appears between the Apocalypse and the apostolic history! In his parting address to the Ephesian elders at Miletus, Acts xx. 29, 30, Paul says, "For I know this, that after my departing shall grievous wolves enter in among you, not sparing the flock. Also of your own selves shall men arise, speaking perverse things, to draw away disciples after them." That these words point to a double danger threatening the Ephesian church, one from without, and another coming from among themselves, cannot be denied. And it is equally certain that by grievous wolves which would enter the church, he meant Judaists; and by those speaking perverse things who should come from among themselves, ethnistic false teachers. Whether we consider the warning of the apostle respecting this double danger to have been spoken by himself or afterwards put into his mouth, —I adhere to the former alternative,—it is the same; in the first case, Paul must have already perceived the germ of antagonistic errors; and in the second, the author of the Acts of the Apostles must have had knowledge of the existence in Ephesus of both classes of error. Now we find again the indigenous ethnistic heresy in the Nicolaitanes; but where are the grievous wolves who enter in, the Judaizing teachers? We can look for them only in those who give themselves out for apostles, and are not. We can here only point to another coincidence, namely, with the Epistles to Timothy, and simply mention also that Paul speaks of the same sort of men as the seer does, when he writes, 2 Cor.

xi. 13, "Such are false apostles, deceitful workers, transforming themselves into the apostles of Christ."

One of the two errors which the seer has in his eye, and against which, with the exception of one place, he everywhere struggles, he describes by *various names*. What do these signify? When the name Nicolaitanes appears, ii. 6, according to xi. 7, it is not to be concluded either that what has been said previously relates to the same, or that the seer must have met with it before. That he desired, according to the opinion of several Fathers of the church and later writers, to designate the adherents of a man called Nicolas, the proselyte of Antioch, mentioned in Acts vi. 5, is conceivable (we may compare the name Antipas, which is decidedly not symbolic, ii. 13); but the comparison of ii. 14 and 15 shows unequivocally that, in perfect harmony with his manner, he sought in the Old Testament an analogy to existing error. This was found in the narrative of Num. xxxi. 15, 16, xxv. 1, 2; and the meaning of the name Balaam, destroyer of the people, not escaping him, he rendered it by the somewhat similar Greek name Nicolas, and so it has come to be a symbolic party name of the Nicolaitanes; and in order not to lose the significant analogy with the history of Balaam, at one time he has said, "them that hold the doctrine of Balaam," and at another, "them that hold the doctrine of the Nicolaitanes." We are prevented from understanding by the woman Jezebel, a woman in Thyatira, who was really called Jezebel, by the meaning of the name, as well as by the striking parallelism with Balaam; even this parallelism, as the change between the expressions, "them that commit adultery with her," ii. 22, and "her children," ii. 23, shows, forbids us to think of a single teacher of false doctrine in Thyatira. Much more does the woman Jezebel describe symbolically the false doctrine which has before been called "the doctrine of Balaam," ii. 14, and "the doctrine of the Nicolaitanes," ii. 15, and that, indeed, on the basis of 1 Kings xvi. 31, xxi. 21–26; 2 Kings iii. 2, ix. 22–37.

But in what do the two false doctrines opposed by the seer *consist?* We get no image of the *Judaistic* error, and doubtless because its effects in the Ephesian church—we may compare the aorist—had been subdued. Still, the expressions which are used with regard to them and to the action of the church against them, —above all, the statement that they say they are apostles, and are not, and are found liars, that they are evil or wicked men;

further, that the church had found it difficult to bear with them, that it had labour with them, that it had shown patience toward them,—fully justify us in finding amongst these seducers exactly the same kind of Judaists as those who, according to the Epistles of Paul, obtained during his lifetime an entrance into the churches founded by him, there to seek the advancement of their covetous and tyrannical aims (comp. 2 Cor. xi., especially vers. 13 and 20; Gal. v. 1–12; Phil. iii., especially ver. 2).

That which then existed in an appreciable stage of development, which was peculiarly dangerous, and for that reason almost exclusively contested, was *ethnistic* error. We can therefore, from the statements of the Apocalypse itself, furnish a probable picture. Certainly the views of expositors differ. While Volkmar admits that the Nicolaitanes, in their opposition to Old Testament regulations, had still (?) some relation to the Paulinism of the Gnosis, he regards them as nothing different, and nothing worse, than open and reckless or coarse Paulites. Ritschl, p. 135, finds in them Gentile Christians who, on account of their Christian knowledge of the nullity of the law, did not submit to the conditions of the apostolic decrees, and, probably in designed opposition to them, sought participation in heathen sacrificial feasts, and married within forbidden degrees of relationship. But Hengstenberg, I. pp. 172, 192, 208, 212 (comp. Neander, p. 475, note; De Wette on ii. 24), explains the ethnistic error of the Apocalypse to be Gnosticism in one of its earliest forms. Let us begin with ii. 24, so far as I can see, a decisive passage, "Unto you I say, and unto the rest in Thyatira, as many as have not this doctrine, and which (οἵτινες) have not known the depths of Satan, as they speak." Among the various expositions of this passage, first, that appears to me futile which makes "the rest" the subject of the verb "speak," and ascribes to it the statement that they "have not known the depths of Satan." By this exposition, the words, "as they speak," would not only be superfluous, but disturbing. The almost universally accepted interpretation, "the depths,—not of God, as the Nicolaitanes say, but of Satan,"—is wholly inadmissible; the passage in ii. 9, "them which say they are Jews, and are not, but are the synagogue of Satan" (comp. iii. 9), should not be quoted as a parallel; to serve that purpose it must have read, "who are the synagogue of Satan, as they speak:" had the seer wished to say what some desire he should, he would have written, "who have not known the depths of God, as they speak." As the words read, and as they only can be literally explained, they affirm that the false teachers give themselves credit for knowing the depths of Satan; and that the seer, who in this direction perceived only theoretical and practical error, ironically and sarcastically describes the faithful Christians, with seeming pity, as those who were certainly not so enlightened and free, really not so blind and wicked, as the Nicolaitanes. In "the depths of Satan" we have, without doubt, after the analogy of 1 Cor ii. 10 and the Gnostic phraseology, to understand the popular recognition of the unfathomable relation of being or mystery of the evil principle; and in the "knowing," according to the analogy of 1 Cor. viii. 1–3 and the Gnostic self-description, the popular idea, the conception or abstraction of the words and deeds of an overreaching speculative thought. If we add that Jezebel says she is a prophetess, ii. 20, and on account of the relation to the Old Testament type (comp. 2 Kings ix. 22), and still more on account of the specific meaning of prophecy in this book, that the Nicolaitanes claimed not only a better insight, but must have affirmed their supposed deeper spiritual disclosures to be realized in an intuitive way through inspiration; and further, that, according to the indisputable word-sense of ii. 24, the Nicolaitanes expressly and specially prided themselves in knowing "the depths of Satan," but that in the nature of the case this was not the only, but the more conspicuous instance, or the most important example, or, *for the polemical design of the seer, the only prominent subject of their pretended "knowledge,"*—there then presents itself as the theoretical side, or as the philosophical foundation of ethnistic error, a lofty speculation in the form of inspiration, which claims to understand the Godhead directly, as also all that is supernatural, and to have a perfectly adequate knowledge of His nature; in a word, though yet in one of its earliest stages of development—manifest *Gnosticism.*

But wherein consists the practical foundation of the error? The Lord says to the rest in Thyatira, "I will put upon you none other burden: but that which ye have already, hold fast till I come. And he that overcometh, and keepeth my works unto the end, to him will I give power over the nations," etc., ii. 24–29. That we are to understand here, not a burden of suffering, but a burden of law, a legal restraint, obligation, or command, is universally admitted by modern expositors (comp. Acts xv. 28). No matter whether the seer, by the assurance of the Lord, desired to guard the faithful from the mistake of supposing that, if one or two Old Testament commands had still a binding force, they must take upon themselves the entire burden of the Jewish law, or (and it is much more probable that the "burden" was a contemptuous expression of the Nicolaitanes, and that the seer spoke ironically) whether he desired to present sarcastically the arguments of the Nicolaitanes, in each case there is a reference to the error of the rejection of the limitations of the law, which the seer desires should be firmly held by Christians. When, from ii. 14 and 20, we see that the doctrine taught and led to eating idolatrous sacrifices and to fornication, the first of these two particulars calls for no remark. There are, however, different views with regard to the second. The older expositors understand the expression in its usual sense; Ritschl, *ut ante*, p. 135, explains it as equivalent to marriages forbidden by the Mosaic law; Volkmar understands it as marriage with Gentiles, possibly also as disregard of other marriage laws of the Old Testament. That which Ritschl adduces in favour of his view, namely, that Balaam and Jezebel did not necessarily lead to unchastity, and that their sin was in tempting the Israelites into *matrimonial* alliances with the Canaanites, does not follow from the passages quoted by him, and already mentioned above; on the contrary, the statements of Num. xxv. 1, 6, 18, xxxi. 16–18, refer to non-matrimonial intercourse between the Israelites and Midianitish women. Jezebel cannot be mentioned as a symbol of the false doctrine which taught and led to fornication, because she lived in the married state with Ahab; but because she insisted upon the impure worship of Baal (comp. 2 Kings ix. 22). That fornication consisted in marriage with the heathen, Volkmar maintains only on the assumption that the Nicolaitanes were Paulites. When he says that by what the Christians of the apostolic times called fornication we cannot understand fornication properly so called, and that it has long been acknowledged that it is marriage contrary to the Old Testament economy, we would say more correctly that, by the fornication of which the seer speaks, and which is represented as a sinful casting away of the burden of the law, we have to understand all that in this relation was forbidden by the law, and thus impurity in our sense of the word, marriage in near degrees of relationship, and with the heathen. By this exposition of fornication, the reference or relation to the apostolic decrees, Acts xv. 19, 20, which comes to light in the "burden," and in connection with "eating things sacrificed to idols," is in no way excluded; it only demands a wider corresponding conception of "fornication" in that decision, which, moreover, even apart from the Apocalypse, shows itself to be against its limitation to marriage in forbidden degrees of relationship (comp. Ewald, *Geschichte des Volks Israel*, VI. p. 437). It is also self-evident that we are not to regard eating things sacrificed to idols and fornication as the only illegalities of the Nicolaitanes, but in a similar manner as "the depths of Satan," as the most striking criteria, as it were the signs, or, in the apocalyptic concrete representation, the only manifestations presented of a recent but universally-developed *Antinomianism.*

But I am unable to see how, according to Baur's statement, *ut ante*, p. 214, the difference of the two standpoints, of the seer and Paul, at least in relation to eating things sacrificed to idols, shows in its whole breadth wherein at this point the much talked of opposition of the former to the latter consists, when the apostle has confessedly written 1 Cor. v. 1–5, vi. 12–20, vii. 12–16, viii. 1–13, x. 6–8 (comp. Ritschl, *ut ante*, p. 136), so long as it is not shown that a failure of motive, in one of the two writers, for a common judgment, influenced their various standpoints. If the seer, like Paul, regarded the eating of meat offered to idols as in itself lawful, he could still not have introduced it into this book. But granted that it was to him not lawful in itself, was it so even to Paul, where it appeared, as here, in connection with heathen immoralities? Much rather does the error condemned in the Apocalypse appear to me to be the free-thinking and essentially Gnostic-antinomian tendency, in a somewhat advanced stage of development. I say an advanced stage, not because of the general difference between 1st Corinthians and the Apocalypse, which is difficult to authenticate, where even "the depths" of our book, certainly alluding to the mode of speech used by the opponents, appear (1 Cor. ii. 10); but only because it is to be supposed that doctrinal error, both in theory and practice, must have further developed during the period between the first Epistle to the Corinthians and the Apocalypse; its results in both respects have become more fully defined, and the error itself more completely shaped into system and party, with which ii. 14 and 20, and especially the strongly pronounced "teach" in the latter place, decidedly agree.

(e.) *Christendom in its Existing Condition.*

When Hengstenberg places the promises closing the letters in which these errors are condemned in close relation with them, I agree with him so far as, according to the peculiarity of the book, the tree of life in the paradise of God, ii. 7, the new name, ii. 17, power over the nations, and the morning star, ii. 26–28, certainly allude to and contrast with the nature, promises, and results of false doctrine. But passing over the fact that we cannot, like Hengstenberg, find the Gnosis of the second century controverted in this book, the data of the letters, even with microscopic research, are too sparing to allow us to hope that a comparison of each promise with the error would lead us beyond the sphere of uncertain conjecture. We therefore ask, What was the *condition* of the churches in general under such temptations of the flesh and the world, such persecutions from Jews and Gentiles, such Judaizing and heathenizing doctrine? The seven letters give us a picture of sevenfold variety. While the church at Ephesus had left its first love, fallen from its earlier state, and was admonished to repent and do the first works, ii. 4, 5; while the church at Sardis had a name as if living, but was dead, and was exhorted to be watchful, and to strengthen the things that remain, and which were ready to die, since the Lord had not found her works perfect before God, and to remember how she had received and heard, and to hold fast and repent, iii. 1–3; while the church at Laodicea was neither cold nor hot, but lukewarm, and said, "I am rich, and increased with goods, and have need of nothing," and knew not that she was wretched, and miserable, and poor, and blind, and naked, and was admonished to be zealous and repent, iii. 15–19,—the poor church at Smyrna was rich, ii. 9; and the last works of the church at Thyatira were more than the first, ii. 19. Against the slanders of the Jews, the church at Smyrna was exhorted to be faithful unto death, ii. 9, 10. The church at Philadelphia had a little strength, and had kept the word of the Lord, and had not denied His name, but had used the door set open before it to repent, iii. 7, 8. The church at Pergamos had held fast the name of the Lord against the persecutions of the heathen, and had not, even in the worst times, sacrificed its fidelity to him, ii. 13. The church at Ephesus, in the midst of severe conflict, had withstood the Judaizing errors which had burst in upon it, ii. 2, 3. The same church had decidedly rejected the errors of heathenism, ii. 6, while the adherents of those errors were found in the church at Pergamos, ii. 14, 15, and were tolerated by the church at Thyatira, ii. 20. Here we must assume, in conformity, on one hand, with the number seven and the typical character of the book, and with the name and concrete features on the other, that in the letters to the individual churches John had in his eye definite historic characteristics, but addressed his book to these several churches, because each of them was a conspicuous type of the varied condition of Christendom generally; we see, therefore, that at the time the book was written, life in Christendom was not dormant, as most expositors briefly say, but that in some churches it existed in full vigour; that in others, compared with what it was in the first Christian generation, it was already in a state of decline; that the pressure of the Jews, and the actual violence of the Gentiles, though leading to severe and dangerous temptation, had nowhere resulted in formal apostasy; and that Judaistic error had, generally, no longer any footing; but, on the other hand, Gentile libertinism had, in some churches, if not numerous, all the more obstinate, ii. 21, and zealous adherents, ii. 20 (comp. ver. 14).

THIRD PART.

PROPHECY.

1. The Beast. The False Prophet. Babylon.

Christianity is nothing, and will be nothing else than the fulfilment of Old Testament prophecy, or the realization of Jewish eschatology. But as Christ has already come, He is also to come again; thus Christianity in one respect is already present, but in another there is an impending fulfilment or realization of the religious ideal. While, for the historians, the evangelists, the first aspect predominates; for the prophet, the seer, the second stands in the foreground. This future aspect, or, as we may now say, this Christian eschatology, in times of extraordinary tension between the kingdom of God and the world, presents itself to the prophets, in the way of inspiration or of intuition, as a revelation in visions and voices, but neither in their abstract universal contents nor in the form of their ultimate realization, but in concrete forms, and, indeed, in the form of the nearest approaching stage of fulfilment, in perfect analogy with the prophecies of the Old Testament. For the Christian prophet, to whom the Messiah and His kingdom have already appeared, the *punctum saliens*, and at the same time the moving force, is obviously the manifestation of Antichrist, according to the condition of which, the reaction on the part of God or Christ in judgment, or otherwise modified, must appear to the seer. From this it follows, that though the statements of our book, in their main substance contained in chap. xiii. and xvii., concerning the beast, the false prophet, and Babylon, or the three antichristian powers, practically or ecclesiastically regarded, in no way constitute its most important contents,—though the Antichrist of the Apocalypse has not entirely passed away with the Roman empire, but in the course of centuries more than one new edition has appeared, and certainly in the future there will be seen the fulfilment of all its essential features,—but rather, from the idea of Antichrist proper to the book, that the least controverted parts of it have for edification immediate and most urgent importance; we must yet not conceal from ourselves the fact that, historically and scientifically considered, we have now arrived at the real kernel of the Apocalypse. We will explain in their order the meaning of the three individual powers in which Antichrist presents itself to the seer.

(a.) *The Beast.*

It is said of the second antichristian appearance: "and I beheld another beast," xiii. 11, and of the corresponding phenomenon, that they "worship the first beast," xiii. 12. But as the author himself elsewhere still describes the first beast simply as "the beast," and as, xix. 20, xx. 10, he places the beast and the false prophet beside each other, it will not be against his sense if we—reserving the exposition of "another beast"—briefly call the first antichristian appearance *the Beast.*

According to xiii. 1, this beast has "seven heads and ten horns, and upon his horns ten crowns, and upon his heads the name of blasphemy;" according to xvii. 3 (comp. xvii. 7), the same is "a scarlet-coloured beast, full of names of blasphemy, having seven heads and ten horns;" but, according to xii. 3, the "great red dragon has seven heads and ten horns, and seven crowns upon his heads." The similarity between the beast and the dragon is remarkable; and the difference urged by Düsterdieck, that the dragon has on his heads seven crowns, while the beast has on his horns ten crowns, is explained very simply on a comparison of xvii. 10—according to which the seven heads of the beast mean seven kings—with xvii. 12, which says that the ten horns are ten kings. Thus there can be no doubt that the beast stands in the closest relation of nature to the dragon, and that the latter is in the eye of the seer the Antigod, and the former the *Antichrist.*

But is it Antichrist in the sense of a single person? John sees the beast rise up out of the sea, xiii. 1, and, according to xiii. 2, he "was like unto a leopard, and his feet were as the feet of a bear, and his mouth as the mouth of a lion." In this description he undoubtedly had in view Dan. vii. 2–7, and therefore, first, he does not intend us to see in the beast a single person, but an *empire.* When expositors dispute whether the beast is designed to represent the God-opposing world-power in general, that is, in all its successive forms, or a single, and, indeed, the last of these forms, it is most decidedly against the first idea, that according to it the seer must have omitted the fourth beast of Daniel, while he gives us to understand clearly enough by the ten horns of his beast that he intended by it that beast as described in Dan. vii. 7. But it does not by any means exclude the supposition that he saw in the fourth beast of Daniel, and consequently in his own, the climax, or a combination of the earlier three; evidently it is not opposed to this that Daniel says, "and it was diverse from all the beasts that were before it;" and it is not merely more expressive, but is also more in conformity with the manner of the author (and, indeed, it is directly indicated by the seven heads, of which, with Daniel, the three first beasts have each one, while for the fourth there are four), if we suppose that he has conceived the form of the fourth beast of Daniel, which is not definitely given, from the prominent features of the three preceding beasts combined, and has therefore endowed his own with the same, than if we suppose that for his beast he sought animal features only in a general way, and so transferred to it those given by Daniel. Thus he does not intend the ungodly power of the world in general, but one of its various phases, therefore a definite individual empire, the latest and most extreme, reproducing in itself all earlier phases of the world's enmity to God; or, the last and most remarkable of all empires, the climax and complement of all that had existed before it: this is the first meaning of the beast.

We find in chap. xiii. and xvii. an entire series of expressions which are in harmony with the above interpretation; and since that with which Weiss, *bibl. Theol.* p. 604, supports a contrary interpretation is inapplicable, namely, that the appearance of the last Ruler directly introduces the final catastrophe, while there is given to the beast, after the healing of the deadly wound, a respite of three and a half years, we may venture to ask, how could the seer, by the beast which had seven heads and ten horns, which mean seven and ten kings, the beast upon which the woman sat, which represents great Babylon, have intended a single personality? Yet, when it is said that the seven mountains on which the woman sits are seven kings: five are fallen, and one is, and the other is not yet come; and when he comes, he must continue a short space: and the beast that was, and is not, even he is the eighth, and is of the seven, and goeth into perdition, xvii. 10, 11,—the seer has doubtless there understood not an empire, but *a single person*. The exposition which finds everywhere only an empire, fails as much as that which finds everywhere only a single person. Are we then to understand that the seer, by the one name of "the beast," wished in various places to describe two entirely different things? This, at all events, follows when we find these two meanings apportioned to the first and second representations in chap. xiii. and xvii.; but while he, xiii. 3, sees one of the heads "as it were wounded to death," he represents the other beast, xiii. 14, as inducing the inhabitants of the earth to make an image to the first beast,—"which (who) had the wound by a sword, and did live,"—implying that to him the one head of the beast was identical with the beast itself; while the angel, xvii. 8, says: "The beast that thou sawest was, and is not; and shall ascend out of the bottomless pit, and go into perdition;" and the same angel says, xvii. 11, "The beast that was, and is not, even he is the eighth,"—the eighth king is identical with the beast whose seven heads are seven kings. What remains, then, but to say that if individual forms of world-power appear to the seer to culminate and unite in an empire which he calls "the beast," so he sees again the particular stages of the development of this empire, the individual rulers of the same, culminate in one prince, which he also describes as "the beast:" as the leopard, the bear, and the lion are contained in the beast, so are the seven heads of the beast contained in the one head. We may say that, as he sees in an individual king the nature of a definite empire, uniting in itself all earlier empires, personified, so also he sees unfolded in this empire the nature of that individual king: this king is to him the empire in person; this empire is to him the king in the form of a kingdom. It is also evidently much easier in the one place to think of an individual king, and in the other of an empire, and it is therefore ever to be maintained that the seer so thought; the empire of which this is the king, the king whose is the empire. That this interpretation has its analogies in the Apocalypse, for example, in "the word of God and the testimony of Jesus," in the woman of chap. xii., and especially in the double meaning of the three and a half years of Antichrist, can here only be mentioned; it may also be pointed out that it is only by our interpretation that the readings αὐτόν in xiii. 8, and ὅς in xiii. 14, very simply explain themselves. But when Weiss (*bibl. Theol.* p. 604, note) says, that by identifying the head with the beast, in order to represent, as with Daniel, a collective idea, the entire allegory of the seer becomes confused, we may indeed much rather refer to the departures of the seer from the original sense of the Old Testament foundation passages than to the supposed confusion of allegory.

But what empire and what king did John intend by the beast? The reply to the first of these questions, if considered without prejudice, can hardly be doubted; by the beast on which the woman sits, which undeniably means Rome, the seer cannot possibly have understood any other empire than the one of his own times, the *Roman empire.* But in what individual emperor does he see the antichristian nature of this empire so fully manifested that he identifies him with the empire itself? He says, xvii. 9–11, "The seven heads are seven mountains, on which the woman sitteth. And there are seven kings: five are fallen, and one is, and the other is not yet come; and when he cometh, he must continue a short space; and the beast that was, and is not, even he is the eighth, and is of the seven, and goeth into perdition." It is generally acknowledged that by the five kings already fallen we are to understand the Cæsars,—Augustus, Tiberius, Caligula, Claudius, and Nero. By the one who is, some expositors understand Galba; on the contrary, Düsterdieck and Weiss believe him to be Vespasian. But when Düsterdieck says that, according to a later historian, the *rebellio trium principum*—Galba, Otho, and Vitellius—reduced the empire to an *incertum et quasi vagum,* and that Vespasian appears as the sixth head of the beast, because he was the first from the *gens Flavia* to establish again the tottering empire, Volkmar (p. 193) justly asks, in objection, whether, a couple of months before the destruction of Jerusalem, about Easter 70,—where Düsterdieck places the authorship of our book,—Vespasian became the founder of a new imperial family? whether, within half a year from his exaltation, he differed in anything from Galba? And with similar propriety he remarks, that it might have been otherwise if this period had been fixed upon from the second or third century—by Dion Cassius and Suetonius;—one might then have seen in Vespasian the founder of a second dynasty after the

Julian, and regarded the three brief reigns as a sad interregnum, and disowned Galba with the other two. There is still another remark; it is inconceivable that, in case John wrote in the time of Vespasian, he should not once have mentioned the three governments intervening after Nero; the ten horns, xvii. 3, vii. 12, which Düsterdieck refers to here, have, as we shall see, an entirely different sense. Thus the king who "is" is Galba, whose period of government was the present of the seer, and the time in which his book was written. After Galba he expected one whose rule would "continue a short space;" after this the beast that was, and is not, will appear, and will be the eighth, but still from the seven. By the one who is not yet come, and who is to continue a short space, Düsterdieck understands Vespasian's son Titus; by the eighth king, who is of the seven, Domitian, whom John regards not only as the individual personification of the Roman Antichrist, but also as the last possessor of the imperial power. But both these meanings fail with the interpretation of the sixth head; and it is especially against them that the important number seven does not take its due position. This takes place only upon the supposition that in the seven heads, or kings, the antichristian nature of the Roman empire gradually and partially unfolds itself; but after this gradual and partial development has been completed, there appears again one from the seven, and brings the antichristian nature of the Roman imperial power to a complete realization; as it is on one side an individual head of the beast, and on the other the beast itself, so it is on one side the eighth king, and on the other one of the seven. Now, when this eighth, of which it is said "he was, and is not," can be identified neither with that which is nor with that which is not yet come, and thus neither with the sixth nor the seventh, the question arises, which of the five emperors from Augustus to Nero, in the sense of an individual personality, was intended by the seer? According to the testimony of history, as also according to the historical background of our book, the answer must be, *the Emperor Nero*. The words, "of the seven," so strongly urged by Düsterdieck and Weiss, neither in the genealogical nor in the decidedly more important sense of an enigmatical indication, as uniting in himself all the seven, and, at the same time, an individual of the number, lead to Domitian, but in the latter sense compel us to think of Nero. With this result the enigmatical number of xiii. 18 perfectly harmonizes, "Here is wisdom. Let him that hath understanding count the number of the beast: for it is the number of a man; and his number is Six hundred threescore and six." It is not necessary to speak of any other interpretations than those of *Λατεῖνος* and קסר נרון. That, on account of the expression, "the number of a man," the number must intend the name of some particular human person, and therefore that only the latter of the two interpretations is possible, cannot be admitted; according to the analogy of xxi. 17 (comp. Isa. viii. 1), the number of a man signifies that the number expresses the name after the manner of a man, that is, according to the numeral value of the letters current with every man. If the choice is to be between two interpretations, the former is to be preferred, because it is within the language in which the Apocalypse was written, and there is not a word by which we are led to think of a Hebrew name; while from ix. 11, xvi. 6, it is evident that the author wrote for Greek readers. On the other hand, it is not to be denied that the second meaning agrees better with the subject—Antichrist—of which it treats, and the question arises, whether the writer by a numeral enigma intended the solution to be sought outside the Greek language. With our view of the beast, it is really perfectly indifferent which of the two interpretations is preferred. Both of them agree with it, and confirm it. As a pure supposition, however, and one to which I do not attach much importance, I may suggest that both meanings may be correct, and that the seer chose the number 666 because in Greek it represented the name *Λατεῖνος*, and in Hebrew the name קסר נרון, so that by its double meaning it might mean the Roman empire as well as Cæsar Nero.

As, according to the view of the seer, the world-power thus flows in four different forms, which are symbolized by the leopard, the bear, and the lion, and the beast which unites in itself the other three, and has appeared in the Roman empire; so—and this with him is the principal thing—the Roman empire appears again in seven representatives, seven individual emperors, symbolized by the seven heads of the beast, five of which belong to the past, one to the present, one to the future, which in a short time Nero and the antichristian nature of the Roman empire will follow as the eighth, yet one of the seven; and as during his life he had done relatively, so then absolutely he will bring that nature into realization and manifest operation. What are the marks which, for John, *distinguish the empire* in general, and the emperor in particular, as the beast or Antichrist? We should not beforehand expect that in the delineation of the beast that which belongs to the empire and to the emperor would be kept asunder. Further, we may assume that in this delineation what has been and what is still to come will often flow into each other. Finally, it should not pass without notice, that since our author regards the beast as the fulfilment of Daniel's prediction of the fourth beast and the little horn, he has borrowed the colours for his description partly from Dan. vii. Still the historical foundation, or the historical point of connection, for the picture of the beast, can be pointed out with tolerable certainty. The dragon stood on the sand of the sea, and from the sea John saw the beast ascend, xiii. 1; as also with Daniel, the four beasts come up from the sea. We will not lay too great stress upon the circumstance that "the great whore" appears sitting upon "many waters," xvii. 1, and that these many waters are explained to be "peoples, and multitudes, and nations, and tongues." But the relation of the sea to this beast, and that of the earth, xiii. 11, to the other, is remarkable. We do not understand the sea, with Düsterdieck, in its natural sense, nor with Volkmar and others as that which covers the abyss, and is associated with it, nor with some, as the sea "at Cæsarea;" but symbolically: the beast ascends from the sphere of the earthly, in contrast with the heavenly, and, indeed, from the sea as the department of earthly movement and earthly occurrences, in distinction from the earth as the department of earthly being and feeling; in other words, John sees the Roman empire arise out of secular history, the agitation and tumult of the nations, and called into being by that enemy of God and man, the devil. It is a beast (*θηρίον*), not a living creature (*ζῶον*), compounded of leopard, bear, and lion, xiii. 2. As Daniel symbolizes the world-empires by wild beasts, in contrast with the kingdom of God which follows, and which is typified by a form like that of a Son of man, Dan. vii. 13, 14 (comp. also Dan. iv. 28, etc.), in order to present those empires in contrast with the beautiful human, humane, and Godlike character of the kingdom of God, as animal, bestial, and brutish, and especially the features of rude force, cruelty, and terror; so there appeared to him all these individual features united into one frightful whole in the Roman empire.—The beast had on his heads the name of blasphemy, xiii. 1; as also, according to xvii. 3, being full of the names of blasphemy. Without doubt, the writer had in his eye the titles by which the Roman emperor appropriated to himself, and permitted to be appropriated to him, divine honours, as Augustus, Divus. Caligula, at least, allowed himself to be saluted Jupiter Latiaris (comp. Krenkel, p. 76).—The dragon gave to the beast "his power, and his seat, and great authority," xiii. 2. As called into being by the ruler of the ungodly world and its history, from the ungodly course of humanity, the Roman power appears to him as the earthly representation or self-assertion, the personal medium or alter-ego of Satan; and his instrumentalities correspond to his origin and significance: power; influence and importance: throne; his all-subduing, irresistible works; and authority, "All the world wondered after the beast. And they worshipped the dragon which gave power unto the beast: and they worshipped the beast, saying, Who is like unto the beast? who is able to make war with him?" xiii. 3, 4. The seer observes what an imposing, overpowering, transporting impression the Roman empire exercises upon men; how the world is astonished at it; that it is amazed by its greatness, power, and glory, and does homage to it; how the world worships the dragon, because he has given power to the beast,—that is, not consciously worshipping the devil, but perceiving, in imperial power and in its individual possessors, supposed manifestations of the divine, it really gives divine honours to the devil; he notices how, in striking contrast to Ex. xv. 11, the world says, "Who is like unto the beast? who is able to make war with him?" xiii. 4, "in blasphemous parody of the praise with which the Old Testament church celebrates the unparalleled glory of the living God" (Düsterdieck), the Roman power is deified as unequalled.—There was given unto the beast "a mouth speaking great things, and blasphemies: and he opened his mouth against God, to blaspheme His name, and His tabernacle, and them that dwell in heaven," xiii. 6 (comp. Dan. vii. 8, xi. 20, 25, 36; Ps. xii. 4). Whether John had any individual thing in his mind, and what it was, cannot be easily made out; probably he perceived, especially in the presumptuous style of the imperial decrees, and generally "in all the language with which Roman arrogance ascribed to itself, not only unlimited authority over the world, but also expressly celebrated with divine predicates and divine honours, the city, the empire, and the emperor" (Düsterdieck), the beginning of the fulfilment of Daniel's prediction of the presumptuous language of the little horn, and, in anticipation, comprehensively ascribed to the beast blasphemies against all holy things, as he really expected them from the personal Antichrist.—"It was given unto him to make war with the saints, and to overcome them," xiii. 7; and, according to xi. 7, "the beast that ascendeth out of the bottomless pit shall make war against them, and shall overcome them, and kill them;" and in xvii. 3 we are told that the beast is "scarlet-coloured" (comp. the red dragon). There doubtless hovered before the mind of the seer in this opposition to and slaughter of the saints, first, the persecution of the Christians by Nero; but, according to his views of the Jews, the Jewish war may be also included in this feature. What the Roman empire had already done in the bloody persecution of the true servants of God—scarlet indicates at the same time both the Roman imperial colour and blood—will reach its climax in the rage of the personal Antichrist; for in this we have mainly to think of the beast ascending out of the bottomless pit, which will neither fear nor spare even the two witnesses—those men of God—Moses and Elias.—"And power was given him over all kindreds, and tongues, and nations. And all that dwell upon the earth shall worship him, whose names are not written in the book of life of the Lamb slain from the foundation of the world," xiii. 8. "They that dwell on the earth shall wonder, whose names were not written in the book of life from the foundation of the world, when they behold the beast that was, and is not, and yet is," xvii. 8. That which the seer has already said, xiii. 2 and 4, of the power and worship of the beast, he sees in the future, and, indeed, as xvii. 8 shows, where he has again chiefly in view the personal Antichrist, through his appearance developed to the uttermost; the already huge power of the Roman empire extended over the known world, and the widely-spread apotheosis of the imperial power become universal, with the exception of the few elect.

By what *signs* has the seer recognised among the various Roman emperors *Nero* in particular as the individual personification of the antichristian power? It is to be doubted whether, by the "beast," he desired to point to his bestiality and brutality,—to the inhumanity which he showed to his mother, and wife, and tutor. But he certainly intended by it to brand the detestable persecutor of the Christians; and this emblem of Rome appears to have been in his thoughts in connection with their persecution (comp. xvii. 16). But just as certainly did the Nero legend, originating soon after his death, and widely spread and firmly believed in Asia Minor, contribute very essentially in two respects to present Nero to John as Antichrist. Düsterdieck justly objects to the assumption of those expositors, according to whom either the seer simply appropriated the contents of the legend, or that it must have originally had the apocalyptic form. The original form was, in fact, not that Nero ascended from the bottomless pit, xi. 7, xvii. 8, but that he would reappear after a temporary concealment among the Parthians. But he should not therefore have called in question the undeniable connection of the apocalyptic statement concerning the beast with the original Nero legend, but should only have demanded the acknowledgment that the seer may have suitably modified the popular expectation respecting Nero, noticed and accepted by him. The ten horns of the beast, xiii. 1, xvii. 3–7, are interpreted by the angel in xvii. 12–14: "The ten horns which thou sawest are ten kings, which have received no kingdom as yet; but receive power as kings one hour with the beast. These have one mind, and shall give their power and strength unto the beast. These shall make war with the Lamb." Düsterdieck's exposition, according to which, in the remaining places, the ten horns are the ten rulers from Augustus to Titus, including Galba, Otho, and Vitellius, and that, on the contrary, xvii. 12–14 signifies ten future kings (comp. Dan. vii. 24), needs no refutation. We are decidedly forbidden to find, like many advocates of the Nero legend, the interpretation in his Parthian allies, by the consideration that the ten kings are symbolized by ten horns of the beast, and also by the statement that they have yet received no kingly authority, but are to receive it with the beast for one hour. It must be evident to every unprejudiced reader that the ten kings signify Roman provincial prefects, *proconsuls, præsides, rectores provinciarum.* The seer reckons, in a general way, ten great provinces in the Roman empire; he had known it after Nero's death, and had seen how the prefects, through their armies, received power as kings for one hour; and the representation is, that when Nero ascends from the abyss, the provincial prefects generally will rise against the seventh and last emperor, and unanimously attach themselves to Nero, and, as his allies and helpers, march as well against Rome as against Christ. When, by a candid exposition, the Parthian allies of Nero, xvii. 12–14, have disappeared, where is there in this book an indication that he sojourned among them, and would return? Certainly John knew of the Parthian allies of the beast, xvi. 12–16; but they come not with the emperor, until then hidden among them, but at his call and for his help. Our author has expressed himself in harmony with the popular faith.—Nero received, indeed, a deadly wound, but was healed; was not dead, but lived, and in due time would come again. But in the eye of the seer Nero lived, if we may call that a life, in the abyss; he went alive down to hell, and from hell would one day return. Thus modified, the Nero legend, in a double respect, helped to stamp him in the estimation of John as Antichrist. Once, and it is not commonly noticed, in this relation Nero forms such an accurate personal representation of the Roman empire, that the seer can in the one almost completely describe the other. When he received a deadly wound, and the same was healed, xiii. 3, did not the Roman empire, in his fall and the cessation of the Julian dynasty, receive a deadly wound also, and did not John expect it would be healed again, xiii. 12 and 14? When he says of Nero that he was, and is not, and shall reappear, xvii. 8–11, is it not true of the Roman empire, which, at the time he wrote, to a certain extent was not? Still, in the esteem of our author, the contrast or *counterpart* which, in his conception of the popular belief, Nero presented to Christ, was much more important than the parallel with the empire. We may notice that Christ "was slain," v. 9, and as the Lamb slain, stands before the throne of God, v. 6; that of the seven heads of the beast, one was "wounded to death," xiii. 3; that the beast had a "wound by a sword," xiii. 14, "a deadly wound," xiii. 3. Christ was "dead, and is alive again," ii. 8 (comp. i. 17, 18); the deadly wound of the beast was healed, xiii. 3–12; it "had the wound by a sword, and did live," xiii. 14. Christ comes from the throne of God, to which He is caught away, xii. 5, upon which He sits, iii. 21. He will come "with clouds, and every eye shall see Him, and they also which pierced Him; and all kindreds of the earth shall wail because of Him," i. 7. The beast will ascend "out of the bottomless pit," xi. 7, xvii. 8, and "they that dwell on the earth shall wonder," xvii. 8 (comp. xiii. 3), and worship the "beast, whose deadly wound was healed," xiii. 12. The antithesis reaches still further, even to the reign of the beast and to the reign of Christ during the thousand years, and closes with a contrast between the casting of the beast into a lake of fire, and the enthronement of the Lamb in the New Jerusalem. On the whole, we may venture to say that the striking contrast between Christ and Nero, as the Nero legend brought it near to the writer, and as in his apprehension of the same it must have forced itself upon him, where not the actually deciding cause, is still one of the chief grounds why Nero was to him the personal Antichrist. As Christ, according to his representation, has already appeared on earth in Jesus, but only in His future coming will appear in His entire significance as the Messiah-Logos; so also the personal Antichrist has appeared in the historical Nero, but will only reach his full manifestation in the Nero ascending from the abyss.

(*b.*) *The False Prophet.*

The second antichristian power, "another beast," as he is called, in distinction from the first beast, xiii. 11, 12, the seer himself explains as the *false prophet*, xvi. 13, xix. 20, xx. 10. The question can only be, whether he understood thereby all false prophecy, or an individual false prophetic personality, or, as under the first beast, both in one. Volkmar, by an "impartial" exposition, has found out that, on account of Rom. xiii. 1–7, the seer regards the Apostle Paul as the other beast. But we reject this "historico-critical" interpretation, not less than Krenkel's interpretation of Josephus, for it is difficult to discover a single feature in the description of the false prophet which points to an individual personality; on the other hand, all is explained on the supposition of false prophecy. But where are we to look for it? The assertion, for example, in Bunsen's *Bibelwerk* (comp. Schenkel's *Bibellexikon*), that, "besides the heathen secular power, the Christian church had another enemy, namely obdurate Judaism, which now with its false Messiahs and false prophets (comp. Matt. xxiv. 5, 24) disturbed the world, seduced many believers, and falsified the genuine Messianic hope: as far as these false prophets prepared an alliance with the Parthians, whence the seer expected Nero, he represents this second beast as a satellite of the first," may appeal with some plausibility to 2 Thess. ii., and especially to ver. 9, etc.; but, notwithstanding, it needs no refutation, for most of the characteristics of the other beast are totally incompatible with Jewish false prophecy. But we preserve an harmonious whole as soon as we acknowledge that, besides the beast, he represents the false prophet as a world-power hostile to God, as God-opposing wisdom and mental power (Lechler, p. 201); that in distinction from Antichrist, in which "heathenism is embodied more as the external force which at the same time opposes Christianity and deifies itself, there is rather represented in the false prophet the fraudulent means which it adopts in order to establish itself as the religion of the world," Köstlin, p. 496; that John by the false prophet had in view "that form of Roman heathen prophecy which was marked as much by magic as by divination, and in this peculiarity, with all its augurs, interpretations of omens, and the like, was a powerful support to the Roman empire" (Düsterdieck); or, as I would rather say, that the seer by the other beast, or the false prophet, intended heathen witchcraft and soothsaying, the heathen religion as divination and magic (comp. "die Astrologen, und Mathematiker, die Chaldäer," Krenkel, p. 80), according to its demoniacal origin and background, its demoniacal arts, and its demoniacal influence upon the mind. By the similarity of the name (comp. ii. 20), as well as by the analogy between the ethnistic error of the Apocalypse and the libertine error, referred to "the last time," of the Epistle of Jude and the second Epistle of Peter (comp. also 1 Tim.), it is certainly not a wide step to say, with Weiss, *bibl. Theol.* p. 604, though in the circle of vision in which the prophet principally moved, false prophecy was above all active in heathen soil, the appearances of a Satanic false prophecy within Christendom could still not be thought to be excluded as far as it tempted believers to heathen immorality, and thereby also led them to allegiance to the empire. We have, however, already remarked in the section on the churches, when considering doctrinal error, that there is not to be discovered the slightest evidence that our author really combined false prophecy in the churches and false prophecy in the world, and we therefore adhere to the interpretation which refers it to heathen religion as magic and divination.

We shall find this view confirmed if we take a closer survey of the *characteristics* of false prophecy. The writer sees "another beast coming up out of the earth," xiii. 11. The heathen religion, or heathenism, is homogeneous and similar in nature with the heathen State or the God-opposing secular power, namely, sub-human, inhuman, and bestial. This other beast came up "out of the earth," not, as Düsterdieck says, because it will operate upon the whole earth and its inhabitants (comp. ver. 12), nor, as Ewald thinks, because there were in Asia Minor so many delusions; but as a parallel to the ascent of the first beast out of the sea. Earth and sea are commonly the antithesis of heaven, of the ideal world (comp. xii. 12); the sea means the ungodly and God-opposing world on the side of movement and development, the history of the world in an evil sense; inasmuch as it is in this that the world-power originates, the earth signifies the same ungodly world on the side of being, consciousness, the spirit of the world in an evil sense (comp. Jas. iii. 15), and therefore heathenism, or the heathen religion, ascends out of it.—The other beast "had two horns like a lamb, and he spake as a dragon," xiii. 11. We are reminded here of the seven horns of the Lamb, v. 6, and also of the dragon "which deceiveth the whole world," xii. 9. But the seer does not refer here either to the lamb or to the dragon; his design is rather, by the other beast having two horns like a lamb, to express harmlessness only in appearance (comp. Matt. vii. 15), and by its speaking like a dragon,—dragon is often synonymous with serpent,—cunning, deceptive power (comp. ver. 14); in a word, in distinction from the mere material violent procedure of the secular power, he characterizes it as more intellectual, and operating with intellectual instrumentalities, but not therefore as a less diabolical power.—The other beast "exerciseth," that is, brings into activity and full operation, all the power of the first beast before him, and causeth, that is, induceth, "the earth and them which dwell therein to worship the first beast, whose deadly wound was healed," xiii. 12 (comp. xiii. 5). Thus the great power which the seer has repeatedly ascribed to the first beast, xiii. 2, 4, 7, is used by the Roman empire only because through its material resources it has religion with its spiritual forces in its service, or "before" it, as a willing helper. The idolatrous homage by which the empire was consecrated and strengthened, it owed to the demoniacal influence of its religion upon the mind. The other beast "doeth great wonders, so that he maketh fire come down from heaven on the earth in the sight of men," xiii. 13. According to xvi. 14, there are "the spirits of devils," who work miracles; our author gives credit to the demon-cultus, the demoniacal witchcraft, for accomplishing these signs (comp. Matt. xxiv. 24), and in its approaching climax of development it will work wonders which will compare in appearance with the greatest miracles of the true prophets, for example, with those of an Elias (comp. 1 Kings xviii. 38; 2 Kings i. 10, 12; Rev. xi. 5). The other beast "deceiveth them that dwell on the earth by means of those miracles which he had power to do in the sight of the beast, saying to them that dwell on the earth, that they should make an image to the beast, which had the wound by a sword, and did live," xiii. 14 (comp. Dan. iii.). If, now, the heathen religion, with its demoniacal power, had already deluded the world, much more will it be so in the expected completion of that power; and as already it consecrated images to the Cæsars for divine homage, as to gods,—it is natural here to think of Caligula, who desired to place his image in the temple, and who coveted divine honours (comp. Hausrath, p. 224),—so with the appearance of the personal Antichrist, it will fully bring the world to set him up as God, and to render him divine honours. —The other beast "had power to give life unto the image of the beast, that the image of the beast should both speak, and cause that as many as would not worship the image of the beast should be killed," xiii. 15. The seer knew, and did not doubt what was said among the heathen about speaking images; and he expected, therefore, that heathen sorcery would succeed in giving life, the spirit of life (comp. xi. 11), to the image of the beast, so that it would speak, and thus be fully manifested to the world in its usurped divinity. And, indeed, in his time it had already happened that Christians were put to death because they refused to pay divine honours to the image of the emperor; so naturally would it be in the future, as John foresaw, that refusal to worship the speaking image, as in the case of Nebuchadnezzar, Dan. iii. 6, would end in death.—And the other beast "causeth all, both small and great, rich and poor, free and bond, to receive a mark in their right hand, or in their foreheads: and that no man might buy or sell save he that had the mark, or the name of the beast, or the number of his name," xiii. 16, 17. The Christians were already variously and seriously hindered in business, because in the Roman empire the heathen religion penetrated and governed all civil relations, indeed in this respect they were under a ban; there needed only one short step more, and as slaves bore the name of their master, priests the name of their god, engraven upon their skin to show to whom they belonged,—the seer combines the two, and in striking contrast with Ex. xiii. 9, 16, Deut. vi. 8, where the precept is given to bind the word of the Lord upon the hand, and to have it between the eyes,—the worshippers of the beast, led by false prophets and religious fanaticism, would willingly place the name or the number of the name of the beast, as a sign that they belonged to him, upon their right hands, or upon their foreheads, or in the most conspicuous places; and those who would not consent to this, Christians included, would be able neither to buy nor sell, they would be shut out from intercourse, banned, marked and robbed of the vital air in civil and social life.

In the consideration of the first beast, we have found how important for this representation of the seer was the remarkable contrast, according to his view of the Nero legend, between Christ and Nero; and at the close of our exposition of the other beast, the question arises, to what, in the view of the seer, did it stand opposed? With this inquiry may be connected another, namely, why in our book is the term Antichrist never used? and to both we reply, that the Roman empire was not to the seer, either generally or in its individual personification, the perfectly exact counterpart of Christ, or the complete Antichrist. In his esteem it lacked too much one chief feature, the religious; he had found this in the heathen religion of the State and of the people, with its witchcraft and superstition; but only the empire in union with the heathen religion was to him the complete Antichrist, the full antithesis to Christ, the first-born from the dead, and Lord of lords, to Christ the faithful witness of God. But the absence of the name Antichrist may also be explained from the peculiarity of the apocalyptic language, and we may refer the false prophet to a concrete antithesis indicated by the name itself, even true prophecy. We have seen, indeed, how Old and New Testament prophecy are one, also how the activity of the Spirit coincides almost entirely with prophecy. It may therefore best express the sense of our author, if we say that the false prophet is the exact opposite of the true prophecy of the Old and New Testament, and as the first beast is Antichrist, so the second beast is

Antispirit. It agrees with this, that in the entire description of the false prophet there is nothing that can relate to Christ, but in more than one feature the antithesis is to the work of the witnesses of Jesus, especially of the two witnesses in the eleventh chapter. It also appears to me, considering the inclination of the seer to contrasts, significant—and Ewald also has called attention to this—that, according to the conception of the false prophet as Antispirit, there appears in xvi. 13 an informal trinity, the dragon, the beast, and the false prophet, in contrast with the divine Trinity of i. 4–6.

(*c.*) *Babylon.*

John saw a woman sitting upon the first beast, xvii. 3; "and upon her forehead was a name written, Mystery, Babylon the Great," xvii. 5. "The seven heads are seven mountains, on which the woman sitteth," xvii. 9. The woman "is that great city which reigneth over the kings of the earth," xvii. 18. There can be no doubt that by the woman John meant Rome, for among the Jews it was frequently designated by the term Babylon (comp. Hengstenberg, *ut ante,* II. p. 142). Thus, according to the views of the seer, it holds a similar position in the history of the New Covenant to that which Babylon held in the history of the Old; or, in other words, that which Babylon signified in its time, was fully realized in Rome.

But in what does the *Babylonian signification of Rome* consist? The great whore sits upon many waters, xvii. 1 (comp. Jer. li. 13; Nah. ii. 9); and the many waters where she sits are "peoples, and multitudes, and nations, and tongues," xvii. 15. The woman sits on "a scarlet-coloured beast, full of names of blasphemy, having seven heads and ten horns," xvii. 3. "The woman is that great city which reigneth over the kings of the earth," xvii. 18. Rome is the capital city, the seat and centre, the metropolis of the Roman empire. "I will show unto thee," said the angel, "the judgment of the great whore," xvii. 1. On her forehead was written, "Mystery, Babylon the Great," xvii. 5 (comp. great Babylon, xiv. 8, xvi. 19, xvii. 5, xviii. 2; the great city, xviii. 10, xvi. 18; and the great city Babylon, xviii. 21; the mighty city, xviii. 10). Rome is a giant city.—"The woman was arrayed in purple and scarlet-colour,"—the former referring, probably, to ruling power, and the latter to the shedding of blood,—"and decked with gold, and precious stones, and pearls," xvii. 4 (comp. xviii. 3, vii. 11–19). Rome is the imperial city, the city of wealth, and pomp, and luxury.—The woman had "a golden cup in her hand full of the abominations and filthiness of her fornication, and upon her forehead was a name written, Mystery, Babylon the Great, the mother of harlots and abominations of the earth," xvii. 4, 5. The angel said to the seer, "I will show unto thee the judgment of the great whore that sitteth upon many waters; with whom the kings of the earth have committed fornication, and the inhabitants of the earth have been made drunk with the wine of her fornication," xvii. 1, 2. Already the angel has said, "Babylon is fallen, is fallen, that great city (comp. Isa. xxi. 9; Jer. l. 2, li. 8), because she made all nations (Gentiles) drink of the wine of the wrath of her fornication," xiv. 8 (comp. xviii. 3, 9, 23, xix. 2). "Mystery," as the position of the word and the sixth and seventh verses show, does not mean that "Babylon the Great," etc., is a mysterious name, but it is itself a part of the name, and rests on the fact, inexplicable to the common consciousness, that Rome, notwithstanding its terrible guilt, stood there continuously so great and glorious. The fornication cannot mean the idolatry practised with Babylon, nor the worship of the secular power, but idolatry or heathen lawlessness generally, with its impurities and abominations (comp. Lev. xviii. 27; Jer. li. 7; Ezek. xvi. 22), to which, indeed, the worship of the beast belonged as a principal feature. It is said, however, "Come out of her, my people, that ye be not partakers of her sins, and that ye receive not of her plagues (comp. Jer. li. 6, 9, 45): for her sins have reached unto heaven, and God hath remembered her iniquities," xviii. 4, 5. Rome appears to our author as the great whore, because it influences the rest of the world, and is at the same time the nourishing medium and starting-point of the Roman state religion, of the heathen spirit; as the mother of harlots, and the other cities as her daughters (comp. Ps. xlviii. 12), because they and the provinces have received and accepted from her the evil disposition; the kings of the earth have committed fornication, and lived wantonly with the woman; she has made all nations drunk with the wine of her fornication (comp. Jer. xxv. 15; Isa. li. 17, 21, 22; Nah. iii. 4; Isa. xxiii. 15, 17); that is, princes and nations are subject to the bewitching influence of Rome, and have surrendered themselves to her abominations. The writer also "saw the woman drunken with the blood of the saints, and with the blood of the martyrs of Jesus," xvii. 6 (comp. xviii. 20, 24, xix. 2, xviii. 6). The persecution of the Christians in Rome by Nero stands before the eye of the seer; but Rome is (comp. xviii. 24) chiefly the central point and head-quarters of unjust persecution and bloodshed, and so may and will be charged to her all the righteous blood shed on the earth (comp. Matt. xxiii. 35; Jer. li. 49).

In the two beasts we have found counterparts of Christ and the Spirit; to what does Babylon stand in contrast? The woman, the whore, is plainly in opposition to the woman in the twelfth chapter, and the Bride of the Lamb in xix. 7, xxi. 2, 9; Babylon the great city, to the beloved city, xx. 9—the holy city, the New Jerusalem, xxi. 2–10; the lot of the woman, xvii. 6, to that of the Bride, xix. 7, xxi. 1. It is significant that Jerusalem is described as the holy city, xi. 2, trodden under foot of the Gentiles; but in xi. 8, as the great city, where our Lord was crucified. Rome, in the view of the seer, is the antithesis of the *holy city, and of the church of the saints; it is to him the place and church of Antichrist.*

2. The Seals, the Trumpets, and the Vials.

For doctrines of less importance, the three series of visions, according to their extent, take an exceedingly significant place in the representations of our book. The first of these, the seal visions, introduced in the fifth chapter, are contained in vi. and viii. 1; the second, the trumpet visions, introduced in viii. 2–6, are contained in viii. 7–13, ix. 1–19, xi. 15–19; the third, the vial visions, introduced in xv. and xvi. 1, are contained in xvi. 2–21.

Let us first, in a few words, and as far as our purpose requires, establish the *sense of the individual visions.* The vision which goes forth from the book of fate, after the opening of the first *seal,* vi. 1, 2, namely, that of the rider upon a white horse, is very variously interpreted (comp. Düsterdieck, p. 250). Many expositors consider the rider to be identical with him who is described in xix. 11, and refer the vision to Christ, and regard it as representing His triumphant progress, beginning with the feast of Pentecost, at the commencement of the Christian church, fulfilling itself in a time of triumph and joy, interrupted at the end of thirty years by the storm of war. I do not understand, however, how, from the circumstance that some of the characteristics both here and there are not of equal but only of similar import, there can be inferred the identity of the two riders; for a certain similarity between Christ going forth to a victorious conflict with His enemies, and a triumphant king or general going out to conquest, leads as little to the identity of the two as the description of the angel in x. 1–3, on account of its similarity to i. 15, 16, iv. 3, leads to an identity between the angel and Christ or God. It is inconceivable how the seer could have represented the Lamb as opening the first seal, and then going forth from it in the form of a rider. When expositors adduce in favour of identification, that since the appearance of Christ Himself opens every vision which proceeds from the unsealed book, it is evident that He guides and controls the course and aim of all events portrayed in subsequent visions, this is a representation of which the seer nowhere gives the slightest trace. Ewald, *ut ante*, p. 174, very properly points to the bow as an emblem of wild war unsuitable to Christ, and also to the fact that the first rider is not wholly unlike the following one. Finally, from the apocalyptic standpoint, the beginning of Christianity was not altogether a period of triumph. I, therefore, do not regard the rider on the white horse as an antithesis to the rider of xix. 11–16, but as a personification of war on the side of victory, with which, as Düsterdieck, *ut ante*, p. 254, acknowledges, it agrees that the third and following verses represent the other side and its consequences. The rider on the red horse, vi. 3, 4, is undeniably, and to some extent, an acknowledged personification of war on the side of bloodshed. The rider on the black horse, vi. 5, 6, indicates both figuratively and literally a partial dearth. The rider on the pale horse, vi. 7, 8 (comp. Ezek. xiv. 21; Jer. xxi. 7, xiv. 12), represents a somewhat devastating pestilence and great mortality. The ground-thought of the four riders appears to be a combination of Zech. i. 7, 8 with vi. 1, 8. The vision after the opening of the fifth seal, vi. 9–11, brings martyrs, who pray to be avenged. After the opening of the sixth seal, John sees a great earthquake, which announces the immediate coming of the final judgments of God (comp. Isa. xiii. 13, l. 3, xxxiv. 4, ii. 10–22, lxiii. 4; Hos. x. 8; Joel iii. 4, i. 15, ii. 2; Nah. i. 6; Mal. iii. 2; also Isa. xiii. 10; Nah. iii. 12; Amos vii. 9). In these six visions we have just the same phenomena presented as in Matt. xxiv. 6–9 (comp. Luke xviii. 1–8) are predicted as the beginning of woe.—The silence in heaven after the opening of the seventh seal, viii. 1, has evidently no independent meaning, but is rather an artistic device, and should represent the anxious or intense expectation of the inhabitants of heaven, who not only, after the exhaustion of the sixth seal, look to the last decisive catastrophe, but from the appearance of the seven angels, to whom were given seven trumpets, conclude that it is near (Düsterdieck, *ut ante*, p. 299). From the seventh seal there proceeds not merely a single vision, but a whole series of visions, which, like the representation of the last day, as the great jubilee, the divine day of the general recompense and restoration of the just (comp. Isa. lxi. 2), as well as on the ground of Ex. xix. 13–16, Isa. xxvii. 13 (comp. Zech. ix. 14; Josh. vi. 3–16; 1 Thess. iv. 16, 17; 1 Cor. xv. 52), associates itself with the *blast of trumpets*. The first four trumpets bring plagues, which affect the whole sphere of the visible world, earth and sea and inland waters, stars and day and night. Substantially, the Egyptian plagues furnish the images for the first five. That which appears after the sounding of the first trumpet, hail and fire mingled with blood, and destructive effects on the land and its inhabitants, viii. 7, reminds us to some extent of the plague described in Ex. ix. 22–25 and vii. 19, 21 (comp. Joel iii. 3). The sounding of the second trumpet is followed by a sign which borrows its image from a volcanic mountain, and produces destructive effects upon the sea and its inhabitants, viii. 8, 9. The third trumpet brings the poisoning of a third part of the rivers and fountains of waters, and thereby the death of many, viii. 10, 11 (comp. Ex. vii. 21–24). The fourth trumpet brings harm to the sun, the moon, and the stars, of which a third part is darkened, and a third part of the light of day and night is withdrawn, viii. 12 (comp. Ex. x. 21–23; Joel iii. 4; Amos viii. 9). These four plagues remind us of Matt. xxiv. 29. That only a third part of each sphere of creation is affected by them, shows that their purpose was only preliminary. As connected with each other, and forming a whole, like the four riders of the seal visions, the plagues of the four first trumpets show that the three following plagues, as three woes, are separated from them. The fifth trumpet brings the first woe, namely, the infernal locusts, as a plague upon the men who had not been sealed, ix. 1–12; and the recollection of the Egyptian and later plagues of locusts, Ex. x. 4–6, Joel i. and ii. (comp. Deut. viii. 15; Ezek. ii. 6, 7; Jer. viii. 3; Job xxxix. 20, 25), all the more causes the plague here described to appear in its supernatural terror. The sixth trumpet brings the second woe, wonderful horsemen, who kill the third part of men, ix. 13–21, and whose description points unequivocally to the Parthians. On the sounding of the seventh trumpet, there arises a song of praise in heaven, which celebrates the end as having already come; the temple of God in heaven is opened, and the ark of the covenant is seen, and there are signs of the judgment of God, which brings the final consummation, xi. 15–19. This symbolic representation is related to the proper contents of the seven trumpets, precisely as the half-hour's silence is to the contents of the seven seal visions; and it is expressly said, x. 7, that "in the days of the voice of the seventh angel, when he shall begin to sound, the mystery of God should be finished." As the seventh seal divides into the seven trumpets, so again the seventh trumpet vision unfolds itself in the seven *vials of wrath.* After the pouring out of the first vial, there fell a noisome and grievous sore upon the worshippers of the beast, xvi. 2 (comp. Ex. ix. 10, 11; Deut. xxviii. 27, 35). The second vial changes the sea into blood, and all the creatures in it die, xvi. 3; this plague is evidently an intensification of that which followed the sounding of the second trumpet, viii. 8. The third vial changes the waters of the continent into blood, xvi. 4–7, and is an intensification of viii. 10, 11. The fourth vial is poured upon the sun, and men are scorched with fire and great heat, xvi. 8, 9, and there is an evident reference to viii. 12. The fifth vial is poured upon the seat of the beast, and his kingdom is filled with darkness, xvi. 10, 11; it is similar to Ex. x. 21, 22 (comp. Isa. xix. 11), and forms a parallel to an earlier stage, viii. 13, 14. The sixth is shed upon the Euphrates, and its waters are dried up, and the way of the kings of the East is prepared, xvi. 12–16. The seventh angel pours his vial into the air, and brings thunder and lightnings of unparalleled severity, as well as other signs of the approach of divine judgments, xvi. 17–21 (comp. Zech.

xiv. 4; Josh. x. 11; Isa. xxviii. 2–17, xxx. 30, xxxii. 19); the manifestations after the sounding of the seventh trumpet are an enhancement, concretization, and progress to the last preliminary judgment on Babylon. But the peculiar contents of the seventh vial consist in this as little as the appearances after the sounding of the trumpet were its peculiar contents; still it is said, "It is done!" xvi. 17 (comp. xxi. 6): "Babylon came in remembrance before God, to give unto her the cup of the wine of the fierceness of His wrath," xvi. 19. Still the seventh vial vision represents only symbolically what is given in the immediate sequel, mainly in the actual fall of Babylon. Thus we may say that all which follows until the advent is the contents of the seventh wrath vial; the seven wrath vials are again the contents of the seventh trumpet, and the seven trumpets are the contents of the seventh seal. Therefore the book sealed with seven seals, which God held in His right hand, and which the Lamb took and opened, v. 1, 7, vi. 1, etc., contains seal, trumpet, and vial visions, or the whole preliminary judgments of God upon the world.

The question arises, what is the *general meaning* of these visions? The subjects as well as the "wrath," for example, xv. 1, xvi. 1, the "judgments," xv. 4, and the righteous judgments, xvi. 5, leave no doubt concerning their character as the avenging judgments of God. On the other hand, it follows from the words of the victors, xv. 3, 4, as well as from the repeated remark, that notwithstanding the plagues, men did not repent, but blasphemed God, ix. 19–21, xvi. 9, 11, 21, that these plagues designed the conversion of the world. It is therefore as great an error to describe the contents of the entire visions as punitive or portentous, as it is to describe the contents of the seal and trumpet visions as more distant and nearer portents; and, on the other hand, the contents of the vial visions as pure penalty. Rather the whole, the seal, trumpet, and vial visions, as vi. 17 especially shows, do contain the avenging judgments of God, but only in the sense of warning, threatening, and alarming portents, preliminaries, and preparations for the great day of the divine wrath, designed for the deliverance of the world from destruction, through which men might have repented, but by which they were hardened (comp. iii. 10). Only on this supposition can the interpretation of the avenging justice of God be applied both to the cry of the martyrs to be avenged, vi. 9–11, and to the drying up of the Euphrates, xvi. 12–14, 16.

For when God allows outrage upon His saints to go unpunished, it is a sure sign that His last judgment is approaching, and so far it is an avenging judgment. The persecution of the faithful is also mentioned, Matt. xxiv. 9, along with war, hunger, and pestilence, as a sign of the end, Matt. xxiv. 33. The inner connection is fully shown in 2 Thess. i. 4–10 (comp. also Luke xviii. 1–8; Phil. i. 28). But so also the preparation of the way for the kings of the East, as well as their assembling in Armageddon, is a sure sign and direct approach of the final decision,—in the sense of the author, a divine avenging judgment.

Another question is, whether the seer has given in all the visions only those things which are *yet future*, or partly the so-called *vaticinia post eventum*. The correspondence between the seal visions and Matt. xxiv. is certainly undeniable, and therefore the admission of an outline scheme is not difficult; but if it be once granted that the seer saw Antichrist not only in the future, but also in the past, in the history of the Roman empire, it would be very strange if the plagues, for him corresponding with the past, were not associated with it. The relation of the fifth seal vision to the persecutions under Nero is then very striking. Further, the remaining seal visions may, without any violence, be distributed to the governments of the various Cæsars; and lastly, according to the usual manner of the seer, it must have been to him in the highest degree significant that the succession of emperors offered the filling up of the apocalyptic sign scheme. We, therefore, with many expositors, understand the rider on the white horse to refer to the victories and triumphs of the Augustan, and of the earlier times of Tiberius; the rider on the red horse, to the time when, especially under Caligula, Palestine became the theatre of the devastating Arabian war, and also of bloody party feuds,—the Parthians threatened the borders, and in the chief city of the world peace was disturbed by intrigues (comp. Hausrath, p. 191); the rider on the black horse, to the scarcity under Claudius, as it prevailed in Syria, in Asia, and most terribly in the year 44 throughout the empire (comp. Hausrath, p. 339); the rider on the pale horse, to the mortality, pestilence, and war which followed the famine (comp. Hausrath, p. 342); the fifth seal vision to the strangled martyrs under the fifth Cæsar, Nero, in the year 64; the sixth, to the most recent past, in which, under Galba, by the universal shaking of the Roman world, all were filled with alarm; and, or instead of this, to the earthquake which visited Asia Minor at that time; to the horrible portents which, according to Plin. *Ep.* vi. 16, 20, Tacit. *Hist.* i. 4, terrified the heathen world. And thus have we come to the time which the seer, as a time of pause and breathless expectation, an anxious, sultry season before the coming storm, represents as silence in heaven for half an hour (comp. Hausrath in Schenkel's *Bibellexikon*, I. 156).

But if the trumpet and vial visions belong to the future of the seer, the question arises with regard to them, whether he expected that future to be *exactly in the manner and order in which he painted it*, or whether he poetically represented it in artistic elaboration of a given scheme. As we have hitherto learned to know our author, it must *à priori* be most probable that both possibilities meet in him. We are led to expect this by the seal visions; for, besides the striking coincidence of the same with the signs of the end announced in Matt. xxiv., the grouping in four and in three visions—the number four representing rapid succession and stroke upon stroke, and the number three representing great and decisive occurrences—is not to be mistaken; and yet this coincidence and this grouping is to John quite historical. Similarly must we conceive also of the second and third series of visions. With perfect justice it is pointed out how for the trumpet and the vial visions, first the Egyptian plagues, and then also other earlier events happening, for example, in Joel's time, have furnished the type; how, between the four first trumpets and the four first vials, there exists a parallel, the first plagues falling upon the land, the second upon the sea, the third upon inland waters, and the fourth upon the heavenly bodies; how the trumpet visions correspond to the seal visions in the numbers four and three, but that, on the contrary, with the vial visions, at the quickening of the speed with which the end hastens on, this distinction falls away; how the seal plagues strike only the fourth part of the earth and its inhabitants, the trumpet plagues the third part, the vial plagues all the worshippers of the beast, and the sea and all that dwell therein; how, finally, the first series of plagues concern Christians, Jews, and heathen, the second Jews and heathen, and the third the heathen only. But through it all a real regulator is not excluded; yet neither with the distant, nearer, and almost present signs of the last divine judgment, nor with the exercise of the patience of the saints, has the true purpose of the writer been seen. But it can be recognised with absolute precision by a comparison of the seal and vial visions (comp. especially, xvi. 10, 12 et seq.). The seer has clearly distinguished three periods of Antichrist,—that lying behind him, that in which the personal Antichrist will manifest himself, and the period between, until the end of the then reigning sixth, and under the seventh emperor. But the preludes of the last judgment, taking equal steps with the development of Antichrist, must also graduate themselves into three periods: the past—seal visions; until the appearance of Antichrist—trumpet visions; the time of the personal Antichrist—vial visions. Thus is simply explained the—so far as I am aware, elsewhere unexplained—threefold series of plagues, with their entire design. Discrepancy between believing anticipation and the artistic creation of what is presented in the trumpet and vial visions, cannot be ascribed to the seer.

3. The Angel with the Everlasting Gospel.

It is said: "And I saw another angel fly in the midst of heaven, having the *everlasting gospel* to preach (εὐαγγελίσαι) unto them that dwell on the earth, and to every nation, and kindred, and tongue, and people, saying with a loud voice, Fear God and give glory to Him; for the hour of His judgment is come: and worship Him that made heaven and earth, and the sea, and the fountains of waters," xiv. 6, 7.

In the section on the gospel we have shown in detail that we are to understand by the term nothing but the proclamation already made by the prophets of the Old Testament and the New, of the completion of the kingdom of God; to the former, by His coming in the flesh, which was still future; to the latter, by the historical Christ. When the seer in the spirit sees an angel who has this everlasting gospel to publish to all the inhabitants of the earth, and when he expressly exhorts them to conversion because the judgment of God is near, it is evident that the angel is only an apocalyptic art device, in a similar manner as the archangel Michael, in the twelfth chapter, for the publication of this message of glad tidings is in reality accomplished by the apostles and other preachers. Its meaning fully coincides with the words of Matt. xxiv. 14:

"And this gospel of the kingdom shall be preached in all the world for a witness unto all nations, and then shall the end come." This close harmony, compared with that already seen to exist between the seal visions and Matt. xxiv., and, moreover, the position of the vision in the contents of the Apocalypse, do not permit us to doubt that the seer saw in the publication of Christianity in ever widening circles, together with warning, threatening and alarming plagues, the admonishing, alluring, and friendly signs and preludes of the approaching completion of things, just as already we have felt ourselves compelled to refer the seven lamps, the spirit, with the lightnings, and voices, and thunders, and judgments, iv. 5, to this double side of the preparation for the end.

4. The Saints in the Great Tribulation.

We have recognised as the time of the Apocalypse the period under the sixth head of the beast, or the sixth emperor, xvii. 10, the period of the sixth seal, vi. 12 et seq. The first of the three periods of Antichrist,—namely, until the death of the fifth emperor, under the sixth and seventh, and under the personal Antichrist, as well as of the three periods of preparatory judgments,—the seal, trumpet, and vial visions, belonged to the past, but the other two to the future of the seer. From this it follows that neither the fortunes, nor the task, nor the consolations of Christians would be essentially different in the future from what they had already been. It may therefore be questionable whether, after a section on the saints and their work, and one on the churches, there should follow another on the saints in the great tribulation, and whether it would not have been better to have presented the whole material either there or here. It may seem all the more questionable when the seer, in the seven letters from which we have chiefly drawn the contents of those earlier sections, has occasionally considered the future (comp. iii. 10); while, on the other hand, in the description of Antichrist, xiii. xvii., the past is included. As, however, the chief contents of the letters would be little suited to this place, so a series of statements in the later chapters would in these earlier sections have been omitted. They require special consideration here.

The Christians have thus far been tempted by the devil

through *persecutions* and by *false doctrine;* but these temptations appear to be frightfully intensified in the visions of the two beasts, chap. xiii. Is not the ever-increasing might of the God-opposing empire, xiii. 2, iv. 7; the ever growing power of its enchantment over the mind, xiii. 3, 4; the influence and operation of the heathen spirit by magic and divination, xiii. 12, 13; the direct persecution by imprisonment, oppression, and death, xiii. 7, 10, xv. 17 (comp. vi. 11, xii. 17, xx. 4),—in a word, the tribulation, i. 9, ii. 9, 10, the great tribulation, vii. 14, the most dangerous temptation for Christians? Moreover, our author foresees that all the inhabitants of the earth whose names are not written in the Lamb's book of life will worship the beast, xiii. 8.

Another, and hitherto much-controverted question, is how the seer conceived of the *relation of the plagues to Christians?* Since the sealing, vii. 1–8, follows only the sixth seal vision, Düsterdieck, *ut ante,* p. 274, does not refer it to the six first plagues, but only to the vision which succeeds it; thus he also thinks that, according to the intention of our author, Christians were not exempt from the preliminary judgments already executed. Weiss, *bibl. Theol.* p. 601, who affirms that Christians were not generally affected by the preparatory divine judgments, stands alone in this opinion: the controversy arises first with the sealing described in vii. 1–8. That we are not to understand by the 144,000 Christian Jews, but Christians as the true Jews, has been shown in the section on the churches. Whether, by the image of sealing, we have to think of the ancient custom of bearing sacred signs impressed on the skin, the bearer thereby acknowledging himself to belong to some god or sanctuary (comp. xiii. 16, xiv. 9, 11, xvi. 2, xix. 20, xx. 4; Isa. xliv. 5), or of the custom which placed the name of the master upon the slave, or of the symbolic signature of Ezek. ix. 4–6, Ex. xii. 7–13, or of the confirmation of a document, Esth. viii. 8 (Krenkel, p. 68, finds in the mark on the forehead a scarcely to be mistaken reference to baptism as the substitute for the "seal" of circumcision, Rom. iv. 2), may remain undecided, though I have no doubt that Ezek. ix. 4–6, probably combined with one or the other, is the foundation passage. What we are concerned to know is whether, with many expositors, we are to find the interpretation of the sealing in the thought that the sealed are to be protected from the coming plagues; or, with Düsterdieck, *ut ante,* p. 280, that by the sealing of those who are the servants of God is meant the unchangeable firmness of their election (comp. Matt. xxiv. 22–24), which was not to be disturbed by the "temptation" (comp. iii. 10) of the last great "tribulation" (comp. vii. 14). In support of his view, Düsterdieck says that it would be contrary to New Testament eschatology (comp. Matt. xxiv. 20–22) if the sealing in the Apocalypse was designed to shelter the sealed from the approaching visitation, so that they should not be smitten like unbelievers, and that it would come especially into conflict with the predictions of the Apocalypse, which could only admonish to patient endurance to the end, and encourage to conflict and victory in every temptation and trial (comp. chap. ii. and iii.), on the assumption (comp. vii. 14) that the servants of God would not be exempt from any of the sufferings which would come upon the world. But since God, Matt. xxiv. 22–24, in the impending tribulation, exercises a sparing regard for the elect, the parallel is rather against Düsterdieck's view. The admonitions and encouragements of our book have a good sense, even if the tribulations of Christians proceed only from Antichrist. Also, according to the analogy of ii. 10 (comp. i. 9), we interpret correctly the "tribulation," vii. 14, as temptation by persecutions; and when the Lord says to the church in Philadelphia, "I will also keep thee from the hour of temptation, which shall come upon all the world, to try them that dwell upon the earth," iii. 10, it surely speaks of the preservation of the Christians from the plagues; that the locusts hurt only the men who have not the seal of God on their foreheads, ix. 4, is seen, by a comparison of xvi. 2 and 10, to be less favourable to Düsterdieck's view, in that the sealed servants of God cannot be touched by a plague coming from the bottomless pit, than the circumstance that they are entirely safe from the trumpet and vial plagues. Moreover, it would be very surprising if the seer had made use of the Egyptian plagues without reference to the protection of Israel. The place in Ezekiel also allows us to expect protection; and it is unmistakeable how, agreeably with the assumption of protection, the plagues from this time intensify themselves. I therefore decide against Düsterdieck, and understand the sealing as a symbol of divine assurance that His servants should not be smitten by the greater plagues which were yet to come.

How does the *task* of the Christian present itself in relation to the second and third phase of Antichrist? John sees those who "had gotten the victory over the beast, and over his image, and over his mark, and over the number of his name," xv. 2. He sees "the souls of them that were beheaded for the witness of Jesus and for the word of God, and which had not worshipped the beast, neither his image, neither had received his mark upon their foreheads, nor in their hands," xx. 4 (comp. xii. 11, 17, xiv. 4). Thus they did not cowardly and faithlessly submit to the antichristian power, with its alluring and terrifying temptations (comp. xxi. 8), but overcame it, whether in prison or by a martyr's death. But what does this include? "Here is"—that is (comp. xiii. 18), here at this place, here belongs, here comes—"the patience and faith of the saints," xiii. 10; "here is the patience of the saints: here are they that keep the commandments, and the faith of Jesus," xiv. 12 (comp. i. 9, ii. 10, xiii. 2, xix. 12, 17, xx. 4). Thus the patience, and as its protection, faith; or faith, and as its protection, patience; or the patience which protects itself in keeping the commandments of God and the faith of Jesus, are the forces by which the victory of the Christian over Antichrist is conditioned,—they constitute the task of the Christian against Antichrist.

But upon what does this patience of the saints rest? What *encourages* it, and helps them to remain faithful in the great tribulation? It is said, "If any man have an ear, let him hear: he that leadeth into captivity, let him go into captivity: he that killeth with the sword must be killed with the sword," xiii. 9, 10. An angel said, "with a loud voice, If any man worship the beast and his image, and receive his mark in his forehead, or in his hand, the same shall drink of the wine of the wrath of God, which is poured out without mixture into the cup of His indignation; and he shall be tormented with fire and brimstone in the presence of the holy angels, and in the presence of the Lamb: and the smoke of their torment ascendeth up for ever and ever: and they have no rest day nor night, who worship the beast and his image, and whosoever receiveth the mark of his name," xiv. 9–11 (comp. xi. 18, xviii. 6, 7). In both places it is expressly said that on account of, or in view of, the severe retribution that threatens Antichrist for its persecutions, and its adherents for their worship of the beast, there is patience or faithfulness among Christians,—that is, Christians, alarmed by the retribution falling upon Antichrist, are moved to a stedfast adhesion to Christianity.

But this is more a *negative*, fear-incentive. The *positive* motive, *consolation,* is far more prominent. We pass over here the reference of xx. 4 to the temptations of Antichrist, and limit ourselves to what immediately belongs to this place. It presents itself for the most part, and in the fullest detail, in the great episode between the sixth and the seventh seal visions. Here especially the servants of God have received divine assurance, symbolized by the sealing of 144,000 from all the tribes of the children of Israel, vii. 1–8, that they should be safe from the plagues of the trumpet and vial visions, as we have shown at length above. They then venture to console themselves in their trials here with the prospect which, as victors over Antichrist, xv. 2, awaits them in heaven, vii. 9–17, xiv. 13 (comp. vi. 9–11). Since we have in various earlier sections already solved several questions suggested in these places, we occupy ourselves here with but one—what is presented in them for the consolation of the Christian? Those "who have washed their robes, and made them white in the blood of the Lamb,"—that is, who, through Him who died for them on the cross, have freed themselves from their sins, and have become holy, vii. 14: "the dead who die in the Lord;" those who enter into fellowship with Christ, and continue in the same until death, xiv. 13 (comp. ii. 10), described in the common expression of our book as those who "overcome,"—are "blessed from henceforth," though not from the present of the seer, or the vision, nor "because the glorious end which the perdition of the enemy and the perfect blessedness of all believers will bring is immediately at hand,"—for the following sentence does not agree with this: the emphasis also lies on the contrast with the foregoing perdition of the worshippers of the beast,—but from the moment of death, immediately on their departure, because they do not, like other men, enter into the death state of the grave, but into the state of blessedness in heaven, xiv. 13. Hoekstra, indeed, with some other expositors, holds it to be most probable that in such descriptions as vii. 9–17, xiv. 1–5, xv. 2–4, xix. 14, the writer anticipates, and that he may have been compelled to it by the arrangement of his book, since here he can have nothing to do with the actual dead; and that he explains this himself when, in the description of the glory of these sleepers, he uses the future, vii. 15–17, as also he permits to appear the souls of those who were not yet dead, vii. 14, xv. 2 (comp. xx. 4). And certainly we do not see how the passages referred to can be regarded otherwise than as anticipatory; only we do not so understand the anticipation as if the seer described beforehand what is only in the final state, but what in that state is really anticipated by the heavenly state, or what will occur for those who are still living here. Hoekstra, p. 383, adds that the writer appears to have conceived of the state of the souls of the faithful as a naturally blessed rest (comp. xiv. 13, vi. 11); but one need not be much versed in the Scriptures in order to know that the death state, in the sense of existence in hades, and happiness are, with a biblical author, two irreconcilable things. We desire to conceive of heaven and the heavenly state as it is in the representation of the author, and we know that, with him, deceased Christians are certainly dead,—some slain and killed,—and that they shall be made alive again; but they, or rather their souls, are not in hades, but in heaven,—not in the hidden lower, but in the hidden upper reality. They have now salvation,—that is, the essentials of deliverance from sin and death,—which God, through Christ, has imparted to Christians, as implied in their grateful ascription of the same to God and Christ, vii. 10. But this salvation or blessedness in heaven has a negative and a positive side. On the positive side it consists in freedom from the sufferings of the earthly life. They come out of the great tribulation, vii. 14; they rest from their labour, xiv. 13, vi. 11 (comp. ii. 2, 3); they "hunger no more, neither thirst any more, neither shall the sun light on them, nor any heat: and God shall wipe away all tears from their eyes," vii. 16, 17 (comp. Isa. xlix. 10, xxv. 8). But while Christians in death leave their sufferings behind them,—and here we come to the positive side of their heavenly happiness,—"their works follow them." Not the reward of their works; still less do their works follow them to judgment to secure their justification; but "their works," that is, what constitutes them Christians, their Christian nature, which subjectively makes them fit for objective blessedness, xiv. 13 (comp. iii. 4). It appears also as a positive element of this blessedness, that Christians have palms in their hands, vii. 10. The symbol is certainly not, as Ewald says, from the Olympian games; for, as Hengstenberg correctly remarks, what follows treats not of victory, but of salvation, and is drawn from the feast of Tabernacles, the harvest festival, and joyful thanksgiving of Israel (comp. Lev. xxiii. 40; Deut. xvi. 14, 15; 2 Macc. x. 7): and, as the same expositor observes, there is probably in vii. 15 an allusion to the tabernacle, in vii. 16 to the trials of the wilderness, in vii. 17 to the scarcity of water; we recognise in the entire picture a heavenly feast of Tabernacles, and Christians, with trials overcome, are in a state of festive joy. Further, they are "clothed in white robes," vii. 9, vi. 11 (comp. iii. 45); as here they became sanctified, or saints, so they are recognised and honoured as such in heaven. They stand before "the throne of God and the Lamb," vii. 9; they are before "the throne of God, and serve Him day and night in His temple," vii. 15. Thus their activity is in the service already carried on by them during the earthly life, the divine service, now freed from earthly limitations, or more definitely the priestly service, the uninterrupted adoration of God. "And He that sitteth on the throne shall dwell among them," vii. 15 (comp. xxi. 3; Lev. xxvi. 11; Isa. iv. 5; Ezek. xxxvii. 27). God, enthroned in glory, will be immediately and personally present with them; the divine Shechinah will no longer be veiled in pillar of cloud or fire. "The Lamb, which is in the midst of the throne, shall feed them, and shall lead them unto living fountains of waters," vii. 17 (comp. Isa. xlix. 10; Ps. xxiii. 2). Thus as by Christ, their atoning mediator,—for this is implied by "in the midst of the throne,"—they were led and protected, and crowned with eternal life here, so yonder there will be leading and protection, only more direct; and the enjoyment of eternal life, but more complete. We therefore find our statements, in the section on the saints and their work, with respect to their expectations, to be confirmed,—namely, that the heavenly promises would add nothing essentially new to those already available for the earthly Christian life. It is evident that the promise of deliverance from tribulation, rest from labour, cessation of suffering, as well as perpetual joy after trial overcome, belong only to heaven. But otherwise the contents of heavenly blessedness are distinguished from those of the promises in the letters only in particular symbolic features, and it is still in nature the same. The Christian has this blessedness at the moment of his becoming a Christian; but what he possesses and does, and is here in conflict and growth, amidst the discrepancy of his real nature with its manifestation in his life, and still more with the conduct of the world, he possesses, and does, and is there, in rest and realization, —not, indeed, in visible, but in a real ideal harmony of the subjective and the objective, of the nature and the appearance, of the inner and the outer, of the estimate and the result. I say expressly, not in visible ideal harmony; for when we shall find also that the preliminaries, as well as the perfect realization, both in the thousand years' reign and in the new world, add nothing essentially new to the heavenly promises; so the fifth seal vision, not only with its question, how long? and its command to rest for a little season until the numbers should be fulfilled, but also with its souls of the slain under the altar, in distinction from "the souls of them that were beheaded," who live, or are partakers of the first resurrection, as well as with its "rest," in distinction from "reigning with Christ," xx. 4–6, points distinctly and expressly to this, that to the state in heaven there will yet follow a higher and highest.

This is the place for the examination of a vision which in its meaning is for Christians in the great tribulation neither properly admonitory nor consolatory, but, under the idea of *exaltation,* partakes of both. I mean the vision contained in xiv. 1–5. That we are to look for Mount Zion in heaven, or to regard it as indicated by the connection as a special local symbol of heaven, and to conceive of the 144,000 as identical with the harpers and singers, has been shown in the section on heaven; and that we are to understand them as symbolizing neither Jewish nor Gentile Christians, but Christians generally, as the true Israel, or the chosen people of God, has been pointed out in the section on the churches. And since the "first-fruits" have been explained in the section on the saints and their works to be the designation of Christians as the divinely-consecrated or sanctified, closely allied to the Old Testament kingly priesthood, there remains to us here only to fix the meaning of the vision as a whole. This presents itself on a comparison with the chapter immediately preceding. John has seen how the first beast ascended out of the sea, how it manifested its enmity to God, and how the world wondered after it; he has seen how the other beast arose from the earth, and operating with devilish temptations, drew the world after it; and then his prophetic eye turns from the world and its antichristian state. Now he sees—not as Weiss, *bibl. Theol.* p. 613, supposes—the Messiah at the central point of the Old Testament theocracy, the 144,000 assembled around Him, with whom He is going forth to the last conflict; but the hill of Zion, the sublime height, the region of salvation where God's dwelling is, in contrast with the sea and the earth, or with this lower world; the Lamb in contrast with the two beasts, and in contrast with the inhabitants of the earth who worship the beast, and have his mark on their foreheads and their hands; the 144,000, the elect host, as Israel, a people of God who have the name of God and the Lamb on their foreheads, who are consecrated to God and Christ, who are His peculiar people, and offer to Him priestly service (comp. iii. 12). And what does the seer hear? While things are going in the world so dreadfully, the chosen host sing—loud as many waters and great thunders, sweet as the voice of harpers, neither silenced nor subdued by alarm and anxiety, nor crying in suffering and distress—"before the throne and before the four living creatures and the elders;" that is, not, as Hoekstra, p. 374, thinks, to do homage to God and the saints (to the living creatures also?), but there, where the ideal reality is, they sing a new song, or a song which is old but yet new, the song of Moses and the Lamb (comp xv. 3), the grateful song of deliverance, which beside them no man is able to learn, because he has not experienced it in himself (comp. ii. 17, xix. 12). Even in this festive, priestly song, this real lyric in the midst of the proceedings of Antichrist, is seen the exaltation of the chosen host above the conflict and the strife. But this exaltation springs from their nature and its activities. Ideally seen in heaven, or from heaven (comp. xii. 11 with ver. 10), they have, in the most marked contrast to the world with its fornications, or idolatrous worship and service of sin (comp. section on the earth and its inhabitants), not defiled themselves with women; that is, in the strongest and fullest sense, they have not committed fornication, have not been unfaithful to God; they have not allowed themselves to be tempted by the world, and have not sinned, "for they are virgins;" that is, what they are according to their nature as Christians, pure, holy, chaste, has in their lives simply perfected itself in gradual development, or in the particular case maintained itself. Certainly many expositors take the words just explained in a peculiar sense, and determine the representation of the seer to be, that perfect abstinence from sexual intercourse belongs to the distinguished sanctity of the 144,000, and that on this account they enjoy peculiar blessedness; which, as Köstlin, *ut ante*, p. 493, observes, is not merely in the spirit of the Old Testament, but (comp. die kolossischen Irrlehrer) is Esseno-Ebionitish Not for the purpose of escaping "the thought prominent in the word-sense," and apart from the impossibility of finding in the Apocalypse any point of connection with Esseno-Ebionitish error, I agree, for the following simple reasons, with the symbolic exposition. The 144,000 are neither distinguished Christians, nor do they enjoy peculiar happiness; even on this supposition, it would be wholly inconceivable that the seer should have imagined 144,000 unmarried Christians, and, according to the literal sense, Christians of the male sex; still less could he have regarded as Christians only those who had not been married. When I do not, with many expositors, place the meaning of these figurative expressions in abstinence from the uncleanness associated with idol-worship, or find in continence an example of all the virtues, but agree, with Baur, *ut ante*, p. 225, who declares it to be at least doubtful whether the unmarried state is not probably a biblical expression for being spotless, the state of moral purity, it is simply on account of the all-dominating contrast to the world in its antichristian spirit; and I find that John has spoken of the idolatry and the sin of the world as fornication, with sufficient frequency, and strength, and clearness, to enable us to see in it the true interpretation of this imagery. It is to be observed that, as it seems to me, the true sense more decidedly presents itself if we begin, not with the first, but with the second member of the sentence—"they are virgins," which is evidently symbolic. The proof would then be, not that they have abstained from fornication, but that they "were not defiled with women;" because of the second definite member, the first has taken a rather indefinite form; by the second the first is explained. "These are they"—so with emphasis begins in the first sentence the description of the exaltation of the 144,000: "these are they," continues the second sentence, "which follow the Lamb whithersoever He goeth," not merely in suffering and death on earth, nor merely to the blessed reward in heaven, but they are everywhere the constant companions or disciples of the Lord, whether He goes to the cross or to the crown. "These,"—for so again the third sentence emphasizes the statement,—"these were redeemed from among men, being the first-fruits unto God and to the Lamb,"—that is, they are delivered from fellowship with the world through Christ; the first-fruits of humanity consecrated to

God and Christ. "And in their mouths was found no guile," that is,—the ψεῦδος is the antithesis of ἀληθινός and ἀλήθεια (comp. xxi. 8, 27, xxii. 15, also ii. 2, 20, iii. 9, xiii. 11, 12, xix. 20), as fornication is the antithesis of purity or holiness,—in contrast with the lies and frauds of the world, or the God-opposing nature of the world, they have shown themselves true in thought and word, in theory and practice, thus in this respect sinless; "for they are without fault,"—that is, therein is completed, or realized only in time, what, apart from time, they are according to their nature and idea; they are made spotless, perfectly righteous. The whole picture has its parallel, not in vii. 9, 10, where the design of consolation decidedly prevails, and just as little in other places where there is the obvious purpose of admonition; but in xii. 10, 11, where the triumph of the faithful over Satan is as ideally anticipated as the protection of the faithful amidst the temptations of Antichrist is in this representation; while in vii. 9, 10 they are really in heaven, they are in xiv. 1–5 there ideally.

Finally, the passage xv. 2–4 belongs to this place. As the words themselves show, and as the connection demands, we must in this scene put emphasis, not on the state of Christians, but upon their words. Evidently the seer aims to intensify the picture of the obstinacy and impenitency of the world, which he represents in the course of the vial visions, and therefore, at the commencement, calls up the expectation of a different issue; but, on the other side, it is equally clear that he desires to soften the impression of the terrible judgments which he is about to introduce, and therefore announces beforehand the final glorious results. But through whom can these results be accomplished? Only through those who as men can sympathize with the plagues, but who at the same time, as Christians, as redeemed, are delivered from them, and can understand them in their divinely intended meaning; thus through Christians, as victors in heaven, or in their ideal state. He sees them standing on a sea of glass mingled with fire, having the harps of God, and they sing the song of Moses and the Lamb; that is, Christians above, after they have overcome all the temptations of Antichrist, look upon the holy and righteous judgments of God, or His works and ways with the world, the contents of the plague visions, as once Israel looked upon the plagues of Egypt and the Red Sea,—indeed, in these visions the Egyptian plagues frequently furnish the type,—they sing the song of the deliverance of their persons, the song of salvation, as the children of Israel once sung it, Ex. xv., in its Christian fulfilment. Christian salvation is essentially that of the Old Testament, the completion once prepared but now begun. According to Hoekstra, p. 380, it is, moreover, the song which Moses and the Lamb first sung, and their followers have learned. But it is not now shared by, but applied to the heathen; it is the grateful adoring *hope* that the judgments of God will accomplish their object, and all the heathen be converted to Him. The tendency of this scene is neither admonition, consolation, nor exaltation, but it presents, as it were by the way, a supplement to xiv. 1–3, especially to xiv. 2, 3, and enables us to recognise the Christian view of the judgments of God on the world as one which, while understanding, admiring, and glorifying Him, lovingly desires and hopes for its salvation.

5. The Holy City in the Forty-two Months.

Every exposition of chap. xi. which understands by the "holy city," ver. 2, or the "great city," ver. 8, the secularized church, is wrecked by the statement of ver. 8, "where also our Lord was crucified," as it is also by the contents of ver. 13; for a city, the tenth part of which is destroyed by an earthquake which slays 7000 persons, can only be a real city; and the real city, where the Lord of the two witnesses was crucified, can only be Jerusalem. At the same time, however, the exposition which in the holy and great city finds Jerusalem in a merely local sense, cannot, to say nothing of other considerations, be maintained before vers. 1, 2. The type for these two verses is Ezek. xl. 1–3 (comp. Zech. i. 16, ii. 1, 2; Amos vii. 7–9; Isa. xxxiv. 11); but the measuring does not here, as in Ezek. xl. 1–3, mean making manifest the contents, but, as in Amos vii. 7, Hab. iv. 6, exception from the destruction which should come upon the unmeasured. When the seer measures "the temple of God, and the altar, and them that worship therein," that is, the priests, but leaves out "the court which is without the temple," he does not say that only the courts of the Gentiles and Israelites should be trodden down of the Romans, and that the temple and the court of the priests should remain uninjured, or, as the besieged believed, "that the Romans would not be able to penetrate further than to the boundary which a Gentile, on pain of death, was forbidden to cross, and that then the Messiah would appear for their deliverance" (Hausrath in Schenkel's *Bibellexikon*, I. p. 161). Is it conceivable that the seer imagines the Romans entering the city as victors, and possessing the temple court, and the temple itself remaining free from destruction or desecration for forty-two months, the whole period of the last tribulation? We may add to this, that the words themselves show that John cannot have had such an idea. The altar, as we have seen in the section on heaven, means the altar of burnt-offering, in distinction from the altar of incense; but the altar of burnt-offering did not stand within the edifice of the temple, but outside in the court of the priests. We may translate *ἐν αὐτῷ*, "at it," that is, the altar of burnt-offering, or "in it," namely, in the temple; and if against the laws of language we do not directly or indirectly insert, in place of the court of the temple, the outer court, the word-sense will always exclude only a part of the court of the consecration, and then the whole court is abandoned to the Gentiles. The word-sense carries us beyond itself; the temple, the altar, and they that worship therein, as well as the court of the temple, must be intended symbolically; the court of the temple, as a symbol of those standing without, not the priestly, but the profane, the non-Christian Jewish people; but the temple, the altar, and those worshipping therein, the priests (comp. the king-priesthood of Christians) as symbols of the saints, the priestly, the Christian part of this people, Jewish Christians. But this interpretation would certainly be denied us, whether it were said, "leave out the court and the holy city, for they are given to the Gentiles," or, "leave out the court and the holy city, for the Gentiles shall tread them under foot forty and two months," in other words, if the court and the holy city were classed together; but nothing hinders us from understanding the words, "and the holy city shall they tread," as an explanation rather than an amplification of the words, "the court is given to the Gentiles." According to Luke xxi. 24, we may venture to assume (comp. Dan. ix. 26, 27, xii. 7) that the treading down of Jerusalem by the Gentiles was a standing eschatological representation and mode of expression; the seer has given its contents first with a view to the Jewish

Christians in the peculiar form: "the court which is without the temple leave out, and measure it not, for it is given unto the Gentiles;" and then he gives the same contents in their statutory, solemn form, "the holy city shall they tread under foot forty and two months." Can we still understand "the holy city," "the great city," to be Jerusalem in a purely local sense? No, the city is Jerusalem, but, as frequently elsewhere, it is at the same time *the representative of the Jewish people.* (Comp. Matt. xxi. 5, xxiii. 37; we may think also of Antichrist as equally representing both Nero and the empire.)

What does *chap.* xi. *say to us of Jerusalem in relation to the Jewish people?* The true people of God, the servants of God, the saints, are, to our author, Christians whether they come from Jews or Gentiles; the believing Jews are to him, in contrast with the unbelieving, the temple of God, and the priests serving in it contrast with the court without the temple. Of those Jews who hate, malign, and indirectly persecute (comp. ii. 9, 10) the true Messiah and His followers, he says: "they say they are Jews, and are not, but are the synagogue of Satan," ii. 9 (comp., as a contrast, Num. xvi. 3, xx. 4, xxxi. 16). "I will make them of the synagogue of Satan, which say they are Jews, and are not, but do lie," iii. 9. But the chapter treats of the Jewish people according as a small part of it was faithful to Jesus, and a far greater part rejected Him, and continued unbelieving. The seer was to "measure the temple of God, and the altar, and them that worship therein;" that is, as Christians generally were protected from the trumpet and vial plagues, vii. 1–4, so should Christians out of Israel be protected from the judgments which were to come upon Jerusalem and the Jewish people (comp. Matt. xxiv. 15–18). On the contrary, the court without the temple was to be "left out," for it was given to the Gentiles, and they should tread the holy city under foot forty and two months; that is, the judgments already predicted by Daniel will burst in upon the non-Christian, unbelieving Jewish people. Whether John, by its being given to the Gentiles, and their treading it under foot, had in mind the destruction of Jerusalem, the words do not expressly say; correctly interpreted, the measuring of the temple is not against it, and just as little, that later the city appears as still existing. When we look at 2 Thess. ii. 4, it is significant that, in connection with the presence of the beast in

Jerusalem, xi. 7, his sitting in the temple is not mentioned; and since John, by its being left to the Gentiles, and its being trodden under foot by them, cannot have meant a mere desecration or damage, we must say that he expected its destruction, and that of the temple, though not giving it prominence, and still less describing it; but with the future of Israel before him, he implies it in the old prophetic and sacred expressions for the conquest, ill-treatment, and spoliation of "the holy city." But in a similar manner as God caused the publication of the gospel to accompany the plagues which fell upon the heathen, so for Jerusalem or the Jewish people He associates with judgments the call to repentance. The Lord will give His two witnesses, that they may prophesy for 1260 days clothed in sackcloth. When the seer speaks of the two witnesses of Christ, he wishes it to be understood that he intended definite personalities known to his readers. But who were they? The expression, "their Lord," proves as little in favour of the disciples of Jesus, who might still live in Jerusalem, as the words, "my two witnesses;" and the description of their activities and their fate is against this idea. It reminds us rather of Moses and Elias. From the report given of the Transfiguration by the synoptical Gospels, for example, Matt. xvii. 1–13, as well as from further statements (comp. Ewald, *ut ante*, p. 293), we know that one or two of the great prophets of the Old Testament, especially those just mentioned,—the law and the prophets, or the whole Old Testament in its two poles,—were expected to appear in actual personalities, as precursors and heralds of the Messiah. This is the original type of the two witnesses. But it is also said of them, according to Zech. iv. 2–14, iii. 1–5, "These are the two anointed ones, that stand by the Lord of the whole earth;" that is, they will, like Joshua and Zerubbabel, made true prophets by the Spirit of God, serve the Almighty, and He will protect and honour them as His. By the two witnesses John thus understands two personalities, in whom, as their designation and destiny show,—corresponding also to the culmination of all things already in existence, which is to happen before the end,—the two testimonies of God, law and prophecy, which were in vain for Israel before Christ, will once more, and in the highest form, personally appear; in whom also, at the same time, their fulfilment, which appeared in unison in Christ Himself, according to their two sides, or, so to say, polarized, consequently the Christian testimony, the apostolate and prophecy, will come into view in a doubly intensified representation, which as a new Moses and Elias, and as a new Joshua and Zerubbabel, will prepare the Jewish people for the coming of the Lord in glory, heralding His approach, testifying of Him, and labouring for Him in word and deed. These two witnesses will prophesy, clothed in sackcloth, 1260 days, equal to forty-two months, the time during which the Gentiles tread down the holy city (comp. Jer. iv. 8; Jonah iii. 5); that is, they will publish the gospel to the Jewish nation for their repentance (comp. xiv. 6). "If any man will hurt them, fire proceedeth out of their mouth and devoureth their enemies,"—probably a combination of Jer. v. 14 and 2 Kings i. 10, 11 (comp. Sir. xlviii. 1–3), "If any man will hurt them, he must in this manner be killed," that is, in the same manner in which he thought to have killed them. "These have power to shut heaven, that it rain not in the days of their prophecy," after 1 Kings xvii. 1; and we may notice the agreement of the three and a half years with those of Elias (Jas. v. 17), and the forty-two months with the period mentioned by Daniel. "And they have power over waters to turn them into blood," according to Ex. vii. 19, "and to smite the earth with all plagues as often as they will," after the plagues with which Moses smote the Egyptians, Ex. viii. et seq., and as it is said later, ver. 10, "these two prophets tormented them that dwelt on the earth." "When they shall have finished their testimony, the beast that ascendeth out of the bottomless pit," that is, Antichrist in the form of Nero, "shall make war against them, and shall overcome them, and kill them," as, indeed, it is generally "given unto him to make war with the saints to overcome them," xiii. 7. Where will that happen? From what follows, it will take place in Jerusalem. Thus Antichrist comes to Jerusalem, and dwells there. One feels tempted to pursue the subject further, and to think of the last manifestation of Antichrist, namely, the works of the false prophet in Jerusalem, and the image of the beast in the temple (comp. 2 Thess. ii. 3, 4); but in view of vers. 1, 2, we adhere to what is expressly said. As the witnesses appear in suffering there as imitators of Christ, as Jesus is slain by the beast as the Roman empire; so they are put to death by the beast as Nero, and this likeness goes still further. "The dead bodies of the witnesses lie in the streets of the great city, which spiritually is called Sodom and Egypt, where also their Lord was crucified." In relation to the Gentiles, Jerusalem is "the holy city," but to the witnesses, "the great city," in a similar manner as Babylon in xvii. 18, analogous also to the temple and the court, vers. 1, 2, as a statement of its profanation and fall; perhaps also as an indication that the greatness is the worthless reason of its godless security, and haughty rejection of Christ and His witnesses. "Sodom and Egypt" (comp. Isa. i. 9–11; Ezek. xvi. 46–49; Jer. xxiii. 14) denote perfect enmity against the true God, His servants, and His people, the radically erroneous position of the Jewish nation. That the Lord of the two witnesses was crucified in Jerusalem, is naturally not a merely local reference; it is said therein that the antichristian enmity of the great city is always the same; that the same hatred which once brought the Lord to the cross, now slays His witnesses, and that because they are His; or that Jerusalem and the Jewish nation stand in the same relation to the beast, and that, as in the crucifixion of Jesus, so also the death of the two witnesses will be shared when the God-opposing, worldly power in it gets the upper hand, and comes to the light.—"They of the people, and kindred, and tongues, and nations shall see their dead bodies three days and a half, and shall not suffer their dead bodies to be put in graves" (comp. Isa. liii. 9). The three and a half days refer, without doubt, first to the three and a half years during which the witnesses testify; they are the climax, the quintessence, the sum of the great tribulation period; but if, in the slaying of the witnesses, there is an unmistakeable analogy with the death of Christ, so we shall find in the three and a half days, though with a certain intensification, an allusion to the time between the death and resurrection of the Lord; and though the intensification of the shame—the lying in the street, and the denial of burial—stands in the foreground, yet, as Ewald, *ut ante*, p. 229, remarks, "according to the sense of the entire prediction, all that is terrible rises here to a point which it did not reach at the crucifixion." "And they that dwell upon the earth," evidently the same as "they of the people, and kindreds, and tongues, and nations," not only the heathen, though preponderating, but the world which worships the beast, ver. 7, Jews and Gentiles, "rejoice over them and make merry, and shall send gifts one to another," as on joyful occasions they were accustomed to do (comp. Neh. viii. 10–12; Esth. ix. 19–23), "because these two prophets tormented them that dwell on the earth;" thus also the world rejoiced at the death of Christ. But "after three days and a half the Spirit of life from God entered into them" (comp. Gen. ii. 7), "and they stood upon their feet" (comp. 2 Kings xiii. 21; Ezek. xxxvii. 10); that is, they rose from the dead as Christ arose; "and great fear fell upon them which saw them. And they heard a great voice from heaven saying unto them, 'Come up hither.' And they ascended up to heaven in a cloud; and their enemies beheld them." The ascension to heaven reminds us directly of that of Elijah, 2 Kings ii. 11; but the seer, as the expression "in a cloud" (comp. Dan. vii. 13; Acts i. 9) shows, had also in his eye the ascension of Christ. By their being seen of their enemies, he points out, as in their resurrection, only in stronger terms by the express mention of their "enemies," the distinction, that what in the case of Jesus seen by His followers, and by them made known to others, happened here before all the world, and directly before the eyes of their foes; that thus the power of God verifies itself, as with Christ, in the glorification of His servants after ignominy and death, but in a much more striking and convincing manner. "And the same hour," in which the two witnesses went to heaven, "was there a great earthquake" (comp. Matt. xxvii. 52, xxviii. 2), "and the tenth part of the city fell, and in the earthquake were slain of men seven thousand,"—perhaps in antithetic play upon 1 Kings xix. 18:—"and the remnant were affrighted, and gave glory to the God of heaven." God, in His miraculous attestation of His two servants, thus sends upon Jerusalem a similar but milder plague than that which fell on Babylon (comp. xvi. 19, also vi. 8, ix. 18), and thereby the city, the Jewish people in the gross, finally becomes converted. When Weiss, with whom in other respects I have come to an independent agreement in the conception of xi. 1, 2, says, *bibl. Theol.* p. 602, "The seer ventures no longer, with Paul, to hope for the final general conversion of Israel, but that, according to the ancient prediction of Isa. i. 9, x. 22, 23 (comp. Rom. ix. 27–29), a remnant shall be saved," much rather, I think, does John see that ancient prophecy fulfilled in the Jewish Christian church intended in xi. 1; on the other hand, in xi. 13, he intends essentially the same which is predicted in Rom. xi. 25–27.

If we gather up the various particulars, the result is this: the seer represents the Jews who brought the Lord to the cross as exceedingly obdurate; the fate of the Christ-murdering city, which, according to ancient prediction, was to be trodden down of the Gentiles during the time ordained by God, apart from individual conversions which will take place here and there, iii. 9, just as little as the wonderful works of the two prophets, or witnesses of Christ, expected in the last time, will of itself lead to conversion; but the wonderful history of the sufferings and the glory of Christ, the intensified and more violent fate of the two witnesses, in union with a relatively modified plague, will at last so influence the Jewish people, who have been prepared by judgments and warnings, that they will cease to be, contrary to their ideal, of the world, and will become a Christian people, a true Israel, and Jerusalem a truly holy city. That the Apostle Paul possibly regarded the fulness — that is, not, as to my astonishment I find that every expositor under Tübingen influence continually misinterprets, as meaning the whole number of the heathen, but as with absolute certainty I affirm, the fulness of the divinely-ordained number which, before Israel's conversion, shall believe—as being greater than the seer represents; further, that he has possibly represented the course of the conversion of Israel differently,—may be the more readily admitted, since the circumstances under which Rom. xi. and Rev. xi. were written make such a difference almost necessary beforehand. But how any one can quote the eleventh chapter of this book in proof of the Particularism of the seer against the Universalism of the apostle—and yet Baur does this, *ut ante*, pp. 211–13; and, on the other hand, how any one can say of Paul, that, in opposition to the seer, he contemplated with equanimity the extinction of Israel among mankind (comp. Schenkel's *Bibellexikon*, I. p. 162),—must appear to a candid reader of Rom. xi. as a sheer curiosity, or a remarkable proof of the power of prejudice.

6. The Impenitence of Men.

"And all the world wondered after the beast. And they worshipped the dragon which gave power unto the beast: and they worshipped the beast, saying, Who is like unto the beast? who is able to make war with him?" xiii. 3, 4. "All that dwell upon the earth shall worship him,"—the beast in person,—"whose names are not written in the book of life of the Lamb slain from the foundation of the world," xiii. 8. The other beast "causeth the earth, and them which dwell therein, to worship the first beast," xiii. 12. The same "deceiveth them that dwell on the earth by the means of those miracles which he had power to do in the sight of the beast, saying to them that dwell on the earth, that they should make an image to the beast," xiii. 14. Indeed, "he caused all, both small and great, both rich and poor, free and bond, to receive a mark in their right hand, or in their foreheads," xiii. 16. Great Babylon "made all nations drink of the wine of the wrath of her fornication," xiv. 8. "And the nations were angry," xi. 18. Thus the earth, the inhabitants of the earth, the men, *the heathen, as a whole and in the gross,* have allowed themselves to be led astray—have *become antichristian, and pursue an antichristian course.*

Therefore follows "the hour of temptation which shall come upon all the world, to try them that dwell upon the earth," iii. 10. God visits them with the growing judgments of the seal, trumpet, and vial visions, but at the same time publishes, in ever-widening circles, among the inhabitants of the earth, the everlasting gospel, that they may be led to repentance, xiv. 6, 7.

What will be the result? According to the vision of the sixth seal, "the kings of the earth, and the great men, and the rich men, and the chief captains, and the mighty men, and every bond man, and every free man, hid themselves in the dens, and in the rocks of the mountains; and said to the rocks and the mountains, Fall on us, and hide us from the face of Him that sitteth on the throne, and from the wrath of the Lamb: for the great day of His wrath is come; and who shall be able to stand?" vi. 15–17. And at the beginning of the vial visions the victors on the sea of glass sing, "Great and marvellous are Thy works, Lord God Almighty; just and true are Thy ways, Thou King of nations. Who shall not fear Thee, O Lord, and glorify Thy name? for Thou only art holy: for all nations shall come and worship before Thee, for Thy judgments are manifest," xv. 3, 4. But do men repent? No. After the judgments of the seals and trumpets have fallen, and slain a large proportion of them, it is said, "and the rest of the men, who were not killed by these plagues, yet repented not of the works of their hands, that they should not worship devils, and idols of gold, and silver, and brass, and stone, and of wood; which neither can see, nor hear, nor walk. Neither repented they of their murders, nor of their sorceries, nor of their fornications, nor of their thefts," ix. 20, 21. And is it better when the plagues of the highest degree have fallen? By those of the fourth trumpet, men "were scorched with great heat, and blasphemed the name of God, which hath power over these plagues: and they repented not to give Him glory," xvi. 9. By the pouring out of the fifth vial of wrath "upon the seat of the beast, his kingdom was full of darkness; and they gnawed their tongues for pain, and blasphemed the God of heaven because of their pains and their sores, and repented not of their deeds," xvi. 10, 11. Even after the outpouring of the last wrath vial, men "blasphemed God because of the plague of the hail; for the plague thereof was exceeding great," xvi. 21.

While the seer thus expects of the Jews, with the self-evident exception of those who in truth are not Jews, but are of the synagogue of Satan, that through God's chastising and persuasive judgments they will, notwithstanding all resistance, at last as a people repent, he also expects—possibly, as Weiss conjectures, on account of a pause in the Gentile mission through the persecution of Nero, but more probably as well on account of his original expectation as his subsequent experience of the heathen world, and, as far as I can see, in perfect agreement with the Synoptists and the Apostle Paul—of men in general, the *heathen in the gross;* but again, with the exception of those who are written in the book of life, and allow themselves to be redeemed by God from among men, though considered from the ideal, we should doubtless expect the opposite, that by all the chastening and persuasive judgments of God, even when the same have reached their highest development, they *will not be brought to repentance.* What remains, then, but that God should judge, or complete His true and righteous judgments, xix. 2, no more for warning and deterring fear, but for severe and rich retribution? xiii. 10, xviii. 6, 7, xi. 18.

7. The Fall of Babylon.

The fall of Babylon forms the transition from the preparatory to the final judgments. For certainly as it constitutes the chief contents of the seventh wrath vial, xvi. 17–21, and so far belongs to the last preliminary judgment, and appears proleptically as a motive to repentance, xiv. 8, it still cannot be denied that it was referred by the seer more to the final judgment, chap. xvii. and xviii., as is shown by the independent description, the absence of every expression concerning continued obduracy, notwithstanding the event, and the immediate succession of the advent. If, instead of treating of the fall of Babylon under "the seals, the trumpets, and the vials," we now speak of it in a separate section, it will be justified when, in conclusion, we quote the remark of Weiss, *bibl. Theol.* p. 506, "as once the fall of Jerusalem was the signal for the closing catastrophe, so it is now, when at the beginning of the last period of tribulation stands the fall of the chief city of the world."

That Babylon, the imperial city of Rome, as the chief city and capital, the home and origin, the local representation of Antichrist, will fall, and, indeed, *for the reward of her sins will certainly, suddenly, and awfully perish,* the seer can hardly proclaim often and strongly enough. "Babylon is fallen, is fallen, that great city, because she made all nations drink of the wine of the wrath of her fornication," xiv. 8. So speaks an angel of her coming doom as already past. The last vial plague "rends the great city into three parts, the cities of the nations fall, and great Babylon comes into remembrance before God, to give unto her the cup of the wine of the fierceness of His wrath," xvi. 19. After that, John says of one of the seven vial angels, "he carried me away in the spirit into the wilderness," and said, "I will show unto thee the judgment of the great whore that sitteth upon many waters; with whom the kings of the earth have committed fornication, and the inhabitants of the earth have been made drunk with the wine of her fornication," xvii. 1–3. He sees "another angel come down from heaven, having great power; and the earth was lightened with his glory. And he cried mightily with a strong voice, saying, Babylon the great is fallen, is fallen, and is become the habitation of devils, and the hold of every foul spirit, and a cage of every unclean and hateful bird. For all nations have drunk of the wine of the wrath of her fornication, and the kings of the earth have committed fornication with her, and the merchants of the earth are waxed rich through the abundance of her delicacies," xviii. 1–3. John heard "another voice from heaven, saying, Come out of her, my people, that ye be not partakers of her sins, and that ye receive not of her plagues: for her sins have reached unto heaven, and God hath remembered her iniquities. Reward her even as she rewarded you, and double unto her double, according to her works: in the cup which she hath filled, fill to her double. How much she hath glorified herself and lived deliciously, so much torment and sorrow give her: for she saith in her heart, I sit as a queen, and am no widow, and shall see no sorrow. Therefore shall her plagues come in one day, death, and mourning, and famine; and she shall be utterly burned with fire: for strong is the Lord God who judgeth her," xviii. 4–8. And again, "A mighty angel took up a stone like a great millstone, and cast it into the sea, saying, Thus with violence shall that great city Babylon be thrown down, and shall be found no more at all. And the voice of harpers, and musicians, and of pipers, and trumpeters, shall be heard no more at all in thee; and no craftsman, of whatsoever craft he be, shall be found any more in thee; and the sound of a millstone shall be heard no more at all in thee; and the light of a candle shall shine no more at all in thee; and the voice of the bridegroom and of the bride shall be heard no more at all in thee: for thy merchants were the great men of the earth; for by thy sorceries were all nations deceived. And in her was found the blood of prophets and of saints, and of all that were slain upon the earth," xviii. 21–24.

The manner in which judgment will come upon Babylon is shown by the angel in chap. xvii. The waters which John had seen, xvii. 1, and upon which the woman sits, are "peoples, and multitudes, and nations, and tongues," xvii. 15, or the manifoldly various nations constituting the Roman empire. The ten horns which he saw, xvii. 3–7, "are ten kings, which have received no kingdom as yet, but receive power as kings one hour with the beast," xvii. 12; that is, the prefects, governors, commanders, and rulers over the various provinces, countries, and peoples of the Roman empire, who, on the appearance of the personal Antichrist, and by their connection with the same, for a short time made themselves independent of Rome, and were raised to sovereign power in a similar manner, only in a smaller measure, as it happened after Nero's fall. These revolutionary sovereigns have but one mind, and give their power and strength unto the beast, xvii. 13. "For God hath put in their hearts to fulfil His will, and to agree, and give their kingdom unto the beast,"—that is, to proclaim Antichrist as emperor, and to subject themselves to him as vassals,—"until the words of God shall be fulfilled," xvii. 17. "The ten horns and the beast shall hate the whore,"—the former, because Rome will not endure their separation and independence; the latter, Nero, because Rome had fallen away from him, and led to his ruin,—"and shall make her desolate and naked, and shall eat her flesh, and burn her with fire," xvii. 16 (comp. xvii. 3, xviii. 2, 6, 8, 18). Thus Antichrist—Nero and his vassals, the angry governors in the Roman empire—will march against Rome, and—as the small example of the Vitellian war, and the greater one of the Neronic conflagration, and the subsequent persecution of the Christians, had to a certain extent given the type—they will, in the most terrible manner, ill-use, plunder, burn, and utterly destroy the imperial city.

How will this destruction of Rome be regarded on earth and in heaven? "The kings of the earth, who have committed fornication, and lived deliciously with her, shall bewail her, and lament for her, when they shall see the smoke of her burning, standing afar off, for the fear of her torment, saying, Alas, alas! that great city Babylon, that mighty city! for in one hour is thy judgment come. And the merchants of the earth shall weep and mourn over her; for no man buyeth their merchandise any more: the merchandise of gold, and silver, and precious stones, and of pearls, and fine linen, and purple, and silk, and scarlet, and all thyine wood, and all manner vessels of ivory, and all manner vessels of most precious wood, and of brass, and iron, and marble, and cinnamon, and odours, and ointments, and frankincense, and wine, and oil, and fine flour, and wheat, and beasts, and sheep, and horses, and chariots, and slaves, and souls of men. And the fruits that thy soul lusted after are departed from thee, and thou shalt find them no more at all. The merchants of these things, which were made rich by her, shall stand afar off for the fear of her torment, weeping and wailing, and saying, Alas, alas! that great city, that was clothed in fine linen, and purple, and scarlet, and decked with gold, and precious stones, and pearls! For in one hour so great riches is come to nought. And every shipmaster, and all the company in ships, and sailors, and as many as trade by sea, stood afar off, and cried, when they saw the smoke of her burning, saying, What city is like unto this great city! And they cast dust on their heads, and cried, weeping and wailing, and saying, Alas, alas! that great city, wherein were made rich all that had ships in the sea by reason of her costliness! for in one hour is she made desolate," xviii. 9–19. So on earth. But in sharp contrast it is said, "Rejoice over her, thou heaven, and ye holy apostles and prophets; for God hath avenged you on her," xviii. 20. "And after these things I heard a great voice of much people in heaven, saying, Alleluia; Salvation, and glory, and honour, and power, unto the Lord our God: for true and righteous are His judgments; for He hath judged the great whore, which did corrupt the earth with her fornication, and hath avenged the blood of His servants at her hand. And again they said, Alleluia. And her smoke rose up for ever and ever," xix. 1–3.

8. The Coming of the Lord.

It is said, "Behold, He cometh with clouds," i. 7 (comp. Matt. xxiv. 30, xxvi. 64). "That which ye have already, hold fast till I come," ii. 25. "Behold, I come quickly," iii. 11, xxii. 7, 22 (comp. Matt. xxiv. 33, 34). "Behold, I come as a thief. Blessed is he that watcheth, and keepeth his garments, lest he walk naked, and they see his shame," xvi. 15 (comp. Matt. xxiv. 42–51; 1 Thess. v. 2; 2 Pet. iii. 10). "The Spirit and the bride say, Come. And let him that heareth say, Come!" xxii. 17. "He which testifieth these things saith, Surely I come quickly: Amen. Even so, come, Lord Jesus," xxii. 20. There needs no proof that in all these places the coming of the Lord in the usual sense of the advent is intended. But in ii. 5, the Lord says to the church of Ephesus, after He has exhorted it to repentance, "else I will come unto thee quickly, and will remove thy candlestick out of his place, except thou repent." To the church in Pergamos He says, "Repent; or else I will come unto thee quickly, and will fight against them"—the adherents of the Nicolaitane error—"with the sword of my mouth," ii. 16. To the church in Sardis, "Remember, therefore, how thou hast received and heard, and hold fast and repent. If, therefore, thou shalt not watch, I will come on thee as a thief, and thou shalt not know what hour I will come upon thee," iii. 3. To the church of the Laodiceans, "Behold, I stand at the door, and knock: if any man hear my voice, and open the door, I will come in to him, and will sup with him, and he with me," iii. 20. We cannot, without doing violence to these passages, interpret them in the sense of Christ's second coming. An unprejudiced comparison of the passages in which the seer speaks of the coming of the Lord (ἔρχεσθαι and ἥκειν), shows that he understood *any personal revelation or energetic self-affirmation of the exalted Christ, as a coming of the Lord;* sometimes it is preliminary, and refers to individual Christian churches, or to members of a church; and sometimes it is final, and relates to all men; at one time it is a manifestation mainly of judicial chastisement, and at another rather of gracious blessing, and only from the connection can it be decided which of these meanings is intended in the particular case. We meet here once more with that peculiarity of our author, which has so often been observed before, namely, that he describes the beginning and the end of an action or state by the same terms, because he regards both as common and equal. On account of this view, every personal energetic interposition of the Lord in the outer or the inner life of the church or the individual is as much a coming of the Lord as His second advent will be; and had there been occasion, he would doubtless have considered Christ's appearance in the world, and the beginning of His public life, as a coming of the Lord, because essentially similar to His second coming.

We are now concerned only with the coming of the Lord in the narrower sense, with His *second advent;* and first, we inquire at *what time* John expected His final appearance. The Gentiles shall tread under foot the holy city forty and two months, xi. 2. The two witnesses shall prophesy 1260 days, xi. 3. The woman is to be nourished in the place prepared for her in the wilderness for the same period, xii. 6; and the same is to happen to her for a time, and times, and half a time, xii. 14. Power is given to the beast to continue forty and two months, xiii. 5. Twelve hundred and sixty days are equal to forty-two months, or to three and a half times, or years; and thus the measure of the time before the end, or until the coming of the Lord, is given. It is figurative time measure; according to the precedent of Daniel (comp. Dan. vii. 26, xii. 7),—equally misunderstood,—the seer describes by these limitations the time before the end, with the enmity of the world increasing to a climax; its persecutions of the devout, ever becoming more insufferable; the divine plagues reaching their most terrible development; the constantly widening publication of the gospel, with a view to repentance, as a troubled respite accurately measured by God, and in its continuance proportionately short. But when expositors—Hengstenberg, for instance—deny to this specification of time all historical meaning, they fail to justify the striking agreement between the historical relations and the symbolic time specifications of the book. The seer would not have written, "Behold, I come as a thief," xvi. 15 (comp. iii. 3), if he had fixed to a day the appearance of the Lord; nor would he have written, "I come quickly," iii. 11, xxii. 7, xii. 20; "which must shortly come to pass," i. 1, xxii. 6 (comp. Dan. viii. 26, xii. 4, iv. 9); "the time is at hand," i. 3, xxii. 10; "the dragon knoweth that he hath but a short time," xii. 12; that the seventh head "must continue a short space," xvii. 10,—if he had expected the end in ten years, or even after thousands. The "speedy" coming of the Lord—undeniable in the face of the doubt and perplexity respecting it which arose at the beginning of the second Christian generation, and which crippled the life of the churches —is the chief occasion of the origin, as well as the chief power in the consolatory aspect of the book. The author is faithful to the eschatological principle expressed in the Synoptists and in the Epistles to the Thessalonians; time and hour, that is, the definite point of time of Christ's coming, is known to God only; but Christians, and especially the prophets, do right, and are in duty bound to observe the signs of the times, and to draw conclusions from them respecting the nearness of the coming of the Lord. Now from these signs John had become certain that He would come *soon*, and had therein found himself justified in explaining the 3½ years, the 42 months, the 1260 days of Daniel, at one time in the sense of 3½ decades, or thereabout, from the ascension of Christ to His second coming, and at another in applying this period in the proper sense to the 3½ years, or near it, of the personal Antichrist, as it were the concentrated 3½ decades of Antichrist in general (comp. xi. 11).

But how will the Lord come? The Apocalypse contains a *threefold representation* of His advent. It is said, "Behold, He cometh with clouds; and every eye shall see Him, and they also which pierced Him: and all kindreds of the earth shall wail because of Him," i. 7. The saying rests upon a union of Dan. vii. 13 and Zech. xii. 10. By the words, "they who have pierced Him," we are not to understand the actual murderers of Christ still living; and we are forbidden to refer them to the Jews, and the "kindreds of the earth" to the Gentiles, as Düsterdieck does, by a double consideration; first, as the absence of a predicate to "they also which pierced Him" shows, it is impossible that they and "the kindreds of the earth" are parallel parts of "every eye;" second, that the only general predicate, "shall see Him," would, by Düsterdieck's exposition, be affirmed of universal man, and then also of the Jews, but the Gentiles shall mourn because of Him. On a closer examination of the passage in Zechariah, the conviction forces itself upon us, that, applied in its original sense to the advent, we can understand by the mourning only a penitent sorrow, and by "they also which pierced Him," and "the kindreds," equally the Jewish people (comp. Acts iii. 11–26); but gradually with the widening of the view beyond Israel into the Gentile world, the subjects of the mourning have become instead of the Jews, unbelievers,—the murderers of Christ, the kindreds of the earth,—and from a penitent mourning ἐπ' αὐτῷ, it has become a fearful mourning ἐπ' αὐτόν (comp. Matt. xxiv. 30). If we thus understand "they also which pierced Him," and "the kindreds," as essentially identical, the supposed contradiction between the statement of i. 7 and other representations of the last things in the Apocalypse falls away, and we have a new confirmation of the fact that the author has throughout amalgamated with his thoughts and descriptions, Old Testament and Jewish Christian expressions and images. Certainly the position of the passage—the author brings forward just at the beginning, in a few strong words, the sum of the whole book (comp. Amos i. 2),—and the use of it,—it consists of a quotation—does not leave us in doubt that John speaks here of the advent in a solemn formula, probably from a writing much read and generally known; it is manifestly to him the Shibboleth of the Christians:—"he cometh" (comp. 1 Cor. xvi. 22) is only the *theme*, the concrete exposition of which is the subject of his prophecy.

The Apocalypse gives *another* representation of the second advent in xiv. 14–20. It is based on Joel iii. 17, 18 and Isa. lxiii. 1–3, and in its first half reminds us of such words as Mark

iv. 26–32; Matt. xiii. 30, 39 (comp. ix. 37, 38). We have shown in the section on the person of Christ, that by Him who sits on the cloud we are to understand Christ Himself; and in the section on heaven, that the altar from which the second angel came, points to the martyrs crying to be avenged, vi. 9, ix. 13, xvi. 7 (comp. viii. 3–5); and in the section on angels, that by the fire over which this angel had power, is meant fire chiefly in its judicial signification, but with an evident allusion to the fire of the altar, to the avenging judgments of God called forth by the prayers of the saints, viii. 3–5. The city outside of which the wine-press is trodden, can be no other than Jerusalem; the distance of 1600 furlongs to which the blood flowed, up to the horse bridles, may be referred to the proximate length of Palestine, as originating in the quaternion, the four corners of the earth. But little as the writer permits the advent actually to appear in xiv. 14–20, just as little does he give us the concrete form in which he expected it. Rather in the harvest as well as in the vintage he brings before us, in a manner suitable to the connection preliminarily and typically, the coming of Christ to judgment in some of its principal features, namely, as harmonizing with the full ripeness of the world, and as beyond measure terrible; and he does it in the parabolic, or, more correctly, in the plastic forms of Old Testament prophetic language, whereby the words, "without the city—even unto the horse bridles," and "a thousand and six hundred furlongs," in their incongruity with the image of the vintage, form the transition to the actual representation of the seer; while, on the other hand, "the wine-press of the fierceness and wrath of Almighty God," xix. 15, in its incongruity with the description there given, points to the earlier and preliminary. Both descriptions in their substantial features are based on prophetic (comp. Isa. lxiii. 1–4), and also, indeed, upon apocalyptic precedent.

Finally, the advent, as John *actually expected* it, is placed before us in the *concrete form* in chap. xix. If we combine the description here given with all preceding indications, we get the following picture. The personal Antichrist having come up from the abyss, the prefects or generals of the empire who had attained independent authority, but who had allied themselves with Antichrist as their head, with united hatred have moved against the imperial city, and devastating, plundering, and burning it, have reduced it to destruction, xvii. 8–10. At the same time (comp. xiii. 2–4), there appears in this the fulfilment, or the last and complete realization, of antichristianity, chap. xiii. Again, as the highest point of this complete realization, John represents, in harmony with Matt. xxiv. 15, 2 Thess. ii. 3–10 (comp. Dan. xi. 31, xii. 12; 1 Macc. i. 54; 2 Macc. vi. 2), thus also in conformity with one of the permanent eschatological features, that Antichrist comes to the holy city which is trodden by the Gentiles, and there slays the two witnesses, and generally fulfils the predictions concerning itself, as far as the then existing locality and circumstances of Jerusalem permit in its last and most awful features, xi. 7–10, chap. xiii., especially vers. 6, 7, 14, 15 (comp. 2 Thess. ii. 4, 9, 10; Matt. xxiv. 11, 24). Immediately after, yet in the last hour, unbelieving Israel in the gross having given glory to God and repented, xi. 13, Antichrist, with his confederates and accomplices, the false prophet (comp. xix. 20) and the authorities of the empire (comp. xvii. 14), as his allies, prepares himself for a final conflict. God has already caused the river Euphrates to be dried up, that the way might be prepared, xvi. 12, for the kings of the East, or the Parthian princes; "out of the mouth of the dragon, and out of the mouth of the beast, and out of the mouth of the false prophet," "three unclean spirits went forth," "unto all the kings of the earth and of the whole world, to gather them to the battle of that great day of God Almighty," xvi. 12–14,—that is, indirectly Satan, directly Antichrist and the false prophet, by their devilish influence have aroused the rulers outside the Roman empire throughout the world who were essentially like-minded with themselves, especially the Parthian princes, who were attached to Antichrist, to the last, destructive conflict. They assembled in "a place called in the Hebrew tongue Armageddon," xvi. 16. Ewald's explanation, Harmagedol, cabbalistic anagram for Roma haggedolah, Roma magna, is wrecked by the form of the reading, as well as by the consideration that "the battle of that great day of God Almighty," xvi. 14, takes place not in Rome, but in Palestine (comp. xii. 7, xiv. 20). It is clear that by this name we are rather to understand Megiddo, which Judg. v. 19, 2 Kings xxiii. 29, 2 Chron. xxxv. 20–24 (comp. Zech. xii. 10, 11), mention as the great battle-field of the Old Testament. But a mere statement of locality cannot be intended, for then it would not be called Armageddon, but Megiddo or Magedon, nor would it be said that the locality was so called in the Hebrew. This addition, as well as the compound name, compels us to notice the verbal meaning, and yet not the etymological meaning of Magedon, which John, on account of its difficulty, would certainly have added in Greek (comp. ix. 11), but only that Armageddon in Hebrew means, hill of Megiddo. It is in the highest degree probable that in this designation the seer refers to Zech. xii. 11, "in the valley of Megiddo,"—valley, symbol of defeat; hill, of victory,—and wishes us to understand that what the heathen once did against Josiah and his people at Megiddo, would now find its counterpart in what they did against Jesus and His followers; but that as once in the valley of Megiddo the theocracy was borne to the grave with Josiah, so in Armageddon, the hill of Megiddo, the Lord would avenge the crime of the heathen. Antichrist, the false prophet, and the antichristian princes of the empire, and the kings of the known world, with their armies, the worshippers of the beast, free and bond, small and great, have assembled, xix. 18–21, on the ancient battle-field of the kingdom of God, which now must have another signification; and against them stand the "called, and chosen, and faithful," the few who have survived all persecutions, and have stedfastly continued to be saints. Then the Lord comes, the heavens open, and upon a horse of brilliant white Jesus appears, who, according to Hoekstra's (p. 382) very good remark, here for the first time acts directly, or presents himself in his proper person, in the exhaustless significance, and in the wholly irresistible revelation of His Messiah-Logos nature, xix. 11–16 (comp. "He who is to come"). "The armies in heaven," the holy angels, xix. 14 (comp. Matt. xvi. 27, xxiv. 30, 31, xxv. 31; 2 Thess. i. 7–10, ii. 8), follow Him clad in garments of shining white byssus, upon horses of the same brilliant colour. When Hoekstra affirms, p. 396, that the "called, and chosen, and faithful," xvii. 14, follow Christ as armies in heaven on white horses, xix. 14, first the subject in these two places is not at all a following in heaven; secondly, the "called, and chosen, and faithful," on account of xx. 4, cannot be conceived as coming on white horses from heaven, but only as opposing the beast and his followers in conflict upon the earth; thirdly, "the armies in heaven," with which Christ comes to the final decision, according to universal biblical usage and standing eschatological representation, do not mean Christians, but the holy angels; nor can the shining white byssus determine otherwise (comp. xix. 8), for the vial angels wear the same, xv. 6. The time has now come when the great prediction of i. 7 is fulfilled, "Behold, He cometh with clouds; and every eye shall see Him, and they also which pierced Him: and all kindreds of the earth shall wail because of Him. Even so, Amen." The beast, and the kings of the earth, and their armies have gathered together to wage war against Him that sat on the horse, and against His army, xix. 19; but what is the issue? "The beast was taken, and with him the false prophet," and were "both cast alive into a lake of fire burning with brimstone," xix. 20 (comp. Num. xvi. 32–34; Isa. v. 14); not being of human nature, they do not suffer an earthly death in order to receive their reward in the judgment of the world; but as hellish or devilish powers in human form, they are judged already, and return condemned to the place whence they came, and to which they belong. But the rest, kings, and captains, and mighty men, horses and riders, free and bond, small and great, xix. 18, worshippers and allies of the beast, the forces of Antichrist, the inhabitants of the earth, are "slain with the sword of Him that sat upon the horse, which sword proceeded out of His mouth," xix. 21 (comp. ver. 15, i. 16),—that is, by the word of His lips (comp. Isa. xi. 4); "and all the fowls," which an angel has already summoned to the great feast, xix. 17 (comp. Ezek. xxxix. 17–20, xxix. 5; Jer. vii. 33; Matt. xxiv. 28), "were filled with their flesh," xix. 21 (comp. ver. 15, xiv. 20).—This representation of the coming of the Lord for the final struggle with His enemies, and of the struggle itself, rests upon a combination of Old Testament descriptions of the judgment, as the conflict and victory of God over the heathen nations assembled against Israel, as, for example, Ezek. xxxix., Zech. xii., Isa. lxiii.; and the expectation of John has clothed itself therein, because it corresponded to the circumstances and relations of his time, and to the course of development which, in his opinion, antichristianity and the divine reaction must take.

9. The Thousand Years' Reign.

John "saw an angel come down from heaven, having the key of the bottomless pit and a great chain in his hand. And he laid hold on the *dragon*, and bound him a thousand years, and *cast him into the bottomless pit*, and shut him up, and set a seal upon him, that he should deceive the nations no more, till the *thousand years* should be fulfilled: and after that he must be loosed a little season." By the conflict of Michael and his angels with the dragon and his angels in heaven, the latter were cast down to the earth; but while the inhabitants of heaven rejoice, there sounds over the earth a woe, because the devil has come down in great wrath, knowing that his time is short, xii. 7–12. We recognise as the meaning of this, that in consequence of the birth and taking away of the promised child, xii. 1–5, or of the appearance, the works, the conflict, the sufferings, and the exaltation of Christ, the power of evil in the ideal reality, and for all living in the same, was overthrown; but since evil feels its defeat to be quickly and unavoidably approaching in the visible or earthly human reality also, it presents in this sphere of existence temptation all the more wicked, and persecution all the more bloody. This short time, with all that it brought with it for antichristendom, on one side the tribulation and patience of the saints, and on the other the persuasive and warning judgments of God, has passed away. The once born and exalted child has now come from heaven in His full Messiah-Logos glory. Antichrist and the false prophet are hurled alive into the lake of fire and brimstone; their accomplices, allies, and adherents, the worshippers of the beast, are destroyed. Now, after the organs of Satan are thus routed, and his kingdom on earth is broken in manifest reality, he himself, the personal absolute ground and originator of all evil, of the God and Christ opposing disposition, is banished from the earth, out of the manifest earthly human reality, into the abyss, the sphere of the sub-earthly, of the anti-ideal and hellish being, and there chained and imprisoned; he can no longer do what from the beginning he has done with such a terrible result, namely, deceive the nations, or the inhabitants of the earth. Christ can now assume His authority in the world, and it may become the kingdom of God and His anointed.

And this will be for a thousand years, xx. 3–6. At this length do eminent Rabbis fix the duration of the Messianic kingdom; and they do so according to a combination of Isa. lxiii. 4 and Ps. xc. 4 (comp. 2 Pet. iii. 8), probably in union with the reasons adduced by Barnabas, that as God in six days created the world, and rested on the seventh, so in six thousand years, as in six world-days, all will be finished, and on the seventh and last thousand, a great world-Sabbath (the Messianic reign) will be celebrated. From the brevity with which the seer treats of this period, it seems to follow that he regarded it as well known, and that it had for him a symbolic value, and signified a long but limited period of time.

After the dragon is cast into the bottomless pit, John sees "thrones, and they sat upon them, *and judgment was given unto them*," xx. 4 (comp. Dan. vii. 9, 10, 22, 27). According to most expositors, the thrones, on account of the passages in Daniel, and the expression "judgment," are not to be considered as those of kings, but only as thrones of judgment, and that the reference here is only to decisions concerning worthiness to share in the thousand years' reign. But then, who are the judges? When God and Christ are excluded by the expression, "judgment was given unto them," one hesitates between the twenty-four elders, the angels, and the apostles. In my opinion, the seer can here have desired to give only either a symbolic intimation that a judgment takes place, so that by "them" no definite persons are intended (comp. Hoekstra, p. 379); or, and I think it is the only correct idea, since the Messianic judgment (comp. xix. 11–21) has been held already, he intends by "them" persons who present themselves in the connection. But what persons besides the saints does the connection represent as surviving the advent? Certainly they cannot sit in judgment on themselves; but has not judgment, in the only pertinent foundation-passage, Dan. vii. 22, the meaning of judging, as the chief power in government? We may compare with this Matt. xix. 28 and 1 Cor. vi. 2, 3. On our view, the following comes here as a suitable conclusion. Finally, in this way only can a great difficulty be removed. When, for instance, some expositors assume that the seer conceives of all Christians as being dead at the advent, they contradict not only the representations of all other New Testament writers, but also those of John himself. The passages i. 7, ii. 25, 26, iii. 11, xvi. 15, xxii. 12, show that, in perfect agreement with 1 Thess. iv. 15–17, 1 Cor. xv. 51, 52, he expected that some Christians would be alive at the coming of Christ. But where, in the view of the thousand years' reign, is there express mention of these survivors, if not in this place? I find therefore here, according to the analogy of i. 7, xi. 2, the solemn expression for the beginning of the authority of the saints who live to see the second advent (comp. Lechler, p. 203, note). That those who sit down upon thrones, and to whom judgment is given, consist only of real saints; that at the advent many who have the name or appearance of such come to shame; indeed, that according to strict recompense the saints, in various degrees, will share in the salvation now to be manifested,—is evident, and follows from the passages referred to above, namely, xvi. 15, "Behold, I come as a thief. Blessed is he that watcheth, and keepeth his garments, lest he walk naked, and they see his shame;" and xxii. 12, "Behold, I come quickly; and my reward is with me, to give every man according as his work shall be" (comp. ii. 23). The contents of this judgment we learn from what follows. The first resurrection presses itself so much into the foreground, that the seer no longer expressly thinks of survivors; but, in the first place, the "judgment" in its real meaning requires that John, like Paul, 1 Cor. xv. 52 (comp. Phil. iii. 21; 1 Thess. iv. 17; also Luke xx. 34–36), must have expected a change of the living; and then the being priests, and the reigning of ver. 6, in comparison with the reigning specially ascribed to the risen in ver. 4, show that in the second half of ver. 5, and still more in ver. 6, the thought has unobserved extended itself from the risen saints to all who share in the thousand years' reign; in other words, that the first resurrection, the blessedness and holiness of those partaking of it, the exaltation above the second death, the being priests and kings, chief features in the self-evident modification of the change, to the seer hold good for the survivors.

In the foreground, however, there is for our author, as also earlier for the Thessalonians, 1 Thess. iv. 13–18, especially ver. 15, and in its position with regard to actual and expected time relations, very intelligibly the question respecting the fate of those Christians who die before the advent. How is it with them? John "saw the souls of them that were beheaded for the witness of Jesus, and for the word of God, and which had not worshipped the beast, neither his image, neither had received his mark upon their foreheads or in their hands; and they lived and reigned (became kings) with Christ a thousand years. But the rest of the dead lived not again until the thousand years were finished. This is the *first resurrection.* Blessed and holy is he that hath part in the first resurrection: on such the second death hath no power; but they shall be priests of God and of Christ, and shall reign with Him a thousand years," xx. 4–6. The seer had in his eye two classes of the dead: first, those who have for the gospel surrendered their lives, the witnesses of Jesus in a special sense, xvii. 6, not only those whose souls, vi. 9, are under the altar, but those also who come after, vi. 11 (comp. xiii. 7, x. 15, xvi. 5, 6, xvii. 6, viii. 24); the full number of those who, according to the will of God, should die; until the completion of which—and therefore until the judgment and avenging wrath of God—those already killed must rest in heaven, vi. 9–11;—then, all other believers who, notwithstanding affliction and threatened death, remain faithful, and have died in the Lord, xiv. 13, xiii. 15, 16; in a word, all real Christians who have died either a violent or a natural death. Hoekstra, p. 392, affirms that the two classes of the privileged are properly only one, the martyrs; the second is particularly mentioned because the writer wishes to give prominence to the then existing persecution, and nothing can be more certain than that, according to the Apocalyse, the privilege of a thousand years' life in glory, prior to the final catastrophe, is awarded to martyrs only, as a recompense for their sacrificed lives. We should agree to this representation if its rejection, as Hoekstra declares, led to the strange conclusion that at the great resurrection day only the condemned will rise. But this is not the case, for to the "rest of the dead" belong, above all, the pious of the Old Testament also. That the second class is not a special one, is not indicated in the least. Not worshipping the beast refers throughout, according to the correct explanation of the beast, not merely to the existing persecution, and is—the exclusion by the author of a Stephen or a James is inconceivable—still again only the concrete form for Christian faithfulness *without* the surrender of life, as the being beheaded for the same is *with* it. While the remaining dead, good and bad, remain dead during the thousand years' reign until the general resurrection, the sleeping saints or Christians live, that is, rise from the dead (comp. Ezek. xxxvii. 1–14), and, indeed, according to i. 5, ii. 8, are thus glorified as Christ, and according to xi. 11, as the two witnesses. This resurrection is called the first, in distinction from the general resurrection of the dead to judgment described in xx. 12, 13. That the seer means by it what Luke xiv. 14 calls "the resurrection of the just" (comp. Luke xx. 35, 36), and what

Paul speaks of as "the resurrection of the dead," Phil. iii. 11 (comp. 1 Thess. iv. 16; 1 Cor. xv. 23), in which is included the change of the living, there can be no doubt. "Blessed and holy is he that hath part in the first resurrection,"—blessed, because, negatively understood, the second death (comp. ii. 11), condemnation, perdition, misery, has no power over them; holy, because, understood positively, they reign with Christ a thousand years; are priests of God and of Christ, and reign with Him; and as the holiness is in various degrees, so is the blessedness (comp. xxii. 12, xvi. 15, ii. 23). Thus, in a word, the entire contents of Christian prophecy, as in detail we have above represented them, will now no longer be tentative, hidden, and suffering from opposition to their manifestation, but a perfected, visible, glorious state, as far as within the limits of the finite it is possible on this earth.

Then is fulfilled that great word: "Behold, I come quickly; and my reward is with me, to give every man according as his work shall be," xxii. 12, the beginning of which points us to the advent and the thousand years' reign, even as the meaning of the other words of reward, xi. 18, point to the judgment of the world and the final state. Both describe the same, but in different degrees or stages, as indeed the judgment of the world and the final state, are in general, the advent and the thousand years' reign in a higher potency; and, as throughout with our author, the higher stages of the development of the kingdom of God, and the Christian life,—like the opposite,—consist only in the intensification of a lower degree. Faithful to the principle of treating the individual features of the promises in the place where the apostle presents them, we refrain from showing how he conceives them *fulfilled in the thousand years' reign;* and since the writer has not mentioned them, we pass over such expressions as "power over the nations," and ruling them "with a rod of iron," ii. 26, 27, which in their meaning belong properly to this place. Nor can even the words, "the marriage of the Lamb is come, and his wife (bride) has made herself ready," xix. 7–9, occupy our attention here, since they have no place in the description of the seer,—although they undeniably point to the advent and the thousand years' reign, preceding them, as it were, like a herald's cry; and although we do not agree with Weiss, *bibl. Theol.* p. 610, in finding it very remarkable that in the earthly completion of the kingdom of Christ the highest union of the church is not realized.

We satisfy ourselves with showing that the contents of the same are to be conceived of as having a temporal fulfilment in the thousand years' reign, that is, the contents of the words: "Alleluia: for the Lord God Omnipotent reigneth. Let us be glad and rejoice, and give honour to Him: for the marriage of the Lamb is come, and His wife hath made herself ready. And to her was granted that she should be arrayed in fine linen, clean and white: for the fine linen is the righteousness of saints. And He saith unto me, Write, Blessed are they which are called unto the marriage supper of the Lamb," xix. 6–9. How the seer represented to himself in detail the *relations, conditions, and activities of the priestly kingdom of Christ and the saints on earth,* he does not inform us. We can only infer from the idea of the priesthood, from xv. 2–4, a description certainly belonging to this connection, and from what follows in xx. 7–9, that He conceived Jerusalem purified and holy, as the local centre, the chief city; the known world, *the orbis terrarum,* as the sphere; the nations which have not taken part in the conflict against the saints, and therefore have not been destroyed in the battle of Armageddon, but have been influenced by the righteous judgments of God, xv. 4, as its inhabitants; Christianity, as the unhindered and blessed power, spreading on every side, penetrating, transfiguring, and glorifying all,—all the heathen will come and worship before the king of nations, xv. 3, 4,—the whole as the fulfilment of all divine promises to Israel and mankind within the limits of finality. He has not finished the picture, because, on the one side, he wished to reserve the Old Testament colours alone available for a higher stage in chap. xxi., and on the other, because it would have carried him beyond the preliminary to the final issue.

But "when the thousand years are expired, Satan shall be loosed out of his prison, and shall go out to deceive the nations which are in the four quarters of the earth, Gog and Magog, to gather them together to battle; the number of whom is as the sand of the sea. And they went up on the breadth of the earth, and compassed the camp of the saints about, and the beloved city: and fire came down from God out of heaven, and devoured them. And the devil that deceived them was cast into the lake of fire and brimstone, where the beast and the false prophet are, and shall be tormented day and night for ever," xx. 7–10. The kingdom of Christ, or of God and the saints, will exist upon the earth for a thousand years; Christianity has a period before it, and indeed a long one, of unimpeded, powerful, and blissful extension and authority in this present world; but this period must one day come to an end: the earth in its present sin-ruined form, or rather state, cannot become the eternal or absolute state, form, or manifestation of the Christian ideal world. Evil, though so long and so extensively kept in abeyance, will once more arouse itself for the struggle with the kingdom of God. After the course of a thousand years, the personal principle of all ungodliness will be loosed from his prison, and, according to the purpose of God, will again become active on the earth; the devil has still a footing there; evil yet exists, and must show its activity in opposition to God and His kingdom. Christianity has spread and triumphed even to the end of the earth; but there are yet heathens who are not subject to it, but who, enslaved and led by the devil, seek to destroy it. Gog and Magog, Ezek. xxxviii. and xxxix., the former the king, the latter the people, but in rabbinical theology the allied nations, the heathen peoples on the border of the earth, or in the extreme north, the heathen nations opposed to the kingdom of God, under apocalyptic names and apocalyptic images, assemble in numberless hosts on the plain of the earth, and surround the beloved city, — without doubt Jerusalem, having now become the holy central point of the kingdom of God, — and the saints who have encamped around it. But, according to the type, Ezek. xxxix. 6, fire falls from God out of heaven, in which, as Hoekstra, p. 381, justly observes, God Himself appears for the first time as acting directly upon the aggressors and consumes them; God interposes with the fullest manifestation of His wrath, and the last rising of evil upon the earth finds a deservedly terrible defeat. Satan will not again be cast into the prison of the bottomless pit, but into the lake of fire and brimstone, whither his two representatives, after they had filled up their measure, preceded him, for now Satan's time also is run out. Evil has realized its last possibility, and has been overcome; there is therefore nothing more for him to do on earth, and he goes into his proper state, namely, that of everlasting perdition.

Ewald, *ut ante*, p. 324, correctly remarks of the millennium, that this hope, in the definite form in which he sees it, did not originate with the seer; perceptibly it appears with him as an *already given*, stedfast, and almost matter of course expectation, while it is nevertheless peculiar, and of the highest importance, and could not, as it were, by the way, thus penetrate the whole circle of such hopes. Only we must go a step further, and entirely give up the view that the seer started from the expectation of the final end described in chap. xxi.; but, as Ewald says, there came to him the representation of a thousand years preceding the ultimate state of blessedness, which would be more glorious and happy than the present, but still not the time of the full end, and that the application to his own circle of the new views and hopes of this thousand years became to him a grand interval, when an earthly kingdom of Christ would reign, at least within the wide sphere of the Roman empire and upon its ruins, the reformed earthly Jerusalem being its central point, where thus, under the strong protection of Christ, now restored to His people, the kingdom of the glorified would begin in a narrower compass, and as the prelude of the universal and eternal glory. Moreover, everything favours the idea that our author proceeded from the expectation of the millennium as the ultimate point of hope, and it was therefore to him originally far richer in contents. As observed above, he has treated it with remarkable brevity, because, on the one hand, he desired to spare the only colours remaining to him for the higher state which was to follow; and still more, on the other, because it would have carried him beyond what was preliminary, to the goal itself. But would he have so spared those colours, and would it have thus driven him forward, if really "the representation of the thousand years' reign of Christ in Jerusalem, with the undestroyed temple as the chief point, formed the centre of gravity to the whole Apocalypse" (Weizsäcker, p. 237), if the earthly kingdom of Christ had not been to the seer much rather an essential and indispensable element of the eschatology, the contents of which were to pass over almost entirely into the heavenly state? Only on this supposition can the brevity and fragmentary character, the enigmatic and almost absolute poverty, of distinctive features in the description of the millennium be explained; only thus can we see why, for example, at xi. 18 it is not expressly introduced; only thus can the expression, sounding so decidedly Jewish, "with Christ," xx. 4, and, above all, the feature of non-citizens in the final state, xxi. 24–26, be cleared up.

Had the seer, starting from the idea of that state, conceived the thousand years' reign not merely as received, but also as essentially the pattern of his hopes, the representation of the same would have been far richer in colour and in detail. We can with less difficulty show the chiliasm of our book to be an exceedingly important idea, if we find independently predicted in it, or at least foreboded, "the Christian time," or "the national church." But it is certainly more correct to say the idea of an earthly kingdom of Christ, originally inherited by the seer, is for us a highly important one; but for himself this idea, on account of that appropriated later, of an absolute final state, is thrown so much into the background, that it might be entirely left out without creating any great blank in his system. His hopes properly rest not upon this earth, nor in the condition of Christ's kingdom, but on the absolute realization of the ideal world.

10. The Judgment of the World.

At the opening of the sixth seal, men "hid themselves in the dens, and in the rocks of the mountains (comp. Isa. ii. 19); and said to the mountains and rocks, Fall on us, and hide us from the face of Him that sitteth on the throne, and from the wrath of the Lamb: for *the great day* of His wrath is come; and who shall be able to stand?" vi. 15, 16 (comp. Mal. iii. 2). On the sounding of the seventh trumpet, the elders in heaven said, "We give Thee thanks, O Lord God Almighty, which art, and wast, and art to come; because Thou hast taken to Thyself Thy great power, and hast reigned. And the nations were angry, and Thy wrath is come, and the time of the dead, that they should be judged, and that Thou shouldest give reward unto Thy servants the prophets, and to the saints, and to them that fear Thy name, small and great; and shouldest destroy them which destroy the earth," xi. 17, 18. After the pouring out of the sixth vial, "three unclean spirits go forth unto the kings of the earth, and of the whole world, to gather them to the battle of that great day of God Almighty," xvi. 14. Of these three passages, the third is connected with the contents of chap. xix. as certainly as the second is with xx. 7–11 or with vers. 12–15. The connection of the first admits of doubt, as the ruin described on the opening of the sixth seal may be understood in a politico-social as well as in a cosmic sense. The great day of wrath (comp. Isa. xiii. 13; Ezek. vii. 19; Zeph. i. 15; Rom. ii. 5, 6), that great day of God (comp. Jer. xxx. 7; Joel ii. 11, iii. 4; Zeph. i. 14; Mal. iii. 2; Acts ii. 20; Jude 6), means with our author, as with other Old and New Testament writers, the *final catastrophe* in which God will fulfil to the world His threatenings and promises in manifest reality (comp. xi. 19). Since, therefore, this final catastrophe in the view of the seer occurs preliminarily at the advent, and fully at the judgment, he can use the names of the great day for the preliminary as well as for the full realization; and we have therein a new example of the peculiarity of the writer, who in his descriptions combines commencement and completion. It would be a mistake to distribute the advent and the judgment to the beginning and the end of the great day: to the author they are the same in different degrees. It would be a mistake also to represent the first degree as preponderating with him; for, as xi. 17, 18 and the parallel of the millennium show, the representation of the seer lives more in the second—in the final and the absolute. A discrepancy, as Weiss, *bibl. Theol.* p. 608, imagines it, when he says that in an earlier vision the eternal kingdom of God and His Anointed, xi. 15, appears directly after the conversion of Israel, xi. 13, at the close of the great tribulation, xi. 2 (comp. xiii. 5); but that here, on the contrary, the kingdom of the Messiah separates itself from the perfected kingdom of God. But such a discrepancy, in view of the unity everywhere else perceptible in the thoughts of the seer, we cannot admit.

"And I saw a great white throne, and Him that sat on it, from whose face the earth and the heaven fled away; and there was found no place for them," xx. 11. The distinction of "the great white throne" from the "thrones" of ver. 4, as well as its agreement with xxi. 5, and still more, the constant description of God as "He who sits on the throne," compels us to regard the above passage as referring to God, but not to God in distinction from Christ. According to the Christology of the seer, it is *à priori* wholly inconceivable that he has represented Christ as having no share in the judgment. To this add that, according to iii. 21, He sits with His Father on His throne; that vi. 16 places together "the face of Him that sitteth on the throne" and "the wrath of the Lamb;" that directly before the announcement of the judgment of the world, xi. 15–18, it is said, ver. 15, "the kingdoms of this world have become the kingdoms of our God and of His Christ, and He shall reign for ever and ever;" that the book of life, upon the statements of which here, ver. 15, depends eternal damnation, is called "the book of life of the Lamb slain," xiii. 8; and that Christ promises to him who overcometh, that He will not blot out his name out of the book of life, but will confess his name before His Father and before His angels; that, according to xiv. 10, where death and hades are cast, vers. 14, 15, with all who are not written in the book of life, the worshippers of the beast shall be tormented with fire and brimstone in the presence of the holy angels and in the presence of the Lamb; and there then can be no doubt that, according to the representation of the author, and, indeed, according to the whole Christology of the book, as well as the indications of iii. 5 and xiv. 10, Christ is to be thought of as concerned in the judgment as its executor, or, more correctly, its *mediator*. But why is not the Lamb expressly mentioned here, with Him who sits on the throne, as well as in vi. 16? According to the author's representation of the judgment (comp. iii. 5, xiv. 10), Christ's place is not in xx. 11, but in the verse following; and that He is not expressly mentioned and personally introduced, admits of easy explanation, since, on the one hand, from its peculiar brevity or sketchiness, similar to that of the scene which immediately precedes, and also, on the other hand, similar to the obvious conditions of the description of the thousand years' reign, other things thrust themselves into the foreground. As there the change of the living, so here the activity of Christ in the judgment was self-evident; as there the first resurrection predominated, so here the general resurrection and the fate of those who rise. Possibly also it may have been for the sake of *formal* distinction; as at the advent Christ only is mentioned, so at the judgment God only.

What is the first exercise of the great wrath of Him who sits on the great white throne? At the opening of the sixth seal "there was a great earthquake; and the sun became black as sackcloth of hair, and the moon became as blood; and the stars of heaven fell unto the earth, even as the fig-tree casteth her untimely figs, when she is shaken of a mighty wind: and the heaven departed as a scroll when it is rolled together; and every mountain and island were moved out of their places," vi. 12, 14; so that all men believed that the great day of His wrath had come, vi.

15, 16: as at the pouring out of the seventh vial "there came a great voice out of the temple of heaven, from the throne, saying, It is done. And there were voices, and thunders, and lightnings; and there was a great earthquake, such as was not since men were upon the earth, so mighty an earthquake, and so great. And the great city was divided into three parts, and the cities of the nations fell: and great Babylon came in remembrance before God, to give unto her the cup of the wine of the fierceness of His wrath. And every island fled away, and the mountains were not found. And there fell upon men a great hail out of heaven, every stone about the weight of a talent," xvi. 17–21; and now these premonitions find their fulfilment in that earth and heaven flee away before the face, from the wrath, of Him who sits on the throne; and there is found no place for them, in other words, in the *destruction* of the whole *present* visible *world.* That we need not understand by heaven here the invisible ideal world, wants only the proof lying in xxi. 2–10 (see the section on heaven). Evidently the world passes away before the anger of God, because it has become the place or kingdom of evil, and is disfigured by sin, and therefore falls beneath the divine judgments. The seer does not give us a description of the destruction of the world. To conclude from the precedents in chap. vi. and xvi., he would represent it almost as it is in 2 Pet. iii. 7-10 (comp. Ps. cii. 27; Isa. li. 6 · Heb. i. 11; Matt. xxiv. 35).

Judgment is executed on the world universally, but it is executed on every individual, and that in two periods,—first, in the *general resurrection,* which the seer himself introduces only as supplementary: "And the sea gave up the dead which were in it; and death and hell delivered up the dead which were in them," xx. 13. That by "death and hell" we are to understand the grave-world on or rather under the earth; and by "the sea," the great watery grave; by the "sea, death, and hell," the universal hidden region of the dead,—has been shown in the section on the earth and its inhabitants. This universal unseen region gives up its contents—its prey, its citizens. But who awakes them? It can be no other than He who, according to i. 18, has the keys of death and hell,—namely, Christ. It is self-evident, moreover, that in this general resurrection the saints have no share, inasmuch as they had part in the first resurrection, and the change at the advent of Christ. Those who rise now are the rest of the dead, who, according to the express statement of xx. 5, live not again until the thousand years are finished.

"And I saw the dead, small and great, stand before God: and the books were opened; and another book was opened, which is the book of life: and the dead were *judged* out of those things which were written in the books, according to their works," xx. 12; "And they were judged every man according to their works," ver. 13; "And death and hell were cast into the lake of fire. This is the second death. And whosoever was not found written in the book of life was cast into the lake of fire," vers. 14, 15. The great declaration of xi. 18 is now fulfilled. When Baur, *ut ante*, p. 208, says, "those who are counted worthy of the first resurrection probably do not come into the judgment of the world," it is so, as he understands coming into judgment. When, on this occasion, the book of life is opened, the saints collectively (comp. xi. 18) are interested in it; but since, by the first resurrection, they are already recognised as registered in the book of life, they are not now judged according to their works; for them the general judgment can be nothing else than the declaration of what they are, the solemn confirmation of what was assured to them by their sharing in the thousand years' reign (comp. xx. 6), Christ's acknowledgment of them as His before His Father, and before the holy angels, iii. 5, the distribution of reward in the highest degree, the completion of that which came to them at the advent (comp. xxii. 12, xi. 18). On the other hand, all the rest of the men, without distinction or exception, are judged according to their works; with respect to which, against Köstlin, who says, *ut ante*, p. 491, "works are what save the righteous in the day of judgment," we refer to the section on the saints and their works. That the books in which the works of every one are written, debt and credit, according to the contents or balance of which every one is judged, are to be, in an inner relation, classed with the book of life, is, as Düsterdieck remarks, *in loco*, perfectly true; but we have already shown, in the section on God, how this inner relation is not so intended that it is according to the works which are written in the books that their names are found in the book of life or not, but so that after the account of each is shown in the book of reckoning, his name is referred to in the book of life; and, indeed, according as the name stands there or not, it is represented how God's eternal predestination or gracious purposes (comp. xiii. 8) has found realization or fulfilment in the works, how the elect are also the justified, and the non-elect are also the rejected; or as Weiss, *bibl. Theol.* p. 610, expresses it, the definite sentence only affirms what has long been fixed in the purpose of God. All those whose names are not written in the book of life, —the case absolutely as seen by God and from eternity,—all those whose works are evil, the same relatively considered from a human and historical standpoint, will now manifestly, as the rejected of God, receive their merited doom; they will be cast into the lake of fire. Thither death and hades—in this place, ver. 14, not to be understood (comp. the abyss), as directly before, ver. 3, locally, but potentially—have preceded them; death is not simply destroyed, but as a devilish power, the auxiliary or instrument of the evil one (comp. Heb. ii. 14, 15), it is abolished for ever, made innocuous, condemned, and annihilated (comp. 1 Cor. xv. 26). What comes to all those whose names are written in the book of life, and what sort of reward they receive for their works, will be shown in the next section. The mistake, for example, of Hengstenberg, as if in the judgment of the world only the condemned appear, needs, indeed, no refutation;—or did the seer think of Moses and the servants of God, the prophets, as appointed to the lake which burneth with fire and brimstone?

11. The New Heaven and the New Earth.

The religious ideas of the seer do not flow into a restoration, but into an *absolute dualism.* With the judgment of the world, the struggle between God and the devil, heaven and hell, the ideal and anti-ideal, is finally decided, and for ever closed. God, heaven, and the ideal, have obtained the victory. The devil, hell, and the anti-ideal, have been defeated. But the devil is not changed, hell is not purified, the anti-ideal is not idealized, nor are they destroyed in the sense of ceasing to exist; but from the final decision they continue eternally without any intervening medium, like earth and heaven, in their present position, in absolute contrast with each other: here, the lake of fire and brimstone; there, the new heaven and the new earth. Heaven and hell are now in visible reality what they were in the hidden reality, or in their ideal, and they have now really what, according to their nature, always belonged either to one or the other.

"This," the lake of fire, "is the *second death*," xx. 14. The second death, a rabbinical phrase, relates to death in a similar manner as the first resurrection, xx. 6, relates to the resurrection of the dead; the first resurrection, the resurrection in the higher sense, is the coming of the saints to the eternal life, which is never lost, xx. 6; the second death, the intensified death, is the coming of sinners to the eternal death, from which there is no resurrection, or to perdition (comp. xvii. 8, 11), which consists not in the "destruction of the wicked," but in the definite loss of happiness, in eternally restless pangs, and perpetual consciousness of consummated death. The beast and the false prophet, their time having expired, are thrown into the lake of fire and brimstone at the coming of Christ, xix. 20; then, after the suppression of the last outbreak of Antichrist, the course of the devil having been run, he is cast in also, xx. 10; in like manner death and hades, after the destruction of this world and the resurrection of all the dead, are assigned to the same place, xx. 14; so also, after they have been judged, are all those who are not written in the book of life, xx. 15; and there, too, must we look for Babylon in her doom, xix. 2, 3. The devil, the beast, and the false prophet, will be tormented there for ever and ever, xx. 10. "If any man worship the beast and his image, and receive his mark in his forehead, or in his hand, the same shall drink of the wine of the wrath of God, which is poured out without mixture into the cup of his indignation; and he shall be tormented with fire and brimstone in the presence of the holy angels, and in the presence of the Lamb: and the smoke of their torment ascendeth up (comp. Isa. xxxiv. 10) for ever and ever: and they have no rest day nor night, who worship the beast and his image, and whosoever receiveth the mark of his name," xiv. 9–11. "The fearful, and unbelieving, and the abominable, and murderers, and whoremongers, and sorcerers, and idolaters, and all liars, shall have their part in the lake which burneth with fire and brimstone: which is the second death," xxi. 8 (comp. ver. 27, xxii. 3, 15). "They said, Alleluia. And her (Babylon) smoke rose up for ever and ever," xix. 3.

But decidedly as the author holds an eternal damnation, and strong as the colours are in which he represents it in his threatenings, he does not place it before us in a special vision as he does its opposite, and that evidently with the highest flight of his plastic poetic power, and with the application of all the gifts at his command.

"And I saw," he begins, "a new heaven and a new earth: for the first heaven and the first earth were passed away; and there was no more sea," xxi. 1. Here the seer had before him Isa. lxv. 17 (comp. lxvi. 22, liv. 9). He probably held (comp. xx. 11, the face), in harmony with Jewish opinions, which meet us also in 2 Pet. iii. 5, x. 12, 13 (comp. 1 Cor. iii. 13), that as the first world came forth from water, it would be destroyed by fire, and the *new world* be formed by the same element. Possibly, on account of the origination of the new world by fire, he conceived of it as being without sea; or thinking of the sea as the birthplace of the old world, he regarded it as ceasing with it; possibly also the absence of the sea in the new, is only to place it in contrast with the old world; but most probably, by leaving out the sea, he simply wishes to express the new in the fuller sense of the word, the ideal, or the perfection of the new world, inasmuch as—on account of its dangers, and the many deaths in it (comp. xx. 13), but chiefly because of its being repugnant to all the ancients—he regarded the sea as an unpleasant feature, and a prominent imperfection of the present state. Moreover, he did not intend the common Jewish representation, that the new world will be new in substance, but that it will be renewed, refined, transfigured, new in the sense of the ideal, and will be related to the old as gold which has passed through the purifying fire is to the unrefined ore. When Baur, *ut ante*, p. 209, declares it to be undeniable that the apocalyptic kingdom of Christ is much below the moral idea of the kingdom of heaven presented by Jesus, because the seer not only teaches chiliastically an earthly kingdom of Christ, but also that the condition of perfection and blessedness following this kingdom will be that of an earthly heaven, and that in the view of the Apocalypse it can only be realized on the material foundation of the final though transfigured earth, not only does the supposed difference between the heavenly kingdom of Jesus and that of the seer, but also Baur's entire conception of the apocalyptic final state, rest upon a gross misunderstanding, only to be explained by a prejudiced judgment. While the old heaven and the old earth were the visible, fluctuating, or contested reality, lying between the ideal and the anti-ideal, the new heaven and the new earth are the ideal reality made visible, or heaven manifested. As the ideas, prototypes, the souls or spirits of all past, present, and future, personal and impersonal sanctities, sublimities, and glories on earth or in this world, or in the first heaven and the first earth, existed in heaven in ideal but hidden reality; and as, on the other hand, all this was in the first world, in manifest but unideal reality; so in the new heaven and on the new earth all this is no more in a visible but ideally inadequate manner as in the first world, nor in a really ideal but hidden manner as in heaven, but in manifest ideal reality. The first has gone, and He who sits upon the throne says, "Behold, I make all things new," xx. 4, 5; and the renewal reaches to everything that can become ideal, because it has an idea: to all which has been in this world, and has had its ideal in heaven. We may compare Rom. viii. 18–21; 2 Pet. iii. 13.

It is therefore an error to identify the new heaven and the new earth with the New Jerusalem, for thereby the understanding of xxi. 24–27 is beforehand rendered impossible. The New Jerusalem is ever only a part of the new world, though according to its meaning as well as in its representation it almost entirely occupies the foreground. It means the people of God, the multitude of the saints, the church, the kingdom of God, in the stricter sense of its completion (comp. Heb. xi. 10, xii. 22, xiii. 14; Gal. iv. 26). For its description two representations offer themselves to the writer, in like manner as Babylon and the great whore present themselves for the description of the church of Satan, namely, a *personal* and a *general* one. The former, resting upon such Old Testament passages as Isa. liv. 1–3, Hos. ii. 19, 20, Ezek. xvi. 7–14, and especially upon Solomon's Song, regards the Messiah as the bridegroom, and the church as the *bride;* the final consummation is the time of the marriage, as an image of the close and indissoluble union between the Lord and the church; the happiness of the heavenly state appears under the image of a marriage feast; and the saints are those who are called to it, the marriage guests. This representation, like those of the coming of the Lord, the harvest, and the vintage, have been used by John before. After judgment has come upon Babylon, he "heard as it were the voice of a great multitude, and as the voice of many waters, and as the voice of mighty thunderings, saying: Alleluia: for the Lord God omnipotent reigneth. Let us be glad and rejoice, and give honour to Him: for the marriage of the

Lamb is come, and His wife hath made herself ready. And to her was granted that she should be arrayed in fine linen, clean and white: for the fine linen is the righteousness of saints. And He said unto me, Write, Blessed are they which are called unto the marriage supper of the Lamb," xix. 6–9. In the proper representation of the heavenly state, this personal description appears at xxi. 2, where John sees the New Jerusalem come down out of heaven prepared as a bride adorned for her husband; and at xxi. 9, 10, where, in significant contrast with the vision of the great whore, xvii. 1, 2, one of the vial angels says to the seer, "Come hither; I will show thee the bride, the Lamb's wife," and then points out to him the New Jerusalem; and at the close of the book the same image meets us once more in the words: "the Spirit and the bride say, Come."

For this description of the people of God in their perfection, John has used, in its rabbinical interpretation, the general picture of the *New Jerusalem* offered to him in the Old Testament. In the letter to the church at Philadelphia, the Lord said: "Him that overcometh I will make a pillar in the temple of my God, and he shall go no more out: and I will write upon him the name of my God, and the name of the city of my God, which is New Jerusalem, which cometh down out of heaven from my God; and I will write upon him my new name," iii. 12. Now in the new world John sees "the holy city, New Jerusalem, coming down from God out of heaven, prepared as a bride adorned for her husband," xxi. 2; and, for the sake of a closer description, it is said, "there came unto me one of the seven angels which had the seven vials full of the seven last plagues, and talked with me, saying, Come hither; I will show thee the bride, the Lamb's wife;" and he led the seer to a great and high mountain (comp. xvii. 3), and showed him Jerusalem, the holy city, descending out of heaven from God, xxi. 9, 10 (comp. xxii. 19).

In keeping with this general representation, John next depicts the perfect state of the church by a description of the New Jerusalem in its *architecture*, after the type of Ezek. xlviii. 30–35. From the great and high mountain to which the angel had led him (comp. Ezek. xl. 2; Rev. xvii. 3), John saw the holy city descend—become realized in visible ideality—out of heaven—the invisible ideal world—from God, with whom the ideal world exists, or with whom in an "ideal manner the final consummation is already prepared long before it is realized at the end of time" (Weiss, *bibl. Theol.* p. 610). "The city lieth four-square, and the length is as large as the breadth;" the ground-plan forms a quadrate (comp. Ezek. xlviii. 16); "the length, and the breadth, and the height are equal;" and the whole is a cube, like the Holy of Holies in the Mosaic sanctuary (comp. Ex. xxvi., xxvii.). And this cube is wonderful in size, for the angel that talked with the seer "had a golden rod to measure the city, and the gates thereof, and the wall thereof," xxi. 15 (comp. Ezek. xl. 3, 5–16); and, according to the measuring of the angel, the extent of the city is 12,000 furlongs in length, and breadth, and height, xxi. 16. The square, the quadrate, the cube, are all symbols of the complete, the perfect, and the universal (comp. Isa. xliii. 3–6); and the specially large proportions point to the remarkably large number of the complete church of God. The material of the city is of "pure gold, like unto clear glass," that is, of pure transparent gold, xxi. 18; the streets of the city consist of the same,—"pure gold, as it were transparent glass," xxi. 21. Around the city is "a wall great and high," xxi. 12; the height of the wall is "an hundred and forty and four cubits, according to the measure of a man, that is, of the angel," xxi. 17. According to Düsterdieck, the relative lowness of the wall is indicative of the security of the city (comp. Isa. liv. 14); and very justly do we see in the size of the city, and the height of the walls, so prominently expressed, a symbol of its safety from every danger. In these walls are twelve gates (comp. Ezek. xlviii. 30–35), three towards each quarter of the heavens, xxi. 12, 13; each gate consists of a single pearl, xxi. 21; and there stand at them twelve angels, as ideal gatekeepers, symbols of divine protection, after Isa. lxii. 6; and the names of the twelve tribes of Israel, that is, of the people of God, are written thereon, xxi. 12 (comp. Ezek. xlviii. 31–35). The twelve gates are for the entrance of the chosen; and their direction toward the four quarters of heaven points to the universal character of the New Jerusalem (comp. Isa. xliii. 3, 4). These walls have twelve foundations, that is, the sections of the walls between the twelve gates are borne by one stone, xxi. 14; and these foundations are "garnished with all manner of precious stones" (comp. Isa. liv. 11, 12), jasper, sapphire, chalcedony, emerald, sardonyx, sardius, chrysolite, beryl, topaz, chrysoprasus, jacinth, and amethyst, xxi. 19, 20 (comp. the stones in the high priest's breastplate, Ex. xxviii. 17–20); and upon them are "the names of the twelve apostles of the Lamb," xxi. 14 (comp. Matt. xvi. 18; Eph. ii. 20–22). "The building of the wall," that is, the superstructure raised upon the foundations, consists of jasper, xxi. 18 (comp. 1 Cor. iii. 10–15). The New Jerusalem is therefore, in extent and amplitude, in beauty of material and form, indeed in every respect, a perfect building; and this perfect building is the image of the final state of the church, as a perfect one, whether considered in its universal importance, in the number of its members, in its inviolability and peace, or in its magnificence and glory.

In harmony with the general representation of the final state, John further exhibits it by a description of the *conditions in the New Jerusalem.* And he does so in a threefold manner. As he saw the New Jerusalem descend, "he heard a great voice out of heaven, saying, Behold, the tabernacle of God is with men, and He will dwell with them, and they shall be His people, and God Himself shall be with them, and be their God. And God shall wipe away all tears from their eyes; and there shall be no more death, neither sorrow, nor crying, neither shall there be any more pain: for the former things are passed away. And He that sat upon the throne said, Behold, I make all things new. And He said unto me, Write: for these words are true and faithful. And He said unto me, It is done. I am Alpha and Omega, the beginning and the end: I will give unto him that is athirst of the fountain of the water of life freely. He that overcometh shall inherit all things; and I will be his God, and he shall be my son," xxi. 3–7. In the final state, those great promises in Lev. xxvi. 11, 12, Ezek. xxxvii. 27, Jer. xxiv. 7, xxx. 22, xxxi. 33 (comp. 2 Cor. vi. 16; Heb. viii. 10), are fulfilled. That God Himself dwells with men is not symbolic, as in the Old Testament, but in nature and disposition He is really and directly near, joined and present with them—"men," the people of God; "God," the God of men; indeed, those great words of 2 Sam. vii. 14 are also fulfilled, and God stands to them individually in the relation of Father, and they stand to Him in the relation of sons. When Hoekstra says, p. 371, "God is never called the Father of men, not even where the opposite, sons or children of God, seems to demand it, xxi. 7; manifestly the writer uses the word son here because the collective people has no singular form to express the individual, and sonship denotes belonging to the people of God," it is admitted that the individuals of the people of God are called servants of God; thus, when God says, "I will be his God, and he shall be my son," and not "he shall be my servant," it is clear that the seer limits the parental name of God to Christ, but considers the relation of Christians to God in its fulfilment not as a servile, but as a filial one; and, on the contrary, precisely on account of the Old Testament prophecy, he would not use for the people of God the names "family" or "house," corresponding to its realization. Then is fulfilled also the prediction of Isa. xxv. 8, lxv. 19; with the first earth, all suffering connected with it, and even death itself, pass away; it is a new and blessed state, corresponding to the new earth. In the closer description of the New Jerusalem, John sees "the glory of God: and her light was like unto a stone most precious, even like a jasper-stone, clear as crystal," xxi. 11. He sees "no temple therein: for the Lord God Almighty and the Lamb are the temple of it. And the city had no need of the sun, neither of the moon, to shine in it; for the glory of God did lighten it, and the Lamb is the light thereof," xxi. 22, 23. It is said "there shall be no night there; and they need no candle, neither light of the sun: for the Lord giveth them light," xxii. 5. But the glory of God is the revelation of His nature as light, and so in the New Jerusalem the prediction of Isa. lx. 19, 20 is fulfilled also; instead of earthly light as a symbol, instead of the sun and the moon as emblematical bearers of the divine light, there is in the heavenly state "the glory of God," and by it the noblest of all light; the glory of God so shines that there is "no more night;" and the light thereof, that is, the light-bearer, mediator, revealer of the divine glory, is the Logos-Messiah. The angel shows to the seer "a pure river of water of life, clear as crystal, proceeding out of the throne of God and the Lamb. In the midst of the street of it, and on either side of the river, was there the tree of life, which bare twelve manner of fruits, and yielded her fruit every month: and the leaves of the tree were for the healing of the nations. And there shall be no more curse: but the throne of God and of the Lamb shall be in it; and His servants shall serve Him: and they shall see His face; and His name shall be in their foreheads . . . and they shall reign for ever and ever," xxii. 1–5. Thus that great prophecy of Ezek. xlvii.

1–12, concerning a stream of living water and healing trees, is fulfilled; also that of Zech. xiv. 11, that no one shall again fall under the destroying curse of the Lord: therefore there is in it the throne of God and of the Lamb; that is, God, relatively Christ, is in the absolute fulness of His being active there. "His servants shall serve Him," that is, their entire activity is a priestly service; "they shall see His face," in other words, they shall enjoy immediately His bliss-giving presence and absolute self-revelation (comp. Matt. v. 8); "His name shall be in their foreheads," they are manifestly His; "they shall reign for ever and ever;" that is, as in their relation to God, so they are in their relation to men and things, the absolute and eternal fulfilment of the prediction of the royal priesthood of Israel, Ex. xix. 5, 6.

If we look at the entire description of the final state in its *relation to the promises* to Christians *on earth, in heaven, or in the thousand years' reign*, we shall find that confirmed which was said in the section on the saints and their works, namely, that the promises in this book are for all stages essentially the same, and that, evidently for the sake of avoiding uniformity, here one, and there another phase, is brought into prominence, and that similar promises made to various stages undergo a corresponding modification in their meaning. What the perfected are, God's peculiar people, priestly kings to God out of all nations, they were from the moment of becoming Christians (comp. i. 6, v. 9, 10); the worship of the heavenly state they already celebrated on earth (comp. v. 8),—even there they were immoveable pillars in the temple of God, and bore the name of God, of the New Jerusalem, and of Christ (comp. iii. 12); already as victors they ate of the tree of life (comp. ii. 7); they had the crown of life, and could not be hurt of the second death (comp. ii. 10, 11); they had power over the nations (comp. ii. 26); their names were in the book of life (comp. iii. 5); they sat with Christ on His throne (comp. iii. 21), and as victors inherited all the promises. As in the New Jerusalem, so also they stood already in heaven before the throne and before the Lamb (comp. vii. 9–15); as here, so there they serve God day and night in His temple (comp. vii. 15); as here God dwells with them, and beams upon them, so there He does also (comp. vii. 15); as here all suffering passed away, so there also hunger and thirst, and burning heat, ceases for them (comp. vii. 16); as here, so God has already there wiped away all tears from their eyes (comp. vii. 17); as here the river of the water of life flows for them, and God gives freely to the thirsty of the living fountains of waters, so the Lamb leads them there to the same (comp. vii. 17); as here there is no more curse, so already the 144,000 virgins were without guile or fault (comp. xiv. 4, 5). In the thousand years' reign the perfected were already priests of God and Christ, and reigned with Him, and the second death had no power over them (comp. xx. 6). And is not the church below already the bride of the Lamb (comp. xxii. 17)? does she not already appear on earth as the true Israel (comp. vii. 4–8)? There is hardly a feature in the description of the final blessedness which has not been recognised by us before, with the obvious exception of those which are conditioned by the peculiarity of the stage itself. All that the saints and people of God were and had on earth, in ideal hidden reality, in process, and amidst suffering,—what they were and had in heaven, in similar reality realized and free from suffering, and what they were and had in visible ideal reality, in finite relations during the thousand years' reign, they are and have in the final state of blessedness, in visible reality, absolutely, eternally, and perfectly.

But is the share in this blessed state *equal for all*, or is it *various?* and if so, in what manner? It is said, "The nations (ἔθνη) of them which are saved shall walk in the light of it: and the kings of the earth do bring their glory and honour into it. And the gates of it shall not be shut at all by day; for there shall be no night there. And they shall bring the glory and the honour of the nations into it. And there shall in no wise enter into it anything that defileth, neither whatsoever worketh abomination or maketh a lie; but they which are written in the Lamb's book of life," xxi. 24–27 (comp. Isa. lx. 3–14; Ps. lxviii. 30, lxxii. 10, 15). The meaning of this passage is disputed. Some expositors understand the ἔθνη to be the heathen. But while Messner, *bibl. Theol.* p. 375 (comp. Hofmann, *ut ante*, II. 2, p. 660), finds indicated the susceptibility of the heathen to conversion in that state, Köstlin sees, *ut ante*, p. 490, in those heathen who "do not come into the holy city itself," xxi. 24, the same of whom it is said, "All nations shall come and worship before Thee; for Thy judgments are made manifest," xv. 4. On the contrary, according to Weiss, *ut ante*, p. 615, the prophetic expectation that only in the millennium would the theocracy include within it the heathen in the gross, so dominates the view of the seer, that in the form of an entirely unassimilative representation it still mingles with the description of the heavenly Jerusalem. Baur, *ut ante*, p. 212, on account of xxi. 12, affirms that, according to our author, Jewish Christians will always form the basis of the Christian church; and, in the ambiguous style already animadverted upon, goes on to say that "the heathen—heathen Christians are intended—stand always only in the second rank; and one does not know—since there can come into the New Jerusalem only those whose names are written in the book of life—whether this category will find its full application in the heathen,"—that is, heathen Christians. A third class of expositors—as Hengstenberg, *in loco;* Lücke, *ut ante*, p. 738; Lechler, *ut ante*, p. 205; Düsterdieck, *in loco*—take the ἔθνη for nations who are allied or belong to the holy city. The last mentioned of these expositors finds described in this passage, with the tone and style of the ancient prophets, the people which shall find entrance into the future city; in general, only those who, as ver. 27, in a positive, exclusive manner affirms, are written in the book of life; but vers. 24–26 would also describe expressly, and agreeably to the ancient predictions, the heathen as such who would find admittance into the city. To Düsterdieck it does not seem justifiable to conceive of the nations and the kings as dwelling without the city; much rather would the "essentially parallel description," vii. 9–12, lead him to think of believers from the heathen as domiciled in the New Jerusalem. The peculiar representation is, according to him, conditioned by the Old Testament type, in the perspective of which that which falls in the earthly period of the Messianic times does not appear definitely separated from that which for New Testament prophecy lies beyond the second coming of the Lord. I cannot entirely agree with any of these interpretations. The naturalization of the heathen in the New Jerusalem would be too peculiarly represented by vers. 24–26; and hitherto the seer has given no occasion for the assumption that, by his leaning to Old Testament types, he has been led in his representation to mingle the citizenship of the heathen in the New Jerusalem and their conversion on this earth with each other. The nations "allied" with and those "belonging" to it are different; the "allied," the apostle has been able to represent not unskilfully through vers. 24–26;

on the other hand, the "belonging" is precisely that which, in distinction from the "allied," the citizen will explain. That the twelve tribes of Israel, whose names are on the gates of the New Jerusalem, are not Jewish Christians only, or the believing Jewish nation, but the true Israel from Jews and Gentiles, we have shown earlier; but of Gentiles who do not come into the holy city itself, in whom the category of the book of life possibly finds not its full application, there is in this place simply nothing said. The conversion of the heathen in the future state has certainly something attracting; since, at the judgment of the world, all the dead from all nations and times arise, and since only those are condemned who by their works cannot stand, and whose names are not written in the book of life, one is disposed to ascribe the representation to the seer. In the final state, the true Israel of all times, the pious of the Old Testament, who believed in a predicted Messiah, and the pious of the New, who believed in a Messiah who had come, and who have kept the faith, form the central point for the multitude of the heathen, who in the course of the thousand years in various lands have longed for the light, and have not found it on earth, but with unsatisfied longing have gone thither. In the New Jerusalem is the perfected church: there is the glory of the Lord, and it shines forth; there the perfected serve the holy God as His priests; but around it is the church, included only in the last stage, which walks in the light streaming from the centre, and brings its glory thither for the worship of God. It would be in harmony with such a conception, that in the New Jerusalem the tree of life bears its fruits for the inhabitants—for the nourishment, strengthening, and maintenance of the eternal life; but its leaves are for the healing and recovery to eternal life of the nations dwelling around and coming to the city for worship, xxii. 2. Nevertheless, satisfactory as this interpretation appears on all sides, it has a defect which outweighs all its excellences, namely, that there is not a single word expressly in its favour; we therefore let it drop. But are, therefore, the contents of vers. 24–27 an entirely unassimilative representation? Köstlin has justly pointed to xv. 4; only he should not have, at least doubtfully, explained ver. 27 as if these Gentiles should not come into the holy city itself. There is also with him at the bottom the false assumption that the final condition of the new world will be again that of the present. The hope expressed in

xv. 4 is, as the ways, judgments, and righteous acts there mentioned, and the kinghood and priesthood of Christians, xx. 4–6, show, fulfilled first in the millennium; while before the manifestations of the righteous judgments of God, individuals from various nations accepted redemption,—v. 9, for example,—and thereby entered the true Israel; then all the heathen, that is, the nations still continuing heathen, will generally, or in the mass, revere and honour the name of God, and will come and worship before Him. But what we find in the millennium existing in a temporary, limited manner, will have place in the new world absolutely. As there the beloved city is the central point of the kingdom of God, xx. 9, so it is here; as there the true Israel is a nation of priestly kings dwelling at the centre, serving God and governing the world, so also in the final state (comp. xx. 4, 6, 9, xxi. 12, xxii. 3–5); as there the heathen nations come, and princes and peoples bring their offerings and receive the blessing, so also in the New Jerusalem, everything there, unlike the earthly prelude, is in the most perfect manner. This representation must certainly appear unassimilative until we perceive the distinction which the author makes between individual heathens and the heathen nations. When he wrote the Apocalypse, the Christian church consisted of a small number of believing Jews and a larger number of believing Gentiles; the latter had for him the same importance as their brethren from the Jews. Christendom, composed of these two elements, was to him on one side the twelve tribes, the true Israel, the 144,000 elect, the first-fruits, the priestly kingdom of God, as well as on the other, the innumerable multitude "of all nations, and kindreds, and peoples, and tongues." But the woman with the twelve stars fled into the wilderness; the existence of the Christian church mainly outside the Holy Land, and its composition, principally of non-Israelites, is for John a temporary condition. He expects in the future that the heathen in the gross will be more obdurate; but that, on the contrary, the Jews will be converted to Christ. The church, consisting of Jews in the gross, and of many, though of individuals only, adopted from the Gentiles, reigns with Christ in the millennium on earth; and—though not expressly stated, but evidently understood—after the general resurrection and the judgment, its number increased and completed by the Christians before Christianity, the true Israel of the Old Testament, it will reign also in the new world for ever. On the other hand, the heathen nations in the gross are converted only after Christ's coming on earth,—not to the saints or to Israel, but they are "Christianized," and in the final state form the population of the new world around the city of God, corresponding, indeed, to the completion of the church of God by the Old Testament "Christians," increased from the "devout" heathen of all times. Little, therefore, as we are to think of an exclusion of the Gentiles from the dwelling-place of God and His priestly people, or from the enjoyment of salvation,—the fruit and leaves of the tree of life, the nourishment or refreshing and healing are the same for different persons,—just as little are we to conceive an identity of those living in and around Jerusalem. As between the New Jerusalem and the new world, so there is, and for ever remains, the distinction between "Israel" and the "nations," the "priest-kings" and the people or kingdom, the centre and the circumference. In conclusion, we find it once more confirmed that the seer is not in harmony with modern categories. Particularism and universalism show themselves to be equal in the Apocalypse; and just as certainly does it appear that the judgments and representations on each side are not contradictory, but are the equally justified features neither of a particularistic nor universalistic, but of a view peculiar to the writer.

THE RELATION BETWEEN THE

DOCTRINE OF THE APOCALYPSE

AND THE

DOCTRINE OF THE GOSPEL AND THE EPISTLES OF JOHN.

INTRODUCTORY REMARKS.

IN the year 1826, De Wette wrote, in his *Lehrbuch der historisch-kritischen Einleitung in die Bibel Alten und Neuen Testaments*, II. p. 355: "In New Testament criticism there is nothing so certain as that if the Apostle John is the author of the Gospel and Epistles, he did not write the Apocalypse; or if this is his work, he cannot be the author of the other writings." This alternative had for a long time, in the esteem of critics, a sort of axiomatic value. Within its limits the contrast has completed itself: while the school of Schleiermacher, as here specially represented by Lücke, Bleek, and Düsterdieck, accepted the apostolic authorship of the Gospel and the Epistles, and, on account of the supposed irreconcilableness of these writings with the Apocalypse, decidedly denied it to be John's, the school of Baur for a long time more or less expressly recognised the Apocalypse as the work of that apostle, and as such used it in disputing the authenticity of the Gospel and the Epistles; and to this day, non-critical theology generally ascribes to the apostle all the writings of the New Testament known by his name, only because tradition is in his favour.

In the meantime there has long been perceived in many critics, even of entirely opposite tendencies, a *departure*, to a greater or less extent, *beyond the earlier alternative.* In his

Christenthum der drei ersten Jahrhunderte, p. 132 (comp. *theol. Jahrb.* 1844, p. 691; *Kanonische Evangelien*, p. 380), Baur declares it to be an error, if, on account of the difference and contrast, we overlook the close relation in which the Gospel stands to the Apocalypse; that it cannot be mistaken that the evangelist, in order to use the authority of John in Asia Minor on behalf of his Gospel, has imagined himself in the place of the seer, and, indeed, that it was not merely an external leaning to a much honoured name, there being not wanting an inner point of contact between the Gospel and the Apocalypse; the latter especially offers so many connecting points for the higher conception of Christianity, that one can only admire the deep geniality and delicate art with which the evangelist, in order to spiritualize the Apocalypse into a Gospel, has appropriated the elements which, from the standpoint of the former, lead to the freer and higher standpoint of the latter (comp. Köstlin, p. 498). Even the ultra-Tübingen Volkmar says (p. 43): "The new form of John or of the Gospel, named by the Catholic Church, 'according to John,' consists in any case only—still thus!—in an idealizing of the last apostle, who in this Apocalypse of Judaism has so freely soared toward God, proclaimed the 'Logos of God,' so fervently testified of the 'Lamb that taketh away the sins of the world.'" Though, for the whole Tübingen school, the origin of the fourth Gospel was, at the earliest, long after the latest conceivable termination of the life of the Apostle John, and thus a fundamental critical article is in the way of the supposition, it cannot be denied that the concession, or, more correctly, the assurance of an inner connection between apocalyptic and evangelic doctrine, notwithstanding the diligent and skilful denial by Lücke, and also by Düsterdieck, indicates a noteworthy step in advance.—From an entirely different side Neander (p. 481, note) cannot recognise the Apocalypse as a work of the apostle; but he finds that it bears witness of an already existing Johannine doctrinal type; and as a sign thereof, he reckons the agreement in the doctrine of the Logos, the description of the living waters, and many things in the superabundant descriptive symbolic expressions. Even the similar apostolic origin of the Gospel and the Apocalypse has gradually found a series of more or less decided defenders. Weiss, in his *Johanneischen Lehrbegriff*, p. x., proceeds upon the supposition of the genuineness of the Gospel, and reckons himself among those who regard the inquiry into the apostolicity of the Apocalypse as in no way closed. But in his opinion, it belongs in any case to another epoch in the life of John, and therefore to another stage in his doctrinal development. The same writer, in his *Lehrbuch der biblischen Theologie des Neuen Testaments*, p. 656, note, expresses his view most distinctly, that biblical theology may be fruitful for the solution of the critical question so far as it shows whether or not there is found in the Apocalypse the connecting point for the development of the doctrine before us in the Johannine theology. Ritschl treats the Apocalypse simply as a work of the apostle, and also regards the Gospel as genuine (comp. p. 48, note), though he finds that, as far as it directly or indirectly represents the standpoint of the Apostle John, it has far overstepped the relative contrast between the original apostles and Paul. Hase, p. 25, without reserve declares himself for the common origin of the Apocalypse and the Gospel from the Apostle John. He finds in the former, instead of a strict Judaistic sense, only Jewish forms; and instead of an entirely sensuous perception, the immanent presence of a clear Christian self-consciousness in gospel predictions and visions,—at least in the form of religious poetry,—over against which there is not wanting in the Gospel the transcendent and the sensuous. With him, the distinction between the Apocalypse and the Gospel is only that of an advance to a loftier height—externally, indeed—occasioned by the divine judgments on the Jewish people, but inwardly by the natural development of the Christian spirit. The Gospel appears to him as a sublimated Apocalypse, only corresponding in its manifold relations and analogies to the higher development of John. Lechler, p. 228, describes the harmony presented by the doctrine of the Gospel and the Epistles on one side, and the Apocalypse on the other, as remarkable; and he calls attention to a few chief points in order to establish the decided recognition "of the unity of the spirit, and, in fact, also of the doctrine of the writings themselves under their different drapery and different aims."

Niermeyer, in his *Verhandeling over de echtheid der Johanneische Schriften*, 1852, crowned as a prize work by the Hague Society for the Defence of Christianity, but known to me only through Lechler's full review in *Studien und Kritiken*, 1856, 4 Heft, has compared the spirit and doctrine of the evangelist and the seer, and has deduced the result that the Apostle John may have, must have, written the Apocalypse, the Gospel, and the Epistles.

I am therefore not wholly without *precedent,* when, starting from the *possibility* that the tradition of the common origin of the writings going universally under the name of John may be in harmony with fact, I compare the doctrine of the Apocalypse on the one hand, and the doctrine of the Gospel and the Epistles on the other, in order to ascertain whether their mutual relations confirm, or rather demand, the acceptance of the identity of the authorship, and thereby—since the Apocalypse was written by the Apostle John—prove also for the Gospel and the Epistles the authorship of the same writer.

Even for such a comparison, the conjecture raised here and there, especially by the Tübingen school, that even the *Gospel* and the *Epistles* may be assigned to *several authors,* is not without importance. In the meantime, apart from the notorious weakness of the evidence for such a suspicion (comp. Grimm in *Studien u. Kritiken,* 1849, p. 269; Düsterdieck, *die drei johanneischen Briefe,* I. p. 57), and from the surrender of the same, almost without exception, by recent critics (comp. Keim, I. 149; Holtzmann in Schenkel's *Bibellexikon,* III. 349), it is open to every man to observe in the result, all those positions which stand or fall with the unity of the authorship of the Gospel and the Epistles. I do not think that the issue will thereby be essentially altered.

Certainly I need for my undertaking some concessions. First, I require to be granted—what, indeed, is commonly admitted—that *the destruction of Jerusalem* lies between the production of the Apocalypse and the other Johannine writings, and therefore that the differences between the two, which can be satisfactorily explained by this event, do not involve different authors. Secondly, it may be granted me beforehand, that a Gospel, especially apostolic Epistles, and an Apocalypse—apocalyptic letters also—are various in their object. Further, that an Apocalypse and a Gospel, as such, must treat of *manifoldly various subjects and on various sides;* consequently there is no proof of various authorship if one writing contain many things of which the other is silent, provided this difference arises from the evangelic or the apocalyptic character of the book. Finally, it may be granted on one side, and on the ground of our representation of the apostolic doctrine, that the seer has not presented his ideas unveiled, but with full consciousness, and to the best of his ability, has clothed them in Old Testament forms of speech and thought; and on the other side, on the ground of obvious fact, that the author of the fourth Gospel has not presented the evangelic material chronologically, but according to premeditated selection and personal views, so that differences between the apocalyptic and the evangelic doctrine, which in the respective writings find sufficient explanation in *the different purpose* and *the different representation conditioned by it*, prove nothing against the identity of the author. When, against these three concessions, I expressly reject the later stage in the doctrinal development of John, asserted so emphatically by many expositors,—as, for example, Ritschl and Weiss (comp. *bibl. Theol.* p. 656),—and, indeed, on the double ground that to me the admission of an essential change in doctrinal views and teachings in the time between the Apocalypse and the Gospel appears to remove the question of the identity of the author from the sphere of investigation to that of pure conjecture, and also because I am certain that an expedient so questionable is not needed, the unprejudiced reader, so far as I am concerned, will hardly have occasion to mourn over conditions too severe. Far rather it may seem to him, notwithstanding the preparation by means of the representation of apocalyptic doctrine, a bold beginning when I endeavour to prove, by a comparison of their teaching, that the notorious "fantastical, Judaizing-zealotic" (Strauss) author of the Apocalypse, and the lauded final reconciler of all the contrarieties of the first and of half the second century, the author of the fourth Gospel, are one and the same apostolic personality.

I expect tolerably general agreement when in this endeavour I do not distinguish between *the doctrine of Jesus in the fourth Gospel and that of the fourth evangelist.* And hardly will any one object that here I do not, with Weiss, discriminate between the great mass of evangelical doctrine and those doctrinal elements, on the one side delivered, but still not perfectly assimilated, and on the other side independent, but not associated with Christ's words. Isolated doctrinal elements, given by the evangelist from memory, may not always be perfectly assimilated or independently realized even by himself; on the other side, individual portions of his doctrinal statements may in his recollection find no point of contact with the discourses of Christ (Weiss, *bibl. Theol.* p. 660).

Both elements bear too little upon our aim to lead us to a special consideration of them.

It will probably be strongly regretted that I do not compare at *considerable length* the spirit or character of the apocalyptic and the evangelical theology; nor is it my intention to deny the truth and high importance of a remark like that of Baur (*theol. Jahrbücher*, 1844, p. 691), that the narrative in the Apocalypse and in the Gospel concerns itself with a great struggle on the part of Christ with Satan, the prince of this world. And when Weiss (*bibl. Theol.* p. 662), among other things, presents as a peculiarity of the evangelist that he sees everywhere only the pervading contrasts of God and the devil, light and darkness, truth and falsehood, life and death, love and hatred, in such a way that he manifestly takes no account of the various stages of the development, because he recognises in each only the nature of that which in a certain measure and degree is realized in it; or when he (*bibl. Theol.* p. 660) remarks that the law and the prophecy of the Old Testament appear to the evangelist as a positive preparation and introduction to Christianity, and, indeed, that the pre-Christian revelation, in its manner and effects, is often brought by him into very striking parallel with the completed revelation in Christ,—we shall have to show, as the most important result of our comparison, that these and other peculiarities are common to both evangelist and seer; only, first, it should not be expected from us —as here and there it has been—that we should speak briefly of originality, genius, poetic flights, depth of emotion, or, on the other hand, of the lack of gentleness and patience, in literary historical categories. Characteristics and parallels of this kind are generally of only doubtful value, and have for the question before us no importance. And, secondly, it will not be required that we class together the common features which we may discover, in a special section; we must desire that the reader in this matter will follow us from point to point with "microscope" and "retort;" and he who has done this will need no summary repetition.

After Weiss, in his Johannine doctrine, has gained the honour of finally establishing the *Old Testament foundation of the Johannine theology*, it may seem proper, in the comparison of the apocalyptic and the evangelic doctrine, to keep the common Old Testament, especially the common original apostolic, and the common properly Johannine doctrine separate from each other. In fact, I have hesitated whether I should endeavour to carry out this distinction or not. Apart, however, from the unavoidable prolixity and repetition associated with it, can there be drawn here a firm and sharp border line? May not the use by the seer and the evangelist of Old Testament representations occurring in other New Testament writings be wholly peculiar? And has not the production of an Old Testament statement, common to the seer and the evangelist, or of a common original apostolic representation, on both sides, under the circumstances, an importance equally as great or greater than the proof of a specifically Johannine characteristic? From this and kindred considerations I have preferred generally to avoid in the comparison the distinction between that which is founded upon the Old Testament and the specifically Johannine, and to credit the reader with a knowledge of the Old Testament foundation of the Johannine theology (comp. Weiss, *der Johanneische Lehrbegriff*, pp. 101–191), and at the same time with a corresponding appreciation of all the individual results of the comparison; and on my part, as far as I am able, so to present and group the various results, great and small, that, by their united force, they may produce a common and decisive impression.

It appears to me self-evident, that in a comparison between the doctrine of the Apocalypse and that of the Epistles and Gospel of John, based on the ground of a preceding representation of the doctrine of the former, that we should maintain the order there followed. The *sections* here will therefore closely correspond in *number and order.*

THE COMPARISON.

1. God.

(a.) *The Nature of God.*

"Little children," writes the evangelist, "keep yourselves from *idols,*" 1 John v. 21. The so-called gods of the heathen are to him just as they are to the seer, according to their appearance, idols, images, the work of men's hands; but according to their significance and nature,—otherwise he would not have written, "keep yourselves from them,"—demons or supernatural evil beings (comp. Rev. x. 20). He presents God, in *contrast with false gods*, as the Creator (comp. Rev. xiv. 7), as the King of nations, xv. 13, as the only holy, xv. 14; so also the evangelist expresses this contrast in the words, "that they might know Thee, the only true God," xvii. 3; and also when he says, "this is the true God," 1 John v. 20 (comp. ver. 21, and John v. 44, the only God). It is true, and obviously so, as Köstlin remarks, p. 483, that the evangelist expresses the contrast with heathenism by giving prominence to the nature, but the seer by calling attention to the attributes of God; and would not an author now change his method of representation according as he wrote prose or poetry? —In the second of the above passages, however, the evangelist's contrast with false gods steps back considerably toward the absolute sense of the "true," and everywhere else it is with him, as with the seer, an entirely different contrast which conditions the statements concerning God. Certainly it is not the same, but corresponds with the statement, that the evangelist emphasizes the nature of God against heathenism, and the seer His attributes; when we find that the latter says of God, what can protect against the *world's course*—consolation and warning; the former, what promise and obligation have in them for Christians against the *nature of the world*, the flesh. If we have grasped this difference in the point of view from which the Apocalypse and the Gospel speak of God, we have with it brought into recognition the difference between evangelical and apocalyptic representation, and the assurance that neither of the two writings will yield a "doctrine of God;" and, moreover, that it is accidental, when the evangelist does not describe God as "the truth," etc.; we shall therefore, beforehand, expect in statements concerning God only infrequent and slight contact between the seer and the evangelist. All the more remarkable, therefore, are the unmistakable traces of relation, and even of identity, which upon a closer consideration press themselves into view.—"God is a *Spirit*," said Jesus to the woman of Samaria, John iv. 24. No even remotely similar statement is to be found in the Apocalypse. If we get rid of the modern fancies respecting this expression of Jesus, and understand it as He Himself presents it in the connection, what else does it contain but the foundation, lying in the nature of God, of the prediction that instead of the worship offered on Gerizim and at Jerusalem, vers. 20, 21, He should be, and indeed already was, vers. 23, 24, worshipped in spirit and in truth? And in what else does this foundation consist than in the statement that "God is a Spirit;" that is, not flesh, or fleshly, in the sense of the material, the sensible, in the sense of space and time, or limitation and finitude; but supersensual, absolute, perfect being; therefore He seeks those who worship Him agreeably with His nature, not outwardly, materially, in symbolical forms, but in the element of the spirit, and therefore in a really corresponding manner. But we remember how frequently and expressly the Apocalypse represents Christians as priests, or priestly kings, for example, i. 6, v. 10; how the prayers of saints are as incense presented to God, v. 8, viii. 3; how the death of Christ is the great passover (comp. the Lamb); how the martyrs are described as slain and sacrificed, vi. 9, xviii. 24; how it is promised to the faithful that he shall be a pillar in the temple of God, iii. 12; and how it places the throne of God and of the Lamb in the New Jerusalem, where His servants render Him priestly service, xxii. 3, 4. If in all this the Christian worship of God in the present, and its perfection in the future, is undoubtedly represented as the worship of God in spirit and in truth, must not the seer necessarily have conceived of God as a Spirit wholly in the sense of the Gospel?—Christ says, "As the *living* Father hath sent me," vi. 57—"as the Father hath life in Himself," v. 26; and the evangelist writes, "This is the true God, and eternal life," 1 John v. 20. In these places God is described as the possessor of absolute life, as the personal absolute life; and we find that this is the sense of Rev. iv. 10, x. 6, xv. 7, vii. 2. Absolute or eternal life is manifestly to the evangelist as important an element in the nature of God as it is to the seer. The living Father of the former points not less decidedly to the Old Testament than the living God of the latter. In John v. 26, the absolute life of God is placed almost exactly in the same relation to death and resurrection as in Rev. vii. 2.—"This, then," it is said, "is the message which we have heard of Him, and declare unto you, that God is light, and in Him is *no darkness at all*," 1 John i. 5. Certainly this is not expressly said of God in the Apocalypse; but if He who sits on the throne is like unto jasper, iv. 3;—if the city needs not the light of the sun, nor of the moon, to shine in it; because the glory of God doth lighten it, and the Lamb is the light thereof, and the nations walk in its light, xxi. 24, 25;—if there is no more night, and it needs not the light of a candle, nor the light of the sun; because the Lord God giveth them light, xxii. 5,—so we have already found in the consideration of these passages in our Representation of Doctrine, that to the seer holiness is the ethical, essential nature of God, and that this holiness is similar in its signification to light, or the nature of light. The statements of the evangelist concerning God as being light, have no other sense than that in His nature and will He is holy, ethically perfect or absolute.—It is said, "God is love," 1 John iv. 8, 16. Nowhere does the Apocalypse affirm this of God, nor does it ever speak expressly of the revelation of the love of God in sending or giving His only-begotten Son (comp. 1 John iv. 9; John iii. 16). But when the evangelist writes, "Behold what manner of love the Father hath bestowed upon us, that we should be called the sons of God," 1 John iii. 1, there answers to it that word in Rev. xxi. 7, "He that overcometh shall inherit all things; and I will be his God, and he shall be my son." That the love of God generally is no strange thing to the seer, we have shown in detail in the proper place.—When Christ says, "My Father, which gave them me, is *greater* than all; and no man is able to pluck them out of my Father's hand," John x. 29, we are reminded less strikingly of the Lord God, the Almighty, than of the Lord of the earth, who will not permit His two prophets to be hurt unavenged, Rev. xi. 4–13; we think of the scene where the four angels could not hurt the earth, or the sea, or the trees, until the servants of God were sealed in their foreheads, vii. 1–3; of the Lord holy and true, to whom the martyrs cry for vengeance, vi. 10, 11; and of the appearance of Christ, as He held the seven stars in His right hand, i. 16 (comp. ii. 10, iii. 10). That God is greater than our hearts, and knoweth all things, 1 John iii. 20, connects itself in meaning with a statement, not indeed concerning God, but Christ, according to which all the churches shall know that He searches the reins and hearts, and gives to every man according to his works, ii. 23. The "*faithful* and *just*" God of 1 John i. 9, and the "righteous" Lord, "which art, and wast, and shalt be," Rev. xvi. 5 (comp. xv. 3, xvi. 7, xxi. 5, xxii. 6), as well as the *Holy* Father upon whom Christ calls, John xvii. 11, and the Lord, holy and true, to whom the martyrs pray, vi. 10 (comp. the thrice holy of iv. 8), need no proof of their relationship.—That *true*, real, the truth, has with the evangelist, besides the meaning of moral truthfulness, still another, will not be disputed. But it is ever worthy of notice that ἀληθινός occurs in proportion more frequently with the evangelist and the seer than with any other New Testament writer; that this word, occasionally with the evangelist, and always with the seer, expresses the contrast to the deceptive, lying, and false in a moral sense; for example, "herein is that saying true," John iv. 37; "His record is true," xix. 35 (comp. Rev. xix. 9, xxi. 5, xxii. 6); that as the seer uses ἀληθινός more in the sense of ἀληθής, so also the evangelist does not distinguish these words from each other (comp., for example, John xix. 35), and that he, like the seer, gives great prominence—positively and negatively—to the moral truthfulness of God (for example, John iii. 33, viii. 26; 1 John i. 10, v. 10). —With regard to the *wrath* and the *love* of God, we may with reason say that, in the prominence given them, they stand with the evangelist in an inverse relation to their position in the Apocalypse. Still, not only is what was said of wrath in the Apocalypse applicable to love in the Gospel, namely, that it necessarily presupposes wrath as its reverse, as is manifest from the contrast of perdition and eternal life, John iii. 16; not only do such expressions as salvation and condemnation point to the wrath of God as a very essential feature in the evangelist's doctrine,—but at least once the evangelist speaks of it very expressly, "He that believeth not the Son shall not see life, but the wrath of God abideth on him," John iii. 36, and thereby satisfactorily shows that only the difference between apocalyptic and evangelical writing has given to the anger and the love of God such a different position. For the same reason, a *symbolic* representation of God is not found in the Gospel; we may, however, mention here its direct tendency to point to the historical, personal, real symbolization or glory of God in Jesus (comp. John i. 14, xiv. 9, xvii. 4; 1 John i. 1–3, etc.). There is no contradiction between the evangelist and the seer when the former makes Jesus say: "Not that any man hath seen the Father, save He which is of God, He hath seen the Father," John vi. 46 (comp. iii. 12, 13, v. 37); when He Himself says: "No man hath seen God at any time; the only-begotten Son, which is in the bosom of the Father, He hath declared Him," John i. 18; and, "No man hath seen God at any time. If we love one another, God dwelleth in us," 1 John iv. 12 (comp. ver. 20); and when the seer, on the other hand, describes how he has seen the glory of God, Rev. iv. 2–6.

For what the seer reports of himself, the evangelist ascribes—expressly with reference to Christ, and on account of Isa. vi., tacitly with reference to God—also to the prophet Isaiah, "These things said Esaias when he saw His—Christ's—glory, and spake of Him," John xii. 41; and as the evangelist expects for Christians of the heavenly state the vision of God in the sense in which the Son sees Him (John xii. 45, xiv. 7, 8, 3 John 11, do not apply here), "we shall see Him as He is," 1 John iii. 2, so the seer writes, "and they shall see His face," xxii. 4.

(b.) *God's Works.*

The *foundation* of the world appears in John xvii. 24 under the same name as in Rev. xiii. 8, xvii. 8, and is referred to in the expression, "before the world was," John xvii. 5; in the sentences, "all things were made by Him (the Word), and without Him was not anything made that was made;" "In Him was life," John i. 3, 4; "my Father worketh hitherto," John v. 17; but it is naturally less frequently and prominently brought forward in the Gospel than in the Apocalypse, for which omnipotent power revealed in the creation, as well as the sole right of God to the world founded thereon, in contrast to the manifest opposition of the course of this world, must have had the greatest significance. Still more is God's *government of the world* kept back in the Gospel; it meets us almost only in the saying of Jesus already quoted, v. 17, and evidently on account of the purpose of the book. The characteristic "shall" and "given" of the seer meets us again with the evangelist (comp. John iii. 14, xii. 34, xi. 51, xii. 33, iii. 30, ix. 4, xx. 9, iii. 27, v. 26, 36, xix. 11, etc.). The relation between God and men is, with the evangelist as with the seer, wholly disturbed; by what means and to what extent, the section on the devil and on mankind will tell. Therefore the activity of God is directed on one side to the deliverance of men from perdition, and on the other to the bringing His glory or Himself into recognition. The evangelist speaks of deliverance, or "salvation," iv. 22, precisely as the seer, vii. 10, xii. 10, xix. 1 (comp. to deliver, John iii. 17, xii. 47, v. 34, x. 9; the deliverance, John iv. 22; and the Deliverer, John iv. 12; 1 John iv. 14, as well the negative and positive contents: shall not perish, but shall live: life, shall have eternal life, of which we shall treat later). The glorification of God is certainly only seldom specially mentioned in the Apocalypse, xix. 1, vii. 12, iv. 11 (comp. xi. 13, xiv. 7, xvi. 9); while the same substantially as well as verbally is very often introduced in the Gospel, for example, in vii. 18, xi. 4, 40, xii. 28, xiii. 31, 32, xiv. 13, xv. 8, xvii. 1, 4; but instead of this, the Apocalypse brings the glorification of God into almost all its episodes; for what is becoming a King, or making Himself a King, or taking the power, etc., of which we find in the Gospel only weak analogies in the kingdom of God, John iii. 3, and in the kingdom of Christ, xviii. 36, 37, but the evangelical glorification in poetic concrete expression? The contact of the two writings at this point is, in fact, very complete. It is true that if the exposition of God's plan with the world is to be taken into account, the Gospel and the Apocalypse, agreeably with their purpose, widely diverge: the Apocalypse has to do with the completion of God's purpose, Rev. x. 7, and therefore describes His righteous judgments (comp. Rev. xvi. 7, xv. 3, 4), and presupposes the revelation of God in Jesus; on the other hand, the Gospel has directly to do with this, and hardly touches the finishing of the mystery of God, for its design is chiefly to show the same as already essentially present, and therefore almost exclusively it describes the work of God in the world, as giving His only-begotten Son, John iii. 16, as sending Him, 1 John iv. 10; as showing what was to be done and said by Christ, John v. 20, xii. 49, 50; as glorifying Christ, viii. 54, xii. 23, xiii. 31, 32; as glorified in Christ, xiii. 31, 32, xii. 28, xiv. 13, etc.—But would there be any difficulty in maintaining this distinction in the points of view, if the seer and the evangelist, in doctrines still to be considered, were in the contents of their statements less frequently in contact than we shall find them to be?

2. The Angels.

When the evangelist reports that "others said, An angel spake to Him," xii. 29, it points only to popular belief in angels; still it cannot be disputed that there is a close relation between the voice from heaven, which the multitude said was thunder, and some the voice of an angel, and the cry of the angel after which the seven thunders uttered their voices, and whose words the seer was about to write, Rev. x. 3, 4, But when the evangelist narrates how Mary Magdalene saw two angels in white sitting in the sepulchre of the Lord,—one at the head, and the other at the feet, where the body of Jesus was laid,—and how they said to her, "Woman, why weepest thou?" the faith of the evangelist himself in the existence of angels is proved. The words of Christ to His disciples, "Verily, verily, I say unto you, Hereafter ye shall see heaven open, and the angels of God ascending and descending upon the Son of man," i. 51, though we may refer the promised experience of communion between heaven and earth, God and men, realized and revealing itself in Christ, agreeably with the connection (comp. ver. 51), only to the miracles of Christ or to His glory generally, show us that with the Jesus of the evangelist there is found the same Old Testament poetic use of angelic representations as are found in the Jesus of the seer. With respect to the genuineness of the words: "An angel went down at a certain season into the pool, and troubled the water: whosoever then first, after the troubling of the water, stepped in, was made whole of whatsoever disease he had," v. 4, I agree with De Wette *in loco;* but if the evangelist wrote these words, or only something near them, he shared in the Rabbinical representation of the Apocalypse concerning angels as spirits of the elements, and at the same time betrays, in a manner intolerably objectionable to such expositors as Lücke, his near relation to the seer. That, with the latter, angels occur more frequently than with the evangelist, Lücke, *ut ante,* p. 740, finds to be natural in an apocalyptic representation after the type of Daniel and the Old Testament generally. The case of the angels as bearers, communicators, and interpreters of God's revelation in the Apocalypse, in which he finds an important peculiarity against the Gospel, has been noticed in the proper place.

3. HEAVEN.

The evangelist, like the seer, describes the *creation* as a compact whole by the term "world," John xvii. 5, 24 (comp. Rev. xiii. 8), and with relation to the sum of its parts by the phrase "all," or "all things," John i. 3 (comp. Rev. iv. 11). It is not surprising that with him the poetic description of the world in its chief divisions is wanting. But the names of those chief divisions serve him to designate *the various spheres of existence;* heaven is the region of the supersensual, the higher and divine; earth, the region of the earthly, lower, and human existence. That he has recognised a third—the hellish, devilish, anti-ideal existence—is implied in the meaning which he attaches to the devil. This, however, will find more direct expression in the chapter on perdition.—The *heaven,* with which we have to do here, comes before the evangelist in a physical, though general sense, only in xii. 28, xvii. 1; but in a tropical sense more frequently, as in i. 32, 51, iii. 13, xxvii. 31, vi. 31–33, 41, 42, 50, 58. In this sense Jesus also calls it the "above," the higher world, viii. 23 (comp. iii. 3, 7, 31, xix. 11); His "Father's house," xiv. 2. He means this when He says: "from the Father," xv. 26, xvi. 28; "to the Father," xvi. 10, 17; "to Him that sent me," xvi. 5; "where He was before," vi. 62; "whither I go," xiii. 33, 36; "where I am," xii. 26, xiv. 3; and others mean this when they say: "from God," iii. 2, xvi. 30. Of apocalyptic appliances and objects in heaven, such as thrones, altars, ark of the covenant, etc., we do not meet with one in the evangelist; but that saying of Christ's, "in my Father's house are many mansions," xiv. 2, shows that the evangelist had the same local symbolic conception of heaven as the region of the ideals of the holy places on earth. That the heaven of the evangelist, like that of the seer, had God, Christ, the Spirit, and the angels for *inhabitants,* needs no proof; nor does it need stating that the twenty-four elders and the four living creatures are not mentioned in the Gospel. That the Christian conquerors, with the evangelist, have their place in heaven, we shall show later. The seer speaks of those who dwell in heaven; so in the Gospel we hear Christ speak of many mansions in His Father's house; and if, with Hengstenberg, we think of the heavenly inhabitants of the Apocalypse as Christians, so far as exalted above the world they live in the sphere of the ideal, we find the parallel in John iii. 13 (comp. i. 18), "No man hath ascended up to heaven, but He that came down from heaven, even the Son of man which is in heaven." The *conditions* and incidents in heaven are naturally not represented in the Gospel apocalyptically; we have comprehensive names instead,—"If I have told you earthly things, and ye believe not, how shall ye believe if I tell you of heavenly things?" iii. 12. But many comparisons may be made in particulars; for example, between the open heaven to and from which angels ascend and descend upon the Son of man, John i. 52, and the heaven of the Apocalypse, whose God has power over the plagues, Rev. xvi. 9, and from which the angels so frequently descend to accomplish God's purposes on the earth; or between the locality where Christ is, and where His servants shall be also, John xii. 26, and the hill of Zion where the Lamb stands, and the 144,000 who follow Him whithersoever He goeth, Rev. xiv. 1–4. Instead, however, of losing ourselves in individual comparisons, we would rather establish the fact that the evangelist, not less than the seer, whether he calls it heaven or uses circumlocution, means the ideal world, or the ideal sphere of existence in the widest and fullest sense of the word; but that evidently, with the former, heaven is mentioned almost exclusively as the place where Christ was before, vi. 62; from which He has come down, iii. 13, xvi. 28 (comp. iii. 2, xiii. 3); in which He is, iii. 13; whither He will go, vi. 62, xiii. 33, 36; and where He will be, xii. 26, xiv. 3. On the contrary, it is mentioned in the Apocalypse chiefly as the region from which proceed God's judgments on the world, and in which the blessed result of the same is already present. The "*new*" of the seer meets us with the evangelist only in the "new commandment," xiii. 34; 1 John ii. 7, 8; 2 John 5. It is only when we understand the "new" of the evangelist in the sense of the seer,—not merely as that which has had no existence before, but also as that which belongs to the ideal sphere,—that all hesitation about the expression of the evangelist passes away; at the same time, it is worthy of notice upon what foundation the statement, "the darkness is past, and the true light now shineth," 1 John ii. 8, is based.

4. The Devil.

Of the *designations* of the evil principle in the Apocalypse, there meet us in the Gospel and the Epistles: "the devil," John vi. 70, viii. 44, xiii. 2; 1 John iii. 8, 10; and "Satan," xiii. 27. We do not find either the serpent or the dragon; "the evil one," John xvii. 15; 1 John ii. 13, 14, iii. 12, v. 18, 19; and "the prince of this world," xii. 31, xiv. 30, xvi. 11 (comp. 1 John iv. 4), are new. We found that the seer would have given the contents of xii. 7–9 (comp. xii. 4) in another form, if there had not been in his memory, on one side, the standing of Satan before

God in heaven from the Old Testament, and on the other, from Jewish ideas, his *fall* and expulsion, as well as the defection of a part of the angels. Closely corresponding to this is the *οὐκ ἑστηκέναι* of the devil in the truth, John viii. 44. Little as in itself it describes his fall, still, in its peculiar form, it can be explained only on the supposition that, according to the conception of the evangelist also, the devil has fallen from God. Certainly,—and so far Köstlin, p. 128, is right in his assertion that, with the evangelist, the doctrine of the devil excludes the thought of his having been a good spirit,—with the evangelist as with the seer, the retrospect to the fall of the devil before the beginning of time is thrust far into the background,—at one time by a religious historical regard to his works from the commencement of the human race, and at another by a, so to say, speculative view of the same as the personal original principle of all evil appearing in time. The devil with him stands to God in a *relation the direct reverse of that of the Logos.* As the Logos is God, and tends to God, and is in constant union with Him, and is the principle of all that is godly in the world; so the devil is antigod, alienated from God, in constant apostasy from Him, and is the principle of all that is ungodly. It appears to us that, with the seer, the devil takes precisely the same position. As the latter does not lack the association of such a conception with that of the creation of all things by God, so with the evangelist the creation and the evil principle stand directly together. There also meets us in the *attributes and activities* of the evil principle a striking agreement between the seer and the evangelist; falsehood and murder, or persecution, are here, as there, the two essential features of his character. The old serpent that deceiveth the whole world distinctly looks forth from the devil, who, "when he speaketh a lie, he speaketh of his own, for he is a liar, and the father of it," viii. 44 (comp. Rev. iii. 9). We may compare also, to tempt, temptation, the tempter, John vii. 12, 47; 1 John i. 8, ii. 26, iii. 7, iv. 6; 2 John 7; Rev. ii. 20, xii. 9, xiii. 14, xviii. 23, xix. 20, iii. 8, 10. The great dragon is unmistakeably the apocalyptic "prince of this world;" his being red finds its interpretation in the words: "he was a murderer from the beginning," John viii. 44 (comp. 1 John iii. 10, xii. 15; Rev. ii. 9, 10, 13). When, in addition to the terms devil and Satan, the "evil one" appears in the Gospel as a proper name of the evil principle, its absence in the Apocalypse is satisfactorily explained by its abstractness. That Satan and the devil are with the evangelist only varieties in language and not in meaning, is shown by a comparison of John xiii. 2 and 27. Naturally we need not expect to find the accuser of the heavenly brethren with him; but, apart from the striking parallel of Rev. xii. 11 and 1 John ii. 13, 14, we shall find the sense of the apocalyptic statement, namely, that until the overthrow of the devil, the pious, in a manner different from the world, were subject to the devil, very definitely expressed in his doctrine.—How the case stands in the eye of the seer with regard to the position of the devil in *heaven*, has been shown in the proper place; the parallel to Rev. xii. 7-9 is John xii. 31, xvi. 11 (comp. John xiv. 30, xvi. 33).—The angels of the devil, is language which belongs solely to the Apocalypse. *Demons* are known also to the evangelist, vii. 20, viii. 48, 49, 52, x. 20, 21; also unclean spirits, though he does not thus designate them, 1 John iv. 1–3.—"The Satan of the Apocalypse," writes Köstlin, p. 495, "has great similarity to the Johannine prince of this world;" and (p. 496), "without doubt the Satan and the Antichrist of the Apocalypse are to be regarded essentially under the presuppositions which have conditioned the Johannine doctrine respecting these enemies of Christendom, and which at the same time make explicable the extreme power and wickedness which are ascribed to them by John."

5. Perdition.

At the first glance, the difference between the seer and the evangelist on the doctrine of the *abyss* seems greater. We seek in vain in the latter for the same or even a similar expression, in vain for the lake which burneth with fire and brimstone, and in vain also for all those existences which the seer represents as coming up from the abyss. And yet Christ speaks there of "the son of perdition," John xvii. 12; He says that those who believe in Him shall "not perish," iii. 15, 16 (comp. vi. 39, x. 28, xi. 50, xviii. 9, xii. 25); and unmistakeably there stands before us the perdition into which the beast of the Apocalypse goeth, Rev. xvii. 8, 11. And what is the "death," for example, of John vi. 50, xi. 26, viii. 51, 52 (comp. viii. 21, 24), except the death of the Apocalypse, ii. 11, xx. 6, 14? Indeed, little as, with the evangelist, an anti-ideal sphere of existence, with its second death, its perdition, opposed to the heavenly ideal sphere of existence, with its eternal life, its salvation, comes into the foreground, it still belongs to his doctrine as essentially as to that of the seer. We may notice, moreover, that as the conception of eternal life, as already manifest in Christ and present in believers, and also that of perdition, as already decided and present with unbelievers, obviously agrees with the Apocalypse; so also the surprise, or overtaking of men by the darkness, and their walking in darkness, whereby they know not whither they go, John xii. 35; 1 John ii. 11 (comp. John xii. 46); the death in sin, John viii. 21, 24; the abiding of the wrath of God, iii. 36; the condemnation, iii. 18; death, v. 24; 1 John iii. 14, v. 16, 17; and many similar things, with the evangelist, agree with a much more concrete meaning—they are the conditions of the abyss in their beginning, present already (comp. John iii. 18) in sin and unbelief.

6. The Earth and Mankind.

The *earth,* in the proper sense of the word, does not occur with the evangelist. Mankind dwelling upon it, whom the seer describes by the names "earth, world, inhabitants of the earth," are called by the evangelist "the world," John vii. 4, viii. 26, xii. 19, xviii. 20. The individuals are "men," which term the seer also has frequently.

In the conception of the *nature of men* there is harmony between the seer and the evangelist. Though the latter often designates by "the flesh" the opposite of "spiritual" life, which is not expressed in the Apocalypse, he still uses the word for the sensible, material, physical, common to men and animals, John i. 14, vi. 51–56; 1 John iv. 2, 3; 2 John 7. But man, as such, has with him also a body, John ii. 21, xix. 38. The living soul, as the principle of animal life, we do not meet with in the evangelist; but we find the spirit as the principle of the super-animal life, John vi. 63. He has certainly the spirit as well as the soul, as the dichotomic description of the inner nature, John xi. 33, x. 24, xii. 27, which is accidentally wanting in the Apocalypse. To the soul, as the sentient life principle of man, Rev. xii. 11, there is an almost verbal parallel in John xii. 25. As a name for the desiring and avoiding life, as a designation of the life which is not extinguished in death, the soul is not used by the evangelist (comp., however, John xii. 25). The heart is with the evangelist the seat of feeling, desire, purpose, resolution,—for example, John xii. 40, xiii. 2, xiv. 1, xvi. 6, 22. He does not mention the understanding.

The expression "the world," or rather "this world," is used by the evangelist instead of the apocalyptic names, "the earth," "the earth and the sea," "the earth and the heaven," "the first heaven, and the first earth, and the sea," for that which lies between the ideal and the anti-ideal, the earthly sphere of existence,—for example, John i. 10, iii. 17, 19, vi. 14, ix. 5, xi. 27, xii. 46, xiii. 1, xvi. 28, 33, xvii. 11–16, xv. 18, xviii. 37; 1 John iv. 1, iii. 9; John i. 9, viii. 23, ix. 39, x. 36, xi. 9, xii. 25, xiii. 1, xiv. 30, xvi. 11, xviii. 36; 1 John iii. 17, iv. 17. But "this world" reminds us of the Rabbinical contrast of this and future aeons; and it thus corresponds more with the apocalyptic "first heaven and first earth," or the first, in distinction from the new heaven and the new earth, or the "new" (comp. Rev. xxi. 1, 4, 5). The other designation of the evangelist for the earthly sphere of being, "beneath," in distinction from that which is "above," or higher, viii. 23 (comp. iii. 31), springs from another view, but has its parallel in the apocalyptic "earth and sea," in distinction from heaven (comp. Rev. xii. 12). Indeed, in surprising agreement with the Apocalypse, the Gospel uses, interchangeably with the expression beneath, and in contrast with heaven, the expression the earth, John iii. 31; and in contrast with the heavenly, the earthly, iii. 12.

As the seer does not expressly say that the first heaven and the first earth were *originally* good, but implies it in his doctrine that God created all things for His good pleasure, iv. 11 (comp iii. 14, Christ the beginning of the creation); so the evangelist does not anywhere speak of the original goodness of this world, but assumes it as self-evident when, according to him, all things were through the Logos, John i. 3, 10. That the evangelist regards the change as having taken place in the same manner as the seer, namely, through the fall and the loss of paradise, is shown when, in almost universal parallelism with the Apocalypse, he says that the devil, who is a liar, and the father of lies, viii. 44, is a murderer from the beginning, viii. 44; that he sinned from the beginning, 1 John iii. 8; and also makes an expressive reference to Cain and Abel, 1 John iii. 12, and to the water, John iv. 10–14, as well as to the bread of life, John vi. 27–35.

The *state of the world*, entering with this change, the seer describes, on its *subjective* side, in peculiar and entirely general language,—unrighteous, unrighteousness, unrighteous deeds, sins; works, in a bad sense. In the evangelist also we meet with peculiar and general expressions,—unrighteous, or unrighteousness, vii. 18; and stronger,—sin, 1 John v. 17; and then the strongest, "transgression of the law," 1 John 3, 4 (comp. vers. 7, 8). Individual acts are called sins, John i. 29, viii. 7, 21; 1 John i. 7–10 (comp. John v. 14, viii. 11, ix. 16, 24, 25; 1 John iii. 8); works, in a bad sense, John iii. 20; evil works, John iii. 19; evil, iii. 20. In the naming of individual sins there is only little agreement between the seer and the evangelist; and it is easily understood, because the former has to do chiefly with the moral state of the heathen world in its concrete features; the latter, on the other hand, chiefly with the moral condition of Christendom in its inner relations. It must appear all the more significant that in the evangelist we meet with idol-worship in a very express warning, 1 John v. 21; that as the transgressions of the second table come into prominence with the seer, especially in murders, sorceries, fornications, and thefts (comp. Rev. ix. 21), so with the evangelist they appear in "the lusts of the flesh, and the lust of the eyes, and in the pride of life," 1 John ii. 16 (comp. generally, 1 John ii. 15–17 and Rev. ix. 20, 21; also "the works of the devil," 1 John iii. 8, and the deceiver of "the whole world," Rev. xii. 9); that murder plays so prominent a part with the evangelist (comp. John viii. 37, xl. 44; 1 John iii. 12–15; comp. also the slain in Rev. vi. 9, etc.); and that lying, so strongly emphasized by the seer, is frequently mentioned by the evangelist (comp. John viii. 44, 45; 1 John i. 6, 10, ii. 4, 20–23, 27, iv. 1, 20, v. 10). But when the evangelist, with unequalled frequency, speaks of the "truth," John i. 14, 17, iii. 21, iv. 23, 24, v. 33, viii. 32, 40, 44–46, xiv. 6, 17, xv. 26, xvi. 7, 13, xvii. 17, 19, xviii. 37, 38, xix. 35; 1 John i. 6, 8, ii. 4, 21, iii. 18, 19, iv. 6, v. 6; 2 John 1–4; 3 John 1, 3, 4, 8, 12, there is still essentially the same view of sin as with the seer, Rev. xxi. 8, 27, xxii. 15 (comp. xiv. 5). Especially instructive is John viii. 46, 47 (comp. vii. 18); the juxtaposition of innocence and speaking the truth, and, John iii. 20, 21, the contrast of doing evil and the practice of truth, or walking in the truth, and "doing" the truth, and "walking" in the truth, 1 John i. 6; 2 John 4; 3 John 3, 4; we may here mention also what has been said of temptation in the section on the devil. Partaking of the sins of others, against which Christians are warned, Rev. xviii. 4, finds a literal parallel in partaking of the evil deeds of others, 2 John 11.

Of apocalyptic *images* for sin, we meet with impurity or contamination, in the history of the foot-washing, John xiii. 4–17, especially ver. 10, as well as in the words: "cleanse us from all unrighteousness," 1 John i. 9, and also in "every man that hath this hope in him purifieth (ἁγνίζεν) himself, even as He is pure," 1 John iii. 3. We are distantly reminded of the image of whoredom by the words to the Samaritan woman, "Thou hast well said, I have no husband, for thou hast had five husbands; and he whom thou now hast is not thy husband" (comp. 1 John iii. 3). Between the words to the Laodiceans, "Thou knowest not that thou art blind. I counsel thee to buy of me eye-salve, that thou mayest see," Rev. iii. 17, 18, and the history of the man born blind, John ix., especially ver. 39, "For judgment I am come into this world, that they which see not might see, and that they which see might be made blind," there exists an unmistakeable connection. The shame of nakedness, Rev. iii. 18, still more, the shame at Christ's coming, Rev. xvi. 15, appears in 1 John ii. 28, "that when He shall appear we may have confidence, and not be ashamed before Him at His coming." The figure of death is very common with the evangelist; for example, John v. 21, 24, 25; 1 John iii. 14. Sin appears to him as slavery, John viii. 32–36. The seer does not describe sin as debt so expressly as the evangelist does, John xx. 23; 1 John i. 9; though, on account of the Old Testament foundation of his doctrine of redemption, the image undoubtedly underlies it. The figure by which the evangelist most frequently represents the state of sin—namely, that of darkness—we certainly at first sight seek for in vain in the Apocalypse; but apart from what is more distant,—the bright and shining garments, Rev. iii. 4, 5, iv. 4, vii. 13, 14,—all that we have heard of light, in the apocalyptic doctrine of God, the light attribute of Christ and the church, and lastly and chiefly, the supremely important position of light in the heavenly state, Rev. xxi. 23, 24, xxii. 5, show undoubtedly that to the seer sin appeared under the image of darkness, and that it was avoided by him as not being from the Old Testament.

With respect to the two chief features in the *objective* side of the world's condition presented by the seer, we find the absence of God (negative) and the wrath of God (positive), with the evangelist, in the oft-recurring emphatic statement that " no man hath seen God at any time," John i. 18, vi. 46; 1 John iv. 12 (comp. iii. 2); and, reasoning from the opposite, in the words concerning the fellowship of Christians with God, 1 John i. 3, 7, their being in God, for example, 1 John ii. 5, as well as in the wrath of God, John iii. 36; but the other feature—the miseries of life and death —meets us in the miraculous narratives of the Gospel,—as, for instance, in the multitude of sick at the pool of Bethesda, John v. 3, and the words of Jesus to the man who was healed, " Sin no more, lest a worse thing come unto thee," ver. 14; in the diseased, vi. 2; in the man born blind, ix. 1–3; in the history of Lazarus, John xi., especially vers. 33, 38; and in the opposite of eternal life,—for example, John xi. 25, 26.

That this condition of mankind appeared to the evangelist *unbroken until the coming of* Christ, appears from the statement that the devil is the prince of the world, and was overcome and cast out by Him; that this state was also, in the eye of the evangelist, *general*,—that is, prevailed through the mass,—is evident from the circumstance that he uses the names " men," iii. 19, " world," xvii. 14, to describe the ungodly race of mankind,—both in closest harmony with the practice of the seer. But as little as the seer does he regard this general state of pre-Christian humanity as being *without exception*. With him also there runs through the whole history the same contrast which now exists between Christendom and the world. As, now, on one side there are the children of the world, and on the other the children of the devil, those who are born of God or from God, and those who are of the devil, 1 John iii. 8–10; so there were before Christ, the children of God, John xi. 52, such as were of God, viii. 42, 47, and also such as had the devil for their father, viii. 44. What is said in 1 John iii. 12, 13, allows us to assume that, according to the views of the evangelist, there flowed alongside each other from the beginning—that is, from Cain and Abel—two entirely different streams, or that two classes of men stood opposite each other, even the children of God and the children of the devil.

But while the expression, "the world," as well as the designation of the devil as "the prince of this world," presents ungodly mankind as a comprehensive whole, as a Satanocracy, the theocracy is more a self-evident assumption, without, however, entirely lacking an express description; as, for example, "He came unto His own, and His own received Him not," i. 11 (comp. Ex. xix. 5; Deut. vii. 6, xiv. 2); "the sheep of this fold," x. 16 (comp. Ps. xcv. 7, c. 3). On the other hand, such words as, "He came unto His own, and His own," etc., i. 11; "behold an Israelite indeed," i. 47; "salvation is of the Jews," iv. 22, show decidedly that, like the seer, the evangelist essentially identified the theocracy and the Jewish people; while the corresponding relation of the Satanocracy and the Gentile world is rather presupposed as self-evident, though wholly distinct, as indeed is indicated by the judgment on the prince of this world, John xii. 31 (comp. 1 John v. 19), with its reference to the Greeks of vers. 20–22. That this essential identification of heathen and Jewish humanity with the kingdom of the devil and the kingdom of God is, in the sense of the evangelist, as little as in that of the seer, an external mechanical one, is seen in that the scattered children of God, for the gathering of which Christ died, taken in connection with the nation, can only mean heathen, John xi. 52, and that those who are of their father the devil, John viii. 38–40, are externally the seed of Abraham, ver. 37.

But is the evangelist's contrast of the *pre-Christian* children of God and of the devil the same as the *post-Christian?* It is true that the darkness has not comprehended the light which shines into it, John i. 5; that the works of men were evil before Christ, iii. 19, 20; that already a Cain had slain his brother Abel, because his works were evil and his brother's righteous, 1 John iii. 12; but the world has come to judgment, and trial, and sentence only because Christ has come, and has spoken, John xv. 22; because He has done the works which no other man did, John xv. 24 (comp. xii. 37); and the Spirit has reproved the world, John xvi. 8–10, and the world has loved darkness rather than light, John iii. 19 (comp. xii. 37–39), and has not believed in Christ because He has told the truth, John viii. 45, but has hated Him, John xv. 18–24. The world before Christ was so far *relatively* without sin, John xv. 22, 24, not yet so hardened and blinded, John xii. 40, nor so full of hatred against the children of God,

1 John iii. 13, 14, nor so entirely of the devil, 1 John v. 19. But we need only to clothe this view with apocalyptic forms, and we have the old serpent and the great red dragon before us, who deceives the whole world, stands threateningly before the woman in travail, and after his overthrow, descends to the earth with great wrath. The world before Christ is more only the *type*, 1 John iii. 12, the *prediction*, John xii. 38–40, of the world since Christ.—On the other hand, the *Old Testament church of God* stands as *high* with the evangelist as it does with the seer. Jesus says of Abraham, he "rejoiced to see my day, and he saw it, and was glad," John viii. 56; of Moses, that he wrote of Him, v. 46; that Moses and the prophets wrote of Him, i. 45; that Isaiah saw His glory, and spoke of Him, xii. 41; and that the Scripture cannot be broken, John x. 35. We may add to this the repeated appeals to prophecy which occur in almost all the important parts of the evangelical history, for example, John ii. 17, vii. 38, xii. 14–16, 38–40, xv. 25, xix. 36, xx. 9, etc. According to the view of the evangelist, as also according to that of the seer, the devout of the Old Testament already had all that is given to Christians in Christ. But they had all, precisely as with the seer, only as prophecy in word and deed (comp. the paschal lamb), therefore yet only in longing hope. I cannot recognise in John viii. 56 a perception of the fulfilment in paradise, where the patriarch still sympathized with the circumstances of his people; the Rabbinical view, that God revealed to Abraham all the future, leads not to a seeing in paradise, but to this—Abraham rejoiced that he should see the day of the Lord,—see in the sense of surviving, sharing in the kingdom of God in its perfection (comp. John iii. 3),—"and he saw it"—saw it in the sense of prophetic vision (comp. John xii. 41),—"and was glad"—a conception analogous to John iv. 23, v. 25. On the other hand, the pious before Christ had, in real actuality, the law with which, in John i. 17, grace and truth is contrasted, which Christ, in conversation with the Jews, calls "our law," John viii. 17, and in conversation with His disciples, "their law," John xv. 25; which mainly describes the theocracy, the Old Testament, less according to its eternally valid side, the word, and the will, and the commandments of God, John v. 38, 39; 1 John ii. 17, iii. 22; less also according to its predictive, pre-representing side, the Scriptures, John v. 39, xix. 36, but more according to its

human, John vii. 22, 23, v. 16–18, temporary, i. 17, imperfect side; therefore Moses, especially in the Gospel, has a twofold and entirely different meaning (comp., for example, John i. 17, iii. 14, v. 45–48, vi. 32, vii. 19, 22, 23, viii. 5, ix. 28, 29). The same evangelist, who represents Christ as dying to gather the scattered children of God, xi. 52, sums up the meaning of Christ's death in His giving power to those who believed on Him to become the sons of God, i. 12; the pre-Christian children of God were not yet free, viii. 32–34, but were under the law, and had not yet grace and truth, i. 17, but stood under God's wrath, iii. 36. Even, therefore, eternal life had failed them; Abraham and the prophets were dead, viii. 52; the Old Testament saints were, like all other men, dead, vi. 49, 58, dead in their graves, v. 28, until the resurrection at the last day, v. 28, 29, xii. 48. But in all this, is not the relation of pre-Christian devout men to Christians given in another form, though in the same sense, as it is by the seer, in the pregnant and travailing woman, in the accuser of the brethren, and in the rest of the dead, who lived not again until the thousand years were finished, xx. 5?

7. Christ.

(*a.*) *The Life of Jesus.*

As the near or more distant relation of Rev. xii. 1–6 to the Virgin Mary, King Herod, the Bethlehemitish slaughter, and the flight to Egypt, accepted by many expositors, has been shown by us to be unfounded, so now we have to affirm a negative agreement between the seer and the evangelist with respect to the *birth and childhood of Jesus.* On a closer consideration, we find also a positive agreement between the two on this point. It is indeed remarkable that the seer writes, "she brought forth a man-child, who was to rule all nations with a rod of iron: and her child was caught up to God, and to His throne," Rev. xii. 5, and thus, immediately after the appearance of the Messiah in the world,—for that is the meaning of the birth of the child from the Old Testament church,—he represents His exaltation to heaven. But is it not precisely the same conception of the life of Jesus in the two periods of His entrance into the world and His departure to heaven, when the evangelist writes, "Jesus, knowing that the Father had given all things into His hand, and that He was come from God, and went to God," xiii. 3; or when Jesus says, "I am come forth from the Father, and am come into the world again; I leave the world and go to the Father"? xvi. 28 (comp. iii. 13, vi. 62, viii. 14). Köstlin, p. 486, finds a difference on this point between the seer and the evangelist, in that the former gives prominence to Jesus especially in His descent from Israel, from the tribe of Judah, and from the family of David, to which the latter is indifferent. The passages which Köstlin, p. 133, quotes in proof of this indifference, John i. 46, vi. 42, vii. 42, 27, are so little conclusive, that Weiss (*johanneischer Lehrbegriff*, p. 153) refers to the last as evidence of the meaning which the Messiahship of Jesus had for the evangelist; but here the consideration is sufficient that the seer does not give prominence to the descent of Christ from Israel out of Judah, and from the Davidic race, but in sacred language to the Messiahship of Jesus on the side of power, and so indirectly testifies that descent to us, as the evangelist does the Messiahship on the other side, which lay nearest to his immediate purpose; but not less emphatically does he imply, and therein also indirectly testify, that Jesus was to him an Israelite of the tribe of Judah and of the family of David.

That there exists no discrepancy between the indications of the Apocalypse concerning the *history of the life of Jesus*—doctrine, miracle, apostleship, conflict—needs only to be mentioned, for the pertinent statements of the Apocalypse are too meagre for a thorough comparison.

In considering the historical declarations of the Apocalypse with regard to the *death* of Christ, we arrived, through the recognition of Christ as the true Paschal Lamb, at the conjecture that, according to the views of the seer, Christ must have been slain at the time of the paschal offering. It is confessedly a still unreconciled difference between the fourth and the synoptical Gospels, that, according to the latter, Jesus was crucified on the first day of the paschal feast, and in the morning; according to the former, on the eve of the passover, and nearly at mid-day, thus at the same time in which the paschal lamb was slain. The position of the heathen world-power in the person of Pilate, and also that of the apostate Jewish people with relation to the death of Christ, as the evangelist represents it, cannot apocalyptically be more strikingly expressed than through the beast which kills, and the great city, which spiritually is called Sodom and Egypt. As the seer says of the Messiah, coming with clouds, "every eye shall see Him, and they also which pierced Him," i. 7, so the evangelist writes, after he has narrated, xix. 32–37, how one of the soldiers pierced the side of Jesus with a spear, "again another scripture saith, They shall look on Him whom they pierced." The common reply to this parallel,—which is all the more important since the passage in Zechariah, which lies at the bottom, is nowhere else applied,—that the expression of the seer may describe mainly the death, that of the evangelist chiefly the piercing of Christ, we have already referred to; but we have there granted that in themselves the words of the seer may be applied as well to piercing the side of Jesus as to piercing His hands and His feet. Therefore, be it as it may, the seer and the evangelist are equal, and alone, among New Testament writers, find in the death of Christ —or shall we say, with Köstlin, p. 497, that the former sees the prediction fulfilled in the advent, the latter in the death of Christ? —a very remarkable prediction fulfilled; will not every unprejudiced reader see in this a striking indication of the identity of the two? According to the evangelist, Jesus, when on the cross, "bowed His head, and gave up the ghost," xix. 30; can it be accidental that the seer never uses of the death of Christ the expression *ἀποθανεῖν*, but always says *νεκρὸς ἐγένετο*, Rev. i. 13, ii. 8? The significance of the time between the death and resurrection of Jesus, which appeared to us throughout the three and a half days of the two witnesses, Rev. xi. 9–11, is, according to John ii. 18–20, not strange to the evangelist. There must have been for him, as well as for the seer, some amount of unseemliness in the burial of Jesus, when he expressly remarks, John xix. 42, that on account of the Sabbath of the Jews, they buried Him there, for the grave was near. The joy of the world, Rev. xi. 20, meets us again literally in the prediction of Christ, John xvi. 20, that "the world shall rejoice."

If it is the Spirit that quickeneth, vi. 63, how can the evangelist have conceived the *resurrection* of Jesus otherwise than that "the Spirit of life from God entered" His body, Rev. xi. 11, and that thereby He was made alive, Rev. ii. 8, xx. 4? There is with him, moreover, in the saying of Jesus respecting the travailing woman, John xvi. 21, certainly the image of birth for the resurrection of Christ! That the evangelist, like the seer, conceived the resurrection body as exalted above earthly limitations, but in no way inaccessible to the senses, even bearing upon it the marks of the death of the cross, follows irresistibly from John xx. 14–17, 19–21, 24–29. The *ascension of Christ* is described by the evangelist in the same words used in the Apocalypse to describe the ascension of the two witnesses, John vi. 62, xx. 17, Rev. xi. 12; for the vision of those raised, and ascending, both have the same expression θεωρεῖν, John vi. 62, xx. 14; Rev. xi. 11, 12. But we may consider the fact of the ascension to be represented by the evangelist as taking place between, John xx. 17, 19, or as begun with the resurrection, and gradually completed—with which, indeed, John vi. 62, in comparison with John xvi. 10 (comp. ver. 17), the absence of a difference between the appearance to Mary Magdalene and to the disciples, even the typical significance only recognisable on this explanation of the desire "to touch" on the part of Mary, better agree; in any case, evangelist and seer are one in this, that they do not, as all the synoptical writers when correctly interpreted (comp. Matt. xxviii. 7; Mark xvi. 7; Luke xxiv. 50; Acts i. 3), conceive of the ascension as having been divided by a long period from the resurrection.

(*b.*) *The Person of Christ.*

"We have been accustomed," says Weiss (*johanneischer Lehrbegriff*, p. 152), "to regard the Johannine Christology as the higher stage of the Christian consciousness, from which there is no longer seen in Jesus the popular *Messianic idea*, as with the Synoptists, but a higher dogmatic knowledge expressed in the doctrine of the divine Word which was made flesh." Against this accustomed view Weiss then shows that the proposition that Jesus is the Messiah cannot be more designedly presented in the synoptical Gospels than it is in the fourth Gospel, especially in the first part (comp. i. 19, 20, 34, 42, 46, 50, iv. 25, 26, 29, 42, vi. 14, 15; Deut. xviii. 15; John vi. 69, vii. 27, 31, 41, 42, 47, 48, ix. 22, 38, x. 24, 36, xi. 27, xii. 13, 15, xviii. 37, xix. 24, 28, 36, 37, xx. 9). "Hardly," he adds, p. 153, "from the Gospel of Matthew, which is generally supposed to be intended to furnish Jewish Christians with proof of the Messiahship of Jesus, can more evidence be brought, even if we consider that all the places elsewhere in the fourth Gospel, in which the fulfilment of Messianic prophecy is referred to, really count under this testimony." Such a design certainly did not lie before this Gospel, inasmuch as it was written for Gentile Christians; nevertheless the great prominence given to the Messiahship of Jesus cannot have been purposeless; and this is pointed out very clearly by the conclusion of the book,—"these are written, that ye might believe that Jesus is the Christ, the Son of God," xx. 31. That which Weiss, to whose exposition in detail we refer (comp. also *bibl. Theol.* p. 680; Weizsäcker, p. 260), says of the relation of the fourth to the synoptical Gospels in the prominence of the Messiahship of Jesus, also applies literally to the relation of the fourth Gospel to the Apocalypse, as a comparison of the pertinent passages of the former with the Messianic statements of the latter, shows at the first glance.

But we must at some length refer to the other Christological feature, the Logos doctrine present in the Apocalypse; and against that which Weiss, *ut ante*, p. 239, especially p. 250, objects to the contrary, we must still maintain that the direct and indirect statements of the evangelist concerning the "Word" imply more than an agreement in expression, even an actual or historical connection with the original Alexandrian doctrine of the Logos; or, in other words, contain the doctrine of the Logos itself, whether for the present we regard it as directly or indirectly from Alexandria. It is obvious that we are not led to this position by prejudice in favour of the unity of the Apocalypse and the Gospel. We might have spared much labour, and still have fully maintained the identity of the two authors, if, with a great number of expositors, we had denied the Logos doctrine to the seer. But we were under the necessity of vindicating this doctrine of the Apocalypse without reference to the Gospel; and the eventuality of a coincidence in this case with the Apocalypse need not hinder us from recognising the Logos doctrine in the evangelist.

Certainly, if it meant so much as to ascribe to the evangelist an *à priori* speculation respecting the nature of God and His relation to the world, or more especially if it meant that the Johannine doctrine comes more or less exclusively from that of Philo, as Weiss, *ut ante*, really appears to think, then would the admission of the Logos doctrine in the Gospel exclude the apostolic authorship. This at least we do not affirm, but rather that the evangelist as well as the seer first recognised the Messiah in Jesus, and only afterward may have found in the doctrine of the Logos the *full truth;* or, in other words, the *perfectly appropriate expression;* or, in still other words, have seen in the language and views of their scientifically-educated contemporaries the *correct translation* of the Messianic idea of the Israelites. Therefore, here as well as there, we leave the question open whether the Logos doctrine came to the evangelist in its original Alexandrine form, or already combined with the Messianic idea, or actually applied to Jesus; or further, whether the evangelist was prepared for the Logos doctrine, in this or that form, by acquaintance with a popular growing Palestinian Christology representing the Messiah; or was prepared only by his own impulse, or especially by a higher testimony on the part of Jesus Himself, to find for his experience of Him a loftier form of thought. As we said of the seer, that since he conceived the Messianic idea in its modern form, so also he must have conceived the Logos doctrine, because otherwise, agreeably with his entire individuality, he must have rejected it, so the comparison of the first and the last words in the Gospel, i. 1 and xx. 31, which finds confirmation in a comparison of the whole prologue with the entire Gospel,—there, it is announced that in Jesus the Logos was made flesh; here, it is shown that Jesus is the Messiah,—proves incontrovertibly that the evangelist also must have found in the Logos doctrine nothing else than the modern scientific conception and expression of the Messianic idea. Weiss, *ut ante,* p. 154, comes very near to this confession; but by his aversion to an *à priori* speculation allows himself, p. 239 (comp. *bibl. Theol.* p. 687), to be led to ascribe to the evangelist an *à posteriori* speculation, which, without connection with the existing philosophic dogma, must have led him in a more remarkable manner to the same result. Little as we can agree with this expositor when he denies the Logos doctrine to the evangelist, we are thankful that, in his interpretation of John i. 1–3 and 1 John i. 1–3 (*ut ante,* pp. 241–244, comp. *bibl. Theol.* p. 689), he clearly shows how, for the evangelist, all that he understands by "the Word" was already given in the Old Testament, Gen. i.; Isa. ii. 3; Jer. i. 4–11; Ps. xxxiii. 6. Thus the very same characteristic which strikes us in the seer, namely, that, with undeniable reference to the Old Testament, no matter to what particular place, he calls the Logos "the Word of God," and with not less striking Old Testament reference affirms the same to be "the beginning of the creation of God," is proved also in the evangelist without reference to the Apocalypse. How important it is at this point to observe that the evangelist takes precisely the same position with regard to the Old Testament which has such an all-pervading influence in the thoughts of the seer! We may especially notice also how characteristically evangelist and seer agree in the circumstance that, as both hold the doctrine of the Logos, so both only once, or seldom, give it expression,—the evangelist, only in the prologue of the Gospel and in the beginning of the first Epistle; the seer, apart from "the beginning of the creation," at the commencement of the last of the seven letters, thus from a high altitude,—only at the appearance of Christ, and, so to say, at the highest elevation. It may be noticed also that neither of them at any time puts the term "Logos" into the mouth of Christ as a description of Himself.

It is evident from what has been said, that just as the seer neither refers Messianic predicates solely to the Messiah, nor Logos predicates solely to the Logos, but both equally to the *Messiah-Logos*, so the evangelist everywhere, when he speaks of Jesus or introduces Jesus speaking, had the Messiah-Logos in both Messianic and Logos expressions equally in his thoughts. With others, he correctly sees from his standpoint, even in the confession of the common Messiah-faith, the sublimest faith in the Logos as a present living germ (comp. the confession of Andrew, John i. 42; of Philip, i. 46; and of Nathanael, i. 49); but there is not a single case in which unhistorically, instead of the accepted Messiah-faith, he puts into the mouth of any one the Logos doctrine itself; a sure proof that wherever he represents John the Baptist and Jesus Himself as uttering super-Messianic ideas, he was not unhistorical, but was certain that by the names and statements which he there used he perfectly reproduced for his readers the real contents of the expressions of Jesus and the Baptist, only in a somewhat different, more comprehensible and significant form,—a form, so to say, Hellenized, after the analogy of Luther's rendering of the Bible into German. And the historical character of the Synoptists being assumed, it may be seriously contended that the Baptist, or even that Jesus in His apprehensions and teaching, went far beyond the popular Messianic idea, and must have said, only in Palestinian or Jewish form, what the fourth Gospel reports of Him. Or does it agree with the statements of the Synoptists, if we assume that Jesus applies to Himself the title of Son of God or Son of man only in a popular Messianic sense? And are not even these and others, no matter whether wholly independent or whether in partial connection with an already existing, loftier Palestinian Christology—the latter is, on the whole, more probable, and especially according to the Messianic idea of the Baptist—referable, from Jesus Himself, to a higher expression of loftiest significance, in which the fourth Gospel preferably presents Him as speaking?

It might certainly very well consist with the fundamental agreement of the evangelist and the seer in Messiah-Logos doctrine, that in *individual predicates* resting on common ground the two writers might not in a single case be in harmony. Yet there is no failure of contact even in particulars. "Jesus Christ," occurring at the beginning and the end of the Apocalypse, meets us in the Gospel only in i. 17, xvii. 3, but in the first Epistle oftener, i. 3, 7, ii. 1, iii. 23, iv. 2, v. 20, also in the second Epistle, iii. 7. Jesus is described as the Christ much more frequently by the evangelist than by the seer; for example, John iv. 29, 42, vi. 69, vii. 26, ix. 22, x. 24, xi. 27, xx. 31; 1 John ii. 22, v. 1, 6; 2 John 9 (comp. John i. 20, 25, iii. 28, iv. 25, 26, vii. 27, 41, 42, xii. 34). The Lion of the tribe of Judah, the Root and the offspring of David, Rev. v. 5, xxii. 26; we find again in the utterances of one of the parties among the people, John vii. 41, 42: "Shall Christ come out of Galilee? Hath not the Scripture said that Christ cometh of the seed of David, and out of the town of Bethlehem, where David was?" The bright and morning star, Rev. xxii. 16 (comp. ii. 28), we have in the glory of Christ, John i. 14, ii. 11, xii. 41, xvii. 5, 22–24 (comp. vii. 39, xii. 16, 23, 28, xiii. 31, 32, xvi. 14, xvii. 1, 4, 5, 10). To the taking away of the child to God and His throne, Rev. xii. 5, corresponds the exaltation of Jesus, John iii. 14, viii. 28, xii. 32, 34; to the "I am set down with my Father in His throne," Rev. iii. 21, the going to the Father of Jesus in John xiii. 1, 3, xiv. 12, 28, xvi. 10, 16, 17 (comp. xii. 26, xvii. 1, 2, 24); to "the Lord of lords and King of kings," Rev. xvii. 14, xix. 16 (comp. i. 5), "the Father had given all things into His hands," John xiii. 3 (comp. iii. 35, xvii. 2). We are reminded of the key of David with which Jesus opens and shuts, Rev. iii. 7, by what He says, John xx. 23, about remitting and retaining sins, and still more by the words, "Him that cometh to me I will in nowise cast out," John vi. 37. Once Jesus describes Himself in the Apocalypse as "the Son of God," ii. 18, and in the Gospel He speaks of Himself in the same manner, v. 19–23, vi. 40, ix. 35–37, x. 36, xi. 4, xiv. 13, xvii. 1 (comp. viii. 35, 36); others also thus designate Him, i. 34, 50, iii. 35, 36, vi. 69, xi. 27 (comp. xix. 7), and so does the evangelist, iii. 16–18, xx. 31; 1 John i. 3, 7, ii. 22–24, iii. 23, iv. 10, 14, v. 9–13; 2 John iii. 9. He is also called the only-begotten Son, John i. 14, 18, iii. 16, 18; 1 John iv. 9. When Christ speaks of God as His God—in which Baur finds a strong proof of the lower Christological standpoint of the Apocalypse—the evangelist has for this also a parallel, xx. 17. In the Apocalypse, Christ calls God His Father, ii. 27, iii. 5, 21; and God is called the Father of Christ in John xiv. 1. In the Gospel, from ii. 16 to xx. 21, Christ often speaks thus; and from i. 14 to xiii. 3, the evangelist does so frequently. According to Rev. i. 6, Christ has made His people priests unto God and His Father; and in John, the Risen One says: "I ascend unto my Father and your Father, and to my God and your God," xx. 17. Is it not remarkable how almost every *Messianic* expression of the seer finds its echo in the evangelist?

In the meantime the two do not separate from each other at all, even in *super-Messianic* predicates. We regard it as significant that the seer, in both places where he speaks of the Son of man, uses, not ὡς, but ὅμοιος; and we must conclude that he desired by this comparison to characterize Christ as not human, but as the human form of a divine being, the Logos having been made flesh; and on what other interpretation can we at all reconcile (comp. Weiss, *bibl. Theol.* p. 677) the passages in the Gospel where Christ speaks of Himself as the Son of man, namely, i. 51, iii. 13, 14, v. 27, vi. 27, 53, 62, viii. 28, xii. 23, xiii. 31 (comp. xii. 34)? The parallel of Christ with God, for example, in Rev. vi. 16, xii. 10, meets us also in the Gospel, v. 17, 19, 21, 23, 26, viii. 15, 17; 1 John ii. 23. We found statements applied in common to God and to Christ in Rev. v. 13, vii. 10, xi. 15, xiv. 4, xxi. 22, xxii. 1; and in the Gospel also, in

viii. 16, 19, x. 30, xv. 23, 24, xvi. 3, xvii. 3; 1 John i. 3, ii. 22, 24; 2 John 3, 9. The identification of Christ with God, as it meets us, for example, in Rev. vi. 17, xx. 6, xxii. 3, is in the Gospel, according to its real ground, the oneness or the inter-community of being, very strongly emphasized, x. 15, 30, 38, xiv. 9–11, xx. 17, 21 (comp. xiii. 31, 32, xvii. 1). When Christ has ascribed to Him in the Apocalypse the same attributes, actions, and states as are ascribed to God, we find examples of the same in the Gospel, and this not merely in the record of miracles, concerning which we may compare Weiss, *bibl. Theol.* p. 684. When the seer speaks of Christ as the Living One, i. 18 (comp. iv. 9, x. 6), so also Christ says: "As the Father hath life in Himself, so hath He given to the Son to have life in Himself," v. 26. According to the evangelist, Christ calls Himself the light of the world, viii. 12, ix. 5; and the writer speaks of Him as the light of men, i. 4–9. He also says of God that He is light, 1 John i. 5. Christ calls Himself the resurrection and the life, John xi. 25; the life, xiv. 6 (comp. 1 John i. 2); and God is eternal life, 1 John v. 20. Christ prays, "Holy Father!" John xvii. 11; and the evangelist writes, 1 John ii. 20, "Ye have an unction from the Holy One," that is, Christ (comp. Rev. iii. 7). Christ prays, "O righteous Father!" John xvii. 25; and in 1 John i. 9 it is said of God, "He is faithful and just." Christ is expressly described as righteous, 1 John ii. 1 (comp. ii. 29, iii. 7); and, John v. 30 (comp. viii. 16), Christ says, "My judgment is just" (comp. Rev. xix. 11). As in the Apocalypse judgment is ascribed equally to God and Christ,—for example, xix. 2, 11,—though the statements of the evangelist referring to the judgment need an inner connection, which we shall endeavour to find in the section on the judgment, we may provisionally point to John viii. 50, where God is the Judge, and to v. 22, 27, according to which Christ judges. The "coming," in the eschatological sense, as stated in the Apocalypse, of God and Christ, likewise requires, as stated in the Gospel, a closer exposition, and it will follow in the section on the coming of the Lord; but we may mention here that, according to John xiv. 18, Jesus comes to His own; according to xiv. 23, He and the Father will come (comp. 1 John ii. 28, 29). The sending of the angel to unfold the future, which Rev. xxii. 6 ascribes to God, and i. 1, xxii. 16, to Christ, has a close correspondence in the Gospel, inasmuch as, according to John xiv. 26, the Father, and according to xv. 26, Jesus, will send the Comforter. The action which at one time is expressed as common to God and Christ, at another as belonging to Christ only,—as, for example, Rev. xxi. 23, xxii. 5,—perhaps needs in the Gospel only the instance already mentioned, xiv. 23, 18 (comp. x. 28, 29). An immediate change of person from God to Christ is nowhere to be found in the Gospel; but there are not altogether wanting passages in the Epistles where "He" refers to God, though before, the subject of discourse was Christ; for example, 1 John i. 9, ii. 3, ii. 29, and also the contrary, iii. 1–3. Divine adoration, which in the Apocalypse Christ so often shares, v. 13, vii. 10, we find again in the Gospel, in the form of the adoration and glorification of Christ, xiii. 31, 32, xvii. 1, 4, 5, v. 23, xiv. 13, xx. 28. Old Testament predicates of Jehovah applied to Christ, we shall naturally not look for in the Gospel, still the sense of some of them is to be found even there. Should His head and hair, white and glistening like wool, Rev. i. 14, signify His eternal vitality, we have already seen how strongly the evangelist declares that, as God has life in Himself, so Christ has life in Himself—is the life. To his eyes as a flame of fire, i. 14, ii. 18, symbolizing the holy indignation of Christ, we may probably find a parallel in John ii. 17. To the two-edged sword which goes out of Christ's mouth, and expresses His magisterial power, correspond the judgment and the judging word of Jesus, John v. 22, 27, xii. 48. With the countenance of Christ shining as the sun in his strength, Rev. i. 16, we may compare His words, "I am the light of the world, John viii. 12 (comp. xii. 35, 36). The falling down of the seer as if dead at the feet of Jesus has its parallel in the prostration of those who came to apprehend Him, John xviii. 6 (comp. xx. 28). As Christ claims to search the hearts and reins, Rev. ii. 23, so it is said that Jesus "knew all men, and needed not that any should testify of man: for He knew what was in man," John ii. 24, 25 (comp. John vi. 61, 70, 71). The rebuking and chastening of those whom He loves, Rev. iii. 19, Jesus shows in the foot-washing, John xiii. 1–3 (comp. John xv. 2). The Spirit of God, symbolized by the seven eyes of Christ, Rev. v. 6, is, as we have seen above, said in the Gospel also to be sent by Him. The feeding and leading to living fountains of waters, Rev. vii. 17, we find again in the

Good Shepherd, x. 11, and in the living water which Jesus offered to the woman of Samaria, John iv. 10–14. In what sense Jesus calls Himself "the beginning of the creation of God," Rev. iii. 14, we discover from the prologue of the Gospel. Also at the commencement of the first Epistle, as well as in Rev. xix. 13, there appears the Logos-name itself; and the "in the beginning," and "from the beginning" (comp. 1 John ii. 13, 14), remind us strongly of "the beginning of the creation of God."

After all this, we may with the fullest justice affirm that the *relation of the Messiah-Logos to God* is with the evangelist the same as it is with the seer,—the Messiah-Logos is equal with God and still under God (comp. John xiv. 9, 28); He is perfectly one with God, and yet distinct from God, John x. 30, vii. 16; He is all that God is, but has become so through God, or has received it from God, John v. 26, vi. 57, xi. 25; 1 John i. 1, 2; He has all that God has, but it has been given Him of God, John vii. 16, 17, xiii. 3, xvii. 8, 22; He does all that God does, but God has given, willed, or showed it to Him, John v. 17, 19–21, 30, 36, xii. 49. The evangelist can also, like the seer, ascribe one and the same thing to God and to Christ; to God as the absolute, and to Christ as the mediate cause; for example, God sends the Spirit, Christ sends the Spirit—Christ prays to God, and at His request the Spirit is sent by God. That we have selected from the Gospel only one or two proofs of this statement will, with our aim, need no apology; it seems to us that the result of our comparison can only gain in importance if we leave the reader to work out the proof of this somewhat optional point. Certainly he who demands from the seer that he should present Jesus to us in detailed discourses concerning His relations with the Father, or, on the contrary, that the evangelist should present Him revealing in Old Testament symbol His Messiah-Logos position, if the two are to be proved identical, would not be convinced even by ten times the number of proof passages; nor could it be proved to such a one that Wilhelm Meister and Faust were written by Goethe.

There only remains for us now to compare the seer's conception of the *various positions* of Christ, the pre-existent, the historical, and the exalted state, with that of the evangelist. To an expositor who affirms that the seer, in his direct application of predicates of pre-existence to the historical Christ, has left unnoticed the distinction between that which is yet to be realized and that which is already realized historically, between ideal and real existence, we have replied, that according to the apprehension of the seer, who contrasts not the ideal and real, but the ideal and the historical reality, the Messiah-Logos is from eternity realized in Jesus *ideally*, but when the time has come, in Jesus *historically*. Is it not remarkable that the evangelist has made himself liable to the same charge of supposed neglect of the distinction between the ideal and real existence as the seer? Jesus says, "Before Abraham was, I am," John viii. 58. "O Father, glorify Thou me with Thine own self with the glory which I had with Thee before the world was," xvii. 5; "that they may behold my glory, which Thou hast given me: for Thou lovedst me before the foundation of the world," xvii. 24. Christ frequently says that He—not the Logos—came forth from the Father, and has come into the world, John xvi. 28, vi. 62. The Baptist says of Jesus, "He it is, who, coming after me, is preferred before me,"—"for He was before me," i. 27, 30. The evangelist says that Jesus "knew that He was come from God, and went to God," xiii. 3, and that Isaiah "saw His glory," xii. 41. It is clear that the evangelist distinguishes, as little as the seer, between ideal and real existence; but to him also Jesus during His earthly life was the Messiah-Logos in historical reality, as during His pre-existence He was the same in ideal reality.—We have recognised as the seer's idea of the relation of the historical to the pre-existing Christ, that Christ in His earthly life manifested His eternal Messiah-Logos glory, and not only in displays of glory properly so called, but also in self-humiliation and self-denial; we said that the picture of Christ's life, according to his views, must contain such contrary manifestations harmoniously beside each other. Does the sketch of Christ's life in the fourth Gospel permit itself to be otherwise characterized? Self-abnegation in the usual sense of the words cannot have been seen by the evangelist in the earthly life of Jesus when he writes, "The Word was made flesh, and dwelt among us; and we beheld His glory, the glory as of the Only-begotten of the Father, full of grace and truth," i. 14. We may compare, moreover, the narrative of miracles from ii. 11 to xii. 37. But, on the other side, there is in the earlier portion of the Gospel no lack of humiliation,—we think of His continued denial and rejection,—and from the foot-washing onward the narrative is eminently one of humility,—the sufferings and death of Jesus,—until the resurrection. Where is the reconciliation of this contrast? Undoubtedly in the view of the evangelist, that the abasement of Jesus, because self-abasement, was really a manifestation of His glory. It is only thus explained that he, so specially and emphatically, in all the sufferings of Jesus, points out their voluntariness, designedness, and the entire absence of constraint; we need compare only a few passages, such as John x. 17, 18, xii. 27, xiii. 3, 4, xiv. 31, xviii. 4, xix. 30, and it is only thus, also, that light is thrown upon the peculiar use of the phrase—being lifted up, for example, in John iii. 14, xii. 32, 34. To the question respecting the humanity of Jesus in the doctrine of the Apocalypse, we must reply that in it Jesus could not be a man in the proper sense, that is, a "real" not an "ideal" man, nor as the head of the human race referable to it; but rather He is regarded as the Messiah-Logos, become like a Son of man, and become like a Son of man that He might make "men" into "inhabitants of heaven," or like Himself (comp. Rev. xiv. 3); and with respect to the doctrine of the evangelist, the question can hardly be answered in any other way. Certainly, the Word is made flesh, and Jesus is "wearied with His journey," iv. 6, and desires to drink, iv. 7; He weeps, xi. 35; He groans in the spirit, and is troubled, xi. 33, 38; His soul is troubled, xii. 27; He thirsts, xix. 28; He is a man, viii. 40, but He is not flesh, born of flesh, iii. 6; He is in heaven, iii. 13; He is from above, and cometh from heaven, iii. 31; He is not from beneath, but from above, viii. 23; He is not of this world, viii. 23; He says, "whoso eateth my flesh and drinketh my blood hath eternal life," vi. 54. It is evident also that to the evangelist Jesus is not a man in the apocalyptic sense of the human, but He has taken a human appearance, flesh in the "ideal" sense of the word, in order to lead men away from the flesh in the "real" sense of the word, to the spirit; to give them life, and to make them like Himself. Neither does the evangelist know anything at all of a head of humanity; the vine and the branches represent something different, xv. 1–8.—We have seen that the seer did not consider the exalted state of Christ as if the divine glory of the exalted One was not before possessed, and only given and received at His entrance upon His exaltation, but that his representation is rather that Jesus had this glory pre-existently, and as given again in His earthly life; but while in the former case He received it in ideal, and in the latter in mixed ideal historical reality, He has, on the contrary, received it as the exalted One in historical, ever perfecting, and, as it were, increasingly historical reality. And just as little does there lie at the bottom of the statements of the evangelist the antithesis of to possess and to receive,—the Messiah-Logos indeed possesses everything as received; with him also, the distinction is that between to receive and to possess in ideal and in historic reality. Only thus conceived has the relation of the exalted to the pre-existent and to the earthly Christ a good sense, when Christ prays, "Now, O Father, glorify Thou me with Thine own self with the glory which I had with Thee before the world was," xvii. 5; and when He also says, "The hour is come that the Son of man should be glorified," xii. 23 (comp. xiii. 31); while at the wedding at Cana He had already manifested His glory, and while, moreover, that glory had already been seen by Isaiah (comp. xi. 4, xii. 28, xiii. 31, xvii. 10). The gradual historical progress of the glory of the exalted One, which we noticed in the Apocalypse, we find again in the promise of Jesus, "He that believeth on me, the works that I do shall he do also; and greater works shall he do; because I go to my Father," xiv. 12; and that "whatsoever ye shall ask in my name, that will I do, that the Father may be glorified in the Son," xiv. 13; and that the Comforter shall glorify Him, xvi. 14 (comp. xii. 32, x. 16). Only the evangelist knows this progress of the historical development, not as the seer, merely in the exalted state, but, as we have just seen, in the earthly sojourn, and, as the prologue shows, in the pre-existent state also. But this progressive historicalness of the ideal reality, with God and Christ, is one of the most striking peculiarities in the doctrine of the Apocalypse; and we need not especially point to the importance of the circumstance, that precisely the same peculiarity, only, in harmony with the design of the book, more extended and complete, distinguishes the evangelist also.

(c.) *Christ's Work.*

When in the doctrine of the Apocalypse we spoke of the works of *the pre-existent Christ,* we affirmed only that the description of Him as the "beginning of the creation of God," and as "the Word of God," implies a pre-existent activity. And what is the entire content of John i. 3, 4 (comp. vers. 9, 10), but an exposition of that which lies in these two predicates of Christ, namely, that He, as the real principle of the whole creation of God, and all revelation of God, has been active from eternity?

What we have mentioned as being, according to the Apocalypse, one of the chief features in the *earthly* work of Christ, namely, the word of God and the *testimony* of Jesus, meets us again in the evangelist in the same sense. Apart from the remarkable agreement of the evangelist with the seer in the frequent use of the words, testify and witness, it is expressly declared by Jesus in the former, that He came into the world to bear witness unto the truth, John xviii. 37 (comp. iii. 11, 32, v. 31, vii. 7, viii. 13, 14, 18, xiii. 21); and as expressly it is also said, "The words that I speak unto you, I speak not of myself," xiv. 10; "The word which ye hear is not mine, but the Father's which sent me," xiv. 24; "I have given unto them the words which Thou gavest me," xvii. 8; "I have given them Thy word," xvii. 14; "As my Father hath taught me, I speak these things," viii. 28 (comp. ii. 26, 40); "My doctrine is not mine, but His that sent me," vii. 16 (comp. ver. 17; John iii. 2, 34, viii. 47, xii. 49, 50). There cannot be a doubt that the evangelist regarded the word of God and the testimony of Jesus as one and the same, only considered from different sides; neither can there be a doubt that therein appeared to him, in historical realization, the general relation between God and Christ. If we must, with the seer, include in the word of God and the testimony of Jesus, the law and the prophets also, so it attains with the evangelist its full meaning only when He who says: "Search the Scriptures, for in them ye think ye have eternal life, and they are they which testify of me," v. 39; "Had ye believed Moses, ye would have believed me, for he wrote of me," v. 46 (comp. xii. 41),—has testified of Himself through the Scriptures and by the prophets, and now does so by His word, viii. 18, as indeed He must have done, as the light of men shining in the darkness, from the beginning, John i. 4, 5, and as the word of God which Jesus teaches (by the Logos-Messiah) must have been spoken also through the prophets or in the Scriptures; the evangelist distinguishes as little as the seer between the Old and the New Testament word of God (comp. v. 38, viii. 55, xvii. 6, 8, 14, 17; 1 John i. 10). It is worthy of notice, moreover, that by the evangelist, as well as by the seer, prominence is frequently given to the preceptive side of the word of God, and that even—who would have supposed it possible?—by the commandments are to be understood, just as with the seer, neither Old nor New Testament commandments only, but the union of both (comp. John xii. 49, 50 (?), xiii. 14, xiv. 15, 21, xv. 10, 12, 14, 17; 1 John ii. 3, 4, 7, 8, iii. 4, 22–24, iv. 21, v. 2, 3; 2 John 4–6).

The *conflict of Christ with the devil*, to which the Apocalypse often refers, certainly meets us frequently in the Gospel. "For this purpose the Son of God was manifested, that He might destroy the works of the devil," 1 John iii. 8; who does not think here of Rev. xii. 1–12, especially of ver. 5! When Jesus says to the Jews, "Ye are of your father the devil, and the lusts of your father ye will do: he was a murderer from the beginning," viii. 44 (comp. v. 16, 18, vii. 19, 20, 25, viii. 37, 40, xi. 53, xv. 18–24); and when the devil put into the heart of Judas Iscariot to betray Him, xiii. 2, and entered into him after the sop, xiii. 27, it is only the historical expression of what is apocalyptically represented in Rev. xii. 3, 4. Christ says: "the prince of this world cometh, and hath nothing in me," xiv. 30 (comp. x. 11–13), and the same is tacitly assumed in Rev. xii. 5. Christ is crucified, but His crucifixion is His exaltation, xii. 32, 33 (comp. iii. 14); and in Rev. xii. 5 the child is caught away to God and His throne. Christ says, "I also overcame, and am set down with my Father in His throne," Rev. iii. 21 (comp. v. 5); and in the Gospel He says, in the manner we have already seen to be common to the seer and the evangelist, "be of good cheer, I have overcome the world," xvi. 33; and His death, is going to the Father, for example, xvi. 28, and is also His glorification, xii. 23, xvii. 5.

We cannot expect to find in the Gospel a representation of the *victory of Christ over the devil* as the seer gives it, xii. 7–12. But do we not find the contents of that apocalyptic scene given by the evangelist? Christ says, "now is the judgment of this world; now shall the prince of this world be cast out," xii. 31. The connection of these words is, that to Christ, His death in the trying, ver. 27, as well as in the saving signification, vers. 28–30, has become fully present; therefore there is also present "now" as completed in the same, the judgment of this world; that is, as through this death, apparently the overthrow (comp. ver. 24), really the exaltation of Christ (comp. ver. 32), this world as the sphere of sin and death is condemned, judged, and ideally destroyed, so—the same thing seen and extended from another point of view; instead of the kingdom, the king; instead of the beginning as present, beginning and end conceived together as future—through the same death the prince of this world is cast out, not from heaven, not from his sphere, not from his authority, but parallel with "the judgment of this world," he is judged, condemned, ruined—in a word, overthrown. According to John xvi. 11, the Paraclete is to convince the world of judgment, that the prince of this world is judged; here appears as completed what in the earlier passages is at one time represented as perfected in the present, and at another in the future. From this point let us now look at such words as John xvii. 15, 1 John v. 18, 19, and we shall not say, with Köstlin (p. 498), that the evangelist assigns the time of His exaltation, the victory of the Son of man and His judgment upon the world, and upon the devil and his instruments, which with the seer begin only with the second advent; rather with the evangelist, as with the seer, the conquest of the devil and his kingdom through the exaltation of Christ in death is accomplished in ideal reality, and will some time—and when, but at the last day?—be accomplished in historical reality. The first half of John xii. 31, like xvi. 11, presents a close parallel to Rev. xii. 7–12; in the second half of xii. 31—similarly as we find it in Christ's predictions of His future coming—the beginning and the end, which in the Apocalypse are assigned to chap. xii. and xx., are conceived together. We recollect how the seer in chap. xii. perhaps does not represent the expulsion of the devil from the ideal world, but the ideal, or subjugation in principle of the devil, in the visionary form of an overthrow of the same from heaven; and we can scarcely refrain from the supposition that the figurative expression of casting out in xii. 31, at the meaning of which from the connection no expositor has yet arrived, will be explained by the presupposition of the scene of the overthrow of the devil in Rev. xii. In any case, the objector to the identity of the evangelist and the seer must grant that this coincidence respecting such a cardinal point is a very important element in the controversy.

That the evangelist regarded the crucified Jesus as the true *paschal lamb* follows, apart from John xix. 14 and the history of the last days, irresistibly from the words: "These things were done that the Scripture should be fulfilled, A bone of Him shall not be broken," John xix. 36 (comp. Ex. xii. 46; Num. ix. 12). On the other hand, the words of the Baptist, "Behold the Lamb of God, which taketh away the sin of the world," refer too definitely to Isa. liii., especially to vers. 4, 7, 11, 12; besides, in this connection they can be associated only with the historical Baptist. But from the manner of the evangelist elsewhere, it is wholly improbable that he would have given i. 29 and xix. 36 as heterogeneous; and it is just as improbable that he has, without any medium, applied the type of the paschal lamb to Christ; the result is this, that in the lamb-representation of the evangelist, as in that of the seer, the type of Isaiah and of the passover are combined, but the latter decidedly preponderating; indeed, the much controverted expression *αἴρειν*, John i. 29, can find its full explanation only when we recognise in the lamb symbol of the evangelist, not less than in that of the seer, a third element, namely, the lamb in its significance as a cleansing sacrifice.

We pass on to individual statements of the meaning of Christ's *death*. In Rev. v. 9, 10, xiv. 3, 4, we found the Old Testament idea of the *sin-offering*, and the other Old Testament idea of an *acquired people* combined, and both mediated by the later idea of the kingdom and claims of the devil. In vain we look in the Gospel for such expressions as "Thou wast slain," or hast permitted Thyself to be slain, and "hast redeemed." But Christ says in His intercessory prayer, "for their sakes I sanctify myself," that is, "present myself as a holy sacrifice," John xvii. 19 (comp. Lev. xxii. 2, 3); "my flesh which I will give for the life of the world," John vi. 51; and, "I lay down my life for the sheep," x. 15 (comp. v. 13). The Baptist says, "Behold the Lamb of God, which taketh away the sin of the world," i. 29. The evangelist writes, 1 John ii. 2, "He is the propitiation for our sins, and not for ours only, but for the sins of the whole world" (comp. 1 John iv. 10, iii. 5, 16). Can such expressions be explained otherwise than by the idea of an atoning sacrifice? The idea of an acquired people appears with special distinctness in John xi. 51, 52, "This spake he not of himself: but being high priest that year, he prophesied that Jesus should die for that nation; and not for that nation only, but that also He should gather together in one the children of God that were scattered abroad" (comp. John x. 11, 15, 16; 1 John i. 3, 7). The parallelism of these passages with Rev. v. 9, 10, xiv. 3, 4, is exceedingly striking. Finally, the kingdom and claims of the devil, from which Christ has delivered His people, appear in John viii. 32–36; and especially the words, "whosoever committeth sin is the servant of sin: if the Son therefore shall make you free, ye shall be free indeed," which, though not standing in express relation to the death of Christ, form the background, John iii. 14, 15, x. 11, 13, xiv. 30; 1 John iii. 8.

Another prominent representation is expressed by the Apocalypse in the words, they "have *washed* their robes, and *made them white* in the blood of the Lamb," vii. 14. When the evangelist writes, "The blood of Jesus Christ, His Son, cleanseth us from all sin," 1 John i. 7 (comp. ver. 9, "if we confess our sins, He is faithful and just to forgive us our sins, and to cleanse us from all unrighteousness"); "this is He that came by water and blood, even Jesus Christ, not by water only, but by water and blood," 1 John v. 6; "there are three that bear witness in earth, the Spirit, and the water, and the blood, and these three agree in one," ver. 8 (comp. John xix. 34, "forthwith came thereout blood and water"),—we have a close parallel to the passage in the Apocalypse; though by the present tense in 1 John i. 7, 9, the purifying operation is not described as accomplished once for all, but as present and continual (comp. Lechler, p. 220). In the passage, "he that is washed needeth not save to wash his feet, but is clean every whit," John xiii. 10, there is expressed, as so often with the evangelist, only the general significance of Christ, that which is given in 1 John i. 7 as the meaning of the one fact in His history, and in 1 John i. 9 as the act of God. The relation of purification, or washing with the blood of Christ, to baptism pressed itself upon our attention in the Apocalypse, so it is not less undeniable in the quoted statements of the evangelist, especially in 1 John v. 6, 7. The reading of Rev. xxii. 14, "who wash their garments," has a value for our comparison, so far as, by its description of the washing as continuous, it would furnish a more expressive parallel to 1 John i. 7, 9, than Rev. vii. 14. If we notice the difference between the evangelic and the apocalyptic method of representation, we shall also observe the similarity of thought between, "Except ye eat the flesh of the Son of man, and drink His blood, ye have no life in you.

Whoso eateth my flesh, and drinketh my blood, hath eternal life; and I will raise him up at the last day," John vi. 53, 54 (comp. ver. 51); and, "all that dwell upon the earth shall worship Him, whose names are not written in the book of life of the Lamb slain from the foundation of the world," Rev. xiii. 8; here Jesus, through His death, the principle of eternal life for all, cannot be overlooked. The two readings in Rev. i. 5, "delivered us from our sins," and "washed us from our sins," appear to us to stand opposed to each other with equal claims; while the washing has its parallel in the second passage quoted from the evangelist in this paragraph, xiii. 10 (*λούειν*), the delivering harmonizes with many of those mentioned before, especially John viii. 34 (comp. 1 John ii. 12). As in Rev. i. 5 the love of Christ to His people is emphatically expressed as the motive for giving His life, so in John xv. 13 (comp. vi. 51, x. 11–13, xiii. 1; 1 John iii. 16) it distinctly appears as the moving cause of His self-sacrifice. Respecting the universal significance of the death of Christ, we may compare Rev. v. 9 (comp. vii. 9, 10, with 1 John ii. 2, John vi. 51, xi. 52). Thus far even Köstlin (p. 486) finds the agreement of the seer with the evangelist, with regard to Christ's work, very remarkable.

In the representation of apocalyptic doctrine, against an expositor who would give to the work of Christ, especially to His death, a merely *typical* meaning in the thoughts of the seer, we had, with the objective, to give prominence also to the subjective side, in its true signification. How would that expositor maintain his position if we should oppose to him the parallels in the typical, from the Gospel and the Epistles? Just as in the Apocalypse Christians are witnesses, and in the word of their testimony, Rev. xii. 11, xvii. 6, imitate Christ, the true witness, Rev. i. 5; so in the Gospel the disciples witness, xv. 27, as Christ has witnessed, xviii. 37. As there, Christians overcame as Christ overcame, Rev. iii. 21, xii. 11; so here Christians have overcome the wicked one, 1 John ii. 13, 14, as Christ has overcome the world, John xvi. 33. There, Christians allow themselves to be slain, Rev. vi. 9, like the slain Lamb; and here it is said, 1 John iii. 16, "He laid down His life for us, and we ought to lay down our lives for the brethren" (comp. John xii. 25, 26). But what need of many examples? He who will see may see, that little as, with the seer, the objective meaning of the work of

Christ excludes its subjective meaning, or the reverse, since both exist in and with each other, so for the evangelist the two sides are related to each other, as different sides of one and the same subject.

We now turn to the *resurrection* of Christ. "Destroy this temple," He said, "and in three days I will raise it up," ii. 19; "as the Father raiseth up the dead, and quickeneth them; even so the Son quickeneth whom He will," v. 21; "the hour is coming, and now is, when the dead shall hear the voice of the Son of God; and they that hear shall live. For as the Father hath life in Himself, so hath He given to the Son to have life in Himself," v. 25, 26 (comp. ver. 28); "this is the Father's will which hath sent me, that of all which He hath given me I should lose nothing, but should raise it up again at the last day. And this is the will of Him that sent me, that every one which seeth the Son, and believeth on Him, may have everlasting life: and I will raise him up at the last day," vi. 39, 40 (comp. vers. 53, 54); "therefore doth my Father love me, because I lay down my life, that I might take it again. No man taketh it from me, but I lay it down of myself. I have power to lay it down, and I have power to take it again," John x. 17, 18; "I am the resurrection, and the life; he that believeth in me, though he were dead, yet shall he live: and whosoever liveth, and believeth in me, shall never die," xi. 25, 26. Of these passages, ii. 19, v. 26, x. 17, 18, are in their meaning strikingly parallel with Rev. i. 17, 18, ii. 8, and there needs only a reference to what has been said in the doctrine of the Apocalypse. The significance of the resurrection of Christ is once stated by the Apocalypse to be that Christ, as risen from the dead, has the keys of death and hades, i. 17, 18; and the same power is ascribed to Him in John v. 21, 25, vi. 39, 40, xi. 25. But when this significance is by the evangelist ascribed to Christ generally, and not merely to Christ risen from the dead, as with the seer, it has its ground far less in the circumstance that Christ, as reported by the evangelist, thus speaks of Himself not yet risen, than in the peculiarity of the evangelist, only recently noticed, that he often states generally of Christ what belongs to Him only according to a definite side of His nature, or rather according to an individual manifestation of His nature; the seer, on the other hand, wholly in keeping with his task as an author, gives prominence precisely to the individual side and the manifesting fact. Should it be said, on the contrary, that the seer looks upon Christ as if only through His resurrection He attains to the keys of death and the world of the dead, it is refuted by a correct exposition of Rev. i. 17; Christ is also to him the first and the last, living for ever, who through His resurrection is only revealed and historically realized as such, but by no means only becomes such. In a similar manner with the seer, as with the evangelist, Christ becomes mediator between God and the world not only through His giving Himself to death, much more is He also the mediator from eternity as the Messiah-Logos, who through His death of love has, so to say, historically realized and actually revealed His ideal as mediator, and, indeed, in the special sense of the atonement. Those who have taken a deeper glance, though only at one point, of the reciprocal courses of thought, as above expressed, will with difficulty still believe in two different personalities.—The Apocalypse ascribes to the risen Jesus yet another meaning; according to i. 5, He is also "the first-begotten of the dead;" and again I content myself with referring to what has been said concerning this expression in "the Doctrine," but especially to the fact that Christ charges Mary Magdalene with a message to His disciples—"Go to my brethren, and say to them, I ascend to my Father, and your Father; and to my God, and your God," John xx. 17, whereby, as the Risen One, He directly claims for Himself the relation of first-fruits to His people (comp. John xiv. 19).

Jesus *exalted*, John iii. 14, xii. 32, glorified, John vii. 39, xii. 16, 23, xiii. 31, 32, xvii. 1, 5, and gone from the world to the Father, vii. 33, xiii. 3, xvi. 5, 10, 16, 17, viii. 21, 22, xiii. 33, 36, xiv. 4, 5, 28 (comp. Rev. xii. 5), with the evangelist, as with the seer, continues the activity existing from eternity, and which has become historical in time. With the evangelist also the universal sphere of this activity is separated from the special sphere of Christendom; the atoning and revealing is also distinguished from the governing activity. If we take 1 John ii. 1 with the second half of ver. 2, we see at once in the advocate with the Father, Jesus Christ the righteous, the Lamb standing in the midst of the throne, and the four living creatures, and in the midst of the elders, the *propitiation for the* world, Rev. v. 6. The Lamb with "the seven eyes, which are the seven Spirits of

God, sent forth into all the earth," Rev. v. 6, according to John xiv. 16, prays the Father, and He gives the disciples another Comforter, that He may abide with them for ever; this Comforter, the Holy Ghost, the Father sends in the name of Christ, John xiv. 26; after He has gone He sends the Comforter to His disciples, John xvi. 7; after His resurrection Christ sends the disciples, as He is sent by the Father; breathes on them, and says, "Receive ye the Holy Ghost," xx. 21, 22; when the Comforter is come whom Christ sends from the Father, the Spirit of truth which proceeds from the Father, He testifies of Christ, and the disciples also testify, John xv. 26, 27. Christ prays even for those who should believe on Him through the word of His disciples, John xvii. 20: He is in the Gospel, as in the Apocalypse, continually the *revealer* of God to the world.—As in the Apocalypse Christ sits with His Father on His throne, iii. 21, so in the Gospel He is glorified by the Father with the glory which He had with Him before the world was, xvii. 5. God has given Him power over all flesh, that He may give eternal life to as many as the Father hath given Him, xvii. 2; the Father has given all things into His hands, xiii. 3. Nor is the peculiarity of the seer, that Christ's *authority* on one side already exists, and on the other is only future, like that of God, wanting in the evangelist. We need only compare John vii. 39, xii. 16, 23, 28, xiii. 31, 32, xvii. 1, 5: He is, and will be glorified.—That the *duality* in the relation of Christ to Christians, according to which He is the deliverer, as well as the head of the delivered, reaches to the exalted state of Christ, is shown by a comparison of 1 John ii. 1 with 1 John v. 16 (comp. John xx. 23), of John xx. 21, xvii. 20, of John xv. 26, 27, of John xiv. iii. 19, xii. 26, xvii. 24, xvi. 23, 26.—The activity of the exalted Christ in the narrow circle of *Christendom* is well distinguished in its individual aspects as little by the evangelist as by the seer. Moreover, the prophetic activity of the exalted Christ, contrary to the Apocalypse, in which He appears to the seer, and speaks through Him to Christendom, recedes in the Gospel. But if we observe, notwithstanding, how the apocalyptic letters begin, "These things saith He" (Christ), and conclude, "the Spirit saith;" if we notice how both are to the seer the same thing; and if we further notice that to the evangelist the works of the exalted Christ and the works of the Holy Spirit are also one and the same,—we shall see in the difference of the two writings on this point nothing more than the prominence of different aspects, conditioned by their design and form. If we take into account, in the comparison, that the evangelist had in his eye, not churches, but individuals, and that, as everywhere else, so here, the punitive works of Christ are thrown much into the background, it will be all the more significant how, with the evangelist, the parallel, xiv. 21, 23, to the words of Rev. iii. 20, presents itself, "He that loveth me shall be loved of my Father, and I will love him, and will manifest myself to him;" "if a man love me, he will keep my words: and my Father will love him, and we will love him, and we will come unto him, and make our abode with him;" and the parallel in the parable of the vine, John xv. 4–6, to the words of Rev. ii. 5, 16, 22, 23, iii. 3, 16; and, for example, that in John x. 28 to Rev. i. 16, ii. 1. For further remarks, I refer to the sections on the Spirit and the coming of Christ.

8. The Spirit.

Apart from the meaning—breath or wind, John iii. 8, the spirit is to the evangelist the opposite of flesh. The flesh is to him first the external, that which is bound by the conditions of time and space, the sensual, then that which is in itself lifeless matter. Agreeably with this, the spirit designates, first, that which is inward, the soul, John xi. 23 (comp. ver. 38); then that which is independent of time and space, the non-sensible, the immaterial, John iv. 23, 24; finally, that which animates, or the life, John xix. 30, vi. 63. In this meaning the spirit is parallel with the "spirit of life" and "the spirit," of Rev. xi. 11 and xiii. 15. More frequently the flesh means, with the evangelist, the mere natural, or the fallen natural life of sin and death. Corresponding to this, the spirit describes with him the principle which influences, changes, and intensifies, which is not natural,—it may be the principle of the *supernatural,* holy, divine; or it may be the principle of the sub- or anti-natural, hellish, or devilish *life.* In the sense of the non-natural generally, without distinction of divine or Satanic, the spirit appears with the evangelist only in isolated manifestations, when it is said: "Believe not every spirit, but try the spirits," 1 John iv. 1. The evangelist means the principle of the subnatural, hellish, devilish life, when he speaks of "Antichrist," 1 John iv. 3; of the "spirit of error," 1 John iv. 6; and of "every spirit that confesseth not that Jesus Christ is come in the flesh," 1 John iv. 3. The unmistakeable parallel to this presents itself in Rev. xvi. 13, 14. More frequently, however, the evangelist understands by the spirit the principle of the supernatural, holy, and divine life, in which sense he speaks of it sometimes expressly as the Holy Spirit of God, John i. 33, vii. 39, xiv. 26, xx. 22; the Spirit of God, 1 John iv. 2; the Spirit of truth, John xiv. 17, xv. 26, xvi. 13; 1 John iv. 6; and in the mouth of Jesus the Spirit is the Comforter, John xiv. 16, 26, xv. 26, xvi. 7. In this sense the seer uses the word spirit in every place except those before quoted. That the spirit is with the evangelist the *life*, and not the revealing principle, clearly follows from his general representations, as well as from many particular statements; for example, John iii. 5–8, iv. 10–14, vii. 38, 39, xiv. 16–19. Naturally, the evangelist does not speak of "the seven spirits;" but when we find that the seer always uses this representation when he wishes to describe the Spirit of God in all the *fulness* of His nature, and as well when he considers the spirit independently of God and Christ, Rev. i. 4, iv. 5, as when he speaks of Him as the spirit which Christ has, Rev. iii. 1, v. 6, there is at least an analogy to the latter in the words of the Baptist: "for God giveth not the spirit by measure," John iii. 34; and in the words of the risen Jesus, "receive ye Holy Ghost"—not "the" Holy Ghost, John xx. 22, both of which may be correctly referred to the distinction of the fulness from the partial, or from the first-fruits of the Spirit. It was evidently permitted to the evangelist to describe the spirit absolutely, as the seer often does, as the spirit of prophecy only in such connections as 1 John iv. 1–3; "the spirits of the prophets," Rev. xxii. 6, are included in the spirits which, according to 1 John iv. 1, Christians should prove whether they are of God.

The so-called *personality* or independence of the Spirit is acknowledged by the evangelist: we have seen that, according to such passages as Rev. i. 5, iv. 5, xxii. 17, ii. 7, xiv. 13, with the seer the Spirit stands over against God, and Christ, and Christians, with full and independent distinctness. By the evangelist there are presented at every point of the apocalyptic relation of the Spirit to *Christians, to Christ, and to God*, the most striking parallels. As in the Apocalypse the Spirit speaks to the churches, ii. 7, etc., and is expressly distinguished from the bride, xxii. 17; so the Comforter, which is the Holy Ghost, will teach the disciples, and bring all things to their remembrance, John xiv. 26; and when He comes He will testify of Christ, and the disciples also shall bear witness, John xv. 26, 27. As the brethren of the prophets have the testimony of Jesus, which is the spirit of prophecy, Rev. xix. 10; so the world cannot receive the Spirit, John vii. 39, but the disciples of the risen Christ do receive the Holy Ghost, xx. 22. In the Gospel the Spirit appears in the same independence with regard to Christ as in Rev. xxii. 17, and in the parting address especially, almost throughout (comp. John xiv. 16, 17, 26). Still, God has not given the Spirit unto him by measure, John iii. 34 (comp. Rev. iii. 1); and the exalted Christ sends the Spirit, John xv. 26, xvi. 7, vii. 39 (comp. Rev. v. 6); the Spirit will not speak of Himself, but He will take of the things of Christ, John xvi. 13–15 (comp. Rev. xix. 10). With the evangelist also, each of the prophets has a spirit, 1 John iv. 1–3 (comp. Rev. xx. 22); Jesus has, and sends the Spirit. As in the Apocalypse the seven eyes of the Lamb describe the Spirit as proper to Christ, and essentially related to Him, Rev. v. 6; so the resting of the Spirit on Christ, John i. 32, expresses the same distinction between Christ and the prophets. In the Gospel the Spirit guides, teaches, and reminds Christians, and makes known what He hears of Christ, John xvi. 13. It is almost the same to the evangelist whether anything is spoken by Jesus during His earthly life or by the Spirit. Jesus says: "I have yet many things to say unto you, but ye cannot bear them now. Howbeit when He, the Spirit of truth, is come, He will guide you into all truth," John xvi. 12, 13. But why are they the same to Him? Not only because the Spirit will not speak of Himself, but will testify of all which He hears; and will take of the things of Christ, and reveal them, John xvi. 13, 14; but also because Jesus will then no more speak in proverbs, but plainly of the Father, John xvi. 25. As the spirit of prophecy is to the seer the testimony of Jesus, Rev. xix. 10; so to the evangelist the sayings, the testimony, the teaching, the monitions, and guidance of the Spirit are the sayings, self-manifestations, and intercourse of Jesus Himself with His people.—The distinction of Christ from God in relation to the Spirit, we did not find in the Apocalypse to be that the Spirit is the divine, which Christ possesses besides His humanity; but rather in that Christ receives the Spirit from God, while God has the same not as received, but in Himself. The same distinction is made by the evangelist, not merely through his christology generally, but it is also expressly stated; for example, John i. 32–34, iii. 34, xiv. 16, 26, xv. 26, especially xvi. 15. The independent position of the Spirit in relation to God appears also in the evangelist, in that the Father sends the Spirit, John xiv. 26, and that He proceeds from the Father, xv. 26. The last-mentioned passage at the same time furnishes a most adequate parallel to Rev. i. 4, 5; *trinitarian* in sense as the seer has thought and spoken, so also has the evangelist, and while not with a weaker, yet, at the same time, not with a stronger emphasis. Köstlin also finds, *ut ante* (p. 488), that with the Apocalypse, "just as with John," the Spirit belongs not only to God, but also to Christ, the Lord of the world, and that He will abide in it through the latter.

Respecting the *activity* of the Spirit, we found in the Apocalypse that the Spirit (comp. Rev. v. 6, 9) was sent forth into the world by the exalted Jesus, or that since Christ's exaltation the principle of the divine or spiritual life has become active amongst men in the widest circles. The connection of the Spirit's work in time and origin with the exaltation of Christ is clearly expressed, John xvi. 7, 8. On the other hand, the evangelist does not speak of the Spirit being sent into the whole world, but Jesus predicts that if He be lifted up from the earth, He will draw all men unto Him, John xii. 32 (comp. xi. 52, also iii. 15–18, x. 16, and xvi. 8),—in which, according to what has been said above, there is no material difference. But when, according to the Apocalypse, men from all nations are made priest-kings through the work of the Spirit, v. 9 (comp. ver. 6), it is remarkable that this Old Testament conception appears directly in the evangelist when he writes, 1 John ii. 27, "the anointing (χρίσμα) which ye have received of Him abideth in you." As the seer refers the entire exalted position of the Christian in relation to God and men to the Spirit, Rev. i. 4, so also he refers the whole Christian salvation to the same source; and what else does the evangelist do when he speaks of the baptism with the Holy Ghost, John i. 33; of being born of the Spirit, John iii. 5 (comp. vers. 6, 8); of the (living) water which Jesus gives, iv. 14; and of the rivers of living waters which flow out from the believer, vii. 38 (comp. ver. 39)? The church as such is far from prominent with the evangelist; but of the seven Spirits and the seven stars, Rev. iii. 1, or of the church as the bearer or possessor of the divine life principle, we are strongly reminded by the words: "the Spirit of truth; whom the world cannot receive, because it seeth Him not, neither knoweth Him: but ye know Him, for he dwelleth with you, and shall be in you," xiv. 17. It is not to be expected, without prejudice, that He will stand forth from His universal activity in Christians and Christendom, with the evangelist as He does with the seer, specially or exclusively as the spirit of *prophecy*. We need not be surprised if the evangelist should generally speak of the works of the Spirit much more sparingly; and it is very significant if, by both writers, the work of the Spirit is so equally emphasized that Köstlin, p. 489, finds himself led to the remark: "we see that the Spirit had even early in the Johannine circles a special importance, a very active existence; we owe to Him the Apocalypse; here was He formed into a personal Paraclete; here occurred not only a general advance of the dogma, but this advance appears always with the assertion that it sprang from direct divine inspiration, and it had therefore a great interest in giving to the principle of this inspiration a concrete form." But far less could it arouse objection if, in the evangelist, we found the teaching and the reminding, xiv. 26, the testimony, xv. 26, and the reproof, xvi. 8–10, the guidance into all truth, xvi. 13, strongly prominent, and, on the contrary, no mention of prophecy. Yet, behold, there Jesus says of the Spirit, xvi. 13, "whatsoever He shall hear, that shall He speak: and He will show you things to come;" and hardly will there be found a better interpretation for these words than the Apocalypse in its general contents, and especially in all it says concerning the relation of the Spirit to these contents. Indeed, I confess that it always occurs to me in the reading of this passage, xvi. 13, that here may be given the key to the solution of the question how one man may have written both the Apocalypse and the Gospel; or can all the sayings resulting from the different mental modes of the two authors stand before a serious consideration of this one statement, certainly at first sight foreign to the Gospel?—When the seven Spirits are sent into all the *world*, Rev. v. 6, the seer regards the Spirit as operative upon the unbelieving; from Rev. iv. 5 we concluded, further, that to him this work consisted in the everlasting gospel going forth with the seal, and trumpet, and vial visions, with its call to repentance, xiv. 6, and therefore is an inner judging and condemning operation upon the world. According to John xvi. 8–11, the Spirit will reprove (ἐλέγξει, comp. Rev. iii. 19) the world of sin, and of righteousness, and of judgment; of sin, because they believe not in Christ; of righteousness, because He went to the Father, and His disciples would see Him no more; of judgment, because the prince of this world is judged. But these are precisely the substantial convicting contents of the apocalyptic everlasting gospel.

9. The Gospel.

Apart from the superscription, which does not come into consideration here, there is neither in the Gospel nor the Epistles the expression *evangel*, nor the word *evangelize*. In the Old Testament and original Christian sense, as the seer uses them, the evangelist could not apply them, when, in undeniable distinction from the seer, he had not to clothe Christianity in the sacred garments of the Old Testament, and as it were to make a retranslation of Christianity into Hebrew; but to clothe it in the drapery of modern speculation, so to say, to carry it over from the Jewish form of thought and language into that of the educated Gentile or Gentile Christian world; therefore to him the prophecy of the Old Testament is not the joyful message of God concerning His mystery, Rev. x. 7, but the testimony of the Scriptures respecting Christ, John v. 39 (comp. ver. 46), or the Scripture which is fulfilled in the history of Jesus, John ii. 22, vii. 38, 42, xiii. 18, xv. 25, xvii. 12, xix. 24, xxviii. 36, 37, xx. 9; and the proclamation to the world is not the everlasting gospel, with its call to repentance on account of the near approach of God's judgments, Rev. xiv. 6, 7; but the witness of the Spirit, and of the disciples of Jesus, John xv. 26, 27, or the publication of the eternal life now manifested, 1 John i. 2, 3, 5 (comp. 3 John 6–8). If the evangelist did not use *evangel* and *evangelize* in their later New Testament meaning,—in negative agreement with the seer,—it may have its ground less in the destination of his writing, and in regard for the reader, than in the fact that these expressions retained for him, as for the seer, their Old Testament original Christian sense.

The absence of the above-mentioned expressions will, moreover, in no way prove that the evangelist has considered the publication of Christianity only from one side, that of modern speculation; we find the *Old Testament* side presented by him as well as by the seer. When, with the evangelist, the Samaritan woman says: "I know that Messias cometh, which is called Christ; when He is come, He will tell us all things," iv. 25; when Jesus says to His disciples: "The time cometh when I shall no more speak unto you in proverbs, but I shall show you plainly of the Father," xvi. 25; and when He says of the Spirit: "He will show you things to come . . . He shall receive of mine, and shall show (ἀναγγέλλειν) it unto you;" when the evangelist writes, 1 John i. 2, 3, 5: "We show unto you that eternal life which was with the Father, and was manifested unto us; that which we have seen and have heard declare we unto you (ἀπαγγέλλειν) . . . this then is the message (ἀγγελία) (comp. 1 John iii. 11) which we have heard of Him, and declare unto you" (comp. also 1 John ii. 25),—who can deny that in all these places the publication of Christianity, though not by the name of evangel or gospel, is yet described with a remarkably close similarity to it—a similarity not springing from modern phraseology, but more from Old Testament expression, corresponding to the Messiah representation in christology?

There occur also in the evangelist, as expressions corresponding to the Logos doctrine, names for the publication of Christianity,—witness and bearing witness,—used of John the Baptist, John i. 7, 8, 15, 19, 32, 34, iii. 26, v. 33 (comp. iii. 11); of Christ, John iii. 11, 32, 33, iv. 44, v. 31, vii. 7, viii. 13, 14, 18, xiii. 21, xviii. 37; of the apostles, John xv. 27, xix. 35, xxi. 24; 1 John i. 2, iv. 14; 3 John 12; of the Spirit, John xv. 26; 1 John v. 6, 7. They are thus favourite formal words of the evangelist. Sometimes witness is changed for confession, John ix. 22, xii. 42; 1 John i. 9, ii. 23, iv. 2, 3, 15; 2 John 7. Can it really be accidental that the same expression is an undeniable favourite with the seer, who speaks of a witness in i. 5, ii. 13, iii. 14, xi. 3, xvii. 6; of witness in i. 2, 9, vi. 9, xi. 7, xix. 10,

xx. 4; and of bearing witness in i. 2, xxii. 16, 18, 20? Can it be seriously denied that here the evangelist and the seer remarkably agree, and agree too in an expression which bears its relation to the Logos doctrine, especially in the case of the seer, distinctly upon it?

10. The Christian Life.

The Gospel and the Epistles present parallels in John i. 7, 9, 12, 13, v. 23, xi. 51, 52, xii. 32, 1 John ii. 2, to Rev. v. 6, xiv. 6, v. 9 (comp. vii. 9). Christianity has not a particular, but an *universal* significance. That the universality, as well as the absolute character of Christianity, is certainly not expressed by the seer objectively, as with the evangelist, by light and truth, but subjectively, as far as Christianity forms for the one God and His Chosen an election of worshippers out of the world, we the more readily grant to Köstlin (*ut ante*, p. 489), since he himself adds that, with John, the latter certainly appears by the side of the former (comp. John xvii. 4, 10). But that relatively only a few had already become Christians, which the seer gives us to understand by his use of the expressions: "the whole earth," "the whole world," "men," "those who dwell on the earth;" the evangelist also says, partly by his use of the term "world" (see above, "the earth" and "mankind"), and partly in such sentences as John i. 10, 11, iii. 12, 19, 32, xii. 37, and many others. To the evangelist, also, the number of Christians in relation to the multitude of the unbelieving is infinitesimally small.—The evangelist, as little as the seer, expects in *the future* the conversion of all men (comp. John xv. 20, and the whole tenor of the Gospel and the Epistles; for example, John i. 10, 11, iii. 19; 1 John v. 10); one could never interpret John x. 16 (comp. xvii. 21 and 1 John ii. 8) in the sense of such an expectation. With the evangelist, as with the seer, universality has only the meaning that Christianity is not bound by any national limits, and therefore he has the promise that Christians will come more or less out of various nations (comp. John xi. 51, 52, xii. 32). The question whether, according to *the purpose of God,* all men should become Christians, the evangelist answers as differently as the seer. On one side it is said: "The light shineth in the darkness; and the darkness comprehended it not," i. 5; "He was in the world, and the world was made by Him, and the world knew Him not: He came unto His own, and His own received Him not," i. 10, 11 (comp. ver. 12); "God so loved the world, that He gave His only-begotten Son, that whosoever believeth in Him should not perish, but have eternal life," iii. 16 (comp. vers. 17, 19–21). And many other passages might be brought to show that, according to the view of the evangelist as well as according to that of the seer, God wills the salvation of all men, and offers it to them; but freely they either accept or reject it. On the other hand, we meet in the evangelist neither the "chosen" of the seer, Rev. xvii. 14, although election with him appears not only in the expression where he represents Jesus speaking of His choice of the disciples, John vi. 70, xiii. 18, xv. 16, 19 (comp. xvii. 14, 16; 2 John 1), nor the book of life, though both image and substance, in numberless references to life, undeniably relate to eternal life; but Jesus says, "All that the Father giveth me shall come to me," John vi. 37; "No man can come to me, except the Father, which hath sent me, draw him," vi. 44; "My Father, which gave them me, is greater than all," x. 29; "Father, I will that they also whom Thou hast given me be with me where I am," xvii. 24, 25 (comp. John xvii. 2, vi. 12). In a comprehensive retrospect the evangelist says: "But though He had done so many miracles before them, yet they believed not on Him: that the saying of Esaias the prophet might be fulfilled, which he spake, Lord, who hath believed our report? and to whom hath the arm of the Lord been revealed? Therefore they could not believe, because that Esaias said again, He hath blinded their eyes, and hardened their heart; that they should not see with their eyes, nor understand with their heart, and be converted, and I should heal them," xii. 37–40. There can be no doubt that in the thought of the evangelist, as in that of the seer, there existed, side by side with each other, the human historical view, according to which God wills the salvation of all men, and offers it to them; but they, freely deciding, believe or become hardened; and the divine absolute view, according to which some men believe and attain salvation, because God wills it, and others do not believe, and are lost, because God hardens them, and has not appointed them to salvation.

As a *condition* or prerequisite of becoming a Christian, there meets us in the Apocalypse, on the part of *God*, His will, or that men in the full sense are called, Rev. xix. 9; in the weaker sense of the word, called and chosen, xvii. 4, written in the book of life. Instead of calling in the weaker sense, we find the appearance of light; for example, in John i. 5, 12, 35, 36, the testimony of the Baptist; i. 7, 8, 32-34, the testimony of Jesus; iii. 11, 32, xii. 49, 50, His works; xiv. 11, and generally, all that whereby, in the evangelist, God requires faith from men. Instead of calling in the pregnant sense of the word, we have the calling and choice, and drawing of God to Christ, vi. 44; the gift of God, vi. 37, x. 29, xvii. 12, 24; in a word, all that wherein, with the evangelist, God realizes His purpose in the salvation of individuals; instead of being written in the book of life, such a passage as: "My sheep hear my voice, and I know them, and they follow me: and I give unto them eternal life; and they shall never perish, neither shall any man pluck them out of my hand," x. 27, 28. Thus we must say that, with the evangelist, only in other words and images, the same prerequisite to becoming a Christian appears on the part of God as with the seer. On the human side, we find in the Apocalypse the will of man, an ear to hear, or a receptive sense for the truth of the gospel; for example, Rev. ii. 7; a thirsting for the fountain of the water of life, xxi. 6, xxii. 17; the feeling that he is wretched and miserable; dissatisfaction with his subjective as well as with his objective condition in the world, iii. 17, 18. Is there not a striking parallel to the "ear to hear" in those words from the evangelist: "Why do ye not understand my speech? even because ye cannot hear my word," viii. 43; "He that is of God heareth God's words: ye therefore hear them not, because ye are not of God," viii. 47; "My sheep hear my voice," x. 27; "Every one that is of the truth heareth my voice," xviii. 37 (comp. v. 25); "The world heareth them. We are of God: he that knoweth God heareth us," 1 John iv. 5, 6? The "thirst" of the Apocalypse has still more striking parallels (comp. xxi. 6, xxii. 17) in the words of Christ to the Samaritan woman: "If thou knewest the gift of God, and who it is that saith to thee, Give me to drink; thou wouldest have asked of Him, and He would have given thee living water," iv. 10; "Whosoever drinketh of the water that I shall give him shall never thirst: but the water that I shall give him shall be in him a well of water springing up into everlasting life," iv. 14. Also the words of Jesus at the feast of Tabernacles: "If any man thirst, let him come unto me, and drink. He that believeth on me, as the scripture hath said, out of his belly shall flow rivers of living water," vii. 37, 38. The feeling of shame, poverty, and wretchedness, as required by the seer, iii. 17, 18, the evangelist describes also, at least indirectly, as prerequisites to Christianity (comp. John v. 40–44, viii. 32–35, ix. 39–41, xii. 43, also v. 6).

We have seen that the seer has nowhere denominated the process of becoming a Christian by the term "faith;" and we have seen also the reason why he studiously avoids this expression. It cannot therefore disturb us when we see the part which the word plays in the language of the evangelist. On the other hand, we shall not miss in the evangelist the Old Testament forms in which the seer represents it as the "fear" of God, giving "glory" to Him, and "repenting." We shall find it worthy of notice how both writers agree in those representations which we have described as common, or, more correctly, as natural to the seer. According to Rev. iii. 3, 10, vi. 9, xii. 17, a man in his view becomes a Christian when the word of God and the testimony of Jesus is made known and offered to him, and he, in the pregnant sense, hears or receives the same, so that it becomes his own; or when he listens to the voice of Jesus. The Baptist says, John iii. 31–33 (comp. ver. 11), "He that cometh from above is above all; . . . and what He hath seen and heard, that He testifieth; and no man receiveth His testimony. He that hath received His testimony hath set to his seal that God is true" (comp. i. 17, 18, v. 24, viii. 31, 32, 43–47, xii. 47–50, xvii. 6–8, 14; 1 John i. 2, 5, ii. 7, 24, iii. 11, v. 10; the hearing His voice, John v. 25, x. 3, xvi. 27, xviii. 37, also viii. 43). Since Jesus is the Word of God, the Light of the world, there belong to this place also the words of the Gospel respecting the reception of Jesus; for example, John i. 11, 12, v. 43, xiii. 20 (comp. xviii. 37, viii. 43); and the recognition of Him, i. 10, and many more. According to Rev. iii. 17, 18, a man becomes a Christian when he feels himself poor, etc., and comes to Christ, who offers to make him rich, etc.; and in the Gospel, Jesus says, "He that cometh to me shall never hunger," vi. 35; "All that the Father giveth me shall come to me: and him that cometh to me I will in no wise cast out," vi. 37 (comp. vers. 44, 45, 65, vii. 37, also iii. 20, 21).

We found *the meaning* of becoming a Christian pointed out in the Apocalypse, in an entirely general way, as being deliverance or salvation (comp. Rev. vii. 10, xii. 10). According to John iii. 17, God has "not sent His Son into the world to condemn the world, but that the world through Him might be saved" (comp. v. 34, x. 9; also the negative, "not perish," John iii. 15, 16, vi. 39, xvii. 12, xviii. 9): "We have seen and do testify that the Father sent the Son to be the Saviour of the world," 1 John iv. 14 (comp. John iv. 22, 42). In particulars we distinctly find the import of becoming a Christian, as represented by the evangelist, just so far agreeing or disagreeing with the statements of the Apocalypse, as his designations of the condition without Christ, and of the work of Christ, agree or disagree with the same. With respect to the stricter definitions of the Apocalypse, there is the entire absence of the Old Testament turning away from all iniquity; deliverance from falsehood (comp. Rev. xxi. 26, 27, xxii. 15) is echoed in John viii. 32, 44, 55 (comp. 1 John i. 8, ii. 4, 21, 22); conversion from fornication (comp. Rev. ii. 21, 22) clearly meets us in the words, "Every man that hath this hope in him purifieth himself, even as He is pure" (ἁγνός), 1 John iii. 3; the cleansing from former impurity (comp. Rev. iii. 4, vii. 14, xxi. 8, 27, xxii. 3, 11, 15), in the passage, "The blood of Jesus Christ His Son cleanseth us from all sin," 1 John i. 7 (comp. 1 John i. 9, iii. 3; John xiii. 10, 11, xv. 2, 3, xvii. 17); the change from wretchedness, etc. (comp. Rev. iii. 17, 18), in the words of Jesus, John ix. 39: "For judgment I am come into this world; that they which see not might see, and that they which see might be made blind;" and John viii. 12: "He that followeth me shall not walk in darkness, but shall have the light of life" (comp. xi. 9, 10, xii. 35, 36, 46; 1 John i. 5, 6, ii. 8, 9, 11); the passing from death unto life (comp. Rev. iii. 1–3), in the words: "He that heareth my word, and believeth on Him that sent me, hath everlasting life, and shall not come into condemnation, but is passed from death unto life," John v. 24 (comp. John v. 25; 1 John iii. 14); deliverance from bondage (comp. Rev. i. 5, v. 9, xiv. 3, 4), in the words of John viii. 31, 36. With the evangelist, when a man becomes a Christian, he passes from a state of alienation from God into one of closest union with Him (comp. Rev. xxi. 3, 4, xxii. 1, 2, with John i. 12, 13, viii. 41, 42, xx. 17; 1 John i. 3, iii. 1, iv. 12, 15, 16, v. 1, 19, etc.); from the misery of the present, with death as its climax, to the possession of eternal life; for example, John v. 25, 40, vi. 51, 57, x. 10, 28, xi. 25, xii. 25; 1 John iv. 9, v. 11–13. If, regarding the same thing from the standpoint of Christ's work, according to Rev. iii. 3, vi. 9, xii. 17 (comp. xix. 10), the Christian has the word of God and the testimony of Jesus; so the evangelist has written to Christian young men because they are strong, and the word of God abideth in them, 1 John ii. 14 (comp. John xvii. 6–8). As the Christian, according to Rev. iii. 21, v. 5, xii. 9–11, is a sharer in Christ's victory over the devil; so also, according to 1 John ii. 13, 14, Christian young men have overcome the wicked one (comp. John xvi. 33, xii. 31). As in the Apocalypse he is redeemed by God from the earth, v. 9, xiv. 3, 4; so the disciples are not of the world, John xv. 19, xvii. 14, 16 (comp. xvii. 6; 1 John iv. 5). As he has washed his robes and made them white in the blood of the Lamb; so, according to 1 John i. 7, the blood of Jesus Christ cleanseth from all sin. As, according to Rev. iii. 5, i. 9, he has experienced the love of Christ, and has been saved by Him; so also we find it according to John xiii. 1, 34, xv. 9, 12 (comp. iii. 16, xvii. 23), 1 John ii. 9. As in Rev. i. 5, 17, 18, ii. 8, he is allied to the Risen One, and through Him is made a partaker of eternal life; so it is also in John iii. 36, v. 21, 24, vi. 39, 40, 44, 47, 50, 51, 54, 57, 58, viii. 12, x. 28, xi. 25, 26, xii. 25, xvii. 2, 1 John v. 11–13. As in Rev. iii. 21, xi. 8, xiv. 4, Christ has become in every respect a type; so also in John xiii. 15, 34, xv. 9, 10, 12, xvii. 11, 14, 16, 18, 21–23, xx. 21; 1 John ii. 6, iii. 3, 7, iv. 17; John xiii. 16, xv. 18, 20. When we find that with the seer all that is implied in becoming a Christian is associated with *baptism* (comp. iii. 4, 5, 18, vii. 9, 13, 14), and that at the same time he unites the baptismal robes and the priestly garments, so John iii. 3–5, 1 John v. 6–8 (comp. ii. 27), show not merely that the evangelist conceived the Christian profession and baptism as essentially connected; but also that as, with the seer, the Old Testament representation of washing and making white the garments is mixed with the other, that of receiving garments, so the evangelist associates with the corresponding New Testament representation of the higher birth, the being born of God, of the Spirit, the other of becoming priests.

Of the *names* and *predicates* by which the Apocalypse describes the meaning of becoming a Christian, that of "*saints*" is wholly wanting with the evangelist,—incomprehensible if the seer used this name entirely in the sense of the Acts of the Apostles and of Paul; but very conceivable and very significant if the seer, as we have seen, used the term strictly after the manner of the Old Testament; and the evangelist, as he must, expressed himself in the style of the New Testament. When the Apocalypse, with the unquestionable purpose of honouring them, calls Christians *servants* of God or of Christ, and in their collective capacity the people of God, it appears at the first glance, apart from the last-mentioned expression, that the Gospel has a very different view on this point; for Christ says to His disciples, "I call you not servants; for the servant knoweth not what his lord doeth: but I have called you friends; for all things that I have heard of my Father I have made known unto you," John xv. 15. But it seems to us that the evangelist here takes the name of servant in contrast with freedom and friendship, just as he (John viii. 34) represents the Jews as replying to the saying of Christ, ver. 33, "the truth shall make you free," "We be Abraham's seed, and were never in bondage to any man. How sayest thou, Ye shall be made free?" To which Jesus answered, "Verily, verily, I say unto you, whosoever committeth sin is the servant of sin," vers. 34, 35. In this sense the seer uses the word, as his enumeration of the individual classes of men shows; for example, Rev. vi. 15, xix. 18. When Christ says, John xiii. 16, "The servant is not greater than his lord; neither he that is sent greater than he that sent him," the servant is there not the antithesis to the free, but to the lord; yet it has not the honourable signification of the apocalyptic servant of God or Christ. It would not have been surprising if the evangelist had altogether avoided this Old Testament name of honour; but it appears in John xii. 26, in the words of Jesus, "If any man serve me, let him follow me; and where I am, there shall also my servant be. If any man serve me, him will my Father honour" (comp. John xviii. 36). The servants of God who serve Him (as priests), xxii. 3, correspond to the true worshippers who worship the Father in spirit and in truth, John iv. 23.—To the *people* of God who are exhorted, Rev. xviii. 4, to come out of Babylon, and not to be partakers of her sins and judgments, correspond, apart from xi. 1, "His own which were in the world," John xiii. 1 (comp. xv. 19, xvii. 6, 9), who "love not the things that are in the world," 1 John ii. 15–17 (comp. v. 19).—

Naturally we do not find any trace in the evangelist of the description of Gentile Christians as *fearing God*, Rev. xi. 18, xix. 5.—The evangelist nowhere calls Christians *priests and kings*, as in Rev. i. 6, v. 10 (comp. i. 9); but when he writes: "As many as received Him, to them gave He power to become the sons of God, even to them that believe on His name: which were born, not of blood, nor of the will of the flesh, nor of the will of man, but of God," John i. 12, 13 (comp. Rev. v. 9, 10); when Jesus says, "The hour cometh, and now is, when the true worshippers shall worship the Father in spirit and in truth," iv. 23; when He promises: "Whatsoever ye shall ask the Father in my name, He will give it you: hitherto have ye asked nothing in my name; ask, and ye shall receive, that your joy may be full," xvi. 23, 24; and "at that day ye shall ask in my name: and I say not unto you, that I will pray the Father for you: for the Father Himself loveth you," xvi. 26, 27; when the evangelist writes: "This is the confidence that we have in Him, that, if we ask anything according to His will, He heareth us: and if we know that He hear us, whatsoever we ask, we know that we have the petitions that we desired of Him," 1 John v. 14, 15 (comp. Rev. v. 8, viii. 3–5); when he says: "Behold what manner of love the Father hath bestowed upon us, that we should be called the sons of God," 1 John iii. 1 (comp. Rev. xxi. 7, xxii. 3–5; Matt. v. 9); and "the anointing which ye have received of Him abideth in you," 1 John ii. 27 (comp. Rev. xiv. 1–5, ὁ Χριστός, and John xviii. 37),—it would be difficult to find another expression, representing in Old Testament form, such fulness of thought, namely as sonship to God, going as it does beyond all natural limits, than that of priests and kings redeemed from the whole natural human race unto God.—We need expect to hear nothing from the evangelist of *first-fruits* redeemed from the world unto God and the Lamb, Rev. xiv. 4; and yet in the words, "The Father seeketh such to worship Him," iv. 23 (comp. the beginning of the verse), there is obviously the same sense as that expressed by the seer, in harmony with his style, as first-fruits.—In describing the *relation* of Christians to *each other*, the evangelist never uses the word "fellow-servant." Not to mention John xxi. 23, the name "brother" meets us in the first Epistle with extraordinary frequency; for example, 1 John ii. 9, 10, 11, iii. 10, 12–17, iv. 20, 21, v. 16, also 3 John 3, 5, 10. When the evangelist writes, 1 John i. 3, "That which we have seen and heard declare we unto you, that ye also may have fellowship with us: and truly our fellowship is with the Father, and with His Son Jesus Christ;" and 1 John i. 7 (comp. ver. 6): "If we walk in the light, as He is in the light, we have fellowship one with another,"—it corresponds to the companionship "in tribulation and in the kingdom and patience of Jesus Christ," Rev. i. 9. When, in the Apocalypse, the heavenly inhabitants, the angels, appear as the fellow-servants of Christians, and the latter as their brethren, Rev. xii. 10, 11, xix. 10, xxii. 9; so in the evangelist the risen Jesus says to Mary Magdalene, "Go to my brethren, and say unto them, I ascend unto my Father, and your Father; and to my God, and your God," xx. 17 (comp. 1 John i. 3).

In the opinion of Köstlin, *ut ante*, p. 490, Christian *life* in the Apocalypse presents from various standpoints many noteworthy resemblances to the Johannine ideas. Let us look at them. The *works* of which the Apocalypse so frequently speaks form, according to this and many other expositors, the chief evidence of the Judaic character of its doctrine. It is singular that the Gospel and the Epistles use the expression in question with tolerably equal frequency. As the Apocalypse mentions the works of God, xv. 3; so the Gospel speaks of His work, and His works, iv. 34, vi. 28, 29, ix. 3, 4, x. 37, xvii. 4 (comp. v. 20). As the Apocalypse speaks of the works of Christ, ii. 25; so does the Gospel, v. 20, 36, vii. 3, 21, x. 25, 32, 33, 38, xiv. 10–12, xv. 24. As in the Apocalypse, the works of the Nicolaitanes, ii. 6; of Jezebel, ii. 22; of men, in an evil sense, xvi. 11 (comp. ix. 10); of Babylon, xviii. 6, —so in the Gospel are mentioned the evil works of men, iii. 19 (comp. ver. 20), vii. 7, 2 John 11; the works of the devil, 1 John iii. 8, John viii. 41; the works of Cain, 1 John iii. 11; also works wrought in God, John iii. 21; and the works of Abraham, John viii. 39. Certainly the passages here quoted from the seer and the evangelist are by no means completely parallel; still the great and wonderful works of God in the Apocalypse, and the works, or the work of God, in the Gospel—obviously apart from John vi. 28, 29—are essentially the same; and though the works of Christ in the Gospel scarcely come into contact with the same in the Apocalypse, there is, with regard to the latter and the works of the devil,—still more, the works of Abraham as well as the works of God, John vi. 28, 29,—in the evangelist an essential similarity of view. The works of men evidently in both writings have the same meaning. But it may be objected that the evangelist nowhere speaks of the works of Christians, and also that it is not said by him that men shall be rewarded according to their works. I think that he who wrote John iii. 19–21, vii. 7, 1 John iii. 11, 2 John 8 (comp. 3 John 8), cannot possibly have been dogmatically hindered from speaking of the works of Christians; if he has not, the reason is that he had no occasion to do so. Nor could much be said of reward according to works by an author who has to say concerning reward generally almost nothing at all. An unprejudiced comparison shows that the evangelist, as well as the seer, describes the activity of each life principle—be it divine, Christian, good; or be it devilish, worldly, evil—by the name of works; and that certainly he has, in harmony with the seer, laid remarkably great emphasis upon the activity of the life principle. Especially do the proper works of God, John vi. 28; of "your father," John viii. 41 (comp. 1 John iii. 8); of Abraham, John viii. 39, compared with those of Christ, Rev. ii. 26; of the Nicolaitanes, Rev. ii. 6; of Jezebel, ii. 22,—throw upon the personal relation of the evangelist and the seer a very strong light.

The activity of the Christian life principle in *general* we found to be expressed in the Apocalypse by the words: "he that is righteous, let him be righteous still; and he that is holy, let him be holy still," xxii. 11 (comp. Rev. xxii. 14, vii. 14). The evangelist writes: "every man that hath this hope in him purifieth himself, even as He is pure," 1 John iii. 3; "if ye know that He is righteous, ye know that every one that doeth righteousness is born of Him," 1 John ii. 29; and "he that doeth righteousness is righteous, even as He is righteous," 1 John iii. 7 (comp. ver. 10). It is to be observed also that in the same connection it is said, "Whosoever committeth sin, transgresseth also the law: for sin is the transgression of the law," 1 John iii. 4. The Old Testament description of individual acts, by which the practice of uprightness perfects itself as "righteousness," Rev. xix. 8, is not found in the evangelist. Also of increase, as in Rev. ii. 19; of inner wealth, as in Rev. ii. 9; of perfection, as in Rev. iii. 2, there is in the Gospel and Epistles hardly any other indication than the saying in the parable of the vine: "Every branch that beareth fruit, He purgeth it, that it may bring forth more fruit;" and in ver. 5, "he that abideth in me, and I in him, the same bringeth forth much fruit: for without me ye can do nothing;"

or in 1 John i. 7, "If we walk in the light, as He is in the light, we have fellowship one with another, and the blood of Jesus Christ His Son cleanseth us from all sin;" and in ver. 9, "If we confess our sins, He is faithful and just to forgive us our sins, and to cleanse us from all unrighteousness" (comp. iii. 2). When, however, many expositors take strong objection to "the standpoint of judgment according to an absolute standard which the Christian should reach" (comp. Rev. iii. 2), other passages, if they are measured by the same rule, such as, "whosoever abideth in Him sinneth not," 1 John iii. 6; "whosoever is born of God doth not commit sin," ver. 9; also the walking in light as He is in the light, 1 John i. 7; the purifying himself, as He is pure, 1 John iii. 3 (comp. τελειοῦν, John xvii. 23; 1 John ii. 5, iv. 12, 17, 18),—must present to them similar difficulty. But is not the Christian life judged according to an absolute standard which it should reach?

Of the *individual* aspects of the *unaggressive* activity of the Christian life principle there meets us in the Apocalypse only one, though certainly all-comprehensive, namely, that of love, to which at one time reference is made more in its relation to God and Christ, at another more in its relation to the brethren; or it is love to God and Christ, which shows itself in love to the brethren, Rev. ii. 4, 19. Instead of in two places, like the seer, the evangelist may be said to have spoken of love in twenty. But has he at any time done so in a different sense? Is it not with him the same love conceived at one time more in its relation to God and Christ, 1 John iv. 19, 20, for example, and at others more in relation to the brethren, 1 John ii. 10, iii. 14, etc.? And is not love to the brethren with him evidence of love to God and Christ, 1 John iv. 11, 12, xvi. 20, 21? Love to the world —the world understood in an ungodly and unchristian sense—is, to the annoyance of several expositors, wanting to the seer from his "theocratic standpoint," nor is it to be found in the evangelist. I refer to John xvii. 9: "I pray for them: I pray not for the world;" and to 1 John v. 16, "There is a sin unto death: I do not say that he shall pray for it" (comp. 2 John 10). That love in the Gospel and in the Epistles is mentioned so very much more frequently can be a difficulty only if the seer had, like the evangelist, the task of giving the testimony of Jesus and its application to life in general.

At the point of *transition* to the aggressive activity of the Christian life principle stands *prayer*. To the thanksgiving of Christians, as we find it in the Apocalypse, though mostly indirectly, iv. 10, 11, v. 8–10, 16–18, v. 12, vii. 10, xv. 3, 4, xii. 10, 11, xix. 1–7, every parallel is wanting in the evangelist. Supplications, which are expressed in part directly and in part indirectly, Rev. vi. 10, viii. 3–5, xxii. 16, agree at best only partially with what appears in John xiv. 13, 14, xvi. 23, 25, 1 John v. 14, 15, as the contents of Christian supplication. If, in the Apocalypse, the prayers of Christians are addressed sometimes to God, sometimes to the Lamb, and sometimes to both in one, so I may point to the "Him," 1 John v. 14, with its reference to "the name of the Son of God," ver. 13; to the "Advocate," 1 John ii. 1; and to the "Lord" and "God" of Thomas, John xx. 28, and to the position of Christ in the Gospel generally. The symbol of incense, which is referred to the prayers of saints, and which ascends with them before God, Rev. viii. 3-5, and which Rev. v. 8 explains as being the prayers of saints themselves, we cannot expect to find in the Gospel or the Epistles. But how the prayers of Christians become acceptable to God, and that they are so, the Lord tells us, "Verily, verily, I say unto you, Whatsoever ye shall ask the Father in my name, He will give it you. Hitherto have ye asked nothing in my name: ask, and ye shall receive, that your joy may be full," John xvi. 23, 24 (comp. ver. 26); and the evangelist says, 1 John iii. 22, "Whatsoever we ask, we receive of Him, because we keep His commandments, and do those things that are pleasing in His sight;" and 1 John v. 14, "This is the confidence that we have in Him, that, if we ask anything according to His will, He heareth us. And if we know that He heareth us, whatsoever we ask, we know that we have the petitions that we desired of Him" (comp. ver. 16). Incense represents the prayer of Christians; incense is given to them, and ascends with them, according to the seer; because, as he expressly says, they are prayers of saints; that is, they are offered in the name of Christ, or because they seek that which God wills,—that is, they are offered according to the will of God. The evangelist writes, "we know that we have the petitions." How otherwise could the seer symbolize the same thought than when he represents the angel as casting fire from the altar of sacrifice upon the earth, and voices, and thunderings, and lightnings, and an earthquake following, Rev. viii. 5? We found that in the

Apocalypse neither the elders nor the angels have a real mediatorial part in the prayers of saints; but that Christians, having themselves become kings and priests through the Lamb, need no other mediator, and that even through their prayers they very truly show their kingly priesthood. So the words: "At that day ye shall ask in my name: and I say not unto you, that I will pray the Father for you: for the Father Himself loveth you, because ye have loved me, and have believed that I came out from God," John xvi. 26, 27, can have no more suitable sense than that Christians, reconciled to God through the eternal mediator, have no further need of a mediator; and, indeed, the evangelist states, as distinctly and decidedly as John xiv. 12–14, xvi. 24, 1 John v. 14, 15 can express it, that Christians, through their prayers, exemplify precisely that which the seer calls their kingly priesthood.

Much richer results than those relating to the unaggressive activities of the Christian life principle are afforded by the Apocalypse concerning the development of the same *against its opposite;* if this is founded in the design of the book, so in the purpose of both writings we see the explanation of the fact that in the Gospel and the Epistles the relation is nearly reversed. Certainly the same dangers and difficulties which, according to the representations of the Apocalypse, meet and ensnare the Christian, have also prominence in the Gospel. If we look at the *temptations* which come from His own *flesh,* we find that the rebuke given by the Lord to the church at Ephesus, because they had left their first love, Rev. ii. 4, and had fallen from their former high standpoint, Rev. i. 5, corresponds to the words, "As the Father hath loved me, so have I loved you: continue ye in my love. If ye keep my commandments, ye shall abide in my love," etc., John xv. 9, 10; "He that dwelleth in love dwelleth in God, and God in him," 1 John iv. 16; "Whoso hath this world's good, and seeth his brother have need, and shutteth up his bowels of compassion from him, how dwelleth the love of God in him?" 1 John iii. 17 (comp. 1 John ii. 15, 16, and further). Who can deny that the evangelist everywhere, in his first Epistle, has contested with the Christian his departure from his first love, or his sinking from his earlier standpoint? Does the Lord say to the church at Sardis, "thou hast a name that thou livest and art dead"? Rev. iii. 1, 2; so also the evangelist writes, and certainly with a view to the condition of his readers, "he that loveth not his brother abideth in death," 1 John iii. 14 (comp. 1 John v. 16). The same church has only "a few names which have not defiled their garments," Rev. iii. 4, and we compare with it the whole connection and background of the words, "every man that hath this hope in him purifieth himself, even as He is pure," 1 John iii. 3; also ver. 6, "whoso abideth in Him sinneth not!" The strong condemnation of the church in Laodicea, Rev. iii. 15, 17, finds its theoretic confirmation in 1 John i. 8: "if we say that we have no sin, we deceive ourselves, and the truth is not in us" (comp. 1 John ii. 4, 9; John ix. 39–41). In the Apocalypse the Lord rebukes the church at Pergamos, because it had "them that hold the doctrine of Balaam," ii. 14, 15; and the church at Thyatira, because it "suffered that woman Jezebel, which calleth herself a prophetess, to teach and to seduce my servants to commit fornication, and to eat things sacrificed unto idols," ii. 20 (comp. ver. 22); and that the danger of false doctrine threatened the readers of the first Epistle is shown especially in 1 John ii. 18–27, iv. 1–6, and not much less distinctly in other passages (comp. also 2 John 7–9). With the words of the Apocalypse respecting the trials which should come upon Christians through the *enmity of the world*, for example, in Rev. ii. 10 (comp. iii. 10), those of the Lord, John xiii. 16, xv. 18–21, xvi. 1–4, 33, xvii. 14, and those of the evangelist, 1 John iii. 13, run parallel. And as there Christians, if they do not stand in the trial, but fear those things which they shall suffer, Rev. ii. 10, and do not hold fast the name of Christ, but deny His faith, ii. 13, iii. 8, and worship the beast, xiii. 8, xv. 16, xx. 4, are fearful and unbelieving, xxi. 8; so here the Lord exhorts His disciples: "Let not your heart be troubled, neither let it be afraid," John xiv. 27 (*δειλιάτω*, comp. *δειλοῖς*, Rev. xxi. 8); says to Peter, John xiii. 38 (comp. xii. 25): "Wilt thou lay down thy life for my sake? Verily, verily, I say unto thee, The cock shall not crow till thou hast denied me thrice" (*ἀρνεῖσθαι*, comp. John xviii. 25–27 and Rev. ii. 13, iii. 8); and to the disciples generally: "Behold, the hour cometh, yea, is now come, that ye shall be scattered, every man to his own, and shall leave me alone," xvi. 32; and the evangelist writes, "Who is a liar, but he that denieth (*ἀρνούμενος*) that Jesus is the Christ? He is Antichrist, that denieth the Father and the Son. Whosoever denieth the Son, the same hath not the Father," 1 John ii. 22, 23.

In the Apocalypse the Lord gives to the fallen *space for repentance* (comp. ii. 21); and where this is not used He comes with His punishment. Köstlin (*ut ante*, p. 492) finds the chief difference between the evangelist and the seer with regard to the Christian life to be, that with the latter fidelity to the faith is so far a work that it will be subject to the measuring rod of the approving or condemning judge; while the former, in the violation of the true confession, gives prominence to its opposition to God, to the truth, to the idea of the Christian, and refers not to a subject for judgment, but to the nature of the case. So far as this distinction really exists, it is explained by the different purpose and form of the two writings. But that the distinction is not universal, and that the seer, by the violation of the true confession, also points to the nature of the case, and the evangelist also to a subject of judgment, is, from such passages as Rev. ii. 4, 15, 20–23, iii. 1, 2, iv. 17, and 1 John ii. 28, iv. 17, to the unprejudiced, clear as the day.—That there is hardly any correspondence to the manifold *calls to repentance* addressed to those who have fallen in temptation, as they meet us in the Apocalypse, besides 1 John i. 9, "If we confess our sins, He is faithful and just to forgive us our sins, and to cleanse us from all unrighteousness" (comp. John xxi. 15–17; Rev. iii. 15–19), arises chiefly from the fact that the seer, in his prophetic character, has to do with the churches as a whole; the evangelist, on the contrary, has undeniably individuals in his eye, who, once fallen, are beyond the reach of his words. A soft echo of the apocalyptic admonition, Rev. iii. 1, 2, "I know thy works, that thou hast a name that thou livest, and art dead. Be watchful, and strengthen the things which remain, that are ready to die," is found in the words of the evangelist, "If any man see his brother sin a sin which is not unto death, he shall ask, and he shall give him life," 1 John v. 16. We may compare also Rev. ii. 5, 16, 22, 23, iii. 3, 16; John xv. 6; 1 John ii. 5, iii. 14, v. 12, and many others.

But as, with the seer, the work of the Christian is not to give way before any temptation, but rather to *overcome;* so, in highly significant parallelism, it is with the evangelist. The heavenly inhabitants say: "The accuser of our brethren is cast down, which accused them before our God day and night. And they overcame him by the blood of the Lamb, and by the word of their testimony; and they loved not their lives unto death," Rev. xii. 10, 11 (comp. the conclusion of the seven letters, and xxi. 7); and the evangelist says: "I write unto you, little children, because your sins are forgiven you for His name's sake. I write unto you, fathers, because ye have known Him that is from the beginning. I write unto you, young men, because ye have overcome the wicked one. I write unto you, little children, because ye have known the Father. I have written unto you, fathers, because ye have known Him that is from the beginning. I have written unto you, young men, because ye are strong, and the word of God abideth in you, and ye have overcome the wicked one," 1 John ii. 12–14. "Ye are of God, little children, and have overcome them; because greater is He that is in you, than he that is in the world," 1 John iv. 4; and "whatsoever is born of God overcometh the world: and this is the victory that overcometh the world, even our faith. Who is he that overcometh the world, but he that believeth that Jesus is the Son of God?" 1 John v. 4, 5. Köstlin says (p. 491): "We find here that, in a similar manner as with John, faith must fight against external and internal hindrances, against human and devilish devices, and maintain itself victorious; but the Apocalypse has only one side in common with John, the conception of the whole as *ἔργον*; the other, that the victory is already achieved, because the divine Spirit poured down upon believers is wanting; the victory is only completed with the successful conflict even unto death; the life is considered from death, and from the result which this shows is judged; only he who has passed safely over has conquered, although probably in xii. 11 there is mentioned the strengthening power of the victorious death of Jesus" (comp. John xvi. 33). But we have already shown, against Düsterdieck, that not only according to representations of their having overcome, otherwise inexplicable, but also according to universal analogy of the apocalyptic conceptions, the passage in question, xii. 11, must be so understood that even in becoming Christians they have overcome the devil in ideal reality, and that this victory is completed from stage to stage until it has reached perfection. To the *νενικήκατε*, 1 John ii. 15, 16, and *νικήσασα*, 1 John iv. 4, corresponds the *ἐνίκησαν*, Rev. xii. 11; to the *νικῶν* of the Apocalypse, the *νικᾷ* and *νικῶν* of 1 John v. 4, 5. Those who compare without prejudice cannot help recognising identity in an entirely peculiar and exceedingly important particular. Certainly the seer does not speak, and cannot as such speak, of "the victory which overcometh the world, even our faith," 1 John v. 4; but is not Rev. xii. 11, in connection with what immediately precedes, wholly the same thought, though in apocalyptic form? Nor does the seer say either "ye have overcome them," 1 John iv. 4, or "who is he that overcometh the world, but he that believeth that Jesus is the Son of God?" 1 John v. 5; but in several of the letters, are not the false teachers, the world, undeniably the objects for Christian conquest? The passages, Rev. xii. 11 and 1 John ii. 13, 14, are perfectly equal in sense and expression; and is it not significant that there the blood of the Lamb, and here the forgiveness of sins for His name's sake; there, the word of their testimony, and here the knowledge of Him and of the Father from the beginning, as well as the remaining in them of the word of God; there, not loving life unto death; here, being strong, and not loving the world,—are the subject of discourse? According to Rev. iii. 21, the overcoming of the Christian has its type in that of Christ; and in John xvi. 33, Christ says the same thing, "Be of good cheer, I have overcome the world;" and the evangelist writes, "As He is, so are we in this world," 1 John iv. 17 (comp. 1 John ii. 6, iii. 3).

Of the *individual phases of the conquest*, and, first, over temptations by *false teachers*, we find again the not fainting in trial, and the enduring for Christ's sake, the not bearing the evil, and the condemnation of falsehood, Rev. ii. 2, 3, at least partially, in the words concerning Diotrephes, 3 John 9, 10; and in those of 1 John ii. 24, "If that which ye have heard from the beginning shall remain in you," etc. (*μένειν*, Rev. *ὑπομονή*, comp. 2 John 6, 9); and also in the admonition, "Believe not every spirit, but try the spirits whether they are of God; because many false prophets are gone out into the world," 1 Jonh iv. 1 (comp. the expressions "lie" and "liar," 1 John ii. 21, 22). To the not bearing false teachers, and hatred of the deeds of the Nicolaitanes, Rev. ii. 6, corresponds the assurance, "If there come any unto you, and bring not this doctrine, receive him not into your house, neither bid him God-speed. For he that biddeth him God-speed is partaker of his evil deeds," 2 John 10, 11. When, in the Apocalypse, Christians are also warned against false teachers, and exhorted to hold fast what they have, and to keep the work of Christ, Rev. ii. 24–26; so the evangelist in view of the same says to his readers, "Look to yourselves, that we lose not those things which we have wrought, that we receive a full reward," 2 John 8 (comp. Rev. iii. 11): the keeping His commandments, 1 John ii. 4; the so walking as He walked, 1 John ii. 6 ; the self-purifying as He is pure, 1 John iii. 6 ; the remaining in Him, and not sinning, 1 John iii. 6 ; the practice of righteousness, and being righteous as He is righteous, 1 John iii. 7 (comp. iii. 6, 24, iv. 17, v. 18),—are all only the apocalyptic keeping the works of Jesus.—In the Apocalypse, Christians are warned against *persecutions*,—not to fear what they shall suffer, but to be faithful unto death, ii. 10 ; they are praised when they hold fast the name of the Lord, and do not deny His faith, ii. 13, 19; when they keep His word, and do not deny His name, iii. 8; when they keep the word of His patience, iii. 10; and hold fast what they have received, iii. 11 (comp. xiii. 10, xiv. 10–12, xii. 11, vi. 9, xx. 4); so the Lord exhorts His disciples not to fear nor be troubled, John xiv. 27. To faithfulness and stedfastness against all persecutions, corresponds continuing in the word of Jesus, John viii. 31, and in Jesus, John vi. 56, xv. 4–10 ; 1 John ii. 24–26 ; to not denying Him, 1 John ii. 23, iv. 2, 3, iv. 15 ; 2 John 7 ; John i. 20, ix. 22, xii. 42, and to keeping (*τηρεῖν*) the word and the commandments, correspond, even in name, the statements of John viii. 51, 52, xiv. 15, 21, 23, 24, xv. 10, 20, xvii. 6 ; 1 John ii. 3–5, iii. 22, 24, v. 2–4, v. 18 ; for as the *τηρεῖν* presents itself both here and there in every shade of meaning (comp. also Rev. xvi. 15 ; 1 John v. 18), it can with difficulty be explained by "the similarity of the times" alone ; finally, the not loving life, meets us in John xii. 25.—Those who overcome, watch against the temptations of *the flesh*, and keep their garments, Rev. xvi. 15 (comp. iii. 3, 4, 17, 18); and the evangelist writes: "keep yourselves from idols," 1 John v. 21 ; and "he that is begotten of God keepeth himself, and that wicked one toucheth him not," 1 John v. 18 (comp. ii. 28). God's people must come out of Babylon, that they may not be partakers of her sins, Rev. xviii. 4 ; with this we may compare 2 John 2 (comp. 3 John 8). Keeping the words of prophecy, Rev. i. 3, xxii. 9, 18, 19, has at least relationship with "heareth us," in 1 John iv. 6 (comp. ii. 24–27).

In the representation of the seer, the activity of the Christian life, though he does not present it in all its aspects, consists in the *imitation of Christ.* The "love" and the "service," Rev. ii. 19, in the highest probability, belong to the "works" of Christ, which should be kept until the end, Rev. ii. 26; and thus Jesus exhorts His disciples, John xiii. 34, xv. 12, to love each other, as He has loved them; and in washing their feet He gave them an example that they might do as He had done to them, John xiii. 15. Persecution there, as here, falls upon the disciples as upon their Master (comp. Rev. xi. 3–8; John xv. 18, 20). As Christ hath borne witness, so also His disciples, John xv. 27; as He gives His life for His friends, John xv. 13, 1 John iii. 16, so do they (comp. Rev. v. 9, vi. 9); as He is not of the world, neither are they, John xvii. 14, 16; as He walks, so do they, 1 John ii. 6; as He is holy, so are they in this world, 1 John iv. 17 (comp. Rev. iii. 3, 4). Here also is the place to point out the circumstance that with the evangelist, as with the seer, the relation of Christ to God is the type of the relation of the Christian to Christ, only with the former it is also the type of the relation of Christians to each other (for example, John xvii. 11, 21, 22); we may compare Rev. iii. 21 with John x. 14, 15, xx. 21, 22, xvii. 18, 21, 22.

That between the *promises* of the Apocalypse on the one hand, and those of the Gospel and Epistles on the other, there exists a surprising similarity, has been acknowledged, even by expositors who separate by a long period of time the various writings from each other (comp. Köstlin, *ut ante*, p. 497). Let us look at some particular features of this similarity. In the Apocalypse is promised nearness to and personal fellowship with God, Rev. iii. 12,—nearness, that is, life and love, even fellowship in nature and dignity with Christ, Rev. iii. 5, xii. 20, 21. To this corresponds dwelling in God, and God in men, 1 John iv. 12–16 (comp. iii. 24); also the words of Jesus, John vi. 37, "Him that cometh to me, I will in no wise cast out;" and John x. 28, "neither shall any man pluck them out of my hand" (comp. ver. 29); also the intercessory prayer, with its acknowledgment of the disciples—for example, xvii. 8, 14, 16; and the promise to come to His people, John xiv. 18–23. The promise of eternal life in the Apocalypse, ii. 7, 10, 11, 17, iii. 5, 12, has numberless parallels in the Gospel and the Epistles. The divine dignity, glory, blessedness, and power, which the Apocalypse promises to the victors, ii. 7, 27, iii. 5, 12, 20, 21, have their analogies in the freedom which comes through the truth, and in remaining as a son in the house for ever, John viii. 32–36; in the saying respecting the greater works which believers shall do, John xiv. 12; and the fulfilment of their petitions, John xiv. 13, xvi. 23–25; 1 John iii. 22, v. 14, 15; and in their sonship, 1 John iii. 1. Especially has the harmony between the promise of the hidden manna, Rev. ii. 17, and the discourse on the manna or bread from heaven, John vi. 31–35, 41, 48, 51, been more or less recognised. Undeniably from the same hand are the promises of the coming of Jesus, and His supping with true Christians, and of true Christians with Him, Rev. iii. 20; and of the love of Jesus, and His appearance with those who have loved Him; of His coming, and that of His Father, to make their abode with them, John xiv. 21, 23. When Christ promises to the victor that He will make him a pillar in the temple of his God, and that he shall go no more out, Rev. iii. 12; so also in John viii. 35 He says, "The servant abideth not in the house for ever, but the Son abideth ever" (comp. vi. 37). The promise, "To him that overcometh will I grant to sit with me in my throne, even as I also overcame, and am set down with my Father in His throne," iii. 21 (comp. ii. 26, 27), comes into close contact with the words of Jesus, "If any man serve me, let him follow me; and where I am, there shall also my servant be: if any man serve me, him will my Father honour," John xii. 26; and also with the prayer, "Father, I will that they also whom Thou hast given me be with me where I am, that they may behold my glory which Thou hast given me," John xvii. 24 (comp. John xvii. 22, xiv. 3). Jesus says, "He that overcometh shall not be hurt of the second death," Rev. ii. 11; and in the Gospel He says, "He that heareth my word, and believeth on Him that sent me, hath everlasting life, and shall not come into condemnation; but is passed from death unto life," John v. 24 (comp. vi. 39, 40, xi. 25, 26). That the promises of the Gospel and the Epistles are, just as those of the Apocalypse, essentially nothing else than the Christian life in the form of promise; that, with the evangelist, the Christian, even in his becoming a Christian, has already what the promises represent as future,—needs no proof (comp., for example, 1 John iii. 1, 2). Naturally, to those expositors who "hitherto have not in the least regarded themselves as on Johannine ground," must "the many parallels which present the glory of the eternal life be all the more surprising;" to us they bring no surprise, but only a heavily preponderating confirmation of the identity which we have traced, even in the more subtle connections.

11. Christendom.

Of the *names* and *symbols* of Christendom—the individual church appears with the evangelist only in 3 John 9, 10—occurring in the Apocalypse, we can expect to find the candlesticks and the stars in the Gospel, as little as the twelve tribes of Israel and the New Jerusalem. The people of God, the woman, and the bride, belong so exclusively to the Old Testament, that if they were absent in the evangelist we should not miss them; and should they be present, we could regard them only as marks of relationship with the seer. But if we do not claim the saying concerning the travailing woman, John xvi. 21 (comp. Rev. xii. 1–3), though it can hardly have been uttered without relation to Messianic woes, there at least meets us undeniably the *bride* of the Apocalypse in the words of the Baptist, "He that hath the bride is the bridegroom: but the friend of the bridegroom, which standeth and heareth him, rejoiceth greatly because of the bridegroom's voice. This my joy therefore is fulfilled," John iii. 29. The bride of which the Baptist speaks is the same Messianic church which is described as the bride by the seer, Rev. xix. 7–9, xxi. 9, xxii. 17. But as Jesus in Matt. ix. 15 speaks of the bridegroom as present, and in Matt. xxv. 1–3 as future; so to the evangelist John the Messianic church is the bride more according to the Old Testament side—the wedding beginning with the already accomplished appearance of Christ; but, on the other hand, to the apocalyptic John the same church is the bride more according to the New Testament side—the wedding imminent with the future appearance of Christ. But how stands the statement of Köstlin (*ut ante*, p. 490) with respect to such an appearance, "above all,—in the Apocalypse,—Christianity in its monotheistic character common to it with Judaism is against heathenism; but still not, as with John,—the evangelist,—in its trinitarianism against Judaism?" Surely, when the same expositor says (*ut ante*, p. 489), "The woman who is the subject of Rev. xii. 1, 2 is the Jewish and Christian church in one person; Christianity is therefore nothing different from Judaism, and can at the most be only a new form of the same," must he not in justice also conclude from John iii. 29 that Christianity was to the evangelist nothing different from Judaism? We rather say, that to the evangelist, as well as to the seer, every ideal was already present typically, or in actual prediction in the Old Covenant, and found its historical realization or fulfilment through the appearance of Christ in Israel, and will find it in a more perfect manner on the appearance of Christ at the last day, but that the evangelist as such must give prominence far more to the historical, the seer as such to the future realization. But if the evangelist is not more Jewish than the seer, because he describes the Messianic church in the Old Testament form as the bride of the Messiah, why must the seer be held to be more Jewish than the evangelist, because he mostly treats of eternal life as future? That Christ has already come to the bride, is as directly associated with the gift of eternal life already bestowed, as that Christ will come to her is connected with the promise of eternal life; the former is the evangelistic, the latter the apocalyptic conception of one and the same thing.

Reserving the evangelic symbol of "the sheep" for future consideration, since the Apocalypse has it only in a later place, we inquire how the evangelist regards the two *constituent elements*, Jewish and Gentile Christians, in their relation to each other. That, according to the Gospel, just as with the Apocalypse, men, not only from the Jews, but from the various nations, had become Christians, and could and should do so in the future, follows not only from such passages as John i. 12, 13, xi. 52, xii. 32, but undoubtedly from the whole tenor of the Gospel, and is universally admitted. The idea, according to which the seer either distinguishes the Gentile Christians as dependants of the Jewish converts, the peculiar people of God, or prefers the latter, through the sealing, as belonging to them alone, or considers Gentile Christians under the name of Israel, only as allies and citizens of the Messianic kingdom, appears to us entirely without foundation. On the other side, we cannot agree with the opinion that the seer makes no distinction between Jewish and Gentile Christians; we have found rather that he distinguishes Christians at one time, Rev. xi. 18, xix. 5, according to their origin, bringing over the pre-Christian relation of Jews and proselytes in the "servants" of God, and "them that fear" His name; at another, Rev. xii. 17, symbolizing, agreeably with the connection, the Gentile

Christians as the "remnant" of the woman's seed, a tacit time distinction of the Jewish Christians as the earlier born. And the evangelist does this precisely in the same way. Not to mention the passage in the intercessory prayer, John xvii. 20–23, which, in our judgment, certainly refers to Gentile Christians, the words of Jesus, "And I, if I be lifted up from the earth, will draw all men unto me," John xii. 32, stand in undeniable connection with the request of the Greeks, John xii. 21–32, and form in that connection a parallel to the fearers of God in the Apocalypse; as also the saying of Jesus concerning the other sheep which He has, and which are not of this fold, but which He must bring, and which will hearken to His voice, and there shall be one fold and one Shepherd, John x. 16, runs parallel with the apocalyptic description of Gentile Christians as the remnant of the woman's seed.

We have seen, however, that the seer *distinguishes* Christians, not merely according to descent and time, but also according to their *importance*. Amongst the servants of God, some are so in an eminent sense; the prophets divide again, into prophets in a narrower sense, and into apostles. From those who have the testimony of Jesus there come into prominence those who have it in an emphatic sense, namely, the martyrs. But we have already shown, in the section on the Spirit, how the evangelist, 1 John ii. 27, recognises the anointing of all Christians; and yet, for example in 1 John iv. 1–3, clearly distinguishes the prophets of the Apocalypse from other Christians; and how in the parting address, for example in John xiv. 25, 26, xvi. 13, on the one side he comprehends apostles and prophets, and on the other distinguishes them, John xv. 26, 27. Indeed, the distinction which the seer makes between prophets, and to some extent apostles, and ordinary Christians, cannot be more forcibly expressed than in the words of Jesus: "Neither pray I for these alone, but for them also which shall believe on me through their word," John xvii. 20. And in order to see martyrdom distinguished in the Gospel from the common Christian testimony, we need only read in connection John xv. 26 to xvi. 4; or is it only accidental that testimony and excommunication and death stand so closely together?

In their common though only scanty indications respecting the *organization* of the universal or of individual churches, the Apocalypse and the Gospel hardly touch each other. That the evangelist, not less than the seer, regards the universal Christian church as a great living unity, is emphatically expressed in the "one fold and one shepherd," John x. 16 (comp. xvii. 21–23, xi. 52); but that which the Gospel contains respecting the office of the apostles, John xx. 21–23 (comp. xiii. 16), and the third Epistle, vers. 5–8, respecting the office of evangelists, and probably also, vers. 9–11, respecting that of the presbytery, has no parallel in the Apocalypse; as, on the other hand, nothing corresponding to the indications of the latter concerning the Lord's day, and the statements with respect to it, are to be found in the Gospel and Epistles.

In the *history* of Christendom the two representations do not at the first glance appear to harmonize. Certainly the contents of Rev. xii. 1–9, especially ver. 12, or the description of the conflict of Christ with the devil, have, as we have seen in the work of Christ, an undeniable and highly significant relation to a view of His work often expressed by the evangelic Christ Himself. But of the history of Christendom after Christ, given in the Apocalypse, xii. 13–17, in its *Jewish Christian period*, in its transition to the Gentiles, and in its, ver. 17, summarily indicated promulgation among them, there is hardly anything in the Gospel or the Epistles to remind us. In the Epistles, or, more correctly, in the Epistle, where the history of the church generally is not in question, this need not surprise us. It is otherwise with the Gospel, which, though in the form of prophecy, treats frequently of the time of Rev. xii. 13–17, but in a very anomalous manner. If we compare such passages as John x. 16, xi. 52, xii. 24, 32, xvii. 20-23, there meets us as a prediction of Christ with reference to the side involved in this question—this: Christ in death, apparently defeated and overcome, but in truth voluntarily sacrificing Himself (comp. John x. 17, 18, xvii. 19) and raising Himself to glory (comp. John xii. 23, 32, xvii. 5, etc.); but through death unfolding a far more comprehensive activity, John xii. 24, extending from the Jews to all nations, or to the whole of mankind, John xii. 32, and gathering from Jews and Gentiles one united church, John x. 16. How differently does this sound from the flight of the woman into the wilderness, there to continue during the time of tribulation! But do not the elders in the Apocalypse sing of those who have been redeemed by the blood of the Lamb out of every people and nation, v. 9 (comp.

xiv. 4)? and does not Jesus in the Gospel say to His disciples, "They shall put you out of the synagogues; yea, the time cometh, that whosoever killeth you will think that he doeth God service," John xvi. 2; and, "If the world hate you, ye know that it hated me before it hated you," xv. 18: "If they have persecuted me, they will also persecute you," xv. 20?—all which, partly from the expression and partly from the connection, refers to the persecutions of the Jews, and predicts just that which is narrated in Rev. xii. 13: the dragon "persecuted the woman which brought forth the man-child." We must therefore say, that when, corresponding with the aim of the two writings in the Apocalypse, the history of Christendom is represented more prominently as persecution through the unbelief of the Jewish world, and in the Gospel not less prominently as the saving work of the crucified and Risen One in the needy Gentile world, there is still not wanting in either of the two the evidence that the other conception was known, and familiar to it.

Respecting the history of Christendom in the *Gentile Christian*, or in the *period* present to the seer, the seven letters furnished us with tolerably exact information. We observe at once that antichristian Judaism, as well as heathenism, has already persecuted the Christians to the uttermost; the former by its calumnies, the latter by open violence, though not in all places with equal vigour. The Gospel offers to this no parallel, and thus directly proves its historical character in that, in its predictions of the hatred and persecutions of the world, it does not pass the breadth of a finger beyond the circle of the historical vision of Jesus, the Jewish Christian period (comp. John xv. 18, xvi. 4). But in the first Epistle we read: "Marvel not, my brethren, if the world hate you," iii. 13; therefore the readers of the evangelist, like those of the seer, have already experienced the hatred of the world. But whether the hating world of the Epistle included Jews and Gentiles, or only Gentiles, cannot by reason of the universality of the expression be decided by it alone; still the whole tenor of the Epistle, and especially its conclusion, v. 19–21, speaks more in favour of the latter view; and that, after what happened between the authorship of the Apocalypse and that of the Epistle, the synagogue of Satan, with its calumnies, was silenced at the time of the latter, is at least not improbable.

The same terrible catastrophe makes it also perfectly explicable that Judaistic *error*, which appears in the Apocalypse already overcome, expelled, and, as belonging essentially to the past, is not mentioned at all in the Epistles of John. When, on the other hand, ethnistic error in the apocalyptic churches impresses us with the feeling that it is still powerful, and, indeed, still threatens to be dangerous, we must, with our belief in the identity of the two writers, fully expect that in the letters of the same man, though written a series of years later, should they occupy themselves with false doctrine in general, the same ethnistic error, be it still in the apocalyptic or in the succeeding stage of development, will meet us. That the three Epistles contend against doctrinal error, and that it is ethnistic in its nature, needs no proof. But a continuity, much less a parallelism with the errors of the Apocalypse, is certainly not discoverable in the errors spoken of in the Epistles by a superficial examination. If we look closely, however, we find that the false doctrines contested in the Epistles were in practice antinomian, like those of the Nicolaitanes: "Whosoever committeth sin transgresseth also the law: for sin is the transgression of the law," 1 John iii. 4 (comp. v. 17); indeed, the whole Epistle is full of evidence that a profession of Christianity and sin are at variance with each other, and is therefore a prolonged proof that his opponents, just as the false teachers of the Apocalypse, desired to unite that profession and immoral conduct with each other. But, since the first Epistle does not, like the Apocalypse, contend against the temptation to eat of sacrifices offered to idols and to fornication, we must take into account that antinomianism may, in the course of a few years, have become generalized; and we must further consider that the seer had before him a pretty well developed antinomianism, and yet for the sake of the Old Testament prophetic form has mentioned only two sides of it, namely, eating of idolatrous sacrifices and whoredom. And is it not, then, all the more significant when the first Epistle gives the warning against immorality in a form so strongly suggestive of these two evils, ii. 12–17 (comp. iii. 7–10)? when he contests the distinction—after the knowledge of the depths of Satan—obviously current with the apocalyptic teachers of error, between "sin" and that "forbidden of God," iii. 4? when he again and again presents as an example, ii. 6, iii. 5, 7–9, iv. 17, the apocalyptic "works" of Christ, that is, the evident fulfilment of the law in Christ, in contrast with the deliverance from the same contended for by false teachers, Rev. ii. 26 (comp. Matt. v. 17–19)? when He says of the commandments of God that they are not "grievous" (βαρεῖαι), v. 3, as the seer speaks ironically of the burden (βάρος) of the same, ii. 24? when, with undoubted reference to false doctrine, he speaks of "sin unto death," v. 16 (comp. ii. 16, 32, iii. 1, 2)? and when he concludes with the admonition remarkable to every unprejudiced reader, "Little children, keep yourselves from idols"? With the antinomian practice there is associated another very important parallel feature, namely, that the false teachers in the Epistles, just as those in the Apocalypse, are represented as claiming inspiration; they were false prophets (comp. Rev. ii. 20, 14; 1 John iv. 1–3). The knowledge which the apocalyptic false teachers claim to have gained in this way is criticised by the seer only in one place, ii. 24, but in a manner which clearly shows the part which "to know" played in their words and deeds. But we may venture to take as granted that the "knowledge," so often occurring in the Gospel and in the first Epistle, had its polemical occasion in the gnosis claimed and glorified by these impostors. While the gnosis of the apocalyptic false teachers was a knowledge of the depths or mysteries which served as a theoretic foundation for Antinomianism, and the gnosis of the false teachers of the Epistle separated the man Jesus and the Christ, or the Son of God, 1 John ii. 22, iv. 15, or denied that Jesus who had appeared in the flesh was Christ, 1 John iv. 2, 3, 2 John 7, and by this docetism also laid a theoretic foundation for antinomianism, the Apocalypse has still no express statement against docetism. But, even apart from the ever-striking coincidence that the Lord rebukes the church at Thyatira as "the Son of God," ii. 18, there needs only a single glance at the first Epistle in order to find again the "knowledge of the depths;" for example, ii. 3, 4, 13, 14, iii. 1, iv. 6, 12–14, and many others; and we need only read 1 John ii. 18–20 to perceive the newness of the form in which the gnosis is contested by the first Epistle; and instead of entering into an hypothesis as to the manner in which the apocalyptic gnosis may have developed into the gnosis of the epistolary form, we point rather to the preceding stage of the former, which, according to 1 Cor. xv. 12 (comp. 33, 34), already denied the resurrection of the dead.

12. Antichrist.

The evangelist writes: "Little children, it is the last time: and as ye have heard that antichrist shall come, even now are there many antichrists; whereby we know that it is the last time," 1 John ii. 18; "Who is a liar, but he that denieth that Jesus is the Christ? He is antichrist, that denieth the Father and the Son," 1 John ii. 22; "Many false prophets are gone out into the world. Hereby know we the Spirit of God: Every spirit that confesseth that Jesus Christ is come in the flesh is of God: and every spirit that confesseth not that Jesus Christ is come in the flesh is not of God: and this is that spirit of antichrist of whom—according to the correct reading ὅ—ye have heard that he should come; and even now already is he in the world," 1 John iv. 1-3; "Many deceivers are entered into the world, who confess not that Jesus Christ is come in the flesh: this is a deceiver and antichrist," 2 John 7. In the first of these passages the evangelist refers the reader to an earlier announcement of the coming of antichrist; in the third to an announcement of the coming of the spirit of antichrist; and of both he says that they now fulfil, or begin to fulfil, themselves. If we compare with this on the one side the prediction of false Christs and false prophets, Matt. xxiv. 24, as well as that of "the man of sin," "the son of perdition," 2 Thess. ii. 3, 4, and on the other the apocalyptic narrative of the beast and the false prophet, Rev. xiii.; if we notice, moreover, how, in the account of false doctrine, "a deceiver and an antichrist," 2 John 7, are classed together, but at the same time are also distinguished, and "read exactly like an allusion to the closely associated picture of Rev. xiii." (Ewald, *ut ante*, p. 364; compare also the "deceiver" with Rev. xiii. 14, as well as the "of (out of) the world," 1 John iv. 5, and the ascent "out of the earth," Rev. xiii. 11), we must agree with those expositors who think the evangelist refers in the passages quoted, not to Christian teaching respecting the future development, or the future of antichrist in general, but to the *prediction of the two beasts in the Apocalypse*, as to one well known to his readers.

The denial of the identity between that which is predicted and that which is accepted may, however, be consistent with this view; for then, according to Köstlin (p. 496), the evangelist has not passed by the prediction of the Apocalypse, but has referred antichrist to the false teachers who in his time were the chief foes of Christianity, so that it has lost the external form, which corresponded to the theocratic view of the world (compare also Weiss, *bibl. Theol.* p. 753). But is there not some misunderstanding here? When we closely examine the related passages of the first and second Epistles, the result is this: the evangelist has by no means explained the prediction of the two beasts in the Apocalypse in the sense of the false teachers of his time, as if it were already completely fulfilled in them; much rather the lying prophets are to him antichrist so far as they are the organs (comp. John vi. 70), the precursors, manifesting themselves in various ways, of the yet future individual personality of antichrist, in whom all will culminate, and, indeed, not so much on the side of persecution—the beast—as on the side of temptation—the false prophets. Far be it from me to wish to deny the difference between the expectation of the Apocalypse and the Epistles on this point. But it cannot be doubted that as the doctrine of the advent remaining in itself essentially the same, has according to the circumstances, in the view of the Christian prophets, taken manifoldly various forms; so also the expectation of the coming of antichrist in its concrete features must follow the development of history within and without the church. Nothing more natural than that John, after he, in the year 68, under the impressions of the Neronic persecution of the Christians, and its subsequent effects, had seen in the Roman empire, especially in Nero, the antichrist, and in the heathen magic and divination the ally of the same, as it were the antipneuma, should, a few years later, subsequent to the destruction of Jerusalem, no more expect antichrist in its earlier form; it is very obvious also that, under the impression of the false doctrine which began to work fundamental disaster in the churches, when it denied the historical Christ, he now saw in *these false teachers*, which earlier he had not associated with false prophets, the *future antichrist chiefly on the side of lying and deception; or also, and more definitely, the future antipneuma either come or preparing the way;* and is it not in harmony with the pervading peculiarity of the seer and the evangelist, when he describes the false teachers as the precursors, the germs, the manifold connections of antichrist, at one time as many antichrists, at another as many false prophets, now as the antichrist, and then as the spirit of antichrist itself?

Had the evangelist perceived, in false prophecy or in false doctrine, as it is affirmed, the present complete fulfilment of the expectation of antichrist, he could not have written, "as ye have heard," "of whom ye have heard;" but he could have written thus if he was the seer to whom earlier the individual phases of the Roman empire were the beast, and to whom now the antichrist and the antipneuma began to manifest themselves in the many antichrists and false prophets.

But it is asked, Why, then, is the *Gospel* wholly *silent* respecting antichrist, when the same, according to Matt. xxiv. 24, was included in the predictions of Jesus? I reply by asking the opposite question: Is there really nothing to be found respecting antichrist in the Gospel? If we compare John viii. 40–44, especially ver. 44, with Rev. xiii., where murder and falsehood, the two works of the devil, are ascribed to the two beasts; if we compare John vi. 70, 71, xiii. 2, 10, 11, xviii. 27, xvii. 12, especially the last mentioned, with Rev. xvii. 8, 11; if, also, we read John x. 8–10, v. 43, and especially x. 5, in its true meaning,—we shall, on the assumption of some connection between the fourth Gospel and the teaching of Christ and the apostles, and in view of the words of John v. 28, 29, not to be explained away, find established what was to be expected, namely, that the representation of antichrist was not at all strange to him. Certainly, on a superficial consideration, the difference between the Gospel and the Apocalypse on this point appears exceedingly great. But we have now several times made acquaintance with the peculiar genius manifesting itself in both, to which the future is already present, and the present is yet future. The nature of antichrist had already for John revealed itself in Cain (comp. John viii. 44; 1 John iii. 12). Cain is evidently to him an incarnation, or an instrument of the devil. Antichrist reached its relative perfection in the Jews, the children of the devil, and in the individual personality of Judas, the "devil," the "son of perdition." And this revelation of antichrist, or of the hostile contrast to Christ, the Gospel presents almost exclusively, similarly as it emphasizes almost exclusively Christ as having already appeared, and the present holiness and blessedness of Christians. But little as it denies or overlooks the future Christ, and the future perfection of the Christian, just as little does it deny or overlook the future revelation of antichrist.

It only keeps itself entirely within Christ's historical circle of vision when it represents Him as saying to the Jews: "I am come in my Father's name, and ye receive me not; if another shall come in his own name, him ye will receive," John v. 43. Or have we not in these words (comp. x. 8), Matt. xxiv. 24, in its —for non-Jewish readers—whole extent of meaning, and therefore the same prediction, the application of which to definite time relations, the Apocalypse gives in the picture of the two beasts?

13. The Last Time.

Though the first Epistle sees antichrist in the denial of the historical Christ, and the spirit of antichrist in its false prophecy, we shall not expect to meet there the *kind of warning and alarming portents and signs of the end which the Apocalypse places before us.* Indeed, as the statements of the Epistle concerning antichrist do not exclude the expectation of its progress to a still greater similarity with the apocalyptic picture; so its conception of the warning preliminaries to the end do not exclude the prospect of yet other and more apocalyptic portents; and he who wrote of the "coming," 1 John ii. 28, and of "the whole world" that "lieth in wickedness," 1 John v. 19, may well have expected, and even seen, avenging judgments hanging over it. But he expressly says only that the appearance of many antichrists is the sign that it is the last time, which corresponds closely with his description of antichrist. The Gospel does not mention the last time, but Jesus says to the Jews: "Yet a little while is the light with you. Walk while ye have the light, lest darkness come upon you: for he that walketh in darkness knoweth not whither he goeth," John xii. 35. Even if he who wrote this did not directly think of Rev. xiv. 10, xv. 1, and xvi. 10, must he not have expected and seen intimations of wrath coming upon the unbelieving, and following the darkness in which they walked?

14. The Call to the World to Repent.

It was shown in the sections on the Spirit and the Gospel that the evangelist has the contents of that which the seer describes by the name of *the everlasting gospel,* in the testimony of the Spirit and of the disciples, John xv. 26, 27; in the proclamation of eternal life by the disciples, 1 John ii. 4; and, above all, in the conviction of the world by the Spirit, John xvi. 8–11. Though he gives less prominence to its publication through the world as a call to repentance, and as a persuasive premonition of the end, it is at once explained from the subordination of eschatology with him, and from the consideration that he gives prominence to the positive side of conversion; moreover, in the Epistles he has only to do with those already converted. There can be no doubt with respect to the question, whether he regarded the Gospel to the Gentiles as a serious friendly call to repentance, and therefore an alluring preliminary to the advent (comp. John iii. 19–21).

15. The Consolation of Christians.

The *great tribulation* of Christians in the Apocalypse corresponds with the climax of antichristianity predicted by it. As the latter, so also the former is naturally wanting in the Gospel. As in the doctrine of the Apocalypse we had largely to supplement the section on the saints and their works, with respect to their sufferings, their vocation, and their hope, from what related to the great tribulation; so in the corresponding section of the comparison we have brought together what relates to it from the Gospel and the Epistles. We might, indeed, have reserved for this place the exhortations and warnings of the first Epistle against error; its parallel, however, is given in the seven letters, not in the admonitions of the Apocalypse, which reach the future form of antichrist.

The earlier comparison must be extended only to two particulars. First, we find the promise, which with the seer is given expressly only for the great tribulation, that true Christians *really enter at death* into the unseen ideal world, *or heaven,* to which ideally they always belonged, also with the evangelist; not, indeed, in the Epistle, but in the Gospel. This distinction is important, as it confirms our idea of the promise. It is the eternal life, 1 John ii. 25, which is present at the moment of conversion, which at death is continued in a higher degree in heaven, and is perfected at the resurrection. On writing the Epistle, the evangelist sees the last time come, and the advent is near, therefore the promise has the form of 1 John iii. 2—heaven is not mentioned; on writing the Gospel he does not see the advent directly imminent, therefore, as the already present possession of eternal life, so heaven also appears in the foreground—fully corresponding to the different forms of the promise in the seven letters, in the prediction of antichrist, and at the close of the Apocalypse. "He that loveth his life," says Christ, "shall lose it; and he that hateth his life in this world shall keep it unto life eternal. If any man serve me, let him follow me; and where I am, there shall also my servant be: if any man serve me, him will my Father honour," John xii. 25–26. But Christ goes to the Father, and is in His exaltation, with the Father in heaven. "Little children, yet a little while I am with you. Ye shall seek me: and as I said unto the Jews, Whither I go, ye cannot come; so now I say to you," John xiii. 33 (comp. vii. 34, viii. 21). Evidently (comp. ver. 36) the inability of the disciples is to be understood of the time then present. "Lord, whither goest Thou?" asked Peter; and "Jesus answered him, Whither I go, thou canst not follow me now; but thou shalt follow me afterwards," John xiii. 36. That this refers to Peter's martyrdom, we learn from the connection and the expression; but the going away of the Lord, as well as the following of the disciple, equally contain the promise of heaven (comp. xii. 26). "In my Father's house are many mansions," Christ says: "if it were not so, I would have told you. I go to prepare a place for you. And if I go and prepare a place for you, I will come again, and receive you unto myself; that where I am, there ye may be also," John xiv. 2, 3. The coming of Christ can here only be in the death of the individual; He goes before to heaven, and comes again to take His people to Himself. "Father," He prays, "I will that they also whom Thou hast given me be with me where I am; that they may behold my glory, which Thou hast given me: for Thou lovedst me before the foundation of the world," John xvii. 24. It corresponds only to the difference between the apocalyptic and the evangelic if the state in heaven is generally represented by the evangelist as being with Christ, as being where He is, but by the seer more in Old Testament imagery. While we at once recognise in those who hate their lives the Christians of the Apocalypse, who "loved not their lives unto the death," xii. 11 (comp. vi. 9, xx. 4, xv. 2, ii. 10); so on the one side there is not wanting with the seer the being with Christ, Rev. xiv. 1, 4 (comp. vii. 17), and on the other, the being honoured of the Father, and seeing the glory of Christ, etc., found in the evangelist, only more comprehensively, is seen also by the seer, Rev. vii. 9–15 (comp. xiv. 1–4, iii. 21). The rest of the blessed dead from their labours, cannot have been a strange idea to him who wrote John ix. 4. As with the seer the Lamb in heaven feeds His people, and leads them to living fountains of water, Rev. vii. 17; so Jesus is represented by the evangelist as here below declaring Himself the shepherd whose voice they hear; as calling them by name, and leading them forth, etc., John x. 3, 4; and when Jesus offers to the Samaritan woman living water, John iv. 10–12 (comp. vii. 37, 38), it is only a new proof that John, to whom the future was already present, and the present was still future, used one and the same image to represent, now the present, and now the future stage.

We must further extend our earlier comparison to another particular. As the seer, xiv. 1–5, describes Christians in their *exaltation above the world*, the sphere of antichristianity; so also they appear with the evangelist as delivered from the world, and superior to it. It is true neither Gospel nor Epistle represents believers as ideally present in heaven; but the joy of Christ fulfilled in His disciples corresponds to singing the new song before the throne, John xvii. 13. As Christians, according to Rev. xiv. 3, are redeemed from the earth; so the disciples of Christ, according to John xv. 19, are not of the world, but Christ has chosen them out of the world, and out of the world God has given them to Him, John xvii. 6, 9; they are not of the world, as Christ is not of the world, John xvii. 16 (comp. ii. 15); they know that they have passed from death unto life, 1 John iii. 14; as Christ is, so are they in the world, 1 John iv. 17. That they have not, according to the Apocalypse, defiled themselves with women, we are reminded by 1 John iii. 3; that they follow the Lamb whithersoever He goeth, by John x. 3, 4 (comp. ver. 9, xiv. 27, 28, xii. 26, xiii. 36–39); that in their mouth is found no guile, by 1 John ii. 21, 22, 27; and of the absolute statements: "they are virgins," "they are without fault," by such passages as 1 John iii. 6, "Whosoever abideth in Him sinneth not;" 1 John iii. 9, "Whosoever is born of God doth not commit sin; for his seed remaineth in him: and he cannot sin, because he is born of God;" 1 John v. 18, "We know that whosoever is born of God sinneth not: but he that is begotten of God keepeth himself, and that wicked one toucheth him not." A careful consideration will show that this coincidence between the objects of comparison in the representation of the ideal Christian nature as a timeless condition is neither accidental nor unimportant.

16. The Future of Israel.

In the Epistles of John there is hardly any reference to be found to the *Jewish nation.* Certainly in the Gospel Christendom is nowhere expressly described as the true Israel. But when it is said that Moses, in the law and the prophets, wrote of Jesus, John i. 45; that Jews would believe in Jesus if they believed what Moses had written of Him, John v. 45, 46; that they would do Abraham's works if they were his children, John viii. 39; that they would love Jesus if God were their Father, John viii. 42; that the Old Testament types and prophecies are fulfilled in Jesus, for example, in John iii. 14, 15, xii. 37–39, xix. 36–39, —there needs no special statement to show that to the evangelist Christendom was the true Israel (comp. John i. 11 with iii. 11). That those Jews who hate and persecute Christ are not Jews, and that they falsely claim the name, and really belong to the synagogue of Satan, Rev. ii. 9, iii. 9, has a close and almost literal parallel in the words of Christ, John viii. 37–41, especially in vers. 39–41, 44, according to which the Jews, because they sought to slay Him, were not Abraham's children, but the children of their father the devil (comp. also John i. 48, "Behold an Israelite indeed, in whom there is no guile"). But it may be objected here, that with the seer the term "Jew" is a name of honour, falsely assumed by the enemies of Christ; but that on the contrary, with the evangelist, the haters of Christ bear the name. True; but there is no contradiction involved in this. In the Apocalypse it would be impossible to use the name in any but a theocratic sense; in the Gospel, on the other hand, while it can be applied as an ethnographic designation (comp. John ii. 6, iv. 22, v. 1, vi. 4, xix. 42), it can be used also as a generalizing description of the representatives of that spirit which really animated the Jews, as a whole, against Jesus,—namely, the spirit of unbelief, as well as of hatred and persecution, which grew out of it. That which the evangelist expresses by his use of the name, the seer gives us to understand in a manner equally clear, when, having mentioned the "holy city," which the Gentiles shall tread under foot forty and two months, Rev. xi. 2, he soon after speaks of it as the "great city, which spiritually is called Sodom and Egypt," Rev. xi. 8 (comp. vers. 9, 10). What John in the Apocalypse calls by the name of Jew, he calls in the Gospel "Israel" and "Israelite," John i. 31, 47, 49, iii. 10 (comp. 1 Thess. ii. 14, 15, and Phil. iii. 5). That to the seer the temple at Jerusalem is still the temple of God, and will be preserved from desolation, Rev. xi. 1, should not in conjunction with John iv. 21 have been adduced by Köstlin, *ut ante*, p. 489, as a proof of the wholly different standpoint of the two writers, when on the one side we have shown in the section on the holy city during the forty-two months that the temple of God and its preservation must be understood symbolically, and on the other side that John iv. 21 combined with ver. 23 and John ii. 16, etc., gives a view which, after the separation of Jewish Christians from the Jewish commonwealth, introduced by the Jewish war, must have been self-evident, from his idea of the priestly kingdom of Christians, to the seer.

What does the seer hold respecting the *future* of the Jewish people? The evangelist represents Jesus as referring only infrequently, and then only generally and slightly, to the judgment of Jerusalem, which, in his idea, had already been pronounced, v. 43, vii. 34–36, viii. 21, 50, x. 1–3, xii. 35, 36; and there is not the slightest indication of the more distant fate of the Jewish people. The former circumstance furnishes us with a striking proof that, from the silence or cursory reference of the evangelist to any subject, we cannot conclude that his personal position was one of indifference or careless avoidance, but rather that, with a view to a definite circle of subjects, he limited himself in the Gospel to the material he had chosen. The absence of all indications respecting the future of the Jews simply leaves it undecided whether, after the experience realized since 68 A.D., he had given up the hope of Israel's conversion; or whether, with changed relations, it had become modified, in a similar manner as his expectation of antichrist. Merely by the way, I throw out the question, whether it is wholly accidental that the seer represents the two witnesses—Moses and Elias—as preceding the advent of Him who had already once appeared, Rev. xi. 3–6; and that the evangelist represents the witness—the Baptist—of Him who should appear (John i. 7, 8, 15) as being asked whether he were Elias, or that prophet (vi. 14, vii. 10; comp. Deut. xviii. 18), John i. 21–25?

17. The World in Wickedness.

Just as, in the Apocalypse, the inhabitants of the world devote themselves to the two beasts; so Jesus predicts that the Jews, in the sense which the evangelist attaches to that term, would receive another if he came in his own name, John v. 43; the evangelist also says of the false prophets, "They are of the world; therefore speak they of the world, and the world heareth them," 1 John iv. 5. But does the evangelist expect its conversion? We have already seen how far he is from that in the section on Christian life; yet we may remark that in the last time he says, "The whole world *lieth in wickedness*," 1 John v. 18. As a whole, he expects nothing from it.

18. The End of the World.

The evangelist does not speak of the fall of Babylon. But, as in the Apocalypse, a voice from heaven exhorts the people of God to come out of her, that they may not be partakers of her sin and her plagues; her sins having reached to heaven, and her iniquities having been remembered by God, Rev. xviii. 4, 5; so the evangelist writes, "The whole world lieth in wickedness" (comp. 1 John v. 18); "Love not the world, neither the things that are in the world. If any man love the world, the love of the Father is not in him. For all that is in the world, the lust of the flesh, and the lust of the eyes, and the pride of life, is not of the Father, but is of the world. And the world passeth away, and the lust thereof; but he that doeth the will of God abideth for ever," 1 John ii. 15–17 (comp. especially 1 John ii. 17 and Rev. xviii. 14).

19. The Coming of the Lord.

We found that in one series of places in the Apocalypse the *coming* of the Lord is intended in the ordinary sense; that in another it can be interpreted only in the sense of His coming at the advent with power; and that, according to a comparison of the passages generally relating to His coming, any personal manifestation or energetic self-affirmation of the exalted Christ, whether provisional or final, whether to judge or to bless, may be understood; indeed, we could not conceal from ourselves that if the seer had had occasion to speak of it, he would certainly have described Christ's entrance into the world, at His birth as well as at His public appearance, as he does the advent, as a coming of Christ (comp. Rev. xii. 2, 4, 5). The evangelist uses the word *παρουσία*, 1 John ii. 28, which does not occur in the Apocalypse. The coming of the Lord, in the usual sense, is undisputed, except in John xxi. 22, 23, a place not directly belonging to the author of the Gospel. The passages in the parting address are very variously interpreted. "In my Father's house are many mansions: if it were not so, I would have told you. I go to prepare a place for you. And if I go and prepare a place for you, I will come again, and receive you unto myself; that where I am, ye may be also," John xiv. 2, 3; "I will not leave you comfortless; I will come to you. Yet a little while, and the world seeth me no more; but ye see me: because I live, ye shall live also," John xiv. 18, 19; "He that loveth me shall be loved of my Father, and I will love him, and will manifest myself to him," John xiv. 21; "If a man love me, he will keep my words: and my Father will love him, and we will come unto him, and make our abode with him," John xiv. 23; "A little while, and ye shall not see me: and again a little while, and ye shall see me, because I go to my Father," John xvi. 16 (comp. vers. 17–19); "And ye now therefore have sorrow; but I will see you again, and your heart shall rejoice, and your joy no man taketh from you," John xvi. 22 (comp. vers. 23, 25, 26). While the first has been mostly regarded as the calling home of the individual in death, and the remainder have been understood sometimes of the resurrection; on one side, indeed, of the resurrection of the body, and on the other of a resurrection in the sense of a spiritual body; sometimes of the gift of the Holy Spirit, and sometimes of continued spiritual fellowship with the disciples,—such expositors as Hofmann, Luthardt, Lechler, p. 224, have recently referred all these places to the advent, and suppose that John xvi. 23–25, by its introductory formula, "Verily, verily, I say unto you," separates between what has gone before, and relates to the time following. Weiss, on the contrary, *bibl. Theol.*

p. 752, understands John xiv. 2, 3 of Christ's second coming and subsequent gathering of the elect to Him; but all the following passages of the reappearance of Christ after death, and the continuance of His gracious presence. To me, none of these expositions are satisfactory; an unprejudiced consideration will show that it is fully as one-sided when most expositors miss the promise of the advent in these passages (we need only compare, for example, John xiv. 2, 3, with Luke xvi. 9; 2 Cor. v. 1–3, Matt. xxiv. 31, 1 Thess. iv. 17, John xiv. 18–20, with Luke xvii. 22; John xvi. 22 with Matt. xxv. 1–3; John xvi. 25 with 1 Cor. xiii. 9–11), as when the others overlook in one or in several of them, a relation to the next coming (comp. again, for example, John xvi. 22 with John xx. 20; John xiv. 2, 3, with John xiii. 36–38); that only can be a correct exposition which gives to both aspects what is justly due. We remember here that we have found only recently that the evangelist speaks of antichrist, and yet describes the false teachers, through whom it reached its full realization, as antichrists; we remember also that, generally, he thinks and speaks of the realization, and of each of the steps leading to it, as one and the same. We cannot therefore remain in doubt for a moment how he conceived the coming of the Lord. He understood by it the advent, the revelation (comp. 1 John ii. 28), the appearance and manifestation of Christ, and in Christ of God, as of a judge and deliverer, for the accomplishment of purposes concerning the world; in other words, precisely the same thing as other New Testament writers mean by the coming of Christ. But as, for example, to him eternal life and judgment are not merely future, but also already present; so in like manner he sees the coming of the Lord, not as imminent solely on the last day, but as an event then perfected, which has been advancing through manifold preliminary stages; and thus he considers the coming of the Lord at every one of these stages essentially as he does the last, and calls it by the same name. Indeed, as in all other relations the already present stands to him in the foreground, and the future completion of the same falls much into the background; as, for example, he brings forward with such emphasis the filial relation to God, the possession of eternal life, in all its phases, as given at conversion, that many expositors have regarded him as the precursor of a doctrine to which he is altogether strange—namely, the doctrine of immanence; so he gives such strong prominence in the Gospel to the coming of Christ already accomplished, and continuing to be accomplished, that many expositors have entirely mistaken the relation of his words to the positive coming of the Lord. In the intention of the evangelist, we have without doubt to understand the expression "to come," which he so often uses of the pre-existent and of the historical Christ (comp. for example, John i. 9, iii. 19, xii. 46, iv. 25, vii. 27, 28, 31, 41, 42, xii. 15, vi. 14, xi. 27, i. 15, 27, 29, 30, iii. 31, vi. 38, 42, 50, 58, viii. 42, xiii. 3, xiv. 28; 2 John 7; 1 John iv. 2, v. 6; John v. 43, xii. 47, x. 10, xviii. 37), in the meaning of the advent, as the coming, which at the first stage is consubstantial with the last. But while it describes the coming simply and unequivocally as having already ensued, it has also, as it appears in the parting address, a manifold sense as future. In each of the places quoted from that address, Christ promises His coming, as it anticipates and is perfected in the advent; in other words, He speaks there everywhere in a double sense. It is for Him—no matter here whether really so, or only according to the representation of the evangelist—the same coming again in which He takes His people to heaven, and in which He gathers them to Himself in the advent; the same reunion, as the same seeing again in the spirit and in the advent; the same revelation of His person; the same coming and dwelling appear in the mystic life-union and in the advent; the same joy after sorrow in His resurrection and in His second coming—it is one and the same thing, the nearest and the most distant; and as the future is at the same time already present, so the present is at the same time only future. That this explanation throws light simply and uniformly upon the words of Christ concerning His coming, will be as little disputed as its homogeneity with one of the chief characteristics of the evangelist. It certainly has also great significance for our comparison; for just as according to it the evangelist sees the coming of the Lord, so also according to our earlier exposition it is regarded by the seer. A comparison of particulars is hardly needed, still the inner relation of Rev. iii. 20 and John xiv. 21, 23 is at all times striking; Rev. i. 17 and xiv. 19 harmonize in a very remarkable manner; of that which John xiv. 18–20, 21, xvi. 16–18, 25 promises, we have an example in Rev. i. 9, 20; and that in the evangelist we find no instance of the magisterial coming of the Lord, has an analogy in its almost entire silence respecting the reverse side of Christianity.

The seer has not stated particularly the *time* of the advent, or calculated the day and the hour; his statements with regard to it are first typical, but from the signs of the times he had inferred the certainty of the Lord's speedy coming. The evangelist writes, "And now, little children, abide in Him; that when He shall appear, we may have confidence, and not be ashamed before Him at His coming," 1 John ii. 28; he therefore expected that he and his readers would see the advent. In 1 John ii. 18 He writes, "Little children, it is the last time: and as ye have heard that antichrist shall come, even now are there many antichrists; whereby we know that it is the last time,"—the last time can only be that immediately preceding the advent, the end of the day then present, the termination of the current period by the appearance of antichrist; and this is also the view of the seer. That, according to 1 John ii. 8, "the darkness is past, and the true light now shineth," should not have been quoted by Köstlin (p. 495) as a proof that for the evangelist in contrast with the seer spiritual darkness was gradually passing away; did he, according to 1 John ii. 17, regard the world as gradually passing away?

Of the threefold *representation* of the advent in the Apocalypse, we need not expect to find the one in the evangelist which gives the concrete ideas of the seer, because for him the premises have taken another form. The symbolic pictures of the advent are also wanting with him; at the most, a slight contact between the prediction of the harvest, John iv. 35–38, and Rev. xiv. 14–16, as well as between the parable of the vine, John xv. 1–8, and Rev. xiv. 17–20, on the basis of the apocalyptic evangelical conception of the advent—as present, and still at the same time future—is discoverable. But that the evangelist also, xix. 37, has the words of Zechariah, with which the seer prefaces his prediction as it were with a motto, Rev. i. 7, we have already mentioned. When the evangelist places the chief emphasis on the fulfilment of that prediction in the piercing of Him who was to be the world's judge, the seer on the other hand emphasizes the fulfilment of the same prediction, in the appearance in that capacity of Him who was pierced; and though there is a little difference in expression, it is fully explained by the necessary distinction of Apocalypse and Gospel; the representation itself is here as there—they shall see Him coming as a judge whom they pierced on the cross.

That to the seer the advent of Christ is the coming of *God Himself*, we have recognised from several indications; for instance, from the difference between Rev. i. 4 and xi. 17, and in several sections, and also in that on the advent, it has been expressly noticed. Weiss, *bibl. Theol.* p. 752, remarks that when the evangelist speaks of God, 1 John ii. 29, as if He had been the subject of preceding observations, it appears that he thought of the advent wholly after the manner of the Old Testament, as the proper coming of the Messiah, in whom God Himself comes to His people.

20. The Resurrection of Believers.

It is evident that we cannot expect to find the name *thousand years' reign* in the evangelist; yet the thing itself, though probably falling back much toward the absolute, and still more to the already present realization of the Christian ideal, we must certainly expect to find as far as he is identical with the author of the Apocalypse; and we are not deceived. The passages relating to this subject are 1 John ii. 28, iv. 17; John v. 25, 28, 29, vi. 39, 40, 44, 54, xi. 23, 24, xii. 48. Without entering into the various views of expositors respecting some of these texts, I affirm that when Christ says, "This is the Father's will who hath sent me, that of all which He hath given me I should lose nothing, but should raise it up again at the last day. And this is the will of Him that sent me, that every one which seeth the Son, and believeth on Him, may have everlasting life: and I will raise him up at the last day," vi. 39, 40; "No man can come to me, except the Father, which hath sent me, draw him: and I will raise him up at the last day," vi. 44; "Whoso eateth my flesh, and drinketh my blood, hath eternal life: and I will raise him up at the last day," vi. 54,—it is evident at a glance that the resuscitation or resurrection cannot be that of the judgment of the world. When, on the other hand, Christ says, "The hour is coming, in the which all that are in the graves shall hear His—the Son's—voice, and shall come forth; they that have done good, unto the resurrection of life; and they that have done evil, unto the resurrection of damnation," v. 28, 29 (comp. the words of Martha, "I know that He shall rise again in the resurrection at the last day," John xi. 24), there undoubtedly lies before us in a passage recently pronounced an interpolation, the last judgment. But then can—as, for example, Weiss, *bibl. Theol.* p. 754, etc., thinks—the resurrection to life, John v. 29, and the resurrection of John vi. 39, 40, 44, 54, be one and the same, the advent and the judgment of the world together? We have still another passage to compare. Christ says, "The hour is coming, and now is, when the dead shall hear the voice of the Son of God; and they that hear shall live," John v. 25. Very unnecessarily there has been much controversy about the meaning of this passage: it can mean nothing else than the first resurrection, in distinction from the general resurrection to judgment; the difficulty is only in the words "now is;" but it is solved at once if we compare, for example, John iv. 23, xii. 23, 28, 30, xiii. 31, and the peculiarity of the evangelist, so often mentioned, in virtue of which, hearing the voice of Christ by the dead at His coming, and hearing the words of Christ by the spiritually dead now, are to him essentially the same thing as the resurrection of believers there, and the passing from death unto life here. The former is the completion, the latter is the beginning or the germ. But if, in John v. 25, the first resurrection, the resurrection of the just, and in John v. 28, 29, the general resurrection to judgment, is meant, can the two be conceived of as externally one or connected in time? What, then, can be the sense of Christ's words, "marvel not at this," John v. 28? But if the two resurrections do not externally come together in relation to time, then the *last* day, when Christ will raise His people, John vi. 39, 40, 44, 54, and when the word which He speaks will judge those who reject Him, and do not receive His words, John xii. 48, of which John v. 25 and v. 28, 29 equally speak, the day of judgment, 1 John iv. 17, cannot possibly be anything else than the great day of the wrath of God, Rev. vi. 17; the wrath of God and the time of the dead, Rev. xi. 18; "that great day of God Almighty," Rev. xvi. 14; in a word, the *great final catastrophe in its twofold degree or realization*, the advent, and what it brings with it—the judgment of the world and what depends upon it—both one and the same in nature, but in time and in degree of actual realization different. When the evangelist uses the name "last day" for this duality, he still intends, in harmony with the view carried out to its consequences,—that the contents of the eschatology in their beginning are realized on every side by the appearance of Jesus Christ,—essentially nothing different from that which is meant by the words of Christ concerning "His day," which Abraham saw afar off, and was glad, John viii. 56; and the comparison of these words fully explains how he could say, "The hour is coming, and now is, when the dead shall hear the voice of the Son of God; and they that hear shall live," John v. 25.

According to this, the *course of things at the advent*, the millennium of the seer, in the representation of the evangelist briefly forms itself in the following manner: Christ will soon appear, or be manifested, even during the lifetime of the evangelist and his readers, 1 John ii. 28. Those then living who have not remained in Him "will be ashamed before" or from "Him," 1 John ii. 28 (comp. Rev. i. 7, xvi. 15); but if they have continued in Him, they will have confidence and joy, 1 John ii. 28, iv. 17 (comp. Rev. xxii. 12, ii. 26, 27, iii. 11), will not have lost that for which they have laboured, but will receive the full reward thereof in its first potency, the beginning of the consummation, according to 2 John 8 (comp. Rev. xxii. 12, μισθός, xi. 18); Christ will then awake believers who have died, or have been slain; they hear His voice and live, John v. 25, vi. 39, 40, 44, 54, xi. 23, 24 (comp. Rev. xx. 4–6); but this resurrection is to be distinguished from the general awakening of the dead, Rev. v. 29, 30 (comp. Rev. xx. 5). That the Apocalypse does not expressly mention Christ in the description of the first resurrection, as is done by the Gospel, can have, according to Rev. i. 17, no dogmatic foundation. But when the evangelist, in the description of the provisional state, perfect within earthly limits, employs not nearly so many features as the seer, it is easily explained by the circumstance that with him almost all emphasis lies on the present possession of eternal life through Christ; and that so far as with him its perfection is still future, his hopes, as essentially do those of the seer, go out mainly to the absolute fulfilment (comp. 1 John iii. 2, 3). Our exposition has, I trust, shown that in this important point also evangelist and seer hold essentially the same views, and are one in the belief according to which the advent and the world-judgment of the great or the last day have a twofold significance.

21. The Judgment.

As in Rev. xx. 11 it is said, "I saw a great white throne, and Him that sat on it, before whose face the earth and the heaven fled away; and there was found no place for them;" so we read in 1 John ii. 17, "The world passeth away, and the lust thereof; but he that doeth the will of God abideth for ever" (comp. 1 John ii. 8). According to the representations of the seer, the sea and hades will then give up their dead: and all the dead without distinction will stand before the throne, and, after the opening of the books, will be judged according to their works. And all whose names do not stand in the open book, as also death itself, will be cast into the lake of fire. In the Gospel, Jesus says, "The hour is coming, and now is, in the which all that are in the graves shall hear His voice, and shall come forth; they that have done good, unto the resurrection of life; and they that have done evil, unto the resurrection of damnation," John v. 28, 29. To an unprejudiced reader there can be no doubt that, according to this, the evangelist, in the most perfect harmony with the seer, expected that after the completion of the earthly kingdom of Christ, and the last judgment upon Satan (comp. John xii. 31), and the passing away of the present world (comp. 1 John ii. 17), the judgment of the world would take place; all the dead who until then remain in the grave will arise to be judged: one class will attain to life, that is, blessedness corresponding to their works (Christians especially will receive their reward in the highest degree, 2 John 8); the other, also according to their works, will be judged and condemned. We have seen that when it is expressly said in the Gospel that all the dead shall hear the voice of the Son, the seer also regards Christ as the executor of the world-judgment, and especially as the awaker of the dead. Nor does the fact that the evangelist expressly mentions how the one class shall come forth to the resurrection of life make any difference against the Apocalypse, when at this place only the condemnation of the other is described, because the "life" of the former was to be described in detail afterward. The judgment to which the guilty arise can, in contrast with "life," mean only the sentence, or the magisterial decision, and giving over to perdition (comp. for example, John iii. 15, 16). Notwithstanding all this, several writers on the doctrine of John, such as Frommann, Baur, Köstlin, Reuss, Scholten, though in various ways, have with equal decision denied to the evangelist any representation of a final judgment of the world. Their special proof of this is John iii. 17, 18. But when, without prejudice, we consider the numerous statements of the Gospel respecting judging and judgment, the observation forces itself upon us, first, that these expressions are used in a twofold sense, sometimes in the sense of magisterial discrimination and decision respecting that which in itself or in its nature is contradictory among mankind, and then in the sense of condemnation and distribution of penalty to the ungodly side of the contrast. We easily see, further, that, as in so many other relations, so also with respect to the judgment, for the evangelist the completion and the commencing principle are one and the same. If we grasp these two points firmly, we shall understand how the evangelist at one time can say that Christ is not sent into the world to judge or condemn the world, for example, iii. 17, xii. 47, 48; and at another, that He has come into the world for judgment—that is, to bring into activity and reveal the inner or contrasting dispositions in the world, John ix. 39; and that the Father has given into the hands of the Son the whole judgment, not merely that which begins with His appearance on earth, but also the final separation and decision, as well with respect to those who awake at the advent, as with respect to all the dead, John v. 22. Still less hesitation can there be, after all the similar things which we have already noticed, when, according to the statements of the evangelist in one place, the unbeliever is by the fact already condemned, and on the other hand, the believer is not condemned, John iii. 18–21; and according to his statements in another, the judgment for both is yet future, 1 John iv. 17; 2 John 8; John v. 29, 30, xii. 48. Being judged in the present as little excludes, but rather includes, future judgment, as the passing from death unto life does the future awakening from death, or the future reception of eternal life; or as the first advent of Christ, His second; or as the being pure, the purifying; or the casting down of Satan, his future overthrow, etc. Moreover, the seer also ascribes to the appearance of Christ in the flesh, not a judging, condemning, but a saving, delivering signification; and that which the evangelist intends when he says that believers are not condemned, the seer also expresses when he says that "he that overcometh shall not be hurt of the second death," Rev. ii. 11, xx. 6.

22. The Final State.

The evangelist knows as little of restoration as the seer. And though, agreeably with his manner, *one side* of the final condition has very little prominence, an agreement with the seer on this point can be shown. Jesus describes the purpose of His coming when He says, it was "that whosoever believeth in Him should not perish, but have everlasting life," John iii. 15, 16; and the being lost—perdition (comp. John xii. 25, xvii. 12)—is also with the seer, Rev. xvii. 8–11, the prominent name for the state of eternal damnation. In the parable of the vine Jesus says, "If a man abide not in me, he is cast forth as a branch, and is withered; and men gather them, and cast them into the fire, and they are burned," John xv. 6; the eschatological meaning of these words cannot be mistaken (comp. Matt. iii. 10, vii. 19, xiii. 40–42), and as little their close relation to the lake of fire and brimstone spoken of in the Apocalypse, Rev. xiv. 9–11, xxi. 8.

The evangelist speaks rather more frequently of the *opposite side* of the final state. He describes it as eternal life, which with him, as with the seer, is entered upon at conversion, but, as we have shown in the section on Christian life, is also the subject of promise (comp. 1 John ii. 25). There needs no proof that the "no more death," Rev. xxi. 4, "the fountain of the water of life," Rev. xxi. 6, the "river of the water of life," and the "tree of life," Rev. xxii. 1, 2, of the Apocalypse, cannot be more appropriately described than by the words "eternal life." Certainly we do not find express mention in the Gospel and Epistles of a new heaven and a new earth; but when Lücke (*ut ante*, II. p. 731) says that there is no trace of a representation of a change in nature, he has overlooked the scope of the words, "the world passeth away," 1 John ii. 17, and, "it doth not yet appear what we shall be," 1 John iii. 2. The marriage of the Lamb with the bride we should expect to find in the evangelist as little as the New Jerusalem.

But of the three chief pictures in which the seer represents the final state of the blessed, there meet us in the evangelist's description of this condition as such, only a few features; on the other hand, we find almost every feature of the state immediately awaiting in heaven, or mainly *of the already present Christian state,* and indeed with such a coincidence as extorts from Köstlin (*ut ante,* p. 497) the remark already quoted: "Hitherto we saw ourselves least of all on Johannine soil; thus the many parallels presented by the glory of the eternal life as ascribed to the present are all the more surprising." "Behold, the tabernacle of God is with men, and He will dwell with them," Rev. xxi. 3. "And the Word was made flesh, and dwelt"—the same expression *σκηνή* and *σκηνοῦν*—"among us," John i. 14. "If any man love me, he will keep my words: and my Father will love him, and we will come unto him, and make our abode with him," John xiv. 23 (comp. John ii. 21). "God Himself shall be with them, and be their God," Rev. xxi. 3. We may compare the places just quoted in the Gospel, as well as John xvi. 26, 27, xx. 17, and the words concerning God dwelling in us, recorded in 1 John iv. 12, 13, 15, 16. "There shall be no more death, neither sorrow, nor crying, neither shall there be any more pain," Rev. xxi. 4; "He that heareth my word, and believeth . . . is passed from death unto life," John v. 24 (comp. 1 John iii. 14, v. 11, 12); "If a man keep my saying, he shall never see death," John viii. 51; "he shall never taste of death," viii. 52 (comp. John xi. 25, 26); "ye shall weep and lament, but your sorrow shall be turned into joy," xvi. 20; "your heart shall rejoice, and your joy no man taketh from you," xvi. 22. "I will give unto him that is athirst of the water of life freely" (*δωρεάν*), Rev. xxi. 6; "If any man thirst, let him come unto me, and drink. He that believeth on me, as the scripture hath said, out of his belly shall flow rivers of living water," John vii. 37; "If thou knewest the gift (*δωρεά*) of God, and who it is that saith to thee, Give me to drink; thou wouldest have asked of Him, and He would have given thee living water," John iv. 10; "Whosoever drinketh of the water that I shall give him shall never thirst; but the water that I shall give him shall be a well of water springing up into everlasting life," John iv. 14. "I will be his God, and he shall be my son," Rev. xxi. 7; "Behold what manner of love the Father hath bestowed upon us, that we should be called the sons of God," 1 John iii. 1 (comp. John i. 12, xiv. 23, xvi. 26, 27, xx. 17). "The fearful, and the unbelieving, and the abominable, and murderers, and whoremongers, and sorcerers, and idolaters, and all liars, shall have their part in the lake which burneth with fire and brimstone," Rev. xxi. 8; "There shall in no wise enter into it anything that defileth, neither whatsoever worketh abomination, or maketh a lie; but they which are written in the Lamb's book of life," Rev. xxi. 27; "And there shall be no more curse," Rev. xxii. 3; "If a man abide not in me, he is cast forth as a branch, and is withered; and men gather them, and cast them into the fire, and they are burned," John xv. 6 (comp. John vi. 64, 66, also 1 John ii. 19); "Whosoever is born of God doth not commit sin; for his seed remaineth in him: and he cannot sin, because he is born of God," 1 John iii. 9 (comp. ver. 6); "We know that whosoever is born of God sinneth not: but he who is begotten of God keepeth himself, and that wicked one toucheth him not. And we know that we are of God, and the whole world lieth in wickedness," 1 John v. 18, 19 (comp. 1 John ii. 5, 9–11, iii. 15, iv. 5, v. 12). The New Jerusalem has "the glory of God: and her light was like unto a stone most precious," Rev. xxi. 11; "The city had no need of the sun, neither of the moon, to shine in it; for the glory of God did lighten it, and the Lamb is the light thereof," Rev. xxi. 23; "There shall be no night there; and they need no candle, neither light of the sun, for the Lord God giveth them light," Rev. xxii. 5 (comp. xxi. 25); "We beheld His glory, the glory as of the Only-begotten of the Father," John i. 14 (comp. ii. 11), xii. 23, 41, xiii. 31, xvii. 1, 4, 5, xxii. 24; "God is light, and in Him is no darkness at all," 1 John i. 5; "The life was the light of men," John i. 4–9, iii. 19–21; "I am the light of the world," John viii. 12, xii. 35, 36; "The darkness is past, and the true light now shineth," 1 John ii. 8. "The nations of them which are saved shall walk in the light of it," Rev. xxi. 24; "the light shineth in darkness," John i. 5; "the true Light which lighteth every man that cometh into the world," John i. 5; "he that followeth me shall not walk in darkness, but shall have the light of life," John viii. 12 (comp. xii. 35, 36). "I saw no temple therein, for the Lord God Almighty and the Lamb are the temple of it," Rev. xxi. 22; "Woman, believe me, the hour cometh when ye shall neither in this mountain, nor yet at Jerusalem, worship the Father," John iv. 21 (comp. John ii. 21); "The hour cometh, and now is, when the true worshippers shall worship the Father in spirit and in truth," John iv. 23. The angel showed the seer "a pure river of water of life, clear as crystal, proceeding out of the throne of God and of the Lamb," Rev. xxii. 1, with which we may compare John iv. 10, 14, vii. 37. "On either side of the river was there the tree of life, which yielded her fruit every month," Rev. xxii. 3; "I am the bread of life: he that cometh to me shall never hunger; and he that believeth on me shall never thirst," John vi. 35. Thus we see almost every feature with which the seer represents eternal blessedness, used by the evangelist to describe the state of Christians here.

But some individual features he applies to the *heavenly state.* "The tabernacle of God with men," Rev. xxi. 3, we find again in the words of Jesus respecting His Father's house, in which are many mansions, John xiv. 2, 3; the whole picture of Rev. xxii. 1–5, only more briefly, meets us in John xii. 25, 26; especially may we compare the eternal life of John xii. 25, and the river of the water of life, and the tree of life, of Rev. xxii. 1–3; as well as the servant and his honour in John xii. 26, and the service and the vision of His face and the inscription of His name on their foreheads, and their reigning for ever, spoken of in Rev. xxii. 3–5.

Only few but exceedingly important particulars in the apocalyptic imagery of *the final blessedness,* are shared by the evangelist. It is said, 1 John iii. 1 2, "Behold what manner of love the Father hath bestowed upon us, that we should be called the sons of God! Therefore the world knoweth us not, because it knew Him not. Beloved, now are we the sons of God; and it doth not yet appear what we shall be; but we know that, when He shall appear, we shall be like Him; for we shall see Him as He is." The language and contents are against the reference of the pronoun "Him" to Christ in distinction from God, and of the "appearing" to the advent in distinction from the absolute finality; the reference to God in distinction from Christ, and to the final consummation of all things, rather than to the advent, is forbidden by what precedes and follows, 1 John ii. 28, 29, iii. 3. We understand therefore by "Him," which corresponds to 1 John ii. 29, the absolute God, provisionally revealing Himself in the advent through Christ, and finally and fully in the completion of all things; but by the appearing, corresponding to the "last day," the consummation coming in with the advent and closing with the judgment of the world, and that which belongs to it, still so that the latter here predominates. Apart, however, from the circumstance that the pronoun "Him" in such a sense cannot be more strikingly symbolized than by the apocalyptic description of God as the Light, and the Lamb as the Light-bearer, Rev. xxi. 23, of the temple, which is the "Lord God Almighty and the Lamb," Rev. xxi. 22, of the throne of God *and* of the Lamb, "and *His* servants shall serve Him," Rev. xxii. 3 (comp. xx. 6, "They shall be priests of God and of Christ, and shall reign with *Him* a thousand years"); and further, apart from the fact that, to the seer, future blessedness in its different stages is essentially the same, only now the preliminary and now the final preponderating in its hopes and promises, there can hardly be conceived more striking general parallels than between 1 John iii. 1, 2, and Rev. xxi. 1, xxii. 5; but in particular, we may notice the parallel between the words, "what manner of love the Father hath bestowed upon us!" and "he that overcometh shall inherit all things, and I will be his God, and he shall be my son," Rev. xxi. 7; also between the words of the Epistle, "We shall be like Him: for we shall see Him as He is," and those of Rev. xxii. 3–5, especially the words, "and they shall see His face."—The evangelist does not speak expressly of the Christianized heathen nations, and their position in the millennium, Rev. xxi. 24–26, nor of the eternal kingship of the servants of God, Rev. xxii. 5; we need only, however, free ourselves from the folly which supposes that the writer of 1 John v. 19 may by the "we" in another place understand all men; we need only understand correctly the extent of the "we," and the being "like Him" (comp. Rev. xxii. 5), as well as the being "sons of God," and the "seeing His face" (comp. Matt. v. 8, 9; Gal. iv. 4–7; Rom. viii. 17), in the biblical concrete sense, and there meets us in the evangelic picture of the final blessedness the apocalyptic distinction between the citizens and the dwellers around the New Jerusalem.

Since, now, it has appeared to us, on a consideration of apocalyptic doctrine, that the seer makes no essential difference between the promises with respect to the Christian condition here, in heaven, during the thousand years' reign, and in the state of eternal blessedness, but regards them as the same promises fulfilled, according to the stage, in different modifications; and since we have found the views of the evangelist to be precisely the same,—it manifestly does not suffice, with Köstlin (*ut ante*, p. 498), to say, "The apocalyptic future state, John has mostly in the present; partly in the person and work of Christ, partly in the life of believers and the church; and the harmony of ideas, though conditioned by different standpoints, is so great that it cannot be regarded as *accidental;*" and, to continue in the words of the same writer, "the promises of the Apocalypse remained treasured up in the consciousness of the church in Asia Minor, and would not be thrown away by John, but spiritualized, and, in a great measure, put into the mouth of Jesus Himself." It is rather a proof of the identity of the two writers, not easily to be shaken, that, with trifling exceptions, the same promises are to be found in one as in the other; and, indeed, as our comparison here and in the section on Christian life will have shown, they present themselves in almost verbal harmony, or rather unsought, force themselves upon us. But if any one is disposed, after all, to think that the seer might have transcendently what to the evangelist might have become immanent, let him compare not only 1 John ii. 25, but also 1 John iii. 1–2, and he will satisfy himself that the evangelist really saw the same promises which were fulfilling, or had fulfilled themselves here, as yet to be fulfilled in the future; if he is still not convinced, let him explain to us how John should have, in the Apocalypse, treated the promises as mainly fulfilled, and in the Gospel, on the other hand, as mainly delaying their fulfilment!

CONCLUSION.

We have endeavoured to represent the relation between the doctrine of the Apocalypse and that of the Gospel and the Epistles of John, at least in its chief points and its most important aspects, upon the natural foundation of apocalyptic doctrine, and the not less intelligible exclusion of the evangelical material lying outside the comparison. That we have thereby not levelled the ground, but compared,—though often minutely, and somewhat after the manner of a thesis, still really compared, —the candid reader will, I hope, generally admit. But what is the *result* of the long and difficult inquiry in which he has accompanied us?

With regard to the *compass* of the Apocalypse on the one side, and the Gospel and the Epistles on the other, we have in our comparison certainly not found remarkably numerous points of contact between the two. We have even, besides the many differences which rest only upon the misunderstandings and inattention of expositors, perceived very few real differences between the doctrine on both sides. But not a single point has met us in which the silence of one or the speech of the other, or in which difference of doctrine, cannot be fully explained by the interposition of the catastrophe of Jewish history, or from the different literary character, or, finally, from the divergent aims of the writings. But, on the other hand, our comparison has shown, first, that in relation to the individuality of the writings on both sides, the *doctrinal contents* of the Apocalypse on the one hand, and the Gospel and the Epistles on the other, are in *surprisingly many particulars one and the same,* only *in different form,* or even merely in other words; so that the representation in one writing appears as an apt translation of the same into the other. It further appears from our comparison, that *numerous most remarkable peculiarities in viewing religious things, from the beginning to the end, equally pervade* the Apocalypse on the one side and the Gospel and the Epistles on the other. Finally, our comparison has shown that the *manner of conception and representation,* which in many places appears through the artistic Old Testament rabbinical form of the Apocalypse, is *the mode of thought and expression of the evangelist;* and that the evangelist, on his part, consciously and decidedly as he uses his material in modern speculative *style,* yet on many points uses *the symbols and symbolical language of the seer.* For the explanation of this relation between the doctrine on both sides, it is not sufficient to point to the Old Testament or rabbinical theology; for the coincidence in each of the three categories mentioned transcends the Old Testament rabbinism common to all the writers of the New Testament, but does not reach in the smallest degree to the individually and specifically Johannine. The assumption of a spiritualizing of the apocalyptic doctrine by the author of the Gospel, consciously or unconsciously, fails before the consideration that the apocalypse itself is only the artistic clothing of that which is understood by "the spiritual."

If, therefore, the relation discovered by us to exist between the doctrine of the two is not to remain an insoluble enigma, we must acknowledge that *the author of the Apocalypse* is also the author of *the Gospel and the Epistles ;* and, indeed, since the origin of the former with the Apostle John is not inconsistent, either with external or internal evidence,—at least the statement of Georgios Hamartolos, brought into notice by Holtzmann and Keim, according to which Papias, an eye-witness of John, reports his death at the hands of the Jews, is more adverse to the residence of the presbyter in Asia Minor than it is to that of John, and is adapted partially to call in question the doubts shared by us with regard to Irenaeus,—that the author is *the Apostle John ;* a result which agrees with tradition, and is confirmed by it, as also on its own side it confirms the tradition. But the acknowledgment, —and I attach great weight to this,—according to the grounds upon which for us it rests, does not need the limitation that the apocalyptic doctrine must be referred to an earlier and lower, and the evangelistic doctrine to a later and higher stage, in the inner development of the Apostle John,—a limitation which, with the relations involved, cannot seriously be made without giving up the authenticity either of one writing or the other; but it requires only, and that very obviously, as an essential correlative, that we grant that the destruction of Jerusalem happened between the authorship of the Apocalypse and that of the other writings.

But heavily as the proof furnished by our comparison preponderates, that the Apostle John, who wrote the Apocalypse, was also the author of the other writings bearing his name, has not the result a much wider bearing? I undertook the labour in the confident expectation that the comparison between the apocalyptic and the evangelical doctrine, in case it resulted in the identity of the authors, and consequently in the Apostle John's authorship of the fourth Gospel, would also *bring the solution of the enigma* how a *disciple of Jesus,* an eye- and ear-witness, one of the trusted three, *could have written this fourth Gospel,* no matter whether with his own hand or by dictation, whether alone or with help. And now at the close I do not find myself to have been deceived in this expectation; the "Johannine enigma" appears to me in the main solved, and I will at least point out wherein the solution consists.

Had critics, often in a prejudiced manner, not much preferred the fourth Gospel to those of the Synoptists, and been blind, often wilfully, to their importance, the *synoptical histories and doctrinal representations* would long ago have been universally regarded, in the best sense of the words, as *traditional and anecdotal.* There would long since have been no doubt that the Synoptists, except with regard to the baptism and the sufferings of Christ, and other individual particulars, are innocent of all chronology, and that they group the historical material at their command, not according to time, but according to essential connection. Long since, also, it would have been recognised, and it would have been a great blessing, that in general they present only original sayings of Christ, but by no means always His original discourses; far oftener, indeed, as a rule, individual utterances and proverbial expressions from longer addresses, often wholly without their original connection, loosely attached to each other according to a theme, or grouped according to the nature of the facts. Once so far, we should have, *à priori,* not merely admitted the possibility that the history and doctrine of Jesus might in reality have reached beyond the synoptical setting; but we should not have hardened ourselves against the unconscious indications of the synoptical writers, that Jesus wrought in Judea, and especially in Jerusalem itself, more frequently and for a longer time; that His works have a still higher significance, and that here and there He may have spoken in other ways than their representations affirm. If we had been so prepared to enter upon the fourth Gospel, a multitude of difficulties would have disappeared, and very many would have been changed into evidence in its favour.

Still the chief difficulty would have remained. For the unprejudiced, it consists in the fact that, when all that has just been said is fully admitted and taken into the account, the manner of representation and expression of the Johannine Christ is manifoldly, essentially, and generally different from that of the synoptical Christ; moreover, a difference manifestly covering itself almost throughout under the manner of representation and expression of the fourth evangelist; therefore historicalness, for the present conceived in the common sense of the word as faithfulness in the direct representation of what happened on the part of the synoptical writers and the fourth evangelist, can be affirmed only of either one or the other; and that he who without prejudice compares the dual representation, cannot hesitate a moment to recognise *the historical*, as above defined, in the synoptical Gospels as a whole, and to the same extent to deny it to the fourth Gospel. But is it not a perfect contradiction: the fourth in distinction from the synoptical Gospels is unhistorical, and the fourth evangelist in distinction from the synoptical writers is a personal disciple of Jesus, the Apostle John? Or can this contradiction be shown to be merely apparent, and the "unhistoricalness" to accord with the authentic?

I reply, "Yes;" and I do so on the ground of my representation of the apocalyptic doctrine, and the comparison between it and the doctrine of the evangelist. We have found that the Apostle John, even before the destruction of Jerusalem, thought and spoke no longer in Old Testament rabbinical, but in modern speculative, Judo-Hellenistic, religio-philosophical style. Briefly, and more strictly, we may say that he thought and spoke as he did afterwards in the Gospel and in the Epistles, or as, in the former, he represents Jesus as thinking and speaking; but that in the Apocalypse he has, as the apocalyptic required, artistically clothed such mode of thought and speech in an Old Testament rabbinical garment. From this follows what is superabundantly confirmed by the peculiarity common to the seer and to the evangelist, constantly meeting us in our researches, of looking at the beginning and the end together, and therefore of describing the most different stages or degrees of development by the same names; that it was *the special gift*, the charisma, of the Apostle John *to distinguish the essence and the form of things; with facility to retain the essence in a variety of forms; to change them, and to put his life into new ones; to carry over the contents of his religious consciousness from one form of representation into another.* But is there not given with this the key to the enigma?

The Synoptists testify frequently enough, expressly and designedly, that the person, works, and discourses of Jesus were often not understood in their true meaning, either by the people or by His own disciples, and thereby candidly characterize the tradition from which they come as not having perfectly grown up to its subject. But the same synoptical writers, on the ground of this fact, undeniably distinguish the trusted disciples from the number of the Twelve, and continually mention as one of them John, the son of Zebedee. With full right we may assume that the Apostle John had not only a richer, but a far loftier, and therefore more correct, conception of Jesus than the majority of the disciples and the original church, and consequently than the fixed anecdotal traditions of the synoptical writers. The contrast between the " Judaism " of John and the " Paulinism " of Paul, on a candid examination of the related passages, especially those of the Apocalypse, is reduced to a wholly justifiable difference, which could in no way hinder John from taking the place of Paul at Ephesus, and in the province of Asia, as, according to a tradition hitherto unrefuted, he did. But here met him,—if he had not before been influenced by it in Palestine,—no matter whether directly or indirectly, a Judo-Hellenistic mode of conception and expression connected with Alexandria, which, for the sake of brevity, we describe after its central point as the Logos doctrine. That such a mode of thought really appeared in Asia, and prominently in Ephesus, in the Jewish and Christian circles of the apostle's time, cannot, from the statements of the Acts of the Apostles respecting Apollos, and the indications of the Pauline Epistles, be doubted. Indeed, a searching comparison of the earliest and the later Epistles of the Apostle Paul would, according to our opinion, give the surprising result, that even he was in that neighbourhood not wholly uninfluenced by the mode of thought in question; that his residence in, as well as his relations with, Ephesus and Asia Minor during the period between the Epistles to the Thessalonians, and, for example, those to the Corinthians, was not merely a matter of time. And could the Apostle John, who was peculiarly predisposed, as much through his higher conceptions of Christ as through his formal gift, to this Judo-Hellenistic mode of thought and speech, exclude himself from its operation? That John, as a Jewish Christian apostle, in the Tübingen sense of the words, " some time after the death of Paul, or after the destruction of Jerusalem, with flying colours went over to Paulinism; that about the year 70 he was certainly a man of sixty, with all the sacred principles of his youth, of his manhood, and of his activities broken down; that in the rending of Jewish bonds he should have, against 'their law,' the hopeless 'law,' outbid even the Apostle Paul himself—standing alone, regardless of consequences, the devout champion of freedom, against the people and the law, with his opposition to the 'Jews estranged from him and from God Himself,' "—even the probability of such a thing is vainly sought, not only by the author of *Geschichte Jesu von Nazara*, but others have never been able to find "a greater mockery of all history and all psychological probability," than the idea of a "fickle transformation of an old Judaist into an apostle of freedom, high above Paul—the one historical man of unyielding principle." Only to many of the others the Tübingen character of the Apostle John, to say nothing of the Tübingen Paul, is not regarded as one of the irresistible results of the scientific examination of apostolic times, but as a wanton perversion of a matter of fact. An apostle who, according to the statement of the rigidly "Judaistic" Apocalypse, considered the Gentile Christians, fully as much as the Jewish Christians, to be kingly priests or priestly kings of God, who will reign at the advent, may perhaps, in the application of the principle, have often differed in his views from Paul,—may, for example, until the destruction of Jerusalem, have thought the conversion of Israel nearer and easier, and the number of the Gentiles to be added to the true Israel to be less; until then he may have generally cherished a more favourable judgment of the Jews, and a less favourable one of the Gentiles,—may even have carried out the apostolic decrees respecting the relation of Jewish and Gentile Christians more strictly and more in accordance with the law than the Apostle Paul; but a difference in principle between him and Paul has been found by prejudice rather than science. Is it, then, still the greatest mockery of all history and all psychological probability, if we believe that the Apostle John had a conception of the historical Christ superior to the manifold and essentially sublime portrait of the synoptical writers, like Paul, who, not less than he, must have drawn such conception from sure sources, except he may have imagined it?—if we believe that an apostle with such a gift for entering into various forms, as it has been shown that he had, in his fiftieth or sixtieth year,—granting what is very improbable, that hitherto he had not been affected by it,—brought to the same Alexandrian Asia Minor form of thought, a sensibility as open as the Apostle Paul did a little earlier, and when somewhat younger?—if we believe that, like Paul, John also found in the Logos the adequate Judo-Hellenistic, modern philosophic, and scientific idea and expression for the Messiah as he appeared to him in Jesus; and that he, not first and alone, but after abundant precedent, borne along by a previous current in Asia Minor, from that central point carried over from the words and works of Jesus, the whole Christ, out of Palestinian Judaism into Jewish Hellenism? It was indeed for him nothing more than a change of form, which, if not already long undertaken and entered upon, had yet long been prepared, and which, with his views of the relation between the exalted Christ and the Spirit, coming equally to the light in the Apocalypse and the Gospel, appeared to him fully justified, and even required.

From this standpoint John wrote the Apocalypse in the year 68. That he could not be generally hindered by it in the conception of an Apocalypse, will not, in view of the eschatological portions in the first Epistle, and the promise in the Gospel of the revealing Spirit, be called in question. In its doctrine, as our comparison has shown, the Apocalypse stands in harmony with the Gospel and the Epistles. But if the representation of the Apocalypse is declared to be irreconcilable with its composition by the fourth evangelist, those who think so overlook in the most inconceivable manner the fact that the apocalyptic has its perfectly definite art form, and must appear in Old Testament types, symbols, images, and expressions; that an Apocalypse in the form of thought and speech seen in the fourth Gospel is as impossible as, for example, an ode in the style of the Kantian philosophy. With high poetic, plastic power, and with the most conscientious faithfulness, John has discharged his task as a seer. Evidently he would at least not have succeeded in equal measure if he had not started from Palestinian Judaism, and made its original forms of representation and speech conformable to the apocalyptic. Certainly he has at the same time — and how could it be otherwise?—not always been able to avoid the expressions and definitions of his Hellenistic doctrinal language. Here and there they appear treacherously through the ancient and sacred garment. The Old Testament forms often do not suffice for the artistic contents they enclose, and the whole almost makes the impression of a disguise, conceived and carried out in a masterly manner.

From the same standpoint, the same John, after the destruction of Jerusalem, possibly in the fourth or fifth year after the Apocalypse, wrote the *fourth Gospel,* to which, again, the first Epistle, no matter whether regarded as a companion letter to the

Gospel or not, stands in the very closest relation. We are, however, concerned here only with the Gospel. That John assumes the synoptical Gospels to be known to his readers, is now universally admitted, though the significance of this assumption is still disputed. But what induced the apostle to add another Gospel to those already existing, and manifestly recognised by him, and in his circle? A twofold reason presents itself from what has been said. First, the synoptical portrait of Christ was in general, with regard to its contents nor its subject, neither false nor distorted; but it was deficient, and its deficiency consisted far less in the absence of the historical material than in keeping back the meaning of that material. As a Paul would have felt, if at his time the synoptical Gospels had existed and been recognised, so must it have been with John and the circles which by him had been initiated into the evangelic history; and in this was given the occasion and the demand for the composition of a new and *more elevated* Gospel. Very nearly related to this is the second reason. Also in its form or representation, the synoptical portrait of Christ was certainly not false, but defective; and this defect consisted not in that the writers had done too much, but more in that they had done too little to bring the history of the Lord out of the Palestinian-Jewish form of representation and speech, as it were out of the original idiom, to that corresponding with the religious culture of the time, so to say, into a universal Judo-Hellenistic form. But where would the necessity of a new treatment of the evangelical material in the above formal sense be felt more strongly than in the circle where, as in Ephesus and Asia, the Gospel neither met a Palestinian-Judo form of thought, nor by its contents could impress the existing thought with its original form, but must *accommodate* itself to the Judo-Hellenistic mode of representation and expression?—The execution corresponds to the double motive which led John to add a materially sublimer and formally more suitable Gospel to those already existing. He does not even nearly reproduce in his Gospel the material already brought together by the synoptical writers, but only enriches and completes it by that which is similar, though he has not a little in common with them; as little does he furnish, presupposing the labours of the synoptical authors, a mere gleaning or supplement, though sometimes he gives a rectification or more accurate definition of synoptical statements. Much rather the peculiar contents of his book presuppose the synoptical narrative, and a choice, resting upon the usefulness of what was there already known, as well as of the many materials still existing only in his own mind, of signs, or of such acts and discourses of Jesus in which, as from lofty heights, the nature, the idea, the glory of Christ, the Logos-Messiah, had, as through symbols, manifested themselves in their chief aspects in word and work. But the representation of these altitudes does not follow simply from the re-statement or reference to what has been done and said, but from the recognition of all in its meaning as a revelation of the glory of Christ. All that Christ did, and what happened in connection with Him, is symbol, and is as such interpreted either by Christ Himself or by the evangelist—sometimes expressly, at other times through the passages referred to Him. But while the evangelist can *interpret* the history only as symbol, he has the doctrine of Christ, which to him in its original form is also symbol, *to carry over* into another form; so that Christ, and even John the Baptist, speak in this Gospel in the language of the evangelist, or of the Hellenism of Asia Minor. In several places the distinction between the sayings of Christ and those of the evangelist is uncertain; and in those of Christ not merely a combination, but also a continuing or developing, as it were a spinning out on the part of the evangelist, cannot be mistaken. But the seer and the evangelist are one and the same Apostle John; as the future, so also the history appears to him in symbols, and the "signs" of the Apocalypse and of the evangelist, at first sight so different, are of essentially similar import. But while John sees, and forms the signs of the *future*, after the manner of the Old Testament, he sees and shapes the signs of the *history* hellenistically; he carries over—and thus only, on the formal side, the relation between the Apocalypse on one hand, and the Gospel and Epistles on the other, is brought to its briefest expression, as, according to its nature, it is most correctly estimated—there, the Gospel backward into the Hebrew; here, forward into the Greek.

But how does it stand with the *historical character of the fourth Gospel?* In the sense in which we have used the words above, the fourth Gospel is and remains unhistorical; our brief character of the same was on one side nothing else than a concrete definition of this unhistoricalness. But then, is fidelity in the direct rendering of one's own knowledge—in reality always a somewhat mediated rendering—of what transpires the only, or even the highest sense of historicalness? There is a meaning of fidelity in which an art portrait, though a master-work,—without disparagement of photography,—follows relatively the shadows, in which indeed we grant to the photograph the predicate "faithful," but deny it to the art portrait. And yet, so far as we know, no connoisseur hesitates to declare the art portrait, in another and higher, in the spiritual sense of the word, truer than the photograph. A similar relation exists in chronicle and written history in its higher style. Now, in some measure this holds good of the historicalness of the synoptical Gospels in comparison with that of John. It is true that the narratives of the fourth Gospel have not in general, as on the supposition of the author being an eye- and ear-witness we should expect, more flesh and blood, or a greater intuitiveness; they are, on the contrary, apart from many lighter and deeper traces of personal recollections, less concrete, and the development, the historical growth, is in them kept back far more than in the synoptical narratives. But what we miss in John it was not his purpose to give. So it is also an incidental matter, though of greatest importance to us, that in the narratives of the trusted disciple we possess such manifold confirmations and explanations, and on the other side emendations and additions to the synoptical report. No; the chief thing is, that in the fourth Gospel we have the authentic testimony to the glory of the Only-begotten of the Father, full of grace and truth,—a testimony through which also the synoptical picture of the life of Christ attains a higher meaning, appears as it were in another light, and indeed is first truly intelligible. It is notorious that all modern writers on the evangelic history who have taken their stand within the synoptical Gospels, must violently cut off not a small part of the synoptical narratives as towering above the synoptical measure of Jesus and His history; but we go from the Johannine portrait of Christ, and, lo, the whole synoptical material organically arranges itself under one leading idea! For our part, we do not hesitate a moment to acknowledge that the discourses of Jesus, according to John, apart from many unmistakeably original sayings, do not make the impression of verbal faithfulness, but often sound like variations of the evangelist after themes from the Lord, often as discourses of the evangelist put into the mouth of Christ. But he has not desired to give them after the manner of stenographic reports, or noted reminiscences, or special points still remembered. Nor does the historical value of his words of the Lord consist chiefly in the addition which, though important, they make to His synoptical sayings. Their characteristic tendency is rather to "glorify" Jesus in His original discourses; that is, to bring to the understanding, in the Judo-Hellenistic form of thought and speech, their meaning, in its height and depth, in its extent and scope, in its spirit and contents, most freely, and yet, as the evangelist is conscious, most truly, because reproduction, arrangement, and transfer are wrought by the Spirit of Christ Himself. There are certainly synopticists who only acknowledge the character of the synoptical collection of Christ's sayings half-way, and notwithstanding know how to distinguish the original words of the Lord, possibly by a wholly subjective norm, or perhaps by caprice. On the other hand, those to whom the synoptical collection of the Lord's words, from discourses more or less original, have become not even original groups of original words or sayings of Christ, and who thereby have freed themselves from the bond of the connection, have then only a great multitude of imperishably glorious but isolated words, which in their isolation are to some extent incomprehensible or difficult to understand. The favoured disciple of the Lord, who in his words of Christ has borne witness to the Spirit from whom all these words and sayings have flowed, comes to the help of such, and, lo, they speak not only more plainly, but much more significantly,—so significantly that we understand how the Apostle Paul could know the Lord's words, without at any time observing a contradiction between them and his Gospel.

This mainly, though, as desirable in last words, very briefly, is my view of *the solution of the Johannine question.* Evidently it does not consist with the prevailing prejudice in favour of the synoptical writers. But it almost seems to me as if synopticism, in its most recent and in every way most complete form, had produced the impression, not on me only, that besides very many positive results, it has realized the negative one, namely, that if a "history," a "life," of Jesus is possible, which for my part I strongly doubt, it is not to be reached in that way! Well, we may take up again the plea of the witness dismissed a few years ago, the plea of the "condemned" fourth evangelist, and restore to him his rights when we have granted him a hearing respecting the historical Christ!—only this should not be in such a way that we are satisfied with a formal recognition of the fourth Gospel, and, after a preliminary declaration in favour of its apostolic origin in the exposition, lay it aside, and hold to the synoptical Gospels alone. It concerns us to weigh with a just balance, and with equal decision to maintain, that in the *form* of the historical phenomena, the originality, the genuineness, the truth, the fidelity preponderate on the side of the synoptical writers, and on the other hand fully and seriously to admit that in *essence*, in the significance, in the soul or spirit of the historical phenomena, even the same predicates belong to John in a far higher degree. Neither of these two sides excludes the other,—John has not written *against* the synoptical Gospels,—each requires the other for a perfect whole, and only together do they give the true historical Christ. I speak expressly of two sides, for we must avoid another fatal error—namely, that of desiring to unite in a mechanical way John and the synoptical writers. We have not therein fragments, torn-out portions, isolated parts of the portrait of Christ, to which John would add the outward complement or filling up; or other fragments from his recollections, so that our task should consist in bringing the various elements together, and by a synopsis in an external sense restore the whole. No; there needs, resting upon historical intuition, a united view, combination, and working into each other, of a higher style, in order from the traditional anecdotal portrait of Christ, given by the synoptical writers, and that given by the Apostle John,—from the most peculiar personal experience, and at the same time with the freest translation into the form of Hellenistic culture, sketched in great general features, and according to a few chief points of vision,—as a necessary companion picture to construct the historical image of the "Mediator!" It would, moreover, be an unfortunate misunderstanding if any one should attribute to me the expectation that in the way pointed out we should suddenly find ourselves before the goal which the "lives" or the "histories" of Jesus have hitherto striven after in vain; the knowledge of Christ will grow as long as Christendom exists. But I am firmly convinced that the normal solution of the present theological crisis—namely, the issue of the present comparatively justifiable contrariety and one-sidedness, in a subsequent higher unity, because in the central question of Christology—is essentially conditioned by a progressive inner reconciliation between John and the synoptical writers, as on both sides faithful witnesses of the evangelic history. To bring one of the indispensable prerequisites of this reconciliation to a final settlement, namely, the acknowledgment of the fourth Gospel as the work of the Apostle John, the foregoing comparison between the doctrine of the Apocalypse and that of the Gospel and Epistles, or—once more to define the actual contents—between the apocalyptic Old Testamentary and the evangelic and epistolary Hellenistic representation of the Gospel by the Apostle John, would, as a *diversion in the Johannine controversy*, contribute its humble share.

THE END.

MURRAY AND GIBB, EDINBURGH,
PRINTERS TO HER MAJESTY'S STATIONERY OFFICE.

Just published, in crown 8vo, price 5s.,

THE

SYMBOLIC PARABLES

OF

THE CHURCH, THE WORLD, AND THE ANTICHRIST,

Being the Separate Predictions of the Apocalypse,

VIEWED IN THEIR RELATION TO THE GENERAL TRUTHS OF SCRIPTURE.

BY MRS. STEVENSON.

'An excellent treatise, containing much clear thought, and written as intelligibly as the subject would permit. To students of prophecy the book ought to be an attractive one; and to every one who desires to have a clearer understanding of his Bible, it will give much valuable assistance.'—*Glasgow Herald.*

'This is a sober, well-written, and instructive treatise on the Apocalypse. It is exceedingly suggestive, and the theory the Author expounds holds well together. The key seems to fit every ward of the lock. This volume is worthy of the most serious consideration of all who take an interest in prophecy.'—*Daily Review.*

'It is quite refreshing to meet with a treatise on the Book of Revelation like this, marked by good sense and reverence. Brief as it is, it throws more light on a difficult subject than many laboured tomes.'—*Methodist Recorder.*

'It deserves careful study from all to whom the Book of Revelation has been regarded as a mystic utterance not meant for them, for it has the great advantage of being comprehensible by the most simple and unlearned.'—*John Bull.*

'Preachers will here find a mine of valuable hints on the spiritual bearing of the symbols which John's Apocalypse contains.'—*Dickinson's Quarterly.*

'We recommend this volume to our readers' study; they will find it characterized by common sense and ability as well as evangelical piety.'—*British Messenger.*

'We can sincerely recommend this volume as a thoughtful, trustworthy guide to the elucidation of a confessedly mysterious book.'—*London Quarterly Review.*

'A book which every one ought to read who seriously and strenuously and, at the same time, sensibly studies the deep but blessed words of this prophecy.'—*Wesleyan Methodist Magazine.*

'Students of prophecy will find this a book worthy of reading. . . . We have no hesitation in saying the author is a person of considerable learning, and that the work manifests much research and ability.'—*Courant.*

THE DEUTERONOMIC QUESTION.

Just published, in crown 8vo, price 5s.,

THE LEVITICAL PRIESTS.

A CONTRIBUTION TO THE CRITICISM OF THE PENTATEUCH.

BY SAMUEL IVES CURTISS, JR.,

DOCTOR OF PHILOSOPHY, LEIPZIG.

CHAPTER I. Introduction.
,, II. The Ordination and Duties of Levi.
,, III. The Inheritance of Levi.
,, IV. The Blessing of Levi.
,, V. The Modern Critic's Bridge.
,, VI. Joshua—2 Kings.
,, VII. The Credibility of the Chronicler.
,, VIII. The Prophets and the Priests.
,, IX. The Authorship of Deuteronomy and the Middle Books of the Pentateuch.

Extract from Preface by Dr. Delitzsch.

THE Author of the following work has made himself thoroughly acquainted with the writings of the chief representatives of this theory, and seeks by means of sober arguments to show (1) that the history of the people of Israel, as it lies before us in the historical books, presupposes a distinction in rank between the priests and the Levites, which reaches back to the time of Moses, and existed throughout all the periods of Israelitish history; (2) that the post-exilic books are in no way favourable to the opinion that the priestly hierarchy is a product of the time of Ezra; (3) that Deuteronomy, where it treats of religious privileges, does indeed assign them to the tribe of Levi, but yet so that these privileges—without contradicting the older legislation, which Deuteronomy recapitulates in an abridged form, and accommodates to changed circumstances—may be relatively distributed to the sons of Aaron and the Levites. He shows—and this deserves special attention—that the post-exilic Chronicles contain passages which in a Deuteronomic manner entirely obliterate the distinction between priests and Levites, while other passages emphasize it.

'A critical and thorough discussion. . . . After long study and large research, Dr. Curtiss comes well armed into the field. Cautiously, candidly, thoroughly, he handles the assumptions, the canons, and arguments of these men, and shows that they have failed to overthrow the authenticity of the Pentateuch, or to disprove its Mosaic authorship. . . . While his criticism is elaborate and searching, it is also clear and easily comprehensible.'—*American Presbyterian.*

'This is a small volume, charged with weighty matter. . . . Dr. Curtiss has argued his thesis with conspicuous ability, candour, and learning.'—*Evangelical Magazine.*

'This work is well fitted to show, by way of sample, how feeble are the grounds on which the main positions of these interpreters rest, and how arbitrary their method of procedure.'—*United Presbyterian Magazine.*

'It is in such minute details that the most convincing evidences of truth are found.' —*Watchman.*

'We give a cordial welcome to Dr. Curtiss' book, on the ground of its own merits. . . . Dr. Curtiss has done the particular portion of work which he has set himself with great pains and apparent success.'—*Church Bells.*

'A fresh and forcible reply to the ingenious and subtle attacks of rationalist teachers on the historic credibility of the Pentateuch.'—*New York Observer.*

'A thorough piece of criticism upon a nice point of internal evidence touching the origin and authenticity of the Pentateuch.'—*New York Independent.*

Just published, Second Edition, demy 8vo, 10s. 6d.,

The Training of the Twelve;

OR,

EXPOSITION OF PASSAGES IN THE GOSPELS EXHIBITING THE TWELVE DISCIPLES OF JESUS UNDER DISCIPLINE FOR THE APOSTLESHIP.

BY

A. B. BRUCE, D.D.,

PROFESSOR OF DIVINITY, FREE CHURCH COLLEGE, GLASGOW.

'Here we have a really great book on an important, large, and attractive subject—a book full of loving, wholesome, profound thoughts about the fundamentals of Christian faith and practice.'—*British and Foreign Evangelical Review.*

'It is some five or six years since this work first made its appearance, and now that a second edition has been called for, the Author has taken the opportunity to make some alterations which are likely to render it still more acceptable. Substantially, however, the book remains the same, and the hearty commendation with which we noted its first issue applies to it at least as much now.'—*Rock.*

'The value, the beauty of this volume is that it is a unique contribution to, because a loving and cultured study of, the life of Christ, in the relation of the Master of the Twelve.'—*Edinburgh Daily Review.*

'The volume is of permanent value, and we trust that its author may favour us with others of like character.'—*Freeman.*

'It is of no mean order as a profoundly devout piece of practical divinity.'—*Wesleyan Methodist Magazine.*

'It was by the first edition of this invaluable book that Dr. Bruce became known to English students as a theological writer. A more scholarly, more helpful book has not been published for many years past.'—*Baptist Magazine.*

BY THE SAME AUTHOR.

In one volume, 8vo, price 12s.,

THE HUMILIATION OF CHRIST

IN ITS PHYSICAL, ETHICAL, AND OFFICIAL ASPECTS.

(Sixth Series of Cunningham Lectures.)

'These lectures are able and deep-reaching to a degree not often found in the religious literature of the day; withal, they are fresh and suggestive. . . . The learning and the deep and sweet spirituality of this discussion will commend it to many faithful students of the truth as it is in Jesus.'—*Congregationalist.*

'We have not for a long time met with a work so fresh and suggestive as this of Professor Bruce. . . . We do not know where to look at our English Universities for a treatise so calm, logical, and scholarly.'—*English Independent.*

'The title of the book gives but a faint conception of the value and wealth of its contents. . . . Dr. Bruce's work is really one of exceptional value; and no one can read it without perceptible gain in theological knowledge.'—*English Churchman.*

'The writer gives evidence of extensive and accurate theological learning in the topics of which he treats, and he shows that he has theological grasp as well as learning.'—*Church Bells.*

In three volumes 8vo, price 31s. 6d.,

A COMMENTARY

ON THE

GOSPEL OF ST. JOHN.

BY F. GODET, D.D.,

PROFESSOR OF THEOLOGY, NEUCHATEL.

'This work forms one of the battle-fields of modern inquiry, and is itself so rich in spiritual truth that it is impossible to examine it too closely; and we welcome this treatise from the pen of Dr. Godet. We have no more competent exegete, and this new volume shows all the learning and vivacity for which the author is distinguished.'—*Freeman.*

Just published, in two volumes 8vo, price 21s.,

A COMMENTARY

ON THE

GOSPEL OF ST. LUKE.

BY F. GODET,

DOCTOR AND PROFESSOR OF THEOLOGY, NEUCHATEL.

Translated from the Second French Edition.

'We are indebted to the Publishers for an English translation of the admirable work which stands at the head of this review. . . . It is a work of great ability, learning, and research.'—*Christian Observer.*

'Marked by clearness and good sense, it will be found to possess value and interest as one of the most recent and copious works specially designed to illustrate this Gospel.'—*Guardian.*

KEIL AND DELITZSCH'S COMMENTARIES ON THE OLD TESTAMENT.

10s. 6d. each volume.

PENTATEUCH, 3 VOLS. . . . . (*Keil.*)
JOSHUA, JUDGES, AND RUTH, 1 VOL. . . . . . (*Keil.*)
SAMUEL, 1 VOL. . . . . (*Keil.*)
KINGS, 1 VOL., AND CHRONICLES, 1 VOL. . . . . (*Keil.*)
EZRA, NEHEMIAH, AND ESTHER, 1 VOL. . . . . (*Keil.*)
JOB, 2 VOLS. . . . . (*Delitzsch.*)
PSALMS, 3 VOLS. . . . . (*Delitzsch.*)
PROVERBS, 2 VOLS. . . . . (*Delitzsch.*)
ECCLESIASTES AND SONG OF SOLOMON, 1 VOL. . . . (*Delitzsch.*)
ISAIAH, 2 VOLS. . . . . (*Delitzsch.*)
JEREMIAH AND LAMENTATIONS, 2 VOLS. . . . . (*Keil.*)
EZEKIEL, 2 VOLS. . . . . (*Keil.*)
DANIEL, 1 VOL. . . . . (*Keil.*)
MINOR PROPHETS, 2 VOLS. . . . . (*Keil.*)

'This series is one of great importance to the biblical scholar; and as regards its general execution, it leaves little or nothing to be desired.'—*Edinburgh Review.*

In two volumes, demy 8vo, price 21s.,

Growth of the Spirit of Christianity,

FROM THE FIRST CENTURY TO THE DAWN OF THE LUTHERAN ERA.

BY THE

REV. GEORGE MATHESON, M.A., B.D.,

AUTHOR OF 'AIDS TO THE STUDY OF GERMAN THEOLOGY.'

'Mr. Matheson's work is fresh, vigorous, learned, and eminently thoughtful.'—*Contemporary Review.*

'A work remarkable for its originality, its lucidity of exposition, its graceful and impressive style, here and there reminding one of Ruskin's, but more sober; its wideness of research and very able analysis deserve, and no doubt will receive, unstinted praise.' *Clergyman's Magazine.*

'These volumes are full of interest to the general reader, and certain to repay careful study . . . . rich in the repressed eloquence which is born of overflowing thought.'—*Spectator.*

'Mr. Matheson has written with very considerable ability, and sometimes eloquence. a book which gives the results of a thoughtful mind which thinks for itself, the fruits of extensive reading, a clear judgment, and a catholic spirit, and often an original intelligence. All this is no little praise to give, and we give it readily.'—*Scotsman.*

'This truly deserves to be called a great book, and will surely exert a powerful and elevating influence on men of thought and culture.'—*Watchman.*

'The work is one of high and unusual merit.'—*Literary Churchman.*

'We should like to summarize this great and subtle and suggestive work.'—*Daily Review.*

'A brief notice of these two volumes can convey but little idea of their full and varied learning, their fine historical insight, and their power of lucid exposition.'—*Baptist Magazine.*

'This work is a contribution of real value to the popular study of Church History.' —*Pall Mall Gazette.*

BY THE SAME AUTHOR.

In crown 8vo, Third Edition, price 4s. 6d.,

Aids to the Study of German Theology.

'The Author has done his work well, and has given us a real help to the understanding of German theology.'—*Princeton Review.*

'A work of much labour and learning, giving in a small compass an intelligent review of a very large subject.'—*Spectator.*

'An excellent and modest book, which may be heartily recommended.'—*Academy.*

'A helpful little volume: helpful to the student of German theology, and not less so to the careful observer of the tendencies of English religious thought.'—*Freeman.*

'The writer or compiler deserves high praise for the clear manner in which he has in a brief compass stated these opinions.'—*Christian Observer.*

www.ingramcontent.com/pod-product-compliance
Lightning Source LLC
Chambersburg PA
CBHW032257280326
41932CB00009B/602

* 9 7 8 3 3 3 7 2 8 3 2 7 8 *